WITHDRAWN

Donated by Paul Krahn

CHAPTER ONE

INTRODUCTION

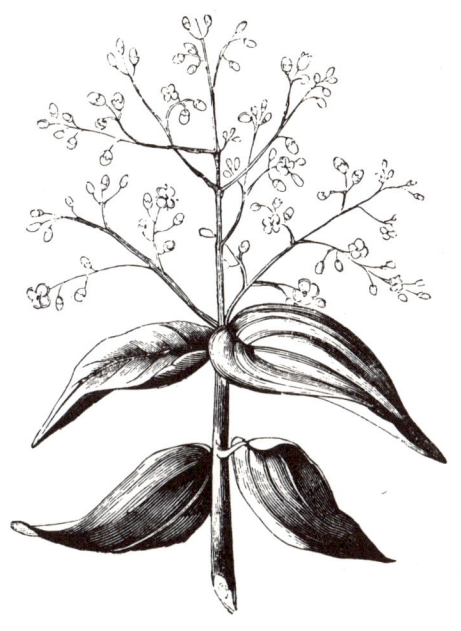

PARADOXES OF PARADISE: IDENTITY AND DIFFERENCE IN THE SONG OF SONGS

by

FRANCIS LANDY

BIBLE AND LITERATURE SERIES

Editor
David M. Gunn

PARADOXES OF PARADISE

Identity and Difference
in the Song of Songs

FRANCIS LANDY

SHEFFIELD
THE ALMOND PRESS · 1983

BIBLE AND LITERATURE SERIES, 7

Copyright © 1983 The Almond Press

British Library Cataloguing in Publication Data:

Landy, Francis
    Paradoxes of paradise. - (Bible and literature
    series, ISSN 0260-4493; 7)
    1. Bible. O.T. Song of Solomon - Commentaries
    I. Title   II. Series
    223'.907   BS1485.3

ISBN 0-907459-16-1
ISBN 0-907459-17-X Pbk

Published by
The Almond Press
P.O. Box 208
Sheffield S10 5DW
England

Printed in Great Britain by
Dotesios (Printers) Ltd
Bradford-on-Avon, Wiltshire

CONTENTS

PREFACE	7
Chapter One **INTRODUCTION**	13
Drush on Rabbi Akiba	13
The Cultural Context	18
Structure and Unity	33
Chapter Two **THE RELATIONSHIP OF THE LOVERS**	61
Introduction: Character and Archetype	61
Androgyny: Fawns and Lilies	73
The Mother and Twins	92
Love and Death	113
Chapter Three **BEAUTY AND THE ENIGMA**	137
Introduction	137
First Episode: 1.5-6	142
Second Episode: 8.11-12	152
Third Episode: 8.8-10	160
Fourth Episode: 1.7-8	169
Postscript: 1.9, 1.15-16	176
Conclusion	178
Chapter Four **TWO VERSIONS OF PARADISE**	183
Introduction	183
Metaphor: The Garden	189
Metaphor: The Tree	210
Paronomasia: Nakedness and Subtlety	220
Dramatis Personae: Serpent and Woman	229
Theme: The Unity of the Body	246
Conclusion	263
Chapter Five **CONCLUSION**	269

NOTES

to Chapter One	279
to Chapter Two	299
to Chapter Three	318
to Chapter Four	328
to Chapter Five	359

LIST OF ABBREVIATIONS	360
BIBLIOGRAPHY	361
INDEX OF REFERENCES	388
INDEX OF MODERN AUTHORS	394
INDEX OF SUBJECTS	400

PREFACE

Writing a book is a little like paying court to a queen of hearts; one might lose one's head. Writing a book on the Song of Songs is especially perilous, since it concerns that which is most painful to man, his most profound gifts, his unfathomable beauty. Writing such a book necessitates distance, separating oneself from what is said, allowing the poem to speak for itself through you, as through others. But it is also a self-discovery; we find ourselves spoken there. A confused bundle of personae, afloat in the twentieth century, hears himself in eternity. Every poet, and I would say every serious writer, writes with his life, as the rollcall of suicides among contemporary poets testifies. Certainly this writer has written with and for his life. Each one of my friends, and all who have aided me in this project, has fulfilled the commandment of "piqquah nefes", saving the soul, literally opening the eyes of the soul. It has been the source of much anticipatory pleasure to acknowledge these debts.

First I would like to thank the Sussex University authorities, under whose auspices I wrote this work, for their patience and trust in me, with affection for the university itself - my sorrow too for its straits - for its unique creativity and its encouragement of imaginative adventure among its graduate students; it was truly good fortune that brought me there. In particular, there are my supervisors: Professor David Daiches, now retired, who made me feel at home, and whose humility and humanity I shall remember with pleasure; and Revd Dr Michael Wadsworth, for the extraordinary thoroughness of his comments, his constant support and concern. I feel especial gratitude to Mr Gabriel Josipovici, who read all the chapters, and whose incisive and constructive criticism proved decisive; and, in a different mode, to the editors of the Journal for the Study of the Old Testament, and to my publisher, Dr David Gunn, who relieved the isolation that pervades graduate studies. Quite apart from their ultimate responsibility for this work, I wish to thank my parents for their excellent proofreading and my mother for her additional labour in compiling, so comprehensively, the indexes. To Dr Jonathan Magonet I owe almost everything. The Prior and friars of Hawkesyard Priory gave me shelter through a particularly excruciating writing block. I have benefitted greatly from the sympathetic advice and generous time of an Egyptologist, Miss Alison Roberts, and hope that our association will continue. I wish to thank Miss Katherine Schardt and, more than I can say, Mrs Rushi Ledermann for their insight and affection.

Francis Landy
June, 1983

Drafts and excerpts of parts of the present work have previously appeared in the following journals: Harvest, Journal of Biblical Literature, Journal for the Study of the Old Testament, Prospice, and Theology.

Transliteration of Hebrew: for typographical reasons spirant forms of consonants are not indicated and no distinction is made between short vowels and hateph vowels.

The translations are eclectic, and not always consistent: I have chosen what seemed appropriate in context, and drawn freely and gratefully from existing versions as well as from my own imagination. Once or twice - in particular, in the case of the "rose of Sharon" - botanical accuracy yielded to poetic familiarity. - F. L.

To the Memory
of Rosalind
My Sister, My Friend

CHAPTER ONE

INTRODUCTION

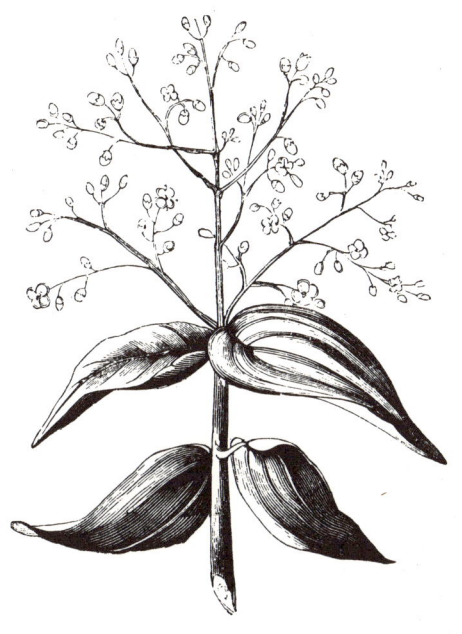

CHAPTER ONE

INTRODUCTION

Chapter One

INTRODUCTION

Drush on Rabbi Akiba

THE first reference to the Song of Songs is also the most radical:

אמר רבי עקיבא: חס ושלום לא נחלק אדם מישראל
על שיר השירים שלא תטמא את־הידים: שאין
כל־העולם כלו כדאי כיום שניתן בו שיר השירים
לישראל: שכל הכתובים קדש ושיר השירים קדש קדשים:

Said Rabbi Akiba: Heaven forbid that any man in Israel ever disputed that the Song of Songs renders the hands unclean (i.e. is holy /1/), for the whole world is not worth the day on which the Song of Songs was given to Israel, for all the Writings are holy, and the Song of Songs is the Holy of Holies. (Mishnah Yadaim 3.5)

How are we to understand this? Attack as the best form of apologetic /2/? Does this already suppose an allegorical interpretation, as many critics assume /3/? Or a mystical one, since the Holy of Holies is the mystery of mysteries? In this connection the argument of Saul Lieberman and Gershom Scholem that the Song is germinal to the Kabbalah is of the utmost interest, that in these early centuries Shiur Qomah speculation, i.e. meditation on the Body of God, developed in part as an exegesis of the description of the Lover in the Song, 5.10-16 (Scholem 1965: 46-52; cf. Lieberman ibid.: 118-26). Many citations prove that even at this time the Song was regarded as supremely esoteric; for instance the Midrash that Rabban Gamaliel wept when Rabbi Akiba passed from the first to the second verse since he had not been worthy to receive its secrets (Lieberman, ibid.: 126). Whether this Midrash is apocryphal, whether the Shiur Qomah tradition was only putatively fathered on Rabbi Akiba /4/, is of course unknowable. Scholem and Lieberman make no claim that this was his original intention. What is true is that Rabbi Akiba was a mystic, who founded the school of minute criticism, famous for his exposition of the taggim, his conviction of the contingency of each letter of the Torah, who put Moses to shame with the subtleties he discerned /5/; he was thus not one to settle for simplistic readings. Moreover, he participated in allegorising, contributing to the Midrash Rabbah. But he was also a lover /6/, whose life gives his statement peculiar authenticity. For it was through sexual love that Rabbi Akiba came to the study of the Torah, and he gave up his life for the love of God, proving in his own flesh that love is as strong as death: "And you shall love the Lord your God with all your heart, and with all your soul, and with all your might." It was he, moreover, who propounded in its most extreme form the view that the love of God is greater than the fear of God /7/ and that "You shall love your neighbour as yourself" is the greatest of all the commandments (Sifra Kedoshim 4.12). Thus human love and divine love are united in the Torah, with which, he said, the world was created (Pirke Aboth 2.18). He was the illiterate shepherd in love with his master's daughter, the revolutionary against imperial secular power, the martyr in the cause of Messianic redemption. If, according to the allegorical interpretation, Israel, the shepherd people, is drawn to the love of the Torah, then he is its epitome; and by the same token, as the most romantic of lovers, he could not but have been sympathetically sensitive to its erotic suggestion. His condemnation of those who trill the Song in taverns and feasts /8/ may well not imply a rejection of its literal meaning, but the vulgarisation of its essential mysticism.

"For the whole world is not worth the day on which the Song of Songs was given to Israel." Which was the day on which the Song of Songs was given to Israel? Rabbi Akiba's view, as argued by Lieberman, is that it was the day of the giving of the Torah, for the sake of which the world was created /9/. Accordingly, "Solomon" is but an acronym for "The King Whose is the Peace" (hammelek šehaššālôm šelô), namely, God /10/.

But the day might be any day, any day on which the Song came into being and was delivered to Israel, and thence to the world. It stresses the point of irruption, the relationship between the poet and time, the world and its articulation in poetry. But this might be true of any poem, the familiar experience that the moment of inspiration is the justification of one's existence, and encompasses the whole of creation. What then is special about the Song?

A felicitous detail lends itself to concomitant expansion: it is the reticent passive that hints at the Midrashic/mystical

Chapter One - Introduction

exegesis: "the day on which the Song of Songs <u>was given</u> to Israel." For it also draws on the universal conviction that poems are "given", that the poet is a listener as well as a creator. As well as God then, we have the Muse.

"For the whole world is not worth the day ..." How much is the world worth? Or is it all vanity? According to the view of the Sages, it is better not to have been born /11/. Thus Rabbi Akiba's statement appears to have been a backhanded compliment. But let us look further, at its context. In our Mishnah the dispute concerning the Song of Songs is coupled with one on Ecclesiastes. The message of Ecclesiastes is that all is vanity, that best of all is never to have been (4.3), and thus accords with the opinion of the Sages; with regard to it, the School of Shammai, that denied the value of life and held that it was best to put a brave face on things /12/, are "meqûlê", in other words they consider that Ecclesiastes is secular commonsense, while the School of Hillel, who argued unavailingly on life's behalf, are "mehûmrê", recognise it as a sacred book /13/, possibly because of its sanctimonious conclusion /14/, possibly because of a genuine appreciation of its religious value. For the Song of Songs, however, all is vanity, except love; for only love is as strong as death, and gives life to the world. Ecclesiastes and the Song thus form a pair; the decision that both are hallowed validates Rabbi Akiba's statement that the world is worthless except for love, the day, i.e. the occasion, on which the Song of Songs was given to Israel. Then it is not the Song but what it expresses that is worthy of such praise; through the Song the day on which it (or the Torah) was given becomes perpetual. Poetry recreates experience; it guarantees love - ideally or historically - against death. But then poetry is inseparable from love; the Song is part of the experience of that day, that part that is accessible to us. Love, as communion, wishes to express itself in language, the vehicle of communication, to make words adequate to gestures, touch, feeling. Rabbi Akiba, through his paraphrase, identifies the realisation in words with the experience; the day is <u>defined</u> as that in which the Song of Songs was given to Israel. One remembers that according to the Talmud God literally created the world with language /15/, that language is prior to substance /16/, and Rabbi Akiba in particular is credited with its minute analysis. The Song, then, as the rebus of the Torah, not only expresses the world, but is the essence of the world; its voice is the reality behind all lovers' gestures. The relationship of language and what it signifies is thus reversed. Instead of poetry being the imperfect vehicle for what is beyond words, lovers' bodies become vehicles of poetry, of music; the love song is the spiritual exemplar of love.

But does it have to be the Song of Songs? Could it not be any love song? One may interpret the title as the Song of which all songs are composed, in which they are all included, as well as perforce all those composed in ancient Israel. Or it could mean the supreme love song, in which case too it could stand as their representative /17/. It is an extraordinary assertion, suggesting on the one hand a collective entelechy of love poetry, of which the Song is the transcription, on the other a touching arrogance, innocent in its isolation from all the great love poets. In its time, in the Ancient Near Eastern tradition, the Song is pre-eminent, and certainly quite original. And yet we can still call it "The Song of Songs", with all our resources, for we can still feel it to be the quintessence of love-poetry, and one of the greatest of love poems.

The concluding conceit - "for all the Writings are holy, but the Song of Songs is the Holy of Holies" - logically develops the argument to the point of paradoxical absurdity. But it should be taken seriously, and brilliantly advances Rabbi Akiba's contention. The Writings, "ketubîm", are not simply the third section of the Bible, as is commonly supposed /18/; the word could refer to all sacred literature, or indeed all literature, and such an interpretation is necessitated by the universal context. The primary reference, I would have thought, must be to the Torah - possibly in the widest sense, to include the Prophets, the Writings, and oral teachings - since only the Torah may be designated holy, and originates together with the Song. The relationship of the Song to the Torah then corresponds to that of the Holy of Holies to the holy things and acts: it is its nucleus. Every practice and word is coded in the Song, as the allegorical approach assumes; but conversely, every word is the exoteric expression of that which is esoterically contained in the Song. Without the Holy of Holies, the holy things are void; without the Song, the Torah is empty. The Holy of Holies is mysterious and inaccessible, except to the High Priest once a year; it is hidden by a veil. Rabbi Akiba was a legendary father of the Kabbalah, who penetrated into the "pardēs" (T. B. Hagigah, 14b). Yet we need not suppose the wiles and wherefores of Kabbalah; it could have a very simple meaning.

With the Torah, and the Song of Songs at its centre, God created the world. The Song of Songs is a love song, the

Chapter One - Introduction

creative discourse of man and woman; man was created in the image of God. At the centre of the Torah, its code of restrictions, its hermetic righteousness, is this act, and this analogy; through love, as through the Torah, the world continues. The purity of the Holy of Holies guarantees the presence of God in the world; the purity of creation, the first commandment "to be fruitful and multiply", the love of man and God, man and man, and sexual relationships, are the central concerns of the Torah. It is very fitting that alongside, or at the centre, of all the disastrous stories, prophetic denunciations, and claustrophobic rules of the Bible there should be this vision of joy. Yet there is also a contradiction. The gay, Dionysiac lyric is fundamentally at odds with the heartless differentiations, the paranoid anxieties, that separate pure from impure, Israel from the nations etc. etc. There is something shocking and refreshing in the juxtaposition Song of Songs: Holy of Holies. The tension is genuine: thematically as well as historically the Song contends with moral disapprobation; it cocks a snook at all Puritans. Yet it points to something essential in holiness, that is stressed repeatedly in the Psalms; that what it preserves, apart from all the corruptions of the world, is the Song that unites all creatures, their perfect relationship - symbolised by the shattered tablets of stone in the Holy of Holies - the dream of justice and universal peace of which Israel is the bearer /19/.

The Song is this song of the creatures, for in it human love and natural love correspond, and the natural world seems to find its voice; it is also the quintessence of love-poetry: the Song in which every song partakes. Can we take the analogy further, and say that every song is holy? Rabbi Akiba would, I imagine, dissent. Only the heretic, Elisha ben Abuya, always had a Greek song on his lips (T. B. Hagigah, 15b). The Kabbalists, however, believed that music expressed the spirituality of a people /20/; and there is the Talmudic notion that each nation has its guardian angel, and its particular aspect of divinity /21/. Somewhere in each song, then, is a trace of its original identity and purpose (the Hassidic masters specialised in rescuing these musical sparks). Israel, in the divine scheme of things, is the light of the world, that which makes the whole world aware of its relatedness; the Song of Songs is the summation of all songs. If each nation has its guardian angel, Israel is rooted in the Shekhinah, that rests in the Holy of Holies, and its music is the Song of Songs. There is something fatefully nationalistic in Rabbi Akiba's statement, with its repeated stress on the word "Israel", as befits his personality. The Song itself is an Israelite poem, intensely devoted to the Land, and part of its contribution to the world's heritage. Yet we are not and cannot be Rabbi Akiba; we can only read it as of universal value, expressing a national but also supranational, human identity, as we shall find in the forthcoming pages.

The Cultural Context

Which was the day on which the Song was given to Israel? The question may seen unimportant, since the Song is a timeless poem, and it plays little part in my investigation. Nevertheless, before approaching the Song itself, it is worth looking at the cultural landscape, so that the Song should speak to us from (or for) its time. No work is totally independent of its circumstances, of the "semantic horizon" (Patte: 18-19), just as it is not entirely explicable by them. Historical awareness cannot be excluded from our reading without distorting it, without making it much less interesting. The Song, for instance, is both polemically and integrally related to its society. The background helps us to understand the Song; equally the Song startlingly illumines the background.

Critics differ widely about the date of the Song, and hence its milieu. Some consider it to be Solomonic /22/, even perhaps emanating from Solomon's court circle, possibly reflecting an actual amorous adventure /23/; others hold that it is as late as the 3rd century B.C. /24/; and still others conclude that it is a compilation, either the work of a single hand (e.g. Rowley 1965: 222), or spanning the whole range of Israelite history, and subjected to substantial revision, analogous to the Greek Anthology (e.g., Gordis 1974: 16-18). In my view, the linguistic evidence overwhelmingly points to a very late date; I see no reason, moreover, for considering it to be a redaction. This will appear in the course of subsequent argument. Both diction and syntax are post-classical, spiced with Persian /25/ and probably Greek /26/ loanwords; they associate the Song philologically with Ecclesiastes (e.g. the frequency of "še-"; the usage in common of the word "pardēs"). Counter-arguments are not compelling /27/. For instance, the appearance of the ancient capital Tirzah in a poem set in the Solomonic age does not necessitate an ancient composition, pace Gordis (1974: 23) /28/; it is part of the literary fiction. Ugaritic lexicography has contributed only a handful of strained readings /29/.

Chapter One - Introduction

Likewise, the Albright-Freedman hypothesis that poems can be dated according to the frequency of two-word parallelisms entirely disregards the rhetorical context and the requisites of genre (especially in a love poem!) /30/. Finally, the suggestion that Persian and Greek loanwords reflect Solomon's trading empire /31/ is far less convincing than that they were absorbed during Persian and Greek hegemony; their currency in Hellenistic times is well-attested, whereas in those of Solomon even their native existence is extremely dubious.

Literary criteria are more elusive than philological data, but far more valuable, since they introduce us directly to the cultural issues. For this reason the decisive determinant in my eyes is the note of nostalgia /32/. Solomon's splendour lacks verisimilitude; the wrangling of the harem, political and social unrest, tawdry actuality. Nor does it sound like mythopoeic adulation (a Biblical Gloriana); for the image of the king in it, as we shall see, is profoundly ambivalent. Solomon's kingdom is objectified, set at a distance from ourselves and the author. We see it as a whole, from our own perspective. In the Song this is achieved through temporal distancing, e.g." ʾappiryôn ʿāsâ lô hammelek šelōmōh" "King Solomon made for himself a palanquin" (3.9) or "Solomon had a vineyard" (8.11) (cf. below, p.153), or the merging of past and present in 3.11, where the daughters of Zion are urged to go out and look on Solomon on the day - located somewhere other than now - when his mother crowned him (cf. below, p.58).

In later times, we know, Solomon and his kingdom became legendary, a Golden Age of temporal and religious fulfilment. Legends take time to grow; the more distant a realm is in time or space the more fabulous its possibilities. Solomon in the Song is a symbolic figure, the type of the ideal lover and of worldly glory. Although it is possible to imagine it as a contemporary document, risking always the conflict with disillusioning reality, it conforms better with his later aggrandisement, and especially the preoccupation with Solomon in the period of the Second Temple and thereafter. Before the Exile, he almost drops out of literary consciousness. This is only to be expected: legend attaches itself to a convenient past. In it are projected all the hopes frustrated in the present: political glory, national independence, under the guidance of a supremely wise and magnificent king. The wish-fulfilling aspiration is clearly much more acute in the period of the Second Temple, when

Israel was a backwater of the Persian Empire and of Hellenistic culture, than of the First, when the two kingdoms were still independent, and in the case of Israel had some measure of grandeur.

These observations are given some impetus by H.P. Müller's reconstruction of the socio-historical background of the Song. He suggests that it is typical of an age of political irresponsibility when, lacking the international power struggles and social concerns of the Prophets, writers reflected on Israel's purpose in an unaccommodating world. One response was a sceptical despair, such as Ecclesiastes, another was hedonism (Müller 1977: 160-1). In both cases, Solomon's kingdom is a symbol of that which has been lost - the island of bliss, of forty years' peace, in Israel's woeful history. It thereby becomes an experimental control for assessing what that history and all worldly power is ultimately worth.

Another approach in determining cultural context and purpose as well as date is literary influence; critics have endeavoured to relate it to one or other literary tradition. For example, Gerleman argues that it is early because of its similarity to Egyptian love lyrics; others have compared it to Mesopotamian poetry, early and late, to Hellenistic models, and found parallels further afield, from modern Palestine to ancient Ceylon /33/. This is very valuable, since the Song did not appear in a vacuum; comparison with other examples of the world-wide erotic tradition will be illuminating. As Fox ("Love, Passion and Perception") says, "To illuminate the distinctive character of an individual poem or of a certain poetic tradition, there is heuristic value in comparing the poem or group of poems with others of the same genre." But one must be careful not to confound congruence with influence, nor to concentrate on resemblances at the expense of differences. Furthermore, the related, especially the ancient, literature presents great problems of interpretation and translation; poetic analysis has hardly begun. Hence there is a high risk that any comparison will be based on false criteria. A case in point is that of John White, whose dissertation on the Song of Songs and Egyptian love poetry is the only full-length study. The correlation with Egyptian love poetry, I might add, is the most commonly adduced /34/, since Egypt was in closest proximity to Israel - and extraordinarily interesting.

White sensitively describes the setting, archetypal content, and atmosphere of the Egyptian love lyrics, as well as the

Chapter One - Introduction

current state of research in the Song; he goes awry when he tries to compare them on the exclusive basis of "topoi", literary fictions, and "Gattungen", literary types or categories. It would appear, according to White, that there are no significant differences, except one, which is totally fallacious, namely that whereas Egyptian love poetry is secular in inspiration, and references to the gods are merely cynical, the Song is a pious work, reinforcing the ideal of God-fearing fidelity /35/. To compare the texts on the basis of their use of the five senses, glorified into "topoi" /36/, or forcing all the metaphors for the lovers into catch-all personae /37/, does not constitute a genuine correlation. White shows no awareness of differences, for example in their sensual imagery, and a blindness to any similarities that fall outside his predetermined categories /39/. Finally, his translation of the Egyptian love songs, which he sees as "the heart of this dissertation" (161), is untrustworthy, as well as unreadable /40/. This then is an example of an intelligent and committed work that is vitiated by form-critical dogma and theological presuppositions.

A far better mutually illumining comparison is offered by Fox, evidently validated by a good knowledge of Egyptian. Fox argues that whereas for the Egyptian poet, love is a psychological state, almost independent of the loved one, to be explored with all the subtlety of his resources, in the Song love is a relationship. Hence the Egyptian poems are monologues, while the Song is a dialogue. Even if love is reciprocated, as in the Cairo Ostracon love song which he calls "The Crossing", "contact between the lovers is only physical" (ibid.: 3), the emotions are private and subjective. In the Song, on the contrary, the lovers influence each other, interanimate each other, for example through verbal echo. Strategic quotation of Donne informs this part of the essay. Another illustration of the contrast is the imagery, for whereas in Egyptian love poetry the descriptions of the loved one, for example in the "wasf" of Chester-Beatty i.a ("The Song of Seven") are literal and unimpressive, those in the Song are very elaborate. Fox's exemplary analysis of the technique of the "wasf" shows how the images are both presentational and representational, combining sensory and affective qualities, so that it communicates a mode of perception of the world, through the eyes of love. This in turn suggests its religious significance. In Egyptian love poetry, in contrast, the imagery is most intense when most introspective. Whereas the Song creates "a private, idyllic universe" (ibid.: 14), the Egyptian poet's ideal is individual felicity.

In my view, Fox oversimplifies these oppositions, and misses the real contrast between Egyptian love poetry and the Song, as well as the real problem of interpretation, namely the symbolic connotation of the images. If, as well as the manifold difficulties of literal interpretation, the poems are misunderstood because the underlying symbolic code is unheeded or unsuspected, comparison will be misconceived. The best discussion is that of Philippe Derchain, of whose work Fox seems unaware. Derchain contends, and demonstrates through a close analysis of the Cairo love songs and various flower and fruit symbols, that only through a precise examination of the emotional overtones of the words, in their Egyptian context, can they truly be translated so as to engage the imagination of the modern reader. In particular, he explores their religious significance, which White minimises and Fox ignores. Love in the love lyrics is pervaded with divinity, inseparable from humanity; the delicious particularity of the foreground is realised in, and takes its seriousness from, a universal vision. For the girl, the Lover is "my god, my lotus", associated, according to Derchain, with the young god Re (76); while for the Lover her figure evokes Hathor. The Lover, who spellbinds the flood, indicated by the same word as chaos (nwn), that separates him from his Beloved, symbolically recalls the rising of the first sun over the primeval waters, the first act of creation /41/. Thus for the Egyptian poet, love is not merely a psychological state but a way of seeing and imagining the world, and participating in its creativity.

Secondly, it is a relationship, despite the absence of dialogue. In fact, in the Song, the lovers speak to themselves, even when they are ostensibly addressing the other. Monologues preponderate over snatches of dialogue. In the Egyptian love poems, communication takes place through verbal echo and shared experience, as in the Song. The Beloved's arms open - a gesture reminiscent of Hathor /42/ - and in response his arms open. He kisses her, and her lips part. She offers him a tilapia fish, symbol of fecundity and evidently of herself, that is quiet in her fingers; three stanzas later his heart is the tilapia, secure in its pond /43/. They think of each other and do so, moreover, through each other's eyes - a surprisingly sophisticated technique. Thus the Beloved imagines the lover looking at her when she bathes fully clothed; her drenched clothes outline her body.

Chapter One - Introduction

Throughout the poems lovers have feelings for each other, testifying to relationship. Fox's statement that contact is only physical denies the feelings communicated between them, for example when they each raise their arms, or when the lips part. Indeed, possibly the very evasion of mendacious, fallible speech directs our mind to these feelings, as truer modes of contact; just as the chastity of language and imagery diffuses sexuality over the entire body /44/.

A third point which now emerges is that the descriptive imagery is not perfunctory, and could only be seen so by one insensitive to its religious implications. For example, the vision of the Beloved at the beginning of the Chester-Beatty cycle is unmistakably assimilated to the overwhelming majesty of the goddess Hathor, "Gold", at the turning of the year, and has justly been compared to the celestial images for the Beloved in the Song of Songs 6.10. Nevertheless, Fox rightly points to the difference: the metaphors for the anatomised body in the Song are far more richly articulated, and far more independent, than their Egyptian counterparts. Whereas in the Chester-Beatty cycle the parts of the body are entirely subsumed in, and emblematic of, the vision of Hathor, in the Song they are logically discontinuous and intensely focussed vehicles for metaphorical freedom. As Fox perceives, they create a world, not, I would say, "a private, idyllic universe", but the world, for example with images of real farming, blessed by love.

This suggests a difference between Egyptian love poetry and the Song, for which Fox provides a clue. Egyptian love poems are affectionate comments, often vignettes, on love as part of life, capturing moments in the social flow; its seriousness is indissoluble from its particularity. In the Cairo love song already cited, the cosmological background - love as a reminiscence of the first dawn - contrasts sharply with the adolescent beauty of the girl's flirtatious daring /45/. The poems are funny, urbane, painfully human, and simultaneously sublime, with constant changes of register and imaginative focus. After the majestic procession of theophanous images of the Beloved in Chester-Beatty i.a, we suddenly see her as an awkward, shy girl, talking to herself. Idealisation alternates with affection, insight and exasperation. Lovers are presented in their social setting, amid their families, going to festivals, bathing, as part of a buoyant and essentially tolerant society. Lovers may be occasionally anguished, e.g. unable to confess their love, but are never alienated. There is an underlying sanity, shared by the lovers, aware of the absurdity as well as the wonder of love. We can almost hear them talking; despite the characteristic reticence of Egyptian writing, some of the poems have a chatty, informal quality. The girl says in the Chester-Beatty cycle, "Truly, he is a foolish one", followed immediately by the self-reflection "But I resemble him" (tr. Miriam Lichtheim). Indeed I would disagree entirely with Fox's comment "We do not learn about the reality of love affairs in Egypt or Israel any more than we discover what love really is today by listening to popular songs" (ibid.: 1-2); in my view we learn much - more than from anything else - about the experience of love and of that society from these poems. In the Song, however, the lovers' world is created more or less in opposition to a repressive society, from which, for example, the mother's house is a refuge; the Song explores ambivalence towards love in its social critique.

This leads to the central issue: for the Egyptian poet love is a part of life on its trajectory towards death - necessary, beautiful, and divinely permeated, as all life is, associated with the young god Re, but nevertheless only a phase in the cosmic process. Egyptian poems are a meditation on the theme of "flighty youth", thrown into relief, for example, by the inclusion of a Harper's Song - a reflection on death - in the Harris 500 collection; there a poignant quotation from Ptah-hotep, "Follow your heart as long as you live", represents a commitment to life from the perspective of death. This explains the undertone of ironic complaisance at the excitement of the lovers, the numerous images of haste, things left undone or half-done, such as the girl's hair in Harris 500 II b.8 (Lichtheim 1976: 191) /46/, and the perfect appropriateness with which in the first Cairo love song (st.2), the girl suddenly imagines the mutual serenity of old age /47/. In the Song, however, the lovers will never grow old; death is excluded from their garden. Whereas for the Egyptian poet both love and death are part of the same necessary cycle, the ambiguous message of the Song is that love is as strong as death, the one thing that is eternal. In support of this contention it fosters an organic vision of the world, and explores everything for its value. In its absolute demands, its profound criticism, and its search for enlightenment, it metaphorically and monistically unites everything in the world in the love of the lovers.

It is much more difficult to compare the Song with ancient Mesopotamian erotic poetry; in addition to the problems of interpretation already cited, we encounter an immense time

Chapter One - Introduction

span, and a generic distance, from the Sacred Marriage hymns of the third millennium to the extraordinary and unclassifiable so-called Divine Love Lyrics of the first. H. P. Müller (1976) describes the Song as a lyric reproduction of myth; whereas in the Sacred Marriage rite king and queen (or priestess) are identified with Dumuzi and Inanna, whose union promotes fertility, in the Song the human lovers are in harmony with but not responsible for the powers of nature /48/. Even if the lover were really Solomon, his royal status would have a purely symbolic function; the lovers are presented in all their humanity. On the individual level, words are not efficacious spells to compel the love of the other - such verbal rape is against the whole spirit of the Song - but descriptive, reflective, anxious, expressing a whole range of linguistic possibilities and ambiguities. Nevertheless, some of the imagery - Dumuzi as king, shepherd and gazelle (Jacobsen 1976: 49), phrases such as "my watered gardens bear honey and wine under him" (ibid.: 42), the invocation of Dumuzi as date-gatherer (ibid.: 34) - does suggest, as J. and A. Westenholz say (218), a common pool of erotic motifs that the Song has inherited. Likewise, the preoccupation with love and death, and the possible Pastoral regression, as the matrix of the lyric voice, are thematically correlated with the Song. It is a millennial resonance, which the Song evokes and which contributes depth to it; it responds to and uses the resources of a sacred tradition, diffused probably through folklore. Moreover, if the Song and Egyptian love poetry have religious implications, the affairs of Dumuzi and Inanna, the consummation of the marriage, the mourning of mother and sister over child, are detailed with a particularity, a humour and depth of grief, expressive of the reality of love and fantasy in Mesopotamia /49/.

Three poems, apart from those associated with the sacred Marriage, have been compared to the Song. The first is the Old Akkadian love incantation MAD.V.8 (Sasson 1973; J. & A. Westenholz 1977), dating from c.2200 B.C.; the principal correlations are the motif of going down to the garden, in which the maidens who do so grow as flowers; the Lover's fragrant oils; Sasson adds the figure of the shepherd. Ancient Near Eastern literature provides other parallels to MAD.V.8 - Egyptian, Ugaritic, Akkadian (J. & A. Westenholz: 212-16). Impressive and mysterious though this poem is, with its interplay of the unattainable and the desirable /50/, its violation of the ancestral garden /51/, and its maternal pathos /52/, the comparison remains very general. Another analogue, suggested by Cooper, is "The Message of Ludingira to his Mother", a highly self-conscious and widely distributed /53/ Sumerian composition of the 2nd millenium, because of its extended metaphors for the mother, the brilliance of the imagery, and its remoteness from any conceivable descriptive utility for the messenger who is thereby supposed to recognise her. One "metallic" sign is compared to the Song 5.10-16; another to the garden in 4.12-5.1. Nevertheless, it lacks the distinctive dissection of the body in the "wasf", an omission not to be accounted for by modesty /54/, and some of Cooper's parallels are unconvincing /55/; besides, a formal letter to one's mother is inherently different from a love poem. The Song of Songs is freer, more intimate, and varied in style. The technical skill and virtuosity of metaphor which they share, as well as some of the material, does however suggest one of its components.

Finally, a structural similarity has been proposed with "The Divine Love Lyrics from Babylon" (Lambert 1959: 7). This is difficult to substantiate, since these are so fragmentary; with their mixture of abuse and praise, solemnity and satirical farce, they are compelling and inscrutable. Certainly the verbal viciousness of the rival goddesses, socially realistic and cathartic as it may be, is very far from the idyllic loves of the Song /56/.

Superficial correspondences with Hellenistic poetry /57/ are likewise few, and can be readily explained as part of a common core of imagery and experience. The knock-about worldliness and discursive techniques of Theocritus are vastly dissimilar to the Song. Yet there is an underlying affinity of pressure and attitude, as if the same forces are operant, though in different forms. One remembers, for instance, that along with Theocritus and Virgil, the Song is a shaping influence on the European Pastoral (Kermode 1970: 35), giving it a religious and liturgical dimension, as well as a stock of images and allusions. I hesitate to call it Pastoral - or indeed to assign it to any genre - especially since it is not literally bucolic; its focus is on the court, and there are urban episodes. Besides, Pastoral did not yet exist (Berg: 25). But there are unquestionably Pastoral episodes, which I will discuss at greater length in chapter Three. In particular, there is the critical reflection on the sophisticated city through reference to the country, which is partly idealised, imagined as a purer and healthier existence. It is combined with a myth of the Golden Age, whether that of Solomon's kingdom, of the Fourth Eclogue, or of Arcadia. Therein, love

Chapter One - Introduction

is the dominant inspiration; song and physical beauty are combined in a celebration that is inherently wistful. It is as if civilisation is returning to its roots, initially indeed as a "novelty" - as Theocritus' Doric was alien to his audience - and then, in Virgil and thereafter, as a controlled artlessness, imbuing the metropolis with the vitality of the country, matching the Mantuan past with the Roman present, for example by projecting Virgil's patrons into the rustic landscape.

The Song, with its liaison between king and country girl, its fertilisation of city by country, conforms then to the Pastoral impulse; as Müller remarks, the urban episodes, and the familiarity with the court, suggest a civil rather than a rural composition /58/. From its aureate diction and wide geographical horizons one may suppose a cultivated audience, with a taste for exquisite words, and a highly-developed poetic vocabulary, drawn from many sources. The sophistication of the Song is now recognised by most commentators /59/. But it is a sophistication that, like the classical Pastoral, uses simplicity as one of its modes or resources; among the allusions there may be echoes of folksongs. This is perhaps clearest, at least most often perceived, in the folkloristic associations of the rhyme of the little foxes in 2.15 /60/.

One sign of the late date and sophistication of the Song is the number of literary styles with which it works. This is not explicable, in my view, by a multitude of sources; it is the conscious absorption, seldom noticed, of a particular manner to make a rhetorical point. We will find repeatedly in the coming pages evocations - though rarely direct quotations - of the whole range of literary forms in the Bible, with the exception of prose narrative - prophetic, parabolic, legalistic, didactic, mythographic. As Barthes and Derrida have insistently argued, literature is constituted of codes /61/. What is impressive in the Song is the individual relation to those codes, that are changed by its voice; to refer to another currently influential critic, Harold Bloom (6ff.), the Song is "a strong poem", in other words an interpretation of previous poems that cannot but misread them. The fallacy of Bloom's approach is the assumption that poems are simply interpretations; they have no mind of their own. It is not that the Song necessarily misreads its sources; it is at liberty to differ from them. Each reference is an oblique comment on the literary tradition, as part of the world the Song inhabits. This is characteristic of a late work, as well as of an educated writer; only when a style has been formed, is part of literary history, can its values be questioned.

In seeking to put the Song on the cultural map, we should inquire as much within the Biblical tradition as to parallels in other languages, particularly since the cultural map does not exist. All the comparisons, even that with Classical Pastoral, are faute-de-mieux; for the great bulk of ancient Oriental love poetry, especially from the period of the Song, has disappeared. For example, nothing survives of ancient Persian love-poetry, whose influence is thus incalculable, but may have been equal to that of Hellenistic culture /62/. Equally distressing is the loss of the entire native erotic tradition. Of this all that remains is the snatch of a love song in Isaiah 5.1: " ʾāšîrâ nāʾ lîdîdî šîrat dôdî lekarmô kerem hāyâ lîdîdî beqeren ben-šāmen" "Now will I sing to my beloved, a song of my beloved to his vineyard; my beloved had a vineyard in Qeren-ben-Shamen", which is very close to "Solomon had a vineyard in Baal-Hamon" in 8.11. Thus, if my dating is correct, the Song uses a stock of poetic conventions at least four centuries old, not only in technique but also in phraseology. Indeed, since Isaiah is clearly using a universally familiar formula for rhetorical effect, it was presumably much older. Likewise, the reference to "šîr kesîlîm" "the song of fools" in Eccl 7.5 (see also Prov 25.19) suggests that there were songs available for fools; when the topic of wine is exhausted, they generally sing of love. The subject matter of folk poetry is very limited. However, this does not mean that the Song was folk poetry, nor that it was a collection of lyrics. Ancient poets had no notion of copyright. What it does mean is that it draws on ancient resources; furthermore that the whole of the erotic lyric tradition had gone into its making. R. Akiba's "day" when the Song was given to Israel encompasses a whole history. In this respect, of course, it is like all literature; there is no book that does not work with multiple echoes.

That love songs were capable of being allegorised is clear from Isaiah's parable /63/; what connotations they acquired during the Biblical period is quite imponderable. Both Goitein (1957: 310-14) and Rabin (1973: 217), for example, are of the opinion that there was a tradition of mystical love poetry, and that even in the Solomonic period the Song communicated an image of divine love, citing the examples of Islamic and Tamil poetry. The latter, Rabin thinks, directly influenced the Song. Another scholar, C. Schedl, who considers the Song to be late, argues that it is an early

Chapter One - Introduction

Kabbalistic poem, whose sonorous, beguiling surface conceals a magic symbolism, an allusive depth, visible only to the adept, full of gematrias and numerological symmetries, like Orphic poetry or Virgil's Eclogues /64/. His illustrations are fascinating but unconvincing; at all events, for an outsider such as myself it is the captivating surface that is of lasting value. Any esoteric significance the Song may originally have had is no longer part of its message, beyond the terms of critical reference. What is possible is to consider the potential audience of the Song, in other words how it may have been received, and its inherent symbolism.

If the Song is a Pastoral, we must suppose an appreciative and readily responsive public. The provincialism of Jerusalem has perhaps been greatly exaggerated. Certainly there were wealthy families /65/; there were "paradeisoi" in the Jordan valley producing balsam /66/, and the cultivation of gardens was encouraged by the possibly recently introduced technique of artificial irrigation (cf. 4.12-5.1) /67/. Thus the luxury of the Song was by no means anachronistic; there were courts, such as those of the Oniads or Tobiads, where exquisite poetry may have been patronised, and at the very least leisured and literate classes /68/. Greek education penetrated these circles very early, testifying to an openness to international intellectual currents, concomitant with political contacts, that probably preceded the Hellenistic era. Educated circles in ancient Israel were limited; the aristocracy, the priesthood, and the Wisdom schools were not yet - and never entirely - dissociated /69/. Moreover, it was an age of extreme cross-fertilisation, from Greece to India, to which a cultivated and enterprising man would have access, mediated, for example, through the Diaspora and through trade and military service, despite religious parochialism. H. P. Müller has commented on the Song as a hedonistic and magical response to political insignificance; to which I add the nostalgic evocation of past greatness and an implicit questioning of its value. Both the Song of Songs and Ecclesiastes relate, in part ironically, to the Wisdom tradition; in the case of the Song this is widely recognised /70/. Both perform the same task, and use the same symbolic figure, the type of the most fortunate man, as a means for testing the worth of limitless wisdom, power and pleasure. Ecclesiastes negates all the warmth and wonder of the Song; in it Wisdom declares itself folly, and exhausts itself in contradiction. In the Song, too, as I will argue, everything is vanity - except love. The Song supplants the one term which if not literally missing cannot quite be accommodated in Ecclesiastes. For according to the Song love alone is as strong as death; it is greater than every pleasure and all political power. The insidious irony that accompanies every reference to Solomon's realm does not apply to the love of the lovers. Here again Wisdom is turned against itself. For the Song uses the techniques of the Wisdom tradition - careful comparison, the classification of experience, exploring and seeking to understand the world - in order to expose its values. If Wisdom, with its love of moderation, was implacably hostile to incautious alliances, the Song counsels abandonment, the submergence of consciousness in bliss, as the only human resource. As a surreal poem, it has a transcendent function, dissolving the boundaries between people, and between them and the world, abolishing mortality for a timeless moment. Surrealism is a return to innocence, and absolute freedom. As we shall see, it also unites man and God.

The 4th-3rd centuries generally were a period of disillusion, in which the hedonistic escape of the Pastoral combined with the profound questioning of values /71/. One is reminded oddly of Plato. For Plato, as for Ecclesiastes, everything was vanity, except for the ideal Forms; by contemplating them, freeing himself from the world, a man could transcend himself. The Song could be seen as an anti-Platonic statement, with its love of the material world, except that it too is a vision of absolute beauty and goodness, it too presents a reality over and against the illusions of the world. Plato would have banned the Song from his Commonwealth; and yet, like the Pastoral, the Song shares the same experience, the same passion, turning away from the world to create a garden, peripatetic or sensual, in which the mind meditates on the ideal, the one working through inference, abstracting the idea of beauty from beautiful things, the other through metaphor, through which all things are expressed and absorbed in the love of the lovers.

In considering then the way the Song was appropriated by its audience, we should beware of a unitary approach: it would strike different ears diversely, it would perform different functions in society. It may well have been sung at weddings, but this would not preclude other uses; there is no evidence that the Song is primarily an epithalamium /72/, and, as Gollwitzer (29-30) has argued forcibly /73/, insistence that it celebrates respectable married love has little textual support. Likewise, the matrix of the theory that it is based on

Chapter One - Introduction

a pagan fertility rite is the assumption, prevalent among Old Testament scholars, that sacred texts must originate in the cult /74/; and is founded for the most part on nothing more than a set of very odd and very general parallels; Schmidt's criticism of its most influential formulation has yet to be rebutted. Pope's recent attempt to buttress the theory through comparison with "marzēaḥ" feasts rests on a false syllogism: the Song opposes love and death; love songs were (perhaps) sung at funeral wakes; therefore the Song emanates from ritual mourning /75/. Nevertheless it did and does have its liturgical function, connected always with fecundity: whether of courtship, in the dances of the 15th Ab - its first recorded ceremonial usage (M. Taanit 4.8) - or of nature, in the spring festival of Passover, or in the induction of the Sabbath, conceived of by the Kabbalists as a mystical marriage /76/. But these are clearly applications of an already existent (and already allegorised) text; they do not explain its original context.

We may suppose, first of all, an aesthetic value: the Song presupposes an appreciation of beauty in the audience, verbal as well as physical, and indeed transports the audience into the world of the Song, as the circle of friends listening to the Beloved in the garden of 8.13. As with courtly Pastoral, it entertains the listeners and induces relaxation and self-forgetfulness, corresponding to the rural retreat that is its principal metaphor. The extraordinary literary sensitivity and philosophic intensity of the period is testified both by the quality of the literature that has survived /77/, and by the title that was given the Song, if it is an editorial rubric, implying that it was valued and preserved precisely because it was the Song of Songs, because of its unsurpassed sensual and lyric beauty.

It suggests, through the Solomonic attribution, that love too is subject to philosophic reflection. We have already explored an aspect of this, the comparison with Ecclesiastes. The correlation with Wisdom literature has been made most recently and conclusively by Brevard Childs, who considers that thereby it entered the canon, for example as an exegesis of the climactic mystery of Prov 29.19: "wederek geber beʿalmâ" "The way of a man with a maid" (cf. J. B. White: 133). Childs contends that it is not human love per se that is celebrated, but Wisdom, and sanctioned love, as part of human experience, arguing from silence, from the absence of permissiveness in the Old Testament. In so doing he misses the mischievous antithesis, between the sensual love song and the rest of the Bible, that has been largely responsible for its fascination, its perennial shock to bourgeois complacence. It is this paradoxical quality - that it is part of yet contradicts the canon - that links it with its literary context. The Song is no more daring or subversive of orthodox assumptions than Job and Ecclesiastes; even Proverbs has its dialectical, self-critical moments /78/. Each of these is complementary, represents a different aspect of the radical critique of Wisdom, the philosophic affinity that most impressed contemporary Greek observers /79/. Comparison can also be made on points of detail. Proverbs expresses society's ambivalence towards love. If the lovers in the Song fear shame, that shame is expressed most forcibly by Proverbs. In contrast to the joy in creation and in sexuality in the Song and in God's speech from the whirlwind, we have Job's puritanical self-vindication in ch. 31, that he has never gazed on a virgin or on the lovely moon passing /80/. Ecclesiastes toys with hedonism. We can look outside the Wisdom tradition too. Both Ruth and Esther are as it were practical illustrations of the Song: Ahasuerus is the king who would give up half his kingdom for love. As in the Song, we have a satire on the pretensions and folly of human power. In these works we have a synthesis of openness and insularity, nostalgic devotion and intellectual daring that would never recur, and that ensured the continued creativity of the Torah /81/.

As I have already remarked, the aristocracy, the Sages, and the guardians of the tradition were not yet dissociated /82/. A few generations later the tension became too great; the division of society resulted in impassable literary chasms. No longer would Sages from the four corners of the earth debate interminably and uncompromisingly in the land of Uz. In the literature of the period we find traces of or responses to all the prevailing philosophical currents - Stoicism, Cynicism, Epicureanism /83/ - and some of its imagery (e.g. the Garden of Epicurus), by which I do not mean to suggest anything so unsubtle as "influence" or literary borrowing. There is abundant evidence of contact with Greek thought and culture, of a creative interaction, both diachronically, with the ancient wisdom tradition, and with the Hellenistic present. This sympathy, compatible with fidelity, is its greatest gift to us. The Pastoral, that fugitive artificial vision of simplicity, with its intense and compassionate irony, was perfectly realised in the three great capitals of late antiquity - Rome, Alexandria, Jerusalem. Geopolitically,

Chapter One - Introduction

Jerusalem, at the imaginative centre of the Song, can hardly compare with its associates, unless we remember its symbolic status, as the joy of all the earth, and its legendary Solomonic glory. Therewith we come to its spiritual significance.

The truest evidence comes from within the poem, and to an exegesis of this I shall devote my book. My contention, briefly put, is that as Wisdom literature the Song inquires into and expresses the nature of love and therefore of man, with a profundity and compression that has rarely been equalled, and in ancient times perhaps only by Sappho. It addresses the human task "lidrôš welātûr baḥokmâ ʿal kol-ʾašer naʿaśâ taḥat haššāmāyim" "to seek and to inquire through wisdom into all that is done under the heavens" (Eccl 1.13), but with joy, that sees everything beautiful in its time (Eccl 3.11). But it also has implications beyond itself, connotative ramifications, in particular involving all the paradoxes and perplexities of Jewish existence. The poem has its nationalistic element, as an idealised portrait of the land of Israel, but in relation to the world; likewise it focusses on the political issue of the monarchy, the alienation of man and the earth, innocence and self-consciousness. As with contemporary poetry, I suggest that it has its self-referential aspect: its subject is the human voice, the possibilities and insufficiency of language /83/. In my last chapter I trace its ambiguous correlation with what I consider to be the central myth in the Bible, that of the loss of Paradise. Finally, like the other Pastoral poems, its is a mystical endeavour, an act of imaginative transcendence, conjoining man and God in the work of creation.

Structure and Unity

The question of the unity of the Song is less crucial than it might seem; one might plausibly consider it to be a collection of very varied provenance, and yet to have a certain generic coherence. Moreover, the question lends itself to confusion between the reader and the poet. One may argue, as does D. J. A. Clines in The Theme of the Pentateuch, that the finished work is more than the sum of its components; that its objective unity on the page, in the eyes of all readers known to us, is a fact of greater import than its hypothetical origins; likewise, we can maintain, with the so-called deconstructionists, that poetic unity is imputed by the reader as much as implanted by the writer. For this reason critics should specify whether they are merely recording their own reaction to the text or inferring from that the author's existence or intentions, a caveat compounded by our awareness of the multiplicity of an author's voices, that every text, especially an ancient one, is the product of a tradition as well as an individual, a complex of quotation and comment, a redaction as well as a new creation. A critic, if he is honest, will pursue correlations and differences as far as they will go, guided however by an inherent tendency towards synthesis, and a presupposition fostered by tradition and the "found unity" on the page.

A further source of confusion is that no critic defines what he means by "poetic unity", an omission that one begins to suspect reflects a certain lapse of the inquiring spirit. Thus the only irrefutable ground for rejecting the unity of the Song, that it lacks logical sequence, rests on a false premise, namely that logical sequence is an indispensable requirement of lyric poetry.

We may accept, with Plato, that organic unity consists of a relationship of the whole to the parts /85/, of which the relationship of the parts to each other is a corollary. From this point of view, the central idea - the head, as Plato calls it - of the Song is clear: it is its vision of love. Insofar as every part of the Song contributes to that vision, it is a unified poem. But it must be emphasised that such unity will only be partial and provisional, since every poem consists of words that are differentiated from each other, every poem is a unity in multiplicity. Moreover, it may be granted to sceptical critics that the Song is an exceptionally difficult poem; it is hard to fathom why one sequence follows another. Disjunction however pervades every level of the poem: the violent conjunction of scenes is reflected in the clash of disparate images. Critics who break up the Song into brilliant fragments are still left with the problem of the fragments. I shall argue in my second chapter that the difficulty of the Song is a necessary consequence of the irreducibility of its subject matter. Stephen Prickett's words are applicable:

> It is simply not possible, in the words of the Preface to the Good News Bible, "to use language that is natural, clear, simple, and unambiguous" about something that is as complex and mysterious as human religious experience. (1981: 114)

Jakobson, in a famous formulation, defines the poetic function as follows: "The poetic function projects the principle of equivalence from the axis of selection to the axis

Chapter One - Introduction

of combination. Equivalence is promoted to the constitutive device of the sequence" (1960: 358). In other words, poetry is not a linear progression; each moment has an element of recurrence, such as metre, rhyme, parallelism. The equivalences across the sequence produce multiple meanings: one word is, as it were, heard underneath the other; in Jakobson's telling phrase, "anything sequent is a simile" (1960: 371). Moreover, correlations develop between different linguistic levels: according to Jakobson again, "words similar in sound are drawn together in meaning" (1960: 371). We must seek organic unity in the dynamic relation of all the parts, i.e. all the linguistic functions, to each other and to the whole, as they all contribute simultaneously to the movement of the poem. Aristotle did a grave disservice to poetics and in particular to critics of the Song by confining organic unity to the level of mythos or plot /86/. But there is a further point: the necessary ambiguity means that the poetic unity does not imply a single truth or meaning; it is commonly a counterpoint of stories and messages. In my third chapter, I will relate this characteristic of the Song to the drama of the aesthetic process, i.e. the assertion of control over instinctual energy.

The Song can perhaps best be categorised as an extended lyric, almost a contradiction in terms, which certainly accounts for some of the difficulties. Lyric poetry, as Northrop Frye has pointed out, is a discontinuous form (1975: 272), whose basic unit is the stanza or strophe, linked to others through association of sound or metaphor, and over great distances. Critics who complain that the Song is episodic, or lacks a clear outline, would in fact prefer it to be a novel, with the continuity of prose. For this reason Rudolph (100) is quite right in arguing that the conjunction of the originally in his view independent lyrics through coincidence of sound is a perfectly valid principle of organisation, though wrong in thinking that it is strange to us.

Especially in lyric poetry, stanzaic forms are often very complex and conventional, with only an uncertain relation to content. If the poem is unified by its voice and vision, its shaping structure presents the poem to us as play - or as Frye (1957: 278) aptly puts it, as doodle. The element of contrivance is in creative conflict with the intensity of feeling. More important, as well as generating semantic correlations, the play is self-justifying, its gratification corresponding to the musical play of sounds, the physical base of the poem. Both then, as well as contributing to coherence, distract attention from it, through abstraction and sensuality. As well as collaboration, the subversion of unity through the contradictory claims of different levels is integral to the poetic process.

Structure implies a centre, an organising principle. But the centre, as Derrida (1978: 278) points out, is never in the poem. The love of the lovers cannot be consummated there; its voice and feeling cannot be formulated in language. Instead we have gestures towards that centre, and the play of words that are always differentiated from each other. The unity of the poem is thus beyond the poem, as well as central to it.

Critical opinion is fairly equally divided between those who think the Song to be an anthology of lyrics, without intrinsic connection, that have somehow fused; those who consider it a collection of songs, but with a unity at the level of redactor or composer (i.e. a "diwan"); and those who believe that it is a single poem /87/. These views are not uniform, and shade into each other; there is an astonishing variety of critical formulation /88/. None of the critics who deny that it is an entity agrees on the number of units into which to divide it; those who see it as a cycle differ as to the principle of organisation; and those who suppose its integrity do so with much diversity. The situation has been complicated in recent years, and the organic approach rendered more respectable, by the increasing awareness of the formal complexity of Biblical literature, reflecting both the willingness to give it the same attention as other literatures, and the realisation that even in narrative the principle of organisation is not on the whole sequential. One may cite, as an outstanding example, Jan Fokkelman's studies in Genesis and Samuel. The consequence of this is that no longer do critics need to feel obliged to seek unity of narrative, a procedure described by Cook (132) as resembling a "thematic apperception test":

> Still there is no necessity to confect for the action some plot more specific than in fact it offers us. The scholars who have done this, Renan and the others, act much like a psychological subject in a thematic apperception test who will produce a whole family history when shown, say, the picture of a young boy sitting in a room that a man is entering.

The only substantive grounds for considering the Song to be a unity is the density of repetition within it (Murphy 1979a: 436). If, as Jakobson proposes, poetry is characterised by

Chapter One - Introduction

equivalence, we have in the Song a profoundly poetic structure. As I have written in a previous article (Landy 1980b: 56):

> The poem is a unity, such as it is, in part because of its thematic coherence, its erotic mode; and in part because of the reappearance of the same elements in diverse contexts, as leitmotivs, refrains, episodes that repeat each other with variations, confluences of images. If the Song is characterised by manic disjunction and extraordinary imaginary flights, each leap is also a reminiscence.

In recent years the unity of the Song from this point of view has been argued most effectively by Roland Murphy /89/, though for a full exposition we eagerly await his forthcoming commentary /90/. He classifies the repetitions as i) refrains, ii) themes, and iii) isolated words and phrases - not always readily distinguishable from each other, concluding after a detailed analysis (1979a: 440):

> What needs to be recognised here is the evidence of the dramatic presentation of love-experiences that continually repeat themselves. This constitutes the argument for unity.

Similarly, if more elegantly, Albert Cook (100) describes the Song as "a patterned if unspecific sequence of action."

The principal objection to this approach is that the refrains and repetitions were part of the stock-in-trade of ancient erotic poets. Marcia Falk (1982: 65), for example, writes:

> But structural parallels are not necessary to account for the presence of these repetitions; they can also be explained by viewing the text as a collection of separate poems derived from a common cultural source. For example, the repeated images in the Song may be conventional stock, much as Petrarchan imagery was the stock of Renaissance poets.

J. and A. Westenholz (218) speak of "a common pool of ancient Near Eastern 'building blocks'," and think that therefore "the Song cannot be dated at all": a striking non-sequitur, since the use of conventional material does not imply no date of composition. Others, such as Pope (1976: 50), invoke the poetics of Ugarit, with singular disregard for difference of genre or context. As Murphy slyly notes (1979a: 436) /91/:

> What if one should urge that the unity was achieved by an editor who locked together several poems by means of these repetitions? Perhaps an adequate reply is that the original poet would have been as expert at this kind of thing ....

The assertion that these were stock conventions is in fact quite unproveable, as well as quite irrelevant. To take up Falk's analogy, Renaissance poets used traditional formulae to give unity and archetypal depth to their poems; refrains, even if they be so-called clichés /92/ - a less apposite technical term I have never encountered - cannot help but echo and reecho in a poem, with a distant resonance: they belong to the genre as well as to the poem. Form-critical analysis, as advocated, for example by J. B. White, is useful insofar as it uncovers these links; in practice, however, as Murphy remarks, it "tends to fragment the Song" (1979a: 441 n.1; cf. 1973), and to result in painfully obvious taxonomy, what Giordano-Orsini calls the "villain" of "analysis without synthesis" /93/. True literary-criticism, however, is concerned with the composition, the interaction, of traditional elements, not their isolation, as Muilenberg argued in a seminal essay (1969). White's further argument for the disunity of the Song, by analogy with the collections of Egyptian love poetry, is fallacious, since both the Cairo love songs and the Chester-Beatty cycle have been shown to have unified structures; other sequences, for example in the Harris 500 Papyrus (Derchain: 79-81) exhibit a certain continuity /94/. This does reveal, however, a common pathology of form-criticism: namely, a tendency to simplify texts, to be unaware of symbolic dimensions, to label rather than understand them.

The analysis of the repetitions in the Song would be an exhausting business, since normally we are dealing with a multitude of equivalences: the Song is an extraordinarily intricate fabric. Roman Jakobson, in several brilliant if controversial analyses, has shown that the structure of even short lyrics is often complex and multiple /95/; in the case of a long poem such as the Song the difficulties are correspondingly greater. For example, the first verse of the poem itself - "yiššāqēni minnešîqōt pîhû kî ṭōbîm dōdeykā miyyāyin" "Let him kiss me with the kisses of his mouth, for your caresses are better than wine" (1.2) - is echoed in two places: 4.10 "mah ṭōbû dōdeykâ miyyāyin" "How much better are your caresses than wine" and 8.1 "'emṣā'ăkâ bahûṣ 'essāqekâ gam lō' yabûzû lî" "I would meet you outside, I

Chapter One - Introduction

would kiss you, and none would despise me"; these in turn generate other correspondences. This brings me to another point: the equivalences need not be exact duplications, nor need they be linguistic. Structural models, for example, have been too self-consciously scientific: sticking to verifiable but superficial correspondences. For real connections are formed on a deep level, between ideas that are often only half-formulated. The logic, in lyric poetry as in dream, is that of association; we work with associative "clusters" of stories, images and phrases, variations of theme and plot, that diverge yet share a common identity. I have elsewhere described the poem as "a communications centre, finding equivalences between the most disparate objects" (Landy 1979: 515), and introduced the two essential elements in the associative process: the "syntagm" and the "paradigm". The first, "the sequence of words as they are combined to form a sequence or story", links unlike objects through contiguity (e.g. lily and apple in 2.2-3); the second, "the class from which a word is selected" links widely separated but congruent passages. For example "apple tree" (2.3) and date palm (7.8-9) both belong to the paradigm of "fruit tree", fawns and doves to that of "gentle wild creatures". By aligning the two axes, we find that "different, even distant, syntagms are ... paradigmatically related" as well as vice versa, i.e. paradigms are drawn together through contiguity.

For this reason exploration of the unity of the Song will be coterminous with this work, for structure can only be approached through content, through the patient discovery of the inner connections of images and sequences. Moreover, structural unity corresponds to and expresses outwardly the unity of action i.e. the union of the lovers, and also to the fusion through metaphor of the lovers and the world. Hence the poem is an organic whole, in which content and form are indissoluble. If, in what follows, I tend shamelessly to separate structure and content, to seek in the Song an abstract pattern - or indeed the barest outline of one - it is not because I am unaware that form arises from content, and is part of it, but because, to repeat myself, it develops autonomously, becomes a pleasure for its own sake; and because of the critical necessity of undoing what is undivided. Any schemata that follow are outside the poem, abstracted from its analysis, and thus pertinent to an introduction. Equally, the ambiguous status of structure - both autonomous (as play) and meaningful - partakes in the pervasive ambiguity of the Song, the subject of my third chapter.

Because of this the shift of emphasis in the last decade from content to form, from trying to demonstrate a unity of action to an aesthetic structural coherence, though a very positive one, has been unfruitful in the case of the Song. I may, for brevity's sake, pass over the earlier and somewhat dull work of Broadribb /96/ and Angénieux /97/, which has been treated by others; in particular, Angénieux has been criticised for his wholesale rewriting of the Song in support of his theory. Instead I should like to turn to two currently influential American rhetorical critics, Cheryl Exum and William Shea.

Of the two, Exum's article is better, to such an extent that she completely undermines her own theory. She divides the Song into six matching poems: 2.7-3.5 : 5.2-6.3; 3.6-5.1 : 6.4-8.3; and 1.2-2.6 : 8.4-14, with bridging passages between them (e.g. 4.12-5.1 foreshadows 5.2-6.3), and a recapitulation of motifs from across the poem in the last verses. Her analysis is very precise and perceptive; unfortunately she produces as many correspondences from outside the bounds of her related units as from within them. As Marcia Falk notes (1982: 66), there are no criteria for dividing the poem where she does. For instance, 2.7-3.5 is an entirely artificial construct, in which two very different episodes coexist in a supposed chiasmus, and combine together at the beginning of 5.2-6.3. Moreover, her divisions cut across well-articulated units. One example, which she does not notice, is 6.1-12; another, which she does (68), is 8.1-7.

William Shea /98/ proposes that the Song constitutes an elaborate chiasmus, with corresponding but fragmentary extremities (1.2-2.7, 8.6-14), more continuous but still mirrored intermediate sections (2.8-17, 7.11-8.5), and extensive paired central sections. It is a far less careful work, whose faults would be tedious to relate. If Exum errs through thoroughness, Shea impresses one with the singlemindedness with which he pursues his goal. The smallest correspondence in the right place is enough to produce a chiasmus (e.g. the word "kesep" "silver" in 1.8-11 and 8.11); while inconvenient echoes are totally ignored (e.g. 3.4, 8.2). The attribution of verses to speakers in the last chapter is totally bizarre, though it suits his theory; and interpretations generally are unsupported /99/. Finally, and more humanly, there is Shea's confession of failure in trying to compare, as he must, 2.1-2 and 8.6-7 /100/!

A very recent article by Edwin Webster, "Pattern in the Song of Songs", suffers from much the same defects. It is

Chapter One - Introduction

difficult to see why he divides the Song as he does, and selects correspondences between certain of his units and not others. It does, however, furnish him with a dubious acrostic: "YHUD H'M 'D YH 'HB", "Judah the Motherland again Yah loves".

It is simplest, in speaking of the structures of the Song, to start with the units of which it is composed, for, whereas the Song as a whole is exceedingly complex, they generally have a very clear and sometimes elaborate formal structure, as indeed is typical of lyric poetry. It will not be necessary to produce more than a few examples.

A. 2.8-17 קוֹל דּוֹדִי הִנֵּה־זֶה בָּא מְדַלֵּג
9 עַל־הֶהָרִים מְקַפֵּץ עַל־הַגְּבָעוֹת: דּוֹמֶה דוֹדִי לִצְבִי אוֹ לְעֹפֶר הָאַיָּלִים הִנֵּה־זֶה עוֹמֵד אַחַר כָּתְלֵנוּ מַשְׁגִּיחַ מִן־
י הַחֲלֹּנוֹת מֵצִיץ מִן־הַחֲרַכִּים: עָנָה דוֹדִי וְאָמַר לִי קוּמִי
11 לָךְ רַעְיָתִי יָפָתִי וּלְכִי־לָךְ: כִּי־הִנֵּה הַסְּתָיו עָבָר הַגֶּשֶׁם
12 חָלַף הָלַךְ לוֹ: הַנִּצָּנִים נִרְאוּ בָאָרֶץ עֵת הַזָּמִיר הִגִּיעַ וְקוֹל
13 הַתּוֹר נִשְׁמַע בְּאַרְצֵנוּ: הַתְּאֵנָה חָנְטָה פַגֶּיהָ וְהַגְּפָנִים
14 סְמָדַר נָתְנוּ רֵיחַ קוּמִי לָכִי רַעְיָתִי יָפָתִי וּלְכִי־לָךְ: יוֹנָתִי בְּחַגְוֵי הַסֶּלַע בְּסֵתֶר הַמַּדְרֵגָה הַרְאִינִי אֶת־מַרְאַיִךְ
טו הַשְׁמִיעִנִי אֶת־קוֹלֵךְ כִּי־קוֹלֵךְ עָרֵב וּמַרְאֵיךְ נָאוֶה: אֶחֱזוּ־ לָנוּ שֻׁעָלִים שֻׁעָלִים קְטַנִּים מְחַבְּלִים כְּרָמִים וּכְרָמֵינוּ
16
17 סְמָדַר: דּוֹדִי לִי וַאֲנִי לוֹ הָרֹעֶה בַּשּׁוֹשַׁנִּים: עַד שֶׁיָּפוּחַ הַיּוֹם וְנָסוּ הַצְּלָלִים סֹב דְּמֵה־לְךָ דוֹדִי לִצְבִי אוֹ לְעֹפֶר הָאַיָּלִים עַל־הָרֵי בָתֶר:

A (2.8) The voice of my love, behold he comes, leaping on the mountains, skipping on the hills. (9) My love is like a deer or a young gazelle, behold he is standing behind our wall, looking through the windows, peeping through the blinds. (10) My love answered and said to me:

B "Arise, my friend, my fair one, and come away.
(11) For behold the winter has passed, the rain has been and gone;

X (12) The flowers appear in the earth; the time of singing /pruning has come, and the voice of the turtledove is heard in our land.

(13) The fig tree reddens/makes redolent its young figs,

and the vines in blossom give forth their fragrance.
B' Arise, my friend, my fair one, and come away.
(14) My dove in the crannies of the rock, in the secret places of the cliff, let me see your face, let me hear your voice, for your voice is sweet and your face is lovely.
(15) Catch us foxes, little foxes, who raid vineyards - our vineyards in blossom.
(16) My love is mine, and I am his, who feeds upon the lilies.
A' (17) Until the day blows and the shadows flee, turn, my love, and be like a deer or a young gazelle on the cleft mountains.

We find then a double chiasmus, one linking the beginning and the end (A-A') of the sequence, the other enclosing the description of the spring in identical phrases (B-B') /10/. In 2.8-9 the Lover comes, and is compared to a gazelle or fawn leaping on the mountains; in 2.16-17 the same image is used of his departure, an association strengthened by the epithet "who feeds among the lilies", since in the corresponding passage in 4.5-6, it is the fawns who feed off lilies. The Lover's seduction is thus artfully highlighted by his arrival and departure, the Lover's words by the Beloved's listening. A less marked concord is between the lattices and windows through which he peeps in 2.9 and the crevices in which she is hidden in 2.14. The inset evocation of the spring turns literally on a so-called Janus-parallelism: "'ēt hazzāmîr higgîa'" "The time of pruning/singing has come", that through the ambiguity "zāmîr" = pruning/song complements both the preceding "hannişşānîm nir'û bā'āreṣ" "The flowers appear in the earth" (i.e. when the vines are pruned in February) and the following "qôl hattôr nišmaʻ be'arṣēnû" "The voice of the turtle dove is heard in our land" as a specification of birdsong (Cyrus Gordon 1978: 59-60). Thus the voices of the lovers merge in that of the spring:

```
        Beloved             A
   Lover              B
 impersonal spring         (turtledove, flowers)
   Lover              B'
        Beloved             A'
```

Both the metaphor and the cohesion of the passage are tightened by the substructure, that links the centre to the periphery, and integrates the two remaining verses into the total composition. The voice of the turtle dove in 2.12 is

Chapter One - Introduction

identified with that of the Beloved as dove in 2.14; "and the vines in blossom [semādar]" in 2.13 is recalled in "our vineyards in blossom [semādar]" in 2.15 /102/. We thus have the following structure:

A	2.8-9 = 2.16-17	Lover comes like gazelle or young fawn on mountains
B	2.10 = 2.13b	"Arise, my love, my fair one, and come away."
X	2.12	Janus parallelism "zāmîr": Description of spring
c	2.14 = 2.12	the <u>voice</u> of the turtle <u>dove</u>
d	2.13a = 2.15	the vines in blossom (semādar)
B'	2.13b = 2.10	"Arise, my love, my fair one, and come away."
c'	2.14 = 2.12	my <u>dove</u> ... let me hear your <u>voice</u> DOVE
d'	2.15 = 2.13a	our vineyards in blossom (semādar) FOXES
A'	2.16-17 = 2.8-9	Lover turns like gazelle or young fawn on mountains FAWNS

B. 6.2-12

This passage too is a perfect chiasmus. I have already analysed its structure as follows (1979: 518):

6.2-3 = 6.11-12		The Lover's descent to the garden - inaccessible
	6.4 = 6.10	Comparison with terrestrial capitals, concluding "terrible as constellations."
	Wasf 6.5-7 4.1-3	Beloved too dazzling
	6.8-9	Her brilliant uniqueness
	6.10 = 6.4	Comparison with celestial rulers, concluding "terrible as constellations".
6.11-12 = 6.2-3		The Lover's descent to the garden - surprised by love.

As in 2.8-17, the central section is divided into two; and likewise, there is a bridging link between it and the periphery, the unusual qualifier "bārâ" "choice, splendid" that couples 6.9 to 6.10. In turn this might reflect the dazzling eyes of 6.5a /103/.

Circularity characterises most of the longer sequences of the Song; and indeed it is a pervasive feature of Hebrew poetry. The last verse of an episode commonly reflects the first, e.g. "hinnāk yāpâ ra'yātî ... kullâk yāpâ ra'yātî" "Behold, you are beautiful, my love (4.1) ... you are altogether beautiful, my love" (4.7). "Mah-dôdēk middôd hayyāpâ bannāšîm" "What is your love more than another, O fairest among women" (5.9) is answered in "zeh dôdî wezeh rē'î benôt yerûšālāim" "This is my love and this is my friend, O daughters of Jerusalem" (5.16). Sometimes the last verse summarises all the images of the preceding sequence (e.g. 5.1); at other times there is a unity of action, such as 3.1-4, where the Beloved's odyssey ends where it began; or an enigma and its solution (3.6-11); or paronomasia e.g. 7.11-14, which begins "lekâ dôdî nēṣē'" "Come, my friend, let us go out" and concludes "dôdî sapantî lāk" "My love, I have stored up for you", with inversion of "NēṢē'" in "ṢāpaN" and repetition of "lekâ" "go" in "lāk" "for you". We shall meet chiasmus constantly as we investigate extended passages closely /104/. However, chiasmus is not characteristic of the extremities of the Song, 1.1-2.7 and 8.8-14, where the units are too small. Nor is it evident in the second dream sequence 5.2-7, precisely because the action there forbids the expected closure, nor - another short sequence - in 7.8-10. Here there is perhaps only the complementarity of the two voices, the Lover's hypothetical excitement in 7.8-10, concluding in "wehikkēk keyēn haṭṭōb" "And your palate like fine wine", being quenched by the reciprocal flow of the Beloved's wine and that voice in 7.10b.

Alongside chiasmus, with its static balance of forces, each passage generates a dramatic tension, a diachronic pressure, that is released at its climax. Thus 3.1-4 concludes with the success of the Beloved's search, 3.6-11 with the celebration of Solomon's wedding, that answers the initial question; 4.12-5.1 with the entry into the garden. 2.8-17 likewise ends with the Lover's parting, coupled with the assertion of their indissoluble unity, "My love is mine, and I am his, who feeds among the lilies". The wasfs are more difficult, since they are defensive displacements of desire; they attempt to freeze the object, to capture it in its perfection; the dramatic energy goes into this unavailing effort. However, the two complete portraits, 7.2-7 and 5.10-16, do in fact have a

Chapter One - Introduction

logical conclusion: in 7.6 "melek ʾāsûr bārehātîm" "A king caught in tresses"; in 5.16, the answer to the daughters' original question. The other wasf, 4.1-7, breaks off after the breasts, leaving a sense of frustration, as in a partial striptease.

Chiasmus, joining the end to the beginning, suggests a unity in time, a perfectly achieved tableau, precariously balancing the elements, and yet within it there is movement, a repeated sexualised explosion of energy. This paradoxical counterpoint, the free perception of order and timelessness when time is at its most insistent, is common to all consummate art. The catharsis and enclosure, however, separate the units from each other: each is a single movement and a complete entity; each is a new beginning. At this point it is not so much the unity of the Song that is in question, as its restlessness; it is not satisfied with any conclusions. Hence one scene is followed by a contrasting scene, whose essential virtue is that it is somewhere else. The inexhaustibility of desire after every climax is evoked by the urgent repeated imperatives and questions that commonly introduce a sequence: "Behold, you are beautiful, my love, behold you are beautiful ..." (4.1); "With me from Lebanon, O bride, with me from Lebanon come" (4.8); "What is your love more than another, O fairest among women, what is your love more than another ...?" (5.9); "Whither went your lover, O fairest among women, whither turned your lover ...?" (6.1); and "Return, return, O Shulammite, return, return ..." (7.1).

C. 3.1-4

עַל־מִשְׁכָּבִי֙ בַּלֵּיל֔וֹת בִּקַּ֕שְׁתִּי אֵ֥ת שֶׁאָהֲבָ֖ה נַפְשִׁ֑י בִּקַּשְׁתִּ֖יו
וְלֹ֥א מְצָאתִֽיו׃ אָק֨וּמָה נָּ֜א וַאֲסוֹבְבָ֣ה בָעִ֗יר בַּשְּׁוָקִים֙
וּבָ֣רְחֹב֔וֹת אֲבַקְשָׁ֕ה אֵ֥ת שֶׁאָהֲבָ֖ה נַפְשִׁ֑י בִּקַּשְׁתִּ֖יו וְלֹ֥א
מְצָאתִֽיו׃ מְצָא֨וּנִי֙ הַשֹּׁ֣מְרִ֔ים הַסֹּבְבִ֖ים בָּעִ֑יר אֵ֥ת
שֶׁאָהֲבָ֖ה נַפְשִׁ֖י רְאִיתֶֽם׃ כִּמְעַט֙ שֶׁעָבַ֣רְתִּי מֵהֶ֔ם עַ֣ד
שֶׁמָּצָ֔אתִי אֵ֥ת שֶׁאָהֲבָ֖ה נַפְשִׁ֑י אֲחַזְתִּיו֙ וְלֹ֣א אַרְפֶּ֔נּוּ עַד־
שֶׁהֲבֵיאתִיו֙ אֶל־בֵּ֣ית אִמִּ֔י וְאֶל־חֶ֖דֶר הוֹרָתִֽי׃

(3.1) On my bed nightly <u>I sought him whom my soul loves</u>; <u>I sought him</u> and <u>did not find him</u>.
(2) Let me arise now and <u>go round about the city</u>, in the streets and squares, <u>I will seek him whom my soul loves</u>; <u>I sought him</u> and <u>did not find him</u>.
(3) <u>They found me</u>, the watchmen who <u>go round</u>

about the city. "Have you seen him whom my soul loves?"
(4) Hardly had I left them than I found whom my soul loves; I grasped him and would not let him go until I brought him to my mother's house, the bower of the one who conceived me.

Here the chiasmus is both sustained and negated by compulsive repetition. On the one hand, we have a circular movement between two locatives: "'al-miškābî ballêlôt" "On my bed nightly" and "'el-bêt 'immî we'el-ḥeder hôrātî" "to my mother's house, to the bower of the one who conceived me", that are both the same and yet comprise a progression from restlessness to rest, from solitude to companionship. Symbolically as well as structurally the last phrase "to the bower of the one who conceived me" represents a return to origins as well as the threshold of new generation; in other words, the structure is both closed and open. The midpoint is the marked juxtaposition of "lō' meṣā'tîw / meṣā'ûnî" "I did not find him / They found me" on either side of the sentence divider of 3.2-3; it is the point of greatest alienation, when not only does the Beloved not find her lover, but she is found by the potentially hostile watchmen /105/. On both sides of this crisis we find the verb "MṢ'" "find" twice repeated: in the first half negatively ("I did not find him"), in the second half positively ("they found me / I found him"). Whereas in the first half she seeks him ineffectually, in the second she purposively asks the watchmen; when she does find him, "'aḥaztîw welō' 'arpennû" "I grasped him and would not let him go" clearly echoes and contrasts with "biqqaštîw welō' meṣā'tîw" "I sought him but did not find him" in 3.1-2. Finally, both she and the watchmen are described as those who "go round about the city", emphasising the circularity and weary repetitiveness of the whole. And yet one phrase remains constant: "'ēt še'āhabâ napšî" "he whom my soul loves", suggesting an unchanging tension between the desperate imperative ("my soul loves") and its object, and that the whole structure amounts to an identical moment. We shall encounter the counterpoint of rhythm and timelessness elsewhere in this thesis. Moreover, the repetition tends to freeze separate moments, for instance the bed and the city, to reproduce the uncanny dislocation of déjà-vu; it alternates with extreme parataxis e.g. the omission of the watchmen's answer, to disturb our sense of time, an oscillation between slow motion and suddenness that is an important component of the somnambulist effect.

Chapter One - Introduction

The parallel passage in 5.2-7 uses the technique of patterned repetition similarly though less densely, and with greater syntactic articulation. There too repetition slows time down; for instance it takes the Beloved three verses to open the door; but in contrast we have not gaps but a sudden compression of time, marked by a paratactic starkly juxtaposed sequence of verbs: "dôdî hāmaq 'ābār" "My love had gone, vanished" in 5.6; "hikkûnî peṣā'ûnî nāś'û" "They smote me, wounded me, took ..." in 5.7; suggesting, instead of the circular dream-work of 3.1-4, a harsh awakening to reality.

The structure of 3.1-4 can be summarised as follows:

A   Upon my bed nightly

B1+2   I sought him whom my soul loves;   [seeking <u>and</u>
         I sought him and did not find him.   <u>not</u> finding]

C   Let me arise now and <u>go round about the city</u>,
         in the streets and squares,

B1+2   I will seek him whom my soul loves;   [seeking <u>and</u>
         I sought him and did not find him.   <u>not</u> finding]

X

B'2   They found me,

C'   The watchmen, who <u>go round about the city</u>.

B1   "Have you seen him whom my soul loves?" [seeking]

B2   Hardly had I left them than
        I found him whom my soul loves;   [finding]

B1+2   I grasped him and would   [grasping <u>and</u>
        not let him go until I brought him   <u>not</u> letting go]

A   To my mother's house,
         to the bower of the one who conceived me

D. 7.8-10

זֹאת קוֹמָתֵךְ דָּמְתָה לְתָמָר וְשָׁדַיִךְ לְאַשְׁכֹּלוֹת:
אָמַרְתִּי אֶעֱלֶה בְתָמָר אֹחֲזָה בְּסַנְסִנָּיו וְיִהְיוּ־נָא שָׁדַיִךְ
כְּאֶשְׁכְּלוֹת הַגֶּפֶן וְרֵיחַ אַפֵּךְ כַּתַּפּוּחִים:
וְחִכֵּךְ כְּיֵין הַטּוֹב הוֹלֵךְ לְדוֹדִי לְמֵישָׁרִים דּוֹבֵב שִׂפְתֵי
יְשֵׁנִים:

A   This your height is like a date palm,
B   And your breasts like clusters.
A   I said "I will climb the palm tree,
     I will catch hold of its fronds,
B   And your breasts shall be as clusters
C   Of the vine, and the fragrance of your nose like apples,
C   And your palate like fine wine, flowing to my love smoothly, stirring the lips of sleepers.

Here, as we have seen, concentricity is minimal; there is only the exchange of the lovers' voices and fluids. Instead there is a divergent development of the single composite image, in which strategic repetition is combined with tacit displacement. The initial conceit - Beloved with breasts = date palm with clusters - is complemented at the beginning of 7.9 by the insertion of fronds in the sequence; the image of breasts can then attain independence. Their specification as clusters of <u>grapes</u> allows for a further bifurcation, the palate as wine substituted for the breasts. Thus an initially clear, tactile image, objectively distant, through a series of metaphorical sleights-of-hand becomes an image of sexual fusion, sustained, as we shall see when we come to examine the passage, by the interchange of breath implied by "werêaḥ ʾappēk kattappûḥîm" "And the fragrance of your nose like apples", and of speech, through the Beloved's words in 7.10.

The links can be summarised as follows:

Beloved + breasts = date palm + clusters
Beloved + breasts = date palm   + fronds
Beloved + breasts = date palm + clusters of grapes
Beloved + breasts = date palm + clusters of wine = palate

A similar structure is to be found in 2.15, as part of the intricate concentric unit 2.8-17, illustrating how different patterns can coexist simultaneously:

ʾeḥezû lānû šûʿalîm
    šuʿalîm qeṭannîm
        meḥabbelîm kerāmîm
           ûkerāmēnû semādar

Catch us foxes,
    foxes, little ones,
        who raid vineyards,
           our vineyards in blossom.

Here the function of the repetition is to create a light two-stress rhythm, whose very naivety, which commentators

Chapter One - Introduction

describe as folkloristic or reminiscent of nursery rhyme, reflects on the artifice of the composition /106/.

The units at the beginning and end of the Song differ from those we have discussed in being much shorter, and lacking circularity. They are not less closed structures, as we shall see in chapter 2; but the structure consists of a single reciprocal movement, as in 1.5-6 or 8.8-10; a dialogue of corresponding voices, in 1.7-8, with imitation of melodic lines; a formally perfect but mystifying riddle in 8.11-12, where each element is reconstituted, but without inversion. 8.13-14 is perhaps too fragmentary to be ascribed to any one pattern. There is only the meeting of imperatives in the middle "hašmî'înî" "Let me hear" / "beraḥ" "Flee". In 1.2-4 all the line-endings are interlinked.

The absence of chiasmus opens out each of these episodes, on one side, to the rest of the poem, and to the possibility of completion elsewhere; there is one single dramatic moment, in contrast to the division of dramatic focus in concentric units. If, for example, "mî zō'ṯ" "Who is this?" in 3.6 looks forward to "ṣe'eynâ ûre'eynâ" "Go out and look" in 3.11, here there is only the bare statement, such as "šeḥôrâ 'anî wenā'wâ" "I am black and comely" in 1.5. It presents us with the Beloved as she is outside the poem, as she is about to enter the poem, and generates a certain expectancy about her; just as the previous dramatic moment - "yiššaqēnî" "Let him kiss me" - shows us the Beloved again from outside and alone with the intensity of her desire, that directs us forward to its consummation. In each case, the immediacy of her impact fades into recollection, reflection and the anonymity of the group. She offers herself and shyly withdraws. From 1.7-8 the lovers engage with each other. The Pastoral exchange of 1.7-8 introduces the Lover, but still self-effacing, out of range of the Beloved. 1.9 is his true appearance, when the dialogue of the poem starts. All these episodes point forward to the relationship, and backward to the past; they have a liminal pathos and tension. In my view they serve to introduce, and finally allude to, the various modes of the Song, like musical subjects, e.g. court, country, pastoral. Those at the end of the Song reflect over its experience /107/. Thus in the little sister, the Beloved sees an image of herself; there is a temporal shift in the last verse, as she recalls her own success /108/. The obscure parable of the vineyard in 8.11-12 is also set in the past; and encapsulates her own history. Finally, at the end of the Song, the Beloved's voice dismisses the Lover; it looks back, and perhaps is telling of their experience to the friends "listening to her voice", and yet to him it is no longer audible; once again we are beyond the threshold.

1.9-2.7 is the only sustained dialogue of the Song, introducing the lovers to each other, and admitting us to their discourse together. The verses are short, and grouped in threes; one triad from the Lover is answered by one from the Beloved, and then they share the units, creating them between them /109/. Each of the groups moreover is constructed in the same way: 1:1+1, in other words is a couplet with a line to cap it:

1.9-11   The comparison of the Beloved to a mare, with pendants and circlets, augmented by the repetition of "tôrîm" and "nequdôt/ḥarûzîm" in 1.11

1.12-14 The lovers compared to spices, with the addition of an extra image for the Lover, syntactically parallel to 1.13 (1:1+1)

1.15-17 Mutual admiration in identical phrases (1.15-16), complemented by their surroundings (1.16b-17)

2.1-3   Exchange of images of the Beloved as flower (2.1-2) capped by one of the Lover as apple tree.

Each of these units then suggests the possibility of elaboration, rapidly cut short, a pattern of expectation and frustration. Only in 2.3 does the image of the apple tree free itself of its immediate rhetorical context, and become the subject of an extended fantasy. It thus introduces the more continuous episodes of the Song.

The structures found in individual episodes may be projected onto the Song as a whole. As Exum and Shea suggest (cf. also Goitein 1957: 298 and Murphy 1979a: 443), and as one might guess from the orientation of the fragmentary material round the coherent centre the most conspicuous feature is chiasmus, as if the poem were a long insertion between matching pieces. Chiasmus, as that which joins boundaries, is most readily discerned in the outermost sections; in other words, those that are not internally organised on that principle. Shea's attempt to see the Song as a palindrome is misguided, because there is no exact correspondence between opposite parts, but recurrence of thematic groups and circles. Nevertheless, there are concentric patterns also within the body of the poem, that direct attention towards its centre. The symmetry is disturbed by the splitting of some passages in the reprise, such as 4.1-5 in 6.5b-7 and 7.4-5, and the convergence of

Chapter One - Introduction

others. 7.12-14, for example, recalls both 1.13-14 and 2.10-13; the latter is also alluded to in 6.11.

The initial and concluding fragments not merely shape the poem, but they complete each other. They are not chiastic, but open to each other; the entire poem is thus bounded by an enormous symmetry. But this is also an inversion. Thus the poem begins with the ascription of the poem to Solomon - whether as subject, dedicatee or composer - and the Beloved's desire for his kisses; it ends with her singing in the garden, and his fruitless desire to hear. If in 1.1-5, he is enclosed in his palace or curtains, the subject of adoring attention, and she is the excluded one, the nervous stranger of 1.5, in 8.13 she is in the enclosed garden, surrounded by the listening audience, and he is excluded. Whereas in 1.7 she fears the company of his friends (ḥabēreykā), now the friends (habērîm) are her circle. The correspondences between 1.5-6, 1.7-8 and 8.8-10 and 8.11-12 are fully dealt with in my third chapter, and need not occupy us here; the movement from absence of self to fullness of self, from the Beloved as the unkept vineyard who keeps those of others to the one whose vineyard is hers to give or withhold, from the cast-out sister to the cared-for sister, provides on the one hand alternative realities - two versions or interpretations of her life - on the other a process that takes place over the poem.

The sequence and paradigm thus interact; the correspondence perceived over a vast distance is also a development, just as it is on the smaller scale of individual passages, contained within a tight construction. The same two coordinates exert contrary pressures on the poem: the one, the space of the poem, tends towards symmetry; the other, its time, moves towards climax. Hence, as in the smaller episodes, there are two structural foci: the centre and the conclusion. The centre is the space, the silence, between the consummation in the garden in 5.1 and the Beloved's awakening in 5.2; a point that, as I have said, cannot be articulated in the poem, and is marked by profound contrast. A similar point is to be found in the centre of the myth of the garden of Eden in Gen 2-3. Round this nucleus are grouped the episodes of the Song. The other focus, the climax, is the credo of 8.6-7, the message that love is as strong as death. To this conclusion all the comparisons and experiences of the Song are adduced; the Song is, so to speak, a giant syllogism. The consequence of the interaction of the two forces makes the recapitulation an intensification, that condenses previous material to complete the circle, and uses it to sustain the climax. Syntagmatically, episodes are telescoped, since only an allusion is needed to make the reference, so that the last chapters have a crowded urgency; paradigmatically, they are concentrated, quintessential state- ments of themes, reflecting the seriousness, the ultimate concerns, of the context.

The climax of 8.6-7 transcends the poem, and has no correlate within it; like the centre, that is absent from it. On either side of it, 8.8-14 corresponds to 1.1-8, while 8.1-5 encapsulates motifs from chs. 2 and 3, contiguous with the adjuration to the daughters of Jerusalem, the most prominent refrain in the Song. In the next chapter, I will look at these more closely. They may be summarised as follows:

A	2.3=8.5b	Beloved under the apple tree
c	2.6=8.3	"His left hand under my head, and his right hand shall embrace me."
d	2.7;3.5=8.4	"I adjure you, O daughters of Jerusalem, by the does and hinds of the field, do not awaken or stir up love until it please!"
B	3.1-4=8.1-2	Finding lover outside, bringing back to mother's house.
d	3.5=8.4	"I adjure you, O daughters of Jerusalem, by the does and hinds of the field, do not awaken or stir up love until it please!"
e	3.6=8.5a	"Who is this who comes up from the wilderness?"
B	8.1-2=3.1-4	Finding lover outside, bringing back to mother's house.
c	8.3=2.6	"His left hand under my head, his right shall embrace me."
d	8.4=2.7;3.5	"I adjure you, O daughters of Jerusalem, do not awaken or stir up love until it please!"
e	8.5a=3.6a	"Who is this who comes up from the wilderness?"
A	8.5b=2.3	Lover under apple tree.

[majorscules = motifs; miniscules = refrains.]

The refrains 2.6 + 2.7 (c+d) and 3.5 + 3.6a (d+e) comprise the sequence 8.3 + 8.4 + 8.5a (c+d+e), enclosed externally by the motif "under the apple tree" (A-A). The "return to

Chapter One - Introduction

the mother's house" (B-B) precedes the refrain d+e in 3.5-6a and the entire sequence c+d+e in 8.3-5a.

As we shall see when we discuss the sequence, the movement here is to bring together single images of the lovers from across the poem, to conjoin them as a pair at the moment of birth before the contention with death, a movement both from absence of self to fullness of self, for instance in 3.6 ► 8.5a, from the instance to the quasi-mythic point of origin (2.3 ► 8.5b) (cf. below, 120ff., 217ff.), all contained within a wistful fantasy. In 8.5b and 8.1 there is an inversion of roles, from Lover to Beloved:

| 1.2 he will kiss her | ► | 8.1-2 she will kiss him |
| 2.3 she is under apple tree | ► | 8.5b he is under apple tree |

the whole sequence comprising a tight chiasmus:

8.1=8.7b	"Who would give, they would not shame me"
8.1-2=8.5b	siblings suckling mother, return to matrix
8.3=8.5a	couple in each other's arms
8.4.	
8.5a=8.3	couple supporting each other
8.5b=8.1-2	lovers together at the moment of birth
8.7b=8.1	"If one were to give ... they would surely shame him"

The Beloved's invitation to the Lover to see the spring in 7.12-14 corresponds to his in 2.10-13. In 2.12 the vines in flower (semādar) give forth fragrance (nātenû rêaḥ); in 7.13-14 the vines bloom, the flowers (semādar) open, and the mandrakes give forth fragrance (nātenû rêaḥ). Characteristically, the Beloved's description is more personal; whereas the Lover dissimulates his amorous interest behind the objective sights and sounds of spring, she focusses on their participation, "We will sleep ... wake early ... look ...", culuminating in the promise "There I will give my love to you". There is a further echo of the passage 2.8-17 in 7.11, "I am my love's, and towards me is his desire", a variation of the refrain "My love is mine, and I am his" in 2.16.

7.11-14 also recalls 1.13-14 through a remarkable lexical cluster "LUN", "KPR", "KRM" occurring within a few words of each other in "nālînâ bakkepārîm naškîmâ lakkerāmîm" "Let us lodge in the villages/henna bushes, let us go early to the vineyards" (7.12-13), corresponding to "between my breasts he shall lodge [yālîn]" in 1.13b and "a cluster of henna (kōpēr) is my love to me, in the vineyards [bekarmê] of Ein Gedi" in 1.14. In 7.8-10 the phrase "wešādayik le'aškōlôt" "and your breasts like clusters" (7.8), elaborated as "your breasts like clusters of grapes" in 7.9, supplements these correspondences with two others: "between my breasts he shall lodge" (1.13) and "a cluster of henna" (1.14) /110/. In 1.13-14 we have:

1.13 ṣerôr hammōr dôdî lî bēn ŠĀDAY YĀLÎN   7.8,9; 7.12
1.14 'EŠKŌL HAKKŌPER dôdî lî BEKARMÊ 'eyn gedî
                                            7.8,9; 7.12,13

1.13 A sachet of myrrh is my love to me;
     he lodges between my breasts.
1.14 A cluster of henna is my love to me;
     in the vineyards (or plantations) of Ein-gedi.

In 7.8-10 we have:

> your breasts like clusters (7.8)
> your breasts like clusters of grapes (7.9)

and in 7.12-13:

> let us lodge in the villages/henna bushes (7.12)
> let us go early to the vineyards (7.13).

The image of the Beloved as a tree, a date palm, in 7.8, corresponds to that of the Lover as apple tree in 2.3; both inspire craving, for apples (2.5, 7.9) and other fruit (dates and grapes, 7.8-10). The relationship between the myrrh and the henna in 1.13-14, the cedar/cypresses to the green forest in 1.15-17, the lily to the apple tree in the wide world in 2.1-3, and the palm tree to the fruit and blossom (henna, vines, mandrakes) in 7.8-14 will be the subject of extensive discussion in the next chapter. I will suggest that the relationship of the lily to the apple tree in the wood in 2.1-3 corresponds to that of the spices (henna, myrrh) of 1.13-14 to the green forest with its cedars and cypresses of 1.15-17, and that the intertwining motifs converge on the protective apple tree of 8.5. Again, the movement from the beginning to the end of the poem results in an inversion of role from the apple tree as an image for the Lover to the palm tree as emblematic of the Beloved, and in both cases attention is redirected to the bed that unites them: the green couch and their houses in 1.16-17, the villages or henna bushes in 7.12, and their doors in 7.14.

Chapter One - Introduction

1.15 "Behold you are fair, my love, behold you are fair, your eyes are doves" is repeated at the beginning of the wasf in 4.1; another connection between chapter 1 and chapter 4 is the admiration and description of the neck with its necklaces in 1.10-11, 4.4 and 4.9. Furthermore, 4.10 closely resembles 1.2-4 /111/. There are very few other correspondences between the centre and periphery of the Song (only 2.16-17 // 4.5-6). However, the tightly knit structure of 1.9-2.3 and its function as a bridge between the fragmentary beginning of the song and its more extended central passages is not elsewhere duplicated. It thus contributes an element of asymmetry that should not be wished away.

So far we have found the following pattern round the climax of 8.6-7:

7.8-14 contains elements of
   i)   1.9-2.3   (lexical cluster, metaphors of trees and plants)
   ii) 2.8-17   (description of spring, refrain)

8.1-5 combines
   i)   2.3-7   (apple tree, refrains)
   ii) 3.1-6a (mother's house, refrain)

8.8-14 reconstitutes
        1.1-8   (absence of self ➤ fullness of self; cast-out sister ➤ well brought-up sister; metaphors and questions; see Ch.3 below)

Now a complication sets in. If the recapitulation is much shorter than the primary material, the concentric structure will be unbalanced /112/. Accordingly, there is an inner chiasmus, composed of much larger units, bounded by the wasfs 4.1-7 and 7.1-7, both of which celebrate the Beloved, and enclose, as the core of the chiasmus, the wasf portraying the Lover in 5.9-16. The pair of wasfs surround a pair of scenes in the garden, whose relationship will be considered in my fourth chapter. Thus an inner pair corresponds to an outer pair. However, chapters 5 and 6 comprise the central narrative of the Song /113/, in which the Beloved seeks her lover, is beaten by watchmen, appeals to the daughters of Jerusalem for assistance, describes him, and tells them that he has gone down to his garden; fading out with his account of how he was surprised by love there. Likewise, ch. 4 is a continuous sequence, as we shall see when we come to examine it. Thus syntagmatic coherence underpins paradigmatic equivalence; the anomalous passage 5.2-7 is part of a unified action. We thus have the following overlapping structure:

A	a 4.1-7	A: Wasf for Beloved	a wasf +
B	a 4.8/12-5.1	B: Consummation in garden	extended metaphor
	b 5.2-8		b narrative sequence
C	b 5.9-16	C: Wasf concerning Lover	ditto
B	b 6.1-12	B: Descent to garden	ditto
A	a 7.1-7	A: Wasf for Beloved	a wasf +
	a 7.8-10		extended metaphor

Ch. 7, moreover, parallels ch. 4; in each a wasf is followed by an extended metaphor; the static description becomes ecstatic enjoyment. This extends the central section into the conclusion, and fosters ambiguities; for example, 7.8-11 is both an appendix to the wasf and the beginning of the recapitulation. Moreover, 6.1-12 is both part of the central narrative (b) that begins with 5.2, and corresponds to the exposition of the garden in 4.12-5.1, enclosing the description of the Lover. Thus the inner chiasmus is doubly focussed, on 5.9-16 and 5.2-6.12. It displaces the centre and diffuses it. The balance is restored through two processes:

i) The shifting of emotional weight to the centre 5.1/5.2. The movement from absence of self - fullness of self which we observed in the outer segments is thus reversed. In the first garden scene the Beloved is the garden, in the second she is excluded from it; in some ways, as we shall see, 6.1-12 is a parody of it. Similarly, the dramatic focus of the narrative is on 5.2-7, after which the action peters out. Thus the emotional centre of gravity of the inner chiasmus, as distinct from the centre of its circles, spatially as well as dramatically coincides with that of the whole poem.

ii) The outer chiasmus (ch. 1.3, 7.8-14) is projected into the inner one; parts of the recapitulation are foreshadowed there. Ch. 6, in particular, is a reflex, often indirect, of the reworking of earlier material in the conclusion. We shall see in my third chapter, for instance, that 6.8-10 is a bridge between the peripheral fragments (1.5-8, 8.8-12); it also echoes and inverts 3.6-11 /114/. 6.11 is in part duplicated in 7.13, and hence corresponds to the description of the spring

Chapter One - Introduction

in 2.10-13; while 6.3 is a permutation of the refrain "My beloved is mine, and I am his, who feeds among the lilies" in 2.16, and is recalled in 7.11. Finally, the wasf of 4.1-5 is split and distributed between chs. 6 and 7; 4.1-3 recurs almost verbatim in 6.5-7, while 4.4-5 reappears in 7.4-5. Thus 6.3 corresponds to 7.11, 6.5b-7 to 7.4-5, and 6.11 to 7.13. 2.8-17 is recollected in 6.3 (= 2.16) and 6.11 (= 2.10-13), 4.1-3 is repeated in 6.5b-7, while there is an echo of 3.6-11 in 6.8-10. Between 2.8-17 and 3.6-11 the missing intermediary is the dream sequence of 3.1-5, whose correlate is 5.2-8. The relationship of ch.6 to ch.7, and ch.3 to ch.5 (& 6) gives internal cohesion to the Song.

The sequence of the Song is generally very simple: it is a series of contrasts. The wooing of the Beloved in 2.8-17 with the sights and sounds of spring contrasts with her nocturnal wanderings in the city (3.1-5), and again with Solomonic splendour (3.6-11). The public wedding is followed by (and implicitly matched against) the intimate formality of the portrait (4.1-7), and the celebration in the garden (4.8-5.1). The Lover's disappearance and the Beloved's humiliation (5.2-7) are compensated for by the amplitude of his description (5.10-16), and the sympathy of the daughters of Jerusalem (6.1). And so on. Parallels develop between contrasting sequences; for instance, the public celebration of the wedding at the end of ch. 3 corresponds to the consummation in the garden at the end of ch. 4. For this reason, perhaps, Albert Cook speaks of the Song as "a patterned if unspecific sequence of action" (100), illustrating it with the parallels between the watchmen and the warriors, and the nocturnal setting of 3.1-4 and 3.6-11 /115/. In other words, he sees configuration in terms of similarity of image or setting. I see it more as a ritual of courtship, in which a formalised gesture from one lover (e.g. an invitation to a walk in the country in 2.10-13) elicits an appropriate response from the other (e.g. ambiguous demurral in 2.16-17). Overture characteristically meets withdrawal, frustration provokes excitation. The lovers pursue each other across the poem, elusive but in touch, changing roles, parting and converging. Thereby they partake of a rhythm, the shared pulse that is the subject of all erotic poetry. The Song consequently resembles the ritual courtship of dance; it would make good ballet.

This directs us to another level on which it is ritual: that of performance. The Song is very conscious of its audience, sometimes hypostatised as the daughters of Jerusalem. This becomes clear if we look at the pattern of rhetorical stances. For example, the Beloved looks at herself objectively in 5.2-7, as if the events happened in a dream, or to someone else: only in 5.8 does the narrative authority break down in stylised hysteria, to be transposed into another mode, that of formal description (5.10-16). In 3.6-11, to give another example, the curiosity and wonder of the question "who is this?" is complemented by the satisfaction of knowing the answer; in the following exposition of the construction of the palanquin, the poet's stance as chronicler of the more abstruse past leaves us unprepared for his sudden return to the present in 3.11, as the instigator of demonstrations of spontaneous joy.

The conative function /116/ is thus split between the audience and the lovers: each word is heard and overheard (Jakobson 1960: 371). As its hypothetical setting, the Song projects a circle of spectators, of which we are part, watching a pair of lovers. Narration, a reenactment, solely addressed at the audience from outside the experience, alternates with urgent imperatives, inviting audience participation (e.g. "sammekûnî bāʲašîšôt rappedûnî battappûhîm" "Stay me with raisin-cakes, refresh me with apples" [2.3]). Gestures too, such as the pervasive imperatives that express the fantasy of omnipotent control, have a self-referential, symbolic function, that leaves the other his essential freedom. They are all part of the performance. The poem oscillates between imperatives and quiet exposition, typical moments in the game of lovers.

In the next chapter, I will examine the sequences leading to the centre and climax. Both are initiated by images of the lovers as siblings (4.8ff., 8.1), in both I suggest that the process towards sexual union is correlated with birth and the encounter with death. Climax and centre thus correspond; the union of lovers unites also the contraries of love and death, order and chaos. The sole lexical correspondences of 8.6-7, from its preface 8.6a, are with 4.8-5.1. "The seal on the heart" recalls the sealed garden of 4.12, and the unique denominative "libbabtinî" "You have ravished my heart" in 4.9. Both centre and climax are isolated in the poem, constructing it between them, along syntagmatic and paradigmatic axes, through their tense opposition. But this is also a powerful attraction. The organic unity of the Song, its union of opposites, is also that of the centre and climax, in the same act. The pause when the lovers meet is the point of articulation of, and the evidence for, its moment of transcendence, symbolised in 8.6 by the flame of God, a divine flow.

CHAPTER TWO

THE RELATIONSHIP OF THE LOVERS

Chapter Two

THE RELATIONSHIP OF THE LOVERS

Voy por tu cuerpo como por el mundo

I go through your body as through the world
(Octavio Paz: Piedra del Sol)

dein goldenes Haar Margarete
dein aschenes Haar Sulamith

your golden hair Margarete
your ashen hair Shulamit
(Paul Celan: Todesfuge)

1. Introduction: Character and Archetype

T the centre of the Song there is a relationship, of which critics have almost nothing to say. It appears as if the relationship of the lovers is not problematic; they are an idyllic couple, of whom nothing can be said, except perhaps to lay a tribute. The lovers are left to their privacy, and to the page they can never leave. Perhaps, though, there is a corresponding objective difficulty: the lovers are not distinct personalities. Old-fashioned character analysis is singularly unproductive. Hence the expenditure of energy on constructing a coherent story, out of which the figures of the lovers will emerge more clearly. However, anecdotal curiosity, the vicissitudes of a particular couple, is but a displacement of the problem of love per se, that threatens to become too personal. We identify with the lovers, who exhaust the possibilities of love. This is the function of the multiple conflicting stories, to make them types of lovers, rather than single persons, a cumulative eidetic portrait. But herein also the Song is faithful to lovers. For lovers are among the most archetypal of human beings. In love, man and woman perform their parts in myth and romance, becoming most elementally human and intensely symbolised; for this

reason love easily lapses into cliché. And yet - and here lies a difficulty - we should beware of treating them simply as archetypes. At all points there is a discourse between the specific and the collective, individuality is constantly on the verge of expression. The question then is of the individuality of lovers as they emerge from the background: the tension between the specific locality and incident and the universal context.

Yet the lovers are only images of the poet, his fictions, his reflections of experience. They have no existence outside the poem, and its impression on the world. This banal truth would not be worth saying except as a prophylactic gesture against the Pathetic Fallacy, mistaking literary characters for real people, were it not that it points to their common identity in the poet. Their affairs, vagaries, emotions, reflect a psychic process, common to all of us, insofar as the poet is not a stranger to us. Yet the poem is now free of the poet, who is, in Jabès' words, on its threshold (1963: 15); it constitutes the entire relationship of the lovers. They create the poem with their love. Imperceptibly, though, they absent themselves from their communication; they cannot touch or feel except outside the poem. Thus they too are on its threshold. We see this in the solipsistic dialogue, two monologues side by side. Even the brief exchanges are scrambled. Ironically, the only people to speak sensibly and to the point are the daughters of Jerusalem!

The poem, created by the love of the lovers, thus separates them and grows between them. It incorporates the whole world between them through metaphor and metonomy. The lovers have an instrumental, syntactic function, communicating the poet's love of the world and realigning the gender of things. For example, 2.10-13 is really a poem about the spring. The poet has a gift for gently and affectionately teasing his lovers through the wiles and pitfalls of coded language, the manipulation of social register; their discourse becomes indirect, allusive, hermetic. They communicate through gesture, tone of voice, with nothing to say. The messages of love are very simple. At this point their love coincides with the non-referential, narcissistic component of language. There is no relationship, merely the play of sounds, the pleasure in creating poetry for its own sake. The physical sensation contrasts with the psychic quest: the signifying totality with unthinking immediacy.

H.P. Müller, in his sophisticated explorations of the magic of the Song, has approached it mostly in terms of homeopathy

Chapter Two - The Relationship of the Lovers

between man and the earth, in other words of a regenerative relationship. I should like to take his insight in a somewhat different direction. He notes that the most ancient poetry is magical speech, like spells or charms, and herein are to be found the religious roots of the lyric. But the lyric is associative, mellifluous speech, a composition of sound and images, whose extreme form is nonsense; just as magic tends to express itself in meaningless spells. In both cases there is an omnipotent regression, linguistic anarchy or ultimate power; man is unconstrained by rules of logic or nature. It is to this point, I hold, that the relationship of the lovers tends, through the poet.

The only critic to have given serious attention to the lovers as internal figures, part of a psychic process, is Leo Krinetzki, under the influence of analytical psychology, in an admirably concentrated and bold - indeed nearly faultless - essay "Die Erotische Psychologie des Hohenliedes" /1/. Its great contribution is to shift the discussion from the illusion of the single man and woman to the internal dynamics of each, from the imaginary real world in which the Song supposedly happens to the blend of fantasy and reality in which we live. Each person, according to Jungian theory, is androgynous /2/; an unconscious female element (the anima) exists in the male psyche, and vice versa. The heterosexual partner in the outside world corresponds to this internal figure, through projection. Thus an investigation of the Song is an exploration of the archetypes out of which the self is constituted, not as a single entity, but as a constellation of personae. Furthermore, it explains the dominance of the woman in the Song, since she also stands for the Great Mother, the primary archetype (1970: 407-16).

Necessarily, since he is limited for space, Krinetzki's application of this material to the Song is sketchy, but nevertheless wonderfully illuminating. He adapts Neumann's archetypal feminine symbol of the vessel, and traces its manifestations in the Song, in images of the vagina/belly, breasts and lips; in the Woman as the containing world; in its complex, enveloping relationship with the Lover. He perceives that alongside the fecund Great Mother there is the Terrible Mother, in other words, her inextricable ambivalence (1970: 411). Likewise the man represents the woman's animus /3/, though this corollary is not greatly developed in Krinetzki's article. Through the concrete symbolic projection of the archetypes into the great world the lovers enter into relationship, not only with each other, but with all creatures.

"Jeder erlebt den andern als etwas so Einmaliges, weil er in ihm 'Die Welt' schlechthin wiederfindet" (ibid.: 416). Thus they become for each other an "ēzer kenegdô" or "helpmeet".

Jungian psychology, especially when stripped of its mystifications, is a valuable critical tool. In particular, it introduces the concept of the Self as a psychosomatic unity, comprising ego and unconscious, personal biography and collective cultural heritage (Fordham: 98ff.). Fundamental to Jung's thought is the conviction that the "ego", the unique centre of consciousness, is only a small part of the Self, and that far more unites human beings than divides them. Hence we can understand each other. The collective unconscious amounts to no more than this, what we possess by virtue of being human beings or acquire from our environment (e.g. as Jews or Christians) as part of an historical entity /4/. In particular, we all have innate drives and a propensity for fantasy - a propensity, in other words, to use our imagination to make sense of the world - which tends to be organised round particular "nodal points", such as the breast mother, the child. These are the archetypes which, according to Jung, can only be represented in consciousness by images; in later life, their symbolic manifestations become very diverse. Finally, there is the process of <u>individuation</u>, the tendency of the Self to cohere, the wish to integrate all its fragmented components, whatever the cost and the resistance. This culminates in the <u>conjunction of opposites,</u> good and bad, animus and anima, ego and shadow. It is this process that I believe we may adduce in the Song; as well as its opposite, since the Self is a dynamic growing system, namely the rebirth of elements, animus and anima, Lover and Beloved, from the matrix, in a continuous cycle of union and differentiation.

There is however the danger, into which I think Krinetzki runs, of mistaking the archetypal symbol for the archetype, the expression for the idea. This is encouraged by the technique of <u>amplification,</u> the interpretation of imagery with the aid of comparative mythology, that leads many analysts a merry dance. For instance, Krinetzki's identification of the Vessel with the feminine archetype (1970: 408ff.), impressive as it is, does not in my view quite fit all the images of vessels in the Song, nor do justice to the symbol's full potentiality. For the subject of the poem is really the self as a self-contained entity that enters into relation with the world, "rounded like a stone", in Stokes's phrase (1971: 406), a vessel full of thoughts, feelings,

Chapter Two - The Relationship of the Lovers

activities. Hence the numerous images of vessels or containers in the poem, such as the garden or the palanquin, refer only secondarily to the vagina or the womb; literally they are images for the self, e.g. "A locked garden is my sister, my bride" (4.12). Only insofar as the self or psyche in the Song is feminine, as in the Hebrew language, is Krinetzki's generalisation acceptable.

For in this self the Lover and the Beloved constitute between them the mother. Maternal love, expressed practically in care and protection, is reproduced between them: it is the archetype of love. Perhaps we should replace the word "parent" for "mother", for it is a long time before the father is distinguished as a separate person, and an independent relationship develops; until then the mother combines the attributes and is the repository of feelings that will later be distributed between the two parents. Nevertheless, if I retain the word mother - and it is with some hesitation and inconsistency that I do so - it is partly because of the actual identity of the mother and the original parent, partly because she is still invested with her elemental qualities - empathy, warmth, cooking and serving food, as opposed to the bread-winning, adventurous father. Thus the lovers project onto each other not only mother and father, reproducing the Oedipal entanglement, but their undivided precursor. This emerges functionally, through mutual caresses, elaborate body-language, whereby the lovers, fragmented into numerous part-objects that coalesce, recognise themselves in the body of the other. Many of the lovers' intimacies have their infantile correlate: images of lips and eyes pass freely to and fro; they feed each other, are incorporated into each other. Thereby a flow of identity passes between the lovers; they become one flesh, their personalities merge, and this synthesis has its own character. Within it the lovers have male and female roles, attract to themselves animus and anima qualities. They are submerged in their relationship, that defines them as human beings, nurses them and, indeed, frustrates them - the primary maternal tasks. Theirs is both a personal collectivity, a sense of belonging together, through their unique empathy, and a contiguity in the collective unconscious. I will try to show how all these symbolic layers can actually be experienced in the Song:

    i)   through the exchange of imagery,
    ii)   the concurrence of voices and actions,
    iii) the invention of a family, as in a novel,

iv) the fusion of all generations in a common matrix, and
v) mythological resonances.

In the last chapter I will explore the most extensive of these, that with the garden of Eden.

For paterfamilias, as has frequently been observed, the Song has only a mother(e.g. Falk 1982: 90; Trible 1978: 158); for fathers we have to look for phallic images or covert allusions. The appearances of this mother coincide with moments of greatest intimacy; the effect is not only of benediction, but of a convergence of maternal and amorous affection, transmitting her influence to the lover. For example, in 6.9 his joy recalls her joy at the Beloved's birth.

The mother, moreover, contributes to the generative process, not only in life, but also in the Song, as part of a structural pattern; the references to her comprise a sequence, with reversions and recapitulations, from traumatic rejection to rebirth. In 1.6, her entry coincides with that of the Beloved, her first self-exposure; expulsion from the nuclear family precipitates the erotic encounter. But in 3.4=8.2 the approach to intercourse is a return to the mother; she presides over its public consummation in the wedding in 3.11; and in 6.9 and in 8.5 she is evoked at the moment of birth. Finally, in 8.8-10 the Beloved herself - according to my reading - takes over the maternal function; expulsion from the family is replaced by responsibility within it. Thus there is a movement from loss to restoration; the mother assists in the reproductive process, from desire to birth and future care.

Love, the true maternal gift, infuses and gives birth to the poem, and is celebrated by it. The personification suggests a slightly rhetorical distance, as if the erotic drive could be awakened and abstracted, in turn indicative of a tension between the personal and the collective, the immense instinctual discharge and the fragile consciousness. This tension will be the nucleus of the third chapter.

The poet with his speech produces this primary relationship, for himself and for us, talking in the air to the imagined memory or hallucination of the mother. It corresponds to his task of recreating the unity of the world, of restoring all fragmented relationships through metaphor. The poet has a conviction of a responsive universe, that his words are not vain; which is not merely, I think, the expectation of a sensitive audience but of an ideal invisible listener. It is an interior dialogue, both in the poet and in his

Chapter Two - The Relationship of the Lovers

personae, which we overhear, whose interlocutor is an internalised "other", originally the parent, with whom the baby experiences a complete rapport. But the Muse is herself a mother, who creates the poet, who feeds him with thoughts and pleasures, whom he discovers within himself and as himself. Thus the poet is both listener and communicator, a participant in a dialogue with himself and with the world.

The lovers are symbolically also twins, whose sibling representations will be subject to some attention; their duality couples - establishes kinship between - opposed terms. Deintegration is essential for the dynamic process to start, out of which relationship develops. The poem is separated from the poet, polarising opposites of imagination and reality, the immateriality of art and the quickness of the flesh. Poetry is thus a twin or complement of the poet, associated with the feminine side; as a fiction, it makes everything possible, and has a transcendent function. One aspect of poetry, as I shall argue in the next chapter, is the ideal of language that achieves perfection, becomes ethereal, pure form or music. Wallace Stevens, for example, in his poem "To the One of Fictive Music" invokes this as "Sister and mother and diviner love / And of the sisterhood of the living dead / Most near, most clear, and of the clearest bloom."

But there is another aspect. The mother also stands for the reality principle (Fordham: 116), that which initiates the baby into the world, the source of thirst as well as frustration. In the Song this is reflected in the association of the Beloved with nature, and especially the land of Israel. Alongside the transcendent function there is the attempt to find words for things, to integrate the real and the imaginary. If the mother and baby form one unit, to which she contributes security and constancy, it is that unity - of man and nature, consciousness and matter - that is at the basis of the Song.

There is also the narcissistic element, to which I have already alluded, a condition without relation, except for the drama of the self as it fragments and integrates, producing sounds for the sheer anarchic pleasure of it, and letting them fall into silence.

Finally, there is the archetype of the child. Both lovers emerge from the sexual encounter as newborn children, in 6.9 and 8.5, in a world regenerated by love. "When two kiss, the world changes" (Octavio Paz).

I will begin with the general characteristics of the lovers, insofar as they can be discerned. Obviously in a lyrical poem, one does not approach the relationship as in a narrative, where characters are distinct, identifiable, in a more or less realistic and continuous story. The lyric is broken up into many snatches or glimpses, typical amorous moments, just as the characters appear through multiple conflicting personae. Yet the fragments are luminous, frequently naturalistic, allowing a reconstruction of personality behind them. One speculates or recognises the situation from one's own worldly wisdom.

The transition from incident to the total composition is more difficult and obscure; nonetheless - to my surprise - a few limited generalisations do emerge, from repeated readings, none of them certain or incapable of qualification, that give us at least a silhouette of coherent figures. They are also structural guidelines, indicating where to put the weight of the poem, enabling us to anticipate and respond to recurring patterns in the dance of lovers. Some of these correspond to Near Eastern conventions; others are more unexpected.

First of all, since it is most obtrusive, is the dominance of the woman as a voice and presence. It is not simply a question of quantity, though the woman has more to say; it is also that the combined speeches of both lovers, with their different styles and concerns, focus on defining her image. Goitein (1957: 301-3) has seen this as evidence for the poet's gender, and posited a poetess /5/, since he or she seems to be far more at home in the feminine psyche than in the male; on the other hand, this could perhaps be explained by projection, the fascination of men with the mystery of women as the unknown part of themselves or <u>anima</u>. No generalisation, however, is absolute; a secondary figure of the Lover develops, in her shadow.

Of the two lovers, only the Beloved is preoccupied with self-definition, from "I am black and/but comely" in 1.5 to "I am a wall" in 8.10. Only she indeed uses the first person pronoun "ʾanî" "I" as if to stress this introversion (Goitein 1957: 302). For example, the redundant "ʾanî" in the marked parallelism at the beginnings of 5.4 and 5.5 - "qamtî ʾanî ... pātaḥtî ʾanî" "I arose ... I opened" - slows down the movement and makes us feel how she participates in it /6/; it has a reflexive quality ("I arose myself"). Likewise, she is much more forthcoming about her adventures; we know about her brothers, her work, her midnight perambulations, her daring. If there is a story in the Song of Songs, it is of her

Chapter Two - The Relationship of the Lovers

self, shaped by suffering, pleasure and self-reflection, that is both proud and self-assertive, and very vulnerable.

The Lover, in contrast, hardly talks about himself at all; there is no self-examination, and hardly any narration. He shows us the Beloved from outside. Formal portraits or wasfs take up much of his time. He typically stands outside the consciousness of the Beloved and is fascinated by it. She is of immense power, capturing his heart with "one of her eyes, one bead of her necklace" (4.9), captivating a king in her tresses (7.6).

The woman is the more interesting because she is the more active partner, nagging, restless, decisive. The man on the other hand is predominantly passive and complacent, as befits a king; his most memorable cry is the fourfold repetition of "šûbî" "Return" in 7.1, imperiously expecting her to come at his bidding. Even when he is stirred into ineffective wooing, we hear it only through her mouth (2.10-13, 5.2); her voice thus mingles with his, and we cannot tell whether it may not be her wish-fulfilment.

This domination by the woman may seem strange in a Near Eastern setting, though it is not hard to discern elsewhere; but there is a price she has to pay, as the victim of humiliation, for breaking traditional restraints; and also as the central figure. For if the Lover is fascinated by her, she is committed to him. His is a possibly embarrassing infatuation, but as king and fawn he is essentially free, like the archetypal lover all over the world. She loves him, but he is only in love with Love. His only reference to it is "How beautiful and fair you are, O Love, among delights" in 7.7 /7/ - Love as a wanton delight or pleasure. He is a fawn among the lilies, carelessly cropping flowers. His stance is characteristically aesthetic: for him Love is something beautiful, he spends much of his time looking at and anatomising the girl, and when he recalls her in 7.1, it is in terms reminiscent of striptease: "Return, return, O Shulammite, return, return, and let us gaze upon you; why do you (pl.) gaze on the Shulammite ...?" followed by a long description of her naked body. The Beloved, on the other hand, would never describe Love as "beautiful": for her it is an infection (2.5, 5.8), not to be rashly contracted, that yet cures mortality; it is of absolute value and all-consuming.

The Lover's meditation has two extreme modes, both of which distance the Beloved, defensively romanticising her. The first is adoration, the cosmic hyperbole, commensurate with sky and earth, provoking delicious trepidation.

Captivation is always the Lover's excuse; but the metaphor of theophany - idealisation into a quasi-divine figure - conceals a castration fantasy, that the dazzled king, symbol of virility, is helpless in her gaze, caught in tresses. Reverence bestows respectability on the dark side of erotic obsession, that harbours also a hidden wish, to be without will, in the other's power.

The other mode of contemplation is the reverse of this: it is an affectionate condescension, expressed in particular through pet names. The plaything is innocent and helpless; the innocuousness of the relationship is stressed by the diminutive "my dove", the attribute "my pure one", the implication of chastity in "my sister". The Beloved is possessed by the Lover, e.g. "lesusātî berikbê par'ōh" "To a/my mare in Pharaoh's chariots I have compared you, my love" in 1.9 (cf. below, 176ff.), corresponding to the actual subordination of women to men, concubines to the king, in ancient times. She is part of his extended personality, subject to his control, exemplified by the idealisation that manipulates her into a figure of disarming purity, immaculate availability, in a relationship in which, for the moment, sexuality is banished. It is coy and tender, with an ironic pretence of childhood that barely dissimulates tremendous repression. The Beloved's repertoire of endearments, on the other hand, is very limited: there is only "dôdî" "my love" and "'ēt še'āhabâ napšî" "He whom my soul loves", a true confession rather than a sweet nothing.

The lover as king has a creative function: he makes the Beloved royal, adorning her with jewellery, constructing her a palanquin /8/, perfecting her image. He is thus man the artisan, the fabricator, owner of gardens. Alongside the meditative gaze, then, and devolving from it, is creative fantasy, equally aesthetic, that changes the world to suit our image. But it always escapes us. The palanquin is founded on the love of the daughters of Jerusalem; the cheeks show through the jewellery in 1.10-11; in 7.3 - an image we shall come to - the workmanship of the thighs surrounds the mystery between them (cf. below, 258). Typically the Lover woos the Beloved, eliminating all improper suggestion, appealing to her compassion (5.2), flattery (2.14), or tempting her to pleasures (2.10-13); in other words, he is still dependent on her will, despite his fantasy of control, reinforced by showers of magnetic diminutives, and despite his status as king. For if he is the perpetual outsider, inveigling her from her portals, he is also the insider, in the

Chapter Two - The Relationship of the Lovers

midst of coteries of women, the centre of the kingdom. The absurdity of monarchy, as well as its isolation, is sympathetically depicted. From the multitudes of queens and concubines, he still says "One is she, my dove, my pure one, one is she ..." (6.9); the diminutive is immediately linked to the superlative, the comparison with the celestial bodies in 6.10. The recognition of her uniqueness cuts through the pomp of sovereignty: it is by virtue of being herself, as at the moment of birth, that she is uniquely prized by him, as himself. This is confirmed by the epithets "yônātî tammātî" "my dove, my pure one" that imply - through the word "tam" "complete, simple" - natural simplicity. At the centre of the Song and of the sumptuous court two human beings meet; beneath all the social pressures, conventional attitudes, sexual differentiations that separate them there is a simple equality. For instance, at the beginning of the Song the Beloved tells us "The king brought me into his chambers" (1.4) - temporarily, it is true, and at his bidding, she has been admitted to his sanctum, and what happened there is undisclosed. She is both outside - one of the maidens - and inside, knowing his intimate secrets. Again, in 5.1, he enters the garden that represents them both; at the end of the poem she dismisses him from it. Finally there are the epithets "dôdî" "my love" but also "my cousin", and "ra'yātî" "my friend", so familiar that they become almost indistinguishable. They present the lovers as bound by ties of kinship and affinity, but essentially equal, essentially companionable. And they remind us of the commandment "And you shall love your neighbour (rē'akâ) as yourself" (Lev 19.18) - the primary duty of human fellowship that is at the basis of the Song.

The Beloved's behaviour is paradoxical: she pursues him, wheedles him, yet chases him away. Her characteristic mode is active, not aesthetic; we have hardly any description, certainly no unmotivated contemplation of the Lover. Her only wasf is elicited by the daughters of Jerusalem; if insufficient as an Identikit, it certainly persuades them of his merits. Otherwise, the only sensual symbol for the Lover is the deer, whose beauty is a complex of a moment, in contrast to the highly articulated, static pictures of the Beloved. She does not adore him as a cosmic superlative; the apparent exception, the wasf of 5.10-16, is stiff and tense, contrasting with his animated, beautifully consistent portraits; there is a certain ambivalence, an over-conscientious definition. Neither does she patronise him, taking him into her affectionate orbit. Indeed it is difficult to say what she sees in him, except that she loves him. If he is overwhelmed by her, she is imbued with love. For its luminous touch on the nerves of love, its inner process, the Song is perhaps equalled in the ancient world only by Sappho.

Perhaps, though, her attraction towards him is to be understood through the situation. The Beloved, as Krinetzki says, is signified by images of enclosure: the home, the garden, even the crannies in the rocks in 2.14. Thence the Lover seeks to draw her. For her, then, as fawn, he stands for everything that is free and open, the whole world from which she has been secluded. There is an anarchic, licentious part of herself, I shall argue below, that belongs to that world; union with the Lover is then an integration of herself. His seduction of her using images of the wind, trees and flowers is consequently not mere rhetoric, for it is with that world that he seduces her. In two remarkable passages, we listen to her listening to him beyond her threshold; the inner temptation alongside the outer persuasion. In one, the sound of her lover knocking coincides with that of her heart beating; it betrays her to humiliation (5.2-7). In the other, his voice is that of the spring (2.10-13), that says "qûmî lāk ra'yātî yāpātî ûlekî lāk" "Arise, my friend, my fair one, and come away"; it is echoed in that of the turtle dove, that only now, as a migratory bird, is heard in the land (2.12).

And yet she does not come. Why? Because what she loves is this essential freedom, which is also a sexual freedom, as "hārō'eh baššôšannîm" "he who feeds among the lilies". In the end she dismisses him: "Flee, my love, and be like a deer or a young gazelle on the mountains of spices" (8.14), in the shape of the fawn, the untrammelled animal. There is nevertheless an ambiguity here: in the sister-verse in 2.17, that closes the rapprochement we have just discussed, and again in 4.6, the Lover's flight to the mountains is introduced by the mysterious circumlocution "'ad šeyyāpûaḥ hayyōm wenāsû haṣṣelālîm" "Until the day blows and the shadows flee". Interpretations differ, but I hold that the relevant hour is evening, since deer are diurnal animals /9/. Thus though the day will part them, at night they shall be reunited. In the Song, as quasi-universally, day and night are metaphors for consciousness and unconsciousness, differentiation and fusion (cf. below, 146). In the Song the lovers are simultaneously indissoluble and inaccessible. A similar set of ambiguities will be discovered in relation to the dialogue of 1.7-8. If for the Beloved the Lover is essentially a fawn, not to be tamed or

Chapter Two - The Relationship of the Lovers

limited - if by captivating him she imprisons him - for the Lover she is essentially untouched and immaculate, even at the moment of possession. The two poles never meet, that in each angle greet. If the Song celebrates sexuality, it also celebrates virginity.

2. Androgyny: Fawns and Lilies

The bodies of the lovers are disassembled and reconstructed in the Song, each constituent metaphorically combining with heterogenous elements to give the impression of a collage, a web of intricate associations and superimposed landscapes that serves to blur the distinction between the lovers, and between them and the external world. As Octavio Paz says in the verse I use as an epigraph, "Voy por tu cuerpo como por el mundo". The appearance of an affair between two independent individuals is complicated by an awareness of the multitude of selves and part-objects that make up each person. From the relationship of the lovers, which I have already discussed, we become entangled in that between their parts; like the poem, we lose the wood for the trees. If one is too frightened of losing the wood one will never enter the forest. Parts of the two lovers' bodies will be found to correspond; an inter-personal unity will begin to develop, through linking metaphors. There is admittedly an element of projection in this, of making the loved one a reflection or image of oneself; this sympathetic imagining of oneself in the other is part of the process of integration that takes place in the poem.

The loss of definition of the single body permits a process of regression and recreation, a fluidity between adult and infantile levels of experience. In particular, it passes the threshold of the relationship with a whole object, and evokes the time - not only of Freud's oceanic feeling - when neither mother nor infant are realised as continuous beings; they are confused, split up into good and bad, and innumerable part objects - breasts, lips, etc. The role of infantile regression in love play and sweettalk is universally familiar (Jakobson 1968: 17). The restoration of infantile bliss is, however, only secondary to its creative contribution to adult sexuality, to the concentration of both lives, the eternity in a flower of love.

In this section, I shall begin to explore the interconnections and cross-references, relying perhaps excessively on the wasfs or formal portraits, marvellous inventories of images, but turning also to more dynamic descriptions and incidents. I shall take an image and proceed to an elaboration of its correlatives and complements, not so much for its own sake, to attempt a total elucidation, but as a gradual introduction to the descriptive techniques of the Song, the familial tensions it perceives between the parts of the body, and its metaphorical landscape. The image is chosen at random, or rather because one critic finds it curious (Murphy 1973: 420); it might however be considered questionable to abstract an image from the centre of the poem, rather than to follow its sequence. It could be argued that the proper starting-point is 1.1 or 1.2, with "the kisses of his mouth", for instance. It will be conceded that a reading inattentive to sequence is unbalanced; nevertheless, reading is gradual and cumulative, slowly recognising correspondences from all parts of the poem. Natural reading may well start from the centre, for example from the waṣfs, with their crisp and very puzzling imagery.

The image is that of 4.5: "šenê šādayik kišnê ʽopārîm teʼômê ṣebiyyâ hârōʽîm baššôšannîm" "Your two breasts are like two fawns, twins of a doe, who feed among the lilies". Although any image would ultimately be equally productive, clearly breasts are endowed with the utmost emotive and aesthetic intensity; their essential ambiguity gives them a special status in the Song. They combine adult and infantile sexuality, visual and oral satisfaction, tactile and erectile qualities. They have active and passive characteristics; active insofar as they give suck, passive in that they are subject to the baby's aggressive rage and hunger. On the adult level, they are conspicuous, attracting attention. As we shall find in the next chapter, ambiguity determines the aesthetic response, between desire and repression, perfect form and explosive energy. The breasts are an ideal entity, reproduced in many forms in art and architecture, in cusps, cupolas, etc. /10/. They combine extension, the roundness of feminine beauty, with altitude; compactness and fullness; centre and circumference. Though the Kleinian ambivalence of the good nourishing breast and the sadistic/persecutory one has little role to play in the Song, the breasts are both rich and maternal and thrusting and aggressive, combining masculine and feminine imagery and functions. They are opposed to the genitals as active, forward projections of the female body, and linked to them through synecdoche.

Breasts are compared to towers in 8.10, as assertive and formidable, expressing the Beloved's impact on the world and especially on the Lover. Besides their visual phallic

Chapter Two - The Relationship of the Lovers

similarity, towers are associated with the masculine world of arms and politics. They protect the integrity of the Beloved against assault, while advertising her attractions. Here then the breasts are primarily containers, hard, redoubtable, elevated.

In 7.8-9, however, where breasts are clusters of dates or grapes, their feminine aspect is evident, their roundness and richness. The harmonious, unified breast is fragmented into numerous taut part-objects, that multiply the experience of bursting the skin and extracting the fruit indefinitely. Here, then, it is primarily an organ of suckling, soft, full, and vulnerable.

Before turning to the central image of 4.5, I would like to discuss, albeit cursorily, the poetic qualities and resources of the wasf, especially the one in which it partakes, namely that of 4.1-5.

The Lover as observer, as poet, in this portrait, translates bodily sensations into scenic snapshots, metonymy into metaphor. The parts of the body are metonymous with the vagina, or with the woman herself; through them, sexuality is diffused over the entire body and thence transmitted, via the imagery, to the landscape /11/. The woman becomes transparent; her figure is superimposed on vivid pictures, of minimal descriptive value. Concentration on her expressive face deflects the imagination from the concealed body; propriety closes the portrait after the breasts. Synecdoche - using the face to represent the person - verges on metaphor i.e. likeness /12/. Parts of the face correspond to parts of the body, and carry with them an unconscious symbolism. Dr. Eli Gutwirth has very kindly furnished me with some medieval examples, in which the length of the nose is directly correlated with character and potency /13/. The metaphors thus have a double function: they ally the face with the active, external world, the setting of the Song, and they impart symbolic information. Through cubist disintegration, the reality of the face dissolves; each part, with its exotic image, is instrumental in a wider synthesis.

The wasf itself, in the continuum of the poem, is isolated; a formal poetic exercise that sets the lovers at a distance from each other. Its intimacy contrasts with the public celebration of 3.11; and the descent from Lebanon in 4.8ff. may plausibly be held to introduce the comparison of the Beloved to a garden in 4.12-5.1, so that ch. 4 as a whole is an extended portrait of the Beloved, interrupted only by sighs and ejaculations. As such, however, the wasf, with its meticulous artifice, is a set piece, that does not participate in the movement of the Song. It has the effect of a still life with its complex absence of main verbs; in it each image is paratactically juxtaposed. If the passage is isolated, distinctively bounded from its neighbours, without logical connectives, each sentence within it duplicates this isolation. There is no syntactic frame, no plot, merely the association of tropes by contiguity. Yet the images within the sentences are buzzing with energy. It is as if the vitality has been displaced from the body to the correlate, with its sexual symbolism. Moreover, the images themselves are intricately related to others in the poem, and conform to its major preoccupations and settings. We have the relaxed pastoral idiom and activity of 4.1-2, the military/political dimension in 4.4, the gentle feral tableau in 4.5. This last is linked to the series through parallelism and complementary contrast. We bring to it from the other verses an expectation of extravagance, unreality, of poetic chimera. For the relationship of the lovers it substitutes the conceit, a self-referential congratulatory medium, which discloses an astonishing depth of meditative fantasy. There is thus a parallel metonymy in the object and the subject; libidinal energy is redirected both to the contiguous simile and to the optical imagination. There is an analogy between the continuity of the eye and the pastoral scene it witnesses and that of the infant (or Lover) and the breast; the flow of milk and the fusion of selves is in accord with the unity of discrete perceptual objects and the mind of the poet, in the field of consciousness.

Sensually "Your two breasts are like two fawns" is an extraordinarily sensitive metaphor, combining colour, warmth, liveliness and delicate beauty. The Beloved's breasts are brown, in motion, in repose, sweet, gentle, etc. /14/. Fawns are food, and fawns are visually delectable. Feliks (77) suggests an analogy between the dappled skin of the fawns and the nipples. In looking at the breasts, the Lover is returning to an undisturbed pastoral idyll. Later we will touch on its paradisal implications; here I am more concerned with it as a recollection of infancy.

The breasts evoke suckling: two sucklings, "twins of a doe",

Chapter Two - The Relationship of the Lovers

grazing among lilies /15/. It is a strange reversal: the breast that gives suck itself suckles (cf. Cook: 122-3). On the one hand it is a clear case of projection; in the breast the Lover sees an early version of himself, since elsewhere in the poem there is a stock comparison of the Lover with a fawn. Visual satisfaction thus corresponds to lactation. At the same time the fawns, grazing among the lilies, are feeding off the earth, which in the Song, as in the Bible in general, has a maternal function, and is associated with the Beloved. The fawns are both "twins of a doe" and feed directly off the earth; there are thus two mothers in view, alternative and complementary. The breasts, then, produced by the woman's body, fawns feeding off the earth and mother, are nurtured by femininity; their relationship to the mother is one of divergence as well as continuity /16/. Hence their partial association with masculinity, the symbol of fawns, for instance. Moreover, in the adjuration "by the does or hinds of the field", the doe, mother of fawns, represents the power that guarantees feminine sexuality.

The meadow dotted with lilies, as in a pointillist painting, reproduces the image. The lilies embellish the earth, break up its texture, create a dynamic interplay; yet they are imparted by it. The preposition "ba" in "hārō'îm baššôšannîm" may mean "among" or "on" the lilies ((Pope 1976: 406), i.e. the lilies are either the diet of the fawns or the context in which they feed, the poetic equivalent of decor. The image then is either naturalistic - fawns grazing in springtime - or symbolic. If the fawns feed <u>on</u> them, then they are the breasts of the earth; in any case, they symbolically set the scene for the feast. If the lilies are red, as suggested by the comparison with the Lover's lips in 5.13 /17/, and fragrant, a metaphorical link with nipples becomes more positive.

Thus the breasts fill the informing eye; the fawns, ambiguous creatures representing both the Lover (2.8, 2.17, 8.14) and part of the woman's body, combine also the infantile function of suckling with the adult pleasure in observation, reflection and artistic creation. In the caress verbally represented by the wasf, the breasts are at once a displacement of the vagina, arousing adolescent attraction, an aid in foreplay, and metaphorically construct an equivalence between past and present, the communion of lovers and that of mother and infant. Here historic and synchronic dimensions merge. Instead of the two lovers, and the objective relationship between them, we have a continuum, between the eye, the breast and the earth, in which the past envelops the present. The identity is shared between them. The maternal images - breasts, earth, doe - bestow the vital fluid; they in turn are reconstituted by the Lover. There is thus an inference of reciprocity, of a life cycle in which they both participate; the Lover, who owes his life and sustenance to his mother, in this luminous recollection of infancy is still absorbed in that mutual rhythm. His energy, his poetic talent, is nourished by her. Now in the form of the wasf, he returns that gift, just as, in the underlying image of intercourse, he restores the vital fluid.

Lilies, as flowers, with their delicate beauty, are associated with femininity. In the Song, they are an image for the Beloved, in 2.1-2, corresponding to the apple tree as am emblem for the Lover in 2.3; the phrase in 4.5 "hārō'îm baššôšannîm" "who feed among the lilies" recurs in the refrain: "My beloved is mine, and I am his, who feeds among the lilies" (2.16 // 6.3). Instead of the fawn "who feeds among the lilies" we have the Lover. Similarly in 6.2 the Lover goes down into his garden to pluck lilies; from the context the lilies off which he feeds may be identified with women (cf. Falk 1982: 104). For the relationship of suckling we have sexual fulfilment.

The Lover/infant projects himself into the breasts that feed him and on which he is dependent; they are fawns, emblems of the Lover. We find the same process in reverse, in the Beloved's portrait of the Lover, in connection with her symbol of the lily. "His lips are lilies, dropping flowing myrrh" (5.13). If the Lover sees himself in her breasts, she sees herself in his lips. Lips are commonplace metaphors for the vagina; we speak, for instance, of the labia of the vagina. This is not only a matter of appearance, but evokes their function as recipients of food and liquid, life-sustaining nourishment. If the breasts/fawns are paradoxically imagined as feeding, the lilies/lips are analogously imagined as giving, both in our verse (4.5), and in its sister verse, (5.13) where they "drop flowing myrrh". Clearly, too, there is a symmetry of metonymy. If for the baby, especially in the early months, the breast is the most important part of the mother, for the mother the lips are the point of most intimate contact with the baby. The whole of the baby expresses itself in the lips; the whole of the mother is available through the breasts, and through them she gives life and love to the baby. In turn, he grasps and in fantasy devours the breast. Thus each incorporated in the other, in the unity of mother and infant, the basis for that of the self and the world.

Chapter Two - The Relationship of the Lovers

The mouth in the Song is associated with sweetness and succulence. Corresponding to the Lover's lips that "drop [nōṭepôt] flowing myrrh" are those of the Beloved, which evoke the same verb NTP "drop" in the lovely paronomasia "nōpet tiṭṭōpnâ śiptôtayik kallâ" "Your lips drop honey, O bride" (4.11) /18/. Parallel to this, in the next phrase we find "debaš wehālāb taḥat lešônēk" "Honey and milk under your tongue" /19/. There are several similar images for the palate - "And your palate like fine wine" (7.10), "His palate is all sweets" (5.16), etc. In each case there is an inversion of function: the palate that tastes food is tasted; the milk of childhood is found under the tongue, not in the breast or udder; honey and sweetness are reminiscent both of childhood and lactation, and correlative with bliss, as in the familiar expression "a land flowing with milk and honey" /20/.

Underlying this is the metaphor of the kiss. "His lips are lilies, dropping flowing myrrh" - apart from colour and fragrance - suggests an association of nectar with saliva; in turn, it is supposed, the superabundant myrrh is an index of his eagerness. As Marvin Pope (1976: 441) puts it, "amative oral activities other than sweet talk" are suggested, as throughout the Song. Moreover, the kiss is a wonderfully sensitive and versatile image for intercourse, as needs no illustration. The Song exploits the pun between "NŠQ" and "ŠQH", to kiss and to drink, which we find also in Gen 29.10-11. For example, in the first verse of the Song itself - "yiššāqēnî minnešîqôt pîhû kî-ṭôbîm dōdekā miyyāyin" "Let him kiss me with the kisses of his mouth, for your caresses are better than wine" (1.2) - the sensation of the kiss and the Lover's mouth is assimilated to that of wine (Lys: 63). In 8.1-2, the kiss (ʾeššāqekā) of which the Beloved is deprived leads to a euphemistic fantasy of hospitality "I would give you to drink (ʾašqekā) of my spiced wine, my pomegranate juice" (8.2).

The interpenetration of selves in the kiss, as in intercourse, is an exchange of delectable fluids, a dissolution of boundaries; to pursue the motif of suckling, the Lover finds under the tongue of the Beloved the milk i.e. life and love received from her mother, and likewise in his mouth she partakes of his. And what they taste is themselves.

To turn back to 5.13, and the description of the Lover: "His lips are lilies, dropping flowing myrrh". She sees in him, from an imaginative and temporal distance, an infant, his lips opening like flowers, his mouth watering; just as he sees in her a primal bliss. In both cases there is an inversion of gender and function, the superimposition of adult sexuality, e.g. in the form of a kiss, on an infantile function. The inversion is confirmed by the context of the image, "dropping flowing myrrh", in the wasf of 5.10-16.

עֵינָיו כְּיוֹנִים עַל־אֲפִיקֵי מָיִם רֹחֲצוֹת בֶּחָלָב יֹשְׁבוֹת עַל־מִלֵּאת: לְחָיָו כַּעֲרוּגַת הַבֹּשֶׂם מִגְדְּלוֹת מֶרְקָחִים שִׂפְתוֹתָיו שׁוֹשַׁנִּים נֹטְפוֹת מוֹר עֹבֵר:

(5.12) His eyes are like doves by brooks of water, washed in milk, sitting by the flood (or fitly set).
(13) His cheeks are like a bed of balsam, towers of spices; his lips are lilies, dropping flowing myrrh.

They are all feminine images /21/. In "His lips are lilies, dropping flowing myrrh", perfuming, if not gilding, the lily, to the natural flower or girl we add the recollection of her haste and clumsiness only a few verses earlier, in seeking to admit her lover: "weyāday nāṭepû-mōr weʾeṣbeʿōtay môr ʿōbēr" "And my hands dropped myrrh, and my fingers flowing myrrh, onto the handles of the lock" (5.5). The phrase "to drop flowing myrrh" is transferred from her hands to his lips. Similarly, at the end of the sequence, the previous image, "His cheeks are like a bed of balsam", is recalled in apposition to lilies in 6.2 "My love has gone down to his garden, to the beds of balsam to feed among the gardens, to pick lilies". In turn it corresponds to the Beloved, the "gan nāʿûl" "locked garden" (4.12), the nursery of spices of 4.13-14. The elaboration of the image of cheeks "migdelôt merqāḥîm" "towers of [or growing] spices", confirms the association with fragrance and the interchange of sexuality /22/. Finally, the extended comparison of the eyes to doves in 5.12 uses a symbol, a pet name, for the Beloved e.g. "my dove, my pure one" (5.2, 6.9), "my dove in the clefts of the rock" (2.14).

Thus on his face, the expressive articulate part of his body, we find animate images of the woman; whereas the rest of his body, though appropriately formidable, is coldly metallic and disjointed. By a curious paradox that which is alive in him and relates to her is feminine.

5.13 is, as it were, a very oblique comment on 4.5. The breasts (= fawns) are sustained by the lips (= lilies) which are those of the lover as a poet who trades kisses. In both verses the lilies have a maternal function, exuding nectar, or as part of the pasture; in both they derive from the earth, that is common to man and woman. Their activity as that which gives suck through the fawns to the Lover is reversed in 5.13,

Chapter Two - The Relationship of the Lovers

where the Lover's greed for kisses is also generous. If the fawns communicate the sweetness of the lilies to the Lover, there is a suppressed collision of the two images from the two wasfs. Finally, the projection of each lover into the other - the Lover into the breasts, the Beloved into the lips - contributes to their union that is the work of the poem.

אֲנִי חֲבַצֶּלֶת הַשָּׁרוֹן שׁוֹשַׁנַּת הָעֲמָקִים: כְּשׁוֹשַׁנָּה בֵּין הַחוֹחִים כֵּן רַעְיָתִי בֵּין הַבָּנוֹת: כְּתַפּוּחַ בַּעֲצֵי הַיַּעַר כֵּן דּוֹדִי בֵּין הַבָּנִים בְּצִלּוֹ חִמַּדְתִּי וְיָשַׁבְתִּי וּפִרְיוֹ מָתוֹק לְחִכִּי:

(2.1) I am a rose of Sharon, a lily of the valleys.
(2) Like a lily among thorns, so is my love among the daughters.
(3) Like an apple tree among the trees of the wood, so is my love among sons; in his shade I sat and took pleasure, and his fruit was sweet to my taste.

In 2.1-3 the lily and the apple are paired together in a competition of comparisons between the lovers. The Beloved among girls is like a lily among thorns; the Lover among young men is like an apple tree among the trees of the wood. The lily of the valleys in 2.1 is solitary and fragile /23/; its calyx and whorl of sepals round the central funnel reinforces the feminine connotation. It is a quiet, naturalistic comment on her Sitz-im-Leben, perhaps a little rueful, addressed half or wholly to herself. The Lover's gallant intrusion spoils the intimacy; the condition of the courtly compliment is that it be artificial, with its disarming absurdity. And then her reply is once more serious, with its sensible comparison of different trees. Moreover, as continually happens in the Song, the formal structure breaks down, and the image develops a life of its own.

Trees as opposed to flowers are manly, powerful and vigorous; and indeed later in the Song we have a tree that conforms to phallic expectation figuratively attached to the Lover. He is "bāḥûr kā'arāzîm" "choice as cedars" (5.15). But the apple tree is an affectionate rather than an impressive tree, associated in the Song with shelter ("in its/his shade I sat and took pleasure") and food ("and its fruit was sweet to my taste") /24/. Clearly the primary reference is to sexual pleasure and more distantly to protection and provision, familiar male (or paternal) roles. Three verses later, his encircling arms substitute the shade of the tree; towards the end of the book in 8.5 she leans upon him. But equally, and originally, as we shall see, the tree has a maternal function: food and comfort come from the mother.

The Beloved is also metaphorically linked with a tree - the date palm in 7.8-9: "zō't qômātēk dāmetâ letāmār wešādayik leʲaškōlôt: ʲāmartî ʲeʻeleh betāmār" "This your height is like a palm tree, and your breasts are like clusters. I said: 'I will climb the palm tree ....'" It is a comparison of height and slenderness combined with pendulous breasts, heavy with fruit. There is perhaps a projective identification of the phallus and the woman /25/. We catch a glimpse of amorous convention: the Lover sees himself as bold and triumphant, sex as an assertion of power. Slenderness is an index of litheness, common to both lovers, reminiscent of the deer or young gazelle. Metonymy, such as the comparison of the neck to a tower in 4.4 and 7.5, suggests it occasionally through analogy elsewhere in the poem. Slimness, the adolescent and somewhat ethereal beauty, whose sexual polarisation is not marked (and sometimes confused) is coupled with breasts, whose sweetness and fullness makes them unambiguously organs of suckling. Moreover, the comparison of height is not with other women, but with a diminutive Lover, who climbs the tree; in relation to him she is the infantile mother, the axis of his world, enormous and central, into whose arms he climbs and to whose legs he clings ("ôḥazâ besansinnaw" "I will catch hold of its fronds").

There is an image of the Lover as a flower corresponding to that of the Beloved as lily: "ʲeškōl hakkōpēr dôdî lî bekarmê ʻēn gedî" "A spray of henna is my love to me, in the vineyards of Ein-Gedi" (1.14). Bright yellow flowers; it is unclear whether the "kerāmîm" are vineyards or spice-plantations /26/. In 4.13 "kepārîm" "henna" or "camphire" blossoms, are planted in the garden of the Beloved. In contrast to the lily wherewith the Beloved defines herself, in essence, as a flower both commonplace and miraculous, here the Lover is defined in relation to her as something exotic, brought to her from the uncanny landscape of the Dead Sea, with its luxuriant crops, in the midst of desolation /27/.This Dead Sea fruit has a miraculous, unnatural quality, reflected in its price. Spice too is a

Chapter Two - The Relationship of the Lovers

paradoxical commodity, with overtones of the supernatural; hence its use in magic and medicine, its place in folklore. This is primarily because of its pervasive subtlety (hence the most precious spice of all: saffron); not being food itself, it enhances food. The Beloved brings the Lover from the alien landscape, and uses him to dye her hair /28/.

In the previous verse there is an exact parallel in syntax and formal structure: "ṣerôr hammôr dôdî lî bên šāday yālîn" "Like a sachet of myrrh is my love to me; between my breasts he lies" (1.13). The "bag of myrrh" is an ordinary female accessory /29/, containing a spice from far away. Once again there is an affiliation of the remote and the close; myrrh likewise is associated with the Beloved. But the ending differs: "between my breasts he lies" /30/. An adult sexual conceit overlays an image of infancy; as in 4.5 and 7.8, the breasts mediate between past and present; the fully-grown Lover is simultaneously perceived cradled between the breasts, tiny as a bag of myrrh. Between "between my breasts he lies" and "in the vineyards of Ein-Gedi", the variant endings of the otherwise symmetrical verses, the distances meet; the heterogenous vineyards - otherwise vineyards are metonymic with the Beloved herself - add their allure to her hair, and thus lay a tribute.

Two flower images, two tree images. The lily in 2.1 is the simple and sublime feminine principle, untouched and unguarded, the identity ultimately desirable, and alone in the world; on it converge images of the vagina, nipples and lips. The milk flows to the fawns and the lips, and is reciprocated in the kiss, as we have seen; the same structure influences the other botanical symbols. The pleasure-giving, sheltering apple-tree, whose fruit drops into the mouth, combines a sexual conception (Tenor) with a maternal function and parental care; the Beloved is both the diminutive infant, sheltered and fed by the tree, cradled in her Lover's arms, and a sexual partner. The milk - the sweet food - is now received from the Lover, who thus stands in for the mother; as in 5.13, there is a reversal of function. This is confirmed also by the paternal aspects of the tree. The Lover is tender, caressing, enfolding. There is nothing more maternal than a good father.

The date palm is also a composite metaphor, combining exaggerated femininity and maternal eminence with a slender figure, into which the Lover projects his own wish for dominance, his own virility. The two trees initiate the process through which life is passed through the generations, from mother to son and thence to the Beloved. But they do so in reverse: whereas the apple tree is enveloping, as part of a community of trees, a wood, the isolated date palm is robbed of its fruit. The Lover is apparently its master, conforming to male assumptions, subverted, as we shall see, in the working out of the image.

The image of henna is as fantastical as that of the lily is natural. The Lover is brought from far away, from the exotic oasis, to become an attribute of the Beloved, to increase her attractions. Once again, we have the dependence of the Lover on the Beloved, lodged between her breasts. The movement from Ein Gedi to the breasts is reminiscent of 4.5, where the fawns, fugitive animals, representative of the Lover in 2.8-9 in his search for the Beloved, are now identified with breasts, and at peace.

The net we are casting will now tighten a little.

In the fantasy that follows the extended simile of the date palm we find familiar images tumbling on top of each other - breasts like bunches of grapes, palate like wine, the fruit of all trees tasted together in a Surrealist banquet. Among them is the following strange image: "werêaḥ appēk kattappûḥîm" "And the fragrance of your nose like apples" (7.9). What is so special about the smell of a nose? The image has caused hasty reinterpretation among sober and less sober commentators alike /31/. It is not a question of love play, the "nose-kiss" of Ancient Egyptians and Eskimos /32/. To discern a particular nose-smell is rare, however.

This leads us to a second question. What is the connection, if any, between the apple tree in this verse and the apple tree in 2.3? How has the latter managed to insinuate itself in the elaboration of its corresponding image, the date palm?

In a kiss, the nose perforce smells the nose; the observation is simple realism. But it conforms to a pattern. We have seen how the mouth tastes the mouth, that which gives suck itself suckles. The olefactory organ is savoured. Only elephant ears can be heard, but love looks are long. Moreover, the inhalation diffuses her fragrance through the body, in rhythmical alternation with the exhalation. She breathes him in also; the juxtaposed nostrils share each others' breath. In a sense, he breathes himself; such lovers would not survive for long /33/. For the breath is also the breath of life. They live through each other, in each other's atmosphere. The continuity of the breath, merging inner and outer, as the underlying rhythm of our lives, is a metaphor for that of lovers, and that of mother and infant, ideally realised in the

Chapter Two - The Relationship of the Lovers

womb. Indeed, the interdependence of the self and the world, the air and consciousness, substitutes that of foetus and mother. We have the sensation of the breath, the smell, that revives infantile memories, and is one of the most pervasive, unconscious and emotive of senses, in common with the respiratory medium. In the Song, it is especially prominent, and we have already touched on instances.

We now come to the second question: what is the relation with 2.3? Simple equation is inappropriate; the masculine signification of the tree in 2.3 cannot be transferred directly to the Beloved's nose; the Lover does not smell himself. It is less an oblique comment than a subsidiary motif. The apple tree in 2.3 is paired with that in 8.5, to be discussed in due course; its fruit, the surfeit of apples, derives from it but is detached from it. In 2.5 apples are sought as the gift of the daughters of Jerusalem, representatives of global femininity, as the remedy for love-sickness. They are the commodity of love, passing in between the lovers; for the Beloved they originate in the Lover, and vice versa. Thus as well as the symbolism of the tree, that defines the dignity, identity, and common humanity of the lovers, we have the fruit, their shared resources, their produce. /34/.

The smell of the apple is in anticipation; there is a slight, subtle contemplative shift. Only in the next verse is the fruit eaten.

Corresponding to this is another image for the nose: "'appēk kemigdal hallebānôn ṣôpeh penê dammāśeq" "Your nose is like the tower of Lebanon, overlooking Damascus" (7.5). As in ch. 4, the extended comparison with a date palm is preceded by a wasf, whose principal characteristic is objective definition. Whereas in the Lover's fantasy in 7.8-10 a medley of half-captured sense impressions overlap, each one of which dissolves the object and trespasses on the neighbouring appearances - so that the compact breast is atomised into grapes, the breaths merge, and finally the dissolving wine flows between the palates - in the wasf of 7.2-7 each item is very clear, perfectly articulated. In 7.8-10 the conclusion is a confusion of tongues, literal and metaphorical: "weḥikkēk keyên haṭṭôb hôlēk ledôdî lemêšārîm dôbēb śipetê yešēnîm" "And your palate like fine wine, flowing to my lover [m.] smoothly, stirring the lips of sleepers" (7.10). Unobtrusively, in mid-sentence, the subject changes from Lover to Beloved, the fantasy is transferred or becomes reality /35/. It is as if she can read his thought, and their identification is so complete that it passes automatically from one to the other.

In the wasf, as in 4.7, the summary is a brief appraisal of value /36/. In 7.10 the Beloved's voice completes the dissolution of boundaries with an image of utter ambiguity: "dôbēb śipetê yešēnîm" "stirring the lips of sleepers" /37/. Sleep is both monistic, associated with death /38/, and undifferentiated; it is both the ultimate fusion with the mother and without relation to her. The reference here is unclear - to the Lover / lovers / all lovers? / to the unawakened world, ignorant of love? /39/ - and blends the paradoxes of the Song, namely that true consciousness is a loss of consciousness, self-fulfilment is through self-surrender.

In the wasf, the features are in sharp relief, uncompounded, each one the focus of exclusive concentration. The images are all more or less visual (Gerleman: 195), in other words, belonging to the most rational of senses. The optical faculty has the farthest range, the greatest definition, and distinguishes most precisely between self and other. There is an air of excessive conscientiousness in exact perception in the wasf, of scientific impersonality, compounded by geographical distance and aesthetic remoteness. The Beloved is far off. The head is part of the skyline, the clarity of outline indicative of the light, the Mediterranean purity, that enables one to see from Lebanon to Damascus, from the centre of the country to Lebanon, and that is a primary symbol for consciousness.

"Your nose is like the tower of Lebanon, overlooking Damascus" is one of the most notorious images in the Song /40/. Marvin Pope (1976: 627) makes the point well:

> If our lady is superhuman in nature and size, then the dismay about her towering or mountainous nose disappears as the perspective and proportions fall into focus.

It is not a huge nose, but well-proportioned and slender as a tower, seen from a distance, against the background of Lebanon and the prospect of Damascus. Scale is provided by the context (from this point of view the nose is rather tiny); it is also that of the wasf as a whole.

The appearance of the nose thus contrasts with its recondite smell, four verses later. It is conspicuous /41/, attracting to itself more than its share of fantasy and folklore. The nose, as the most prominent and central feature of the face, helps determine its character. In the Beloved's case, it is high, elegant and distant. If in 7.9 apples and

Chapter Two - The Relationship of the Lovers

breath are shared between the lovers, here it is admired from afar. Noses are intrusive (someone who is "nosey") and affectionate, associated with pertness and play e.g. nose-kisses. If the lips are familiar erotic metaphors for the vagina, the nose may be compared to the phallus /42/. The emphasis on slenderness, on altitude, is, I think, decisive. The nose matches the nose in a parody of combat, in which the man's aggression is reinforced by the woman's resistance. The struggle need not be enacted physically; the gestures of noses can be very expressive /43/.

The tower, associated with military strength as well as erection, characterises the forward breasts in 8.10, as we have seen. Elsewhere in the Song, notably two phrases earlier, it depicts the Beloved's neck; there is thus a direct link between neck and nose:

צַוָּארֵךְ כְּמִגְדַּל הַשֵּׁן עֵינַיִךְ בְּרֵכוֹת בְּחֶשְׁבּוֹן עַל־שַׁעַר בַּת־רַבִּים אַפֵּךְ כְּמִגְדַּל הַלְּבָנוֹן צוֹפֶה פְּנֵי דַמָּשֶׂק:

Your neck is like the ivory <u>tower</u>; your eyes are pools at Heshbon, by the gate of Bat-Rabbim; your nose is like the <u>tower</u> of Lebanon, overlooking Damascus. (7.5)

The image of the neck describes part of the woman, but its connotations are masculine; this is clearest in the most elaborated of the references, in 4.4: "kemigdal dāwîd ṣawwā'rēk ..." "Like the tower of David is your neck, built in winding courses; a thousand shields are hanging on it, all the weapons of the warriors". David is the father of Solomon, the putative Lover and author of the Song, and he is also the prototypical hero /44/. It is I think the only allusion to a father in the Song. As a fortification the tower is both formidable and defensive: in 8.10 it manifests the Beloved's boldness and asserts her integrity; in 4.4 it is graced with the trophies of or garrisoned by a thousand soldiers /45/; in 7.5 it protects the kingdom. As we have seen, breasts and noses alike are sexually ambiguous, representing a masculine projection as well as a feminine function. This is sustained by contiguity: 7.4, the verse previous to ours, is a slightly curtailed repetition of 4.5, with its image of breasts = fawns, that in turn follows that of the neck and tower in 4.4 /46/. The long, slender neck is a somewhat erratic signifier, that essentially confers grace and dignity on the bearer; in this it resembles the date palm in 7.8. Thus we find, corresponding to the cluster of feminine images on the face of the Lover, a set of masculine ones associated with the Beloved. Very noticeably, the Beloved's mouth or lips are not depicted; nor is the Lover's nose.

צַוָּארֵךְ כְּמִגְדַּל הַשֵּׁן עֵינַיִךְ בְּרֵכוֹת בְּחֶשְׁבּוֹן עַל־שַׁעַר בַּת־
רַבִּים אַפֵּךְ כְּמִגְדַּל הַלְּבָנוֹן צוֹפֶה פְּנֵי דַמָּשֶׂק: רֹאשֵׁךְ
עָלַיִךְ כַּכַּרְמֶל וְדַלַּת רֹאשֵׁךְ כָּאַרְגָּמָן מֶלֶךְ אָסוּר בָּרְהָטִים:

7.5 Your neck is like the ivory tower; your eyes are pools at Heshbon, by the gate of Bat-Rabbim; your nose is like the tower of Lebanon, overlooking Damascus.
(6) Your head upon you is like Carmel; and the fringe of your head like purple; a king is caught in tresses.

Subtending these detailed observations, however, is an extended image, that subtly and completely reverses the appearance of distance, in that it is permeated with the Lover, and expresses their interpenetration. That which is hardly and ambiguously accomplished through wild dissolution in 7.8-10 is here an undramatic fact.

The image is that of the kingdom, the Beloved as the land of Israel /47/. The images are topographical, even where the referent, like the ivory tower, is unknown. Together, they compose a collective portrait - the tower of Lebanon sticks up like a nose, the head protrudes like Carmel /48/, the eyes glitter like pools, from a bird's eye perspective. The localities are all northern and peripheral; geographical inference would situate the Beloved's pudenda around the centre of the country, near Jerusalem /47/. The images give an impression of the life of the country - the watchful tower, the populous city, the exploitation of the sea. The military outpost in the far north, the remote city on the edge of the desert, the uncompromising headland, assert boundaries, the limits of the land, and also the possibility of influence beyond it, for example in the sea, or through trade, the busy traffic of Heshbon (it might be helpful to keep the exact images in mind: "Your eyes like pools in Heshbon [i.e. treasure, wealth] by the gate of Bat-Rabbim [lit. the daughter of the multitude] ... Your head like Carmel, its fringe of hair like purple [i.e. murex]"). The land is secure in its strength and prosperity; we have the abundant harvest in 7.3 as an illustration.

The image of the Beloved as the land of Israel is a specialisation of that of the Beloved as earth or earth-mother, our starting-point in 4.5. It is to be found elsewhere, especially in 6.4, the comparison with Jerusalem

Chapter Two - The Relationship of the Lovers

and Tirzah, and in the wasf of 4.1-5, with its pastoral activities and Tower of David. In contrast, the Lover, in his wasf, is associated with remote sources of metals - Tarshish and sapphires. The luminosity of the description of the Beloved, and hence the apparent love for the land of Israel, is augmented by the interdependence of the images. The tower is erected against the sky; the whiteness of its ivory in 7.5, and its shimmering decoration in 4.4, make it conspicuous from afar. The eye, on the other hand, is an image of profundity; light is reflected in the water. We thus have an interplay of height and depth, the duplication of images in the central pool, surrounded by likenesses of towers. In the following verse, the head is framed by hair just as Carmel is bordered by the dark sea; Krinetzki (1964: 216) attractively suggested that the hair glows in the sun. The radiance is seductive and irresistible. There follows an unexpected subversion: "A king is caught in tresses" /50/. And this suddenly is the point. The king is bound to his kingdom, to the royal purple: it expresses his power and wealth, is imbued with his personality; in turn, his wealth, prestige etc. only derives from its resources. This fusion is that of the lovers.

שָׁרְרֵךְ אַגַּן הַסַּהַר אַל־יֶחְסַר הַמָּזֶג בִּטְנֵךְ עֲרֵמַת חִטִּים
סוּגָה בַּשּׁוֹשַׁנִּים: שְׁנֵי שָׁדַיִךְ כִּשְׁנֵי עֳפָרִים תָּאֳמֵי צְבִיָּה:

7.3 Your vulva is a round crater - let the mingled wine never be lacking! your belly is a heap of wheat, hedged with lilies. (4) Your two breasts are like two fawns, twins of a doe.

As in 4.5, the fawns in 7.4 are associated with the feminine emblem of the lilies in 7.3 /51/, adjacent to the image of the vulva. The lilies that grace the harvest are indicative of the dependence of man on the earth, the people on the land, analogous to that of infant on mother, man on woman. If the expressive features represent the external defences, the belly connotes the internal economy. There is the same gratification of appetite as in 4.5 where the fawns feed among the lilies, of which the earth is the unfailing provider; it is reciprocated in adoration and adornment. If in 7.5-6 the woman is formidable and captivating, here she is bountiful, submissive and joyous (Soulen: 189-90); the previous image "Your vulva is a round crater - let the mingled wine never be lacking" /52/confirms, through the image of intoxication and "mingled wine", the dissolution of selves, the infantile clinging of the Lover to the inexhaustible cup of the

Beloved, and completes the metaphorical fusion of sex and suckling, teat and vagina - the vagina is now, as it were, the breast.

An underlying pattern is beginning to emerge, in which in the shadow of the distinctive features - the face, the date palm, etc. - and masked by the clarity of light, is the opposite configuration. The articulate face is a displacement of the body. It asserts the pride and dignity of the woman, her unassailable identity /53/, but it contends with and is permeated by the union of the lovers, whose separate symbols, expressive of their uniqueness, merge, as do their bodily functions; apples are shared under the apple tree and date palm; a few verses later (7.12) we also find henna-flowers, evoked by the Beloved for a tryst. Contrariwise, the Lover's face, with its lively feminine imagery, conducts the repressed energy of the statuesque body. There is the mechanism of projection or, conversely, mutual recognition. But there is also another process involved: a split between appearance and reality, a fusion despite appearances. Between them the lovers create a composite lover; each of them engenders his own child.

Lebanon, on which the Beloved's nose is situated, is an important signifier in the Song. The appearance of Lebanon is associated with the Lover - for example, we have "his appearance is like Lebanon" in 5.15 - as is the height and strength of its familiar timber - "choice as cedars" (ibid.). But the fragrance of Lebanon is feminine: "werêaḥ śalmōtayik kerêaḥ lebānôn" "And the fragrance of your skirts is like the

Chapter Two - The Relationship of the Lovers

fragrance of Lebanon" (4.11). The Lover is enveloped by the scents emanating from the herbs and cedar trees as he walks there. The clothes fit the body as the forest clothes Lebanon, suggesting an analogy between the Lebanon and the woman: the woman as the source of effluvia, the Lebanon as the soil on which vegetation grows, from which the sap is transmuted into perfume. The Lebanon is part of the earth that is personified in the Beloved. In 7.5, too, Lebanon is the connection between the nose with its tower and the earth; it represents the substance of the face and is part of the woman's body.

The palanquin of love, in 3.9, is made out of the wood of Lebanon: "Solomon made himself a palanquin, from the trees of Lebanon". In part this is an ironic reflection, since the palanquin is truly fashioned with the love of the daughters of Jerusalem; all the king's power and wealth - his dominion over cedars - provides only the outer framework. On the other hand, the panelling, with its resin, is both a tribute to the value of love, and subtly permeates the chamber with the scents and colours of Lebanon. In 1.17 too the houses of the lovers are of cedars /54/. And in 8.9 a cedar construction - palisade or plank - reinforces or frames the door of the Beloved. There it is both a masculine intrusion and a feminine assertion, whose ambiguities we shall explore when we investigate that passage in Chapter Three. In each case, then, cedar is bisexual - the house shared by lovers, the palanquin built by Solomon and paved by the daughters of Jerusalem, the adolescent girl whose changes are both physical and social. Likewise it is associated with both lovers in the Song: its appearance is masculine, mighty and imposing, its essence is feminine. Thus we come to the derivation of masculine from feminine imagery, as part of the reconstitution of the mother.

Moreover, the context is familiar from our previous discussion: "nōpet tiṭṭōpnâ šipetôtayik kallâ debaš wehālāb taḥat lešônēk wereaḥ śalmōtayik kereaḥ lebānôn" "Your lips drop honey, O bride; honey and milk are under your tongue, and the fragrance of your skirts is like the fragrance of Lebanon" (4.11). The kiss accompanies the image of Lebanon in 5.15-16 also: "His appearance is like Lebanon, choice as cedars. His palate is all sweets ...." The cycle between mother and infant, breasts and lips, the craving for satisfaction, for the exploratory tongue, is cancelled out by this relaxed participation in the life of the mother, supported rhetorically by the slowing down of the line: "wereaḥ śalmōtayik kerêaḥ lebānôn" "And the fragrance of your skirts is like the fragrance of Lebanon". The previous verse, too, follows the same pattern: "How lovely are your caresses, my sister, my bride; how much better are your caresses than wine, and the fragrance of your oils than all spices" (4.10). Dionysiac intoxication, the flow of liquid between the lovers, gives way to quiet breathing. It is paralleled by 1.1-4, where it is the Lover whose caresses are better than wine, and whose ointments are sweet. We have another instance of the reciprocity of lovers. The scent of the clothes corresponds to the fragrance of the apples in 7.9; there, likewise, the continuity of breathing, that flows uninterrupted between and through their lives, sustains and validates the accompanying orgasm; their momentary encounter is also a lasting concord. 7.8-10, with its intensity and dissipation, matches 4.8-11 in relation to the previous wasf; in both there is a sudden image of fragrance. Aggression is in search of tranquillity; to return to our primal idyll, the quietness of fawns feeding off lilies.

We have come to the turning of many ways. We have discerned various inversions of imagery: the breasts as fawns, the man's lips as lilies; each lover discovers himself intricately constellated in the other. The sustenance of life passes from the lilies to the fawns, from the female to the male, and thence back to the Beloved; there is a cycle, an unfailing spring. The Beloved sits under the apple tree; its delight is breathed by the Lover in 7.9. The differentiating features in 7.5-6 conceal and permit the interaction of king and kingdom, the discourse of fawns and lilies in 7.3-4. The rapprochement of lovers, the confusion of selves, as more and more complexes of images are built, leaves their essential identities untouched, and diffused. The milk passes from the mother to the lover and back again; both lovers seek in the other their first love, their mother. For the Beloved the sheltering apple is predominantly maternal, combining sex and suckling, as do the Lover's lips. There is a general metamorphosis of imagery; the lilies feed the fawns, feminine fragrance is concealed in masculine appearance, as we have seen in the case of Lebanon. For both lovers derive from and reconstitute the primordial bisexual mother, the ambivalent archetype to which we now turn.

3. The Mother and Twins

In 4.5 there is one phrase that has not yet been explored: "teʾômê ṣebiyyâ" "twins of a doe", that introduces us to the whole realm of sibling relationships. The repeated word

Chapter Two - The Relationship of the Lovers

"šenê" is unnecessary, as ruthless critics have noticed /55/. The verse could have read "šādayik koʿopārîm teʾômê ṣebiyyâ hārôʿîm baššôšannîm" "Your breasts are like fawns, twins of a doe, who feed among the lilies", without significant loss of meaning. The insertion of "šenê" before the predicate and complement balances the sentence as follows: 2-word Noun Phrase + 2-word Noun Phrase + 2 word Noun Phrase + 2-word Participle Phrase in apposition. I think its function is more than prosodic. Redundancies are useful guides to deeper levels of meaning (Ohmann: 1964). In this case the tautology reinforces the duality of breasts, of twins; "two" as an underlying motif in the sentence. By an odd regress, it is reflected in the structure: a twofold repetition of two: "Your <u>two</u> breasts like <u>two</u> fawns ...."

Recurrence draws attention to the musical quality of the word, by reducing its informational load. A good example is "werêaḥ śalmōtayik kerêaḥ lebānôn" in 4.11. It becomes a refrain, with a diffused connotative intensity. "Šenê šādayik kišnê ʿopārîm teʾômê ṣebiyyâ" "Your two breasts are like two fawns, twins of a doe ..." isolates the concept of two from particular objects and helps generate an alliteration on initial "š": "Šenê Šādayik kišnê". It also works in other ways.

Twins, in our verse, as rarely in life, are ideal progeny, expressing a perfect symmetry of left and right breasts, contributing to that of the two sides of the body. The twins are equal in age and in their claim on their mother; very possibly they are identical. Certainly there is an inference of equality, in size and beauty (Pope 1976: 470; Gordis 1974: 86) /56/. The two sucklings match two paps; a mother with twins is an ideal family unit, as is illustrated by a plaque from Ugarit (cf. Pope 1976: Plate XI). Parturition makes two complementary units of the single self. Duality in the Song is usually that of the lovers, whose union effects the integration of all natural oppositions. But here the two are not sexually polarised. The Lover recognises in the breast a "double". Doubles are uncanny; twins are often associated with magic /57/. A double in the world is a familiar part of oneself in whom everything unknown is projected.

The pair of fawns at the breast symbolise undifferentiated

opposites, sharing in the identity of the mother, who comprise a whole.

This is confirmed three verses previously:

שִׁנַּ֙יִךְ֙ כְּעֵ֣דֶר הַקְּצוּב֔וֹת שֶׁעָל֖וּ מִן־הָרַחְצָ֑ה שֶׁכֻּלָּם֙ מַתְאִימ֔וֹת וְשַׁכֻּלָ֖ה אֵ֥ין בָּהֶֽם׃

(4.2) Your teeth are like a flock of ewes, about to be shorn, who have come up from the washing; all of whom have twinned, and none are bereaved among them.

It is clear from the context that this image is of ideal fecundity, with a perfectly constituted flock, and a content shepherd. "mat'îmôt" gives an impression of a whole flock, all identical, perfectly white and woolly, multiplying geometrically, a collective and busy maternity that contrasts with the intimate but equally maternal scene witnessed in 4.5. No rams are in evidence. As an image for teeth it is distinctly odd yet ingenious; the upper and lower jaws are even and match each other, as do the breasts. The verse is full of puns and word-plays: mat'îmôt "twinned", for instance, is not only a play on "tamîm" "perfect", but internally symmetrical, with its repetition of "m" and "t" - MaT'îMôT. Surrounding it are two words almost identical but opposite in meaning: "šekkullâm ... wešakkulâ" "all of whom ... bereaved"; the one encompassing the totality of sheep, the other evoking a private, inconsolable absence (here, because it is in the negative, "none is bereaved", it is the absence of absence). Before that we have a curious apical alliteration, that is cunningly varied: "ke'ēder haqqeṣûbôt še'ālû min-hāraḥṣâ" "Like a flock of ewes, ready to be shorn, who have come up from the washing". The primary nouns "qeṣûbôt" "ewes, ready to be shorn" and "raḥṣâ" "washing" alliterate on "qṣ"➤"ḥṣ", "ḥ" being a continuant form of "q". In 6.6, where the verse is otherwise repeated verbatim, we find "ke'ēder hāReḤēlîm še'ālû min-hāRaḤṣâ" "Like a flock of ewes that have come up from the washing". There is, in other words, the same two-letter alliteration, but using a different permutation of letters: "rḥ" instead of "q/ḥṣ" (reḥēlim ... raḥṣâ).

But the strangest alliteration is on "šinnayik" "your teeth". It brings us back to "šenê" "two". The wasf is pervaded with puns on this word /58/: "šinnayik" in v. 2; "šānî" in "keḥûṭ haššānî śipetôtayik" "your lips are like a scarlet thread" in v. 3; "šenê" in v.5, and the "šôšannîm" "lilies". Moreover, if we look at the sister-verse in 7.4, there is an analogous set: "sûgâ

Chapter Two - The Relationship of the Lovers

baššôšannîm" "hedged with lilies" in v. 3; "šenê šādayik kišnê ʿopārîm" in v. 4; and "ṣawwāʾrēk kemigdal haššēn" "Your neck is like the ivory tower" in v. 5. All these are foregrounded, in initial or final positions; "haššēn" "ivory" in 7.5 also parallels the second "šenê" in 7.4. They thus contribute to the frame of the wasf; each verse, apparently totally discrete, is linked through paronomasia, the sound patterns that dissolve sharp visual imagery. The connections formed are at first sight baffling, which leads one to suspect that they are entirely fortuitous. In fact, they express the hidden dynamic of the wasf, its inarticulate structure.

Through the shared subject of lips, the colour sänî "scarlet" is linked to "šôšannîm" "lilies", assuming that the latter are red; it is opposed to "šinnayik" "your teeth", white and glistening. "Šenê" would seem to be without a correlative; nevertheless, 4.2 and 4.5 comprise a pair of images of twins, and share the dual form - "šinnayik" and "šādayik". In contrast, 4.3 is a duality that has fused: "Like a scarlet thread are your lips [śipetôtayik]". We thus have an interesting pattern of correlation and contrast.

We may go further. If 4.2 and 4.5 are distinct dual images, images of differentiation from a single mother, against the background of the productive earth, those of 4.3 are all of splitting or halving. Instead of 2 we have 1/2. What is noticeable in the lips is the crack between them. A "scarlet thread" is perhaps an unfeminine image, certainly compared to "šošannîm", and has received some surprised comment /59/. It appears singularly tame in this surrealist passage. Reduction, however, imparts intensification; the pressure on the lips heightens their colour. Red is an unfailing bait, as the cosmetics industry appreciates; we have lipstick, rouge, nail varnish, each shade with its own subtle message; bright red clothing is flagrant, as opposed to cool and sober blue. In the Ancient World, apart from being the colour of sin in Isaiah, scarlet is attractive and passionate; it is the essence of Ishtar in Lambert's Divine Love Lyrics from Babylon (1975: 123); in Egypt, the crimson of carnelian is the colour of passion as opposed to the sleek blue of faience /60/. Its role in enhancing Anat's potency and beauty preparatory to her bloodthirsty or venereal orgies is likewise familiar /61/. Thus, amid the proliferation of the other metaphors, the restrained image of the lips, as part of the objective delineation of the face, is of a narrow entrance into the interior of the Beloved, her sexual promise; the following phrase, "ûmidbārêk nāʾweh", completes the process: "And your speech is lovely". It is both her speech, expressing her desire for him, and the seductions of her voice, and by extension of poetry; the interchange of gender that we have traced among the senses is also that of thought and feeling /62/. The last phrase in the verse continues the sequence: "kepelaḥ hārimmôn raqqātēk mibba'ad leṣammātēk" "Like a slice of pomegranate is your temple behind your veil". It picks up and magnifies the colour of the lips and also the motif of splitting - the slice of pomegranate, pink and white with multiple seeds, suggests liquid sweetness behind the modest veil, analogous to the translucence of the wasf, the intricate net cast over images of dissolution.

In 4.5 the lilies are multiple and profuse on the meadow, like the pomegranate seeds in 4.3; the scarlet that shows through the lips with which they are paired is likewise fluid and pervasive; it represents the inner intensity of the Beloved, that resists control. Like the penetrated lips, the lilies are pasture for the fawns; corresponding to the intrusive breasts, the sharp teeth are mandibles. Thus there is a whole set of correspondences. In 7.3-5, too, the red of the lilies, scattered in profusion in the corn, contrasts with the single eminence of the white tower, with which it alliterates (šôšannîm ... haššēn). If the former are loosely abandoned, signifying, literally and metaphorically, the completion of the harvest, the latter has an unapproachable dignity. In both cases the alliteration serves to couple opposites, the fawns to lilies, the teeth to lips; more abstractly, red to white, the distinct to the indefinite.

Alliteration interlaces the extreme articulation of images characteristic of the wasf with an abstract musical sensuality, generating similes, a play of colours, voices, fusions and divisions. There is an active coherence, an implicit syntax, subtending the discrete images. It itself is organised into opposed groups: v. 4 has its own independent alliterative intricacy (e.g. "migdal ... māgēn"; the play on "t", "l" and "p" in "bānûy LeTaLPiyyôt ʾeLeP hammāgēn TāLûy 'ālāyw": ltlpt ... lp ... tl) and the rhyme "bānûy ... tālûy"). The distance interposed between the observer/speaker and the Beloved, through images of screens, such as the "veil" of 4.1 and 4.3, through the Pastoral idiom, the infantile temporal perspective, is compounded by this solipsistic pleasure in the pattern of sounds for their own sake, that yet couples and merges the distinct images, perceiving deeper interconnections, and moreover couples his voice to hers: "and your speech is lovely".

Chapter Two - The Relationship of the Lovers

Four times in the succeeding passage we find the phrase "'aḥōtî kallâ" "my sister, my bride", which critics explain, for the most part, as a conventional idiom (cf. Pope 1976: 480-1). Lys (180-1) suggests a possible mythological background, for instance in the love of Tammuz and Geshtinanna; Cook (119) an imagined violation of the prohibition of incest, as an expression of freedom:

> All intimacies, even forbidden ones, and all familial arrangements, even impossible ones, shower their attributes on the pair whom erotic joy expands into the multiple possibilities and heightened identities of union.

Yet it is very different from the conventional epithet, and far removed, as Lys implies, from its mythic origins. In Egyptian love poems the terms brother and sister are universal, and there are no others for lovers, so that apart from a general analogy of affection, it has minimal significance, equivalent indeed to "dôd" and "ra'yâ", as in our context Gordis (1974: 31-32) reductively suggests. It may be that there is Egyptian influence here; if so, the image has been transformed, brought back to life. In the first place, the coupling of "'aḥōtî" and "kallâ" entails an oxymoron; it spells out the incestuous implications that had been suppressed in the pallid cliché. Secondly, only in this passage (4.8-5.1) - with the exception of the following verse (5.2) - do we find this endearment, remarkable in a Song full of pet names. It suggests that it has a distinctive function, a particular colouring, endorsed by repetition, that contributes to the unique character of this sequence.

It is a psychoanalytic cliché that repression is strongest where desire is greatest. This gives an edge to Cook's observation, since what is being freed is one of the earliest frustrations. A sister is a first playmate; with her, far more than with the overpowering parents, one learns about human relationships as equals. Within the family they activate male and female components, complementing each other (which is perhaps why children's books tend to imagine the ideal family as girl, boy and parents); their union then perfects it, and closes it. Incestuous couples, as in inbred royal families, may feel themselves to be too good for the world /63/. In the Bible, incest is associated with sterility, not only in the savage incest laws, but in the ancestral myths. The patriarchal couples border on incest, and have recurring problems of barrenness. A family that only marries within itself cannot relate to the world, cannot contribute to a fecund society. It is an example of the pattern of imperfection, necessary for change and transformation, which we will find in the story of the Garden of Eden.

With the "sister-bride" we find a conjunction of opposites: the sister who has shared one's life, and the bride, the stranger with whom one is about to begin and beget new life; we find an outsider, whose origins are one's own. The identification of sister and bride, the ideal state, can in our world occur only through metaphor; the sister-in-law is symbolically adopted into the family, in her the Lover may recognise his sister. The passage concerns the bride who comes from Lebanon; in it the word "kallâ" is repeated six times. Whether she is really a sister or not, though it seems unlikely, is beside the point; what matters is the resemblance, and the vicarious fulfilment of incestuous desire. It adds another correspondence to those we found in the previous section. The king and the kingdom, likewise extending to Lebanon, are here brother and sister, an endogamous entity. We saw that the exchange of imagery between the lovers created a composite personality. Of this relationship the kinship of brother and sister is the clearest example. It is capable, moreover, of infinite extension (as in Job 17.14: "immî waʾaḥōtî lārimmâ" "My mother, my sister, the worm").

The first appearance of the phrase illustrates the tension between the two mutually exclusive terms:

לִבַּבְתִּנִי אֲחֹתִי כַלָּה לִבַּבְתִּנִי בְּאַחַד מֵעֵינַיִךְ בְּאַחַד עֲנָק מִצַּוְּרֹנָיִךְ׃

(4.9) You have ravished my heart, my sister, my bride; you have ravished my heart with one of your eyes, with one bead of your necklace.

The verb "libbabtinî" is ambiguous: it may be a loss of heart or an access of strength /64/. The heart, that is his consciousness, is intimately connected with hers; they have a shared identity, either because, as a bride, she has overwhelmed his rational, ordering senses with her unassimilated presence, or because, as her sister, their lives have always been bound together. The immensity of her presence, the combined brilliance of the jewels and the eye /65/, as well as the violence of the verse, suggests the former; while the other possibility is suggested more placidly, in the background, by the lovely pun between "ʾaḥōtî" "my sister" and "ʾaḥat" "one" /66/ and the metaphor "with one

Chapter Two - The Relationship of the Lovers

bead of your necklace", suggesting that, like the necklace, they too are indissolubly linked together.

There is an image of the Lover corresponding to that of Beloved as sister:

מִי יִתֶּנְךָ כְּאָח לִי יוֹנֵק שְׁדֵי אִמִּי אֶמְצָאֲךָ בַחוּץ אֶשָׁקְךָ
גַּם לֹא־יָבוּזוּ לִי: אֶנְהָגְךָ אֲבִיאֲךָ אֶל־בֵּית אִמִּי תְּלַמְּדֵנִי
אַשְׁקְךָ מִיַּיִן הָרֶקַח מֵעֲסִיס רִמֹּנִי:

(8.1) Who would make you like a <u>brother</u> to me, who sucked my mother's breasts? I would meet you outside, I would kiss you, and none would despise me.
(2) I would lead you, I would bring you to my mother's house, you/she would teach me, I would give you to drink of my spiced wine, my pomegranate juice.

As in 4.5, two sucklings suckle their mother's breasts; although they are not specifically twins, clearly there is an equivalence of size and status, analogous to that of the breasts in 4.5. It is moreover an identity of experience; the lovers share their earliest memories, the same sustenance and flesh.

Both 4.5 and 8.1 are similes: /67/

Your two breasts are <u>like</u> two fawns ...
Who would make you <u>like</u> a brother to me.

In both cases the comparison separates subject and conception; in 4.5 a formal marker, here it is a disorientatingly tentative analogy, that makes the imagined state yet more hypothetical. The correlative license to sucking the same mother's breasts is kissing in public: "I would meet you outside, I would kiss you, and none would despise me". The kiss communicates oral sweetness; the gift of the breasts, and with it that of life, is transmitted between the lovers. Thus the cycle between the generations is completed; from the mother they turn to each other.

The second verse reverses this: from the streets she brings him back to the matrix. It also casts the simile in doubt: in what sense is he like a brother? Is it that they share the same house or that they may be openly affectionate? Clearly there are limits to social tolerance, since she seeks privacy for further intimacy; on the other hand, she leads him and brings him to <u>her</u> mother's house, suggesting perhaps that it is unfamiliar to him, that he has to be admitted. Hence neither possible comparison works; he remains a quasi-brother, and

8.2 goes some way to restoring the reality of lovers who are strangers, with whom commerce is risky and clandestine. But this stranger is inducted into the family; the maternal nest replaces kinship ties in the scurrilous world. To this house he is a stranger - she brings him and guides him there - and there he receives hospitality. The Lover is thus introduced into the family, he becomes a quasi-brother not genealogically, but as a member of the household. The parallel with "who sucked my mother's breasts" is apparent. As the "twins" are fostered by the mother, so do the lovers return to her house for intimacy and drinks. As hostess, surrogate mistress of the house and its juices, the Beloved has a maternal function, with intensely erotic connotations, the spiced wine and pomegranate liquor combining the sensations of intoxication, fragrance and the quenching of thirst that are elsewhere associated with both sex and suckling. She gives a draught of the "'asîs rimmōnî" "the juice of my pomegranate", namely herself, reminding us of her definition as a "pardēs" -"park" or "paradise" of pomegranates in 4.13 /68/. The sexual metaphor is reinforced by the pun "'eššāqekâ/'ašqekâ" "I would kiss you/ I would give you to drink", suggesting an equivalence between the kiss and the drink, the external affectionate gesture and the warming liquid passed between the lovers. Correspondingly, the Lover is assimilated to the figure of the mother, through the ambiguity "telammedēnî" "You [m.]/she will teach me" /69/; as the one who initiates her, he adopts the part of the mother, through whose guidance the child enters the world. Equally, the mother may teach her either literally or metaphorically; either as a real mother, worldly-wise and experienced, or as the spontaneous feminine gift. Thus the stranger is adopted as a brother; love, an alliance outside the nuclear family, paradoxically restores it.

The simile "Who would make you like a brother to me?" sets the Lover at a distance; it is compounded by the rhetorical idiom "mî yittenekā" "Who would make you?" Only in fantasy, with its infinite possibility, can he ever be "like a brother". The audience, alerted and dismissed by the question, are part of the public social world that pours scorn on lovers. Yet she modestly does not even wish him to be a brother, merely <u>like</u> a brother. The simile reveals a vague non-identity, that the image of the relationship is not quite adequate, that the Beloved does not want her Lover to be her brother, only a quasi-brother, with whom sex would not be incest /70/. Such a relationship was at the mother's breasts,

Chapter Two - The Relationship of the Lovers

before the knowledge of taboos and the distinction of categories. For the Beloved this is always only a fantasy; the Lover is perennially a stranger, for whom she has to run the risk of an open encounter. The family is reconstituted provisionally, and still as a possibility, a wish-fulfilment.

"My sister, my bride", however, repeated affectionately and intensively, is an entirely positive celebration, truer than the fact that a wife cannot be a sister. It exposes the paradoxical duality of women to men, that they represent an unfamiliar part of the self. All wives are sisters, in the human family; the ideally loved sister, for example in children's games, is also the original wife.

The phrase "my sister, my bride" is central to the extended metaphor of which it is part; the hesitation "Who would make you like a brother to me" is peripheral, and soon is forgotten in the developing fantasy. This may be conveyed through the syntax. "My sister, my bride" is a still and functionally isolated part of the sentence, that merely calls forth her presence; symmetrically embedding it are duplicated verbs and images, that as it were radiate from it:

libbabtinî 'aḥōtî kallâ libbabtinî	(4.9)
mah-yāpû dōdayik 'aḥōtî kallâ mah-ṭōbû dōdayik	(4.10)
gan nā'ûl 'aḥōtî kallâ gal nā'ûl	(4.12)
bā'tî legannî 'aḥōtî kallâ 'ārîtî môrî	(5.1)

You have ravished my heart, my sister, my bride,	
You have ravished my heart ...	(4.9)
How beautiful are your caresses, my sister, my bride,	
How much better are your caresses ...	(4.10)
A locked garden is my sister, my bride,	
A locked fountain ...	(4.12)
I have come into my garden, my sister, my bride,	
I have gathered my myrrh ... /71/	(5.1)

At the centre of each sentence, then, is the Beloved.

In 4.5, in the image of suckling twins the Lover sees in the Beloved's breasts an earlier version of himself; between them the lovers contain an animal innocence. The twins are undifferentiated, a mere complementarity of left and right; in them all dualities can be reconciled, created and sustained by the fusion of the lovers, the Lover's gaze, the Beloved's milk. In 8.1 the shared past is likewise an ideal image, to be created or invented by lovers. Here in 4.12-5.1 the coupling "my sister, my bride" is an essential attribute, intricately connected with the rest of the sequence.

The two overlapping images, Lebanon and the garden, are opposites, and interdependent: the wild mountains, the cultivated garden. From the Lebanon the lovers come:

אִתִּי מִלְּבָנוֹן כַּלָּה אִתִּי מִלְּבָנוֹן תָּבוֹאִי תָּשׁוּרִי מֵרֹאשׁ אֲמָנָה מֵרֹאשׁ שְׂנִיר וְחֶרְמוֹן מִמְּעֹנוֹת אֲרָיוֹת מֵהַרְרֵי נְמֵרִים׃

(4.8) With me from Lebanon, O bride, with me from Lebanon come, hurry/ look down from the peak of Amana, from the peak of Senir and Hermon, from the dens of lions, from the mountains of leopards.

Lebanon, as we have seen, is associated with both, with the Lover for appearance, with the Beloved for fragrance. Yet it is strange to both of them, an ambiguous territory, the extreme edge of the kingdom. If in the poem the king and the kingdom comprise a unity corresponding to that of the lovers, it is the verge of the national collective identity, of which theirs is part. There is a double perspective, since "ʾittî" "with me" /72/ implies that the Lover/speaker escorts the Beloved, while the imperative "Come" followed by "hurry/look" /73/ confers a distant point of view, compounded by the singular verb. We would expect a companion to say "let us go" rather than "come". The Lover would be the destination of her journey, accordingly; the view from the mountains encompasses the whole land of Israel, the land of the Song, round which they are grouped in an arc /74/. Lys (178) protests somewhat archly against too particular a travelogue "à moins d'être une géante (une déesse) posant un pied sur chaque mont?" /75/ Nevertheless, there is something clearly larger than life about the verse, to which commentators have been right to attribute mythological

Chapter Two - The Relationship of the Lovers

echoes /76/. The foreclosure of space contributes to the grandeur of the woman, as the mistress of the mountains, the forbidding landscape. Climbing mountains, especially sacred ones, has a mystical aspect, that no part of the earth should be inaccessible to man. She thus dominates nature, apparently unafraid and unharmed, among dens of lions, the mountains of leopards. The note of triumph is sustained by the list of conquered peaks, the dotted rhythm, by repetition and alliteration, e.g. the permutation (a) "tāŠûRî MēRoŠ 'aMāNâ MēRoŠ ŠeNîR weḥeRMôN" (ŠR mRŠ mn mRŠ ŠnR Rmn) followed by (b) "weḥeRmôn mimme'ōnôt 'aRāyôt mēhaReRê nemēRîm" with its ringing "r" sounds, supported by nasals.

In the next verse the distance between the lovers abruptly dissolves; from the remote parts of Lebanon the Beloved enters the heart.

לִבַּבְתִּנִי אֲחֹתִי כַלָּה לִבַּבְתִּנִי בְּאַחַד מֵעֵינַיִךְ בְּאַחַד עֲנָק מִצַּוְּרֹנָיִךְ׃

(4.9) You have ravished my heart, my sister, my bride, you have ravished my heart with one of your eyes, with one bead of your necklace.

The impact is overdetermined by paronomasia between "lebanôn" and "libbabtinî"; the antithesis suggesting a sudden analogy of subjugation, an implosion of energy; Lebanon is as it were concentrated in his heart. The hyperbole - "with one of your eyes, with one bead of your necklace" - intimates overwhelming majesty. A literary analogy is Sappho's Ode "Poikilothron' athanat' Aphrodita" "Richly enthroned immortal Aphrodite" with its tremendous pressure on the human heart and its conjuring of distances /77/ ("mê m'asaisi mêd' oniaisi damna, potnia, thumon" "Break not my spirit, Lady, with heartache or anguish" [tr. Page]).

Then in the last verse before the image of the garden, after a relaxation of tensions, concentrating on her maternal and intoxicating caresses, Lebanon is adduced once more, in an odd parenthesis between kisses.

נֹפֶת תִּטֹּפְנָה שִׂפְתוֹתַיִךְ כַּלָּה דְּבַשׁ וְחָלָב תַּחַת לְשׁוֹנֵךְ וְרֵיחַ שַׂלְמֹתַיִךְ כְּרֵיחַ לְבָנוֹן׃

(4.11) Your lips drop honey, O bride; honey and milk are under your tongue, and the fragrance of your skirts is like the fragrance of Lebanon.

The association with diffuse, enveloping femininity needs no further elaboration; Lebanon represents the essence of the Beloved, clothed by herbs and trees. Thus there is a vivid paradox: the Beloved leaves herself.

4.8   Beloved leaves Lebanon
▼
4.11   Beloved = Lebanon

In the next chapter I will discuss the relationship between ambiguity in the Song and its aesthetic correlate as a conflict between the desire for fusion and the necessity for differentiation. Of this this passage provides an excellent illustration. The divergent meanings are kept in counterpoise, not quite resolving; the lovers are urged to leave Lebanon together, an alien, ambiguous territory, which yet symbolises both of them. The double perspective is maintained throughout. The enormous, intractable mountain, home of the gods /78/, is infused into the heart, the seat of consciousness; "libbabtinî" implies both loss of self, surrender to the Beloved, and self-renewal; the rare verbal form of "lēb" "heart" in the intensive mode (Piel) imbues the heart with a vital, energetic quality, as if it only truly exists in motion, as part of the interchange of lovers; as if the supposition of its stability is illusory. In the next verses the motifs of suckling and intoxication - honey and milk under your tongue, your caresses like wine - appear as metaphor, in an adult reciprocal context, and mitigate being swamped by her presence through metonymy, exclamation and reflection; they enable him, in other words, to recover some of his composure. Finally there is the image of the fragrance of Lebanon, which both envelops him and is reflexively observed by him.

The development of the image of the garden is similar in structure. In 4.12 the garden is the Beloved: "gan nā'ûl 'aḥōtî kallâ gal nā'ûl ma'yān ḥātûm" "A locked garden is my sister, my bride, a locked pool, a sealed spring". The garden, unlike Lebanon, is enclosed, safe and fertile. It has most frequently been understood to be a banal reference to virginity /79/. This may only be one of its implications. The potentiality of a metaphor, while not inexhaustible, is usually multiple: otherwise it would be superfluous. A garden is private, secure, and beautiful; in it nature is humanised, like the girl, whose genetic endowment is perfected through culture. She, like the garden, is her own creation, fostered by her parents and society, secluded, both as a girl in the ancient world and

Chapter Two - The Relationship of the Lovers

as a human being with an innate sensitivity and capacity for growth. She is enclosed in her person, protected by the defences that preserve her identity, her unique privacy. The implications of the metaphor will be more fully worked out in the fourth chapter. Here I would like to concentrate on it as an extended image of the relationship of the lovers, and hence as a microcosm of the poem.

"A locked garden is my sister, my bride, a locked pool, a sealed fountain." She is an enclosed garden, but she is also a sealed spring /80/. The link between the two is suggested by the paronomasia "gan ... gal" /81/ "garden ... pool, source, fountain", and the ambiguity of "šelaḥayik" "your shoots/canals" in the next verse /82/. There is an ingenious phonological metaphor here: "gal" "pool" substitutes the liquid "l" for the vibrant "n" of gan. Visually the participles "locked/sealed" arrest the dissolution of the garden into water; we know that the frozen ondulation must loosen, the garden must open. The surface tension, the pressure behind the Beloved's careful self-containment, promises the contrary: the springs will flow, the lovers merge. In the background of the discreet girl is a pervasive fecund element, a potentiality for flow, the "animula vagula". H.P. Müller has perceptively noticed how the syntax imposes tranquillity: in 4.12-15, according to his reading, the only verbal forms are these two passive participles: "locked" and "sealed", ironically intensifying inertia /83/.

The spring is that which waters gardens, that is responsible for their perennial and gorgeous flourishing. She is thus both a garden, a cultural/instinctual compound, and a small part of one. As a garden, she has extension, enclosed in a physical body which she does her best to protect against injury and the vicissitudes of time; a place in society; a biography, selected and understood through memory; a personality. The products of the garden, spices and fruits, make her attractive, a cultural commodity. As a spring, however, she is the irrepressible life force, the informing spirit of the garden. Thus she is both subject and object to herself; the totality of the self and something obscurely recognised, an elusive essence in each particular.

The spring flows from Lebanon: "maʿyan gannîm beʾēr mayim ḥayyîm wenōzlîm min-lebānôn" "A fountain of gardens, a well of living waters, flowing from Lebanon" (4.15). This is most curious. Does the garden grow round the spring, or does the spring rise elsewhere? A spring by definition is a headwater, a beginning. Hence there is a double focus. The Beloved is both the garden and not the garden, but its nucleus; this nucleus is both central to the garden and at distance from it; and to make matters yet more complicated, the Lebanon symbolises the Beloved in 4.11, and from it she comes in 4.8. She is spring, garden and Lebanon; intrinsic and separate from herself; moving from herself, as a spring from its source in Lebanon, and animating herself through this movement.

A further source of ambiguity in 4.15 is the plural "A fountain of garden<u>s</u>, a well of living waters". This may be an inflated plural for singular, or suggest that the evidently magnificent garden portrayed in 4.13-14 is a complex of gardens, as perhaps in 6.11, or that the fertile influence of the stream spreads to others, in other words that the Beloved's life animates those beyond her. Or it may be unlimited - the spring of all gardens - in other words she is transpersonal, pan-horticultural, living water common to all of us, consonant with her symbolic function as a universal figure /84/.

Up to this point the subject has been the Beloved, enclosed within herself, considered abstractly, as in a wasf. In 4.16 the garden becomes an image, the focus, of the lovers' relationship. From being closed it becomes ever more open.

עוּרִי צָפוֹן וּבוֹאִי תֵימָן הָפִיחִי גַנִּי יִזְּלוּ בְשָׂמָיו יָבֹא דוֹדִי לְגַנּוֹ וְיֹאכַל פְּרִי מְגָדָיו:

(4.16) Awake, O north wind, and come, O south, breathe upon my garden, let its spices flow forth, let my love come into his garden and eat its/his precious fruits. /85/

At the centre of the verse there are two suffixes: "gannî" and "gannô", <u>my</u> garden and <u>his</u>. No sooner does she take possession of her garden i.e. her identity, the most precious thing she has, than she sacrifices it, a familiar but complex irony (cf. Falk 1982: 102). For it is not quite selfless. It is not clear that the garden is any the less hers for being his. On the contrary, their individuality, social and sexual maturity, is completed through their union. "Mine" and "his" are in conjunction, joined by the garden that grows between and around them; they emerge at this moment, and contribute to a composite entity. Moreover, the garden may always have been "his"; it was for his sake that the fruit ripened and the spices grew redolent. Sociologically, too, virginity is a sexual

Chapter Two - The Relationship of the Lovers

value, privacy awaits discovery. Paradoxically, the garden fulfils itself through self-surrender: the Lover eats its fruit, breathes its spices.

The Lover's penetration is an image of the sexual act, as most commentators have said /86/. He possesses the garden, conforming to the familiar subordination of women, and he is incorporated by it. The masculine intrusion corresponds to an infantile dependence; the reversal of functions is imparted through a metaphor of feeding, off "the precious fruits". The Lover is contained in the Beloved/mother, returning to an evocation of the womb; her availability recalls suckling. Krinetzki (1970: 410) aptly examines the vessel/container as an archetypal symbol for the mother, as exemplified by the garden. The Lover is then an outsider, who finds his origins in the garden; the Beloved is both mother and maiden. The instigation of awakening at the beginning of the verse "Awake, O north wind, and come, O south", the stirring of the atmosphere, so that its spices flow, rouses also the dormant garden, is a sexual restlessness. The openness to the winds foreshadows that to the Lover. The Beloved too is doubly present; as well as being the garden, she comes from outside it, as the spring that waters it. The garden then grows between the lovers, and it is an image of their relationship. Therein they project themselves, the one as mother, the other as infant, in a symbiosis in which the garden is consummated by welcoming the Lover; and the Lover is entirely sustained by the garden.

The sequence began with the Lover inviting the Beloved to leave Lebanon, associated with both of them, symbol of the archaic bisexual mother. Here the Beloved invites the Lover to re-enter the garden, the matrix. The inception "With me from Lebanon come" is structurally closed by "May my love enter his garden". Similarly, in 8.1-2, the Lover is a stranger, who reconstitutes the original family, and is symbolically adopted into the matrix.

The Beloved invites him to "eat his precious fruits", a reference to his mouth-watering description of her as "a paradise of pomegranates with precious fruits" in 4.13. Similarly, "yizzelû beśāmāyw" "may its spices <u>flow</u>" reflects "wenōzlîm min-lebānôn" "<u>flowing</u> from Lebanon" in the previous verse (the only occurrences of the root "NZL" in the book), and reminds us that the fragrance of her skirts is as Lebanon. The Beloved, in other words, will be incorporated in him, as well as enclosing him, assimilated in his bloodstream. There is a flow of vitality from the Beloved to the Lover, stimulating his appetite. He devours her, "his precious fruit", thus completing the sexual cycle, the exchange of identity; yet she remains constant, inexhaustible. For she is the spring that waters the garden. Because of the unfailing spring, the garden is verdant. In the Beloved the spring is an emission from the earth, the natural mother in the Song, and thus a source of fertility and health that comes from outside the relationship. She draws from her experience; part of her consciousness is detached, bound to earliest memories, generating the garden, yet still secluded from it, or rather in it. Only through being herself can she give herself. Through the sap of the trees and the fruit the spring feeds the Lover: he absorbs the purity of the water, the chastity represented by the garden.

The last verse is a celebratory coda, a free recapitulation, closing the sequence:

בָּאתִי לְגַנִּי אֲחֹתִי כַלָּה אָרִיתִי מוֹרִי עִם־בְּשָׂמִי אָכַלְתִּי יַעְרִי עִם־דִּבְשִׁי שָׁתִיתִי יֵינִי עִם־חֲלָבִי אִכְלוּ רֵעִים שְׁתוּ וְשִׁכְרוּ דּוֹדִים:

(5.1) I have come into my garden, my sister, my bride, I have gathered my myrrh with my spice, I have eaten my comb with my honey, I have drunk my wine with my milk: eat, O friends, drink and be drunken, O lovers.

It is a song of greedy exploitation, of masculine triumph, expressive of satiety. This catalogue of satisfactions is the culmination of the process, the consummation of the enclosed garden. The keynote of the verse is "î", as Müller remarks: /87/ "I entered ... I gathered ... I ate ..." Fertilisation is appropriation; the ego, the possessive, divisive centre of consciousness, can only be selfish. The powerful verbs - the active "qals" that emerge for the first time - represent a phallic thrust. Yet the assertion of the ego verges on dissolution. Underneath the array of inflections - "bā'tî", "gannî", etc. - the verbs evoke sensations of intoxication and confusion. He absorbs the essence of the Beloved, quenching his thirst, consuming sweetness; she comprises his plenitude. The allusions to 4.10-11, as well as to the spice-garden, knit the sequence together; they remind us of her active role in the relationship - her caresses in 4.10, her lips that dropped honey in 4.11 - and its infantile correlate, the dependence of the Lover in 4.11 on the milk of the Beloved. The emphatic succession of verbs likewise has a chiastic resonance: whereas

Chapter Two - The Relationship of the Lovers

he now violates and gluts himself on her, in 4.9 it was <u>she</u> who ravished his heart: "libbabtinî". Her power becomes his.

The symmetry and stillness of 4.12-15, with its nominal structure, bursts in 4.16-5.1 in a proliferation of verbs. The sealed spring is loosened. Actions and gestures tumble over each other, without forethought, as if all delay were intolerable. An example of the subtle festination and the vivid sense of timing is the syncopation "yābōʾ dôdî legannô ... bāʾtî legannî ʾaḫōtî kallâ" "May my love come into his garden ... I have come into my garden, my sister, my bride". Past overlaps with future /88/; the Lover anticipates the Beloved's wish; alternatively, desire and fulfilment are simultaneous.

Moreover, the verbal mode changes from desire to fulfilment: from the improbable imperatives "Awake, O north wind, and come, O south" through conjectural wishes to the active verbs of 5.1; corresponding to this is a development from the ethereal to the carnal, from winds and vapours to the lovers, from awakening and breathing to eating and drinking. With these verbs, the active mode combines with a passive function: the Lover is the recipient of nourishment as well as the aggressive intruder.

The concluding exhortation "Eat, O friends, drink and be drunken, O lovers" has been much emended and disputed /89/. Marcia Falk (1982: 123ff.; cf. Gerleman: 162) - whose interpretation of the whole passage is rather similar to mine - considers that it is a reflection by a third party, such as the poet, witnessing the joy of the lovers. The reasoning is plausible; nevertheless it is not decisive. There is no indication that the Lover stops speaking, that it is not he as poet who reflects on this scene /90/. The friends and lovers include all who participate in the Song, and in the garden of Love. It now becomes a universal image, as the lovers are universal figures. Its linguistic expression is the garden of poetry, namely the Song itself, as an emblem of civilisation. The metaphor will form the basis of my fourth chapter.

The lovers hurry down from Lebanon, which, wild and voracious, threatens to devour them. Yet its lower slopes are fragrant, and it is the source of the spring that waters the garden. That which is barren gives life to the world, a transformation to which we shall return. As the origin of the lovers, whose association with the archetypal bisexual mother has already been explored, it represents the matrix, now alien to them, an ambiguous inaccessible terrain. It is sacred, the home of the gods, in other words, the meeting point of heaven and earth, the primordial parents; as such it excludes man, and is mysterious.

Lebanon and the garden are in apposition, polarising nature amenable to man and hostile to man, unfailing abundance and utter desolation. They represent twin aspects of the Beloved, the archetypal Mother, from whom the two lovers - brother and sister - are differentiated. As the origin of life, the stream that feeds the gardens, Lebanon represents the womb, which we must leave in order to live. The womb is a cold, uninhabited region, precultural, inhuman, whose ravenous denizens - lions and leopards - are unremitting enemies of man. Their appetite contrasts with the fecund hunger of the Lover in 4.16-5.1. Alongside the bountiful, idealised mother is the terrible mother, who devours her children, as does the earth in death /91/; the ambivalence of the Beloved/mother in the Song as in life is a familiar theme, illustrated by Pope (1976: 161ff.) and Krinetzki (1970: 413), and will be the subject of the next chapter. The Beloved as garden reconstitutes the womb, as a bountiful, fertile enclosure, irrigated and vernal. There she meets her lover, in the sexual act generating new life; they are enclosed in that womb, as brother and sister, infant and mother. She too is part of the garden, as its spring. Therefore one must leave the womb in order to enter the womb. In 4.8 they leave Lebanon, as siblings in the womb of the original parent; in 4.16-5.1 they generate life in their turn. The persistent ambiguity makes them strangers in the world. The king and the land, the pure water, are united only through the voice of the imagination and of poetry. Death feeds life, nature culture; the Beloved has her roots in Lebanon, the ancestral past. Thereby she sustains the garden, and admits the Lover.

The integration is most concisely expressed in the equivalence "'aḥōtî kallâ" "my sister, my bride". Its structural encapsulation at the heart of the sentences in which it occurs has already been attested. In the passage as a whole, too, it unifies the image of the garden, as a frame. The initial situation, "A locked garden is my sister, my bride", chimes with "I have come into my garden, my sister, my bride" in 5.1, its resolution. He has taken possession of the enclosed garden "my sister, my bride"; the endearment is central to the Lebanon sequence - the shock of the encounter, her caresses - which is enclosed by "kallâ" "bride", in 4.8 and 4.11, a non-incestuous attachment. Bride becomes sister-bride, sister-bride becomes bride. We can represent the structure as follows /92/:

Chapter Two - The Relationship of the Lovers

	4.8:	kallâ		
	4.9:	ʾaḥōtî kallâ	4.12	ʾaḥōtî kallâ
Lebanon:			The Garden:	
	4.10	ʾaḥōtî kallâ	5.1	ʾaḥōtî kallâ
	4.11	kallâ		

4.8-5.1 is also the central garden of the Song, not only as its most coherent and intricately elaborated image, the focus of all the tensions we have been exploring, and as, more or less, the actual centre of the poem, but because here the relationship is consummated. 5.1, the fulcrum, the midpoint of the poem, divides it into two; it is followed by a silence, and a new, disagreeable beginning. For this reason nowhere else is the Beloved called bride, and otherwise only in 5.2, in a mock-echo, is she called "sister". The terms are crucial. As a bride, coming from Lebanon, transformed into the garden, she represents the union of opposites; the Lover is perpetually a stranger. As sister, she reminds us of our common origin, the complementarity of man and the earth, culture and nature. Through marriage, and its linguistic equivalent in metaphor, the family expands indefinitely. As human beings, the lovers enact in each other their earliest experiences, and are bound by their common humanity, beyond self and other. Herein too we find the imprint of man's existential ambiguity: as a natural creature,, with a capacity for transcendence.

Finally, let us look back. We found three instances of the sibling relationship at the matrix: 4.1-5, the fawns feeding off the mother, 8.1-2, and 4.8-5.1. In each case there is a regression to a time before relationships and prohibitions, to the pastoral idyll in 4.5, an animal innocence, to the breasts in 8.1-2, to the paradise of pomegranates in 4.13, a garden where everything is permissible. We have seen how under the carefully formalised framework there is a pattern of union and differentiation, intermittently perceived through the alliteration of the wasf, in the play on the Beloved's body; through a retreat from society into the womb of the mother's house in 8.1-2, whereby society continues, and through the complex and consistent ambiguity of 4.8-5.1. What remains is to touch on the relationship between the wasf and its consummation in the garden. The wasf, as we have seen, is a highly artificial, hierarchical portrait, concealing the integration of lovers. Both chapters 3 and 4 end with an epithalamium; in between there is this tight, and very tense, passage enclosed by the word "beautiful", in which the Lover attempts to analyse his Beloved objectively, with aesthetic detachment. In the next chapter I shall argue that beauty is essentially ambivalent, a partial defence against anarchic primitive drives, an articulation of the image to prevent its destruction. The relationship between the static portrait and the extended dynamic metaphor corresponds with that between the catalogue of spices in the garden - its tranquil exposition - and its consumption.

The wasf ends in flight "to the mountain of myrrh, to the hill of frankincense" (4.6). Gerleman (158) is right, I think, to associate this with the land of Punt, a fabulous country, like spice islands, far away /93/.

Through the refrain, 4.5-6 = 2.16-17, it evokes the image of the Lover as fawn in 2.17, bounding on the hills and mountains /94/, a free agent, attracted to but never at home in the domains of the Beloved; he is also the poet, fancy free, whose verbal ingenuity and license is denied reality. But here the flight to the vapours of fantasy is in fact a flight to Lebanon. The poet goes to the frankincense hill, the aesthetic resort, the poem goes to Lebanon, through a clever paronomasia. "Lebõnâ" - "frankincense" - and "lebānõn" is another conjunction of opposites: fantasy and reality, tropic and tundra. From Lebanon he calls forth the Beloved, for Lebanon mediates between this world and that, as a frontier territory, between earth and heaven, life and death. Its slopes are fragrant with forests, as the Beloved's clothes transmit her presence; its rain gives life to the world, though it is barren. The mother's affection, the fragrance and security of her clothes, the air she breathes, conceals the reality of her gift of life, that it is life-and-death, death as a concomitant of life, from which we come. In the next section, I shall be concerned with this, the basic relationship of the Song, the contrary and complementary forces and impulses of creation and destruction, the love of life and the drive towards death, consciousness and unconsciousness. For there in the womb of the archetypal bisexual mother, opposites are reconciled, split-selves are integrated.

Chapter Two - The Relationship of the Lovers

4. Love and Death

The tension in the Song between the desire of the lovers to unite and the inevitability of their parting is that also between their voice and the silence into which it vanishes, and between love and death - the ultimate parting, the unbroken silence. Everything created by the Song is a defence against it, or an expression of it. Yet death is not mentioned except once, and then towards the end of the poem. It appears in disguise, metonymically, the invisible presence behind everything transitory, in every threat to the lovers and their world.

Perhaps I am wrong: there is no awareness of death in the Song except for this one verse: it is a Biblical legend of Siddhartha. This indeed is the point, since one can scarcely suppose a writer who was ignorant of death except as an irony; as in the Pastoral, he constructs a perfect world as a retreat and a sidelong comment on his own. Death is alluded to on its fringes, in the lions and leopards of Lebanon, the watchmen patrolling the walls against the city's eventual destruction, the vague "terror of the night" (3.8). Only at the end of the poem, in 8.6 is it personified as part of the language, incorporated as the antonym of love, and hence of the Song.

We have the image of our death inside us, setting a limit to our lives and our capacities, threatening us with oblivion. Against its fear we more or less struggle, seeking to integrate life and death, death as part of life. One cannot venture on the one without arriving at the other; the battle to survive is also against internal destructive forces. We have the wish for Nirvana, the death-wish in Job, and in the Egyptian Dialogue on Death; the desire for rest, to make life complete and whole. Death is also a return to non-existence, an undifferentiated fusion of consciousness and unconsciousness, associated with the womb, sleep and love.

In the Song, as far as I can tell, there is no wish for death, in the sense of annihilation; death is that which is most feared, on the periphery of its consciousness. On the one hand, as Müller (1977: 161) says, it is a "spielerisch-hedonisch" escape, on the other it explores the possibilities of absolute pleasure and absolute value. Furthermore, as we shall see, there is a constant process from life to death and vice versa; life and death are inextricable. If there is no wish to die - in the sense of Job or Keats, as an escape from an intolerable existence - and if death remains for ever inimical to the world of the Song, there is a transformation of death into life, non-being to birth, between Lebanon, the womb they had to leave in order to live, and the garden they create between them.

In this section I hope to explore the climactic opposition of love and death in 8.6-7. It is generally recognised as the grand credo /95/, to which all the painstaking comparisons of the Song have contributed. Love, through metaphor and simile, is the sum of all pleasures; the lovers represent all the creatures and life-forces in the world; now they and that which animates them are set against death, in the context of birth.

I will begin by reverting to 8.1-2, the adoption of the Lover as a quasi-brother in the nuclear family. It is paralleled by and to some extent abbreviates 3.1-4, in which the Beloved leaves her bed, finds her lover "outside", in the streets and squares of the city, and brings him home. In particular, 3.4 has an identical action "to bring ... to my mother's house", amplified however by the synonymous parallelism "to the room of my conception".

עַל־מִשְׁכָּבִי בַּלֵּילוֹת בִּקַּשְׁתִּי אֵת שֶׁאָהֲבָה נַפְשִׁי בִּקַּשְׁתִּיו
וְלֹא מְצָאתִיו: אָקוּמָה נָּא וַאֲסוֹבְבָה בָעִיר בַּשְּׁוָקִים
וּבָרְחֹבוֹת אֲבַקְשָׁה אֵת שֶׁאָהֲבָה נַפְשִׁי בִּקַּשְׁתִּיו וְלֹא
מְצָאתִיו: מְצָאוּנִי הַשֹּׁמְרִים הַסֹּבְבִים בָּעִיר אֵת
שֶׁאָהֲבָה נַפְשִׁי רְאִיתֶם: כִּמְעַט שֶׁעָבַרְתִּי מֵהֶם עַד
שֶׁמָּצָאתִי אֵת שֶׁאָהֲבָה נַפְשִׁי אֲחַזְתִּיו וְלֹא אַרְפֶּנּוּ עַד־
שֶׁהֲבֵיאתִיו אֶל־בֵּית אִמִּי וְאֶל־חֶדֶר הוֹרָתִי:

(3.1) On my bed nightly I sought him whom my soul loves; I sought him, and did not find him.
(2) "Let me arise now and go round about the city, in the streets and squares, I will seek him whom my soul loves"; I sought him and did not find him.
(3) The watchmen who go round about the city found me "Have you seen whom my soul loves?"
(4) Hardly had I left them, than I found whom my soul loves; I grasped him and I would not let him go, until I brought him to my mother's house, to the bower of the one who conceived me.

In 8.1-2 we saw that the movement is from the siblings suckling at their mother's breasts to their adult counterparts, exchanging kisses; the mother's house, in which both lovers have a maternal function, reconstitutes the breast,

Chapter Two - The Relationship of the Lovers

conforming to their expanded horizons, both through the syntactic and semantic coupling in equivalent positions in the sentences of "yônēq šedê ʾimmî" "who suckled at my mother's breasts" with "ʾel-bêt ʾimmî" "to my mother's house", and through oral excitation: milk - kisses - spiced wine, pomegranate juice. 3.1-4 represents regression to an earlier stage still: to conception and birth, "to the bower of the one who conceived me". The Lover is eliminated altogether as an active partner; he is led passively by the hand, "I grasped him and I would not let him go". But like 8.1-2 there is a circular structure. The solitary bed is a place for sleep, for reabsorption into the primal unity, preceding the differentiation of self and other; sleep as a return to the womb - not to speak of a foreshadowing of death - is a commonplace (cf. Fordham: 112). But the Beloved cannot sleep, for she lacks "him whom my soul loves"; only through their fusion can it become complete. She seeks him, her solitude emphasised not only by the darkness and the unhelpful watchmen, but by her curious objectivity: she observes her internal debate, the actions and impulses of her "soul", as if to illustrate the discord within her. She finds him, and brings him home "to my mother's house, to my conceiver's bower". The Beloved will conceive where she was conceived. This may be a simple euphemism: the chamber of conception is the vagina (so Krinetzki 1981: 116); in guiding him there, she is assisting the exploratory lover. The mother's house, "the chamber of conception", is more emotive than this, however; on the ancestral marriage bed the lovers meet. In other words, she is reenacting the intercourse of her parents, and hence of all parents, returning to her own origins to generate new life /96/. Thus we move from the solitary bed to the ancestral bed, from restlessness to fusion not only with her Lover but with her parents. There is a metaphor here: at the matrix history repeats itself. The lovers meet, becoming parents in their turn, at the site of intercourse, in the womb of the generations. The ancestral seed is renewed between them; the dead conceive, and are conceived, in the nursery of the future.

3.1-4 breaks off at this point, at the threshold of intimacy; 8.1-2 continues with the lovers' overtures in the house: "you/she would teach me; I would give you to drink of my spiced wine, my pomegranate juice". The expectation that "ʾel-ḥeder hôrātî" "to my conceiver's bower" will balance ʾel-bêt ʾimmî "to my mother's house" is suspended; there is a sense of elision: "ʾel-ḥeder hôrāti" is mentally inserted alongside "telammedēnî" "you/she would teach me", and the two variants play against each other. This is a favourite technique of the Song. Here they are complementary: the confluence of suckling overlays the sotte voce impregnation. The lovers form the matrix, both in the sense of the womb, the conception-site, and the breast, the life-support. As in the garden, in which the Beloved is "my sister, my bride", here the Lover is fictively a brother, as well as a stranger, in the collective body.

In 8.3, following this scene of growing excitement and activity, there is a brief still-life: "śemō'lô taḥat rōšî wîmînô teḥabbeqēnî" "His left hand under my head, and his right hand would/does embrace me" (8.3). The lovers are tranquil, apparently motionless; enfolded in her lover's arms, the Beloved is protected and in repose. The womb-like fantasy, in which the Lover is again maternal, is expressed through complementary opposition: left and right, supporting and encircling. The two halves of himself come together to enclose the Beloved. The concurrence in the single identical moment is now, in contrast, a timelessness, indefinitely protracted. The great womb of the mother's house in the wide world is replaced by the Lover's arms, in a blank temporal and physical setting.

8.3 is identical with 2.6: the urban dream-sequence of 3.1-4 combines with the reminiscence of the sylvan retreat of 2.3-6, and perhaps of the timbered houses and verdant bed of 1.16-17, to produce a shading of city into forest, that at the tenebrous centre of the stony and oppressive city is the reciprocity of lovers and the ancestral bed, as well as a syntactic metaphor - that the peace of the lovers is detached from all context. Both 2.6 and 3.4 precede the refrain that follows: the exhortation not to awaken love until it please. 2.6 is provoked by the desperation of the previous verse, the love-sickness of 2.5 caused /97/ - or is it compensated for? - by the memory or fantasy of this enfolding, either under the apple tree or in the tavern of 2.4 (lit. house of wine) /98/. Here in 8.3 the refrain completes the perfect accord in the mother's house - the mother's house (bêt ʾimmî) replaces the tavern (bêt hayyāyin) in 2.4 - and links it with the apple tree in 8.5b; traumatic loss is now communion.

The phrase "for I am lovesick" in 2.5 recurs at the end of the dismal parody of the adjuration in 5.8, after the reenactment of the dream-sequence of 3.1-4 has ended in humiliation. The fear of shame in 8.1 is thus a postscript to experience; only through his being "like a brother" can it be

Chapter Two - The Relationship of the Lovers

neutralised. Likewise the sinister and censorious setting at night is relinquished; brother and sister meet and kiss by chance about their business in the familiar daylight, under the disappointed eyes of scandal-mongers. Thus the concord in 8.3 is still shadowed by wish-fulfilment.

הִשְׁבַּעְתִּי אֶתְכֶם בְּנוֹת יְרוּשָׁלָםִ מַה־תָּעִירוּ וּמַה־תְּעֹרְרוּ אֶת־הָאַהֲבָה עַד שֶׁתֶּחְפָּץ׃

(8.4) I adjure you, O daughters of Jerusalem, do not awaken or stir up love until it please.

In the refrain that follows 8.3 the guarantors are omitted; probably "the does and hinds of the field" of 2.7 and 3.5 are absorbed into the Beloved, the incarnation of Love, and into Love itself. The contraction contributes perhaps a sense of urgency; the artful allusion is traced back to its source. The exclamation forestalls closure, as always; it distracts us from the lovers to the message of love, introducing a level of abstraction. Its ambiguity is sharpened by the substitution of the particle "mah" for "'im"; "mah" may be a negative, i.e. "do not", as Pope (1976: 661) and others (e.g. Lys: 281) posit /99/, but it is also exclamatory and interrogative (Levinger: 89) - "How you awaken!" and "Why do you awaken?". On the one hand, it is a warning to refrain from meddling with love, whose unpredictable terrors have been amply illustrated; on the other, it testifies to its compulsion. It is also a promise, implicit in "until it please", of maturity, that Love will be ready /100/. The intensity of the desire and of the necessity for restraining it appears through the repetition of the verb "mah-tāʿîrû ûmah-teʿōrerû" "do not awaken or stir up", which is also ironically reflexive, since it is they who will awaken through love.

The injunction not to awaken love is followed by a pause; out of it comes a question: "mî zōʾt ʿōlāh min-hammidbār mitrappeqet ʿal-dôdāh" "Who is this who comes up from the wilderness, leaning on her beloved?" (8.5a). It is unanswered, for there is no need for an answer, just as the wish that occasioned the sequence is unanswered. The two questions echo each other: "mî yittenekâ" "Who would make you?" and "mî zōʾt" "Who is this?"; and thus 8.1 is linked with its inversion at the end of the passage (ʾim yittēn "If a man would give" in 8.7). But "Who would make you" and "Who is this" are opposites: the first is expressive of despair, the constraints on lovers, the second of wonder. "Who is this?" answers "Who would make you?" as wonder answers despair;

the perpetual surprise that makes anything possible. Out of the wasteland comes the Beloved; to the observer it is like a mirage. She comes from the land of death, where there is nothing, to life, foreshadowing the coming encounter. It also indirectly answers the questioning admonition to the daughters of Jerusalem: here is love awakened, whose attraction is self-evident. There are distant echoes of 1.5-6, where likewise the daughters of Jerusalem, as yet inviolate, are contrasted with the Beloved, the dark outsider; there too she is associated with the desert, through the simile "like the tents of Kedar".

Two other passages begin with "mî zō't" "Who is this?", which is thus foregrounded. In 6.10 "<u>Who is this</u> who peers forth as the dawn?" the wonder is equivalent to that of the light that comes from darkness, the wonder of creation, and explains her transcendence above queens and concubines in the previous verse; in 3.6 an identical formulation to ours introduces the description of Solomon's bed or palanquin. As here, it follows the conjuration not to awaken love. There the effect is of a violent contrast with the interrupted urban assignation, and an expectation, fulfilled in 3.11, of an illustration of amorous awakening, of a conjunction of the desert and Solomon; here the effect is of anticlimax. Instead of the splendid panoply, we have two lovers arm-in-arm, and the scene breaks off. There is an implied equivalence between the Lover and the palanquin, the mutual support of lovers and all Solomon's riches; "mitrappeqet ʽal-dôdāh" "leaning on her beloved" equals and is weighed against 3.6-11. Throughout the recapitulation, exchange of identity leads to reciprocity; each scene that earlier had a single protagonist now admits the other. In 3.1-4 the Lover was completely passive, but in the parallel passage in 8.1-2 both lovers act maternal parts; in 8.5b both are sheltered by the tree. In this citation she leans herself upon him, perhaps intentionally exaggerating her weariness; the two lovers form one unit. In 3.6-11 both are, in a sense, absent: the Beloved, obscured by clouds of smoke, is inoperant and unremarked; Solomon is the destination and the designer of the palanquin, enclosing the Beloved in an artificial structure. If in 3.1-4 she inducts him into his house, here she is ensconced in his establishment, shaped according to his liking.

In 8.5, leaning upon his arm, she says:

תַּחַת הַתַּפּוּחַ עוֹרַרְתִּיךָ שָׁמָּה חִבְּלַתְךָ אִמֶּךָ שָׁמָּה חִבְּלָה יְלָדַתְךָ:

Chapter Two - The Relationship of the Lovers

(8.5) Under the apple tree I awakened you; there your mother travailed with you; there she who gave birth to you travailed.

    The apple tree is an image for the Lover in 2.3, in whose shadow the Beloved is sheltered and feasts; now the roles are reversed, for it is the Lover who is under the apple tree and the Beloved awakens him there /101/, bending over him as he sleeps. In 7.8-9, it is the Beloved who is likened to a tree, the impressive date palm the diminutive Lover climbs and whose fruit he eats. The two trees have a maternal aspect: the kind, protective Lover in 2.3, the elegant, quasi-phallic, dominating Beloved in 7.8-9. If, as in 7.8-9, it is associated with the Beloved, as the one who wakens and overshadows the Lover, its specification as an apple tree couples it with 2.3; sensorily, its spreading branches and knotted craggy boughs oppose it to the slenderness and formal economy of the date palm. Thus the tree is endowed with the qualities of both lovers, and both are subordinated to it.

    The tree recalls birth, the beginning of life as well as of love. Sexual awakening and birth are coupled together; the Beloved projects herself sympathetically into the mother at the moment of birth, just as, for his part, the Lover does in 6.9. The mother is the one who opened his eyes to the world, whose beauty is concentrated in the Beloved; the latter opens his eyes to herself. The tree however is sexually ambivalent. Behind the mother is the father, the act of procreation; the paternal principle is incarnated in the son. There is thus an equivalence between Beloved and mother, son and father. If we compare 2.3 with its complement in 8.5, sexual pleasure under the tree is realised in birth; behind the conventional simile in 2.3 is an inherent potency.

    8.2 and 8.5 are thus symmetrical counterparts; in both love is a return to the matrix, a regeneration at the source of life. The two lovers return to the mother's house; sexual awakening is a reminiscence of birth. The stranger-Lover in 8.2, Beloved in 8.5 - enters the umbilical circle and renews the cycle. There are different mothers - his in 8.5, hers in 8.2 - in other words, each lover penetrates the core of the other. Corresponding to the identification of the Beloved with the mother in 8.5 is the assimilation of the Lover to her mother through the ambiguity of "telammedēni" ("you/she") in 8.2. If in 8.2 the lovers are incorporated as complementary twins in the mother's house, in the womb of human generation, here the landscape opens out. Between tree and earth human generation takes place in the womb of nature; man is a sibling of the spring.

The Beloved speaks these words, identifying with his mother at the moment of birth, whereas the advent of the palanquin is ironically a celebration of maternal love - the bride is completely eclipsed at her wedding:

צְאֶינָה וּרְאֶינָה בְּנוֹת צִיּוֹן בַּמֶּלֶךְ שְׁלֹמֹה בָּעֲטָרָה שֶׁעִטְּרָה־
לּוֹ אִמּוֹ בְּיוֹם חֲתֻנָּתוֹ וּבְיוֹם שִׂמְחַת לִבּוֹ:

(3.11) Come out and look, O daughters of Zion, on King Solomon, on the crown with which his mother crowned him on the day of his wedding, the day of his heart's rejoicing.

It is a public affair, a dynastic triumph; one may even recall Solomon's troubled succession, and Bathsheba's anxious part in it. The spouse is reduced to a political insurance. Hence her total neglect in the description of the palanquin, which is just an expression, subverted by "paved with love", of Solomon's magnificence; her only value is as a metonymy, as part of his display, and for this reason, too, the eye is caught by the attributes of his power: the diadem, the royal sovereignty.

In 8.5, leaning on his arm, she contains the memory of the shadow where she awoke him; the palanquin is replaced by her speech. She comes into her own, restoring the true relationship of mother and son, and a natural innocence. The wedding celebrates the vainglory of the kingdom and the mother's possessive identification with the son: it represents the hold of the ancestors, from whom it was inherited. The Beloved, by bringing him back to the matrix, renews them.

The apple tree represents the generative principle to which the lovers must return, as the Lebanon is the womb they must leave. In the passage of which it forms part, descent to the matrix encloses the embrace of lovers: 8.3 parallels 8.5a, just as 8.1-2 corresponds to 8.5b. The lovers, whose opposition and growing identity I discussed in the second section, meet under the apple tree that symbolises their union; their two paths conjoin. Each recreates the matrix, in which both mothers are present: 8.5b, the scene of the Lover's birth, matches 8.2, where the Beloved was born. The two mothers bring together a difference of setting: the city and the spring, nature and culture. In between, in compressed formulae, two other landscapes clash: the desert, death from which life comes, and the wild, Dionysian forest, that provokes extremities of passion and abandonment. There is a sudden concentration of scenes, in preparation for the culminating propositions, a

Chapter Two - The Relationship of the Lovers

summary of evidence, summoning both lovers, both mothers, life and death, city, country, desert and forest. Under the apple tree, out of this confusion, there is a birth, the stillness emphasised by the sparseness of detail of the two-word parallelism. The birth points towards the future, and to a capacity for wonder: a human being opens his eyes to the world for the first time. In this silence we hear the credo.

שִׂימֵ֚נִי כַֽחוֹתָ֨ם עַל־לִבֶּ֜ךָ כַּֽחוֹתָם֙ עַל־זְרוֹעֶ֔ךָ כִּֽי־עַזָּ֤ה כַמָּ֨וֶת֙
אַהֲבָ֔ה קָשָׁ֥ה כִשְׁא֖וֹל קִנְאָ֑ה רְשָׁפֶ֕יהָ רִשְׁפֵּ֕י אֵ֖שׁ שַׁלְהֶבֶתְיָֽה׃
מַ֣יִם רַבִּ֗ים לֹ֤א יֽוּכְלוּ֙ לְכַבּ֣וֹת אֶת־הָֽאַהֲבָ֔ה וּנְהָר֖וֹת לֹ֣א
יִשְׁטְפ֑וּהָ אִם־יִתֵּ֨ן אִ֜ישׁ אֶת־כָּל־ה֤וֹן בֵּיתוֹ֙ בָּאַהֲבָ֔ה בּ֖וֹז יָב֥וּזוּ לֽוֹ

(8.6) Set me as a seal on your heart, as a seal on your arm, for Love is as strong as Death, Jealousy as hard as Sheol, its sparks are the sparks of fire of the flame of God.
(7) Many waters cannot quench Love, nor will the floods overwhelm it; if a man were to give all the substance of his house for Love, they would surely despise him.

Scarcely one word of this passage occurs elsewhere in the Song; the new forces - death, Sheol, fire, God - give the Song a different dimension. This is compounded by the dropping of conventions - for the first time the Song seems to speak through its own voice and not through its personae. This is its message to the world, affirmed directly, and not through riddles, the enigmatic jigsaw of the Song. As Rosenzweig (201-2) says, for the first time the "I" falls silent. Yet the apparently clear statement is full of difficulties.

To begin with there is the strange introduction: "śîmēnî kahôtām 'al-libbekā kahôtām 'al-zerô'ekā" "Set me as a seal on your heart, as a seal on your arm". It is the Beloved speaking; the grand statement is in her mouth. To what extent then is it objective, and not an expression of her personal experience? To what extent does her voice fade into that of the poet? It has the ring of an ultimate truth certainly, that transcends the world of the lovers, and it would be permissible to suspect a concurrence of the Beloved and the poet; but nevertheless there is still the implication of subjectivity, the possibility of contradiction.

The preface is problematic both in itself, and in relation to the sequence. It is composed of two stichs, intensified by two-word parallelism (kahôtām 'al + part of the body) and governed by the imperative "śîmēnî" "Set me" /102/. It thus forms a prosodic pair with the end of 8.5:

> šammâ ḥibbelatekā 'immekā
> šammâ ḥibbelâ yelādatekā
> śîmēnî kahôtām ʽal-libbekā
> kahôtām ʽal-zerôʽekā

> There your mother travailed with you
> There she who gave birth to you travailed;
> Set me as a seal on your heart
> as a seal on your arm.

"Set me" - the imperative, at once urgent, demanding, and insecure - introduces a compressed formulation of all the ambiguities of identification and difference in the poem. She both commands him and is utterly dependent on him; as a seal, she wills to be his instrument. She is both independent of him, with her own words, and she wishes to be part of him - a very tiny if essential part of his body. We feel the pain of autonomy, the desire for unity, and its insurmountability. The tone of the message is correspondingly uncertain, with an elegiac timbre. We may detect a note of resignation, at the inevitable or imminent parting of lovers; he should retain a keepsake of her, an authentification of her existence even in her absence /103/. Underlying the insistence is anxiety, that he will forget her.

Yet the image suggests the opposite: indissolubility, fusion. A seal is a sign of identity, wherewith the person conducts his affairs. She is thus impressed on his heart, i.e. his feelings and thoughts, as his identity; she governs his relations with the world. No closer fusion can be imagined.

There is another meaning of "seal" linked with another verse in the Song. It is the seal as a sign of completeness, of a covenant between them. The king's seal closes and gives authority to his decree. The Lover's seal binds their relationship. In 4.12 the Beloved, the "maʽyān hātûm" "the sealed spring", is sealed against the Lover; here they are sealed together in the world.

The repetition emphasises the urgency and difficulty of the request - will he hear? can he accede? - that the process of the Song, whereby the lovers progressively become internal images, outwardly foreshadowed in the first verses by the claim "The king brought me into his chambers" (1.4) should be completed. The seal preserves a document, of which the Song is the sole record. Hence the anticlimax "as a seal on your arm" is faintly untoward. Continuity of heart and hand,

Chapter Two - The Relationship of the Lovers

thought and action, as suggested by Levinger (90, 91) or an echo of the supporting arm in 8.5 (Lys: 286) /104/, are possible, but do not explain the minimising effect, the bathos that in fact distracts attention, following the line of the arm away from the vital centre, as a momentary decoy, that leaves us unguarded.

If in 4.9 she is infused in his heart - "libbabtinî" - here she wishes to leave her imprint behind her. For Love is as strong as Death: "kî-ʽazzâ kammāwet ʼahabâ" (8.6).

Love and Death are antonyms - the creative and destructive powers - alike in strength, irresistible and universal; they resemble each other, moreover, in that both offer fusion, final integration. For the ego, then, they are equally threatening; its defences, e.g. its city walls, its moral code, contrive only a temporary and partial resistance. Love threatens dissolution in the other - who represents all others - Death is the dissolution of consciousness. Against such allies the heart is helpless. Yet they are also enemies. The comparative particle k suggests not simply an equivalence but an opposition: their strength as tested against each other. If Death overcomes all opposition, it must inevitably engage Love, dissever all ties of affection; if Love is of infinite value, it must encounter the ultimate fear, the threat to existence. If it is to be better than wine, it must promise more than forgetfulness. Moreover, both Love and Death are incarnated within us, as a psychic potential; hatred coexists with attachment. The warring forces interlock throughout our variegated lives. What is of interest, though, is the connective adjective "ʽazzâ" "strong", which alliterates with "zerōʽekâ" and thus provides a point of contact with the preamble. "ʽAz" has connotations of fierceness and durability /105/. It testifies to the intensity of the struggle, of which the often cited conflict between Baal and Mot in the Ugaritic epics, using the same qualifier, is only an example /106/. The ferocity of the instinctual forces over possession of the heart witnesses to its importance as the centre of consciousness, and justifies the tone of the subsequent assertions. It is only because they are so fierce that the spark of the flame of God can be struck. Love and Death are often thought of as gentle and insidious; their contention is defined, through the adjective "ʽaz", as an indestructible energy that flows through the sequence, taking different forms, establishing the propositions as dramatic, dynamic "states of affairs".

We can now see the logical connection with the Beloved's plea in 8.6a: "Set me as a seal on your heart, a seal on your arm, <u>for</u> [or <u>that</u>] Love is as strong as Death". The conjunction "kî" is either relative (i.e. "Love is as strong as Death" is the seal) or, more probably, explicatory (i.e. "for"). The imminence of estrangement, e.g. the end of the poem, the constant self-definition and differentiation of lovers, gives urgency to the appeal, that there must be an imprint of this, both in their lives and permanently, that their hearts are twin, that that which binds people is as strong as that which parts them. If the heart in Biblical anatomy corresponds to the emotional and rational intelligence as well as to the life of the body, their union animates them in their separate lives as their existential centre. Love is, the metaphor suggests, the heart of life. If the heart is helpless against love, it cannot live without it; it is its only resource against destruction.

The diffident subordination of the following dicta to the preamble, while obviously a syntactic formality, since they far outweigh the occasion, serves to integrate the abstract statement with the action, to make it part of the dialogue of the lovers, as well as suggesting a wider implication: that "kî" is the causal connection between it and the whole poem, that the climactic assertions validate.

In the context it is coupled with the memory of birth, both formally, through the two-word parallelism, and as part of a narrative continuum: her lien on him is convincing because she awoke him at the matrix, she has always been part of him. In 8.4, for the third time, the daughters of Jerusalem are abjured from awakening love; on each previous occasion the issue is avoided, or at least only illustrated indirectly, through parable: the Lover's seductions in 2.8-17 are inconclusive, the palanquin is the scene of self-glorification, the gratification of Solomon's heart (simḥat libbô), the delusion of grandeur. Now in 8.5 she awakens him; the verb, in the intensive form ('RR), obviously recalls the previous injunction. Love is awakened, but in the post-natal stillness, the tranquil empathy on the verge of differentiation, there is not only Love: there is also Death. Death is brought to the surface for the first time in the Song, in the context of birth. Elsewhere, the nocturnal watchmen on the walls, the sixty men-at-arms, stand symbolic guard against a vague "fear of the night" that does not materialise. If, according to the Kleinians and others, Eros and Thanatos are inherent in man, death is the source of our deepest anxiety and our earliest repression. For this reason, perhaps, it does not appear until this point. Death and Love, coexistent and irreconcilable, are

Chapter Two - The Relationship of the Lovers

conjoined in birth, in new life. There is perhaps a small play on words to support this: the mother's pangs (ḥibbelatekā ʾimmekā) anagrammatically form the seal on the heart (kaḥôtām ʿal-libbekā).

"Qāšâ kišʾôl qinʾâ" "Jealousy is as hard as Sheol" parallels "For Love is as strong as Death" syntactically and semantically also. "Qāšâ" "hard" is equivalent to strong; Sheol is the place of Death; qinʾâ is interpreted by many commentators as "passion". Yet each term subtly modifies its predecessor, so as to be almost a parody of it. The principal opposition is between "ʾahabâ" "Love" and "qinʾâ", which in sexual matters normally means suspicion of infidelity; it is hard to justify any other interpretation, except on the assumption of synonymity /107/. It is a subtle opposition, since jealousy is part of love's pathology; it is always a sign of estrangement and insecurity, a loss of the innocence that trusts implicitly. "Qāšâ" has a distinctly negative connotation compared to "ʿazzâ" /108/; it is hard in the sense of "hard to bear", "difficult to withstand", whereas "ʿazzâ" is strong and fierce. Jealousy is thus harsh and bitter as Sheol, whose insatiability is proverbial (Prov 27.30, 30.16), just as obsessive jealousy endlessly seeks morbid gratification. Other comparisons suggest themselves, for example both jealousy and Sheol are parasitic, on love and life respectively; jealousy is in a sense the ghost, or shadow of love, as reflected in its conventional physiognomy. The paroxysms of jealousy resemble infernal torments. Here we come to a difficulty: how to understand Sheol? Jealousy suggests a violent, passionate suffering, much like the hell of later Jewish/Christian tradition, and there may have been some such foreign influence. But Sheol in the Bible is very different: it is tenuous, shadowy, dominated by imagery of unrelieved darkness and grief. Despair is its only residual emotion /109/. "Qinʾâ", which is always raging /110/, and Sheol are thus antithetic, juxtaposing, and suggesting a conflict between, extremities of anguish and melancholia. Jealousy still rankles in the grave. Ecclesiastes is contradicted: "gam-ʾahabātām gam-śinʾātām gam-qinʾātām kebār ʾābādâ" "Their love, their hatred, their jealousy, have all alike already perished" (Eccl 9.6). The obstinacy and endless duration of Sheol - the hardness of oblivion - contends with jealousy's unassuageable fever /111/.

But Sheol and Death are also antithetic. If Death is a fierce energy, a destructive force equal to Love, it leaves behind a cold desolation, the indestructible wraith. Sheol is non-death, as well as non-life, phantom-existence, not non-existence. Instead of fusion, it brings only solitude, perpetual isolation from (or in) the mother.

The imperative "Set me as a seal on your heart" thus has another implication: only by being inseparable can they never be jealous. It is a freedom resulting from security, that their separate lives are interwoven, implicit in the Beloved's insistence that her Lover is hers, even though he feeds among the lilies, a combination of loyalty and liberty prudent when dealing with a fictive Solomon. It may be reciprocal: she too is sealed in his heart during her separate adventures.

The four terms, Love, Death, Jealousy and Sheol, are still more closely related. For Jealousy is Love in the service of Death, self-destructive and murderous. It arises from desolation, the frustration of love, and it produces it. It is this waste, "the pity of it", as Othello says, that is as spectral and irretrievable as Sheol; an isolation in the delusive shadow of Love, as Sheol is in the shadow of Death (Job 10.22).

The referent of the next phrase - "rešāpeyhā rispê ʾēš šalhebetyâ" "Its sparks are the sparks of fire of the flame of God" - is strictly ambiguous: it may be either "ʾahabâ" "love" or "qinʾâ" "jealousy", which is frequently coupled with the divine flame. On the other hand, the principal subject of the verse and the Song is Love, which alone would merit this supreme praise. It hardly matters since it is clear that jealousy and love burn with the same flame /112/. As a sexual metaphor, fire is more than ardour, or even sensual warmth and pleasure; it suggests an analogy of friction with the sexual act, and of creation /113/. The spark of new life is kindled between the lovers. But it also unites them; everything combustible enters the flame. Fire is the purest and climactic image of the fusion of the lovers, in which they are destroyed and recreated as a single flame. It thus concludes the work of integration, of careful correlation, that we have pursued through the poem. The flame of love, its creative drive, arms it and secures it against death - it is "ʿaz" - but nevertheless destroys. It is, as it were, a double-agent acting for love and death, the energy released by their struggle. All the images and words of the poem have gone into its making; struck between the contraries in the poem that grows between them, it is unwavering, the constant transition from creation to extinction, perceived in a moment of incandescence, in which matter bursts into flame, sensation becomes conscious. The imagination of that moment is the substance of poetry; poetic sparks fly in the

Chapter Two - The Relationship of the Lovers

flame of God. For fire is also a symbol for culture, the achievement of the ego, that appropriates instinctive and destructive forces for its own ends. The pyrotechnic technique was one of man's earliest discoveries; therewith, at the hearth, fire becomes the matrix, indivisible from the maternal functions of cooking and warmth. As a light, warding off predators, it establishes the human circle, the small centre of consciousness in the difficult world.

But this is also the sacred flame, the "šalhebetyâ", the flame of God. Commentators tend to eliminate the divine reference, either through reduction to hyperbole /114/, or textual surgery /115/, out of misguided prurience; it is no argument that this is his sole entry /116/, or that sexuality is inconsistent with sanctity /117/. The erotic drive is the divine flame, through which the world continues in being; the lovers, in whom all creatures are united, through creating new life, perpetuate his work. It is the moment of transcendence, in which the distance between the meditation and the poet vanishes. There is only the creative speech and act in which they share.

Fire betrays God's presence throughout the Bible; substanceless, and shapeless, it is his element, the nearest approach to his image. To interpret "šalhebetyâ" as chance lightning does not do justice to it in the context of the Song as a whole or of this verse, with its confrontation of eternal forces /118/. For in Israel, in the dialectics of king and kingdom, the flame of God is constantly alight only on the altar at its centre; it communicates between heaven and earth. Possibly there is an allusion to Solomon's legendary/symbolic role as builder of the Temple. In the sanctuary, the union and differentiation of lovers is a collective process; there, symbolically, the wealth of the kingdom is reduced to ashes, merged with the divine flame, and renewed. God, the source of life, is indwelling in the land, and guarantees its continuance. The shrine is thus the matrix, an inner confine, and the hearth, the generative flame. There the king and the Beloved participate in the creative current, that infuses the lovers at the centre of their world.

God is likened, paradoxically, to a flame that does not consume, for instance in the Burning Bush, or in the destroying yet vivifying flame of Deut 4. If all matter is destroyed in time, it is timeless, a changelessness in change. It is not the ultimate ideal reality devoid of the world, but the reality of the world, the eternity of love despite death.

This is perhaps exemplified in the reference to the divine name, which is only a suffix, has no existence apart from the visible immaterial flame, the love of the lovers and the voice of the poem. It is a semi-vowel and an open vowel, disappearing into silence. Moreover, the name of God which it curtails, the YHWH, is the name of existence: "He Is" or "He causes to be", the verbal form suggesting an imageless intangible energy in everything evanescent /119/.

The divine flame burns in the dissolution of Sheol; it alone authenticates existence, as the YHWH, the inexhaustible spark of life. The love of the lovers thus returns us to the beginning of creation.

The gravity and movement of the verse is alleviated but also more deeply impressed through somewhat obtrusive sound-patterns; the grand contestants must still enter the game of poetry. The recurrence of stress on alternate syllables /120/ in the first two clauses corresponds to their syntactic and semantic parallelism, unifying them in a didactic couplet:

kî ʿazzâ kammāwēt ʾahabâ
qāšâ kišʾôl qinʾâ

For Love is as strong as Death
Jealousy as harsh as Sheol

But it is also an antithesis, phonemic as well as lexical, for "qāšâ kišʾôl qinʾâ" is distinguished by its far heavier consonantal texture, and its dense internal alliteration (qš kš q). "Q" or "k" is the optimal plosive; each word begins with a burst of intense energy - qāšâ, kišʾôl, qinʾâ. "Š" compounds this with an obstruent - qāšâ, kišʾôl. Each word is maximally divided from the other by its tense onset - qāšâ/kišʾôl/qinʾâ; the accumulated energy is released into the stressed final syllables with their long open vowels protracted, in "šʾol", by the liquid "l". The ensuing rhythm is ponderous, each word articulated separately, with cluttered unstressed and held stressed syllables, as if to emphasise the hardness of "qāšâ", the weight of Sheol, the grievousness of "qinʾâ". In contrast, the prosodic texture of "kî ʿazzâ kammāwet ʾahabâ" "For Love is as strong as Death" is light, with its many open syllables and its syncopation of "ʾahabâ".

"Rešāpeyhā rišpê ʾēš šalhebetyâ" "Its sparks are the sparks of fire of the flame of God" drops the alliteration on "q"; that on "š", in the second position, thus becomes dominant, and links the two dicta:

Chapter Two - The Relationship of the Lovers

qāšâ kišʼôl qinʼâ
rešāpeyhā rišpê ʼēš šalhebetyâ

It is a straightforward onomatopoiea: the noisy fricative "š", without formant structure, mimics fire, both audibly and as a synaesthetic metaphor, especially when, in "rišpê", it is combined with the sharp plosive "p" in an impressive consonantal cluster. The "p" of "rišpê" dams the sound of "š" that gathers behind it, and releases it with great force. "R" replaces "q" in the initial position, conducive to a more fluid texture, which, in conjunction with the common denominator "š" (qš - rš) suggests a transformation of the previous phrase: the bitterness of Sheol is fuel for the flame, which absorbs all contraries into its compass. The image of leaping flames is supported by the high-pitched compact vowels "e", each of which carries rising stress: rešāpeyhā rišpê ʼēš. "Rišpê" and "ʼēš", especially, flow into each other, suggesting a metaphorical correlation: the flame catches from the one to the other, from the sparks to the fire. Rhythmically the phrase is characterised by compression: from "rešāpeyhā" to "rišpê" to the monosyllable "ʼēš". Pope (1976: 670-71) concludes thence that the four-syllable "šalhebetyâ" is rhythmically otiose, either too long or too short for the verse, and omits it. In fact, the double stress "rišpê ʼēš" can only be followed by a pause, a moment of suspense, resolved in the long climactic apposition: "šalhebetyâ", introduced by the same fricative consonant "š", linking it and its antecedent: "ʼēš" with "šalhebetyâ". There is thus a chain of elisions: "rišpê ʼēš šalhebetyâ", bridging the gap across markers of stress and sentence structure.

"Šalhebetyâ" "the flame of God" is the apex of the credo, and of the Song. The momentary silence into which the Name dissolves presages a tumultuous conclusion, and a new element:

מַיִם רַבִּים לֹא יוּכְלוּ לְכַבּוֹת אֶת־הָאַהֲבָה וּנְהָרוֹת לֹא יִשְׁטְפוּהָ

(8.7a) Many waters cannot quench love, nor will the floods [or Rivers] overwhelm it.

"Many waters" is, as most commentators say, a mythographical expression (cf. May 1955: 18); the poet assumes an epic manner, drawing on its numinous formulae. The many waters, like the rivers of the next phrase, are the primeval ocean, the Chaos which God subdued to create the world. The verb "lekabbôt" "to quench" suggests a continuing implicit metaphor of divine flame, emanating from Love, at the centre of the verse; like God, it is imperishable amid the mighty, anarchic waters. An obvious analogue is Psalm 93, where the majestic breaking of the mighty waters is transcended by the majesty of God; or the Song of the Sea, in Exodus 15, where the language of triumph over the abysmal Sea ironically celebrates the instrumentality of the Sea in the victory over Pharaoh.

Chaos threatens us with dissolution in the primordial element, it is an ultimate reversion, a tendency to atomise in everything formed. Chaos, inherent decay, is thus not essentially different from Death or Sheol: all three are enemies of Love, and their images coalesce. Keel (1978: 54-55) has wisely warned against too rigid a classification of ancient Oriental cosmography. Thus Pope's insistence (1976: 673) that these are the waters of Death, as distinct from those of Chaos, is without basis. The transformation confers not a change of thought but a greater inclusiveness. Up to this point the Song has more or less stayed within the bounds of creation, the universe as experienced in the lovers: now it is contrasted with a primal negativity. "Many waters" suggests numberless waves cancelling each other out, and incoherent voices, the restless incessant surge that ever subsides. As a symbol for Chaos, the multitudinous Sea is the element that surrounds us, with its discordant, Siren voices, from which God, the formant principle, separated the land and all structured things; the rancour of the sea, its implacable dissidence, pounding against the land, is thus the grudge of the unformed for the formed, death for life. In our lives, Chaos is the tendency to disintegrate inherent in human organisation, social and individual; with their many faces, and clamorous voices, "many waters" is a frequent image for factional politics /121/. As the principle of erosion, it is linked with time, especially if one takes into account the parallelism "rivers". The sea's efforts, its leaping waves, are spent unavailingly in a struggle against love, through which life continues. For this reason the verse stresses "Many waters <u>cannot</u> quench love": that it strives and fails /122/. For Love, the erotic drive, is that which burns in the desolation, that gives light to the world; it taps inchoate instinctual energy to create life, to form and give a soul to the world in darkness. The irredentism of chaos is thus an envy of life, of everything shaped and centred.

"Many waters" is paired with the irresistible torrent of "Rivers" or "Floods", essentially everything that destroys Love in time. The parallelism is more or less synonymous,

Chapter Two - The Relationship of the Lovers

conforming to prophetic exactitude; combining synchronic and diachronic axes, the continuous uproar of the sea with the rush of the rivers. Its main function, however, is prosodic; at this point, indeed, rhythm predominates over alliteration as a melodic feature, though the latter is represented by the nice coupling: "lōʲ yûkelû lekabbôt" "cannot quench" (l kl lk).

If "rešāpeyhā rišpê ʲēš šalhebetyâ" is a long line, too long for Pope, "mayîm rabbîm lōʲ yûkelû lekabbôt ʲet-hāʲahabâ" is an extraordinarily long line for the lyric, as if to illustrate the amplitude of the thought and the confusion of genre. Its principal function, however, is mimetic: the movement, protracted through the cumulative verbal cluster "lōʲ yûkelû lekabbôt", culminates in "ʲahabâ" and it spends itself in the last syllable /123/. It is the force of the sea vainly striving against love; moreover, the rhythm itself is of a long sea breaker, set in motion by "mayîm rabbîm" "many waters", gathering strength through "lōʲ yûkelû lekabbôt" "cannot quench" to its crest in "ʲahabâ" "love". But this is followed by a much shorter line "ûnehārôt lōʲ yištepûhā" "Nor will the Rivers overwhelm it", in which the same syntactic components are straitened. There is the same rhythm breaking on its last syllable, a short wave. But because of the brevity, the division of units is ambiguous, for the second line may be appended to the first, as an outrider. We then have one very long or two overlapping waves, with a double climax, on "ʲahabâ" and "yištepûhā", "love" and "overwhelm it".

We have moved from the two forces in conflict in man, to their exhaustion in Sheol, the shadow of death alongside the shadow of love, and thence brought together the theological and national dimensions of the Song. The two drives meet for a moment in the divine flame. A further opposition comes into play: Creation and the Uncreated. From the careful construction of equations and antitheses in the previous verse, with its formal sententiousness, its balance of predicates, peculiar to Wisdom literature /124/, whose achievement is a cautious and static order, we come to verbal excess, primordial energy and motion, which is defined both as an impotent fury and a devastating inundation, reinforced by the strident consonantal cluster of "yištepûhā". Far from being the spirit of God moving on the waters, Love is a solitary light in all that commotion. But what I think is important is the composite picture. For Love is also a violent perturbation, an overthrow of the senses, especially common sense, for example, in the intensive "libbabtinî"; it too is associated with waters, e.g. the "waters of life" in 4.15, or the beautiful image of eyes as sources of waters in 5.12. But the beating of the heart, when the two hearts flutter together, in "libbabtinî", or when the heart's waking is coordinated with the Lover's knocking in 5.2, like an orgasm, is centred round a stillness, a perfection e.g. in the image, in the next episode, of "kemôs'et šālôm" - for which we await the next chapter.

The conclusion that God is Love supposes a duality - that all the negative forces, Death, Sheol, and Chaos, are excluded. But it is a provisional and ambiguous duality, for the opposites are interdependent, creativity implies destruction. Love seeks to integrate Death, as Death swallows life.

Following the credo, there is an ironic aside: the line stretches even further, and verse collapses /125/:

אִם־יִתֵּן אִישׁ אֶת־כָּל־הוֹן בֵּיתוֹ בָּאַהֲבָה בּוֹז יָבוּזוּ לוֹ׃

(8.7b) If a man were to give all the substance of his house for love, they would surely despise him.

It is a return to the social dismay of 8.1, rounding off the passage: the sceptical "mî yittēn" "Who would make [lit. give] you?" in 8.1 is answered by the romantic hypothesis "'im yittēn" "If one would give"; the conclusion, that only in the realm of impossibility would they not shame me, "lō' yābuzû lî", is confirmed by the inevitable consequence: "bôz yabûzû lô" "they would surely shame him". "Lô" must, I think, refer to him, so as to correspond with "lî" ("me") in 8.1 /126/. In the sequence, then, we have passed imperceptibly from the wishful fantasy of 8.1-3 to the personal and cosmogonic myth of origins in 8.5 and 8.7, the underlying archetypal reality, to eternal verities, only to return sharply to the surface, the petty social discriminations with which we started /127/. The dissociation is expertly handled; but more to the point, it illustrates the true nature and pervasiveness of the chaos of the previous statement. Since love is worth everything, a man who gave all for love would be vindicated. It exposes both the illusions on which society is founded, the hopelessness of the credo, and the cost of male freedom, that values power and exploitation instead of love. There is, moreover, a possible literary echo. In Prov 30.16 all the elements that we have summoned - Sheol, the womb, water, and fire - comprise a paradigm of insatiability. Of each it uses the same word as in our verse: "lō''āmerâ hôn" "It does not say 'Enough!'" If a man

Chapter Two - The Relationship of the Lovers

does not give his wealth, his "hôn", to Love, where will it go?

After the credo, the Song has nothing more to say. There are only a few difficult fragments, little parables of the union and differentiation of the lovers, the induction and transformation of the Beloved in the social world. The lovers find themselves in each other, in autonomy from each other, in their imminent parting. Social satire, with elements of parody, mingles with affirmation. The complexities of these episodes will be the subject of the next chapter, as well as their contribution to the concentric structure of the Song. Finally we return to the garden, only to leave it:

הַיּוֹשֶׁבֶת בַּגַּנִּים חֲבֵרִים מַקְשִׁיבִים לְקוֹלֵךְ הַשְׁמִיעִנִי: בְּרַח
דּוֹדִי וּדְמֵה־לְךָ לִצְבִי אוֹ לְעֹפֶר הָאַיָּלִים עַל הָרֵי בְשָׂמִים:

8.13 O you who sit among gardens, friends listening to your voice, let me hear.
(14) Flee, my love, and be like a deer or a young gazelle on the mountains of spices.

At the centre of the Song the two lovers meet in the garden, an image of the sexual act in the womb of the archetypal mother; now at the end they are parted by it. The Lover is free to roam the mountains; in his freedom he typifies the son who has left his mother, life in the world - outside the Song.

CHAPTER THREE

BEAUTY AND THE ENIGMA

Chapter Three

BEAUTY AND THE ENIGMA

> Denn das Schöne ist nichts
> als des Schrecklichen Anfang, den wir noch grade ertragen,
> und wir bewunden es so, weil es gelassen verschmäht,
> uns zu zerstören.
> For Beauty's nothing
> but beginning of Terror we're still just able to bear,
> and why we adore it so is because it serenely disdains
> to destroy us.
> (Rilke: Duino Elegies I
> tr. Leishman and Spender)

Introduction

IN essence this chapter is a close reading of four of the most difficult passages of the Song, endeavouring to show that the difficulty, far from being an insuperable obstacle, is in fact part of the meaning, and contributes greatly to its beauty. The four episodes, symmetrically situated at opposite extremities of the Song, are linked through close correspondences of imagery and thematic material. The relationship of the ambiguity of the Song to its beauty and the ambivalence of love which we discerned in the last chapter will be the principal subject of enquiry.

Critics have been quick to note the beauty of the Song, but few have made any attempt either to analyse it, or to consider it as an integral part of its composition. They ignore it as purely decorative, and turn to more serious matters. Similarly, while individual ambiguities, paronomasias etc. have received attention, they have not been perceived as more than an occasional device, or rhetorical ornament. Pope links the ideas of Beauty and Terror, but in a mythological context. For him the Beloved is simply a manifestation of the black, beautiful, passionate, bloodthirsty, venereal and virginal goddess who appears everywhere under different names - Anat, Ishtar, Kali in India, the Black Madonna in Europe, the Shekhinah in the Kabbalah. What is not clear is whether he regards this as the literal meaning, and therefore the Song as a cultic poem dedicated to a demonic goddess, or whether it is a subliminal paradigm. This is because he never escapes from his fascination for the arcane and primitive, never extracts from it its human meaning. Beauty and Terror are externalised as attributes of ancient mysteries, instead of being comprehended as very intimate feelings.

Albert Cook (142, 145-146), too, has alluded to this relationship, somewhat cryptically and indecisively. At one point he seems to regard Beauty and Terror as alternatives: the Beloved chooses to love rather than to terrorise; at another, love apparently appropriates terror. But nowhere does he treat Beauty and Terror as more than a chance conjunction.

The most sensitive interpreter of the aesthetics of the Song is Leo Krinetzki, who pays a great deal of attention in his earlier commentary to its alliterative patterns and their possible significance; for the most part his observations consist, however, of simple impressionistic correspondences, that do not affect the Song's intrinsic meaning. It is unfortunate that this preoccupation with word-music does not appear in his later work. He recognises, commenting on 6.4, the association of Beauty and Terror as corresponding to the Good and Terrible Mother respectively (1981: 179; cf. 1970: 411-412). It would be interesting to correlate, on a sophisticated level, sound values e.g. synaesthesia with his now Jungian interpretation.

H. P. Müller (1976: 25) also has a passing mention of the coupling of Beauty and Terror in 6.4 and 6.10, as divine attributes projected onto the Beloved; it does not however figure greatly, as it could, in his analysis of the transformation of mythic speech and lyric speech, of beauty in the service of the divine (1977: 158).

Beauty in the Song is an all-pervasive quality, that one cannot separate from the love of the lovers, the world they inhabit, or the language in which the poem is written. The three levels signify each other: the beauty of the lovers parallels that of the world, and both are expressed, exist only through the speech that describes them. Moreover, this beauty is contagious, passes from one level to another. Lyricism persuades us to accept the possibility of this beauty, because we imagine it emanates from a supreme inspiration; a golden language imitates a golden age. At the same time

Chapter Three - Beauty and the Enigma

it confers its gold on that age. Similarly, we are persuaded of the beauty of the lovers through their comparison with beautiful things; but equally their metaphorical equivalents are graced through association with the lovers, they acquire a human beauty. For instance, when the Beloved is compared to Jerusalem and Tirzah, we learn something about Jerusalem and Tirzah as well as the Beloved.

The beauty the Song celebrates is very powerful, and consequently frightening, as we have found in the last chapter; a king is caught in its trammels in 7.6; the heart is overwhelmed in 4.9. In 6.4, the verse I have just cited, the comparison of the Beloved with the beauty of Jerusalem and Tirzah is followed by the mystifying "'ayummâ kannidgālôt" "terrible as constellations" /1/, and the plea "Turn your eyes away from me, for they dazzle me" /2/. This in turn reflects the contrary impulses towards fusion and differentiation, self-surrender and self-possession, that we have already considered.

Poetry depends on ambiguity for its richness. A poem is a counterpoint of multiple meanings, its essence is "multiplex, polysemantic", as Jakobson (1960: 370) says. The discussion in the previous chapter amply illustrates the depth of symbolic association in the Song. Critics who confine themselves to a flat, one-dimensional interpretation, a paraphrase in other words, consequently err as greatly as allegorical expositors, who substituted a spiritual for its carnal meaning. For love is of infinite significance. Everything in the poem is implicated in the love of the lovers; for example, Jerusalem and Tirzah are its subject, as well as the Beloved. Human love is part of the fertility of nature, and both are expressed through the love of language.

The love of the world, man and language correspond to each other in the Song through metaphor; they also implicate each other. Language preserves all that is left of the poet, his characters, and his world; as a sexual metaphor, it is an intercourse of vocables; in it, the world finds expression. The lovers create the poem out of their love; they care for and cultivate nature, the gardens and vineyards of the Song, just as they cultivate speech, loving the world, finding words for it, using it to describe their love. Nature pervades language sensually, as sound; its fruit, honey etc. sustains the lovers, and reproducing itself "after its kind" it sympathetically stimulates them; they are part of the spring.

The language combines two main functions, the <u>intellectual</u> function and the <u>emotive</u> one. The <u>intellectual</u> function refers to the analysis of the phenomenology of love I discussed in the last chapter; on the natural level, this manifests itself in what one might term "a grammar of the senses". The emotive function calls for the reader's participation in the experience of the lovers, his empathy. Ideally, the <u>signifiant</u> is identified with the <u>signifié</u>, the world of the poem is sensuously apprehended in its word. Thus the poem is a <u>synthesis</u> of the three levels we distinguished, language, man and nature; its basic form is metaphor. As more and more words are found to be equivalent, so does the poem come to be a tautology.

For this reason, a feeling of paradox pervades all the language of the Song. Fundamentally, it attempts the impossible: to communicate in language what is beyond language. Language is an intermediary, temporal and physical, while love is a fusion beyond speech. Moreover, direct experience cannot be expressed in language, yet poetry - all poetry - tries to recreate sensations, to make words "say" something, as well as signifying it. Hence the language of the Song is very difficult when one tries to comprehend it intellectually, and very simple and compulsive if one engages in it with one's feelings. This paradox is analogous to that of love, that two can become one and yet remain distinct /3/. The relationship of language and the world reflects, too, the paradoxical status of man, who is both natural and cultural, part of nature and apart from it.

At this point we may make a distinction between an ambiguity and an enigma. An enigma may be defined as a negative ambiguity. Whereas an ambiguity has a double meaning, an enigma arises from an unanswered question. It occurs wherever speech is reticent. Ambiguities, however, frequently generate enigmas, whenever they result in a puzzling contradiction. Between the horns of a paradox dwells an enigma.

Within the limits of its paradoxes the Song is wholly enigmatic. We never know quite what happens or whether anything happens, and all the anecdotal energy that we devote to the construction of the narrative results either in false solutions, or in frustration. There is no single truth in the poem, only an inexpressible reality. Yet the poem tempts our imaginative, constructive efforts through its prodigality with clues, the promise of the brilliant fragments of narrative that compose it. Even these little dream-sequences, however, are riddled with doubts and ambiguities. They rarely have a beginning and an end, are reminiscent of snatches of radio plays that one switches on and off. They modulate the

Chapter Three - Beauty and the Enigma

one to the other abruptly, without transition. Internally, they often turn on key double-meanings which, when examined, are found to derive from the central paradoxes. We will be looking at some of these in due course.

The enigma then is a feature of the narrative code of the poem, its dynamic forward movement that always turns back on itself, becomes timeless. On the other hand, its ambiguities are a set of concomitant meanings, synchronic processes. Movement in stillness, stillness in movement are the recurrent subjects of poetry, the "real place for wonder", as Northrop Frye puts it (1957: 88). He continues that the mystery of the poem does not emanate from "something unknown or unknowable in the poem, but something unlimited within it". I confess I do not quite understand this, for the unlimited is surely always unknowable. In "great poems", however, the mystery becomes as manifest as possible, somehow finds expression, without thereby becoming the less mysterious. The great poet never lets the mystery alone. To adapt Wittgenstein's formulation, the poet always speaks where he should be silent.

Beauty can only be experienced at a distance /4/, in objects contemplated separately fron oneself, preserved intact and ineffable. Thus Beauty is always the result of tension between desire and control, instinctual energy and repression. In its pure form the desire is to unite with, to integrate, to destroy the otherness of the other. It can be dangerous, expressing itself, for example, in the rite of "sparagmos", the rending of the living body. Yet it is essential to life. Hence the ambivalence of Beauty, as the object of desire. Because men project their emotions onto the source of arousal, the destructive, sadistic impulses evoked by Beauty are attributed to Beauty itself. It is Beauty that causes men to "lose their heads", and is responsible for dangerous explosions of irrational feeling. One might say - a popular myth concerning rape or sadism - that the victim deserves what she gets, for she provokes it through her very presence. Then the beautiful woman becomes the bad woman, the temptress, mingling polarities of adoration, fear, and fascinated contempt.

Ugliness is in fact not very far from Beauty, as Anton Ehrenzweig (1965: 68-81) has argued with an abundance of examples. Aesthetic values are extraordinarily volatile. For Ugliness is a rejection of the elements that Beauty disguised. Beauty becomes ugly when it is too threatening, too terrible. The most awe-inspiring works of art are those where the tension is greatest, the ugliness most nearly unbearable (e.g. "King Lear"), and the aesthetic triumph consequently most breathtaking.

Man is fatefully attracted by mystery, for he seeks in it his ultimate answer. Hence the profusion of mystery cults and oracular utterances. Yet he also fears it, because the ultimate mystery is death. Knowledge is thus acutely perilous, for it promises an integration of good and evil, a mastery over chaos. For this reason knowledge carries with it a sense of beauty. It is a rhythmical alternation of an intense curiosity, which is but one manifestation of the erotic drive, with an ability to stand back and perceive a whole object. We can now see the relationship of ambiguity and ambivalence, meaning and value; for it is meaning that one most values. Ambiguity always arouses feelings of ambivalence, for it both conceals and reveals; this is true even when it is relatively empty of emotive content, as in trivial puns. When it expresses conflict or unsuspected depth, aesthetic admiration is stirred by the integration of different psychic levels, the successful formulation, at a distance, of intimate disturbances. The ambiguity enables unacknowledged subversive wishes to be fulfilled surreptitiously, often through heavy disguise. Octavio Paz (1975: 3-5), for example, has pointed out the metaphorical link between anus and sun in Spanish Gongoresque poetry.

Beauty then becomes enigmatic, and not only because of the unanswered question, "Will she be mine or not?" This merely expresses it in practical terms. It is enigmatic because of the powerful charge of repressed feeling, the wish to destroy it and the wish to preserve it. Beauty is thus very close to mystery, which knowledge seeks to penetrate. Mystery is beautiful when it is not terrible. Beauty is never very far from Death either, for we long to humanise what we most fear.

First Episode: 1.5-6.

שְׁחוֹרָה אֲנִי וְנָאוָה בְּנוֹת יְרוּשָׁלָ͏ִם כְּאָהֳלֵי קֵדָר כִּירִיעוֹת שְׁלֹמֹה׃
אַל־תִּרְאוּנִי שֶׁאֲנִי שְׁחַרְחֹרֶת שֶׁשְּׁזָפַתְנִי הַשָּׁמֶשׁ בְּנֵי אִמִּי נִחֲרוּ־בִי
שָׂמֻנִי נֹטֵרָה אֶת־הַכְּרָמִים כַּרְמִי שֶׁלִּי לֹא נָטָרְתִּי׃

(1.5) I am black and comely, O daughters of Jerusalem, as the tents of Kedar, as the curtains of Solomon.
(6) Do not look on me, that I am dark, that the sun has burnt me; my mother's son's were angry with me; they made me a keeper of the vineyards; my own vineyard I did not keep.

Chapter Three - Beauty and the Enigma

Stripped of explanations and comparisons, the passage consists of two clauses:
1. I am black and comely
2. Do not look on me.

With the first the Beloved announces herself, to the reader as well as to the daughters of Jerusalem. In fact, for them words are superfluous; her beauty speaks for her, calls attention to itself. And what does she/it say? "Do not look on me!"

This presentation and withdrawal is not only pointless; it is paradoxical because Beauty is essentially something to be looked at, only exists in the eye of the beholder. Furthermore, one normally introduces oneself to initiate conversation, in this case, the dialogue of the poem, but her extreme shyness, self-effacement - especially when the whole poem is dedicated to the vision of the Beloved - is the reverse of sociability.

Both clauses, too, are wholly enigmatic:
i) The conjunction wĕ in "I am black and comely" may also mean but. She may be a dark beauty or a beauty in spite of her darkness /5/.
ii) Her embarrassment is caused by her darkness, but is this enviable or contemptible, ugly or beautiful /6/?

The alternatives are linked to each other; if we think of darkness as antithetical to beauty, we suppose hers to be a fear of contempt; if they are complementary, it is of the malice of envy.

Envy and contempt are in fact dialectically related, in two ways. One is simple and secondary; contempt is a defence against envy, wherewith one comforts oneself, like the fox in the fable, by pretending that the other is not admirable (Salzberger-Wittenberg: 124). The other way is fundamental: that envy makes one wish either to emulate the other or, if that is impossible, to destroy the other; envy is the source of the most bitter hatred, one of whose weapons is disgust (Segal 1964: 27). The envied object becomes the pariah. These apparently contradictory functions reinforce each other, to ensure that envy is always accompanied by denigration.

Similarly, the paradox that Beauty says "Do not look on me" in fact expresses its essential ambivalence, as the product of desire and repression. What it shows can only be seen indirectly.

To quote the epigraph, "Beauty is the beginning of terror we are still just able to bear" because it is a guise (vision, "gestalt") dolling up what we cannot bear to see - our naked anger, frenzy, greed. Beauty is a neutralisation of terror, imposing on it shape and structure, articulating it - finding words as guises for gazer and gazed - to exorcise it (Ehrenzweig 1965: 68-70). Whether the Beloved is beautiful or ugly, humiliated or adored, depends on the success of this process, which is, in fact, a filter. "Throughout the ages almost everyone who has asked for literary clarity has actually been asking for a moderation of light, in order to protect the retina from shock, within a routine penumbra" (Lopez Velarde) (Paz 1976: 78). Ugliness and Beauty, like envy and contempt, are linked terms, twin aspects of the aesthetic process, psychic distance - "I am black and comely".

In the Pastoral, courtly tradition, darkness of skin is ambivalent, while the conventional beauty is fair /7/. Hence the synonym in English. A white complexion is delicate, unspoilt; and readily merges with the symbolism of whiteness as purity. The unspoilt, delicate girl is virginal, carefully raised within society to await her husband. The dark girl - whether Theocritus' "sunburnt Syrian", Virgil's Amyntas or Menalcas, or the "nut brown maid" - is available, and consequently less idealised and more enticing /8/.

In our passage, conventional fair beauty is represented by the daughters of Jerusalem whom the beloved addresses, since she is conspicuous among them; it is the beauty of the city, of civilisation. The Beloved comes from outside "society"; her darkness is an index of class, like an accent. It is caused by sunburn, and rustic toil (1.6). For this reason it inspires contempt. But if it is beautiful, it is also enviable.

This envy is at the root of the Pastoral, that accomplishes, in an innocuous, dreamlike setting, a complete inversion of social values. In the Pastoral, envy is creative, expressing a longing for identification, and a real empathy. The Beloved, with her dark beauty, signifies the hidden longing of the daughters of Jerusalem.

For if theirs is civilised beauty, hers is natural beauty, associated with sun and soil, and change. It incarnates in man the beauty of creation, and is the evidence of our intrinsic perfection. Civilisation, founded in repression, resists this faith, without which it would have no validity. As the amoral, uncivilised Beauty, the Beloved stands for the integration of good and evil, the totality of man and the world. She is thus the living presence of the irresponsible, untamed part of the daughters of Jerusalem. One may illustrate this by imagining their social situation; then the Beloved becomes a wish-

Chapter Three - Beauty and the Enigma

fulfilling image of freedom and sexual license, activity and open spaces, of all of which they are deprived, enclosed in the city.

Her dark beauty is threatening because it is seductive, despised and worshipped for the same reason. Provoking sexual desire, it is the irreductible enemy of common sense, that says "Deceptive is charm, vain is beauty" (Prov 31.30). It negates moral codes and political hierarchies; to refer to the royal persona, a king may fall in love with a country girl, who is worth his capital cities, Jerusalem and Tirzah. This subversiveness is characteristic of the Pastoral, that idealises the rustic, uncorrupted by civilisation; for it thereby charms away, and ironically confirms, the reality of the peasant, his poverty, exploitation, coarseness, and incipient hostility. Peasants are usually discontented; the Pastoral, if taken literally, incites revolution.

The split-off self threatens a similar revolution within the daughters of Jerusalem. Virginity protects the self against intrusion; it remains a preserve and a mystery. Its corollary is the collective pride of the daughters of Jerusalem, and their concealed individuality. It expresses the fear of the one fate that is really worse than death: the loss of one's identity (Frye 1976: 78). However, erotic desire threatens to overwhelm this carefully brought-up, demure integrity, to submerge one self in the other, with rapturous abandon.

The two types of beauty, fair and dark, city and country, may now be identified with what Nietzsche describes as the Apollonian and Dionysiac poles of the aesthetic experience. The Dionysiac urge, subversive, irrepressible, is contained by Olympian detachment, psychic distance. The rest of my comments on our phrase "I am black and/but comely" will explore the implications of this tension as it relates to the Beloved and the daughters of Jerusalem.

If darkness of complexion is an index of class, and explicitly linked with the opposition of the country and city, this is not its total symbolic meaning. Darkness is a very powerful signifier, attached to our earliest memories /9/. To begin with, it evokes the colour of the soil, and superimposes on the country/city dichotomy that of nature and culture. It is an obvious extension of the paradigm that the country girl should speak for the earth on which she works and with which she is in constant communion, as that the city girl should speak for the civilisation in which she has been raised. Furthermore, the identification of the Beloved with the earth is confirmed repeatedly within the text of the poem, through the metaphorical association of her body with landscapes and harvests. As an idea, an essential attribute of the earth is fertility, that expresses itself in man through the sexual drive. The dalliance of the lovers is one aspect of vernal excitement. Mythologically, in the Bible, the earth is the mother, from which the human race is formed (Gen 2.7), and from which it feeds. Likewise, as we have seen throughout the poem, the Beloved is associated with a mother-figure (e.g. 3.4, 3.11, 8.2, 8.5).

We are absorbed in the mother in the womb, our first darkness. The light/dark antinomy is associated with the cycle of night and day, consciousness and unconsciousness, life and death. In the darkness we cannot distinguish self and other. The Dionysiac impulse, according to Nietzsche (1956: 29) is the release of Thanatos, the will-to-die, to revert to a primordial undifferentiation, an oceanic pleroma. This is because Death is the concomitant of Life as process, the earthly/maternal cycle of decay and richness. Darkness, earth, fertility and decay recall ineluctably a most emotive process, excretion. Anal disgust is coupled with aesthetic idealisation in the creative work of the body (Ehrenzweig 1965: 79-82; Rickman). At the epicentre of explosive pleasure and extreme repression, defecation combines with genital sexuality and Dionysiac dissipation to form one pole of the aesthetic experience, the Dark Beloved. In contrast, the daughters of Jerusalem stand for a conservative civilisation, that excludes, for example, the vitality and subversive restlessness of the "lower classes". All its energies are devoted to its self-preservation, to a resistance to change and mortality (cf. city walls, soldiers, manners, agriculture). The daughters of Jerusalem attempt not to embark on life, so as to escape inevitable shipwreck.

The polarity may be formulated in the opposition of two terms that are usually held to be interchangeable: purity and innocence. Purity implies impurity, an already corrupted world. The fair daughters of Jerusalem, untouched by the sun, are fearful, since to the pure all things are impure. Innocence, however, precedes good and evil, in the garden, for instance; its ambivalence is in fact integration.

The relationship of the Beloved with the daughters of Jerusalem is an important structural element in the poem. From being an uncertain and casteless outsider she becomes the leader of their circle. She advises them, speaks for natural, spontaneous love; and when she is humiliated by the guardians of public morality (5.7), they aid her and comfort

Chapter Three - Beauty and the Enigma

her, calling her "the most beautiful among women". If, as Northrop Frye (1957: 43) claims, comedy is essentially characterised by social cohesion, this induction presents the cooperation of country and city, Thanatos and Eros, innocence and purity, and all the contraries we have cited, in mutual dependence.

The Dionysiac character of the Beloved may be further illustrated by a glance at Marvin Pope's list of mythological prototypes (1976: 311-318): Black Madonnas, virgin goddesses, Anat, Ishtar, Kali etc. that combine homicidal glee with an insatiable sexual appetite, to be the subject of dangerous adoration, at the centre of cultic circles.

With the images "as the tents of Kedar, as the curtains of Solomon" /10/ the Beloved supposedly illustrates her dark beauty; but in fact they draw attention away from it. The artifice of language disguises her challenge and reinforces her plea to be admitted into civilised society; part of the persuasiveness and reassurance of the Pastoral is imparted by the fiction that countryfolk speak mellifluously. But as ornamentation, the images surreptitiously widen the symbolic discourse of beauty and terror, at one remove.

The tents of Kedar are black and rich in the waterless desert; a chromatic correlation reinforced by a pun (K̆edar: black). But the simile works mainly through contextual connotation, a comparison of the situation of the Bedouin and that of the Beloved. Like her, they are exposed to the fierceness of the sun, and, like her, they are strangers to urban civilisation, subject to contempt and admiration. They are a menace, as raiders, and therewith virilely attractive, endowed with simple, tough virtues. The idealisation of nomads, free of the taint of civilisation, appears, for example, in Jeremiah's description of the Rechabites, and the general Prophetic interplay of desert and settled land, ancient faithfulness and contemporary perversion /11/. Thus it adds to the Pastoral opposition of country and city that of desert and fertility, an amplification that is in fact subversion for city and country are now one unit:

City / Country : (City + Country) / Desert.

The country, personified in the country girl, is compared with the desert, and yet is aligned against it. Through cultivation, the fields emerge from the desert, just as life comes from death. The Beloved thus mediates between the city and the wilderness. In the same way, the nomads are those who are able to survive, and indeed grow rich (cf. Isa

21.16, Ezek 27.21) in the desert, who can colonise the wilderness, through the shelter of their tents, their darkness. Thus the image combines the threat of destruction (raiders, desert, non-nature) with the hope of integration (virtue, innocence, humanisation).

The curtains of Solomon are at the opposite extreme. They are a metonymy for his palace, and hence for the beauty and splendour of his kingdom. They isolate the king as an individual behind the manifestations of his power, sexual and political; yet he is at the centre of society, the object of all its attentions. Moreover, it is especially the enigmatic inaccessible person who is attractive, the source of sexual intoxication.

Extremes meet. Both king and nomad are in some sense unconstrained by society and its laws, representing an irresponsible freedom; both mingle polarities of fear and romantic desire. This symmetrical opposition to the daughters of Jerusalem, as well as their syntagmatic coupling as images for the Beloved, establishes a hidden link, on a geographical axis (desert - country - city - palace), parallel to the transformation of the Beloved from rural outsider to leader of the circle, and royal mistress.

The attributes common to Solomon and Kedar are those that essentially characterise dark beauty, with its Dionysiac ambivalence, coming from outside society, incarnated and worshipped within it. Yet the Beloved is not like Solomon, but merely like his curtains, defined in terms of the other. She is the mediator, in other words, between the king and the kingdom, between the desert and man.

1.6 explains the Beloved's bashfulness by means of a story: "Do not look on me, that I am black, that the sun has scorched me; my mother's sons were angry with me; they made me a keeper of vineyards; my own vineyard I did not keep." The enigma is displaced, first synchronically, through simile, and now diachronically, through narrative. Like the comparisons, the anecdote entertains the listeners, rhetorically seduces them; they unconsciously obey her command, not to look on her. The paradoxical state is accounted for, but only in terms of paradoxical events. Events supposedly speak for themselves; hence the Beloved appeals to an objective but confused authority, exposing society's double-mindedness, its own ambivalence.

Historically contempt/envy turns into persecution; the Beloved fears rejection because she has so much suffered it. She is driven out of her family, tormented by the sun, and

Chapter Three - Beauty and the Enigma

even exiled from herself - "my own vineyard I did not keep". Yet she is made the keeper of the vineyards! The wry irony of the sequence turns on this transformation of the neglect of one's own vineyard into the care of others, of the rejection by the brothers into social responsibility. In the Song wine is a recurrent sexual metaphor; grapes are the fruit of Dionysus, tended by the intoxicating Beloved. The metaphorical equivalence of sex and alcohol, vagina and vine, makes her the source of drunkenness, the seductive sorceress, ever-available and by the same token abandoned, both by herself and by her family. Sociologically, forsaken women are both exploited by society and excluded from it; in terms of the Pastoral, the tender of grapes works to free others of care, to make society irresponsible and light-headed.

The sun that ripens the grapes burns the woman; through its virulence the rage of the brothers becomes a cosmic violence /12/. Yet it is because of this combined malevolence that she is darkly beautiful, as the victim of the sadistic cycle, attraction through hatred. Stranger still, the sun, the source of light and splendour, causes darkness in women, while the daughters of Jerusalem are fair, because they have been shielded from it. There is thus a correlation between the city, to which she says "Do not look on me", and the intent gaze of the sun, just as there is between homelessness and sexual availability, and between the cultivation of intoxication and the social exclusion of its mediators. Wine always has more or less subversive connotations. The light of the sun is the light of the world through which the Beloved passes; in its eyes innocence is darkened.

The brothers are impelled by considerations of family honour, or else jealousy. The Beloved through her intrinsic seductiveness presents the potentiality of illicit love. Within the family, the play of desire and repression is especially perilous, and is complicated by competition for maternal affection: hence the paraphrase "my mother's sons ...." For the first time, the incest motif appears in the Song, albeit as a traumatised banishment of the forbidden sight.

At this point jealousy is experienced as outrage, that the family refuses the shelter it should provide against a hostile world. Fraternal rivalry turns into complicity, to maintain a delicate balance of familial relations, based on the myth that infantile innocence = purity. The Dark Beloved is expelled from the family, as the source of defilement. Here other considerations arise, that will figure in subsequent episodes, namely family property and the sociology of gender.

To summarise the work so far: the antinomies of the dark beauty that account for its enigmatic character, since it suggests the possibility of integrating the unacceptable, are projected spatially onto the spectrum from desert to king, and historically in the growth of the Beloved, from an unburnt child in the midst of the family to a burnt dispossessed woman in the midst of society. The issues will be seen more clearly, in relief, as it were, if we turn to a passage (6.8-10) that is in all respects an inversion of ours. I will not discuss it in all its details, despite its fascinating richness, but merely concentrate on a few points of comparison.

שִׁשִּׁים הֵמָּה מְלָכוֹת וּשְׁמֹנִים
פִּילַגְשִׁים וַעֲלָמוֹת אֵין מִסְפָּר: אַחַת הִיא יוֹנָתִי תַמָּתִי
אַחַת הִיא לְאִמָּהּ בָּרָה הִיא לְיוֹלַדְתָּהּ רָאוּהָ בָנוֹת
וַיְאַשְּׁרוּהָ מְלָכוֹת וּפִילַגְשִׁים וַיְהַלְלוּהָ: מִי־זֹאת הַנִּשְׁקָפָה
כְּמוֹ־שָׁחַר יָפָה כַלְּבָנָה בָּרָה כַּחַמָּה אֲיֻמָּה כַּנִּדְגָּלוֹת:

(6.8) There are sixty queens, and eighty concubines, and maidens without number.
(9) One is my dove, my pure one, one is she to her mother, radiant /13/ to the one who gave her birth; the daughters saw her and called her happy, the queens and concubines, and praised her.
(10) Who is this who peers forth as the dawn /14/, fair as the moon, radiant as the sun, terrible as constellations?

Here the dark Beloved is brilliant and pure (tammātî), adored at the centre of society instead of being outcast from it. She is seen and praised by the daughters, queens and concubines, instead of fearing their contempt and begging them not to look on her. She is radiant as the sun, giving light to the world, the source of joyfulness. "The daughters saw her and called her happy." Envy is strangely absent, though richly deserved.

There is one constant factor linking 1.5-6 and 6.8-10: hers is a natural beauty, as opposed to the cultural beauty of the queens and concubines. She is a dove, a wild creature of the rocks. The most remarkable structural feature of the passage, however, is the fusion of two moments at the furthest remove: the moment of birth with royal intimacy. This is the ultimate image of integration: a "hieros gamos" of king representing society with newborn baby. Opposed to it

Chapter Three - Beauty and the Enigma

were all the forces of 1.5-6: the brothers/the daughters/the sun. But here the brothers are absent; she is her mother's unique child. The sun, instead of tormenting and darkening her, has met its match: it is she who is "as radiant as the sun" and gives light to the world; indeed the accumulation of celestial bodies, sun, moon and stars, may imply her superiority.

There is consequently a progression from the innocence of birth to adolescence; from the all-pervasive vital beauty to the cast out beauty, repelled because it is too attractive. If the dark beauty in 1.6 tends the fruit of Dionysus, the resplendent beauty of 6.9 is the source of ecstasy. In a sense, she is the king's "baby", his protegée, and shares in his licentious freedom and privilege. The luminous beauty, darkened in the eyes of the world and the sun's glare, corresponds to the splendour of the king, hidden behind curtains.

Let us pause for a moment to look at the images of the last verse: "Who is this who peers forth as the dawn, fair as the moon, radiant as the sun, terrible as constellations?" We have the emergence of day, the coexistence of beauty and terror; but still more powerful is the combination of moon and sun, rulers of day and night, in her person. The integration of dark and light takes the form of an ordered alternation in Genesis and in common experience; the two luminaries introduce the calendar, days, months and seasons. At this point the Beloved transcends society and becomes a cosmic figure, immortal yet human, commensurate with the cycles of time and the immensity of space. /15/.

I have not the scope here for a full survey of the syntactic structure of 1.5-6, nor do I think it would contribute greatly to this particular argument. Nevertheless, one or two observations may be of interest.

The passage begins with a magnificent assertion of identity: "šehôrâ ᵓanî wenāᵓwâ" "I am black and comely ..." "This is what I am", it seems to say, "Good and bad, rustic, persecuted; take me or leave me." It ends with dispossession: "My own vineyard I have not kept." This forward movement in the surface of the text, fullness of self ➤ loss of self, is reversed in the syntactic structure: the main clauses are at the beginning of each sentence, and the subsequent units refer back to them. The similes in 1.5 "illustrate" the dark beauty; the sequence of events in 1.6 is subordinated to and explains her reluctance to be seen. In this case, syntax and logic correspond: the temporal sequence is from the end of the verse to its beginning. In both main clauses (I am black and comely ... do not look on me) the Beloved is powerfully present; the symbolic context fills in her background and claims our sympathy. There is thus a movement from loss of self to fullness of self. Paradoxically, it is through being dispossessed, leaving her family etc., that she finds herself; she becomes the keeper of vineyards, socially responsible, indignant, fascinatingly mysterious. In contrast, the well-mannered collectivity of daughters may seem colourless. Yet it is her individuality that courts degradation. Hence her proud annunciation is placatory, hoping to win an unassuming place in the world. This brings us to our opening enigma, that Beauty says "Do not look on me!"

Second Episode: 8.11-12

כֶּרֶם הָיָה לִשְׁלֹמֹה בְּבַעַל הָמוֹן נָתַן אֶת־הַכֶּרֶם לַנֹּטְרִים אִישׁ יָבִא בְּפִרְיוֹ אֶלֶף כָּסֶף: כַּרְמִי שֶׁלִּי לְפָנָי הָאֶלֶף לְךָ שְׁלֹמֹה וּמָאתַיִם לְנֹטְרִים אֶת־פִּרְיוֹ:

(8.11) Solomon had a vineyard in Baal-Hamon; he gave the vineyard to keepers; each one would bring for its fruit a thousand pieces of silver.
(12) My own vineyard is before me; yours, O Solomon, the thousand, and two hundred for the keepers of its fruit.

This passage has especially intimate links with 1.5-6, because of their lexical and metaphorical correlations: the unique phrase "karmî šellî" "my own vineyard"; the

Chapter Three - Beauty and the Enigma

occupation of "nōtēr/nōtērâ"; the play of my vineyard over against those of others; the figure of Solomon. It contrives to be even more enigmatic. In it, however, beauty undergoes a significant transformation.

The parable sets up a mystery: whose is the vineyard? Are the vineyards in 8.11 and 8.12 one and the same? Is the vineyard - "karmî šellî" - the Beloved, as in 1.6, or is it something else?

Am I justified in calling it a parable, at least without indulging in a truism, since every action in poetry is metaphorical, simply by virtue of being in a poem? Unlike the other narratives in the Song, however, which are more or less pertinent to the affairs of lovers, the vicissitudes of Solomon's vineyard can only be understood as a similitude. The lease of one of Solomon's vineyards would hardly be immortalised in a love poem simply as a business record. In addition, it signals itself as parable through its setting in an indeterminate time, its semi-legendary protagonist, its formulaic opening, and its apparent triviality. But if it is a parable, what does it illustrate?

In fact, the parable becomes enmeshed in paradox, belongs to what James Williams calls "the Wisdom of Counter-Order". The promise of narrative simplicity relaxes the reader, tempts and traps his anecdotal interest. In this way the parable is subversive /16/.

It is also disturbing because it breaks its own rules. It begins like a ballad, a footnote to history. Yet in the next verse it becomes sharply personal. We do not know whether the first verse is set long ago, in the fabulous age of Solomon; it was his, "kerem hāyâ lišlōmōh", because he and it are no more; or whether he is alive and active, as the second verse suggests, and it has merely passed out of his possession. When the past tense is replaced by the present, Solomon is addressed directly, the first possibility is eliminated; we may imaginatively participate in that distant era, as the player enters the drama. The result is a foreshortening, a fusion of mythic time and real time, in which the present becomes fabulous. This in fact is one of the tricks of the parable: it entertains us at a distance with what apparently does not concern us, and then shows that we are involved, for example when David discovers that he is the subject of Nathan's parable.

The emblematic nature of the tale - its quality of fantasy, if you like - is intensified by the clearly allegorical overtones of the vineyard's location in the otherwise unknown Baal-Hamon /17/, lit. Lord/Baal of the multitude/wealth. The introductory formula: Vineyard + was + to So-and-So + in Allegorical Place Name is found also in Isaiah's Parable of the Vineyard, itself a love song (Isa 5.1):

kerem hāyâ lîdîdî beqeren ben šāmen
My beloved had a vineyard in Qeren-Ben-Shamen

A variant occurs also in the Song, in 3.9:

ʾappiryôn ʿāśā lô hammelek šelōmōh
Solomon made himself a palanquin

In both these cases, likewise, the carefully distanced past vanishes: the vineyard is Israel, whom the Lord denounces; the daughters of Zion go out and gaze on Solomon (3.11).

The traditional introduction is a signal to the listener; he knows that he is listening to parable, to a form communicated through the singer. Through the ritualised formula, like "Once upon a time", the singer establishes his credentials, is invested with the authority of the automomous, and therefore ever present, past. Parable, Northrop Frye tells us, is a subsidiary form of oracle (1957: 56).

Several critics attribute 8.11 or both verses to the Lover or poet /18/, both of whom are identified with Solomon as one of their personae. There is no indication however of a change of speaker between 8.11 and 8.12, nor between 8.10 and 8.11; parsimony suggests that both 8.11 and 8.12, the exposition and development of the parable respectively, are part of her story. In the first verse her voice merges with that of the parable; in the second she projects herself and dramatises herself in its imaginary past. In 8.13 she is the singer, singing her own story. In other words, she is the observer and narrator of the events she experiences: the self splits into subject and object.

Solomon participates in the poem in two ways: as persona of the Lover and as sovereign. These generate the ambiguities of "kerem", the "vineyard", to which we now return.

Society cultivates intoxication in the vineyard; in the Song both it and its product wine have powerful erotic connotations. The vineyard at Baal-Hamon may well be the Beloved, the source of sexual intoxication, "the only one" (6.9). On the other hand, it may be his kingdom, the source of Dionysian luxury and power /19/.

The name Baal-Hamon, Lord of Wealth or of the Multitude, draws attention to this second possibility: analogous to it are the allegorical place-names Heshbon and Bat-Rabbim in 7.5. But the toponym has another connotation, that of displaced

Chapter Three - Beauty and the Enigma

local deities. Might there be a suggestion of fertility? Or of hubris?

If the vineyard is the Beloved, then one may suppose that 8.11 and 8.12 are contrasted: "Once upon a time," she says, "I was Solomon's vineyard; now I am my own." The difficulties start when one wonders what Solomon is doing giving her to "keepers", especially if the latter bring a thousand pieces of silver for her fruit. The third stich may mean that they <u>give</u> or <u>receive</u> the silver; or it may simply be an impersonal statement of value: <u>one would give</u> ... /20/. Some critics have accordingly sought to identify the keepers with hired eunuchs, a clearly apologetic construction /21/. The first possibility, that they give the silver, is both more daring and more realistic: Solomon has used her in political barter, instead of wearily consigning her to the harem. Although betrayal of their love is outrageous in the Song, in sober history it is merely sensible. Thus we encounter a profound opposition:

Way of the World+ | Values of the Song‾
[+ = valued positively; ‾ = valued negatively]

If the vineyard is the kingdom, analogously those who tend its grapes are ministers, officials. He delegates responsibility in quest of the true, valuable vineyard, that of the Beloved. Consequently, the opposition is reversed:

Way of the World‾ | Values of the Song+

In the eyes of the world, a hedonistic king who fails to care for his kingdom is unworthy of his throne: we may catch here a resonance of the traditional criticism of Solomon. But the painstaking work of the Song is to show that love is worth all pleasures and riches, for it alone is as strong as death.

A similar opposition between the ways of the world and the values of the Song has been found a few verses earlier in the sketch of the man who gives all the substance of his house for love and is accordingly despised.

"My own vineyard is before me", in 8.12, is an echo of "My own vineyard I did not keep" (lō' nātārtî) in 1.6. Now she is the keeper of her own vineyard, not those of the community; unlike Solomon, whose vineyard others maintain. Supposing this to be a declaration of independence, there is a disjunction between past and present, the vineyard that was Solomon's and is now hers. But if she is her own mistress, he equally has disengaged himself from her, handing her over to the "nōtrîm", in a mutual withdrawal. Self-possession is thus in the face of exploitation, and the consequence of rejection.

In 1.5-6 we noticed an underlying movement from loss of self to fullness of self, which is dynamically effected in the transformation from social outcast, who squanders her potential, to king's mistress and social luminary. Self-possession results from sexual consummation. The whole space of the poem separates "My vineyard is mine" from "My own vineyard I did not keep". If nothing else, the Song tells of the discovery of oneself through love. In a sense, this inversion of 1.6 in 8.12 encapsulates the total experience of reading the poem.

She may therefore be her own through being his, or having been his. Self-possession is a product of conjunction, instead of separation, as the daughters of Jerusalem would have it.

These contraries implicate the following clause "hā'elep lekâ šelōmōh" "Yours, O Solomon, the thousand", which is likewise totally enigmatic. She may offer him "the thousand"; or tell him to keep the thousand he offers. The free gift from the fullness of herself complements the sense of pricelessness, that a woman who can be bought does not value herself, and is therefore valueless. The "thousand" either identifies her vineyard with Solomon's, or else establishes an equivalence; her vineyard is worth the kingdom, all he has to offer. If the thousand pieces of silver are the hireling's wages, she permits the king himself to be her retainer, when she says "The thousand be yours, O Solomon". The two images, her vineyard and his, the Lover and the kingdom, represent a perpetual motion, whereby the king continually abandons his kingdom for the truly valuable Beloved, the source of fertility, only to use her in the service of the kingdom. Analogously, the Beloved preserves her vineyard so as to bestow it freely; through bestowing it she fosters it.

The questions we formulated at the beginning of this section - Whose are the vineyards? Are they the same? The Beloved or the kingdom? - cannot be truly answered, for each alternative is dependent on the other.

The last phrase, "And two hundred for the keepers of its fruit" is weird. I do not propose to guess at the significance of the opposition 200|1000 /21/. If the keepers are ministers (second alternative), or lovers (first alternative), they too are expected to participate in Solomon's joy or rejection. An analogous instance is 5.1, where friends and lovers are invited to feast in the Lover's garden. For love is socially dynamic; his intimacy gives pleasure to the king's entourage, as in 6.8-9, where the queens and concubines rejoice in the

Chapter Three - Beauty and the Enigma

Beloved's light, even though the king enjoys her exclusively. On the other hand, if "the thousand be yours" is a rejection, then pointedly included in it is the whole hierarchy.

The enigma in this passage serves to present two quite different stories simultaneously, and to show their incompatible and inextricable coexistence. We have found therein two reversible oppositions: The way of the world/the values of the Song, and conjunction/disjunction. The two may be superimposed: in a loveless world self-fulfilment is narrowly egotistic, coldly repressive; people are valued according to political status. The Pastoral opens the self to the other, sophistication to coarseness. In the poem, where metaphors unite the most discrete components, the play of conjunction and disjunction becomes exuberantly insistent.

In 1.5-6, the first pole was represented by the daughters of Jerusalem, the second by the Beloved. The oppositions of Dionysus and Apollo, integration and differentiation, that we found there clearly correspond to those we have just formulated, the poles of lascivious abandonment and worldly calculation.

There are, however, differences, both in structure and in substance. In 1.5-6 the sequence of events is clear: the beauty that does not wish to be seen, the burning and tormenting of the Beloved, and so on. The enigma is, as it were, intrinsic. Here it invades the superstructure, undermines the narrative. There we have the directness of speech, a present that invokes the past; here we have a faraway parable, a past that becomes present. The present is obscure, as the Beloved's plea is transparent. The voice of the parable, of traditional wisdom, is paradoxical, unintelligible. Its autonomous time invests the speaker with sanctity, with mystery. The Beloved, as the medium for that voice, makes its past her present, both as a comment on life in sequential time and as an affirmation of the timelessness in which love participates. We remember the ambivalent status of the oracle as the chthonic voice of Apollo, subversive of commonsense and fixed truths, and yet the authenticating voice of a static society.

The movement from dispossession to fullness parallels a temporal shift: from the moment before to the moment after. In 1.5-6 the Beloved has not yet been admitted into society; in 8.11-12 the timeless erotic moment is juxtaposed with its passing. The parable looks back with wistful hindsight. The passage from before to after is that from innocence to experience, to a passé dignity from envied despised beauty.

Beauty now reappears, in disguise. For though all its perplexities the theme of the parable is plain: it is the metamorphosis of grapes into money, of love into a commodity. In time, the transience of ecstasy becomes social currency; for instance, sex is institutionalised as marriage. Silver, because it is imperishable, is a resource against disaster, a conservation of energy, accumulated through commonsense, caution, foresight. Work is converted into silver, silver into pleasure; silver filters, and postpones the exuberance of pleasure. As a defensive reserve, it paradoxically betrays man's insecurity and impermanence. Therewith he manipulates his surroundings and controls the sources of pleasure, constructing his magnificent, defensive civilisation. Whereas in tending the vineyards, man participates in the process of nature, and enjoys the sweetness of the earth, through the Midas touch he makes process changeless; his greed becomes repressive, abstract. The transformation of Dionysiac intoxication is symbolised by a change of colour, from chthonic darkness to glittering whiteness.

For silver is beautiful, is a source of pleasure in itself. The beauty of silver is distant, indestructible. It has the purity of repression, and consequently is the root of corruption. For mastery of silver makes all pleasure available, postponed, imagined, and finally squandered. The agent of repression conceals in its splendour infinite wish-fulfilment. Entirely similarly, the fairness of the daughters of Jerusalem is protected against their own desire.

Avaricious greed, miserly retention, conspicuous waste: the metaphorical language of money is derived from the nutritional cycle. Money is inedible, symbolic food. The anxious polarities of thrift and expenditure, manic extravagance and tight control, correspond to a phase of money as ex- crement /23/. We thus witness the transformation of dark, foetid excrement into bright, incorruptible silver.

For silver is death in the service of life. If the dark Beloved represents the power of integration of life and death, the transformation into silver renders death immutable, tame, a changeless quantity.

A strange thing happens. The means of repression comes itself to stand for the thing repressed. Money becomes the agent of Dionysus, the instrument of social change, of life as process. And as is the way with such instruments, it enslaves its master. So man loves and is dominated by matter, as

Chapter Three - Beauty and the Enigma

Marx's concept of alienation suggests (Marx: 175-185). From being the means of obtaining pleasure, it becomes the compulsive pleasure itself.

Neurosis mistakes the surrogate for the source, symbolic food for real food. For reality is terrifying, mysterious, and ultimately deadly. The transactions of society, whereby love enters the poem, grapes the greengrocer's, ensures the diffusion of Dionysiac intensity. The single conjoined moment enters disjunctive time, inspiration becomes commonplace. The nuclear sentence in the passage is "hāʼelep lekâ šelōmōh", "Yours, O Solomon, the thousand". All the others provide the setting; the last phrase is a tag or bobtail. "The thousand be yours, O Solomon", through its ambiguity, combines both poles in a harmonious relationship. It expresses self-validating pride, an assertion of identity worth all the silver in the world. But the pride comes out of receiving the homage of the world (Solomon, silver) and self-surrender, out of their fusion. The passage puts that which is beyond value in the market-place; it is like the child's question "How much do you love me?" The random hyperbole, as well as being evidence for the metaphorical nature of the vineyard, clearly demonstrates the nonsense of equation. And yet sadly it happens: women become tokens, beauty is traded, wine merchants prosper.

In 6.9-10, the Beloved undergoes an apotheosis, from darkness to brilliance, a solar figure at the centre of society. As Marcia Falk (1982: 125) points out, the word for "moon", "lebānâ", emphasises its whiteness. She is, as it were, living silver /24/. The figures of the moon and the sun combine lunar periodicity with solar plenitude. Moreover, the last image in the sequence, "terrible as constellations", projects her wonder onto the patterns of fixed stars, in perpetual revolution. One thinks of Ps 8.4: "If I look at the heavens, the work of your fingers, the moon and the stars that you have established", and its sense of the littleness of man. Now it is she who is equal to the cosmos. Astrology, which was known if not monotheistically sanctioned in Ancient Israel /25/, is founded on an intuition of predestination, that everything is foreknown and therefore preexistent, and of a secret correspondence between things, by means of which our destiny is coded in the stars; now the stars are coded in her. She becomes a figure of Fate, the mystery of life and death, terrible and wondrous, accepted as pattern. Thus she integrates the forces that silver neutralises.

Third Episode: 8.8-10

אָחוֹת לָנוּ קְטַנָּה וְשָׁדַיִם אֵין לָהּ מַה־נַּעֲשֶׂה לַאֲחוֹתֵנוּ
בַּיּוֹם שֶׁיְדֻבַּר־בָּהּ: אִם־חוֹמָה הִיא נִבְנֶה עָלֶיהָ טִירַת
כָּסֶף וְאִם־דֶּלֶת הִיא נָצוּר עָלֶיהָ לוּחַ אָרֶז: אֲנִי חוֹמָה
וְשָׁדַי כַּמִּגְדָּלוֹת אָז הָיִיתִי בְעֵינָיו כְּמוֹצְאֵת שָׁלוֹם:

(8.8) We have a little sister, and she has no breasts. What shall we do for our sister on the day when she shall be spoken for?
(9) If she is a wall, we will build on her a turret /26/ of silver; and if she is a door we will enclose her with boards of cedar.
(10) I am a wall and my breasts are like towers; therefore I was in his eyes as one who found peace.

This passage immediately precedes 8.11-12, and so it might seem odd to discuss it after it; this is because 8.11-12 exhibits closer lexical correspondences with 1.5-6: "karmî šellî" etc. 8.8-10 uses different materials, yet it combines the image of silver from 8.11-12 with the theme of familial relationships in 1.5-6 and 6.8-10. Its relationship with 1.5-6, the starting-point of our discussion, is one of antithesis, as will appear; yet it offers the possibility of harmonising the disjunctions that until now have been our principal concern.

The first ambiguity concerns the speaker, who could be the brothers of 1.5-6, sisters, or the Beloved herself /27/. I consider it to be the latter, since the other views would involve introducing new characters without textual authority, a bad critical procedure. Moreover, it necessitates supposing a "flash-back" (Lys: 294) or poor eyesight, to account for the discrepancy between the non-existence of breasts, as seen by the "brothers", and their full development, as declared by the Beloved. This precipitates the invention of stories, romances woven round the text /28/. My view is simply that the Beloved speaks, as a member of her family, about her little sister, who is growing up.

In 8.8-10 the enigma is overt, instead of appearing through a paradoxical action, as in 1.5-6, or an ambiguous metaphor, in 8.11-12. It is an unanswered question: "What shall we do on the day she shall be spoken for?"

The text contemplates two hypothetical futures: that she be a wall and that she be a door. If the metaphors had a clear, culturally defined meaning, it has been lost. Once

Chapter Three - Beauty and the Enigma

again we meet our ambiguous "wĕ": "If she is a wall ... and/but if she is a door". They are thus either adversative and/or complementary.

That there is some opposition is evident from 8.10, in which the assertion "I am a wall" explains the Beloved's success. What remains unclear, however, is whether "wall" and "door" are two kinds of beauty or character, both of which are of value, or whether they are contrasted. In the latter case, if the wall wins the Lover's favour and is crowned with silver, the door would correspondingly be unattractive.

The older critics saw in this a straightforward opposition of virtue: the wall is an unassailable woman, the door is open to all comers. Tur-Sinai (1943: 19 n.2), followed by Gordis (1974: 100) and others, remark that "wall" and "door" are traditional synthetic parallelisms; like the wall, the door is normally barred, and consequently they believe that both are expressive of a chaste reserve.

This ambiguity is compounded by that of "nāṣûr" in the last stich. It may mean to "enclose", but also to "adorn", "fashion", or "besiege" /29/. Taking only the first view, the older critics found here confirmation of the brothers' cruelty (and their own attribution), in a diabolical punishment for the girl's imprudence, namely, seclusion in a cedar cubbyhole; Krinetzki (1964: 250) puts forward essentially the same interpretation in a milder form: if the brothers feel that she is a bit too vivacious, they will sedulously protect her. If, however, "nāṣûr" means "we will adorn" or "fashion", it parallels "nibneh" "we will build" in the first stich, and the two images are complementary.

The parallel superstructures, the turret of silver and the boards of cedar, have a dual function, as fortifications and embellishments. Accordingly, both "wall" and "door" are ambiguous, as only Albert Cook (149) has perceived. The turret is seen and glitters from afar; the planks are carved from costly wood. The Beloved is an attractive fortress; attractive and barred presumably because she is worth defending. However, if the wall tipped with silver and the door barricaded with cedar share the qualities of being rich and formidable, they are also antithetical.

Silver is conspicuous, the parapet catches the eye; analogously, the Tower of David in 4.4. glitters with the thousand shields of the warriors, that both repel attack and are a splendid ornament. Cedar, however, is strong and dark, associated, as we have seen, with smell and masculinity. The materials are appropriate to their tasks; for in a defensive network walls are visible, doors are concealed.

If the door raises the question of chastity, clearly it corresponds to the vagina; like the vagina, the door may be open or closed. If, in 8.10, the relationship of the breasts to the person is that of the tower to the wall, the tenor of the latter is equally transparent: it is the body, in which the "I" is contained. The body is conspicuous, the vagina is secret. The one attracts aesthetically, at a distance; the other communicates chemically, unconsciously, especially through smell, whose pervasiveness annuls differences.

At puberty, "the day when she shall be spoken for", the body expresses itself by developing breasts, the vagina through the growth of pubic hair, to which the planks of cedar may be compared , as the towers are compared to breasts. Both are powerfully erotogenous, the pubic hair through concealing the genitalia, the breasts through announcing their presence. Therein may be discerned the relationship between them: the breasts, like the face, make sexuality aesthetic; they refer metonymically to the reticent vagina, that in them expresses itself socially, discreetly. The pubic hair, by screening the vulva, makes it mysterious, inexpressible; and hence initiates the process of linguistic diffusion. If the body represents a sexual potential, common to both man and woman, the vagina is the essence of femininity. At puberty, the emergence of breasts feminises the body, while the pubic hair disguises the vagina.

If in 1.5-6 Beauty comes from outside civilisation, here it is enshrined in its centre; it is, as it were, a city under siege. The wall and the door are complementary and antithetical, activating opposite poles of the aesthetic experience. The wall contains the door, without which it could not be entered; if in this case, the wall divides self and other, the door provides the means of communication, either open or closed. The wall differentiates, the door unites, like the body and the vagina, that stand for Apollo and Dionysus respectively. The one is transmitted to the conscious eye, that appraises objectively, the other to the sensitive nose, in whose reactions disgust and ecstasy are inextricably mingled.

No woman, of course, is all vagina or all figure; the schematic metaphors isolate qualities that are always mingled in real life, that manifest themselves with different emphases. Wall and door are different types of attractiveness, that yet have a complementary relationship. It is with pride that the Beloved asserts that she is a wall and not a door, and that therefore she met with the Lover's

Chapter Three - Beauty and the Enigma

approval. For the wall is bold and manifest; on the other hand, the door is secret. The relationship between wall and door is that between body and genitalia, the one articulating the other.

If the theme of 8.11-12 is the transformation of grapes into money, here it is the process of ripening. In her little sister the Beloved recognises herself, and her own progress from childhood through puberty. The little sister is an image of herself, in the sequence of generations; in this sense she is "a flashback", as Lys says /30/. Instead of incestuous jealousy and expulsion from the family, puberty here leads to identification.

The child is irresponsible, like Solomon or the Bedouin in 1.5; like the dark Beloved, she comes from outside society and has to be initiated into it. Before she has breasts no one talks about the little sister; it is not yet the day when, literally, "it shall be spoken about her". Puberty makes her a point of general interest, the subject of gossip and intrigue. For especially the adolescent presents the question: "Whose shall she be?" It is quite possible that "bayyôm šeyyedubbar bāh" "the day when she shall be spoken for" idiomatically alludes to marriage negotiations, though the evidence is slender /31/; its range of reference is far wider, however, embracing every gossipy context in which her name might be mentioned. For behind this question there is another, more pervasive one - namely, "What shall she be?" - which one asks of a child more as an expression of wonder and an excuse for fantasy than for a sober answer. If the vagina/door is an unanswered question - is it open or closed? /32/ - the plain wall signifies the absence of questioning, that she has not yet become the subject of speculation. Only when mediation occurs, when the body is sexualised and the vagina concealed, do the questions become active, tangible.

The little sister does not answer these questions, and in fact does not talk at all. She is completely passive, the subject matter of discourse, not the speaker. No doubt there is a sociological reference here. The question of sexual choice is formulated by time and by others, by <u>the day</u> on which <u>it shall be spoken</u> about her. The family adorn and manipulate her, with turrets of silver and planks of cedar. They participate even in her physical development, an idea that is less bizarre than it first seems if one considers the elaborate beautification of nubile daughters in many cultures. Her body is appropriated by the family, as a social asset. The identification of the Beloved with the little sister as an image of herself leads to her transformation into an image of herself, the image the family imposes on her. She is almost literally gilded, to become social currency, decked with silver and cedar.

The little sister corresponds to the fair daughters of Jerusalem: light-coloured, sheltered, dependent. In her, the Beloved contemplates an adolescence in which the family acts as a bridge between the child and the public world, which becomes, as it were, its extension, entered through peaceful transition, instead of abrupt violence. The little sister is then an "altera ego", in whom she recognises, not her own past - for there is no single story in the Song - but a different one.

The images of 8.9 foreshadow the uncertainties of the future; there is no knowing what the little sister will be. Whereas the Beloved appears to control the little sister, to dress her like a doll, in reality all she can do is respond to the child's unfolding disposition. Nothing more can be said about the child's future; she turns to her own past, perhaps as an example of a successful journey, possibly for assurance against those limitless perspectives. The "altera ego" now becomes herself: she presents herself as a wall with towers. The contrast little sister/dark Beloved reverses itself: she is a wall and not a door, chaste - if that is a connotation of wall - well-formed, defended. The dispossessed woman is now self-possessed, i.e. possessed by the family. Yet therewith she attains a forthright independence: the breasts are like towers, dominant, assertive. As in 1.5, she thrusts herself forward, with the first person pronoun: I am ('anî) a wall, just as previously she had said "I am ('anî) black and comely". Yet she fulfils herself in the eyes of the other: "... therefore I was in his eyes as one who found peace". "Kemoṣe'ēt šālôm" can have three meanings, the first two of which are antithetical and complementary:
  i)   to find peace
  ii)   to bring peace
  iii) to surrender, of a city /33/.

Peace is the completion of the process, a perfect integration of self and other. Dionysiac intensity ends in tranquillity, when the desire becomes fulfilment. For the desire is for tranquillity, the absence of desire, in a stable and blissful harmony. Dionysus wishes his own negation or catharsis, in which Apollo, the serene, differentiating principle, is likewise integrated. "In his eyes" may be a synecdoche for himself: her individuality is fostered for his

Chapter Three - Beauty and the Enigma

good opinion. But it may also mean literally his eyes, because they are beautiful; by gazing at his eyes she finds peace. For eyes have a dual function, corresponding to the differentiating and de-differentiating principles. They are observers, through which we become aware of the objective world, in all its manifold difference; yet in them man feels he gets behind appearances, that the subjective personality becomes manifest. The exchange of eyes, like sexual intercourse, annuls differences, communicates without words, "where we cannot speak", where words are unnecessary, obstructive, or deceptive. The beauty of eyes is especially interesting, for they can only unite without touching, at a psychic distance; their objective separateness is the condition for their fusion. "In his eyes" she finds peace, because there objectively - through vision - she is absorbed in the other. Yet likewise she gives peace, for his eyes are filled with her presence. She looks at his eyes that look at her/hers; in him she finds a reflection of herself, of their mutual reciprocity. This is also an image of surrender - the third ambiguity of "môṣeʾēt šālôm"; the city is fortified, the girl is trained for this moment, when culture gives way to nature. The Beloved, through her upbringing, preserves the child through the family into the adult world; innocence survives in the guise of purity. She remains a combination of dark and light, in which the darkness is expressed through the light, as the eyes reveal the mysterious person.

The city surrenders to the Lover, of whose persona as king we have had several illustrations. If in 1.5 he is hidden behind curtains, and in 8.11-12 has to choose between vineyards, here the curtains/wall are the city, and the fusion of love becomes an image of political harmony. In 1.5, the king is both the centre of society and inaccessible to it, as the source of Dionysiac energy. Here he enters the kingdom from outside, and the city relinquishes its defences. The positions are thus reversed: in 1.5 the king personifies the city, and the Beloved is the rural outsider; here the Beloved is the city, and the king the stranger.

There has been a fourth suggested meaning for "kemôṣeʾēt šālôm": that it is the emergence or sparkling of the Evening Star, Shalem /33/. If so, she is the intermediary /34/ between night and day, as in 6.10. There is a complementary link between the two passages, as Dahood and Schoville point out: Shalem in our verse is matched by "šāḥar" "the dawn star/the dawn" in 6.10 /35/. She is the messenger of the tense serenity of twilight, the cosmic conflict and harmonious alternation of light and dark. On this interpretation, "in his eyes" may simply mean "to him"; but if taken literally, his eyes would become a metaphor for the sky in which she shines, a brilliant divine point in his immensity. The moment of consummation then reconciles two extremes: plenitude with particularity. This recalls the opening paradox, that lovers can be distinctly aware of each other and yet merged with each other. It revives the oceanic feeling of earliest infancy: the emergency of consciousness from infinite space.

The little sister, like the daughters of Jerusalem, is cultivated in the midst of society; her beauty is the result of careful nurture. It is the beauty of civilisation, as opposed to the wild, subversive beauty of the Beloved in 1.5. If in 1.5-6, the Beloved is a threat, and in 6.8-10 is adopted and adored, here the threat is disguised, innocence is preserved through change, and once again the Beloved presents the promise of fulfilment. The ways of the world thus subtly confirm the values of the Song; the citadel is elaborated so as to be abandoned in love. There is continuity between infancy, puberty, and sexual consummation; an untroubled adolescence whose cost is self-effacement.

Beautifying hides and heightens sexual attraction; postponing it at a distance. Yet it may be enjoyed, by the girl as well, as fantasy. She is turned into an artistic whimsical ornament, seductive and elusive. On the level of language, this is the work of the Song; on that of nature, it may be any object that catches the fancy, the world as metalanguage used by the lovers. The transformation of love into silver that we have discovered is here mediated; love becomes art, and is therefore preserved for its time and for ever. But there is also sadness: that women become marital objects, that they are fussed over and grow to be something "in his eyes", according to one of its ambiguous meanings.

The enigma here is that of the future - the realm of fantasy "par excellence" - and it is expounded through a parody of legal formulae. Law dreams of controlling the future; it regulates the appropriate response to circumstances, in clear and definite language. Here it classifies the future under two categories, which might be equivalent or

Chapter Three - Beauty and the Enigma

opposed; moreover, as we have seen, the second apodosis is utterly inconclusive. The expectation of a clear directive is thus confounded; whereas law deals with practical reality, the language here is metaphorical. If a metaphor signifies a person, in law abstractions replace the individual. There is, however, another perspective, that is both a perception and a criticism. Our verse cannot be taken seriously as law, with its stereotyped formula "If so-and-so ... then such-and-such", because of its sheer incommensurability. How does one set about building a silver parapet on a person, or declare her "wall" or "door"? The point is not so much that these are metaphorical, but that the law itself has a poetic function. In particular, as the medium of repression, it paradoxically activates some of society's darkest sadistic impulses. The family's behaviour towards the little sister, whether it locks her up, fashions her, or festoons her, expresses through the ambiguity of the verbs the ambivalence of its relations. As in 1.6, a wicked little sister is a challenge, to be coped with through a mingling of aggression and affection. And from all the energy that is devoted to constructing her in the family's image, she emerges: "I am ..."

Syntactically, the passage is a progression from negation to affirmation, from passive to active. The opening verse couples a qualified, minimised subject - "We have a little sister" - with a negation - "And she has no breasts"; this is followed by a clause expressive of the absence of action and bewilderment - "What on earth shall we do for our sister?" In a doubly subordinated position, as a relative clause enclosed in a prepositional phrase, is the most powerful verb in the sentence [8d] "bayyôm šeyyedubbar bāh" "on the day when she shall be spoken for". But it is in the passive mood: it is action done impersonally to the little sister, the opposite of action done by her.

Thus we have four units:

8a ʾāḥôt lānû qetannâ Diminished Noun Phrase (+NP)
we have a <u>little</u> sister

8b wešādayim ʾēn lāh Negation (-NP)
she has no breasts

8c mah naʿăśeh laʾaḥōtēnû Absence of action, questioning
what shall we do for our sister (-VP)

8d bayyôm šeyyedubbar bāh Passive (-VP)
on the day when she shall be spoken for?

167

Moreover, 8b is coupled with 8d: the day when she shall be spoken for is the day when she has breasts. The transformation from ⁻NP - ⁺NP, from being without to being with breasts, leaves her exposed to attention, to being the recipient of action, and results in passivity. Now if we combine 8a and 8c, we have the following sentence: "What shall we do for our little sister?" The sister is thus the passive object of both action and speech.

8.9 alternates a nominal phrase with a verbal phrase, combining wonder with busy activity. We now know what they will do, but the little sister is still passive. The negation of 8c becomes positive, while the passivity of 8d is unchanged. What is most distinct about the verse, however, is its careful symmetry. The formulae are identical in every particular, even to the two-word construct that is the object of each action:

9b   nibneh ʻālêhâ <u>tîrat kāsep</u>   VP(VP + (PP) + NP)
9d   nāṣûr ʻālêhâ <u>lûaḥ ʼārez</u>   VP(VP + (PP) + NP)

We will build on her a turret of silver;
We will enclose her with boards of cedar

and on which each concludes. As we know, in content they combine complementarity with antithesis, to produce an ideal synthesis. The clauses are constructed as artfully as the city; they are in themselves evidence for the playful, inventive character of their alternative futures. Dependent on "What shall we do?" bewilderment turns here to fantasy.

In 8.10 the subject emerges from this complex of questions and conditional clauses; it asserts itself very plainly and boldly:

10a ʼanî ḥômâ   I am a wall
10b wešāday kammigdālôt   And my breasts are like towers.

We find here an echo of the beginning of v.8: "We have a little sister and she has no breasts." Both combine two Noun Phrases. But here the negatives have turned positive, and the subject speaks. In time, and as a consequence (ʼaz), she transfers herself to the other:

10c ʼaz hāyîtî beʻênāyw   Therefore I was in his eyes
10d kemōṣeʼēt šālôm   As one who found peace.

These are both Noun Phrases and Verb Phrases, and strongly affirmative. In 10c the verb "hāyîtî" ("<u>I was</u>") is both action and copula; in 10d, "kemōṣeʼēt", as <u>participle</u>, is both verb and noun. Moreover, both protagonists are the subjects, or rather

Chapter Three - Beauty and the Enigma

they are the shared subject: "I was ... in his eyes", as they are through the various ambiguities, the permutations of giving and receiving, in "kemōṣe'ēt šālôm". Finally, 10b and 10d are linked through their similes, underlined by alliteration: "KaMMigdālōt ... KeMōṣe'ēt šālôm": like towers that give and receive peace.

The movement from negation to affirmation, from absence of self - fullness of self, coupled with the cyclic recurrence of 8ab in 10ab, and the integration of syntactic components in 10cd, corresponds, as we have seen, to the thematic patterning of the passage. In 1.5-6 we found a syntactic current from loss of self - fullness of self runs counter to the surface movement from fullness of self - loss of self. As in other respects, 8.8-10 is in opposition to 1.5-6; syntax and content are in concord, as the girl with the city.

	Subject	Attributes	Verb	Address	Mode
8	Little Sister	no breasts	no action	no speech	Passive, Object
9a	Wall		build		Active, Object
9b	Door		enclose		Active, Object
10	I	+wall +breasts		speech	Active+Passive Verb+Noun

Fourth Episode: 1.7-8

הַגִּידָה לִּי שֶׁאָהֲבָה נַפְשִׁי אֵיכָה תִרְעֶה אֵיכָה תַּרְבִּיץ
בַּצָּהֳרָיִם שַׁלָּמָה אֶהְיֶה כְּעֹטְיָה עַל עֶדְרֵי חֲבֵרֶיךָ: אִם־לֹא
תֵדְעִי לָךְ הַיָּפָה בַּנָּשִׁים צְאִי־לָךְ בְּעִקְבֵי הַצֹּאן וּרְעִי אֶת־
גְּדִיֹּתַיִךְ עַל מִשְׁכְּנוֹת הָרֹעִים:

(1.7) "Tell me, you whom my soul loves, where do you graze, where do you rest your sheep at noon, for why should I be like a wanderer by the flocks of your friends?"

(8) "If you know not, fairest among women, go forth in the sheep tracks, and pasture your kids by the shepherds' huts."

1.7-8 corresponds to 1.5-6 as 8.8-10 does to 8.11-12, both syntagmatically and through its recombination of materials. Like them, its meaning is extremely elusive; yet in it we return to our starting-point, to the place of beauty in the world, the heat of the sun, and the motif of shame.

Rhetorically, however, it is a development on 8.8-10, in that an overt question meets a paradoxical answer. Whereas in 8.8-10 the question "What will she be?" is unanswerable, here the reply makes the enigma more perplexing.

In her Lover's presence, the Beloved is preoccupied with his absence. She tries to fix the next rendezvous, which is the result of separation: the two lovers have different paths in the world. A whole morning has to be endured. Furthermore, even in the present she lacks assurance that he is really there, that he is really listening. Almost all of the first half of her sentence is taken up with conative expressions, whose principal function is to elicit attention /36/. This indeed is the sole function of "haggîdâ lî" "Tell me" followed by the vocative, "you whom my soul loves"; the epithet combines flattery with an inkling of the urgency of the message and the responsibility of the recipient to listen kindly. The alliterative doubling of "'êkâ tirʿeh ʾêkâ tarbîṣ baṣṣāhorāyîm" "Where do you graze, where do you rest your sheep at noon?" intensifies the question; the repetition implies anxiety that the question would not be heard the first time, not taken seriously. Another fear is that the Lover is reluctant to answer and hence needs pressing, a suggestion prompted by the second hemistich. For there the Beloved complains of her neglect, and demands to know the reason for her still hypothetical ill-treatment. In this way the indirect accusation of indifference is combined with one of undeserved callousness, so as perhaps to ensure a comforting answer, such as righteous protestation.

The lover's reply /37/ begins with a strange conditional: "If you know not, fairest among women ..." If she knew, she would have no need of asking. To all appearances, the clause is redundant. Perhaps he insinuates that she should know, and therefore her winning artful question is merely conversational; he proceeds to match her, both in the symmetrical artifice of his utterance, and in its euphuistic ambiguity. For by the end of the verse we still do not know whether he has revealed his whereabouts. "Go forth in the sheep tracks", for instance, sounds like the advice of a good detective, but we have no means of telling whether it is his sheep she should follow, nor whether she was adept at distinguishing his sheep tracks from those of any other. But the crucial ambiguity is "by the shepherds' huts". Is this phrase synonymous with "by the flocks of your friends"? If so, will he be there, among his friends? The combination of these alternatives produces the following possibilities:

Chapter Three - Beauty and the Enigma

A. If "by the huts" is not "by the flocks" and the shepherds graze far afield, then it seems likely that he is arranging an intimate colloquy.
B. If "by the huts" <u>is</u> "by the flocks":
    a) He is with them, a shepherd among shepherds, and invites the Beloved to join their amicable company.
or b) He is not there, and leaves "the fairest among women" to be a <u>wanderer</u> ('ōteyâ), as she feared in the first verse.

The guessing-game - Does she know? Does he tell? - leaves the question of their meeting again open, indeed for the rest of the poem. The alternatives comprise two realities: the uncertain divisive future and the assurance of love. She may know where he will be, simply because he always has his lunch on the same spot, and their meetings are recurrent; or it may be intuitive knowledge, as Albert Cook (117-118) suggests, citing the emphatic "ethic dative" "lāk" (lit. "if you do not know <u>for yourself</u>"). This is compatible with ignorance; for intuition is a connectedness between parties, whatever their physical separation. In a sense, it is a statement of simultaneous presence and absence. The dialogue, however, reveals their lurking absence, even when physically present. The ambiguities preserve a necessary distance, enabling them to be in touch without finally meeting. In this way absence even when present is in apposition with presence when absent, and the moment of contact is diffused through subsequent adventures, through memory, through intuition. Absence when present and presence when absent mediate between conjunction and disjunction.

This process takes the lovers into society, where they meet or are separated, an enigma communicated, as we have seen, through the alternative meanings of "by the shepherds' huts". Joviality (Ba) is a middle term between separation by society (Bb) and intimacy within society (A). The Conjunction (A) implies an opposition between <u>shepherds' huts</u> and <u>friends' flocks</u> (i.e. lovers/society) which are in fact paired, since the shepherds return to their huts each night. The lovers are alone, at the site of sleep, the pastoral centre at the point of departure for the shepherds' wanderings, and hence for the question "Where will you be?" This corresponds to the possibility of meeting, intuitively, while apart, of simultaneous presence and absence. The lovers are at the centre of a society that is apparently unaware of them.

The mediant possibility, that they meet in company, requires a dissimulation, wherewith their love is acknowledged, but constrained; possibly recognised and welcomed by society, but not too openly. This coexistence corresponds to the absence when present of the dialogue, to conversation- al allusiveness.

The third possibility (Bb) requires more examination, especially of the Beloved's complaint "For why should I be like an "'ōṭeyâ" by the flocks of your friends?" /38/. The word "'ōṭeyâ" is obscure, and has been variously interpreted: as a "wanderer", a "prostitute", a women "veiled" in mourning or with darkened sight, or even "one picking lice" /39/. Beauty is grief-stricken, astray, for sale, disconsolate or bored, because of her Lover's absence. Here society is the scene of repression, where lascivious women attract shame, as in 1.5-6, and are sexually exploited. The Beloved's complaint is voiced as a question: "Why should I be like a wanderer ...?" She is on the fringe of masculine society, to which the Lover belongs, as a "friend". If he dismisses her, he makes her into a victim of the mockery to which spurned sexual partners are subject. He becomes a collaborator with his "friends", since it is his refusal to tell that is the occasion for her desperate search and exposes her to abuse. On the one hand, he is an adoring lover; on the other, a member of the fraternity that despises women. Her knowledge is of the love that survives despite conformity; and her grief is that this love is not found among "friends", that it is separate.

The three possibilities are variants of the same opposition that we found in 8.11-12: the ways of the world and the values of the Song. In the eyes of the Song and the Lover she is 'the fairest among women', the head of the female hierarchy, unique and splendid in 6.9; but as a 'friend', he turns her into an "'ōṭeyâ", a vagabond, prostitute, etc., dispossessed and hence valueless. The three stories can be collated accordingly:

A: The values of love at the unconscious heart of society.
Ba: Love becomes socialised ... Love ➤ way of the world.
Bb: Love rejected by society ... Way of the world ➤◄ values of the Song.
[➤◄ = opposed to; ➤ = congruent with]

There is in truth no answer to the Beloved's protest, and I would agree with Phyllis Trible (1973: 43-48) in seeing this as an essential part of the subversive message of the Song. In this episode, however, the transformation becomes a means of integrating the Beloved into society, of reconciling received attitudes with anarchic desire. If, in 8.11-12,

Chapter Three - Beauty and the Enigma

intoxication turns into silver, and in 8.8-10, beauty becomes art, here the Beloved is a shepherdess. She is an economic asset, contributing to the wealth of the community, and in this way parallel to the keeper of vineyards in 1.6. But the terms are now inverted. To begin with, the Beloved cares for her own kids, which are a sign of her status, not those of others. Whereas she is made into a keeper of vineyards through disapprobation, she now becomes a shepherdess among shepherds, a comrade of those whose ill-treatment she feared. If the shepherds are paradigmatically related to the brothers, as male collectivities who torment the Beloved, she now returns to the family, one might say to the fold. The sexes are equal in their employment, in their social roles, whereas in 1.6 the Beloved was driven out because she was forward i.e. acted sexually as a male.

It is because she "knows" the value of the Lover, that the Beloved searches for him and risks humiliation, assuming the guises of the "'ōteyâ"; her confusion, "not knowing", is a function of true knowledge. The shepherdess follows the same path, but has a place in society, where she might find the Lover. The lovers are parted by the day and its tasks, society and time, and it is there that the Beloved envisages their meeting, at noon, while grazing. The heat of the sun reverses its emotive value: that which darkens the complexion is now the ally of love. Its fierceness causes them to seek shelter, and is conducive to drowsiness and amorous suggestion, while the flocks graze together, an image of their langorous discourse. If the day is associated with conscious differentiation, and sunlight with the objectivity of vision, the centre of the day and the excess of sunlight bring about a reversion to unfocussed half-consciousness, parallel to the relationship (A) between the friends' flocks and the shepherds' huts, which the lovers visit at noon when the occupants are away, but which are the centre of their activities. The siesta in the middle of the day is parallel to intimacy at the heart of society.

Diurnal love thus corresponds to a flooding of consciousness, and reproduces the transformation between solar darkness and brilliance, which we discerned in 6.8-10.

However, the fundamental difference between the two occupations, the keeper of vineyards and the shepherdess, is that between them intoxication becomes continuance. The dark Beloved tends the fruit of Dionysus, which we connected with her sexual hoard, while the shepherdess takes care of the sources of wool, milk and meat, society's clothing and nourishment. Animal lascivious energy /40/ is tamed and put to use, while in the vineyards and vats society turns natural sweetness into Dionysiac subversion.

Whereas in 1.5 the Beloved's is a tale of exploitation in a stratified community, and exemplifies the interaction of city and country through conformity and violence, the commonwealth of shepherds is egalitarian, and associated in the Pastoral with sweet amours, tolerance, and sympathy with nature (Kermode 1972: 16). The earth gives freely, as in the Golden Age; the shepherds are its untroubled and paternalistic masters. In contrast, the agriculturalist toils for its harvest; he is the base of civilisation, while the shepherd stands somewhat outside it.

It would be inappropriate to dwell on the image of the shepherd in the Pastoral, since apart from this passage it hardly occurs in the Song of Songs /41/. The shepherd is characterised by an intimacy with wildness. His flocks graze on the hills; he is sustained by and knowledgeable of the rough terrain. He is an image of harmony, of nature beneficent to man, and man at ease with and respectful of nature. He is a master of tranquillity and of song, of a natural simple order. It is for this reason that the work is so enviable, as an agent of integration, as well as because of its lazy recurrence, that promotes a sense of timelessness.

The Beloved as "'ōteyâ" disturbs this serenity, as well as our idealisation of pastoral virtue. She is only like an "'ōteyâ", however; in reality, she is a shepherdess, and the most beautiful of women. The three terms, "'ōteyâ", shepherdess, and fairest of women, form a continuum, uniting extremes of beauty and ugliness, envy and contempt, which in 1.5-6 are represented by the Dark Beloved. The "'ōteyâ" is wildness in action, the Dionysiac spirit that haunts the fringes of the Pastoral. "The fairest among women" is reminiscent of 6.8-10, and the splendour of the court; the phrase is associated with the daughters of Jerusalem, who employ it in 5.9 and 6.1. Through her beauty she represents the city (Jerusalem and Tirzah in 6.4), man's achievement when liberated from subsistence. Thus they stand for wildness and civilisation respectively, Dionysus and Apollo, licentious subversion and sophistication; in other words, all the tensions underlying the Pastoral. Yet the Beloved is also a shepherdess - a middle term, like the daughters of Jerusalem - whose kids are in complementary antithesis with the Lover's sheep. Between the contrary pressures of the striving for civilised perfection and the craving for a return to original innocence

Chapter Three - Beauty and the Enigma

is a simple conservatism, motivated by neither ambition nor regression.

The Lover's compliment "hayyāpâ bannāšîm" "fairest among women" contrasts with "šeʲāhabâ napšî" "whom my soul loves", with which the Beloved addresses him. "Fairest among women" is a gesture of objective appreciation, that perceives her relative to others, no matter with what superiority. It contributes to the enigmatic quality of the Lover's speech, that sets her at a distance, both desirable and detached. "Whom my soul loves" defines their relationship, without regard to others; whereas beauty refers to appearance, "whom" implies that she loves him for himself, with her "soul", not her looks. She speaks objectively of her "nepeš", as if love were something that happened through her, that forces her to become an "ʷōṭeyâ", a victim of shame. Unconscious Dionysiac possession thus meets objective, if flattering, appraisal, to produce the quandaries of knowing and not knowing, simultaneous presence and absence, that pervade the dialogue.

If the dialogue measures the distance between the lovers, revealing fear, rage and evasiveness in its sweet phrases, the lovers hear each other's voices. If they are present, and not absent to each other - concerned about the future - this is the sole content of the dialogue: the voice that speaks it. It is surprising how much of lovers' talk consists precisely of this: voice, that speaks beyond the differentiations of language /42/. The superfluity of language in the lovers' discourse - "Tell me", "If you know not", with its redundant "lāk" etc. - has, on the one hand, a conative function, that activates attention; less obtrusively, it transfers it from the thoroughly obscure message to the sound, from tenor to vehicle. The seductiveness of the voice is aided by the mellifluousness of the language; communication becomes play. In the Beloved's speech, we have, for instance, the alliterative parallelism already cited: "ʲêkâ tirʲeh ʲêkâ tarbîṣ baṣṣāhorāyîm" (ʲêkâ tr ʲêkâ trbṣ bṣr); in the Lover's reply there is the rhyme of "ʷim lōʲ TEDeʕI LAK ... Ṣeʲl LAK beʲiqebê haṣṣōʲn U-Reʕl" ... "If <u>you know</u> not ... <u>go forth</u> in the sheep tracks, and <u>graze</u> ..."

The repartee has in fact the character of a duet, with its symmetrical construction and counterpoint of meanings. As in a duet, the voices intertwine, merge and separate. Moreover, the voices couple with that of the poet, to fashion the poem.

In the Classical Pastoral, the shepherd is a metaphor for the poet, whose songs he sings. It is a return to an archaic language, in which sound, meaning, and sensory experience are only just differentiating, a return to a pasture where the poet writes in time to the eternal recurrence of the words, in a tranquil intoxication, uniting the twin poles of the Dionysiac encounter. Poetry is a listening, to the earth, to things, controlled and critical. William Berg introduces his illuminating discussion of the Pastoral with the following quotation:

> Often I am permitted to return to a meadow ...
> an eternal pasture folded in all thought. /43/

Postscript: 1.9, 1.15-16

Beauty in the Song is communicated principally by metaphor, a complex system of alliance between the inexpressible self and the definable universe. The work of comparison obscures the reality of the person by clothing her in images. In this way, it contributes to the aesthetic process, that distances the object of desire. The images are intricate compounds of objective sensory and emotional correlations and deeply disturbing symbolism. We find a good example in the verse immediately following the passage we have just discussed:

לְסֻסָתִי בְּרִכְבֵי פַרְעֹה דִּמִּיתִיךְ רַעְיָתִי:

(1.9) To a mare in Pharaoh's chariots I have compared you, my love. /44/

A horse in fine fettle is an exhilaratingly beautiful animal /45/, especially when richly caparisoned, in other words, when it is metonymically identified with its owner, and shares in his value. A good example is the aesthetic function of the horse in the equestrian statue. The horse and its rider form a unit, especially in warfare, in the heroic code of chivalry. The horse combines the two tendencies that have been the subject for our discussion: it extends the man's vitality through its courage, strength and endurance; through his control, he demonstrates his mastery of heroic energy. Moreover, the cult of heroism, for instance, heroic poetry, is itself a defence, an aestheticisation of terror, since it glorifies violence. This military connotation is confirmed by the setting in our verse, where the mare is harnessed in Pharaoh's chariots.

As Marvin Pope (1976: 338) remarks, mares are likely to cause disarray in battle, and in general steeds were stallions. The sex of the horse in our verse may primarily have been

Chapter Three - Beauty and the Enigma

suggested by the sex of the Beloved, to whom the verse is addressed /46/. The choice of a military image, and of a noble vigorous creature to describe the Beloved, however, induces a transfer of phallic energy, that in a woman is doubly threatening. A woman who is as powerful as a man endangers his supremacy; Pope gives many examples of this archetypal emasculating figure /47/. An anomaly is a marked term, intensifying - through contrast - the attributes of its contradictory components. The mare in battle is terrifying, partially because it is so attractive /48/.

The point, however, is that this energy contributes to royal display; in the poem it is diverted into the game of comparison. The mare is submissive; as an image for the Beloved, it hints at her proper subservience, as a member of the king's entourage /49/, an adornment to his court, on whom he hangs his tropes and jewellery, the gold and silver pendants and chains of 1.10-11. Like the little sister in 8.8-10, she is beautified, and thereby concealed behind silver. "How beautiful are your cheeks in pendants" (1.10a). What is concealed is the freedom and wild delight of the mare, and the overwhelming attraction of nakedness.

If the last syllable of "lesusātî" be a first person possessive suffix, then it increases the emphasis on her status as possession, which is allied to the king's self-satisfaction in these lines, and his wish to manipulate her according to his fancy.

With the last words, suddenly a sense of reality returns: "I have compared you, my love". The past (or perfect) tense reveals the inadequacy of all comparison, that is superceded by the truth. What is this truth? That she is "ra'yātî", my friend and equal. The epithets "ra'yâ" and "dôd" reduce all the personae to a simple human equation. The terms are both tautologous and separate, and in them aesthetic distance turns to human recognition:

הִנָּךְ יָפָה רַעְיָתִי הִנָּךְ יָפָה עֵינַיִךְ יוֹנִים:

הִנְּךָ יָפֶה דוֹדִי אַף נָעִים אַף־עַרְשֵׂנוּ רַעֲנָנָה:

(1.15) Behold, you are beautiful, my love, behold you are beautiful; your eyes like doves.
(16) Behold you are beautiful, my love, yes, lovely; also our bed is green.

The Beloved looks from her loved one to the bed where they will be united, in touch with and cradled by the verdant flourishing of nature. The natural and human levels are metaphorically identified, and also logically, as an image of the womb from which new life develops. The Lover looks at his loved one's eyes, a mode of communication that precedes language, and combines objectivity with an interchange of identity. Their voices, moreover, merge into an inarticulate expression of wonder. Beauty here is just set at a distance with the exclamation "hinnāk" - "There you are!" - and brought into relation through the twin terms "ra'yâ" and "dôd". They turn away from this marvellous gaze to the whole green world between them, in which they unite. Out of this develops the language of the poem, whose virtuosity, through enigma, ambiguity, and metaphor, returns us always to that first astonishment. The whole poem may be seen as a giant tautology, repeating constantly "hinnāk yāpâ ra'yātî, hinnekâ yāpēh dôdî", "Behold you are beautiful, my love", "Behold you are beautiful, my love", and the act of which no words can be spoken. And out of this comes the creative flame that gives life to the spheres, natural, human, linguistic, and divine.

Conclusion

The beauty of the world of the Song is the metaphorical equivalent of the love of the lovers. Yet it comes from outside that world, and threatens to subvert it. Beauty is a stranger, a gift, taking us by surprise, wonderful and terrible; our civilisation devotes itself to being hospitable to that gift, and controlling it. The transformation of beauty and its resistance to change has been the subject of this chapter; in various forms it is the basis of society, agricultural, pastoral, urban, commercial. Thus it participates in and is the object of the creative process. Love shows itself in beauty, that binds us to all things, in their autonomy. Aesthetic experience is thus mystical experience; the message of the Song could be expressed as "God is love, perceived in the beauty of the world." It comes from the periphery to the centre, from the desert to the shrine and royal bed; from lifelessness to where life is renewed. The stranger of 1.5 is the city of 8.8-10 and the vineyard of 8.11-12, from which the king is ambiguously excluded. It is then man who is in exile from beauty; it is beauty where he is most at home.

In the next chapter I shall be looking at the story of the garden of Eden, as the point where this exile began. In the garden, Dionysiac beauty, and the enigma that goes with it, is incarnated in the serpent, the avatar of rational thought. As we have seen, beauty is a secondary articulation that exerts formal control over libidinal energy; the garden is the scene

Chapter Three - Beauty and the Enigma

of its precipitating trauma. The two forms of beauty, the beauty of intoxication and order, interact; there is a dialogue between the daughters of Jerusalem and the Beloved, and also a transformation, e.g. from change to changelessness, darkness to whiteness, grapes to silver. Apollo has his chthonic voice, Dionysus his calm. Civilisation is founded on this transformation. Yet there is also a point of meeting between them, a relaxation of the ego; this is the Pastoral. The lovers look in each others' eyes and say "hinnāk yāpâ ... hinnekâ yāpēh" "Behold, you are beautiful ... behold, you are beautiful". The doves to which the eyes are compared fly to and fro. They are united in their love, and just apart; there is no desire, no tension between them. At this point beauty is not enigmatic, for there are no questions, merely the unquestionable "hinnāk ... hinnekâ".

CHAPTER FOUR

TWO VERSIONS OF PARADISE

Chapter Four

TWO VERSIONS OF PARADISE

גן עדן מה הוא אומר: עורי צפון ובואי תימן הפיחי
גני יזלו בשמיו יבא דודי לגנו ויאכל פרי מגדיו:

The Garden of Eden: What does it sing? "Awake, O north wind, and come, O south, breathe upon my garden, let its spices flow forth, let my love come into his garden and eat his precious fruits" (Song of Songs 4.16).(Pereq Shirah)

Introduction

THE theme is very simple: the primordial couple in Eden lose their Paradise for the same reasons that the couple in the Song regain it. I will argue that the detailed correspondence of thematic material is so extensive that the Song constitutes an inversion of the Genesis narrative. It manifests itself also on the plane of expression, in metaphor, especially the symbols of garden and tree. Both texts find their complement in the other, and, moreover, imply the other. The Genesis myth points outside the garden; the Song goes back to it. Their opposition conceals a hidden identity, for the Song is not merely a commentary on the garden of Eden, but a reenactment, almost a hallucination of it.

We must beware of the Intentional Fallacy. There is little evidence that the relationship I am about to suggest played any conscious part in the poetic composition, though one may suppose a very deep familiarity with the myth from the cultural background. What the comparison does is to help us understand both texts from a different perspective. It is not an exclusive relationship, nor, in the Structuralist sense, closed. Many aspects of both texts are not duplicated in the other; for example, the serpent does not figure in the Song. There is the irreducible difference of genre. Likewise, the Song may profitably be compared with many books, both within the canon and outside it. What makes the comparison with Eden especially meaningful, however, apart from its very detail, is that the search for Paradise is the ultimate quest. Our vicarious pleasure on reading the Song becomes part of a much greater wish-fulfilment; and like all wish-fulfilment, it is ambivalent. This chapter is then a reformulation on a mythical plane of the tensions we have discussed previously, between desire and distance, separateness and fusion. In the Song Paradise is tangible, all-pervasive, yet we are excluded from it, just as we are from the experience of the lovers. The duality is bridged - more accurately, transcended - by the imagination, wherewith we can project ourselves into the other, while remaining ourselves - a somewhat ponderous paraphrase of Bernard Harrison's brilliant "necessary duality of self-transcendence" (1981: 208).

This chapter is not quite undiscovered country, since the reference to Eden has often been made, in passing or at length, by other critics, e.g. Lys: "Le Cantique est rien d'autre qu'un commentaire de Gen. 2" (52); or Cook (120-1). What is new is the detail of the comparison and its structural formulation. Some approaches are typological, as, for example, Krinetzki in his earlier commentary (1964) and more recently Northrop Frye (1982: 107). For Barth, the two texts comprise "a Magna Carta of humanity" (1960: 291, 293), a vision, unique in the Old Testament, of innocent eros, in which the covenant between the sexes, unbroken by adultery or shame, transparently expresses that of God and Israel. The reference of both texts is thus eschatological, to a redeemed and consummated humanity.

> According to the Song of Songs, the Old Testament knows finally a proper meaning and seriousness of the sexual relation as such. That is why it ventures, in the voice of the prophet, to describe the connexion between YHWH and Israel in terms of the relationship between man and wife. (Barth 1958: 319)

From an explicitly but unobtrusively feminist standpoint, Phyllis Trible (1973, 1978) has also matched the two texts, using the techniques of rhetorical criticism; to date, hers is by far the fullest and most penetrating survey. According to her, "The Song of Songs redeems a love story gone awry" (1978: 144); she uses Gen 2-3 as "a hermeneutical key" to unlock its secrets. Correspondences are found on the planes of flora and fauna, sexual and familial imagery; some of these will be found in the succeeding pages. The discussion of animal imagery in the Song as an inversion of that of Eden is

Chapter Four - Two Versions of Paradise

especially akin to my observations. In general, however, her analysis of Gen 2-3 is far more thorough and percipient than that of the Song, which lacks all sense of ambivalence; quotation and breathless enthusiasm compensate for insight. The levels of comparison are also somewhat mechanical. We differ also, not only in details of interpretation of Gen 2-3, but in my greater concern for the connotations of words and symbols, in contrast to their lexical (rhetorical) structure.

A fascinating study of Gen 2-3 from a structuralist perspective, edited by Daniel Patte, has recently been published in the journal Semeia, too late to be fully integrated into the creative work of this chapter /1/. The contributors discuss different aspects of the text in the belief that its meaning results from the convergence or otherwise of different textual systems and interpretative strategies; one may note in passing a distinct dependence on Greimas' actantial scheme. The text has no unitary meaning, according to Patte, in his introductory essay - this being the illusion of conventional literary-critics - merely transitory meaning-effects, that can be no more explicated than the glitter of a jewel (4, 20); structuralism, accordingly, restores to the text its mystery. One wonders whether literary-critics are as convinced of its transparency as he supposes. The essays are divided into analyses of the intrinsic organisation of the text - narrative, symbolic, semantic - and its participation in a communication process, e.g. its deictic markers (Hugh C. White) and its techniques for eliciting the sympathy of the audience, in an essay by a rhetorical critic, Thomas Boomershine, that promises an interesting dialogue between the two approaches. The longest, most formidable, but also most penetrating analysis is that of Patte and Parker, who attempt, through the rigorous application of semiotic squares, to establish the semantic horizon of the text, the deep, largely unconscious values that permeate the text and focus it. Other illuminating contributions are those of David Jobling, who examines its myth-semantics, borrowing oppositions and isotopies familiar from Levi-Strauss, and Hugh White, on deictics, whose emergence, he contends, are indicative of alienation. His work has affinities with that of Scriabine, of which he seems unaware. The volume is impressive for its creative excitement, its focus on ultimate concerns, its numerous insights, both textual and methodological; its faults are an insistence on scientific technique to the detriment of the imagination, and a tendency (since meaning is an aesthetic, relational effect, a mystery beyond interpretation) to ignore it in the fun of their expertise. In practice, however, even the most rigorous exponents, such as Patte/Parker, are far more subjective, free, and consequently rich in their insights than appears at first sight, and also closer to the traditional literary critic in the coherence they find in the text, resulting from the steady relation of systems and parts.

Two other structuralist analyses are by anthropologists, Morris Freilech and Edmund Leach (1969). Freilich, in a discussion to which I shall refer extensively, criticises Levi-Strauss' view that myth is a vehicle for the suppression of time /2/, and contends that it is typically an explanation of the conversion of what he calls the Smart into the Proper, in other words of the intelligent but timeless techniques for manipulating reality into the irrational cultural conventions wherewith a community maintains its sanity and enters history. His analysis however loses touch with his thesis and is moreover highly selective. Leach, in a discussion celebrated out of proportion to its size, proposed that Gen 2-3 participates in a structural set with the other primeval stories to mediate complementary oppositions, in this case incest and sexual origins, life and death. His observations are too brief to be more than suggestive; first published in 1962, they are primarily of historical interest.

Boomershine's article in Semeia, in which he discusses the narrator's adoption of inside and outside views to manipulate audience response, may be compared with a rhetorical-critical essay by Alan J. Hauser, in the recent volume Art and Meaning which examines devices for intimating emotional distance between the characters in the narrative; intimacy in ch. 2 is succeeded by alienation in ch. 3. His theme and many of his perceptions coincide with those of White, in the same Semeia volume. A more successful rhetorical-critical analysis is that of Phyllis Trible, in whose view a symmetrical inversion of life and death, integration and discord, surrounds the central trauma. The subordinate created worlds of ch. 2 - human, plant, animal - rebel against God, who is absent from the central scene; a restoration of divine authority leads to their mutual estrangement. A cyclical pattern is perceived also by Walsh and A. J. Williams (1973: 359ff.); for the latter the structure is focussed on the central figure of the serpent, the subject of his thesis. Its function is to provide a man to till the earth, outside the garden. Walsh's is a superb literary study; he examines the myth as an inversion of the motif of the quest for the centre.

There have been some good recent literary-critical

Chapter Four - Two Versions of Paradise

analyses: two brief essays by Kenneth Gros-Louis, in the volume Literary Interpretations of Biblical Narratives (1974), comparing the conceptions of God in Gen 1 and 2, and the fraught dynamics of the Garden of Eden; and a perceptive account by Michael Fishbane (17-23), followed by a fascinating survey of the transformation of the motif in the prophetic writings, a study that has points of contact with Northrop Frye's recent book, The Great Code (1982). The best, though incidental, discussion is by Robert Alter in his comprehensive examination of Biblical narrative technique (The Art of Biblical Narrative [1981]), who demonstrates the conscious artistry with which Gen 2.18-25 has been composed from traditional materials (27-32), and how the syntactic difference between Gen 2.1-4a and Gen 2.4b-7, which he analyses beautifully, exemplifies the different outlook of their respective authors (141-147). It is curious to note that Trible (1978: 75) dismisses 2.4b-7 as merely tedious.

Two other studies should be noted. The first, by Alonso Schökel, details very precisely the convergence of sapiential and covenantal motifs in Gen 2-3; he proposes that using mythic elements the narrator meditates therein on the origins of universal evil and the nature of wisdom in a story that is an archetype of sacred history, following the pattern of covenant, disobedience, punishment and reconciliation (cf. Boomershine: 117). Paul Ricoeur in The Symbolism of Evil seeks to compare Gen 2-3 with the tragic vision, Orphic myth, and sacred kingship; he argues that it is essentially anthropological, concentrating on man in this and every instant of time, and the ambiguous coexistence of sin and innocence within him, original goodness and radical evil. Its existential pertinence is reminiscent of, and contrasts with, the essays of Joseph Soloveitchik, for whom Gen 1 and 2 represent majestic, unconditioned man and solitary man respectively.

Many other approaches will be referred to in the coming pages; a comprehensive bibliography is to be found in Westermann's commentary. Several authors attempt to integrate Gen 2-3 with the rest of the primeval history; the work of David Clines and Patrick Miller is especially notable. Some scholars associate the myth with an anti-sapiential tradition (e.g. Mendenhall, Barker) and postulate a late date (for a contrary view see Daube); others interpret it in terms of power (Coats) and ecology (Duncan).

If Genesis 2-3 is an aetiological myth, concerned with the beginnings of culture, it is peculiarly comprehensive, as if the narrator (J) wanted to relate all the conditions of our life to a single traumatic event /3/. There are other aetiological clusters in Genesis, each arising from a traumatic fixation, but none have the same inclusiveness or cultural importance as Gen 2-3. In contrast, and with perhaps literary economy, Gen 1 is remarkably chaste in its aetiological formulations: it establishes time and the Sabbath. The relationship between Gen 1 and Gen 2-3 is uncertain /4/; especially since the dating of both has recently been called into question /5/.

It is my view that Gen 2-3 presents a fundamental ambivalence, not only somewhat conventionally towards culture, but also towards man and within God, and implicating the whole of creation. Gen 1 is an ordered progression, a closed structure that is virtually a separate book; Gen 2-3 introduces a radical doubt, and a story that never ends. Gen 1, like a continuo, assures us throughout the Bible with its constant rhythm; Gen 2-3 is a set of misadventures and inspirations (Fishbane: 15). It is both a Fall and a Rise (Daube: 60-61): a fall from bliss but a discovery of man's quest for knowledge and immortality that will lead, among other things, to the Song of Songs. It is not true that "the Yahwist" had a negative attitude towards culture /6/; what emerges from his conception is that it is inherently compromised. To give one tiny example: the invention of music and metalwork in Gen 4 is not less beautiful or seductive because it is associated with murder (cf. Fishbane: 27); as in the Song, beauty is ambivalent. Wisdom is both good and bad, godly and subversive. Furthermore, as Ricoeur points out (237), Christian exegetes in particular concentrate excessively on the nature of Adam's sin, on the "moral" of the tale. The word "sin", with its many synonyms, does not occur in the text, a choice not without stylistic significance. The act is apparently innocuous, and human beings, on whose astonishing innocence the narrator concentrates his ironic and compassionate gaze, cannot fail to be taken in. The crime, with Eve's thoughts and the serpent's prompting, is the innermost of concentric circles. Radiating from it, along paradigmatic axes, are questions, growing more profound the wider the circle. Why did God tempt man? Why did he create the tree and the serpent? Why did he create man imperfect and solitary, and why did he make redundant animals? What is the nature of the ambivalent knowledge he seeks to hide from man? These questions are posited by the text. For example, the serpent is not only specifically God's creature (3.1); he is his messenger who communicates temptation, the spokesman for the tree

Chapter Four - Two Versions of Paradise

that enshrines God's secret power. The serpent symbolises a side of God (the tempter; good-and-evil) he refuses to recognise: serpent-tree-God comprise one paradigm; woman, man and God another. Looking further than this, beyond the outermost circle, there is another question: Why did God create the universe? Why did he create man? His statement "It is not good for man to be alone" (2.18) ignores the one relationship that has mattered to man up to this point, that with God himself; it may also be an indicator of God's own need, his own loneliness, out of which he created the universe. Man is then in God's likeness, his companion, "ᵉēzer kenegdô", in his dissatisfaction, in the complexity of a relationship that is never fulfilled: as in the Song of Songs.

In the succeeding pages I will proceed from shared metaphors - the garden and tree - to puns: and thence to the difficult and tentative comparison of characters and themes, in particular the theme of unity in multiplicity /7/.

Metaphor: The Garden

I will begin with the first part of the story of the garden of Eden (Gen 2.4-15), that in which the man is created and the garden planted. It is essentially a descriptive context from which the drama develops. From a consideration of the archetypal meaning of the garden, cultural, infantile and artistic, I will proceed to the form it takes, both in the garden of Eden and the Song of Songs. The comparison of the characteristics of both gardens will be succeeded by an excursus pursuant to one in the text on the rivers of Paradise. I will then focus on the place of man in the two gardens, and their human meaning. This discussion will be complicated by the relationship between the principal episodes in the Song, that have very different structures. Finally, I will apply my findings to other images in the Song, and thus work out the paradigm of the Garden.

The garden is essentially private, protected against the elements, against weeds and wildness. It is nature perfected by culture, enclosed also from the fields, where man cultivates for subsistence. It is an index of riches, of liberation from necessity. This is especially true of the magnificence and complexity of the garden in the Song, that associates it with the royal paradigm. However, in it culture returns to nature; it is a place of retreat and relaxation. The Lover goes there to see the spring.

The garden is man's first organisation of the world, demarcating good and bad, his own and the other. He begins to cultivate nature to please his senses, to arrange it according to his taste. It is the prototype of civilisation, of man's first small attempts at agriculture, of the delight in creation that distinguishes gardening from hunting and gathering.

The garden is a contained world, intimate and limited, that man can control. Its scale makes it accessible and secure, a combination of earth and home, the first colony in childhood, which the child explores safely.

The garden is cultivated aesthetically, in other words symbolically. One goes into the garden to see the spring, or the grass, or to lose oneself like a green thought in a green shade, and its action is as sympathetic metaphor. Gardening is a formal art, flowers are emblematic. It is this that gives it its value in poetry, and that we shall explore in the coming pages.

The garden is thus a metaphor for poetry, as an enclosed space within language that tries to encompass the world, as a civilised achievement that returns to nature for inspiration (Berg: 5). The movement is in fact identical to that of the Pastoral.

The Garden of Eden is both secluded and universal, primordial and inaccessible: "wayyiṭṭaʽ yhwh ʼelōhîm gan beʽēden miqqedem" "And God planted a garden in Eden eastwards/from of old" (2.8) /8/, a small, humanly manageable world. This limitation by God already makes us feel that the world is a human place, in contrast to Gen 1, where man is God's terrestrial counterpart. Nature begins in a garden, undifferentiated from culture. In origin then it is not yet wild, and its spontaneity is divine; it is an ideal order. In it

Chapter Four - Two Versions of Paradise

God planted ("wayyaṣmaḥ" = "made to grow") "every tree lovely to look on and good to eat" (neḥmād lemarʲeh wetôb lemaʲakāl) (2.9), combining subsistence and delight. An exclusively fruitarian diet is somewhat hard to balance: presumably there was an abundance of nuts in the garden. Fruit, in our world, is associated with sensuous pleasure, not subsistence, with natural sweetness and refreshment. Like all food, fruit is overladen with cultural values and symbolic meanings. Through its function here, proffered by bountiful nature at the beginning, it recalls lactation. It is superfluous food, not substantial but delicious.

The dream-diet combines with an aesthetic function: "every tree lovely to look on". The eyes articulate and interact with the world, finding in it shapes and colours desirable (neḥmād) in themselves, as a second order, contemplative pleasure. The trees acquire beauty through fantasy, the poetic gift of metonymy and metaphor; they become an intellectual object.

The two functions, looking and eating, correspond to the twin poles of the aesthetic process I discussed in the previous chapter: desire and distance, Dionysus and Apollo. Eating fruit tends towards gluttony, Dionysiac indulgence, an excess of pleasure over sober nourishment; the food is absorbed and becomes part of the bloodstream. Sugar is correlated with ecstasy, as a source of concentrated energy, as well as with the taste of infantile food. Sweetness and bliss are metaphorically interrelated, as hardly needs illustrating. Correspondingly, looking preserves the loved object at a distance. Looking at trees and eating their fruit harmoniously combines both poles: absorption and differentiation.

The garden is enclosed, an island of life, planted in an earth where everything is still potential. Outside it is history and death. It is planted "miqqedem" "in the former time", "in illo tempore", from which we are excluded. Or else it is always eastward. Throughout the myth we are aware that outside the garden the earth is barren, that death is present both there and implicitly in the tree, that we are outside the garden. In contrast, the order in Gen 1 is universal: there is nothing outside it.

The garden in the Song of Songs is much more richly elaborated. It, too, is "lovely to look on and good to eat". The obvious difference is that it is part of man's creative achievement in time. In it culture not only returns to nature, but attempts to restore it to its original perfection. If the garden of Eden precedes the differentiation of nature and culture, the garden of the Song represents their convergent cooperation. The garden likewise is cut off from the world: it is "a locked garden" (gan nā'ûl - 4.12), excluding wild nature and social cares. At the same time, the enclosed garden modulates, for instance through refrain, into a vision of the world in springtime: it becomes universal /9/, like the garden of Eden. Thus the enclosed garden and the world correspond: hostile nature almost vanishes, to be evoked and partially neutralised at the fringes of civilisation - for instance, in the tents of Kedar, the lions and leopards of Lebanon.

Above all, death is excluded from the garden, both explicitly, as a place of perpetual life, "living waters" (mayim ḥayyîm), and implicitly, as part of the rhetoric of the Song. For the garden is defended ultimately against its own inevitable destruction.

The garden of the Song is more diverse than the garden of Eden. There is a list of its products in 5.1 - wine, milk, honey, fruit and spices - representing the versatility of man's exploitation of nature. As the garden of culture, the garden of the Song improves nature, making it conform to human wishes. The return of culture to nature combines with a contrary movement, that turns nature into culture. But there are other differences also. As well as pomegranates and precious fruits, the "pardēs" is the repository of exotic spices:

שְׁלָחַיִךְ פַּרְדֵּס רִמּוֹנִים עִם פְּרִי מְגָדִים כְּפָרִים עִם־נְרָדִים:
נֵרְדְּ וְכַרְכֹּם קָנֶה וְקִנָּמוֹן עִם כָּל־עֲצֵי לְבוֹנָה מֹר וַאֲהָלוֹת עִם כָּל־רָאשֵׁי בְשָׂמִים:

(4.13) Your shoots/canals are a paradise /10/ of pomegranates, with precious fruits, cypress and nard.
(14) Nard and saffron, sweetcane and cinnamon, with every incense-bearing tree; myrrh and aloes, with all species of spices.

The list persuades us that there is no spice tree, or perhaps fruit tree that is omitted, that it is a Noah's Ark of the vegetable kingdom. Like the garden of Eden, in it all species are represented, in a confined space. In this sense too, i.e. symbolically, it is universal /11/. But the acquisition and cultivation of these spices is at immense cost and labour, it is a supreme cultural achievement. Moreover, spices are specifically cultural commodities, whose function is to make nature acceptable by disguising it and thereby enhancing it, to make food palatable and women attractive. They are

Chapter Four - Two Versions of Paradise

subtle and invisible catalysts, refining crude (e.g. sexual) smells and tastes. Between the twin poles in the garden of Eden, eating and looking, they interpose the arts of cooking and perfumery.

The Lover goes down to the garden "lirʿôt baggannîm welilqōṭ šôšannîm" "to graze in the gardens and to gather lilies" /12/ (6.2), and in 6.11 "to see whether the vine had blossomed, the pomegranates were in flower". Flowers, like spices, are not found in the account of the garden of Eden. They are indices of time, unlike the trees "lovely to look on", whose beauty is constant. The Lover goes to watch the spring, and to anticipate the harvest. Moreover, gathering lilies is an act of Dionysiac wanton possession, that lays waste the fragile beauty and preserves it in culture, in wreaths and vases. Like spices, then, it has artistic connotations, and mediates between eating and looking. But unlike spices, flowers are not catalysts, nor are they useful: they are intermediaries between nature and culture, between man and woman, incorporated by the self and beheld distinctly as an object.

The garden of the Song is a more complex version of the garden of Eden, reenacted through the substances of illusion. At this point we do not find an inversion of the myth, for both texts have the same metaphorical frame, but the careful trompe d'oeil in the Song is an unstable and tense displacement, and thus necessarily ambivalent.

Moreover, the garden is now only a small part of the world, at the end of many generations, human and cultural. Its relations with the world are complex and ironic, for the world outside is momentarily apparently equivalent to the garden. This point - the paradigm of the garden in the Song - is one I shall return to later. The seemingly superfluous seclusion of the garden reminds us of its isolation in time, as a mnemonic fragment of the beginning, distorted as all memory is, in a differentiated world.

Before turning to the place of man in the garden, to its all-important human meaning, we shall first complete the description of the garden in Gen 2.10-14:

וְנָהָר֙ יֹצֵ֣א מֵעֵ֔דֶן לְהַשְׁק֖וֹת אֶת־הַגָּ֑ן וּמִשָּׁם֙ יִפָּרֵ֔ד וְהָיָ֖ה לְאַרְבָּעָ֥ה רָאשִֽׁים׃ שֵׁ֥ם הָֽאֶחָ֖ד פִּישׁ֑וֹן ה֣וּא הַסֹּבֵ֗ב אֵ֚ת כָּל־אֶ֣רֶץ הַֽחֲוִילָ֔ה אֲשֶׁר־שָׁ֖ם הַזָּהָֽב׃ וּֽזֲהַ֛ב הָאָ֥רֶץ הַהִ֖וא ט֑וֹב שָׁ֥ם הַבְּדֹ֖לַח וְאֶ֥בֶן הַשֹּֽׁהַם׃ וְשֵֽׁם־הַנָּהָ֥ר הַשֵּׁנִ֖י גִּיח֑וֹן ה֣וּא הַסּוֹבֵ֔ב אֵ֖ת כָּל־אֶ֥רֶץ כּֽוּשׁ׃ וְשֵֽׁם־הַנָּהָ֤ר הַשְּׁלִישִׁי֙

חִדֶּקֶל הוּא הַהֹלֵךְ קִדְמַת אַשּׁוּר וְהַנָּהָר הָרְבִיעִי הוּא פְרָת:

(2.10) And a river flows out of Eden, to water the garden; and thence it is parted, and becomes four heads.
(11) The name of the first is Pishon; that is the one that compasses the whole land of Havilah, where there is gold.
(12) And the gold of that land is good; there is bdellium and onyx stone.
(13) And the name of the second river is Gihon; that is the one that compasses the whole land of Cush.
(14) And the name of the third river is Tigris, that flows east of Assyria. And the name of the fourth river is Euphrates.

The passage is a strange intrusion into the narrative; the four rivers play no further part in the story /13/. Even more interesting, they are spoken of in the present: even now they have their origins in Eden. This frustrates the search for the exact location of Eden, quite a pastime among critics /14/. Eden exists still, but it cannot be identified in space. Instead it becomes a poetic idea: the source of all the great rivers, the origin of life.

The garden is watered by a river (2.10), which is both abundant, since it feeds the world's great rivers, and perpetual. Rain, on the other hand, is seasonal, chancy, and random in distribution. Rain falls everywhere, rivers are confined to their courses. In the garden of Eden rain is not mentioned, a fact that is forced upon our attention by a conspicuous loose-end. In v. 5 it tells us that in the beginning there was no grass "kî lōʾ himṭîr yhwh ʾelōhîm ʿal-hāʾāreṣ weʾādām ʾayin laʿabōd ʾet-hāʾadāmâ" "for the Lord God had not caused it to rain upon the earth /15/, and there was no man to till the soil". It then describes the creation of man, but not of rain. Instead an "ʾēd" /16/ rose up from the earth (2.6). Rain remains in suspense throughout the story, associated as it is with the unpredictable earth following the expulsion from Eden, with the seasonal time, and global distribution. Rain, like death and time, is outside the garden.

In the Song, as we saw, the garden is nurtured by the "living waters" (4.15) of sources and springs (4.12,15). Its waters are controlled and exploited by man through dams (gan nāʿûl) and irrigation canals (šelāḥayik) /17/. In chapter 6,

Chapter Four - Two Versions of Paradise

too, the garden is in a river valley, a "naḥal" /18/. The spring or source is unfailing and pure, indissolubly linked with the garden through paronomasia (gan ... gal) and as a metaphor for the Beloved. It is abundant, sufficient for several gardens (4.15), and perennial. It is through the springs that the gardens are especially favoured, experience perpetual vitality. Outside, the earth is moist because the rain has been and gone (2.11), in an evocation of spring notable for its many temporal images (2.10-13). The world of the Song, then, is our world, subject to seasons, responding to rain; but enclosed within it there are gardens, privileged and protected, close to the source of life, the "mayim ḥayyîm" "living waters", just as the garden of Eden grows round the source of the rivers. In 6.2 and 6.11, likewise, the Lover goes down to his garden, which is planted round the stream or river-valley; an image not only of fertility, but of shelter.

The garden grows round the spring: "A source of gardens, a well of living waters ..." (4.15). The construct form, "maʿyan gannîm", implies not merely that the spring is for the benefit of gardens but that it generates gardens. The verse concludes "flowing from Lebanon" /19/. There is thus a double focus: the garden and Lebanon. The winter snows are transformed into bountiful streams, probably connoting refreshing coolness (Lys: 197). In reality, too, as a rain-catchment area, Lebanon gives rise to several rivers. It may seem strange to associate the cold and inhospitable mountains with the garden of Eden, and yet, like the garden of Eden, Lebanon is naturally luxuriant, the habitat of the choice trees (5.15, 3.9). Like the garden, it is fragrant with herbs and spices (4.11). In the second chapter, I found that the Lebanon is a bisexual image, associated with both lovers; it is the place of origins, whence they come in 4.8, and fosters the garden; it represents both the primitive bisexual mother and the hostility of the womb. Eden too is the now inaccessible and deadly matrix of mankind, and the source of the living waters. The four great rivers of Eden suggest four directions, that the fountain head splits four ways, and hence its universality. This is confirmed by their distribution: Kush and Havilah in the south-west, Euphrates and Tigris in the north-east. The latter two are familiar and regular, and hardly merit description in the text; the former are remote and exotic countries /20/, cut off from the rest of the world by encircling rivers, the Gihon and Pishon, whose real existence is doubtful and cannot be separated from mythological elaboration. Thus two actual rivers complement two symbolic rivers /21/.

Patte/Parker observe that in contrast to the undifferentiated "*ēd*", the rivers divide the earth into regions and thus give it order (67). They compose a mandala, a symbol for the self, cohesive, yet with a capacity for division and interaction. Rhetorically it is self-contained, with its prolepsis linking 2.8 and 2.15, bounding the description of the garden from the rest of the narrative, and within it the topography of the four rivers. The mandala, isolated and certain, is a sign of identity, a fingerprint or imprimatur at the beginning of the Bible. Here the rivers part, here history begins, and man becomes multiple. As long as the garden is there, even if it is inaccessible, it has a protective influence. Somewhere in the world is safe from time and vicissitudes. Internalised, it is an indestructible core.

We have found a second equivalence of Eden: Lebanon, transformationally linked to the garden. That this is not entirely fanciful is suggested by Ezekiel 31.3-9, in which Lebanon and Eden are functionally identical, and in which the motifs of tree and river are likewise intertwined. Michael

Fishbane (17) likewise proposes that Eden was situated upon a cosmic mountain, adducing in addition to these considerations the streams' downward flow in our passage.

A very clear illustration comes appropriately from Assyria (see on left; cf. Keel 1978: 118, fig.153a). A little more elaborate is a relief, in which the mountain god holds two trees, and is flanked by four rivers divagating from anthropoid fountains (Keel 1978: 117, fig. 153; cf. figs. 185 and 188). Or there is the celebrated wall painting from Mari (see opposite page). Othmar Keel comments:

> The two rectangles) are flanked by two trees (or treelike emblems), four cherubim, and two bulls. One foot of each bull is planted on a mountaintop. The two mountains probably indicate that the center of the court is located on a mountain. The two fountain deities in the

Chapter Four - Two Versions of Paradise

lower of the two ... rectangles correspond to the two mountains. A stream with four branches (cf. Gen. 2.10) rises from the vessels held by the deities. A stylised plant grows out of the stream. This is the place from which all life issues. In the center of this region, in the upper rectangle, stands Ishtar. (Keel 1978: 142-4)

The garden with its spring is self-sufficient, self-fertilised; it needs no rain, nor any cultivation; hence it is enclosed. The spring comes from the earth, and feeds it, generating new life; not only is it perpetual, but it is part of a cycle of self-perpetuation /22/. Rain, however, is celestial in origin; it is a mode of dialogue between earth and heaven. The earth is fertilised from outside, dependent and insecure, subject to the ambivalence of relationship.

In 2.5 "for the Lord God had not caused it to rain upon the earth" is parallel to "and there was no man to till the soil". The falling of rain corresponds to the interaction of heaven and earth that made man; both are the work of God. Instead "an Jēd' rose up out of the earth" and "a river came out of Eden" /23/. Thus a self-fertilised, autonomous earth opens up to engage in relationships; just as the enclosed garden of the Song opens up to include the Lover, and then all lovers. At this point, there is the curious phrase "'ûrî ṣāpôn ûbôʾî têmān hāpîḥî gannî yizzelû beśāmāyw" "Awake, O north wind, and come, O south, breathe upon my garden, let its spices flow

..." (Song of Songs 4.16) /24/. The centripetal attraction of the winds that surely represent all winds inverts the centrifugal divergence of the four rivers in Genesis. Or rather, it traces them back to their source in Eden, for the sake of the diffusion of spices, so that the atmosphere of Eden should be mingled with that of the world.

Weather in the Song is usually ambivalent - the scorching but soporific sun of 1.6 and 7, the nocturnal dew, soaking and seductive, in 5.2. Rain likewise is unpleasant but beneficial. The most important characteristic of the rain in 2.11 is that it is now over: "For behold, the winter has passed, the rain has been and gone", leaving the world clearer and fresher than before.

Like Eden, then, the garden is sustained by perennial, terrestrial water, flowing from the lifeless matrix. Outside it, the world achieves perfection through time and rain. The winds return to the garden from which the rivers issued. But the garden also participates in the seasons, with its flowers and blossoming trees. It is part of the weathered world, uniting changeless time and cyclical time, open both to rain and man. Its integrity is fostered, through dams and irrigation canals, for the sake of those outside it, so that its influence should be felt in the world. In this, as we shall see, it is analogous to the Beloved, to the little sister disguised and protected, whose fate we discussed in the last chapter.

"Wenāhār yōṣēʾ mēʿēden lehašqôt ʾet-haggān" "And a river came out of Eden, to water the garden." Is it suggested that the river came from outside the garden, from the barren world, just as both stream and lovers come from Lebanon? We then meet with a double regress, that coincides with a curious detail concerning the first man.

The garden is man's first home: "wayyitta yhwh ʾelōhîm gan beʿēden miqqedem wayyāśem šām ʾet-hāʾādām ʾašer yāṣār" "And the Lord God planted a garden in Eden eastward, and he put there the man that he had formed (wayyāśem šām ʾet-hāʾādām ʾašer yāṣār)" (2.8). It is apparently an ideal first environment, fulfilling man's needs and abolishing his anxieties; outside it, as we have seen, are death and time. Yet the text quietly indicates that man does not originate in the garden, since God put him there /25/. Man was created before any other creature, or even vegetation. Preceding the memory of Eden is one of an inconceivably bleak and desolate world. Man already knows what is outside the garden, and hence cannot be entirely at home - entirely unafraid - in Eden. The description of the earliest phase, however, does

Chapter Four - Two Versions of Paradise

not imply despair: it is too brief. In it man simply becomes "a living soul", and then he is transported to Eden. No sooner does he wake up than he finds himself in a garden. Yet there is still a consciousness that there was something, or rather nothing, before this plenitude.

But the garden that man enters is also solitary, with ideal objects but no subjects, except the man himself. It is a solipsistic domain, whose external images enter and make up the man's consciousness. In contrast, before he was placed in the garden we have the unimaginable self that nothing constitutes. There is thus no rivalry, no awareness of the other, a relief from social tension that is at the same time an obscure lack of fulfilment, that becomes explicit in 2.18.

Several verses later, following the description of the garden, the narrative goes back on itself and repeats this central action: "wayyiqqaḥ yhwh ʲelōhîm ʲet-hāʲādām wayyanniḥēhû began-ʿēden leʿobdāh ûlešomrāh" "And the Lord God took the man, and set him in the garden of Eden, to work it and keep it" (2.15). After the digression of 2.10-14, the reminder is tactful to the reader. The chiasmus serves to arrest the narrative, to enclose the garden syntactically as well as spatially. Nevertheless, the repetition of the identical moment is undermined by subtle variations, and difference of context. V. 8 is near the end of a cadence ("wayyîṣer - wayyippaḥ - wayyiṭṭa' - wayyāśem - wayyaṣmaḥ" "And he created - breathed - planted - put - caused to grow") whose focus is God's creative act and solicitude, and which leaves man safely in the garden. In contrast, by resuming the narrative, v. 15 makes us aware that it has not ended. Implicit in v. 8 is a feeling of relief; subtending v. 15 is a question "What next?" In the following sequence there is an underlying insecurity - the tree that must be protected, the creation that is imperfect. This thematic difference shows itself in the detail of the verses and their relation to their context. In v. 8 the apparent redundancy, "ʲašer yāṣār" "which he had created", refers back to the main point of the sequence - God's creative act - and binds it together; it is emphatically theocentric. To this the blissful description of the garden is an elaborate coda, illustrative of God's goodness and man's fortune. V. 15, however, adds two significant words to the nuclear sentence: "leʿobdāh ûlešomrāh" "to work it and keep it". The description is then also an introduction: the perfect garden must be kept and maintained, if it is not to deteriorate; it is fundamentally insecure.

"To work it and keep it" - two overlapping, semi-synonymous functions, through which man creatively interacts with the garden, making it something new and human. Work requires aesthetic foresight and imagination, whereas keeping or guarding (lešomrāh) denotes observation, judgment, and an awareness of limits. With its fundamental meaning of "watch", it corresponds to the earlier "lovely to look on", but is more self-reflective. "Work" and "eat" are likewise a pair, as active verbs, coupled with the passive "watch" and "look".

Working and watching, man lives for the sake of the garden. That is his function, to be a gardener, according to v. 15. In v. 8 God has planted the garden for man's sake. He finds himself in an ideal order, "everything fair in its time", as Ecclesiastes says (Eccl 3.11), and he fulfils his purpose within it by changing it, playing about with it, adapting it to his own taste and ingenuity. Aesthetic delight (v. 8) leads to aesthetic motivation. In 3.17-19 man is destined to eat bread in pain and with the sweat of his brow. This toil, and the boredom that goes with it, was apparently unknown in the garden. It is a fundamental misconception that the garden was a place of passive harmony, to be thankful, for instance, "that by means of sin and the Fall we managed to get ourselves expelled from that place" /26/. It was a place of essentially imaginative activity.

"La'abōd" has connotations of worship and service. In the Babylonian myths of creation man is created to serve the gods (Pritchard ed.: 36). Here he serves the earth, with a labour and a love that will soon become pantheistic. Trible (1978: 85-86) notes the multiple connotations of the root "'bd", and the interdependence of power over the earth and nurture of it. In her scheme, work participates in the unfolding of Eros. By working on the soil, man comes to identify with nature, to participate in its process. Work can be a mode of self-transcendence, of contributing to a greater cause. Solipsistic man becomes selfless man.

"To work and keep/guard" are for the moment honorary, light duties. There is little to guard against, when there is nothing outside the garden, and within it, perhaps a little pruning of the perfect trees. Nothing is said about the work until after the story is over. But the phrase anticipates something more serious: it leads us to expect a use for these functions of working and watching, it points outside the garden, where they will be needed in earnest.

For "le'obdāh" participates in another chiasmus: in 2.5 nothing grew because "there was no man to till the soil" (la'abōd). At the end of the passage, in 3.23, man is cast out

Chapter Four - Two Versions of Paradise

"laʕabōd ʼet-hāʼadāmâ" "to till the earth". In between we have a garden planted by God, an anomaly that mediates between absence and existence /27/, and that is necessary if man is to survive and learn. Here all the conditions of the world enclosing it are transposed. Grass, which is not yet existent in 2.5, and on which man will subsist from 3.18 onwards, is then in significant contrast to the trees that characterised the garden. Likewise, as we have said, rain is in abeyance throughout the story, and is contrasted with surface water. Finally, instead of God producing rain and man working the soil, we have God working the soil and the "ʼēd" rising by itself. When man joins God in tending the garden, he initiates the second part of the mediation, the transition to normality.

The garden in the Song is a difficult and extended metaphor, a terrain that both lovers inhabit, from which they are both excluded, and which they share. There are two scenes set in the garden, forming a chiasmus round chapter 5, and antithetical to each other. Both are concentric in structure, with the same basic development: the enclosed, private lover who opens out, blossoms, to the power of love. But in each scene it is a different lover who figures: the woman in 4.12-5.1, the man in 6.2-12.

The human meaning of the metaphor can be clearly discerned in both passages: it is the self, or part of the self, that is inaccessible, apparently self-generated, that is fostered through being protected, and is the product of culture as well as nature: its beauty signifies that of the lovers, of human, civilised perfection. Accordingly, the image of the garden in 4.12-5.1 was examined at length in my second chapter, where it exemplified the interchange of identity between the lovers, the sealed self that consummates itself, paradoxically, through self-surrender. Hence the passage is packed with ambiguities of possession - is the garden "his" or "hers" in 4.16? - and definition - is she the garden or merely the spring that waters the garden, is she a subject or object to herself? In what follows I will try to avoid the fate of the fool in Prov 26.10, and concentrate on three topics: the description of the garden as a metaphor for the Beloved; its relationship with the parallel passage, 6.2-12; and a comparison with the place of man in the garden of Eden.

In 4.12-5.1, the Beloved is the garden, a heady correlative compounded of scents and round, firm objects, the pomegranates of 4.13. Her image is diffused and departicularised, we sense her as an animating spirit, an atmosphere or personality, flowing streams or wind-stirred air. The pomegranates are enclosed gardens in miniature, numerous part-objects, decomposing the body of the Beloved; within they are messily succulent. Even a tiny detail - "šelāḥayik" "shoots" or "canals" - draws attention to the extent or extremities of the garden, away from the centre, the genitalia, the Beloved as a sexual object.

In 6.2-12, in contrast, the Lover is not the garden, nor is he even its denizen. He is a visitor, who goes there to divert his mind, as an adjunct to a complex, urban civilisation. This garden is setting rather than subject, a made place in the mind, where the Lover goes to pick flowers and be otherwise careless. It is less serious than the garden in 4.12-5.1, or the garden of Eden - it is one of his many possessions, or even gardens (6.2), hence its specificity, as nut garden /28/. In it things happen, whereas the focus in 4.12-5.1 is on the imagery and energy of the garden itself, as the Paradisal Beloved. The king goes down to his garden, putting him beyond the reach of the Beloved and her friends /29/: it is a sign of the royal prerogative, like the royal curtains in 1.5, which I discussed earlier (above p. 131), or Ahasuerus' sanctum in Esther: the king must not be disturbed at the centre of society. In contrast to the garden of love in 4.12-5.1, it is an escape from love, a place for solitary contemplation and innocent pleasures, such as picking flowers. Here the king loses his formality, returning to nature, to childhood, to erotic irresponsibility. A childhood preserve, I suggested, is one of the connotations of the garden. In his descent to this refuge we encounter another persona: that of Lover as fawn, grazing among lilies, our starting point in chapter 2. King and fawn, the Lover combines in himself the extremes of wildness and civilisation, seclusion and exposure: the king is both the most public and the most mysterious of figures.

If this garden is a retreat within civilisation to an idealised childhood or animal innocence, if, symbolically, it is a separate enclave of the mind to which one may descend sometimes ("Often I am Permitted to Return to a Meadow" - Robert Duncan), the garden of 4.12-5.1 represents a genuine integration of male and female, nature and man, close to the sources of life. It is then an already existent archetype, to which the Lover comes; a garden which has never been opened, which has never entered into relation with the world, and of which the garden of 6.2-12 is a formulated echo. The return to the garden in ch. 6 (childhood, innocence) is an artificial reenactment of the true return in ch. 4; but as it develops it becomes ironically serious.

Chapter Four - Two Versions of Paradise

For love surprises him in the garden. Already we can see this in the first verses, that the retreat, the innocence, is compromised. It is the Beloved who speaks. She says "dôdî yārad legannô" "My love has gone down to his garden" (6.2), and we accept the fait accompli, that she cannot pursue him into the garden. But she imagines him there, among the flowers and spices, in an act of sympathetic possession. Moreover, she asserts "'anî ledôdî wedôdî lî" "I am my beloved's and my beloved is mine" (6.3), that despite his sequestration, his apparent rejection of her, they still mutually belong to each other.

The Lover goes down, she says, "lirʕôt baggannîm welilqôt šôšannîm" "to graze in the gardens and to pick lilies" (6.2): lilies, as we have seen, are an emblem for the Beloved. She is, as it were, Flora, and the gathering of flowers has a natural erotic significance, not only in the Song of Songs. The plural "šôšannîm", lilies, universalises it: as well as flower picking, the king has the pick of women, as the Song reminds us, time and again. Going to the garden to pick lilies, among the plantations of spices (laʕarugôt habbōśem), thus has a slight sexual suggestion, which is amplified in the succeeding verses. The key words "lirʕôt" and "šôšannîm" are repeated in 6.3, capping the formula "'anî ledôdî wedôdî lî hārôʕeh baššôšannîm" "I am my beloved's and my beloved is mine, who <u>feeds among the lilies</u>", and binding the passage together.

But they have lost their literal meaning. No lover actually grazes among lilies /30/; the refrain applies a particular formal imagery, established in the poem. The fawn is a persona of the Lover (2.9, 2.17, 8.14), the lily of the Beloved (2.1); the fawn nibbling among lilies is a lover metaphorically feeding among women. Refrains are particularly susceptible to allegorical interpretation; recurring in differing contexts, they accumulate deposits of meaning /31/. The formal epithet in our verse, however, unbalances the refrain: if he is hers, "dôdî lî", how can he promiscuously graze among women? This is in fact a point of extreme tension in the Song. It amounts to an affirmation that she possesses him, absolutely and mutually, even though he is "hārôʕeh baššôšannîm" "he who feeds among the lilies".

Likewise, although in 6.2 he apparently prefers "flowers" to herself and the daughters of Jerusalem, she declares that they are reciprocally indissoluble. Picking flowers, moreover, is a whimsical, dilettanteish pastime, and effectively contrasts with the absolute seriousness of their love. Her assurance is confirmed later on in the chapter by no better authority than the Lover himself, as the theme recurs of the Beloved's uniqueness among many women.

For the voice now switches, from the Beloved to the Lover. Inset between the two accounts of the descent to the garden that frame the chapter are two short meditations and two apostrophes to the Beloved. As Levinger (74) and Falk (1982: 124) have inferred, the formal construction indicates coherence of action, that the whole chapter is as it were enclosed in a garden. Thence the Lover speaks, and thinks about his Beloved. The refuge, where he would escape from love, and indulge in innocent pastimes, turns out to be illusory, for his obsession pursues him even there. He addresses his Beloved as if she were present: "You are beautiful, my love ..." (6.4). He is dazzled by her eyes in 6.5, and recoils "Turn your eyes away from me ..."; he constructs a beautiful poem about her, which suddenly breaks off. Evasiveness and desire are thus intermingled; even the poem is both a tribute and a screen, that hides her in images.

In the second meditation the Beloved is compared to other women, to queens and concubines (see above pp. 150f.). She is inducted into society, into the enchanted circle of the king's court. Here the shift of images is complete: the garden with its lilies is fully transposed into an intimation of royal pleasure, for which indeed the royal park is a suitable setting; at such times especially he may not be disturbed. The king goes down to relax, to escape from the world and love, seeking vicarious satisfaction among flowers and women, and he finds that his love is incomparable. In Chapter Three, in discussing this passage, I found that its central image is a hieros gamos of king and newborn child. The Beloved then offers the true return to the sources of life, to the original garden, as in chapter 4, at the very simple generative centre of royal display and culture. The queens and concubines admire and praise the Beloved; like a chorus, they surround her, and are in a sense dedicated to her. Thus the opposition we have discerned between the two gardens, the quiddity and the archetype, is overcome; the one exists in the context of the other.

In 6.11-12, the descent to the garden is recapitulated, this

Chapter Four - Two Versions of Paradise

time from the Lover's point of view /32/; unfortunately, it is badly mutilated. The Lover goes down to the garden confidently and officiously, to inspect the progress of the spring, as the master of his domain; a complacent preamble to the succeeding convulsion. For he is not even master of himself "lō' yāda'tî napšî šāmatnî" "I did not know / my soul set me" /33/ (6.12). The incoherence that follows, "markebôt 'ammî nādîb" "chariots of my princely people", /34/ is presumably contingent, yet reflects, through a remarkably appropriate serendipity, the disturbance of the narrative. There is no doubt that "my soul", like the Beloved's "heart" in 5.2, likewise opposed to the "I", represents the power of love and the unconscious, the Dionysiac imperative that is belied by the conscious artistry and control with which man cultivates the garden. Thus chapter 6, which begins on a note of resignation, with the definition of limits, ends with their destruction, that sweeps away the royal redoubt.

As well as being related diachronically, the two gardens develop different features of the Genesis myth. The genetic relationship between the gardens of chapter 4 and chapter 6 is in fact the same as that between the garden of Eden and the Song of Songs, between the primary myth or symbol and the secondary evocation. Chapter 4 corresponds closely to the physical imagery of Eden; it is the primordial garden planted in the Song of Songs. It has the stream, trees, and is associated with birth and the origins of life. Yet on the human plane there is an astonishing inversion. The garden of Eden is man's first home, where he is put by God; he likewise enters the garden of chapter 4, which is the Beloved. Man's solitude, of which God complains in 2.18, is now perfect intimacy: the first home is the matrix.

What the Song does is very simply to substitute the Beloved for the garden of Eden through the metaphor: "A locked garden is my sister, my bride". The equivalence makes human generation into an autochthonous creation, articulating the metaphor already implicit in the myth of Paradise, for instance in the sweet fruit. The metaphor bridges our world and the original world; between the incompatible terms there is the mediation of the Beloved, who both belongs to our world and is the other. In her, Paradise can be re-experienced, through the arts of culture, poetry, perfumery, etc. But she also represents something much more ancient: the natural world from which man grew, and on which he feeds.

Chapter 6 activates a quite different component of the

scene in Genesis. It concerns man's task in the garden: "to work it and watch it". The king goes down to the garden to observe the progress of the spring, "to see whether the vine had blossomed, the pomegranates were in flower" (6.11). He fulfils his commission of protecting and fostering the kingdom in miniature, in his own possessions, for example, in his vineyard at Baal-Hamon in 8.11. Like Adam, his task is not onerous: the king, as gardener, is a figurehead, a symbolic functionary. Adam is training for his task in the world; the king is escaping from his task in the world. The pompous descent to the garden thus has a half-satirical import, compounded by the following irony: as we might expect, he is not even master of himself, of his own possessions.

The garden reappears in the Song just before its end:

הַיּוֹשֶׁבֶת בַּגַּנִּים חֲבֵרִים מַקְשִׁיבִים לְקוֹלֵךְ הַשְׁמִיעִנִי: בְּרַח דּוֹדִי

(8.13) You who sit among gardens, friends listening to your voice, let me hear.
(14) Flee, my beloved ...

The garden of the Beloved now excludes the Lover, whereas it incorporated him in 4.16-5.1. But, to our surprise, it is not an enclosed or solitary garden; there are "friends" there, whose role as admirers and participants corresponds to that of the "dôdîm" and "rēʻîm", the drunken "friends" and "lovers" in 5.1. They listen, however, with attention to the separate voice, maintaining a certain distance. The Beloved is she who sits or dwells among gardens, the human presence whose voice speaks for the garden, gives it meaning and intangibly fills it. It is an articulating spirit at the centre of all gardens, and functionally identical to the "maʻyan gannîm", the spring or source of gardens in 4.12-5.1. The mythical identification (Beloved = garden, spring) is rationalised into a humanly accessible situation (Beloved in the garden with her voice). The voice is the only explicit paradigmatic equivalent of the garden, organising and enclosing natural sounds in language. In particular, it is the voice of poetry, of which the garden is a natural and very early image. The audience listens to the Beloved's voice, and the Lover wishes to join them, because it is beautiful, and everything she speaks is poetry, "ki qôlēk lʻārēb ûmarʼêk nāʼweh" "For your voice is sweet and your appearance lovely" (2.14).

The formal circle implies a recitation, of which the Song itself is the only example. To us the Beloved's voice is

Chapter Four - Two Versions of Paradise

indissolubly linked with that of the Song, whose audience we are. Thus the Song concludes with a self-reference; to put it more exactly, with a reference to the genus of which it is the exemplar, as the <u>Song of Songs</u>. The performance becomes part of the poem, and the Lover is excluded /35/. This is very strange, because nominally he is the composer of the poem/garden, for whose sake it opens out in ch. 4, and at the very least he contributes to it. There is in fact a chiasmus between the first verse and the last, between "The Song of Songs that is Solomon's" and "Flee, my beloved", between "yiššāqēnî" "Let him kiss me" (1.2), and "hašmî'inî" "Let me hear" (8.13). At the end the poet and the poem must part, and he enters the audience, becomes one of the friends.

The Song, like the Beloved, interprets the original garden to ourselves, and brings it to life between us. It too is an intermediary, through which it enters history, becomes universal property.

The paradigm of the garden, with this exception, falls into two classes. The first are the natural images, the wider garden of the world. There are the vineyards in particular, but also images of harvest and herding /36/. These vineyards have to be enclosed and protected, against foxes in 2.15; like the sealed garden, they are associated with the Beloved's self (1.6, 8.11), and are beautiful in springtime. Without repeating earlier material, we need only look at the two passages in which one lover invites the other to take a walk in the spring (2.10-13, 7.12-14). There is a sympathetic interaction: the lovers are at the centre of the season, which flourishes for their eyes, and is celebrated by their voices. Its fecundity is the background to their love (Krinetzki 1964: 129-130; 1981: 103); they participate in the spring by admiring it and being loving creatures. Moreover, they are the summation of its beauty, equivalent through metaphor to the whole of creation. Thus the two versions of Genesis are reconciled: the enclosed, human garden is the world.

The other category of paradigmatic images is that of civilisation. In the Song it is represented by two settings, besides the garden: the city and the palanquin. Like the garden, both are ideally splendid, both are enclosed against wild nature, protected against destruction. The city is surrounded by walls and patrolled by watchmen, against enemies without and subversion within; sixty men at arms guard the palanquin from "fear in the night" /37/. At the heart of each, too, there is the generative power of love: the Beloved at the centre of the daughters of Jerusalem, for example; the palanquin whose "midst" is paved with their love /38/.

If in the garden nature is perfected by culture, for pleasure as well as necessity, and the city manifests a society, the palanquin is constructed out of trees. Yet society is also repressive, as we have seen; its achievements can only be maintained at the cost of its more anarchic wishes. The Beloved is beaten by the watchmen because she is shameless (5.7), lovers cannot kiss in the street (8.1). The lovers retreat to the Beloved's mother's house, to the room where she was born (3.4, 8.2), an enclosure where they are safe, in the protective embrace of the mother. The relationship between house and city is the same as that between the garden and the world: between the ambivalent, seasonal terrain and the secluded matrix.

The implication, noted above, is that each act of intercourse repeats that of one's parents, and so all parents, that each act of conception takes us back to our birth, and so history is confounded by a series of identical moments.

In another respect, too, city, palanquin and field differ from the garden, and emphasise the cyclical revolutions of time; for all of them evoke the night, the shadow of the day. This is especially so in the case of the city, since both urban episodes are nocturnal. The city at night is eery, unfamiliar, desolate /39/, except for the sinister watchmen; above all, it is the place of loss, where the Lover cannot be found. Even in 3.3, where the watchmen appear to be friendly, they chance upon her - "meṣā'ûnî haššōmrîm hassōbebîm bā'îr" "The watchmen who go round about the city found me" - highlighting the loss of her lover, through the keyword "mṣ'" "find": "biqqaštîw welō' meṣā'tîw" "I sought him but could not find him" (3.2) that occurs at the end of the previous verse. Then, when she does find him, she takes him back to her mother's house, forcibly, "I grasped him and would not let him go" (3.4), back to the inner sanctum, the permanent home.

The empty, annihilated city, with its normally crowded streets and squares (baššewāqîm ûbārehōbōt), in these somnambulist sequences hovers Cavafy-like between reality and dream; if to the waking Beloved it represents active, social vitality, the scene of her daily communication, here it represents the emptying of consciousness, and reveals the substratum of fear, that her Lover will be lost for ever, she will be abandoned for ever. The circularity of the search ("'āqûmâ nā' wa'asôbebāh bā'îr ... haššōmrîm hassōbebîm bā'îr" "Let me arise now and go round about the city ... The

Chapter Four - Two Versions of Paradise

watchmen who <u>go round about</u> the city") captures the sense of frustration and constriction, when repetition becomes purposeless.

The "fear of the night" that afflicts the palanquin is only touched on for a moment; it explains the presence of the guard in 3.7 while rendering it ineffectual. Nothing can defend against fear of the dark, which is ultimately a fear of annihilation, as Lys rightly says (157); the phrase "against fear in the night" is one of the first dissonant suggestions of the encounter with death at the climax of the poem. Against it clamour the repeated images of day in the last verse of the passage: "the <u>day</u> of his wedding, the <u>day</u> of his heart's rejoicing" (3.11), which cannot be dissociated from the palanquin paved with love, or true perfection.

The night spent in the fields (or villages) in 7.12 is much more innocuous, suggesting escape, perhaps elopement, from the city, and dreamlike wish-fulfilment. It has an element of special daring. The oppressive weight of the city is contrasted with the adventurous night in the fields, and the peace of the garden.

The paradigmatic equivalents I have cited all have one feature in common: they are associated with or identified with the Beloved, not the Lover. For example, the Beloved is compared to a city with towers in 8.9-10, which the king enters from outside. Likewise the palanquin has been made by Solomon for his bride; it is saturated with the female presence: "tôkô rāṣûp ʲahabâ mibbenôt yerûšālāim" "its midst is paved with love of the daughters of Jerusalem". The opening phrase of the passage is ambiguous: "mî zō'ṯ" in 3.6 may either mean "Who [fem.] is this?" or "What is this?" If we turn to the agricultural paradigm of the garden, the vineyard is a metaphor for the Beloved and her intoxicating gifts, shared with or withheld from the Lover (8.12); and she is associated throughout with fertility, fruit and flowers. Finally, the garden of poetry is inhabited by the Beloved; the Lover/composer is just within earshot.

Thus the garden of the Song is an inversion of that of Eden, despite its great similarity. Whereas in Genesis, woman is a secondary creature, taken from man's side, here she represents the original garden, which man reenters through his elaborate culture, the exercise of his tasks of working and watching. As king, he is a symbolic functionary, like the first man, responsible for his kingdom as Adam is for the garden. Whereas death, like rain, had not yet penetrated the garden of Eden, it is precariously excluded from the garden of the

Song, where rain and spring correspond. The garden of the Song, like that of Eden, gives life to the world; reciprocally, it attracts the winds. Whereas, in Jobling's formulation, the Genesis myth attempts to express the semantics of inside using the language of outside, in the Song poetic language enables us, always ambiguously, to return inside. However, the garden of Eden, as we shall see, is riven with contradictions, that complicate the relation with the garden of the Song. In the next section, I shall turn to the first of these: that between the two trees in the midst of the garden.

Metaphor: The Tree

In the description of the garden there was one detail I omitted:

וְעֵץ הַחַיִּים בְּתוֹךְ הַגָּן וְעֵץ הַדַּעַת טוֹב וָרָע:

(2.9) And the Tree of Life in the midst of the garden, and the Tree of Knowledge of good and evil.

The tree is the central symbol in the myth, the tree and its spokesman, the serpent. What's more, the trees are at the centre of the garden, which grows around them. They are qualitatively different from the other trees, no longer existent in nature, and with a clearly allegorical significance (Hugh White 1980: 93). Yet their abstraction, and their special place in the story, should not betray us into falsely isolating them. The two trees share a generic identity with the others, and correspond to their two functions: lovely to look upon and good to eat. The first is equivalent to knowledge, the second to life. We eat food to live, we look at the world and come to understand it. The two trees represent the arborial experience, in essence, in consciousness.

Trees are stately, longlived, constant landmarks. Their great age, as well as their deep-rooted strength, associates them with immortality, and hence the Tree of Life has many counterparts (James). Frequently, trees are sacred, endowed with a cult as the immemorial vitality of the shrine that constantly renews itself /40/. The Tree of Life is thus explicable as well as traditional. It bestows immortality, as we learn from 3.22, and is quite unambiguous. It is at the centre of the garden, perhaps a "temenos", as Soggin suggests (1975b: 172-3), the spot most removed from the external desolation and corruption; and the essence of the garden, its everlasting vitality, is concentrated in its fruit. By implication, as the climax of the sentence, the fruit of

Chapter Four - Two Versions of Paradise

immortality is the fairest to look upon and the best to eat, of all the trees in the garden. The ageless immortals are ideally beautiful, since they are free from all corruption; eternal youth and pleasure is the best of the gifts bestowed by the garden.

But the verse continues after this climax, with a phrase that would have puzzled a comparative mythologist in antiquity: "weʽēṣ haddaʽat tōb wārāʽ" "And the Tree of Knowledge of good and evil". It is a phrase in apposition, an afterthought; and yet commentators have ground their teeth over this tree, which is unexampled elsewhere, and which is a new development in mythological thinking.

But why is it a <u>tree</u> of knowledge? There is no obvious metaphorical correlative between knowledge and trees, as there is between eternal life and trees. In my view, the explanation can only be a perceived connection between life and knowledge, that the two stand in dialectical opposition to each other. In other words, it is only a <u>Tree</u> of Knowledge because the other is a Tree of Life, and the metaphor is a vehicle through which the relationship is articulated.

It is an important point, because for a long time some critics have attempted to assign the two trees to separate traditions /41/. According to them, the original story is that of the Tree of Knowledge, and a secondary tale, borrowed largely from Mesopotamian sources, has been tagged on to it. What I am striving to show is that the conception of a Tree of Knowledge is dependent on that of a Tree of Life, since out of this context it is a meaningless metaphor.

Moreover, the Tree of Knowledge is functionally, and perhaps was originally called, a Tree of Death, as Mattiteyahu Tsevat has brilliantly argued /42/; stylistically complementing the Tree of Life. A Tree of Death is clearly an anti-tree, the negation of the tree's natural significance, associated, in Tsevat's Ugaritic text, with the ophidic underworld /43/. The transition from death to knowledge, which Tsevat explains in terms of narrative probability and economy, is more puzzling. For why is death associated with knowledge? Abraham Ronen traces this to prehistory, to man's awareness of death as part of his growing self-consciousness, thus confirming the myth's essential truth fulness (1975: 99-103). To understand it better, we must consider the nature of knowledge, as defined in the story.

It is "knowledge of good and evil". These are inclusive terms, as Soggin and Vawter stress /44/. But it is not simply universal knowledge (Von Rad: 79), the wisdom which

Ecclesiastes despises and Job celebrates /45/. It is awareness of a universe divided into good and bad, of the ambivalent contraries that make up existence /46/. Hence the first knowledge is that of nakedness, of the disturbing duality of gender.

Moreover, it is knowledge of good and evil that is desirable; man wishes to know evil so as to understand it and overcome it. Knowing death is an essential part of knowing evil: it is its absolute form. Consequently knowledge, and the aesthetic anxiety that drives it, is ultimately preoccupied with death, with coming to accept it and master it. Hence the ritual elaboration of death, the attempt to make it beautiful, and its uncompromising mystery, as that which resists understanding and is beyond experience.

In this respect, then, it is a statement of fact when God says "on the day when you shall eat of it you shall surely die", since death is the ultimate knowledge /47/. But the warning does more than that: it sows the idea of death as a tantalising mystery in the mind of man. Death is already planted in the garden, at its very centre, and in the guise of the longest-living thing, the tree. As the one certainty, death resembles immortality, and the differentiating characteristic of human wisdom is that it is transmitted from generation to generation through language, transcending death and time. More to the point, life and death are inseparable, and very nearly the same substance. At the heart of the primeval garden we find twin trees, that correspond to Eros and Thanatos in man. The two trees grow together at the centre of the garden, and yet in the Tale they are mutually exclusive. The one is permitted when the other is forbidden, and likewise they participate in different scenes /48/. They correspond to man's two deepest wishes: for immortality, and for experience. The first is rooted in the fear of death, which is also a fear of life as a creative and destructive process; in its pursuit man constructs a changeless society, like that of Plato's Republic (Popper: 86-99). The second - man's curiosity - is extraordinarily daring, and risks everything for the truth. It is characterised by "an opening of eyes" to oneself and the other, and to life. Thus the two desires contradict each other in the world, as in the garden of Eden. For only God can be both immortal and know "good and evil" (3.4, 3.22). This is a most perturbing attribute. God knows that his creation is good and evil, inherently flawed and amoral. His self-projection is thus ambivalent, and suggests a duplicity in God, that explains the contradictions in the account of the creation /49/.

Chapter Four - Two Versions of Paradise

There is one further detail about the fruit of the Tree: it makes man like God, "knowing good and evil". God combines immortality and knowledge, because he is transcendent and immanent, both changeless and a dynamic participant in the processes of life and death. Man too is preoccupied with what is beyond him, including the death he cannot directly experience. Both he and God stand outside creation, and imagine the lives of its creatures. Man too possesses "the duality of self-transcendence", as God's partner and interlocutor.

In the Song there are many trees, as if to document the likeness to Eden (cf. Trible 1978: 154). The house of love and the palanquin are constructed with cedars and cypresses (1.17, 3.9); the garden is filled with incense-bearing trees (4.14); pomegranates and fig-trees flower in springtime (2.12, etc.); the Lover's appearance resembles cedars (5.15); the Beloved is like the date palm (7.8). All these trees serve the lovers, recompensing man for his service in Genesis. In one case the resemblance goes further - the apple tree. Extended analysis will be obviated by the prominence of this image in the second chapter.

כְּתַפּוּחַ בַּעֲצֵי הַיַּעַר כֵּן דּוֹדִי בֵּין הַבָּנִים
בְּצִלּוֹ חִמַּדְתִּי וְיָשַׁבְתִּי וּפִרְיוֹ מָתוֹק לְחִכִּי:

(2.3) Like an apple tree among the trees of the wood, so is my love among sons; in his shadow I sat and desired/ took pleasure, and his fruit was sweet to my taste.

The Beloved is among young men as in a forest, enveloping and half-perilous, quite the contrary of the casual young man among the flowers in the previous verse. Among trees, however, the apple is not especially imposing, unlike, for example, the virile cedars of 5.15. It is distinctive for its gifts and its low shadowing branches, a particularly affectionate relationship with man. It/he protects her from the sun that burns her in 1.6, from change and activity. She sits passively in his circle, and felt passion (ḥimmadtî), using the same verb as that for the loveliness of the trees (neḥmād) in Genesis. As a sexual metaphor, the fruit gives life, in a protective embrace; a return both to the womb and to the garden, among the trees. Here I would merely like to recall its function in the regeneration of life at the matrix. This is confirmed two verses later, when its fruit cures love-sickness: "śammekûnî bāʾašîšôt rappedûnî battappûḥîm kî ḥôlat ʾahabâ ʾānî" "Stay me with raisin-cakes, refrain me with apples, for I am lovesick" (2.5). In the garden of Eden, eating the fruit brings death and suffering into the world; here it is a restorative. There it causes the separation of the lovers; here it heals their absence.

In 8.5 the image of the apple tree recurs:

מִי זֹאת עֹלָה מִן־הַמִּדְבָּר מִתְרַפֶּקֶת עַל־דּוֹדָהּ תַּחַת הַתַּפּוּחַ עוֹרַרְתִּיךָ שָׁמָּה חִבְּלַתְךָ אִמֶּךָ שָׁמָּה חִבְּלָה יְלָדַתְךָ:

Who is this who comes up from the wilderness, leaning upon her beloved? Under the apple tree I awakened you; there your mother travailed with you; there she who gave birth to you travailed.

The tree presides over birth and the awakening to love; as throughout the Song, the Beloved imaginatively identifies herself with the mother. The recollection is of human origins, in a paradisal landscape, in the open, under fruit trees. Like the apple tree of 2.3, it is a Tree of Life, but it is also a Tree of Knowledge, where the Lover "opens his eyes" to the Beloved. As in 2.3 and 2.4, its fruit is the fruit of love, and, as in 2.7, love is an awakening. In other words, the two trees of Paradise are now one, no longer mutually exclusive but indivisible. This is illustrated in the next verse, where true knowledge is that love is as strong as death (8.6), is of immortality.

The inversion is thus complete: the fruit that cures love sickness bestows knowledge and immortality. But both scenes are viewed in a temporal perspective. In 2.3-7 the past is intensely realised, but in a distant present "Stay me with raisin-cakes, refresh me with apples, for I am lovesick", the collective, anonymous audience magnifying the absence of the loved one. The apples and raisin cakes are whimsical surrogates, that cannot actually cure love sickness /50/; only the source of the metaphor, the Lover himself, can do that /51/.

In 8.5 the Beloved is reminiscing from the wilderness, leaning on her Lover's arm. Now he is an adult, and the dependence is either reversed, or else they support each other, in an inhospitable landscape. On this journey she carries the memory of the original Paradise with her /52/. Moreover, the fragment duplicates the beginning of 3.6-11, the description of the palanquin. The palanquin is also seen in its ascent through the wilderness, surrounded by warriors against the "fear of the night"; at its centre there is the love

Chapter Four - Two Versions of Paradise

of the daughters of Jerusalem. The lovers replace it as a paradigmatic equivalent of the garden, closing the circle: the garden that grew between them in 4.12-5.1 is now the memory of birth under the apple tree, shared between them on their journey.

The prohibition of the Tree of Knowledge bounds the garden from within as well as without (Patte/Parker: 72). It sets the tree apart, linguistically; not only is it biologically the purveyor of evil, but functionally, apparently arbitrarily, it stands for being naughty, it introduces the idea of rebellion and trespass into the world. God gives no reason for his command; he merely asserts his authority (Westermann 1974a: 89; 1974b, 304; Brams 13). In doing so, he raises the crucial question of power and obedience, that will determine the coming course of the story (Coats: 230). Regulation ensures infringement, in our world and in the fairy tale, where the arbitrary or incomprehensible command is infallibly broken. Thereby man discovers his freedom /53/, his intolerance of frustration, ultimately the wish for the world to be open to him, of which curiosity, the desire to know good and evil, is one of the principal vectors. But man is not yet curious; in presenting him with a mystery, like a "koan", God very subtly rouses him (Fishbane: 18). It is difficult to imagine the mind of man at this point, with a vestigial memory and consciousness of absolute desolation, and correspondingly an ideally nourishing and dependable world, where he imaginatively cooperates with God; and now to be told that the partnership is illusory. The two halves of the sentence are in fact complementary: "wayeṣaw yhwh ʾelōhîm ʿal-hāʾādām lēʾmōr mikkōl ʿēṣ-haggān ʾākōl tōʾkēl" "And the Lord God commanded the man, saying: 'Of every tree of the garden you may surely eat'." Our first reaction may be gratitude, but mingled with surprise, that he was not free to eat at his pleasure, that food is a concession by God /54/. Suddenly it is revealed that man has no independence, no rights, and that his harmonious enterprise in the garden, where he fulfils his purpose in creation by changing it, is part of a rigorous divine order. The prohibition thus breaks the harmony; instead of man's imagination having as its object the immediate environment, it turns in on himself and the other, the limits of his world.

Yet nothing happens. The narrative expectation is raised and disappointed /55/. It does not occur to man to eat of the tree; instead he is fully occupied naming animals, etc. Before the tension provoked by God is realised in action, two other destabilising elements have to be introduced: the serpent and woman /56/.

In the Song of Songs, on the contrary, the apple tree protects the lovers from the rest of the world. "In his shadow" - in his circle - "I sat and took pleasure", in the wild wood. Likewise, the apple tree is preserved as a memory in the wilderness; "under" it, birth and sexual awakening continue to foster the lovers in the contrasting terrain.

Moreover, there is no prohibition there; it is the only area of the world outside politics, the realm of power and disobedience that was initiated in the garden of Eden. It is the point where the mother wakes the child, and the lovers are in equilibrium. At birth there is no issue, no tension, to disturb the relationship of mother and child. And likewise between the lovers power is subsumed in mutual possession. "My beloved is mine and I am his." The conflict between love and politics is something I have noted throughout, for instance in discussing 8.11-12. As a small illustration, in our passage we have "wediglô ʿālay ʾahabâ" "And his banner/look upon me was love". If we read "diglô" as "banner", the superb martial symbol shelters and is in the service of love. According to the other reading, "look", the active male initiative "He brought me to the house of wine" turns to passive admiration /57/.

In 2.7, however, there is a prohibition, that also precedes the parallel passage in 8.5: "I adjure you, O daughters of Jerusalem, by the does and the hinds of the field, do not awaken or stir up love until it please" /58/. The daughters of Jerusalem, addressed always in the absence of the Lover, are outside, uninitiated. Love, then, and the knowledge it gives, is still inviolable. In 2.5 the desperate imperatives - as if she would die without raisin cakes and apples - are symptomatic of her love sickness. Here the didactic imperative is evidence of her knowledge /59/. Her teaching, the enlightenment she gives, is paradoxical: the wisdom of love is not to awaken it. Similarly, in 8.4 the adjuration contrasts tellingly with the key verb "I awakened you ..." The memory of the primordial past is juxtaposed with reverence for its undisturbed integrity. The Tree of Knowledge remains then intact, a private resource, like the garden, the fountain, and the other recollections of Paradise, that is yet ever-active in the world, always spontaneously awakening. The point of the oath is that the daughters of Jerusalem are all potential lovers, who must not spoil love, if it is to flourish.

Similarly, <u>knowledge</u> in the Song is an unknowing. This can

Chapter Four - Two Versions of Paradise

be seen most clearly in the one occurrence of the verb, 6.12, where, as we saw, knowledge is a sudden Socratic awareness of ignorance. Elsewhere in the Song, the false security of the "I" is ambushed by the demands of the "nepeš" or "heart", e.g. "I am sleeping, but my heart wakes". In the oath, love that pleases is gratuitous, taking us by surprise, coming unsummoned from ourselves. It is associated with animal nature, the earth, and sexuality, "bișbā'ot 'ô be'ayelôt haśśādēh" "by the gazelles or hinds of the field". In 8.5, the awakening under the apple tree has just this quality of innocent occurrence; she fortuitously happened on the Lover there. It illustrates "love that pleases".

The relationship between the apple trees in the Song, between 2.3-7 and 8.5, duplicates that between the Song and the garden of Eden. The apple tree in 2.3-7 has a social and naturalistic setting, characterised by quite sophisticated changes of register, from the courtly exchange of compliments in 2.1-3 to the cultivated abandonment of 2.5. 8.5 is a quasi-mythological fragment, in which the motifs of birth and awakening are explicitly stated /60/. The tree there is an originating symbol, whereas in 2.3 it is a self-conscious metaphor, and the likeness is a convenient fiction. In 8.5 it is <u>the</u> apple tree, here it is one of the familiar trees of the wood. The Lover is now an adult, becoming a tree in his turn; between him and the infant there is the same distance as that between 2.3 and 8.5. For the Beloved he substitutes that protective tree, performing the same functions, becoming one might say, its human manifestation.

Externally, the two images - the garden and the tree - have an identical structure in the Song of Songs. A mythological or archetypal prototype is correlated with a secondary elaboration. Like the apple tree in 2.3-7, the royal garden in 6.2-12 is an artificial reformulation of the original garden of 4.12-5.1.

In both cases, the garden is an inclusive, undivided image: the scene of action. In both passages involving the tree, however, there is a sharp division: between the desert and the tree in 8.5, wandering and repose; and in 2.3 between delicious memory and lovesickness. The tree is elusive, exclusive. The similarity expresses opposite tendencies. The mood in 2.3-7 is frantically dislocated, with constant changes of tense, imagery, and address; and the brooding on delight only aggravates lovesickness; it exemplifies extreme disjunction. In 8.5, however, the memory is contained within the couple, in the desert; there is a complementary integration. Here the situation in which the Beloved/mother woke the Lover/infant is transmuted completely into the mutual support of lovers. The apple tree is not the Lover, but the love and the awakening that they share, that still protects them and feeds them.

In 4.12 the Beloved is identified with the garden, in 2.3 the Lover with the tree. The tree grows in the garden, from the earth in 8.5, where the Lover is born, at the intersection of male and female forces. The tree and the garden are complementary, as vertical thrust and horizontal extension, axis and circle. The tree has an obvious and frequent phallic connotation, while the garden is the matrix and the container of delight. In terms of the myth, it is with knowledge that man imaginatively cultivates the garden.

The tree embodies the virile energy, like that of the fawns, that animates both lovers and gives life and creativity to the garden. It is shared by both lovers and grows between them, like the garden, in their garden. The inversion of lovers sheltered - the Beloved in 2.3, the Lover in 7.8-9 and 8.5 takes us by surprise, if the allusion is recognised: that underlying the dissociation there is reconciliation. It is part of the harmonising recapitulation in the Song. The two scenes set in the garden interact quite differently: the archetypal garden precedes its counterfeit, in the time of the poem as well as history, and is part of the same dramatic sequence: they collide explosively at its end, when the royal escapist garden is fused with that of the Beloved.

If the Song of Songs enacts a return to the garden of Eden, in which the Beloved replaces the garden, and is the presence behind all its forms, the tree is not only its male complement, but it relates to it in a subtle and simple way. In Genesis it forces the crisis, the divergence of man's imagination and God's creation, and potentialises the many points of tension in the account of the garden. Here it is the place where the lovers meet, and that sustains them. In Genesis the two trees are separate and contradictory, here they are one. For whereas in Genesis knowledge is of death, here knowledge is of life, of immortality. The Tree of Death has become a Tree of Life. David Clines has noted a similar inversion in a different literary context, that of Psalm 19 /61/.

The Tree of Life is not eaten in the garden of Eden. Man shows no interest in it, and as with the Tree of Knowledge, his indifference is impressive. The Tree of Life is mentioned in 2.9, and left in suspense until 3.22. In all this time, man

Chapter Four - Two Versions of Paradise

could have eaten of its fruit, and won immortality for us all. Possibly, Eve simply made an error of judgment, eating of the wrong tree in the wrong order. Even after his lapse, if he had become truly wise, man could have quickly repaired his omission. This indeed is the force of 3.22: "And now, supposing he stretch forth his hand and take also of the Tree of Life ..."

Before the catastrophe, there is no motivation for man to eat of the Tree of Life. Animals that do not know death do not desire immortality. After it, it seems, man is totally preoccupied with his nakedness and guilt. Consequently, he chooses the wrong strategy, trying to cover himself and hide in the bushes. What is most interesting, however, is God's apparent carelessness. He delivers the curses, including that of mortality, clothes man and woman, and suddenly remembers, as an afterthought, the Tree of Life. He too, like man, has forgotten its existence. In the tale as it stands, it is a last incalculable irony /62/.

Man leaves the Tree in the garden, and goes forth into the world possessed of the fruit of knowledge. But there the fruit has a reversed significance. 4.1 begins "wehā'ādām yāda' 'et-ḥawwāh 'ištô" "And the man knew Eve his wife". Knowledge is now that which unites, not that which separates man and woman. Moreover, from being the agent of death it becomes the instrument of life. Thus the implication we will find in 2.24 is confirmed; sexual knowledge brings us back to Eden.

In the Song of Songs, in 8.5 the lovers are wandering in a barren land, like Adam and Eve after they have left Eden. Between them they
bring the memory of their origins, the Tree of Life and Knowledge. But, as in Genesis, it is secluded in a mythic context. The Tree of Life is recognised in the Lover, but still inviolable. Finally, the parallel with the palanquin suggests that the lovers are on the way to Jerusalem, at the end of the long barren ascent from the Rift Valley /63/. The climax of 3.6-11 is the royal wedding; that of 8.5 is the affirmation of love. In the historical perspective of the Song, Solomon and Jerusalem represent the acme of achievement, the cultural reflex of Paradise. The progress of the lovers takes them from the primordial garden, the place of birth, through the desert to its civilised enactment /64/; it embraces the entire span of the Song. Corresponding to this temporal span, embracing the whole of history, is the socio-geographic spectrum, from the desert to the capital city, the tents of Kedar to Jerusalem.

Paronomasia: Nakedness and Subtlety

The story of the garden of Eden, and the whole of the Bible, turns on a pun:

וַיִּהְיוּ שְׁנֵיהֶם עֲרוּמִּים הָאָדָם וְאִשְׁתּוֹ וְלֹא יִתְבֹּשָׁשׁוּ: וְהַנָּחָשׁ הָיָה עָרוּם מִכֹּל חַיַּת הַשָּׂדֶה אֲשֶׁר עָשָׂה יְהוָה אֱלֹהִים

(2.25) And they were both of them naked ['ărûmmîm], the man and his wife, and they were not ashamed.
(3.1) Now the serpent was more subtle ['ărûm] than any of the beasts of the field that the Lord God had made.

The pun reveals a connection where none might be thought to exist, between two terms that in our world are mutually exclusive. Nakedness and subtlety are antithetical: subtlety ('ormâ) implies foresight, a clever disguise or displacement of intention or desire; nakedness is unsubtle, a brute statement of what we are. The pun is quite unambiguous; in each verse the meaning of the word is clear. It is their juxtaposition that makes it problematic.

The seriousness of the pun is underlined by context and content: the greater the weight of meaning attached to it, the more momentous it will be (Landy 1980a: 14-15). Humour always has its serious face, as we have known from Freud onwards; it converts into laughter humanity's most unac-

Chapter Four - Two Versions of Paradise

ceptable wishes and fears. Hence cruel jokes, gallows-humour, smut. It is natural, then, that humour begins when man becomes subversive or subtle, when his deeply destructive wishes (e.g. his rivalry with God) and dangers become manifest. Puns in particular have a highly emotive charge, since they threaten to reduce language to nonsense, the simplest form of humour, according to Freud (1905: 174-5) /65/.

But here there is no humour, merely two factual statements side by side. It is before humour, before the convulsion that gave man his wit and his grievance. This is probably why commentators have not done justice to it /66/. Moreover, it is told by the narrator at his most ironic /67/, his most impersonal. What we experience is something else: it is curiosity. Why should two such dissimilar concepts be expressed by the same word, and be placed strategically in such proximity? The wonder and the import of the pun is compounded by two other factors: it is a marked term, in the Structuralist idiom.

The first is the concepts themselves, whose confusion, whose juxtaposition, presents the central issue in the story. Man is innocently naked because he has not eaten of the Tree of Knowledge; the immediate consequence of his acquiring knowledge is that he knows that he is naked. The serpent is wise, subtle ('ārūm), clearly possessed of a species of knowledge. He knows, for instance, that the fruit of the Tree will make man like God. The conflict is essentially that of the impact of the knowledge of good and evil on nakedness. .

Secondly, it bridges the very centre, one might say the "eye" of the story, the still point between two movements. 'Arūm/'arūmmîm may be spatially six words apart, but the distance is syntactically enormous /68/: 2.25 ("And they were both of them naked, the man and his wife, and they were not ashamed") concludes the account of creation, the achievement of the garden; 3.1 ("And the serpent was more subtle ...") begins the account of its dissolution. Between them there is an unmitigated pause, heavily poignant, where the reader/listener may rest for a moment, so as not to lose too soon the sensation of fulfilment. On either side there is the pun that suggests a certain overlap, a déjà-vû, that the comfortable hiatus is treacherous.

Moreover, there is the Brobdingnagian reversal of our familiar assumptions. Animals are subtle, man is naked. Through the Tale man becomes subtle, and animals naked. Thus the pun focusses attention on a crucial transformation of function, on the ambiguity through which one incompatible term slides into the other.

The narrator records as one of the differences or anomalies of Eden: "And they were both of them naked, the man and his wife, and they were not ashamed." Nakedness is shameless; or there is as yet no shame, no boundary between man and woman /69/. The separated selves are not yet a problem. Why they should be emerges clearly from the preceding verses. First let us consider it in the abstract.

Nakedness in man is primarily a signifier, quite unequalled in intensity, as goes without saying - though Westermann, for example, finds shame inexplicable (1974b: 321). Good is on the right track, I think, when he correlates nakedness with helplessness, except that this need not exclude a sexual interpretation, as Good implies /70/. On the contrary, sexuality is especially vulnerable; as if to illustrate this, fig leaves cover only the genitals. Moreover, the defence is essentially symbolic, for it affords no physical protection: it is a sign, a gesture. For nakedness threatens immediate dissolution into "one flesh" (2.24), to undo the finely balanced differentiation so hardly achieved in the preceding narrative.

Shame is curiously both transitive and intransitive, something one feels in oneself and towards another person. It is expressed through modesty, an aversion of the eyes, a refusal to meet the gaze, interrupted by the state of confusion known as blushing, which is both a defiant protection, a rush of blood, and indicative of inner turbulence. The lowering of eyes directs attention to the ever more complex gravitational field between man and woman. On both sides there is a terror of exposure and a refusal to look too closely. But therewith develops the fascination with nudity, as the sign of the other as he/she is, in essence, simply.

At this point subtlety comes in. Through subtlety, cleverness, forethought - all the attributes suggested by '"ārûm" - man cooperatively creates his culture, through the sublimation of libidinal energy. By averting his eyes, he is forced to look upon the world in between the lovers, man and woman, and to enter into dialogue, a mode of indirect, cultural communication. The dialogue is a shock, that makes him aware of the other and interpret it; it initiates the intricacies of gesture and allusion, the play of metonomies and metaphors, through which we habitually talk to each other. But even more (and thereby) it makes us aware of the unfathomability of the other person, and consequently of

Chapter Four - Two Versions of Paradise

ourselves; so that what man really wishes to know is nakedness.

But shame has another function: it is a means of avowal. A blush indicates that something has been touched beyond the boundary, and attaches value to the person. Moreover, through subtlety unacknowledged desires may be expressed subtly, in disguise: hence the complex metalanguage of lovers.

Thus eating the fruit presents both the object of knowledge (Truth, the naked body) and the terrified reaction to it. Man opens his eyes - "wattippāqaḥnâ 'ênê šenêhem" - only to deprive them of their sight. We can now see the ambiguous relation between the quality of subtlety and cunning, represented by "'arûm" and knowledge. "'Ormâ" in the Wisdom tradition has both positive and negative connotations, it is both the agent of knowledge and its antagonist /71/; but in both cases it opposes one kind of knowledge to another. Through subtlety man comes to knowledge, and through subtlety, sewing figleaves, hiding in the garden, he attempts to deny it. Therewith begins the pull of obsessive attraction and desperate repression that conditions his reflexes in the world. 2.25, when man was naked and not ashamed, precedes this contention, and is for that reason unimaginable.

These themes should be familiar from the previous chapters: the pun neatly compresses the ambiguity of the Song. The Song is a return to a world where man was naked and unashamed, to birth, to the true knowledge afforded by the tree in the garden, but it can do so only through subtlety, the interplay of gender, the aesthetic process. It remains language, allusion, communicating in the interstices of the words, to us who are outside the experience. It goes from metonym to metonym, employing all its extraordinary poetic resources to transcend language (Paz 1969: 44-46). As I suggested earlier, the poet always speaks where he should be silent.

Linguistically, nakedness can only express itself in silence, "the heart of light" (T. S. Eliot, "The Wasteland"). Between lovers silence can either represent a failure of communication or total communion. We have for instance the significance of the eyes gazing into each other. Melanie Klein says:

> However gratifying it is in later life to express thoughts and feelings to a congenial person, there remains the unsatisfied longing for an understanding without words - ultimately for the earliest relation with the mother. (1963: 100)

Philosophically, too, the poem is a quest that meanders through the senses so as to make all experience participate in that of the lovers. The quest is an inexhaustible labour, that is a form of love play, of caresses designed to draw a response, to induct nakedness into society and language. Wooing the truth weaves the tissue of language around it, beautifies it, comparable to the induction of the Dark Beloved into society, in 1.5-6 etc.

At the same time there is a reverse process in the Song. The lovers draw apart, construct screens of images in which to shelter. We find a pattern of hide-and-seek, fusion and definition, flickering between recollection, immediacy, and anticipation. Subtlety is employed with remarkable versatility between the lovers both persuasively (e.g. 5.2) to procure delight and as a means of dalliance, whether to prolong the pleasure or to decline advances. In 1.7-8, for example, where the Beloved fears being an "'ōṭeyâ", we found that a whole range of subtle devices measures the distance between the lovers.

In particular, shame is the great enemy of the lovers. We have found metonymic displacement onto secondary sexual features; an array of metaphors, that distract attention, and superimpose the body of the Beloved onto that of the world; the transformation of darkness into brilliance, of spontaneity into civilisation; the refusal to be explicit, to reach the point of sexual climax; and the mystification of the enigma. The "wasf" is a painstaking poetic dissection of the Beloved's body that curiously turns nakedness into an abstraction, and robs it of tension and vitality. In particular, it is an effort of control, most intense when most under pressure, as when the girl's thighs and vulva are imagined as works of craftsmanship, owing their existence to the artist, possessed by the eye as the bowl - "'aggan hassahar" - is possessed by the drinker (7.2-3). On the other side, there is the statuesque Lover, whose head is gold, his belly ivory, his thighs alabaster. The images make him impenetrable and cold, and incapable of motion, in other words, safely exalted.

This formal detachment is ever imperilled by subsidiary details; it is ever in a state of tension. One finds that the Lover's features express all the plasticity and energy that is sealed in the body. And then each image is divided against itself. The gilded hands are inlaid with "taršîš" /72/; the belly encrusted with sapphires /73/. It suggests depth and cracks, surface within surface and an inner resonance. The fluidity is carried by the extraordinarily seductive sound of the verse

Chapter Four - Two Versions of Paradise

(which is typical of the entire sequence) - "yādāw gelîlê zāhāw memullā'îm battaršîš, mē'āw 'ešet šēn me'ullepet sappîrîm" "His hands are rods of gold inlaid with tarshish-stone, his belly is a plaque of ivory covered with sapphires" [5.14]) - with its intricate alliteration of "l" and "š". Likewise, in the description of the Beloved, the images are <u>containers</u> of uncontrollable excitement. On the periphery of vision, we have sexual emblems such as the lilies in 7.3, with which the corn i.e. the formulated landscape is bordered.

The suggestiveness of inarticulate symbolic pressure and the euphemistic metalanguage through which it is expressed brings us to the question of shame. Shame is primarily a function of society in the Song; first of all, through the conventions of art, the things a poet may not say. The lovers only feel shame in a social context, and time and again it hinders their fulfilment. But I do not think it ever interposes itself between the couple when they are undisturbed by outsiders in the Song. Nakedness causes perturbation, and an aversion of the eyes; but not shame. For shame, as we have seen, is intrinsically linked with envy; moral disapprobation of the lovers is in proportion to repressed desire. We may see this, for instance, in the ferocity of the watchmen in 5.7, who personify the vigilance of the law, that imposes shame and prohibition, and yet who are human beings, with an ambivalence towards licentiousness. In the parallel passage in 3.3 the girl asks them "Have you seen whom my soul loves?" apparently expecting a sympathetic answer. Though their reaction is not recorded, it may be inferred that patrols were not always disapproving, and might even assist lovers.

The intimacy of the lovers corresponds to the imagery of the garden and its paradigm. This is the sphere of true knowledge in the Song, the knowledge of life and nakedness. Society imposes shame because it is ignorant, because it has forgotten the true value of love. In its eyes, one who gives all his substance for love has committed the greatest folly, and "they would surely despise him" (8.7). In the Song then, man is fallen because he is ignorant. Love remains a private matter: lovers cannot kiss in the street (8.1). Yet they can only meet through the public world, running the risks of nocturnal adventures, and its hostility remains a perpetual frustration. In 8.1 and 5.2, as we have seen, and especially in the formulaic equivalence "my sister, my bride", this is represented by the prohibition of incest.

Yet society enshrines shamelessness at its heart, in the

person of the wanton king, and with the moral support of the daughters of Jerusalem, who comfort the Beloved and exalt her as head of the alternative hierarchy, as the "fairest of women", just after she has been humiliated by the watchmen (5.9). This is part of the process of integration in the Song, the union of the Dark Beloved and the king, nature and culture.

If shame clothes a person, shaming disrobes him. The watchmen strip the Beloved of her mantle, her "redid" (5.7), as a sign of her shamelessness, but also of society's latent desires and fears, just as the brothers assist the sun in darkening her in 1.6.

The Beloved especially is the victim of shame; it is she who fears being despised in 8.1 and 1.6, and it is she who is beaten. The Lover, on the contrary, seems quite immune from reproach for amorous exploits. Only if he surrenders himself to love, as in 8.7, inverting male dominance, is he shamed. All this fully conforms to Mediterranean mores, where the lover is expected to be bold, and the girl shy /74/. Thus in 5.7 all our sympathies are with the Beloved in her travail; in 8.1, as in 1.7, the unfairness of traditional values is communicated through the rhetorical fantasy, with its note of petulance, and through the final allusion to herself alone as vulnerable to aspersions: "gam lō' yābuzû lî" "they would not despise me". The imbalance is indicative of a corrupt and cruel society, that has forgotten the original identity of man and woman.

The pun in Genesis is itself subtle, an ingenious reflection upon its subject. It superimposes one concept on the other, in much the same way as the ambiguities in the Song of Songs. In fact, it is a poetic device, and as such works against sequential language, robbing it of its clear definition. Poetry, even the clearest, is an alchemie du verbe, working with sound against sense, recreating the world in the human image. In particular, it impresses itself allophonically, beneath or in between the words, bestowing a certain aura and striving, in the spell of the Pathetic Fallacy, to achieve a miraculous empathy with the sensual world. Thus language undoes itself, and attempts through subtlety to express nakedness.

We can see this in the consideration of language in the Garden of Eden. God brings Adam the animals to name:

וְכֹל אֲשֶׁר יִקְרָא־לוֹ הָאָדָם נֶפֶשׁ חַיָּה הוּא שְׁמוֹ׃

Chapter Four - Two Versions of Paradise

(2.19) And every thing that the Man would call it, each living soul, that is its name.

Each creature has its fixed designation, implicitly not an arbitrary configuration of sounds, but an essential part of its being /75/. The text asserts unambiguously "that is its name", as if there can be no other. A certain point of ambiguity is whether Man perceives this identity, or imparts it. At any rate, naming is the human contribution to their creation, and the only assignment that specifically devolves on man in the garden, through which he "works it and keeps it" /76/. Classification and onomastica will remain human preoccupations /77/, illustrating the importance of this primary task, through which man symbolically possesses the inarticulate world, is even responsible for its identity, and introduces it to the imagination /78/.

Nevertheless, this is not yet a language. Things are defined in their particularity, but without relation. Only when woman is created can language begin, since language is essentially combinative. Then we get names that are not discrete, but syntactically expressive. We have "ʾādām/ʾādāmâ", "ʾîš/ʾiššâ". Language now escapes from parsimony, the strictness of magical formulation: both man and woman in the narrative have two names, as does God. The excess of words over things permits poetic transcendence, since vocabulary is unlimited. Jakobson considers parallelism to be the basis of poetry, allowing the manipulation of synonyms for pleasure, to invent new meanings (1960: 368ff).

We find an illustration at the very first opportunity. We do not hear Adam speak until the woman is created. Then he says:

זֹאת הַפַּעַם עֶצֶם מֵעֲצָמַי וּבָשָׂר מִבְּשָׂרִי לְזֹאת יִקָּרֵא אִשָּׁה
כִּי מֵאִישׁ לֻקֳחָה־זֹּאת׃

(2.23) And now this - bone of my bone, and flesh of my flesh. This shall be called Woman [ʾiššâ], since from man she was taken. (2.23)

Critics have long perceived in this a rudimentary poem, characterised by metre, chiasmus, and parallelism /79/. The two expressions, "ʿeṣem mēʿaṣāmay ûbāśār mibbeśārî" "bone of my bone and flesh of my flesh", are a complementary paraphrase for the whole person, like "good and evil" in the universalist interpretation /80/. The repetition and variation amplify the statement, with purely emotive effect; the duplication of language suggests a surcharge of meaning, contained within the metrical structure. The second couplet overlays syntactic correspondence with lexical inversion; it begins and ends with "zō'ṭ" "this", while the differentiating couple, whose phonological correspondence occasions it, meet in the middle:

Lexis:	A		B	B		A
Sentence:	lezō'ṭ	yiqqārê	'iššâ	kî	mē'îš	luqohâ zō'ṭ
Syntax:	PP	Passive			PP	Passive

Instead of redundancy, we have antithesis, repetition in a mirror. Each phrase in the first couplet may similarly be divided: "'eṣem//mē'aṣāmay", "bāśār//mibbeśārâ" /81/; each describes the splitting of identical terms. The poetic structure metaphorically reflects the theme of the poem, the first wondering perception of diverging likeness.

In the Song of Songs, we came to the same moment at the end of the last chapter:

הִנָּךְ יָפָה רַעְיָתִי הִנָּךְ יָפָה עֵינַיִךְ יוֹנִים: הִנְּךָ יָפֶה דוֹדִי אַף נָעִים

(1.15) Behold, you are fair, my love, behold you are fair, your eyes are doves.
(16) Behold, you are fair, my love, also pleasant ...

Only the suffixes, and the slight projection of "hinn-āk/ekâ" distinguish the lovers. The convergence of cultural poles, the Song of Songs and the garden of Eden, is instructive of the whole process. In the Song it is a sophisticated inarticulacy, a triumphant admission of failure. The naming of woman in Genesis represents an original naivety. The most conspicuous word is the demonstrative pronoun "zō'ṭ" "this". Adam keeps saying "this", like the Israelites naming manna; seeing and trying to define it for the first time. Furthermore, it is completely impersonal. He does not say "I call you Woman", but "This shall be called Woman, for from man she [lit. this] was taken". It suggests that he cannot conceive himself yet as an active subject. It takes us back to a very early linguistic phase, before the mastery of shifters /83/. The events seemingly take place of their own accord between the persons, at the point of division.

Poetry thus begins with the creation of woman, the first relationship. It expresses incommunicable emotion and elemental mystery: "this". We find the first perception of likeness or metaphor of causation; "'iššâ" too is the first mnemonic sign, that from man she was taken /84/.

There is a second illustration. At the end of the passage,

Chapter Four - Two Versions of Paradise

the woman is renamed Eve, "ḥawwâ", "the mother of all that live" (3.20). There may be a surreptitious pun on a synonym for the serpent (ḥwt, ḥiwia', etc.) /85/. If so, it does not imply that the woman should be identified with the serpent. Like "ʿārûm/ʿarûmmîm" it mediates contraries. The woman and the serpent are antagonists between whom the pun suggests a transfer of power, of essence. The new name inverts the old: she who was taken from man is now the universal mother. More remarkably, the serpent, the instrument of death, now fulfils that function. Life or being (ḥwt) is expressed by the same word as serpent.

The imagination and foresight that man needed to tend the garden in 2.15 now becomes autonomous, and is redirected to different, often subversive, ends. But there is another point also. Nakedness does not merely threaten sexual dissolution. There is a fear that if we look too closely, we will find both good and evil, an incarnate malice. It takes the form of the serpent, whose subtlety enables it to become manifest. This destructive principle will introduce the next section.

Dramatis Personae: Serpent and Woman

The Serpent is "subtler than any of the beasts of the field that the Lord God had made". The text, through its use of "ʿārûm", presupposes intentionality, that the serpent knew the answers to his questions and deliberately provoked the Fall. To understand this singleminded and selfless hate one must go back a few verses. And one must understand his nature.

Investigation has so far proceeded mostly from the standpoint of comparative mythology. This is perhaps because of the paucity of internal and Biblical evidence, though A. J. Williams devotes his thesis to determining its function as defined in the story. But this must be supplemented by the eye of the critic; "the first step", John Armstrong remarks, is "to look at it". According to his attentive fantasy (34-6) the unpredictable, sinuous serpent "approaches the verge of amorphousness" /86/. The mythological/ psychoanalytic evidence is of value, but only insofar as it fits the text, with which we engage our perceptions.

The snake is poisonous, destroying man painfully and subtly from within, with a tiny wound. It is the most insidious of natural perils, unseen and unmotivated. Moreover, whereas normally the human life enters the animal that devours him, here the animal essence is transmitted to the human. Snakes are associated with metamorphosis - examples are legion, but most horribly in Dante's Malebolgia. The venom, secreted from within, is its principal attribute. It becomes the <u>venomous</u> serpent, incarnate antilife.

And yet it is beautiful. Its beauty is Dionysian, a whirl of patterned marking and iridescent colour that is also a camouflage, escaping into the background. It requires an effort of attention to distinguish it, or more usually a surprise, chancing on it in repose and unexpectant. The inarticulate offers itself to us innocently and miraculously, contained in a living body. There is both attraction towards the unformed, and a fearful neutralisation of it, manifest in the mixture of thrill and detachment in the aesthetic process.

In Jungian psychology (Jung 1959b: 189, 234, 244-5 etc.), the serpent is a symbol for the most deeply unconscious part of the self, with its own coldly instinctual wisdom and healing capacity; it is that which connects, and hence incarnates the tension between opposites (1959b: 247). "Traditionally the snake stands for the vulnerable spot in man: it personifies his shadow ...", for example, it thus comes to represent the sexual complement, the animus or anima (see Dyke for dream-illustrations).

The mass of mythological material on serpents is so extensive that theses have been written on it, e.g. A. J. Williams, The Significance of the Gen. 3 Serpent. Karen Joines' short article is thus welcome /87/. She documents three functions of the serpent corresponding to the Genesis myth: immortality, wisdom and chaos. The destructive principle perpetually generates new life; it is associated with the child, the spirit of rebirth. The other two terms, chaos and wisdom, through which man makes sense of the world,

Chapter Four - Two Versions of Paradise

are normally antonymic. Ophidic wisdom, however, is the knowledge of chaos, or that chaos produces; it is characteristically esoteric, and gnomic, for example, in the Delphic oracle.

The convergence of description and myth is clear: the venomous formlessness of the serpent is a metaphor for seditious chaos. The connection between chaos and vitality is reproduced in the birth of the very young instinctual child, the figure of the future (Jung & Kerenyi: 113), of the life cycle, who is also, as we know, in the grip of terrifying destructive impulses. He is furthermore a very beautiful, marginal creature between life and non-life (the sense of miracle on seeing a newborn baby), as between man and animal.

But children are not wise; nor are serpents. They are mysterious, and thus the source of secret knowledge. Observing children, we travel back to our own origins, our inner determinants, just as in the serpent we come to the edge of our articulate vision. If it is a symbol for the psyche, its wisdom is subtle, pervasive, and often contrary to conscious intentions. It points out what is unknown in man - his secret self.

The serpent embodies the Dionysian duality of life and death, the beauty of change, and the abolition of contraries. In particular, it is the visible sign of man's most intolerable wish, to destroy what is human, the trappings of culture, the reasoning, differentiating intellect, in other words subtlety; for underneath there is nakedness, threatening dissolution, and it is nakedness he stands for.

In the garden of Eden, the serpent manifests himself under the aspect of shrewdness: "And the serpent was more subtle than any of the beasts of the field ..." (3.1). Its wisdom is that it instinctively grasps and exploits the woman's unconscious desire, to be equal to God; it exposes and puts into words that part of herself of which she is still unaware. Moreover, it holds forth the prospect of knowledge, which it may or may not possess, and is thus the source of wisdom, of man's scientific promptings. Its knowledge is esoteric, contained magically in the fruit of a tree, and it is defined in the enigmatic phrase "good and evil", a formula which, typically of mystery, generates infinite interpretation. With its forked tongue, it introduces doubt and the opacity of language. To the serpent, and henceforth to the imagination, everything is possible, an open question. It takes the part of the deceiver, like many seers and oracles, for this is the way of the unconscious, that expresses its subversive message subtly, and in disguise. But more profoundly, we are left in doubt as to whether he is really a deceiver (i.e. the deception is that he is deceiving) /88/. Everything he claims comes true: Man acquires knowledge, becomes like God, and does not die. What he does is to introduce the plurality of meaning; the intrinsic ambiguity, and hence deceptiveness, of the world /89/.

Now the anarchic implications are clearer. The serpent incites rebellion, tempting the Woman to "become like God", to overthrow the established hierarchy. He does this by presenting her with the confusion of the world, that the unthinkable is possible. He transmits his venom to us, which is not merely mortality, but a permanent dissatisfaction. Man becomes a curious, analytic creature, reducing forms to constituents, syntheses to hypotheses. The world becomes deceptive, a mesh of appearances hiding structures, and multiple. The archetypal Man moreover breaks up into individuals, only provisionally and imperfectly organised in society; the human world is fissile and fractious. At bottom there is death, that both stimulates man's critical endeavour /90/, and has a lasting attraction. The serpent's gift of mortality promises integration of animate and inanimate, and a final resting point. It evades us and provokes us, and willy-nilly compels us. If the love of the truth is most characteristically human, it is destroyed by death - or internalised death - that is its ultimate object.

For this reason, the serpent is an agent of regeneration to refer to Joines' schematisation. It is he who mediates between the garden and the world, and assists in the delivery of the human race. He contains also the possibility of imaginative integration, for, in the garden, his is the voice of hope and ambition: we shall become like gods, we shall know good and evil. This hope does not vanish with the Fall, for mankind does not die, as the serpent truthfully promised. As well as the venomous mortality of the serpent, man also inherited his various beauty: the versatility of imaginative creation.

The serpent speaks, and in this respect differs from the species in our world, as in its posture, which was probably upright, and its less bestial diet: presumably, in contrast to dust, it shared the fructarian sustenance of man. Its loquacity occasions no surprise; we recognise it as belonging to a genre, shared by children's stories and South American myths, but surprisingly rare in the Ancient Near East /91/. In South

Chapter Four - Two Versions of Paradise

American myths, typically, the animal (jaguar, tapir, etc.) is the master of some distinctive human skill, such as cooking or making fire, and is divested of it, often through marital complications; it then becomes hostile to man, loses its language, its means of communicating with him, and its previously ambiguous status. An inherent potentiality in the world thus becomes a human acquisition, the substance of thought, existent in time. In our myth, the serpent is the master of knowledge, i.e. all culture, to which man will attain; as a result of the Fall there is enmity between him and Woman, instead of their discourse.

The genre is naturalistic, since it concerns the evolution of man from nature; the serpent - the "nāḥāš" - is a species to be found in our world, small enough to be spoken with. In contrast, there are the vast and formless archetypal monsters of cosmogonic myths, that concern the evolution of the world from chaos /92/.

The serpent is a marginal creature, intermediate between man and animal, and yet superior to both, through its sapience. In Freilich's exciting theory of myth, which he illustrates with the story of the garden of Eden, it is the marginal, lonely creature, the anomalous term that cannot be integrated, that gives the myth its dynamic /93/. He calls it the Nonsense-in-Myth-Strategy: that the clues to the message, as in dream-analysis, are to be found in apparently nonsensical details (Freilich: 209-12). In this case, he says, the serpent, the marginal creature, introduces uncertainty; he makes man marginal in his turn, "a limit of the world", as Wittgenstein says (Tractatus: 5.632).

Freilich's theory has much to recommend it; nevertheless in my view unsurprising components are, on the face of it, as worthy of consideration as arresting eccentricities. The story is one whole, all of whose elements have functional importance. Moreover, in his particular analysis, Freilich isolates progression and differentiation at the expense of regression and integration. In other words, he fails to recognise the work of the combinative poetic principle, for instance the paradigm of the serpent, to which we now turn.

The serpent communicates the message of the animals; in fact, it is an animal, one of "the beasts of the field that the Lord God had made". The reference reminds us of the creation of the animals, and sets the temptation in a wider context. Animals were created to be partners of man, to assuage his loneliness (2.19-20). But they are not partners for man: "ûleʼādām lōʼ māṣāʼ ʽēzer kenegdô" "And for Man, he did not find a helpmeet like unto him" (2.20). Instead they are living evidence of the failure of the attempt, and his imperfection alone /94/. Woman then supercedes the animals, succeeding in being a partner where they were inadequate. But woman is man, a divided self. Man is thus still alone, amid the volatile frustrated creatures, his original companions.

The serpent then has reason to resent the woman, a hatred that implicates both man and God, who rejected him. It is in the first place jealousy, that the woman supplanted him. Jealousy, enmity towards a rival, is a comparatively mature and rational emotion, developing first and archetypically with the Oedipal child (Klein 1957: 32); it is preceded by envy, the hatred of the loved object because it is withheld from us. The envious person cannot bear other people's happiness or autonomy. It is a more total and despairing impulse than jealousy; its only gratification is destruction /95/.

The serpent's motives are of course hidden from us, and to a certain extent enigmatic. We can only deduce them, I suggest, from his actions and situation /96/. The serpent is an excluded creature, as we have seen, with a grievance against the whole order of creation. It is sharpened by his intelligence and percipience; no animal is so aware of his deprivation, exacerbated by his superiority. He employs his talents to ruin the happiness of the human couple and disturb the divine equilibrium, that cannot survive his chagrin. His is thus the voice of envy, with which he instigates man. But to diagnose the serpent's condition as envious is insufficient, since it does not allow for his ambivalent complexity. Envy is inseparable from desire; it is precisely because an object is loved that its denial is hated. Envy may be confused with love, both with defensive idealisation and manic greed. The serpent's envious attack on the lovers takes the form of seduction, apparently altruistic, even selfless (indeed, envy is characteristically satisfied with Schadenfreude, without benefit or even with injury to oneself). Thus he achieves the object of his jealousy, detaching the woman from the man, taking revenge on him, attracting her. Jealousy may embrace both partners in the relationship, as in the Oedipal triangle; nevertheless, in our text the interest of the serpent in the woman is mainly, if not exclusively, instrumental. Here we come to the transformation into love; through seducing the woman, the serpent reaches the man. In other words, the excluded animal once more participates in relationships, fulfilling his purpose, through the woman. The effect,

Chapter Four - Two Versions of Paradise

however, is to estrange the woman from the man, in the embarrassment at nakedness; she absorbs and comes to represent the animal world /97/.

This leads us to a further difficulty. Why did God create the animals, fallacious partners of man? The error contains a core of insight. Animals are partners of man, with which we share the animate, sensual world /98/. Yet they are differentiated from man by everything man lacks: their inherent spontaneity, their freedom from culture. They are natural creatures, for whom nakedness is not shameful. They remind man of his origins, not only palaeontologically, but in terms of the myth, of his irrecoverable innocence. That man cannot find his complement among them is indicative of the cost of being human. Throughout history man's relation with the animals will be compounded of exploitation, distrust, and a hidden yearning. In Messianic Prophecies history will close with their reconciliation.

Adam gives names to the animals, drawing them into the human family (Duncan: 192). Some of them will stay, as pets or livestock, fulfilling their function as an "ʿēzer", a "help" to him, but in a subordinate position. "ʿEzer kenegdô" however implies complementarity, an opposition of equals. The animals cannot match (kenegdô) the overture, to refer to a poem ("Prayer") by Abraham Shlonsky (my transl.):

> Many times now have we probed with our speech
> Among all your creatures - but they could not understand.

Instead they make overtures to the woman. The woman is the messenger for the animals, man's erstwhile companions, and contrariwise, as a human being, reestablishes that relationship: she turns from the man to the serpent.

The serpent makes the unthinkable possible, that man should be like God, partake of the tree and not perish. Listening to the animal, ironically she contends with God, opening to the suggestion from below to surpass herself. The enclosed carefully graded categories threaten to become a continuum. For thought trespasses, with its absurd ambition and its compromised sources. New thoughts have a Dionysian, subversive quality, coming as they do from outside the human frame of reference. Their discoverer mediates between the human and non-human domains; he is associated with divinity, and has a somewhat mantic quality /99/.

At the moment of conception, the thought is almost naked, unencumbered with commentaries, and intoxicatingly beautiful, with a "beauty we are only just able to bear". It emerges from the encounter with the world around man, so that the serpent represents thought as well as the psyche, the natural impulse to think, to gain knowledge, despite every prohibition, as well as the object of thought: man himself, and his world. It is a dual impulse, that both isolates man from other creatures and enables him to consider them; both a reversion to their original relationship, a vicarious consummation, and the occasion for their decisive breach.

The Song of Songs is a great human effort to understand and communicate natural beauty; here we find its origins, in Beauty itself, in the Serpent. The ambivalence of Beauty is inherent in the dual principles of life and death, the insidious promise of the serpent and his fatal seductiveness.

Animals in the Song participate in the relationship of the lovers through metaphor; the lovers symbolically adopt the animal kingdom /100/. In them the abortive union of Genesis is fulfilled; they are quite literally "kenegdô", a figurative complement. It is their authority that the Beloved invokes to protect the inviolability of love. The animals - the deer and gazelles - have a benign supervisory function, to safeguard the Beloved's teaching (2.7, 3.5). Her wisdom, based on her experience and status as the supreme lover, expresses itself as deference to natural forces and creatures. They communicate sexual energy, as we have seen, man's physical endowment. In the lovers, animals represent a surcharge of instinctual wisdom, and energy. Like the serpent, the Lover is a composite creature, animal and man, nakedness and subtlety. But the access of animal wisdom restores him to harmony. Its association with divinity as the innate vital principle is imparted through the adjuration of 2.7 and 3.5, with its paronomasia and solemnity /101/, as well as through more general cultural considerations, appertaining to the typical animals of the Song. Whereas in Genesis it suggests that man eats of the fruit, provoking human initiative, here wisdom consists of restraint, patient inhibition: "Do not waken or stir up love until it please" /102/. Wisdom in the Song, as we have seen, is an unknowing, a surrender of cleverness and foresight. Animal wisdom then is correlated with the wisdom of the Song, opposed to the way of the world (cf. pp. 137-39).

If we investigate the fauna of the Song more closely, the inversion becomes clearer. It is a distinction between two different types of wisdom. There is no serpent in the Song; no hermetic creature. The serpent's words, double-edged, fork-tongued, introduce the hermetic quest /103/: to become

Chapter Four - Two Versions of Paradise

like God, and to know his secret intentions. They remain mysterious, fraught with malevolent background. The serpent is worldly-wise ("Ah, God knows ...!"), deceptive. Yet the knowledge he claims reveals an affinity with God. He is thus a sacred creature, whose language is wilfully enigmatic. It is composed of half-truths - man will not die immediately or altogether, only in one sense will become like God - and reflects, as we have seen, a profound ambivalence. The enigma, such as whether the serpent or God are telling the truth, initiates man to the opacity of language, as Scriabine says /104/, and to the hermetic secret, such as the fruit of the tree.

The animals principally aligned with the lovers are the fawn and the dove. I will concentrate here on the comparison with the serpent, and their Paradisal association. In contrast to the serpent, they are gentle, not poisonous nor hostile, and shy. They suggest a quiescence, an absorption in the present peacefully grazing among lilies or refreshed by pools of water. Whereas in the garden of Eden, animals are intrinsically dissatisfied and unfulfilled, here they possess an unthinking contentment, while it is man who is driven by his desire and contrary wishes. It is he who is excluded, through his self-consciousness, from nature, rather than the animals who are excluded by man. The animals live before history, in the timeless unchanging world of the garden that the Song persistently tries to establish. Moreover, the fawn and the dove have especially strong infantile and blissful connotations. In the Song, the fawn is an image for the breasts (4.5, 7.4), the dove corresponds to the newborn child (6.9). Both are in retreat from man, the dove "in the clefts of the rock" (2.14), the deer with its proverbial swiftness and justified timidity. Its repose is rare and tense; at any moment it might become aware of our presence. We thus experience what it was like before fear interposed itself between men and animals. Here it is safe, between the lovers /105/. Its beauty is always about to vanish; in that it arouses man's most sadistic impulses. Sadism is linked with envy, as was the case of the Dark Beloved, since the fawn possesses what the hunter most lacks: gentleness, spontaneity, grace. Hunting is a measure of man's exclusion from Paradise, and is linked, Northrop Frye remarks, with metamorphosis (1976: 105). Between the lovers, the fawn is safe; for they contain its wildness and nakedness. The pasture in 4.5 - whether or not the fawns actually eat the lilies - is idyllic, and hence poignant. Fawns are not often so fortunate. In temporary conjunction with the garden in springtime, the world has achieved perfection. Accordingly the wild fawn has his tame counterpart within the garden, the king/lover, "who feeds among the lilies" (2.16, 6.3).

The dove in the clefts of the rock is cajoled into appearing, suggesting a bond between man and nature, desert and civilisation, that underlies the spectrum between the tents of Kedar and the curtains of Solomon in 1.5. Similarly, the fawn/Lover is not running to escape from man, but towards the Beloved; the Lover as fawn "leaping on the mountains, bounding on the hills" (2.8), is carefree with a sure-footed vigour. It is an irresponsible and sure-footed delight in his body that the Beloved imagines, and that invites her to share the spring. The voice of the dove in 2.14, however, is detached and reticent. It is pleasant, "ʿārēb", and plaintive, speaking to man and soothing him. Its message, in the Bible generally, is of a sympathy between man and nature, and especially a sharing in sadness /106/. The voice is correlated with that of the Beloved as singer in 8.13; through verbal echo as well as paradigmatic convergence. The Beloved's voice is both that of dove and singer; to both the Lover wishes to listen, and cannot. Birdsong and poetry, the garden and wilderness, correspond, as with the fawn; the lulling musical voice that is the Beloved's natural not cultural gift. Like the voice of the turtledove in spring (2.12), it brings life to the poem, animating its significations. Thus it too is associated with a recondite wisdom, namely that of the poem /107/. The poem is itself hermetic, a coded allusive text conjuring a mystery beyond words. Whereas the serpent's wisdom is speculative and intuitive, an intellectual rebellion against the facts of existence, that of the animals is an innocent acceptance. It is an innate rapport, an effortless skill that the Song cultivates, and that is the goal of the hermetic quest.

Thus the serpent, fawn and dove are characterised by complementary opposition. The serpent is more subtle than the other animals, with his combination of opposites, death and renewal, wisdom and chaos. He launches man on his career as a self-reflecting stranger. His ever-changing beauty, as the most open of structures, contrasts with the firm lines and harmonious proportions of the deer, and the formal simplicity of the dove. Their perfection arouses nostalgia; in a Paradisal retreat, it shatters as soon as they become aware of our presence. Both fawn and dove project the paradigm of the garden into the untamed environment;

Chapter Four - Two Versions of Paradise

they are secure and tranquil, free from mortal apprehension and liberated from necessity. They represent the garden in the world, with its extraordinary vulnerability. The Song, with its polymorphous subtlety, a work of civilised suggestion, takes its strength from animal resources. It is the familiar Dionysian regression, characteristic of the Pastoral. The king, the most sophisticated of men, is a fawn, who goes down to the garden that is safe from death and time; the royal union in 6.9 is also that of ideal creatures, fawn and dove, of the human and natural orders. Analogously, the animal consummation takes place in a human setting, between the breasts or eyes.

The relationship between the fawn and the dove is parallel to that we discerned between the two gardens. The fawn is in haste to reach the Beloved, a restlessness that is only appeased when "he feeds among the lilies", in a maternal ambience. It corresponds also to the inversion of masculine and feminine imagery, the identification of the Beloved with the garden which the Lover enters.

The fawn, the creature of perpetual motion, and the dove, with its inaccessible song, are complementary figures, for energy and stillness, day and night, purity and innocence. The serpent disrupts the apparently perfect wholeness of Paradise; the fawn and the dove, never quite reaching it, unite it.

The two other animals associated with the lovers require little attention: the mare, compared with the Beloved in 1.9, and the raven, mentioned in passing as an image for the Lover's hair (5.12). The latter is quite insignificant, coupled with the doves in 5:13 to produce the familiar black/white antithesis /108/. The former has been examined in a very different context; its ambiguity of gender relates it in a general way to the problem of androgeneity that we will discuss later. It illustrates the civilised exploitation of Dionysian energy, for instance in the licensed "sparagmos" of warfare. It is on our side of Paradise, a human instrument of pride and aggression. The fawn and the dove are visions of uncorrupted innocence, more wistfully compelling and more persuasive emblems for the lovers, in their innocence.

Other animals in the Song, the lions and leopards of 4.8, are in our world voracious and intractable. Here, however, in the original nexus of Lebanon, the home of lions, the Beloved is unafraid /109/. Its association with Eden needs no further discussion (see p. 196 above). The coexistence is a reminder of the preexistent harmony between man and beast, when man had dominion over animals, from the point of view of historical estrangement. It is therefore fragile, and irrecoverable.

Finally, there are the foxes: אֶחֱוִי

לָנוּ שֻׁעָלִים שֻׁעָלִים קְטַנִּים מְחַבְּלִים כְּרָמִים וּכְרָמֵינוּ סְמָדַר׃

(2.15) Catch us foxes, little foxes, who raid vineyards; our vineyards in blossom.

The foxes are guileful, riddling creatures in fable and proverb; and thus comparable to the cunning serpent. Like the serpent, they are associated with theft, unremittingly hostile to man /110/. Their threat however is minimised; they are little foxes, easily caught. In folklore they are frequently foolish /111/. On the sexual level, where in the Song keeping vineyards is equivalent to preserving virginity, the verse mingles the thrill of fantasies of rape with the power to avert it, an assertion of human strength. The vineyard is an image of civilisation, as we have seen, like the garden, eroded by nature and time; here for the only time in the Song the enmity of the wild beasts is enacted. As in the garden of Eden, the object of envious greed is the woman. The attack however fails; and the foxes are caught, and appropriated: "Catch us foxes ..." As with the lions and leopards in 4.8, it has an air of enchantment; in reality, foxes are not easily caught; Levinger suggests that it is a nursery rhyme (34). The woman calls upon unspecified others /112/, perhaps the community at large, to be "noṭrîm", to protect her vineyard,

Chapter Four - Two Versions of Paradise

whose inviolability is threatened; an inversion of 1.6, where she guards those of others, but has neglected her own. The foxes become attributes of the Beloved, things attached to her ("'eḥezû lānû" "Catch for us") /113/, possibly amatory conquests, evidence of her power. At the same time they reveal her helplessness, and her need for assistance. The civilisation that the vineyard symbolises and the Beloved guards is both triumphant and vulnerable. The ambivalence of the Song towards it is especially acute /114/. The verse ends with an assertion of seductiveness: "ûkerāmênû semādar" "Our vineyards in blossom". The phrase in apposition suggests both a causal link with the raid, and a self-reflection evoking qualities of tenderness and possibly assurance.

Animals in the Song by and large constitute an idealised Paradisal grouping, a natural commonwealth in which the lovers participate, and which miraculously is neither persecuted by man nor at odds with him. The lions and leopards on the fringe of the civilised world are at peace with the Beloved; her beauty disarms them. We thus find a civilised regress, a powerful statement of natural virtue. The lovers integrate and speak for wild life, through metaphor, through nakedness and spontaneity. Domestication provides one form of mediation with civilisation, whether in the guise of the Pastoral, in which human life and amours are attendant on the slow grazing of the flock, or the harnessing of the mare. But another form of impingement is that of the foxes, whose greedy destructiveness is transformed into strength, energy and song. Here an implacable conflict is recognised; animals are still envious and excluded. Yet the Song, the nursery rhyme, is affectionate; hence the diminutive "little foxes" /115/; and the peril is neutralised through displacement and wish-fulfilment.

In the Song there is no serpent: this is the first inversion. Instead there is the Dark Beloved - the spirit of change, life and death, perilous beauty. She is the instrument of regeneration, of a restoration of Paradise. Nevertheless, as we have seen, she is symbolically associated with evil, for example when she is cast out and her reputation blackened by her brothers in 1.6. Thus the two items - serpent and woman - that are separated in the myth are fused in the Song.

In the myth the relationship between the woman and the serpent is essentially one of opposition: the serpent is male while the woman is female; the serpent acts the part of the seducer, who corrupts the woman under a show of friendship. Yet, as we have seen, his success depends on a rapport, a certain identification; he knows the woman's secret wish, and he symbolises the psyche, the "other" self. The dialogue between them, one of the most masterly and appropriately subtle in the Old Testament (Westermann 1974a: 91), is very illustrative of the difference between them. It displays an astonishing series of non-sequiturs and disjunctions. The serpent asks "'ap kî-'āmar 'elōhîm lō' tō'kelû mikkōl 'ēṣ haggān" "Did God really tell you not to eat of any tree of the garden?" (3.1) /116/. He pretends to be stupid so as to put the woman offguard, and appeal to her didactic authority /117/: it is calculated to make her believe that she is doing her duty, enlightening and instructing the animals. The first step in seduction is to pretend to be harmless. But then in v.4 the serpent drops the pretence; ignorance turns to wisdom, and he now instructs her. The astonishing import of his words blinds her to the transformation. But she hardly appears to notice them; they are not admissable, even now. Even the serpent drops out of her thoughts. The discontinuity of the dialogue is baffling. At this point the text reaches its subtlest. She now has to choose whom to believe, the serpent or God (Coats: 231). She does not make up her mind; in fact has no basis for doing so /118/. If we have an impossible decision to make we tend to be swayed by irrelevant factors. Instead of deeply considering, she looks at the tree, whose fruit is appetising and attractive:

וַתֵּרֶא הָאִשָּׁה כִּי טוֹב הָעֵץ לְמַאֲכָל וְכִי תַאֲוָה־הוּא לָעֵינַיִם
וְנֶחְמָד הָעֵץ לְהַשְׂכִּיל

(3.6) And the Woman saw that the tree was good to eat, and that it was delectable to the eyes, and the tree was lovely for insight.

Through his minute concentration on her thought processes, the narrator teaches us sympathy. For the first time we enter the interior of another human being, an experience very different from that of Adam's performative act in 2.23 as it is from the apportioning of guilt in the rest of the chapter. The narrator takes care to help us understand rather than judge, to show us how innocent Eve is /119/. For the first time we become aware of unconscious motivation. Eve looks, feels appetite, contemplates; all natural human propensities. She breaks the prohibition almost absentmindedly, in a welter of desires and sensations and in the end takes the fruit quasi-automatically /120/. The question of obedience is not faced. Instead of a malignant sinner, we have an innocent,

Chapter Four - Two Versions of Paradise

i.e. undisciplined, child, responsive to her inner promptings. This is overdetermined by an echo, a reference back. "That the tree was good to eat and that it was delectable to the eyes" recalls "kol-'ēṣ neḥmād lemarʲeh wetôb lemaʲakāl" "Every tree lovely to behold and good to eat" in 2.9, in other words the first creation of the garden. Thus the beauty and succulence of the fruit is indicative of man's delight, paradisal sweetness, when the aesthetic poles of eating and looking, absorption and differentiation, were harmoniously combined. As we have seen, looking implies an intellectual or imaginative activity, that already in its inception the garden is subject to change. In a sense, then, the woman is merely responding to its function of stimulation and satisfaction; the Tree of Knowledge at the creative centre of the garden represents the essence of arborial experience (see above p. 210). It is a flashback to innocence, that makes us aware yet again of how inherently compromised is the perfection of the garden. The opposites that are so clearly distinguished are here confused: "And the woman <u>saw</u> that the tree was good to eat ..."; the appetite is aroused by the senses: "wekî taʲawâ-hûʲ lāʲēnayîm" "and delectable to the eyes". But to the rhythmical complements "lovely to behold and good to eat" is added a third term - "weneḥmād hāʲēṣ lehaśkîl" "And the tree was lovely for insight". The quality "neḥmād" ("lovely") is thus transferred from the appearance to the idea. It suggests a step beyond the tidy harmony, that the intellect is looking beyond edible and visual satisfaction, that it is transcending the immediate physical context /121/. Yet it is still tied to nature: "the <u>tree</u> was lovely for insight". We thus find captured with delicate precision the moment of parting, just as in Adam's poem on his wife in 2.23. And then the sequence concludes swiftly "wattiqqaḥ mippiryô wattōʲkal" "And she took of its fruit and ate" /122/, an action preempted by the previous wondering. Again, the emphasis is on the simplicity of the act, almost a reflex, whose consequences are incalculable; in other words, the irony of human weakness, her extraordinary innocence /123/.

Eve has been much maligned by critics and theologians. For example, Cassuto says that the cunning of the serpent is that of the Woman /124/. On the other hand, feminist critics have rallied to her defence: "If the woman be intelligent, sensitive, and ingenious, the man is passive, brutish and inept" is one instance (Trible 1973: 40; 1978: 113). But what is remarkable is how clearly her femininity emerges from such a brief dialogue /125/. She is garrulous, charmingly illogical, in that she fails to notice the serpent's fancy footwork, and generous, giving the fruit to her husband. Her well-known expansion of God's command in 2.17 in 3.3 is another example of this generosity; its significance is I think less intellectual than emotive: she is anxious to please, to be forthcoming /126/. Ricoeur characterises the eternal feminine as "the mediation of weakness, the frailty of man", (254), inherent in the structure of finite freedom, quoting one of Hamlet's most neurotic lines. But there is another side to this. Essentially she is open, curious, seeing both sides of the question. She is Goethe's, not Ricoeur's, "Ewig-Weibliche", the spirit of creative dissatisfaction, for whom everything "is but a likeness", polysemantic, a ripening potential (Das Unzulängliche/Hier wirds Ereignis). The tree becomes the instrument of insight (lehaśkîl), rather than the object of contemplation; insight that looks beneath the external appearance, finds hidden connections. If the serpent speaks for the psyche, he represents a radical doubt, an intolerable ambiguity; the perception that God's warning could be a "likeness", that everything could be true or false. This has already been anticipated, as has been pointed out, by a subtle modification in 3.3. The mandatory penalty "môt tāmût" "You shall surely die" in 2.17 is replaced by uncertainty: "pen temutûn" "Lest you die". This acts as a bridge for the serpent's emphatic denunciation "lōʹ-môt temutûn" "You shall not die" (3.4) (Walsh: 165).

Walsh perceives two ambiguities in the serpent's speech, which are not only "ultimately irreducible", as he says, but quite meaningless /127/. Thereby he misses the ambivalence for which the serpent speaks, that of "good and evil", false and true, God's contradictory intentions. The serpent himself is an entirely ambiguous figure. By turning to him, the woman asserts her individuality, stepping outside the primordial couple, just as syntactically and functionally she breaches the limits of the garden through her act. Each closed unit then becomes open - as Freilich says, she is a symbol of creativity (215), that is itself a product of Ricoeur's frailty or weakness, of human imperfection. Characteristically, Freilich overstates his case, failing to see her unique complexity /128/. For development consists in reversion to an earlier stage of creation. The woman through the serpent reopens the question that was shelved in 2.17 (see above pp. 215f). The serpent activates the tree that was planted by God /129/. All three mediate the same phallic generative power. By turning to the serpent, the woman taps the source of creative

Chapter Four - Two Versions of Paradise

energy, which she then communicates to her husband: "And she gave to her husband with her, and he ate" (3.6). Thus the secondary creature becomes the matrix, "the mother of all that live".

The dove is white, innocent, with a clear outline; associated with love and grace, it is the very opposite of the serpent. In the midst of the court (Song of Songs 6.9), the dove represents a pet wildness, part of the transformation of the dark outcast to social luminary that took place in the last chapter. The dove is a symbol of the integration of good and bad, innocence and purity, whose distinction was the work of the serpent. If the Dark Beloved incorporates the daemonic, Dionysian qualities of the serpent, a challenge to a closed society, the transfiguration in 6.9 reintroduces it as divine, the creative centre of society. As we have seen, the repressed often appears in the guise of its opposite. This may be illustrated by the respective messages of serpent and dove. The serpent "opens our eyes" to the ambiguity of the world, its plurality and uncertainty. The dove, the Song itself, uses ambiguity to restore the cohesion of the world, to perceive likeness, integrate good and evil. However, its voice is seductive beyond signification, "the play of differences"; it is the voice that speaks, sadly and compassionately, the human voice in the Song, the natural migrant voice in the spring or wilderness, the maternal voice to the child, the mother in the Song and myth, "of all that live".

Theme: The Unity of the Body

Bendt Alster writes, in his analysis of "Enki and Ninhursag":

> The whole myth is an exposition of a logical problem: supposing that originally there was nothing but one creator, how could ordinary binary sexual relations come into being? (1978: 19)

This problem is the basis of myth, Alster claims, as well as of Structuralist thinking about it /130/, an insight that is not original, but clearly formulated, and geographically close to our concerns. As part of the introduction to the monotheistic Bible, Genesis 2-3 is of especial interest in this discussion. It may be seen as a succession of parallel stories, each one working out the implications of the original problem. We will discuss two of these - the story of man and woman, that of man and God - with reference to a third - man's bond with the earth. The issue, however, is the universe as an indivisible whole. Each story corresponds to the other, and has its effect on the other.

The body of the title of this section is the human body, that subdivides into sexes, at the centre of the universe, and whose constituents are in perpetual tension; also the body of the earth, from which man is taken; and the body of God, in whose image man is. I will proceed through a digression on narrative technique to a discussion of the Song, where the images are confused and correlated, and thence to my conclusion.

Semantically, the word "'ādām" is ambiguous: shifting between the human species and its male component. Hardly ever, and I believe only in Ecclesiastes 7.28, is it differentiated from woman; hardly ever does it refer to man as an individual, rather than to human nature /131/. Hence the Midrashic contention, little referred to by orthodox scholars /132/, but enthusiastically adopted by feminists /133/, that Adam was androgynous.

Trible summarises the evidence correctly (1973: 35):

> Ambiguity characterizes the meaning of "'adham" in Genesis 2-3. On the one hand, man is the first creature formed (2.7). The Lord God puts him in the garden "to till it and keep it", a job identified with the male (3.17-19). On the other hand, "'adham" is a generic term for humankind. In commanding "'adham" not to eat of the

Chapter Four - Two Versions of Paradise

tree of the knowledge of good and evil, the Deity is speaking to both the man and the woman (2.16-17). Until the differentiation of female and male (2.21-23), "'adham" is basically androgynous: one creature incorporating two sexes. /134/

I would like to add one or two comments.

וַיַּפֵּל יְהוָה אֱלֹהִים תַּרְדֵּמָה עַל־הָאָדָם וַיִּישָׁן וַיִּקַּח אַחַת מִצַּלְעֹתָיו וַיִּסְגֹּר בָּשָׂר תַּחְתֶּנָּה׃ וַיִּבֶן יְהוָה אֱלֹהִים אֶת־הַצֵּלָע אֲשֶׁר־לָקַח מִן־הָאָדָם לְאִשָּׁה וַיְבִאֶהָ אֶל־הָאָדָם׃

(2.21) And the Lord God caused slumber to fall upon the man, and he slept; and he took one of his ribs/sides, and bound flesh underneath.
(22) And the Lord God built the rib/side that he had taken from the man into a woman, and he brought her to the man.

What matters is not that man is hermaphrodite, but that the female element in him is undeveloped. The "ṣēlā'", whether it be "rib" or "side" /135/, has to be constructed into a woman; in itself it is without sexual characteristics. The woman's creation activates the male side or "ṣēlā'"; henceforward man (or the text) will think in terms of sexual relations. Up to that moment sexuality is dormant, indefinite and global.

In the Song of Songs too we have found that the immature little sister's passage through puberty is marked by the differentiation of male and female characteristics and the entrance into language; social dialectic is paralleled by that of the body. Similarly, the attractions of the lovers are mediated through strong contrasts of gender between primary and secondary features. But herewith the Song inverts the events in Genesis: whereas in Genesis man is the subject of the transformation, in the Song it is the woman, and puberty in man is neither cited nor symbolically significant.

Woman is a secondary creature, taken from Adam /136/; but in 3.20 she is called Eve, the mother of all that live /137/. In the Song of Songs she is likewise identified with the mother, and with the earth from which all life comes, whereas there is no father; the male principle is secondary and derivative. Thus there is another inversion: the primacy of man in Genesis is reinterpreted as that of the woman, the primordial bisexual mother.

No sooner do the two halves separate than they strive to unite: God brings the woman to the man - "wayebiʲehā ʲel hāʲādām" - creating a narrative expectancy. But the text is careful to project it into the future: "Therefore a man will forsake his father and his mother and cleave to his wife, and they shall be one flesh" (2.24). It is deferred right through the narrative of the garden with great subtlety and evasiveness. Only when they have left is the relationship immediately consummated: "And Adam knew Eve his wife" (4.1). Paradoxically, in the harmonious totality of Eden the two selves cannot be integrated; only with its loss are they reunited.

If Eve is the mother, from whom all life comes, this union is a reversion to the source of life /138/. In contrast, in 2.24 a man cleaves to his wife to find the lost part of himself, through which he establishes his separate identity. Maturity is correlated with regression, just as in the Song adult sexuality is also the experience of infancy. Eve is the universal mother, in whose womb we share. She has another maternal function: that of feeding with the fruit (3.6), associated with suckling (see above p. 191). Thus she both nourishes him and absorbs him. The two aspects of the relationship, two stages of the process, are perhaps reflected in the ambiguity of 2.24. The precondition for cleaving (dābaq be-) is separateness, however strong the adhesive; becoming "one flesh" is a complete dissolution. In these verses Adam asserts the fundamental identity of man and woman, despite their separation. In 3.20, however, although Eve is recognised as the mother, the name sets a formal distance between her and Adam /139/; she is as it were of a different substance, without etymological relation. "ʲīš - ʲiššâ", the synchronic pair, becomes "ʲadām - ḥawwâ", the lineage, separate in time: "A man forsakes his father and mother, and cleaves to his wife ..."

The name dignifies the woman: she is the matriarch, object of veneration in ancient times, providing sustenance, and dominant. It is she who is the active partner; the man accepts the fruit without demur /140/. Moreover, in 2.24, his need for her compels him to seek her out. She is apparently impregnably superior. Why then does the text define her future relationship as follows: "weʲel-îšēk tešûqātēk wehûʲ yimšol-bāk" "And to your husband shall be your desire and he shall rule over you" (3.16)? It is not simply to be explained as a curse, a punishment that overturns her previous eminence, since it precedes 3.20; and besides both this and 2.24 are

Chapter Four - Two Versions of Paradise

proleptic, anticipating the relations of men and women in our world. Instead it points to an intrinsic contradiction: she is subordinated to man as a secondary creature who is at the same time primordial.

The myth accommodates these contraries by postulating change, through the projection in time. The relations of man and woman are dynamic and versatile, as in our world. Looking at the text, we feel an impress of the entire range of human emotions.

3.16 nevertheless must be understood in context, as part of the new order. Phyllis Trible correctly understands the apothegm as a critique of conventional male dominance:

> This statement is not licence for male supremacy, but rather it is condemnation of that very pattern. Subjugation and supremacy are perversions of creation. Through disobedience the woman has become slave. Her initiative and her freedom vanish. The man is corrupted also, for he has become master, ruling over the one who is his God-given equal. (1973: 41; cf. 1978: 128)

Love, identification, turns into measured authoritative distance /141/, an imposition of the will, with its attendant frustration and rage. And yet woman is condemned to love her husband: "we'el 'îšēk tešûqātēk" "And to your husband shall be your desire". In 2.24 it is man who goes in quest of his wife; in 3.16 it is the woman who desires him. "Tešûqâ" is a rare and curious word; however, nearly all agree on its meaning /142/. It is as yet unsatisfied desire, that dominion serves to repress and perpetuate. The preposition "'el" is a feeler, a direction, in contrast to "be-" in 2.24. The desire is for something that is not there, an apprehended image of her husband. The word "'îšēk" is perhaps a clue: it is for her husband as her other self, for his desire for her. In other words, the "tešûqâ" is a yearning for the time of sexual equality and innocence; it testifies to the loyalty of positive feelings despite domestic tyranny (Trible 1978: 128). The two statements - 2.24 and 3.16 - "Therefore ... a man shall cleave to his wife and they shall be as one flesh" and "To your husband shall be your desire, and he shall rule over you" - are both projected into our world, and coexist there. They represent the poles of innocence and experience. Underneath the apparent injustice and cruelty of marital relations man still seeks out his wife and the sexes are equal; the woman's "tešûqâ" is a persistent reminder of this beginning.

It is a critical commonplace that poetic justice is at work

in the curses /143/, from this point of view the woman's fate is less anomalous than it appears /144/. For it was she, through the serpent, who introduced the question of power, the wish to become like God. She is now the victim of power. Mendenhall observes interestingly that in ancient times "women have very often been in the peculiarly dangerous situation of being in a position to exercise enormous influence with virtually no public responsibility" (332). The parallel with "tešûqâ" in Gen 4.7 becomes clear. There man rules over sin; here he rules over his own anarchic hubris /145/.

In the Song of Songs the curse is revoked: man and woman become one flesh, and their relationship is equal. Indeed, the Beloved is the more active, at least the more vocal partner, in contrast to the submissiveness traditional in conservative societies. Power politics and its corruption of love is experienced in the Song, as we have seen; but at its centre - in the garden - is the love of the lovers.

Moreover, in the Song it is the woman who does not leave, but is forsaken by her family, in 1.5-6; her search for her lover, risking exposure to disgrace, and the ire of authoritarian figures, such as the brothers or the watchmen, is an ever-repeated motif. It is she who cleaves to her lover: "I found whom my soul loves; I grasped him and I would not let him go ..." (3.4). In contrast, the Lover is elusive and disappointingly somewhat passive. Despite all the complexity of the Song, it is predominantly the Beloved who seeks, it is her "tešûqâ". Moreover, instead of sexual union disrupting parental bonds, as in Gen 2.24, it completes them: the climactic moment of Solomon's wedding is his coronation by his mother, expressing her joy, and a recognition that her work has now reached fruition (the happiest day in a Jewish mother's life); the Beloved takes her lover back to her mother's house (3.4, 8.2), and she - according to one reading of the ambiguous verb "telammedēnî - participates in their amorous education. Thus the cycle begun in Genesis is completed; there the man leaves his house and cleaves to his wife; here the woman is the more active partner, and the couple are restored to their parents.

Power in the Song is complex, because it falls into two categories. The first is the power of "wehû' yimšol-bāk" "And he shall rule over you" (Gen 3.16). We find this exemplified again and again, almost unconsciously, in the dialogue, as when the Lover is cagey about his whereabouts in 1.8. The Beloved becomes one of the Lover's possessions, his accoutrements, such as his mare, or his dove: his epithets

Chapter Four - Two Versions of Paradise

either communicate the Beloved's attachment - "dôdî" "my cousin"; "'ēt še'āhabâ napšî" "he whom my soul loves" - or his freedom. The central image of king is that of supreme male sexual authority, a power that rules over everyone (wehû' yimšol-bāk) in the kingdom. Nevertheless, as we have seen, there is a second kind of power, that of the Beloved, who traps kings in her hair (7.6), who is the equal of armies and constellations (e.g. 6.10) - it is the power of love, for whose sake Solomon - in the Bible as well as, ambiguously, in the Song - is prepared to abandon his kingdom, just as a man forsakes his father and mother. Thus the Song juxtaposes both kinds of authority; it reminds us of the Dionysiac imperative, even in a formalised repressive society; just as the myth projects both forms of heterosexual relation into our world. Within this context, it reverses the process; the return, the "tešûqâ", is the work of the woman.

"Tešûqâ" is the only direct verbal link between the two texts /147/, the only piece of evidence of conscious influence. We thus need to look at it, with a due sense of proportion. It occurs once in the Song, and nowhere else in the Bible except in the story of Cain and Abel, sixteen verses from our text, in Gen 4.7. But in the Song it is the man's "tesûqâ" that is for the woman: "'anî ledôdî we'ālay tešûqātô" "I am my beloved's and upon me is his desire" (7.11), instead of the woman's "tešûqâ" for the man. In the Song it is a distorted echo of the formula "'anî ledôdî wedôdî lî harô'eh baššôšannîm" "I am my beloved's and my beloved is mine, who feeds among the lilies" (2.16, 6.3), where it expresses the perfect reciprocity of the lovers in the garden, despite the lilies. Here, in 7.11, it suggests something other than mutual possession: "I am my beloved's", but he is not mine, only his "tešûqâ" is for me /148/. If she is his, why does he long for her? It illustrates the paradoxical imbalance of their relations. "Tešûqâ" is both less and more than reciprocity: it is desire without commitment and a yearning for the unattainable. It may simply be a physical desire, or a loyalty, that leaves him essentially uninvolved. "Tešûqâ" is then on the threshold: it yearns for her from outside, in contrast to the innocence of "'anî ledôdî" "I am my beloved's", through which the woman cleaves to the man. The innocence is exploited, love is a diversion. And yet it excludes man, from "'anî ledôdî wedôdî lî", from perfect cleaving. Throughout the Song the Lover appears on the Beloved's threshold, he never refers to himself as the Beloved's; it is her garden that becomes his, but not vice versa. He never offers himself or surrenders himself, or sees himself as possessed by her. As we have seen, on his descent into the garden he finds that of the Beloved. The extremes are measured by the distance between "ʾanî ledôdî" and "tešûqatô", between the identity of man and woman in 2.24 and their inextricable incompatibility in 3.16. We do not know whether the Beloved is right in her assertion "ʾanî ledôdî wedôdî lî". As long as it may be so, she effects the return, from 3.16 to 2.24, from the Song of Songs to Genesis.

In the Song, in 8.5, paradisal birth is accomplished through suffering, intensified by repetition:

שָׁמָּה חִבְּלַתְךָ אִמֶּךָ שָׁמָּה חִבְּלָה יְלָדַתְךָ׃

(8.5) There your mother travailed with you, there she who gave birth to you travailed /149/.

The Beloved's sympathy with the mother, with the sensations of birth, at the moment of recollection of sexual awakening, makes of the two one event: the pain of birth and the ecstasy of rebirth. In 6.9 the delight of the mother in her newborn child is conflated with that of the Lover: "bārâ hîʾ leyôladtāh" "Radiant is she to the one who gave her birth." The mother's pains are a sign of a great event: the Lover himself, a divine human being, is coming forth into the world /150/. The pain is replaced by the pangs of maternal and sexual love, the bond of care and affection; for the son it is the basis of gratitude for the gift of life. The Beloved's imagination goes back to the moment of separation of mother and infant at the moment of sexual convergence; mirror images of the same process. The convulsion of childbirth, the woman's travail, is itself a metaphor for orgasm /151/. In 8.5, love is an awakening from sleep (see above pp. 119f.), analogous to birth; in Gen 2.21 God puts man to sleep to separate woman, presumably so that he should be without pain /152/. Unconsciousness, a regression to primordial union, is a preliminary to further differentiation. In 8.5, at the point of intersection of earth and tree, the infant wakes to discover a mother. The tree is the paternal protector, associated as we have seen with the Tree of Life; the earth is the archetypal mother of whose substance we are made; tree and earth meet at the centre of the garden.

In Genesis 2-3, however, travail is a consequence of the curse:

הַרְבָּה אַרְבֶּה עִצְּבוֹנֵךְ וְהֵרֹנֵךְ בְּעֶצֶב תֵּלְדִי בָנִים

Chapter Four - Two Versions of Paradise

(3.16) I will greatly multiply your pains in childbearing; in pain you shall give birth to children ...

The pain, like the labour of tilling the soil in 3.17-19, is unmitigated and intolerable. But then, in 3.20, the pattern of reparation asserts itself: childbirth is the precondition of maternity, of being the mother of all that live. As in the Song of Songs, the curse turns into a blessing, is part of the blessing. From another perspective, that of the correspondence of punishment and crime, Eve has been the midwife of the human race. The narrative is a painful birth, at the end of which the couple, their eyes opened, are driven from the enclosed garden into the world. This trauma she henceforth enacts in her own body.

In the next verse, 3.21, the rapprochement of God and man continues, in a poignant symbolic gesture that at the same time defines the relationship of men and women:

וַיַּעַשׂ יְהוָה אֱלֹהִים לְאָדָם וּלְאִשְׁתּוֹ כָּתְנוֹת עוֹר וַיַּלְבִּשֵׁם:

(3.21) And the Lord God made for the man and his wife vestments of skin, and he clothed them.

In 3.7, clothing signifies estrangement. Man and woman hide themselves from God among the trees of the garden, and from each other with their leaves. They open their eyes and conceal their bodies, establishing boundaries, zones where they must not look. Fear turns quickly into hostility; Adam declares: "The woman whom you gave to be with me, she gave me from the tree and I ate" (3.12). Rage, fear, guilt, blind the opened eyes /153/. Adam dissociates himself from woman, casting the blame on God for creating her, with some justice. He no longer recognises their partnership, that she is "bone of my bone, flesh of my flesh" (2.23) /154/. Clothing is then a sign of rejection and hatred, of an aversion from one's image. In 3.21, however, clothing defines the formal distance between man and woman and the desperate resource becomes a permanent institution. Therewith the triangular relationship between God, man and woman is reestablished (Von Rad: 94; Westermann 1974a: 104 etc.), with certain constraints and limitations, without the immediacy and intimacy of Adam's naming woman in 2.23, or God's creation of man in 2.7. God clothes man; whereas in 3.8 they hid from his presence, here he makes them clothes so as to enable them to face each other without shame /155/. It indicates the restitution of divine favour, his commiseration for their embarrassment, and a wish for human relations to continue. Once more they are man and wife, equal partners, "ʾādām weʾištô". The verse conspicuously echoes 2.25: "And they were both of them naked, the man and his wife (hāʾādām weʾištô), and they were not ashamed" /156/. Both conclude a narrative unit, the beginning and the end of the story. Nakedness has now turned to subtlety, bliss to sorrow, unimaginable innocence to disastrous experience. They are man and wife still, and their relationship is now much surer, more credible, despite or because of their tensions and sufferings.

It would not do to undertake a history of clothing in the Bible, where paradoxically it is transformed into an instrument for self-assertion. In the Song, clothing is of little importance, and has been discussed in part (see above p. 226). Stripping a girl, in 5.7, is an act of humiliation that reduces her to shamelessness; the veil, however, is an allure (4.3, 6.6), that encourages speculation, and possibly the badge of a prostitute in 1.7 (see above p. 172). In descriptions, clothing either disguises her appearance in order to communicate her essence, in the phrase "werēaḥ śalmōtayîk kerēaḥ lebānôn" "and the fragrance of your garments is like the fragrance of Lebanon" (4.11); or else it is marginal to the naked body, sandals in 7.2, jewels elsewhere. And there is the "kuttōnet", the cloak, in 5.3, which the sleeping Beloved has removed, contrasting privacy and propriety, as in Genesis.

One further possibility needs to be noted: Adam and Eve gird themselves in fig-leaves; God clothes them in the skins of animals. The one is associated with the Tree of Knowledge, the other with the excluded creatures /157/. The knowledge with which man clothes himself is also the instrument for the cultural exploitation of animals /158/. The animals, to their cost, enter into and make possible the relationship of man, woman and God, as in the rest of the Bible.

The "ʾadāmâ" motif has been at the centre of some recent critical interest, e.g. by Patrick D. Miller (34-42), A. J. Williams (1973: 365-6), and Jerome T. Walsh (173), whose work requires no duplication. Miller is interested in the

Chapter Four - Two Versions of Paradise

correspondences: Man is taken from the earth and to it he returns; he is the precondition for its fertility and it is cursed for his sake. Death thus restores the original unity of man and the earth, while the curse ensures their continued dissociation. I would like to add one or two observations.

The first is the relationship with Eve. Eve is the mother of all that live, metaphorically verging on the earth, from which all life comes. The relationship with woman is a precise parallel to that with the earth /159/. Man rules over the earth, whose creatures are ambivalently hostile and frustrated, characterised by the primordial longing of their abortive creation. The same pain, "'eṣeb", "'iṣṣābôn", /160/, mars the fertility both of the earth and woman (3.16, 3.17). The earth too is ambivalent: its close relationship with the serpent is communicated through the duplication of the word "'ārûr" "cursed", in 3.14 and 3.17, referring to both the serpent and the earth; the twice-repeated stress on the serpent's origin, as "a beast of the field" (3.1, 14); and the latter's subsequent diet and posture "on your belly you shall go and dust you shall eat" (3.14) /161/. As we have seen, the serpent is essentially endowed with chthonic wisdom. Likewise, the fruit and thus the temptation of the tree is the product of the earth. The conscious dissociation of man and the earth and his exploitation of it corresponds to his forsaking his father and mother and becoming an adult. The ideal relationship of man and the earth, in the garden and thereafter, is as a partnership, "leʽobdāh ûlešomrāh" "to work it and keep it" (2.15), just as it is with man and woman. The subsequent crabbing of that relationship is likewise symptomatic of the recriminations of man and woman in 3.12, 16 etc. (Clines 1978: 75). Secondly there is the same rhythm of creation, disruption, followed by partial reparation that we saw with man and woman. Just as the curses are parallel and contiguous, so too there is a climactic convergence of compensations: man is reintegrated with the earth in death ("for dust you are and to dust you shall return") /162/, and in the next verse he recognises subordinate woman as the universal mother. Hence life and death principles are identified: the matrix of the earth generates and receives life; Eve, in its image, is responsible for death and is impregnated with all living creatures. At this point there is a quite unexpected irony: death, which throughout the narrative has been God's ultimate deterrent, is now a relief from unremitting toil /163/, and a reconciliation with one's true nature. The poetic balance is very insistent, as Walsh shows (168, n.20):

עַד שׁוּבְךָ אֶל־הָאֲדָמָה כִּי מִמֶּנָּה לֻקָּחְתָּ
כִּי־עָפָר אַתָּה וְאֶל־עָפָר תָּשׁוּב:

Until you return to the earth,
>For from it you were taken;
For dust you are,
>And to dust you shall return (3.19)

Yet it is still ambivalent, still the penalty we most fear. After all our labours, all we have to anticipate is death /164/.

In the Song of Songs the Beloved is associated with images of the earth e.g. the land of Israel, and with the mother. On the one hand, it is set firmly in history amid generations; on the other, it embodies man's autochthonous beginnings. Now the land is blessed, not cursed, for man's sake; the lovers are at the centre of the spring. The relationship of man and the earth is essentially one of celebration, and even where agriculture is exhausting and exploitative, as in 1.6, it introduces the Dark Beloved into society.

In the Song of Songs, notoriously, the name of God does not appear except perhaps in a particle of a word; elsewhere there are divine references - as in the oaths - but curiously understated or in disguise. God cannot be separated from flame (šalhebetyâ), fawns or gazelles (biṣbā'ôt ûbe'ayelôt haśśādeh), and most of all lovers. In Genesis, in contrast, he is a distinct person, yet one whose breath infuses man, and the story is preoccupied by their likeness and difference, identity and non-identity. He is "YHWH 'elōhîm", a totality of divine forces, personal and impersonal. The two names, a formulation almost unique in the Bible /165/, suggest a union of dualities, for instance of the Tree of Life and the Tree of Knowledge, that can only be possessed simultaneously by God. The Song of Songs may be perceived as a sidelong stratagem for attempting that union, of the two trees, of two people, of man and God. Its recurrent theme is the divinity of man, the Beloved as the union of cosmic forces, the Lover composed of precious metals from the far parts of the earth, his appearance like a statue, no longer flesh and blood, and with pagan theomorphic associations. Between them, the lovers generate the "šalhebetyâ", the divine creative flame, though which the world is regenerated. It may be conceived as a hieros gamos, but without - and this is essential - the sacral context devoid of human affections (cf. Lys: 51-53; Müller 1977: 161). In Gen 1 sexual relations mediate the

Chapter Four - Two Versions of Paradise

divine blessing, they imitate, producing after their kind, without originality. In the Song of Songs, the flame of God is that of sexuality, into which everything is drawn, metaphorically, poetically, and reforged, which burns even in Sheol, and which cannot be quenched. In Gen 2-3, the "knowledge" of man and wife is part of the knowledge that makes man like God, a partner of God; hence Eve's declaration on giving birth to Cain: "qānîtî ᵓîš ᵓet-YHWH" "I have obtained/created a man with YHWH" (4.1) /166/. There, however, unlike Gen 1 and the Song of Songs, the emphasis is not on sexual relations; it is on what happens when man turns his eyes away from his nakedness.

Partnership between man and God is the recurrent form of the relationship, in Gen 2-3. Man and God cooperate in cultivation, according to 2.5, God with his rain, man with his effort, the one the sky-creature, the other the earth-creature; this finds its immediate application in the garden, where man's task is to work it and keep it. Then when God creates the animals, it is man who names them: "And he brought them to the man to see what he would call it" (2.19), a demarcation of responsibility that is duplicated in the case of woman. Creating and naming: the imaginative capacity that complements the divine order. In chapter 3 the partnership breaks down: man farms the earth, as intended, but the earth is recalcitrant; instead of the mutual assistance of God and man, rain and agriculture in 2.5, and complementing it, the joint participation of spirit and dust, sky and earth, in the creation of man in 2.7, we have the repudiation of the earth by God in 3.17, marked by the word "ᵓarûrâ "cursed", the opposite of the keyword "bārûk" "blessed" in chapter 1, and man's continued service - and enslavement - to it as a somewhat bitter reminder of his estrangement. Man is sent out to work the soil in 3.23, but only as an exile, apart from God's presence. The concentric pattern between "ᵓadāmâ" (2.5) and "ᵓadāmâ" (3.23), and "ᵓabōd" (2.5) and "ᵓabōd" (3.23) /167/, marks an ironic inversion. Rain falls still and man works, and grass grows - the conditions of the blessing are satisfied - but also thorns grow, and with hardship does man eat bread. With this, and especially the curious phrase "beṣēʽat ᵓappekā" "by the sweat of your brow", the meteorological uncertainty, heat, drought, and the impassive stubbornness of the soil is evoked: a broken, inextricable relationship, precisely like that of man and woman in 3.9-16 /168/.

Yet man in Gen 2-3 wants to be like God; not

complementary and different, but like him. In Gen 1, the position is clear: man is like God (beṣelem demût tabnîtô" - as it says in the Jewish marriage ceremony) and performs his functions on earth. God names, not man; and God makes everything grow after its kind. There is no independent necessity for man; no task that is his alone other than as God's shadow or deputy, to fulfil his need for a mirror-image.

It is an interesting paradox that in Gen 1, where God is most transcendent, man is in his "ṣelem", his likeness, whereas in Gen 2-3, where God is anthropomorphic, he is pathetically anxious to assert his difference. In the Song of Songs, "the human form divine" - in Blake's words - is most purely seen as the "ṣelem", the image of God; its divine and mythological associations have been sufficiently discussed. This indeed is the heart of the Jewish mystical interpretation: through contemplating perfected human beauty we contemplate the image of God himself. But therewith the body transcends itself; it becomes virtually transparent. Through the Beloved we see Jerusalem and Tirzah, sun, moon and constellations. It becomes a vehicle, for imaginative rapture, for a poetic and metalinguistic exploration of the self and the world. Images of transparencies pervade the poem - the slice of pomegranate, itself suggesting depths of confused richness, half-hidden behind the veil (4.3, 6.6); the references to eyes, associated with faraway stars and messenger doves, expressive of the inner world; the ornate and quasi-objective descriptions that lapse into mute gestures of wonder. The sense of the object experienced largely through sight gives way to that of presence and atmosphere, communicated through smell. The body, then, at the centre of creation, recedes into something outside it: a wonder, a peace perceived in his eyes in 8.10, the occasion for the love that survives death and time, and that is preserved in our poem. That which "is dust and to dust shall return" is in the image of God and unites in the divine flame; the references, especially in the key passage 8.6-7, are both cryptic and ambiguous, as we have seen. Nevertheless, I would suggest that the Song of Songs, in its artlessness, touches on very dangerous and interesting theological considerations.

One detail may be cited. In 7.2, the inturnings of the Beloved's thighs are described as "kemô ḥalāʾîm maʿaśēh yedê ʾommān" "like chains, the work of a craftman's hands". On one level, there is a simple though presumably unconscious reference to her true creator /164/ - what a lovely creature she is - a variation on the comfortable

Chapter Four - Two Versions of Paradise

"maʻaśēh yedê YHWH "the work of God's hands". But there is a second, more disturbing, echo, over-determined by assonance: "maʻaśēh yedê ʾādām" (cf. "maʻaśēh yedê ʾommān") "the work of man's hands", familiar from prophetic polemics against the production of idols. This could be dismissed as fanciful and immaterial were it not for a persistent flirtation with idolatrous imagery in the Song, for instance in the description of the Lover, the adjuration "by the does and gazelles of the field", the inexplicit mythological references. This is not to make it into a pagan poem, since in each case the pagan image lacks precision and fades into something more human or conventional, but it raises a suggestion: is the adoration of women idolatrous? And beyond this, there is a truth: the woman is the work of a craftsman, the poet, who matches God's work of creation. And looking deeper still, it is only the inturning of the thighs, the chains, that are the work of the craftsman: there is the space between them, the goal of masculine endeavour and poetic definition, inescapably that which the poet cannot say, the craftsman cannot create. The clear distinctions that elsewhere the Bible seeks to affirm between pure monotheistic worship and numinous polytheism is here, and in the Song generally, immaterial; it is pantheism, with a touch of transcendence.

The differences in formulation and conception of Gen 1 and Gen 2-3 are perhaps too great for useful comparison /170/, notwithstanding the reverberative contrast of key terms. Essentially it is a contrast between a perfect concept of God and one contradictory, composite, and much more interesting. God in Gen 1 is unified, unambiguous, in no way immanent. The universe is perfect, and static; man is created in one piece, as a binary whole. Between him and God there is a fixed distance, between substance and shadow, thought and expression. The word "demût" implies that man is but a semblance /171/. In Gen 2-3 man is a composite creature, half perishable, half divine, in a universe that is defined as composite, both good and evil. God's first distinctive attribute is his knowledge of its imperfection. In Gen 1, however, his insight is that the universe is very good. The two Gods are perhaps irreconcilable; nevertheless, there is a shock of recognition when after the repeated "And God saw that it was good" in chapter 1, we hear the admission "It is not good" in 2.18. (The word "ṭôb" "good" is in fact a key word, a touchstone, both linking and determining the differences between the two accounts.) Whereas the likeness of man and God in Gen 1 interposes no question of rivalry, and preserves the harmonious hierarchy of creation, in Gen 2-3, imparted through the much more flexible particle "k" ("kĕʲlōhîm" "like God" [3.5], "keʲaḥad" "like one" [3.22]), it implies parity of status and qualitative similarity that abolishes the difference between man and God. Whether this likeness is the same on which both texts turn is an open question. Here it clearly relates to the divine part in human nature, the spirit of God in man trying to return to its proper domain. The particle "k", again, implies not identity but proximity, just as when man retraces his androgynous path, the result is not identification but affinity: "wehāyû lebāśār ʲeḥād" "And they shall be as/for one flesh". Moreover, man's challenge to God's supremacy is taken seriously, in 3.22; God shows himself fallible and threatened. This raises the vexed question of anthropomorphism. Whereas in Gen 1 man is a semblance of God, and by implication the whole universe is a shadow or construct of his reality (cf. Scriabine: 45), here God is an image of man, not only in the sense of human possibilities, but indeed, ironically, "as one of us". It seems to me, however, that the anthropomorphism is less naive than it appears; that it is a poetic device, a metaphor in other words, through which the narrator can present his view of divinity. The personality of God, walking in the garden, to take the allegedly crudest example (e.g. Vawter: 81), is set in a shifting perspective. It is suggested inferentially through the varying backdrop. It introduces the mysteriousness of God, dynamic and intangible, through a variety of techniques of indirection /172/. This mystery reflects on the certainty of chapter 1, where God (the God of the philosophers) is rational, determined, and uninvolved. Here he is both in the human situation and appraises it from outside. The image of God emerges from a number of sources:

a) The use of verbs. God is experienced through his actions, through events, as the dynamic impulse, especially "wayyîṣer" - that which creates, makes things grow, and "wayeṣaw" - that which ordains, defines limits, that which establishes the conditions of the world, spontaneous, generative, and formative. It ensures that God is more than a large human being, walking in the garden, since he is responsible for creation and inhibition. Secondly, it defines God not as a thing, but as a process.

b) The specific attributes, knowing good and evil and living for ever. These are abstract qualities, that play no part in the complementary relation with man; through them God is set apart from the world, with his objective knowledge and

Chapter Four - Two Versions of Paradise

immunity from change. By aspiring to be like God in these respects (and not e.g. by making rain or creating animals) man becomes likewise otherworldly, with his quest for knowledge and immortality.

c) Most interestingly, a concealed metaphor: "lerûaḥ hayyôm" "in the breeze/the cool of the day", in which the human couple hear God walking /173/ (3.8). The wind is both sonorous and stirs the leaves in which they are hiding. It should bring relief as part of the natural daily cycle, but in fact presages change and breaks the suspense. Using our imagination, we can feel the wind on Adam and Eve's skin as they are hiding, how it seems to probe them, while the leaves murmur, everything suggests "Where are you?", and the breeze arouses fear as it brushes the skin. The sound of the wind is thus assimilated to God's voice, and to the passage of the day. Breeze and evening, unobtrusive, pervasive, gently moving, are both images for the plastic, dynamic indefinable God suggested, experienced through the verbs. The same image occurs in the Song of Songs "Until the day blows and the shadows flee" (2.17, 4.6), in an uncertain context; there the transition between day and night is associated with that between the fusion and isolation of selves, amid the shifting shadows. There too the spirit (rûaḥ) of the lovers is identified with the diurnal cycle.

d) The nomenclature "YHWH ʾelōhîm", both personal and impersonal, suggesting both the totality of divine forces, as in Gen 1, and a specific mysterious identity. The omission of the "YHWH" by the serpent and woman is most easily explicable on stylistic grounds: it makes their conversation less cumbersome. Encapsulating it, the narrative is more conspicuous in its formality, and in its assertion of the identity of God's individuality and the cosmos.

e) The final scene in the heavenly court: "hēn hāʾādām hāyâ keʾaḥad mimmenû" "Behold, the man has become as one of us" /174/. This removes us from the human scene to a divine equivocation, and explicitly provokes the question of the unity of purpose and identity of God, out of which the narrative develops. Furthermore, it is a link with Gen 1, whose climactic achievement is likewise introduced by an address to the divine assembly, "ʾelōhîm" in the plural (1.26). There it is an expansive gesture of confidence, the audience is introduced (or we are brought into it) for the sake of the applause; here it is anxious and deliberative. The correspondence magnifies the contrast, which affects the content. There the assembly is convoked to make man in their image; here it is the reverse: it is to frustrate that ambition.

There is one seminal ambiguity: is God part of his creation or not? It is mediated through the first verse: "beyôm ʽaśôt YHWH ʼelōhîm ʼereṣ wešāmāyim" "On the day of God's making earth and heaven" (2.4). He acts from outside, establishing the first duality of heaven and earth that will unite in man. But in the next verse he is the sky creature, corresponding to man, the earth creature. He produces rain from clouds, materialising from the sky, while man, emanating from the earth, works the soil. This duality is that of man also. God breathes into man the breath of life. The incipient identity and intimacy of God and man is never so clearly expressed. The breath may be a celestial counterpart to his earthly substance, so that man is truly a union of earth and heaven. But the ambiguous identity of God makes man ambiguous also. The "breath of life" is part of the world, man's celestial component, and it also stands outside it, as "a living soul", a conscious being.

The Song of Songs is one of the books of the Bible most remote from this issue of the likeness and difference of man and God, and therefore only the most general comparison can be made. It is an illustration of Gen 1.26, the image of God in man, achieved through metaphors, and puns, yet it is quite without ambition; the lovers fulfil their divine potential simply by being themselves, in accordance with the blessing: "perû ûrebû ûmilʼû ʼet-hāʼāreṣ wekibšuhā" "Be fruitful and multiply, fill the earth and subdue it" (Gen 1.28). The Song itself with its honesty and its knowledge of good and evil is immortal. It reconciles perfection and imperfection, the two accounts of creation. As we have seen, in its search it remains just ambivalent. Love is as strong as death, it cannot be extinguished in time. The myth in Genesis ends with the cherubim and the "lahat haḥereb hammithappeket" "the flame of the twisting sword" (3.24), that excludes man from the garden /176/. The sword and the flame have a destructive potency, through which man remains mortal. In the Song of Songs, the "salhebetyâ" is ignited between the lovers, and gives life to the world. The cherubim guard the divine presence, that cannot be seen, on pain of death. In the Talmud, they are represented in a sexual embrace. In the Song, through their sexuality the lovers return to the garden and eat of the Tree of Life. The flame grows between them, though it excludes us, who are outside the garden. In it we feel the destructive power of love through which we live.

Chapter Four - Two Versions of Paradise

Conclusion

Man wishes to become like God, to transcend his nature, for instance by eating of the Tree of Life; the divine breath in him seeks its origin, just as the earth reclaims its substance. The cherubim, ministers of the creative and destructive flame, exclude him. For man is essentially a hybrid: his body, compounded of contraries, is his most precious possession, in defence of which he will construct his elaborate civilisation. In the Song of Songs, the body participates in the divine flame, in a process of fusion and rebirth; its apotheosis in language, i.e. in spirit and breath, is the work of the poem. The contradictory claims of Genesis are here in part, and through imagination or illusion, resolved: if in Gen 1 man is in the image of God, here precisely through the imagination he becomes divine. The structural perfection of Genesis is founded on fracture; the quest for the centre /177/ fails because there are two centres of the garden, the trees of life and death, the latter divided into good and evil; man is both a stranger to the garden and at home there; God is both immanent and detached. The narrative develops through sidetracks and false solutions, that ensure that there will be no rest to man's attempts and inquiries. Yet it also projects its conviction into our world, that man and woman will reunite in love, and that the garden still survives; the Tree of Life is preserved inviolate. In the Song of Songs the inversion is complete: the dualities are unified, the two trees become one, the garden as the Beloved exists still in a corrupted world. Yet it is ever frustrated; shame intervenes between the lovers; satire and affirmation are equally balanced. As we have seen, beauty is enigmatic, the product of desire and repression, creation and destruction.

The path I have had to follow has been long and arduous, and at times I have missed my way, illustrating the fact that comparisons are odious. Each text has its fascinations, and constantly asserts its individuality. Moreover, the more deeply enmeshed the critic becomes, the more he is aware of the manifold paths and interconnections, involving not only our two texts, but many others. Finally, there is the difference of genre. The narrative is a work in time; it expresses its preoccupations through constructing a story, a parable. The lyric poem is a mosaic of fragmented stories, existing simultaneously; a description of a moment. The elements carefully distinguished in the story (God, man, serpent etc.) are metaphorically correlated. Synchronic and diachronic modes of expression complement each other; but also lead in opposite directions.

We began with two images, the garden and tree, common to both texts, and whose relationship in the myth is complementary. Both are duplicated in the Song, that thereby internalises its relationship to Eden.

The garden of Eden is an enclosed first home, a fertile womb in which man is prepared for his task in the world. It is self-sufficient, perfect, yet subject to change. The garden of the Beloved opens out to the world, and to the royal garden where the Lover descends to meet it; both are subsumed in the garden of poetry. The gardens of nature and culture blend in the person of the Beloved, "the mother of all that live"; the one a stimulus to culture, the other a reversion to nature.

The two trees contradict each other, in the garden and in the world: the wish for immortality and the wish for knowledge. By planting them God reveals his own duality. In the Song the trees are united: the Tree of Life is the Tree of Knowledge, in a paradisal birth. The Lover, the apple tree in 2.3, whose fruit cures sickness, is protected by it in 8.5; the reversal restores the phallic image to the parental one, the incidental tree in the wood to the archetypal world tree, human generation to autochthonous origins. It is remembered between the lovers, supporting each other in the desolation outside the garden, in their path in the world.

We then turned to puns, to the homonymous opposition between nakedness and subtlety, that is reversed in the Song, where nakedness is celebrated through subtlety. Whereas language in the myth is discrete, and establishes things in their particularity, language in the Song is metaphorical, combinatory, and through puns and all its other verbal delights communicates a reality beyond language, and is itself amatory. Puns in the myth point to the language of the Song. Yet shame intervenes between the lovers, imposing a necessity for words, for screens, for ingenuity.

The connection of the serpent with the Song is more tenuous, since it moves away from the shared resources of metaphor and word play to the narrative constituents of situation and character. The serpent is the Dionysian animal, vital and fatal, combining chthonic wisdom and chaos. It destroys the equilibrium of the garden, articulating its repressed tensions, and it exacts the animals' revenge. In the Song, the perilous Dionysian beauty, repressed in Gen 3.15, is transferred to the woman; the lovers represent the animal kingdom. Envy turns into gratification, contempt into praise,

Chapter Four - Two Versions of Paradise

but only at the cost of sublimation, of darkness into whiteness, of excluded serpent into the contained paradisal fawns or doves; and the minimised foxes.

Finally, we reached the theme of unity and binary opposition, which Bendt Alster sees as the basis of all myth. We looked at the rhythm of division and partial reconciliation of man and woman, man and the earth, man and God. In Genesis, woman is a secondary creature, derived from man, as his companion; in the Song, she is the Beloved, the archetypal mother. The two selves seek to reunite, to become once more solitary; a process repeated in the Song, where the lovers are in flight to and from each other, irresistably attracted and separated. The curse on sexual relations is revoked; it is man's "tešûqâ" that is for the woman, and they are equal partners, despite the continued dominance of men in the world. Likewise, the curse on the earth is annulled; it flourishes in springtime and corresponds sympathetically and metaphorically to the lovers. In both cases, the myth projects its antithesis outside the garden: Eve is the mother of all that live, no longer a secondary creature, while the earth, the universal mother, reclaims its own, in an act of final integration. In the Song too, we have found the conflict between integration and differentiation, between death and life, associated with the Beloved as the universal mother. As man and woman and man and the earth are identical and distinct, so too the "šalhebetyâ" that is created between the lovers excludes them in Gen 3.24. The likeness of man and God, the breath that flows between them, is in the Song a work of imaginative recreation. They are both self-conscious, at the limits of the world, neither identical with nor apart from it. The Bible is a record of their interaction, of their mutual desire and frustration. Their voices merge, however, in its speech.

CHAPTER FIVE

CONCLUSION

Chapter Five

CONCLUSION

T the centre and the climax of the Song are two antithetical elements, water and fire, the spring of the Beloved and the flame of God, in which the antinomies of the Genesis narrative - masculine/feminine, terrestrial/celestial, human/divine - are realised most purely, and which are dynamically linked through ambiguity. If, at the centre, the world of the Song is fed by the spring, at the climax it is absorbed in the flame; the poetic process thus describes the tense passage between immanence and transcendence, between the Beloved's identity with the world, whose celebration makes the Song among the most pantheistic of poems, and the aspiration/temptation to overcome its finitude and become substanceless, like the flame. Both terms - water and fire - are liminal, marking the limits of poetry; both are projected into the very centre. The spring rises in the garden and in Lebanon, the ambiguous matrix that mediates between earth and heaven, Israel and the nations; the fire burns in the inaccessible centre of the kingdom, associated in 7.3 with the vulva or navel, whose alcohol, liquid fire, mingled by the lovers, shall never be lacking. Fire and water: two primary images of poetry, namely the Pierian spring, the animating spirit of the garden, fed by the waters of death, and the incandescent moment, the metaphor of metaphor, in which all the substances, the diverse images of the Song are consumed and through which they flourish, and which unites life and death. The mighty waters are harnessed to irrigate the garden; likewise, the destructive element fire is tamed in the service of culture. Water is transparent, fire is substanceless. The creative flame burns with the aquatic fury of chaos. Both are associated with a moment of silence, the syllable "-yâ" at the threshold of silence, with the central aporia: are structurally germinal, and unassimilable; flow, light, energy present in all the words of the poem.

Rabbi Akiba went into paradise, and alone emerged unscathed. He said "When you come to the place of stones of pure marble, do not say 'Water, water', for it is said 'Liars shall not endure in my sight'." (T. B. Hagigoh 14b) /1/ Water is deceptive, light is deceptive. To be trapped in a mirror, to try and enter and drink from a mirror is a profound image for the loss of self (hence its pervasiveness in folklore) /2/, and clearly the adept on his path has to be careful. The cost is that Rabbi Akiba never really entered paradise, went through the looking-glass; he distinguished between image and image, light and light, and continued to the source of images and lies. "Liars shall not endure in my sight" he says, and we turn away and look at the visible material world, as the lovers look away from each other's eyes and the whole green world grows betwen them. Nothing endures in his sight: the whole realm of change and separateness is implicated. And yet it only exists in his sight. In Nachman of Bratslav's awesome parable /3/, the whole world is invisible to God, since its time cannot register on his retina. In his absence the world can come into being. And there we can speak, words partial, incorrect, half-truths, using all the resources and duplicity of language to say something that should not be spoken. God creates delusions, and needs delusions, to affirm his existence. Through poetry and song, he speaks to us and through us, with our voice, and in his silence.

The mistake against which Rabbi Akiba warned was to say "water" or "marble"; to say "this" or "that"; for metaphor unites everything. In the Song water is transmuted into fire that burns between the lovers, that is created by them. If the lovers come from the spring, and the Beloved is identified with it, they generate the flame. They link earth and God, as in Genesis.

The water gives life to the earth, the fire illumines it. There is another quotation, for which I am indebted to Gabriel Josipovici. "Light is the lion that comes down to drink." /4/. The visual clarity and beauty of the Song, its intensity of consciousness and aesthetic drive to see and understand, is also gentle, as the lion that comes down to drink. The lion personifies animal pride, beauty and power; he sees his image in the water and breaks it. Likewise light and water reflect each other, enter into each other. Man sees himself in the earth, God sees himself in his image in man, and comes down to drink.

At the end of the poem the composer must bid farewell, and leave the Beloved singing in her garden; the poem must be left to its own devices. The separation of the poet from his Muse, that part of himself to which he is compelled to

Chapter Five - Conclusion

listen, and which is all we know of him, is represented as a fantasy of freedom: "And be like a fawn or a young gazelle on the mountains of spices" (8.14), ambivalent, not only because of the cost of silence, and poet's stormy affair with his craft, but because we follow him on his flight; we, like him, are both inside and outside the poem. With the last word it is completed, nothing more can be added, and it returns to the silence from which it came, an integration that is also parturition. I am now in an analogous position. I do not pretend that this work is completed, and am conscious of the levels of signification and aspects of interpretation I have not touched. Likewise, there is a fantasy of freedom, mingled with a little regret. But the Song of Songs, from which I am exiled, and which is a poem of exile, remains with me, just as in 8.14 the poet/lover too carries its voice with him, in the fragrance of the mountains of spices. It remains as a memory, a point of reference, somewhere where I learnt this trade.

More serious than the failure of interpretation, since no one can be perfect, or would wish to be, are its limitations; originally I had hoped to correlate the meaning of the Song, its complex of signs, with its experience, observing that the understanding is often baffled while the heart is seduced, that the Song works as much on the senses as on the intellect (to understate). An analysis of word music, visual effects, etc., would accompany exegesis. One would go from the narrative fragments to the discrete and brilliant images, to the sensations they evoke, and thence to the patterns of phonemes, finally to lose oneself in allophones and a plenitude of sound in which speech cannot be distinguished, and then in nothingness. But this might not only be deadly, it would be attempting the hermeneutically impossible: to penetrate beyond interpretation through interpretation. As Frank Kermode argues in The Genesis of Secrecy, the exegete is always outside the door of the parable, excluded by the cherubim from Eden. Yet inside it there is nothing, just as in the Holy of Holies - to hark back to Rabbi Akiba's dictum with which I began this thesis - there is nothing, except a memory /5/. In the Song of Songs there is only the sexual act, of which there is nothing to say. The meaning of this act and the mystery develop beyond the keyhole; they are our work of self-reflection and understanding, and entirely accessible to us, through its language. What it communicates sensually, I can only hope to have expressed indirectly, through the sympathetic care I give to my own writing, as homage and reflection, and dialogue with the poem.

My objective in this thesis has been to provide as full a reading as possible of the Song, to free it from the limitations of traditional theological and biblical-critical procedures. The question is not how to adapt it doctrinally, nor to provide it with a safely distant historical niche. Rather, it is how does it speak to us, what is its visée on the world; as one of the great human affirmations, how does it speak for us. For this, we need all our imaginative and critical resources, including psychoanalysis, whose contribution to human understanding has been inestimable. As a poem concerning people at their most intimate, the Song especially is close to its insights. However, quite apart from the limitations of my reading, psychoanalysis has been an instrument, not a director of research. Everything that I have said is a no doubt partial exposition of what is said by the Song, whose complexity and unfathomability still astonish me, and account for its greatness; the Song is my only teacher. This in no way detracts from the necessary subjectivity of the reader, through which alone he can understand the Song, through relating it to his own experiences, and discovering and interpreting his own life thereby. Only in this way does it continue to be creative. Reading the Song is thus partly a work of self-understanding, partly motivated by curiosity e.g. why does it have such a powerful influence on Western literature, an openness to the other that returns one to oneself. This brings me to the paradoxes of the Song.

The theme of the book is the process of fusion and differentiation, the paradise that only exists in the world through being inaccessible to it, or is only accessible outside its limits, through imaginative transcendence. The union of lovers, and that of the Self in the poem, is accomplished by the poem that parts them; at the same time they are indissoluble, sealed in each others' hearts, and unattainable. They are absent when present, present when absent. Each consummates himself in self-surrender. The human paradox is that the source of our existence is elsewhere (respectively in the mother, God, nature, non-life), and we both need to make contact with it, to integrate our origins, and to free ourselves from them. Our individuality is at odds with our identity. My subtitle "Identity and Difference in the Song of Songs" refers both to this identity that we find in and with the other, the community to which we belong, and our isolation within ourselves; to the affirmations of language, in which each

Chapter Five - Conclusion

distinctive particle is defined by its divergence from the others, is a minute statement of being, surrounded by silences (cf. Derrida's aphorism "Death strolls between the letters" [1978: 71]), and its syntactic function, that dissolves meaning through metaphor, the multiplicity and unity of the world it presents. Man is both a creature, and alienated from creation; like God in his transcendence and immanence, his partaking of the world, and difference from it; and unlike him, in his mortality and helplessness. The Song, with its interplay of the temporal and the time-free, its creative delirium and immortal pretensions, thus in part, and through fantasy, conjoins them.

I began with the relationship of the lovers, both as archetypes in the human psyche, the collective personality - as it were the Adam Kadmon - projected by the Song, and as individuals, noting the centrality of the woman and the insubstantiality, shadowiness of her lover; corresponding to this is the primacy of the Mother archetype, and its correlation with the Muse. I then entered the forest of part-selves, the multiplicity of relationships comprising each person, exploring the patterns of the imagery, the mechanism of projection, the discovery of oneself in the other. Thereby an androgynous personality develops between the lovers, a continuum of identity that envelops both of them, but which also separates them. I started with a key-verse (4.5), borrowing a technique of Lévi-Strauss (1970: 1) /6/, which combined the motifs of sex and suckling, adult and infantile sexuality. Both lovers were found to originate in, to recall the mother; both relived in the relationship their first love, a transference of riches between the generations, as between the lovers, that finally brought me to the bisexual image of Lebanon. There followed a discussion of the nuclear family in the Song - the mother and twins - the pattern of diverging likeness, and hence the first ambiguity and frustration in the poem, as in life. Incest is driven into the wish-fulfilment of fantasy and metaphor; the siblings must find their semblances in the world. They can only reconstitute the womb of archetypal bisexual mother through leaving the womb, a process from Lebanon to the garden, from death to life, from barrenness to fertility, at its structural centre. Thereby I introduced the integration of Eros and Thanatos, order and energy, that is the subject of my third chapter, and of the climactic credo. Love is as strong as death - the ambivalent message of the Song - but love is <u>like</u> death (kî ʰazzâ KAmmāwet ʲahabâ), threatening dissolution and desolation.

Love is like God, metaphorically love is God. This identification - initially shocking to Jewish ears - of the human and the divine, the creative impulse in man and the world, raises a question implied but never asked in the Song: what is Love? Subject and object, delight and terror, creative and destructive, it is both human and a transforming presence, like a guest; to be described by techniques of indirection, as God is in Genesis, a continuous assurance in everything moving. And like God, it is ambivalent, promising integration and differentiation, the union of contraries.

The second chapter explored these ambiguities from the point of view of the aesthetic tension between desire and repression, distance and fusion. Whereas the second chapter focussed on the relationship of the lovers at the structural foci, the third concentrated on the gnomic periphery. The ambivalence towards beauty - as that which threatens social order and the differentiating consciousness, as well as the object of its desire - generates ambiguity; beauty is adopted and worshipped by society, but in disguise. Hence the pervasive ambiguity and irresolvable enigmas of the Song, traceable to death, the final mystery. As in the garden of Eden, the quest for knowledge is fraught with mortality and sexual ambivalence. Likewise, the fragmentary episodes on the edge of the Song direct us outside it, structurally and thematically, with a perspective towards the future or past, and through the citation of different genres, and thus serve to introduce the wider literary context of the final chapter. Four peculiarly intractable examples are used to illustrate the vicissitudes of beauty in the Song and its relation to insoluble ambiguity or enigma. In the first, 1.5-6, beauty dissimulates itself, says "Do not look at me"; dark, Dionysiac beauty is both cast out and exploited by society, as the source of intoxication. In 8.11-12 beauty is turned into money, social currency; it becomes an instrument of policy, as well subversive of it. In 8.8-10, natural beauty is inducted into society and into speech, as a family asset, concealed artistically through the beautification of the body, a transition from dissimulation to allusion, from traumatic rejection to integration. Finally, in 1.7-8, beauty is admitted to society, but remains on its fringes, as shepherdess and "ōteyâ". In all four episodes, the poetic vision is far more diffused than in my first expository chapter; from being preoccupied by the lovers themselves, and their mutual self-discovery, we look at the world they inhabit. The rustic treatment of fallen women; the opposition of city and coun-

Chapter Five - Conclusion

try, desert and court; royal administration and irresponsibility, familial nurture, all receive attention, exemplified by the intimate yet spectacularly public celebration of 6.8-10. In particular, we have, as the social ambiance projected by the Song, the Pastoral, the reversion to a simpler, more innocent mode of existence, that implicitly comments on our own. This suggests a further reversion, to the original innocence of the garden of Eden.

In the last chapter, we saw the garden and tree forming a whole that is destroyed by linguistic subversiveness - by, for example, paronomasia and the serpent's half-truths, envy, curiosity, and the ambivalence of God; duality coexists with unity. The story of the garden of Eden is a mirror-image of the Song; each is reflected, sees itself as well as its antithesis in the other. Each finds its identity in the other; the garden of Eden is the mythical prototype of that of the Song, which expresses fully its living presence, in the Biblical compendium, and our literary experience. Paradise formulates the paradox that our identity is founded in difference. We leave what we love in order to live.

NOTES

NOTES TO CHAPTER ONE
Introduction

1   All sacred writings communicate impurity, i.e. the hands must be washed before touching sacred food; otherwise it cannot be eaten. Hence "render the hands unclean" is a circumlocution for "to be canonical" (M. Kelim 15.6; M. Yadaim 3.2-5 etc.).

2   Gordis (1974: 1) writes, "The warmth of his defence testifies to the vigour of the challenge to which it was subjected, probably stronger than in the case of Esther, Koheleth and Job". There is no evidence for this; the very late tradition (Aboth de R. Nathan 1.2) that Proverbs, the Song of Songs and Ecclesiastes were suppressed (genûzîm) "until the men of the Great Synagogue interpreted them", does not suggest that it was more threatened than the other Solomonic writings. In our Mishnah, Yadaim 3.5, its inclusion is more assured than Ecclesiastes, since there are no dissenting voices. Michael Wadsworth has suggested to me that the status of the "ketûbîm" in general was subject to much controversy in the 1st century, especially with regard to their public reading and exegesis. It is clear that the composition of the "ketûbîm" was not finally settled until the following century (Encyclopaedia Judaica: "Bible" IV. 825).

3   Cf. Gordis 1974: x-xi, 1; Marvin H. Pope (1976: 19) Goitein (1957: 308-9). Gordis, however, sympathetically postulates an underlying, possibly unconscious awareness of the sanctity of human, sexual love "in consonance with the basic Hebrew conception of the organic unity of the human person" (1974: x-xi), citing various references. It is surprising how little close attention has been given to Rabbi Akiba's utterance, considering its enormity and that it is the first direct mention we have of the Song, though, as commentators have noted, there are possible prior quotations of it e.g. in "The Life of Adam and Eve" (Lys: 25, citing Robert and Tournay [25 and 444]).

4   As with most of the Hekhalot literature, the Shiur Qomah was in part pseudepigraphically attributed to Rabbi Akiba, one of the half-legendary patrons of Merkabah mysticism (Scholem 1965: 36 n.1). It is however held by Scholem to be contemporaneous with or to precede the time of Rabbi Akiba (1965: 37-8).

5   T. B. Menahot 29b. On Mt. Sinai Moses found God tying "taggim" (tittles) to the Torah (cf. T.B. Shabbat 89a). In the "pargod" or Divine Veil, woven out of all events, he saw Akiba expounding the taggim, and could not understand him. Likewise there are many citations of his alleged capacity to interpret every particle in the Torah e.g. the significance of the acc. particle "'et" in Gen 1.1 (Gen. Rabbah 1.14, T.B. Hagigah 12a), said to derive from his teacher Nahum of Gimzu.

6   For the romance of Rabbi Akiba's life see T.B. Nedarim 50a, T.B. Ketuboth 62b-63a. A shepherd in the employ of the fabulously rich Kalba Sabu'a, he fell in love with his master's daughter, Rachel, who married him against her father's wishes. All sources agree on his

Notes to Chapter One - Introduction

total illiteracy, and violent hatred of scholars (Fischel: 15); she persuaded him to leave her to study; according to the Midrash, he learned the letters alongside his little son, being persuaded that it was possible for him when he watched water wearing away stone (Aboth de R. Nathan 6.15). Hence perhaps their mystical importance in his eyes. In extreme old age he supported the Bar Kochba revolt, believing Bar Kochba himself to be the Messiah. He died, torn to shreds with iron combs, reciting the Shema. When his disciples, or according to other versions, the Roman governor, Tinneius Rufus (T.P. Yeb. 14b), wondered at his endurance, he said that only now did he understand what it meant to love God "with all your soul" (Deut. 6.6) (T.B. Berakhoth 61b): "All my life I was troubled about the verse "with all thy soul", (which means) even if He takes your soul. I said: When will it be granted me to fulfil it?" (ibid., quoted by Urbach 417).

7   Urbach 416-17. The emphasis on the extremity of the love of God led to a cult of martyrdom, as its most perfect expression, succinctly formulated in Rabbi Akiba's phrase: "ḥabibim yissorîm" (suffering is precious) (T.B. Sanhedrin 101a).

8   Tosefta Sanhedrin 12.10: "He who trills the Song of Songs in banqueting-halls and makes it a kind of air has no share in the world to come".

9   One may adduce his extraordinary statement: "If the Torah had not been given to us, the Song of Songs would have sufficed to guide the world" (Aggadat Shir Hashirim, ed. Schechter 5, ed. Buber 4).

10 T.B. Shebuoth 35b, Shir Hashirim Rabbah 1.2.1.

11 "Our Rabbis taught: for two and a half years the School of Shammai and the School of Hillel engaged in debate, the former declaring that it had been better for man not to have been created than to have been created, and the latter maintaining that it was better for man that he was created rather than not created. They decided, upon voting, that it had been better for man not to have been created, but now that he has been created, let him examine his past deeds; others say, let him consider his future actions" (T.B. Eruvin 13b).

12 cf. Aboth 1.16: "Shammai used to say: '... Receive everyone with a cheerful expression'".

13 "R. Shimeon says 'With Ecclesiastes the School of Shammai are "meqûlē" and the School of Hillel are "meḥûmrē" '." (M. Yadaim 3.5)

14 As suggested for example by the discussion in T.B. Shabbat 30b. However, according to Lev. Rabbah 28.1, cited by Fischel (40-1), Ecclesiastes was in fact suspect because of its invitation to hedonism in 11.9a-d, and finally approved because of the conclusion to that verse "and for all things God shall bring you into judgement".

15 See Urbach: 196-201. Bezalel knew how to combine the letters with which the heavens and the earth were created (T.B. Berakhot 55a); according to T.B. Menahot 29b God created the world with a He and the heavens with a Yod, the subtlest of letters. The fullest expression of this theme is in the famous and delightful Midrash of the Alphabet (possibly 7th c.), in which the letters come before God clamouring to be chosen, except for the Aleph, which is too shy. God creates the world with the Bet, and begins the Ten Commandments

Notes to Chapter One - Introduction

with Aleph ('Ottiyot de Rabbi Akiba. Wertheimer Vol. 2: 397-403). "By Ten Sayings the world was created (M. Avot 5.1).

16 Scholem writes "To them (the Kabbalists) ... language in its purest form ... reflects the fundamental spiritual nature of the world" (1955: 17).

17 The superlative is the most natural interpretation of the title (Pope 1976: 294; Lys: 61 etc.). There is no reason, however, why the construct should not also mean "the song composed of songs", especially if one supposes that it is a cycle, like Levinger (8). This is supported by R. Hiyya's view, reported in the Midrash (SSR 1.10), that it is constituted of Solomon's 1005 songs.

18 Lys: 25, and others.

19 Most obviously in Psalms 96-100 where the Song of all the earth is combined with the vision of justice or the catalogue of lauding creatures in Psalm 148. For the perpetuation of the vision of universal song in the Psalms in Merkabah mysticism see Scholem (1955: 62). Its most beautiful and most idiosyncratic expression is perhaps the Pereq Shirah, that solemnly records the songs of all creatures, from the heavens and the earth to flies and gnats.

20 E.g. Moses Cordovero (Shiur Qomah 10): "the peoples of the earth are birds of various plumage, each with its own type of music, and its song". The idea is most fully developed among the Hassidim e.g. the stories and discourses of Nachman of Bratslav, expressed from Lurianic times onwards by the subtle parody of gentile songs in Hebrew words as a mode of "tikkun" or reparation.

21 A concept already adumbrated by Ben Sira 17.7.

22 Especially Israeli scholars e.g.Segal: 481-3; Levinger: 16; S. D. Goitein (1957: 304-5); and Rabin (1973: 215-219). Gerleman (69-70) likewise dates it to the "Solomonic enlightenment", on the basis of Egyptian parallels.

23 Goitein suggests that it was composed by a female singer at Solomon's court, since its originality consists in its narrative movement; the idea for this, he thinks, would be most likely to come from experience (1957: 301). Hyam Maccoby (58) even identifies the Beloved as the Queen of Sheba (= Hatshepsut!).

24 Most comprehensively advocated by H. Graetz: Schir Haschirim oder das Solomonische Hohelied (1871) 40-91. Cf. also H. L. Ginsberg, JPSA: 3.

25 Of these, the most uncontroverted is "pardēs" (from "pairidaeza") in 4.13 (cf. Eccl. 2.5, Neh. 2.8), whose currency in Hellenistic Palestine is attested by non-Jewish sources from Theophrastus onwards. Other terms deriving from Iranian, according to Lys: 12, are "nard" (1.12, 4.13-14), "karkōm" (saffron) (4.14) and "'egōz" (nut) (6.11). The first two, however, are Sanskrit, and hence could have entered the language at any time, even if they are not otherwise attested in the Bible; while an alternative etymology of "'egōz" from Ugaritic "'rgz" is proposed by Pope 1976: 574-7 and Dahood 1963-74 I: 290; XI: 362; cf. Schoville 1970: 93 for further references. In the absence of any precise information on the meaning of "'rgz", and its philological distance from "'egōz", the argument remains circumstantial, as Pope admits. M. D. Goulder suggests that

Notes to Chapter One - Introduction

"'argāmān" (purple) (7.6) may be of Iranian origin (Sequence and Precision in the Song: 40, somewhat ineptly, since it is found in Ugaritic (Cyrus Gordon 1965: 365 no. 340) and is Anatolian, according to Pope 1976: 444.

26   Of the four Greek loanwords cited by Graetz - "kōper" (henna) (1.14, 4.13, 7.12), "talpiyyōt" which he interprets as "telopis" "conspicuous" (4.4), "'appiryōn" (palanquin) (3.9) and "mezeg" (mixed wine) (7.3) only "'appiryōn" (= Gk. "phoreion" with a prosthetic Aleph) still carries conviction among the majority of commentators, despite objections that the prosthetic Aleph is redundant (Levinger: 16). Proposed alternative etymologies are not lacking e.g. from Old Iranian "upari-yāna">"aparyan", (Widengren 1955: 112), supported by W.F. Albright (1963: 2); but see Rundgren, for a powerful criticism. Rundgren explains the form as a cross between "piryōn" and "'afiryōn". Gordis (1974: 21 n.74) derives "'appiryōn" from Sanskrit "paryanka" (whence "palanquin"), in line with his view that 3.6-11 is an actual wedding song for Solomon, reflecting his trading connections (see also BDB: 68; while Gerleman characteristically provides an Egyptian derivation from "pr" = house. Other suggestions include "ap" + "rion" (a hypothetical Hebrew word) by Tur Sinai (1951: 384) and various Akkadian correlatives, involving more or less substantial emendations, by older critics (e.g. Wittekindt). Gk. phoreion is the Sept. translation and "'appiryōn" = wedding litter is attested in the Mishnah (Sot. 9.14) etc. Isserlin: 60, notes that whereas the word "phorein" is first instanced c.300 B.C. the object it represents is found from 500 B.C. onwards. Rabin even speculates that it could be Mycenaean Greek (1973: 215). The frequent argument that the loanwords were introduced during the course of transmission seems to me to be forced as well as hypothetical. A scribe would be unlikely to replace a common Hebrew term with an abstruse foreign one. Besides, it is difficult to imagine how the sentences might otherwise have read. For instance, "pardēs" fits perfectly into 4.13: "šelaḥayik pardēs rimmônîm ʿim perî megādîm kepārîm ʿim nerādîm" "your shoots/canals are a paradise of pomegranates with precious fruits, camphire and nard", with an alliterative pattern based on p,r,d, and nasals: PRDs Rmnm ʿm PRy mgDm kPRm ʿm nRDm

27   The relative particle "še-" occurs as early as the Song of Deborah (Jud. 5.7), and is found in cognate languages such as Phoenician. It has been suggested as evidence of a northern or dialect origin of the Song (e.g. Pope 1976: 33), since, supposedly, it occurs mostly in northern texts (cf. BDB: 979). There is little support for this, e.g. from the Northern Prophets, and instances are too few to generalise from. However, only with Ecclesiastes and the Song does it become frequent, and its exclusive use in the Song conforms with post-classical Hebrew. This remains the best explanation. Another factor that in my view determines the choice between "'ašer" and "še" is genre and style: "'ašer" suits historical narrative such as Esther, while "še" is most apt for lyric compression, and has a powerful alliterative function e.g. "šellišlōmōh" (šlšl) "that is Solomon's" in 3.7. We see another example of this in Ps. 137.8-9:

Notes to Chapter One - Introduction

"'ašrê šeyyešallēm ... 'ašrê šeyyō'ḥēz" "happy is he who repays ... happy is he who grasps", where "še" obviates the cumbersome repetition "'ašrê 'ašer". Pierre Auffret (1980: 368) points out the paronomasia between "yerûšālayim" (vv. 6,7) and "'ašrê šeyyēsallēm".

28   Robert and Tournay (233) at the other extreme, see in this an intentional euphemism, reflecting the hostility between Jews and Samaritans; possibly this would postdate the destruction of Samaria in 310 B.C. Pope (1976: 560) proposes, "with diffidence and without expectation of immediate acceptance", that "ktrṣh" should be understood as a verb "thou art pleasing", with an asseverative k, and Jerusalem should be deleted, since he finds the comparison with cities difficult. Freedman objects, according to Pope, that the parallelism is perfect and the comparison no more difficult than with deities. The terrestrial capitals, Jerusalem and Tirzah, complement the celestial rulers, sun and moon, in the parallel verse in 6.10. The Beloved is metonymically associated with cities throughout the Song e.g. the comparison of her eyes with pools of Heshbon in 7.5, or of her body with a wall with towers in 8.8-10.

29   The major study is that of Schoville. See also Avishur. As J. B. White (38) remarks, Schoville has been lacking in proper caution in gathering signs of possible influence; nevertheless, the results have been exiguous. Avishur's work consists mostly in the collation of parallel pairs and types of parallelism, and is consequently very general.

30   Albright (1963: 3 and n.3). Kugel (1981a: 38 n.101) remarks "There is something disturbingly circular about this hypothesis". The two-word parallelisms in the Song normally reflect the intensity of the lovers' emotions. Even on Albright's own terms the two-word parallelisms in the Song are demonstrably later than the Bronze Age, since he considers that paronomasia is only a later feature of Hebrew poetry; those in the Song, however, are marked by intense word-play (e.g. "lebānōn ... libbabtinî" "Lebanon ... you have ravished my heart" in 4.8-9).

31   This argument is common to all who would date the poem early, cf. Rabin (1973: 208ff.). There may well have been trading links between Solomon and India, as Rabin and Gordis (1974: 21) suggest; but there were far closer contacts during the Hellenistic period. In any case, the very existence of Tamil Sangham poetry a thousand years before the earliest recorded example is hypothetical in the extreme.

32   H. P. Müller (1977: 157), elegantly calls this a "'zweiten' Naïvetät".

33   Comparisons have been made with modern Palestinian love poetry (cf. Pope 1976: 56-66); pre-Islamic Arab poetry (Seale: 53-74); and the Gita Govinda, recently translated as The Love Song of the Dark Lord by Barbara Stoler Miller. Pope (1976: 85) traces the comparison to Adam Clarke in 1798. A specialist in Sanskrit, Dr Fred Morgan, has suggested to me, with special reference to the Gita Govinda, that the Song is the nearest approach in Judaism to Indian spirituality. Alonso Schökel and the Mexican poet Eduardo Zurro have produced a beautiful comparison of the Song of Songs with the

Notes to Chapter One - Introduction

traditional poetry of Spain, illustrating the persistence of amorous poetic conventions over the entire Mediterranean area.

34   For Gerleman it is crucial to the understanding of the Song; for example, he explicates the imagery (e.g. eyes = doves) as references to the conventions of Egyptian art (68-72 and passim). Goitein uses the relationship extensively in his interpretation; he sees the Song as a development of Egyptian love poetry (1957: 301). Robert/Tournay similarly hold that the Song imitates Egyptian love poetry; and Grelot (51) suggests that its influence could have persisted into the post-exilic era. J. B. White (67-68) briefly summarises the recognition of parallels by Egyptologists. Cooper (157) also notes that more parallels have been found with Egyptian than Mesopotamian love poetry.

35   J. B. White: 132-34. White appears to infer, from Hermann's contention that there is no <u>exclusive</u> sacral basis for the imagery of the Egyptian love songs (White: 68), that there are no religious connotations whatsoever. In fact, Hermann devotes considerable space to those implications. The admittedly common references to the gods are explained away through irony, and finally dismissed as insignificant. In the Song, however, despite the absence of the name of the divinity, the Sages ("these wise men") expressed their recognition of the God-given nature of love and the virtues of mutuality and fidelity; a contention supported by two quotations from Proverbs. Exactly the same argument could be applied to Egyptian love poetry.

36   The "topoi" (or themes) of Egyptian love poetry, according to White, are i) seeing ii) hearing iii) touching (which includes kissing, embracing etc.), iv) smelling, breathing, tasting v) the heart vi) love-sickness vii) friends and enemies viii) animals and plants. Similar topoi, not surprisingly, are found for lovers in the Song.

37   J. B. White (109-114, 146-48), following Gerleman (60-2), adopts Jolles' theory of archetypal postures into which lovers of all ages project themselves: namely the "king" (which makes do for Jolles' "Ritter Travestie"), the "shepherd" and the "servant" fictions. The most diverse material is ingeniously fitted into these categories, with single-minded assiduity. For instance, there is, admittedly, no king in the Egyptian love lyrics, but there is at least the horse of a king (J. B. White: 110)! The servant-fiction in the Song is represented, among other things, by the seal on the lover's heart in 8.6 (ibid.: 147)! The jackal pup in Papyrus Harris 500.i.4 (which according to Derchain should be translated "wolf" with the same erotic connotations as in English) is apparently an aspect of the shepherd-fiction (J. B. White: 114). If the terms are sufficiently redefined e.g. if the shepherd-fiction includes the whole of the animal kingdom, anything can be categorised as anything. The use that White and Gerleman have made of Jolles' theory has been extensively criticised by Fox (Scholia to Canticles 6). According to Fox, the persona is projected on to the text as a whole, and is adopted by the audience, not the character. For there to be a royal fiction, for example, the lovers would actually have to be royalty. In my view, the lovers adopt all sorts of metaphorical guises, which are linked paradigmatically, and

Notes to Chapter One - Introduction

can be graded according to frequency and emphasis. Thus in the Song the "royal" parody is quite important. On the other hand, it is no use pretending that there is a servant-fiction, or anything analogous to it. In Egyptian love-poetry, incidentally, the rhetorical point is that the lover is not the beloved's servant, and is denied that intimacy (e.g. in the second Cairo Love Song, which Fox [1980] calls "Wishes"). This is an instance where form-critical zeal overlooks contextual relevance.

38   For example, it might be significant that Egyptian love-poetry but not the Song uses synaesthesia e.g. "Pomegranate wine is hearing your voice" (Papyrus Harris 500 c.2, Lichtheim 1976: 192). That the lovers in both Egyptian love poetry and the Song see each other and are attracted by the sight is surely less important than what they see, as communicated through the images. White makes no attempt to examine these, unlike Fox.

39   For example, there is a well-established persona that has escaped the attention of White and his predecessors: the lover as god or goddess. The equivalents in the Song are the theomorphic connotations of the portrait of the Lover in 5.10-16, and the Beloved's appearance in 6.10, with its celestial imagery, comparable with the rising of the morning star at the beginning of the Chester-Beatty cycle.

40   He excuses the style on grounds of accuracy. However, a detailed examination of some of the translations has shown that they are vastly, and at times inexplicably, inferior to those already published by Lichtheim and Simpson. For example, in the Cairo Love Song no.1 (which Fox calls "The Crossing") st.4, he omits two lines completely, one of them crucial ("the crocodile has become a mouse to me"); and gives no explanation for so doing. At other times, he ignores significant lacunae; many hypothetical interpretations are not indicated as such in footnotes. A very interesting, if unreliable version is John L. Foster's Love Songs of the New Kingdom (1975), an attempt to translate Egyptian love poetry into a modern free verse idiom. Foster justifies his approach (1971) as an attempt to communicate the excitement of Egyptian love poetry. Despite much criticism from Egyptologists, and its evident faults, Foster's re-creation of the love poetry is very appealing.

41   The river in the Cairo love song (st.4) is specified as a devouring flood (1.2) in which lurks a crocodile called "dpy" "the consuming one" (Derchain: 68); love tames the water and transforms the crocodile into a mouse. For the interpretation see Derchain (71-2). He points out also that the closure of an impassable gulf between the lovers, a motif we find also in the Song, is reflected in the image of the lover as a god, idealised and inaccessible, who suddenly becomes intimate and human.

42   Cairo love song st.5/6. I owe the information that the gesture is emblematic of Hathor to Alison Roberts.

43   Much discussion has gone into the significance of this gesture. As Derchain (75) points out, it is not characteristic for fish to feel safe in people's fingers; thus this reinforces the symbolic suggestion. The exact connotation of "mnḫ", which he renders "that feels safe" is unclear; Fox (1980: 103) translates "nice", White (188) "well-behaved".

Notes to Chapter One - Introduction

For the tilapia as a symbol of fecundity see Derchain (75); the sexual association of fish is widespread. Derchain suggests that the fish is held quite free in the open palm, in a gesture of offering such as we find in paintings of divers. Fox argues that the tilapia is his heart, which seems unwarranted in context (1980: 106). What we do have is the exchange or fusion of imagery. By analogy, the tilapia would be her heart.

44 Fox analyses the mutuality of relationship and the delicacy of the language in the Cairo love songs perceptively in his 1980 article (106-7). It is puzzling that his forthcoming article "Love, Passion, and Perception" should be less sensitive to these aspects of the poetry. For example, Fox examines in detail the verbal echoes between the lovers as a technique in the Song, in contrast to Egyptian love poetry. Precisely such a technique, however, is described in his account of the Cairo love songs.

45 In the Cairo love song st.3, the girl dives into the river fully clothed; Derchain (72-3) discusses its coquettish significance as an index of class, since diving was a menial but skilful profession.

46
> My heart thought of my love for you,
>   When half of my hair was braided;
> I came at a run to find you,
>   And neglected my hairdo.
> Now if you let me braid my hair,
>   I shall be ready in a moment. (Lichtheim 1976: 191)

47 Fox (1980: 106) rightly says that this wish transcends the erotic. "I will be together with you / even when there comes to pass the day of the elder" does not necessarily refer to death, as Fox assumes (1980: 107, n.17.) Derchain (70) divides the sentences differently: "Je veux faire l'amour tant que passent les jours. Le repos sera pour la vieillesse".

48 Cf. also Müller (1977: 160-61).

49 For the history of the cultic interpretation of the Song, see Rowley (1965: 223-29) and Pope (1976: 145-53). Kramer (1969: 85-106) provides very few convincing parallels. Despite criticism from Schmidt and Rowley, in my view incontrovertible, the theory has proved surprisingly persistent. There is simply no evidence that the Song ever was a Tammuz liturgy, quite apart from the fact that we possess none from Canaan. That they may share a common thematic background, and use some of the same images, is only to be expected, since they share the same cultural horizon. As Rowley wrote, "the way of letters to all but devotees of Tammuz is very hard" (237). Another sensational extrapolation from the Mesopotamian material is that the Song contains love magic (Tur Sinai, passim). This idea has won cautious support from Gordis (1974: 32-3). Perhaps unfortunately for would-be lovers, the argumentation seems to me to be contrived (e.g. "mêšārîm" (1.4, 7.10) = "meshuratim" = "potency" (Tur-Sinai 1951: 369)) and the practical value uncertain.

50 The dialectic is to be found, for example, in the haunting line: "āḥuz pāki / ša rūqātim" "I have seized your mouth, so far away", followed by images of the eyes and vulva. At the end of the poem the

Notes to Chapter One - Introduction

line is transformed into "āḫuz pāki / ša dādi" "I have seized your mouth so fit for love" (J.& A. Westenholz: 203, 211-12).

51 aśhit / kiriiś Suen
  abtuq ṣarbatam / (y)ūmiśśa (?) (l.17-20)

  I vaulted in to the garden of Sin,
  I cut off branches for her day ...

Suen is the father of Ishtar, the goddess of love, and hence of the sexuality represented by the girl and her garden. The reading of "u-me-iš-sa" as "yumiśśa" "for her day" is not very satisfactory, as J. & A. Westenholz admit. The alternative "ummiśśa" "for her womb" (or rather "of her mother") proposed by Gelb (MAD.V), would support the ancestral context. This reading too is dubious (cf. J. & A. Westenholz: 209).

52 As in the Song, in the central "stanza" of the incantation, quite eerily, the Beloved is transformed into a mother:

  You shall go round me among the boxwoods
   As the shepherd goes around his flock,
  The goat around her kid,
  The ewe around her lamb,
  The jenny around her foal. (l.21-24)

Similarly, the first image of the poem is that love is the child of Ishtar, "sitting on her lap, in fragrance of incense" (l.4-5).

53 Trilingual versions (Sumerian, Akkadian, Hittite) have been found at Boghazkoi and Ugarit (Cooper: 158).

54 Cooper (161) writes that "it would be very unseemly to describe one's mother in such specific terms". Inhibition, to say the least, is uncharacteristic of Mesopotamian love poetry. Cooper, moreover, immediately suggests that the tenor of the passage is erotic, and the "mother" is perhaps not a real mother at all, but a manifestation of the goddess Inanna. l.15-16, however, present her as attentive to Inanna, and generally she partakes vividly in the life of her town and her family. The simplest explanation of the lack of detailed bodily disintegration is that it does not interest the poet; he is concerned to communicate her vivacity, common sense and piety.

55 For example, Cooper holds that "the second sign" of "The Message of Ludingira" and the description of the Lover in the Song 5.10-16 are both extended metaphors of a statue (160). In the Song, as I hope to show, this is but one of its possible connotations. In "The Message of Ludingira" only two lines refer to a statuette:

  An alabaster statuette, set on a lapis pedestal,
  A living rod of ivory [Civil: "figurine"],
   whose limbs are filled with charm

The others in the second sign, beginning:

  My mother is brilliant in the heavens,
   a doe in the mountains, a morning star abroad at noon ...

have no possible correlation with the Song 5.10-16. Furthermore, as Civil (7) pointed out in his more thorough analysis of "Ludingira", two of the lines emphasise her animation (l.29 "But she is alive, a breathing thing", and l.31 above). Cooper omits the former line on the grounds of its obscurity (160), which seems no greater, at least according to Civil's discussion, than many of the lines he translates freely. Cooper's article is, moreover, highly selective; he chooses those passages that best suit his comparison. In the context of the "Message of Ludingira" as a whole, this is less convincing. It also misses the rhetorical point of the wasfs in the Song, the correlation of one particular member with one particular, highly articulated scene, in tension with others; here there is merely a catalogue of images.

56   Jacobsen (1976: 232) thinks that this was merely an Assyrian political/religious feuilleton. However it is difficult to deny the beauty of the concluding sequence:

> You are the mother, Istar of Babylon,
>   The beautiful one, the queen of the Babylonians,
> You are the mother, a palm of carnelian,
>   The beautiful one,
>   who is beautiful to a superlative degree,
> Whose figure is red to a superlative degree,
>   is beautiful to a superlative degree.
>   (Lambert 1975: 123, l.18-22.)

The scatological abuse, with its correlation of the anal and the genital, its dazzling sensual and olefactory imagery, suggests ecstatic regression, which is at times wonderfully funny (cf. B. Foster: 79). There may also be ironic reflections on the status of women in such lines as:

> You are the good housewife - create a family;
> You are the fool - process wool.
>   (Lambert 1975: 109, l.19-20.)

and a possible night of misrule:

> In the ritual of Zarpanitum,
>   By night there is not a good housewife,
> By night there is not a good housewife,
>   By night a married woman creates no difficulty.
>   (ibid.: 109, l.5-8)

57   The influence of Alexandrian pastoral on the Song was advocated originally and most fervently by Graetz, but not by most recent scholars, except for the occasional citation of parallels; Robert Graves, however, in his altogether eccentric edition, attributes its composition to a Jew in a Palestinian coastal city with close Alexandrian contacts, and a supply of magic mushrooms; cf. also C. Gebhardt, who compares it to the Idylls (cited by Pope 1976: 36). Conversely Peter Jay has suggested a possible influence of the Song on Alexandrian models. It may be noted that Derchain (66-67) suggests a thematic contiguity at least between Egyptian love poetry and the Alexandrian anthology.

58   P.160; cf. Rudolph 1977: 113, Eissfeldt 1965: 490. On the other

Notes to Chapter One - Introduction

hand, Gordis speaks of the "rustic simplicity" of some of the lyrics (1974: 24). While I would dispute both the description and Gordis' atomistic approach, it is clear that the Song, like all Pastoral, draws on the resources of the country, and that rigid categorisation is to be avoided. City and country were mutually dependent; the city in ancient times was never far from the farm. The relationship is central to the song. An interesting recent article by Gary A. Herion "The Role of Historical Narrative in Biblical thought: The Tendencies Underlying OT Historiography" has examined the tension between city and country as reflected in the Biblical interpretation of history and myth. He too stresses the continuum and cross-fertilisation of city and country.

59   For the consensus see J. B. White (54-55). The characterisation of the Song as folk poetry developed with the Romantics and was most forthrightly advanced by Morris Jastrow, who resists any attempt to ascribe subtlety or insight to the Song. This is maintained by Rudolph: 105 and even as recently as J. & A. Westenholz: 219. The literary craftsmanship of the writing is argued at length by Gerleman (54ff) and demonstrated conclusively and in detail by Krinetzki. White's cautionary note that there is "no internal evidence" for the inference of an educated circle is unnecessarily unenthusiastic; for what Krinetzki, Exum etc. have shown is precisely the degree of sophistication, based on internal evidence, that has contributed to the Song.

60   Yair Zakovitch discusses some of the associations (1975: 292-3, n.5). See below, ch.4 n.111, for further references.

61   Roland Barthes' tour-de-force "S/Z" is the most systematic exposition. Derrida's insistence on the primacy of the text over the individual voice, the illusory "parole originaire", that the text has no "centre", is always heteronomous, is always a play of signs referring to other texts, relates his practice to that of Barthes, and to the general Structuralist notion of "bricolage". His marvellous essay on the history of metaphors in philosophy "White Mythology" (1974) results in a similar subversion of its assumptions:

> There is therefore no properly philosophical category to qualify a certain number of tropes which have conditioned the structuring of those philosophic oppositions which are called "fundamental", "structuring", "originating". (1974: 28-29)

62   With its immense Diaspora, the Jewish community, one supposes, would have been especially receptive to cross-cultural influences. We know little of contact between Jews of Palestine and Babylon and Persia at this period, but there is no reason to suppose that it was not fairly intense, as later; otherwise it is difficult to account for the sense of common identity, homogeneity of practice, and rapid diffusion of sacred literature. The impact of Iranian dualism on Jewish thought and eschatology is generally recognised; court circles in Israel (e.g. the Oniads, Tobiads), with their international culture, may well have been correspondingly open to poetic as well as linguistic trade.

63   See p. 153. Critics have, on the whole, been surprisingly

reticent about the parallel. Tur-Sinai built it into his anecdotal theory. Albert Cook (112) reads it as a public application of the words to the Song.

64   For numerical symbolism in the Eclogues, see Berg (108-9).

65   Martin Hengel (1974: 49) discusses the conflict between this class and the poor from the time of Nehemiah onwards. He possibly exaggerates the extent to which Judea was economically and politically a dead end (for a contrary view, see Morton Smith: 57ff). Nevertheless, its relative isolation in proximity to major trade routes was clearly influential in its survival as an insular yet creative entity (cf. Hengel 1974: 43). Certainly by the 3rd century B.C. Jerusalem was no small city (Hengel: 53). Nehemiah's forcible settling of country folk in Jerusalem may have been motivated by political considerations, as Smith suggests (148); if so, it may have been less underpopulated in the 5th century than is otherwise assumed (Hengel: 53).

66   The spice gardens of Ein-Gedi, though founded in the time of Josiah (Pope 1976: 554), flourished especially in the Persian and Ptolemaic periods (Hengel 1974: 45).

67   Hengel 1974: 46-47. Though one should be cautious of argument from silence, this would tend to confirm the late dating of the Song. Gottwald (1980: 656-660) however, considers that the development of an efficient water-conservation and irrigation system, rendered possible by the newly-discovered technique of waterproofing cisterns at the beginning of the Iron Age, was the material base for the Israelite revolution. It is, nevertheless, extremely difficult to date irrigation systems, as Gottwald notes (1980:792 n.592). For the able exploitation of water in the Early Bronze Age and the Bronze Age settlements in the Negev, see Thompson (1978: 18-20, 26ff). There was extensive field irrigation in the Beth-Shean valley (ibid.: 14).

68   The evocation of the splendour of Solomon perhaps drew on contemporary models. The exquisite gardens of the Song suggest an analogy with Esther: the word "ginnâ" "garden" in 6.11 is elsewhere applied only to Ahasuerus' garden in Esther 7.8 (ginnat habbîtān); both are royal, both specialised, so as perhaps to distinguish them from ordinary gardens. Finally, the gardens in the Song are associated with Persian loanwords: "pardēs", "ᵉgōz". It may reflect the pretensions of the aristocracy who patronised the Song, following imperial fashion; the world of the Song would thus be an idealised projection of the aspirations of the audience. Such imitation is supported by what we know of the court of the Tobiads (cf. Hengel 1974: 267-270).

69   The alliance between the aristocracy and the priesthood (e.g. the Oniads) persisted until the destruction of the Temple; Morton Smith ascribes the Wisdom books to these groups (157ff). But this history of a millennial struggle between separatists and assimilationists is a vast over-simplification, necessarily tending to accentuate conflict and class, and to reduce differences to abstractions. Even at the height of factional struggle some Pharisees came from priestly, aristocratic circles. Leo Perdue, in a recent monograph, has shown that Wisdom circles were not indifferent to

Notes to Chapter One - Introduction

cult and law; we should not disallow the possibility of contrary trends within the same person, let alone class, and that conflict arose within a consensus. Otherwise, it is difficult to account for the absorption of these books into the canonical tradition. Uniformity was never an absolute desideratum of Judaism.

70 Most commentators make a sidelong reference to this relationship, without being very specific what it is (e.g. Gordis 1974: 13-16; J. B. White: 55-56, 132-34; Lys: 55). The ascription is largely founded on its attribution to Solomon, and its inclusion among the "ketūbîm", alongside Job, Proverbs and Ecclesiastes, as we found in the list of books originally proscribed as "mesālîm" in Aboth de R. Nathan. There is little attempt to relate it in depth to the Wisdom tradition. Gordis (1974: 13-16) takes its quality of wisdom in a secular sense, referring to the skill of composition; others hold that it permitted its incorporation in the canon (e.g. Krinetzki 1981: 26-28, J. B. White: 54-55), since Wisdom was dedicated to probing human experience as part of the created order (cf. also Childs 1979: 578-9). Childs (1979: 574) claims that Israelite wisdom was essentially didactic, not philosophical, in support of the contention that it was not secular; the distinction, however, is not entirely clear to me.

71 Berg: 8. In Greece too, there was a loss of political independence, with accompanying demoralisation. Cynicism, Stoicism and Epicureanism originated at this time, diverse reactions to a negative perception of life as illusory or evil; all these movements had close connections with Palestine (cf. Hengel 1974: 84-8); and have their correlates in the Biblical tradition.

72 The theory that the Song celebrated a marriage week had considerable vogue at the turn of the century, following the researches of Wetzstein and others, but is now largely abandoned, because of the lack of any convincing evidence. Pope (1976: 141-45) and Rowley (1965: 210-12) provide good summaries. In recent times, the association of the Song, in whole or in part, with wedding celebrations has been postulated principally by various form-critics, anxious to define its Sitz-im-Leben; cf. Murphy (1973: 416) for discussion, especially of Würthwein, and Krinetzki (1964). Murphy himself has passed through a phase (1961: 55-6) in which he considered it to be a wedding songbook. Krinetzki (1971: 179, 1981: 11) has since modified his views. Goulder holds that the Song is a nuptial drama. Other proponents are Fuerst (166-67) and Webster (87); the evidence, however, is singularly slight and the tone distinctly apologetic.

73 For an excellent summary of views see J. B. White: 25-26. White (27) however doubts whether a poem advocating unmarried love would ever have entered the canon. This surely begs the question. It seems to me also that he is unjustified in inferring the exclusivity of love in the Song on the basis of 2.16 and 6.3; I will argue in the course of my thesis that there is a tension between the uniqueness of the love of the Song and the temptations of promiscuity, as formulated by Solomon's wives (6.8), or the maidens of 1.4.

74 Kirk's criticism of the tendency of the myth-and-ritual school of Biblical scholars to explain every myth as an aetiology of a ritual

Notes to Chapter One - Introduction

(12-13) seizes upon one aspect of a pervasive fallacy: to situate every text in a specific and generally cultic context. For example, almost all the scholars cited by B. Festinger's 1981 article, "A Decade of German Psalm Criticism", suffer from this tendency. To give an example: "According to Delekat (1967), the suppliants are people who seek protection from creditors and personal enemies in a sanctuary where they write their prayers on a wall" (Festinger: 93).

75   Pope 1976: 210-29. Pope does not do himself justice when he claims that "it is beyond the scope of this present effort to attempt any systematic account of funeral cults in the ancient world" (1976: 228).

76   Among Jews, the Song is generally recited on the intermediate Sabbath of Passover; this custom can be dated back to the 6th century (Gordis 1974: 6). The Kabbalists introduced the reading of the Song as the preface to the Friday night service. This practice has taken root among Sephardi but not Ashkenazi Jews. M. D. Goulder (Sequence and Precision in the Song: 46-52) proposes an original liturgical setting at Pentecost, as part of a grand lectionary cycle whose convolutions are expounded in his brilliant but highly controversial The Evangelists' Calendar.

77   Hengel 1974: 107. The boundaries of the literature of the period, and the dates of books such as Job and Ruth, are much disputed. My list coincides with Hengel's: Proverbs, Job, Jonah, Ecclesiastes, Ruth, Esther.

78   James Williams (1981) argues that Proverbs is characterised by an aphoristic wisdom of order, in other words one that works from the authority of tradition, seeks to define the general and typical, and assumes the basic coherence of the world. The wisdom of counter-order, exemplified by Ecclesiastes and the sayings of Jesus, works from individual experience, uses paradox to subvert generalisation, and is sceptical, anarchic or mystical. This is a valid contrast, and a valid contribution to Biblical studies. Nevertheless, it is not quite absolute, since Proverbs also partakes occasionally of the wisdom of counter-order. Williams does not adequately acknowledge this in his analysis of quotations. An example is 26.4-5:

> Answer not a fool according to his folly,
>   lest you be likened unto him.
> Answer a fool according to his folly,
>   lest he be wise in his own eyes.

Here the point is not merely that there are different ways of looking at things, as Williams (1981: 37) argues, but that they cancel each other out; all clichés are questionable. Another instance, not raised by Williams, is 17.27-28:

> He who is sparing of his speech is knowing;
>   he who conserves his mind is understanding.
> Also a fool who is silent is thought wise.

A commonplace is set up and neatly demolished.

79   The earliest Greek reports unanimously represented the Jews as a nation of philosophers, and were extraordinarily curious. There is

Notes to Chapter One - Introduction

an account of a meeting between Aristotle and a Jew in Clearchus, which Hengel (1974: 257) regards as fictitious. Theophrastus, Aristotle's successor, believed Jews to be contemplatives, devoted to the study of the heavens; others, such as Megasthenes, found an affinity with Brahmin philosophy, and others again, beginning with Hecataeus, were interested in Judaism because they thought it embodied the ideal social order. In general Greeks selected those aspects of Judaism that most appealed to them, or projected into Judaism their own wishful thinking. For example, they identified the monotheistic God of Moses with the god of the philosophers, and often contrasted the "pure" Mosaic religion with its perversion in the Judaism then current. Nevertheless, there is abundant evidence of real knowledge, concern, and dialogue (see Hengel 1974: 255-61 for references).

80   Job 31.26-27. The common assumption among commentators that the reference is to an act of worship (Pope 1973: 235; Dhorme: 462-3; Perdue: 177), while not inappropriate, pays insufficient attention to the detail of the language, the qualification of the moon as "yāqār" "precious", the paronomasia of "wayyipt", with its overlapping roots PTH "seduce" and YPH "beautiful", which suggests that the temptation to worship was aesthetic, and to the immediate context, with its exaggerated perfections and exorbitant penalties. One is reminded of R. Jacob's dictum in Aboth 3.9: "A man who studies as he walks and interrupts his study and says 'How beautiful is tnat tree!' ... it is as if he has forfeited his soul".

81   Morton Smith ascribes the Song and related books to what he terms "the gentry", who were opposed to the exclusivity of the Jerusalem priesthood and indifferent to the old Israelite literature; he describes their products as belletrist. However, he somewhat undermines this position by claiming that they came from that part of the gentry that was most sympathetic to Judaism, and that through the works can be traced their gradual reconciliation with the "separatist" party (Smith: 157-63). This does not explain how they constitute the tradition of the period. I would not agree that they are indifferent to the old Israelite literature, as is shown by the use of quotation in Jonah (Magonet 1976: 65-84). Nor would I classify these works as "belletrist", with its somewhat patronising implications. Nor can they be sharply divided from the supposedly Levitical Psalms. Finally, Morton Smith's ascription of works to parties or a period for which there is very little evidence is in my view hopelessly abstract (for a similar criticism see Hengel 1974: 113).

82   Cf. Hengel's estimate that "In all probability, groups of the priesthood, the Levitical writing schools, and the lay nobility shared in producing this rich writing" (1974: 113). Even in very late Second Temple times Pharisees often came from priestly and aristocratic circles.

83   A quite disproportionate number of philosophers actually came from Palestine (Hengel 1974: 83-85).

84   For poetry itself as the true subject of Hellenistic Pastoral, and especially the Eclogues, see Berg: 5-6 and passim.

85   "Every discourse must be composed like, or in the likeness of,

Notes to Chapter One - Introduction

a living being, with a body of its own, as it were, so as not to be headless or feetless, but to have a middle and members arranged in fitting relation to each other and to the whole" (Phaedrus 264 C, tr. Giordana-Orsini).

86   Cf. the discussion of the Poetics in Giordano-Orsini: 77-78.

87   Examples of the first group are Gordis 1974: 16; Gerleman: 59-60; Falk 1982: 62-80; Fohrer: 303; Eissfeldt: 486; Pfeiffer: 708; perhaps its most extreme formulation is that of Landsberger. Landsberger believes that with one or two exceptions the Song consists of miniatures, linked through catchwords, and that even coherent sequences are really catenas of independent poems. Other representatives are to be found in White: 32-33; Lys: 20; Rowley: 221-22. Proponents of the second view include Levinger: 8-9; Lys: 23-24; Rudolph: 100; Rowley: 222. Krinetzki (1981: 16-18) divides the Song into six "Liedgruppe". Levinger, Lys, Tournay and Rowley envisage a unity of composition. Levinger, for example, attributes the sequence to the poet, in a retrospective arrangement of his works; while Rudolph perceives the unity on the level of redaction (cf. also Eissfeldt). The view that the Song has an intrinsic coherence takes several forms e.g. that it is a drama or allegory. It will be discussed in more detail below. Far more scholars actually working on the Song are convinced of its unity than is generally believed; the critical orthodoxy or assumption that the Song is an anthology is belied if one examines the literature. This may be a circular argument, since precisely those scholars are attracted to the Song who are inclined to take it seriously, or it may reflect the human tendency to create wholes out of experience. My contention is that it is this very process of the integration of fragmentary reality that is at issue in the Song.

88   Lys (20-21) lists the number of units into which different critics divide the Song as follows: Pfeiffer 9, Siegfried 10, Haupt 12, Reuss 16, Budde 23, Eissfeldt 25, BC 27, Gordis 28, Gerleman 32 ... Another list is given by White (32-33); the difference is discussed by Falk 1982: 68; Gordis 1974: 17 n.64 etc.

89   Murphy wavers - and has vacillated through most of his professional career (1977: 488; cf. 1949, 1953) - between seeing the Song as a loose collection of poems with a long prehistory, whose relative unity is the work of an editor (1977: 488 and 1979b: 101) and the more positive approach of his article "The Unity of the Song of Songs" (1979b: 436), where indeed he effectively demolishes the redactional hypothesis.

90   In the Hermeneia series (Fortress Press - it will be 1984 or 1985)

91   1976: 50. Loretz and Avishur have been particularly assiduous in tracing parallel parallelisms cf. also Schoville passim. J. B. White is sensibly cautionary (42). Kugel (1981a: 25-40) provides a balanced evaluation, and warns against focussing too much on the "fixed pair" in the comparison of texts, since it is often the point of least poetic interest.

92   Cf. S. Gevirtz (9-10) and Schoville (65-6) (on 2.16 = 6.3) etc.

Notes to Chapter One - Introduction

for this term. Cyrus Gordon in his section on "cliché" in UT 134, however, remarks that "their frequency lends them a poetic flavour akin to that of a refrain". Kugel warns against imposing "modern day notions of originality on ancient texts", citing the example of medieval poetics (1981a: 29-30).

93   Giordano-Orsini (21) contrasts the villain with the "hero" of organic unity; in other words, the poem as a synthesis of interacting parts, and that itself is a participant in other wholes, such as the poet's life, a literary corpus etc. He contrasts this with the New Critical endeavour. His book is a very compelling study of the development of the idea of organic unity in Greek philosophy.

94   Other examples are the Turin love songs (Simpson: 312-15), in which three beautifully characterised trees comment on the lovers beneath them, and the Papyrus Harris 500 IIc (17-19), in which the stanzas are linked together by puns on the names of flowers (Lichtheim: 192, Simpson: 308-9).

95   The most famous of these are analyses of Shakespeare's Sonnet 129 (Verbal Art in "Th'Experience of Spirit", 1971), and Baudelaire's "Les Chats" (with Lévi-Strauss 1970). Critics have included Fowler (1975), Culler (1971) and Riffaterre (1970). These critics object that Jakobson treats all structures, the most obscure and the most prominent, as equivalent; there is no sense of a structural hierarchy. Correlatively, there is little attempt to distinguish them on the basis of their poetic significance i.e. the correlation of sound and sense, their contribution to the entire effect of the poem. Finally, Jakobsonian analysis is purely descriptive, leaving us with a feeling "So what?" (Guiraud discussion 1971: 22); it tells us nothing of a poem's value, and indeed risks confusing complexity with quality. These criticisms are very acute, and have led Riffaterre, Fowler and others away from the New-Critical analysis of the text alone to the response of the reader (and hence to deconstruction). All this is salutary, but it could be argued - not that Jakobson does - that undiscernable patterns foreground and inflect others that are more prominent. Ehrenzweig devotes much of his 1947/65 study to the influence of these unconscious structures, like brushstrokes in painting. Secondly, perceptibility is a variable, that develops with repeated reading, for example in the mind of Jakobson, Lévi-Strauss etc. Thirdly, as Hrushovski points out, poems are characterised by sound and syntactic play for its own sake; patterns may be semantically neutral (1968: 417-19). Again, the attitude of the reader, his recognition that this is poetry, is determinant. Finally, whatever his limitations, his lack of discrimination, Jakobson did enable poems to be analysed more thoroughly and exactly than ever before; his analyses, moreover, unlike those of some of his followers, are always inventive, brilliant and perceptive.

96   Broadribb divides the Song into five fairly arbitrary major sections which he claims are linked through repetition of phrase and action, and strophaic equivalence (his line-division however is a bit hazardous). For Broadribb, the Song is not a "wedding" or "love" song but associated with the New Year festival. His thesis has received little attention among subsequent critics.

Notes to Chapter One - Introduction

97 Angénieux protests against the unscientific procedure of basing structural analysis on content, and proceeds to a detailed classification of refrains and repetitions, bounding and linking separate poems, in a harmonious synthesis. He argues, on the basis of his reconstruction, for a theological/allegorical interpretation.

98 Shea's is an extreme example of a tendency manifest in recent years to see chiasms everywhere in the Bible, a sort of magical key for unlocking its structures.

99 For example, he takes the singular vocative of "hayyôšebet bagganîm" "you who sit among the gardens" in 8.13 as a feminine plural participle, referring to the daughters of Jerusalem, and attributes the verse to the Beloved. Even granted that some of the versions differ - though none of them offer the <u>feminine</u> plural! - this is a quite extraordinary, and blithely unsupported, exegetical licence. He does not comment on the feminine singular "qōlēk" "your voice" at the end of the verse. Presumably the Beloved is talking to herself. He thus gives himself a chiastic parallel with the daughters of Jerusalem in 1.5. By attributing 8.13 to the Beloved, he creates a unit spoken by her in 8.12-14 that corresponds to another in 1.2-7. That this division cuts across two well-defined episodes, namely 8.11-12 and 1.7-8, is unremarked. Contrariwise, he silently obliterates the thematic contrast between 1.2-4 and 1.5-6, as between 8.11-12 and 8.13-14 (Shea: 383).

100 The arbitrariness of Shea's approach is illustrated by the fact that he distributes the dialogue of 2.1-3, in which 2.2 parallels 2.3, not only between distinct units, but between major sections of the poem. He toys with the idea of attributing 8.7 to the Lover, thus making the climax of 8.6-7 into a duet, to correspond to the dialogue of 2.1-2. This idea is abandoned, since no poet is perfect, though he concedes "that very imperfection is part of their art"! (Shea: 384).

101 The chiasmus is examined thoroughly by Exum (54-55), but not, ironically enough, by Shea, who is concerned only to find correspondences with ch.7, and breaks up ch.2 accordingly. Falk (1982: 20-25) finds several independent poems within it, illustrating effectively the flaws of the anthological approach.

102 Exum (54) observes a further symmetrical opposition of sight and sound linking 2.12 and 2.14. In 2.12 blossoms are seen, turtle doves are heard; in 2.14 the initial wish to see and hear her is inverted when her voice is followed by appearance (marʾayik + qōlēk : qōlēk = marʾēk); the motif of voice recalls "qôl dôdî" "the voice of my lover" at the beginning of the passage. Another correspondence that Exum notes, linking the beginning to the middle, is "hinnēh" "behold". "Hinnēh zeh bāʾ" "behold he comes" (2.8) is coupled with "hinnēh zeh ʿōmēd "behold he stands" (2.9), and recalled in "kî hinnēh hassetāw ʿābār" "for behold the winter has passed" (2.11).

103 Exum divides 6.1-12 into different units (5.2-6.3 and 6.4-8.3). Thus while she perceives the parallel between 6.2 and 6.11 and infers from it that it is the Lover who goes down to the garden in 6.11 (Exum: 66), the total structure escapes her. It is, however, noticed by Levinger (74) and in part by Falk (1982: 124-26).

104 A striking Egyptian parallel is the Chester-Beatty Papyrus I

Notes to Chapter One - Introduction

1.a ("The Song of Seven") in which each stanza begins and ends with a reference to or a pun upon its number.

105   The ironic contrast of "I did not find him / they found me" is noted by Krinetzki (1981: 115) and Exum (56). Krinetzki observes that the tension of the passage is spun out by phrases such as "in the streets and squares". In view of this contrast, Rudolph's deletion of "I sought him and did not find him" in 3.2 is singularly unfelicitous (137).

106   See Exum (54 n.26) for references; one might add Levinger (39) and Zakovitch (1975). Exum thinks that the verse might be attributed to the daughters of Jerusalem on the basis of the repetitive style, analogous to 5.9 and 6.1. However, in 5.9 and 6.1, it is whole questions that are repeated, not individual words linking short phrases. I concur, though, that the Lover's wish to hear her voice in 2.14, complementing her anticipation of his voice in 2.8-9, which she hears in 2.10, suggests the change of speaker.

107   Exum (75-77) calls it a "recapitulation of motifs". Similarly, in her view (73-75) the first section, 1.2-2.6, is an introduction, anticipating the motifs of the poem, and forming an inclusion with the concluding fragments.

108   Murphy (1977: 492), however, despairs of finding any coherence among them.

109   Exum points out that 1.15-17 and 2.2-3 have the same structure, in that "the woman reproduces the form of the man's speech and continues her account" (Exum: 72).

110   An excellent parallel, observed by Exum (73), is between 1.16a "Behold, you are beautiful (yāpeh), my love, also fair (nā'îm)" and 7.7: "How beautiful (yāpît) and fair (nā'amt) you are, O love among delights".

111   In 1.2-3 the Lover's kisses are desired "kî ṭôbîm dōdeykâ miyyāyin "for your love is better than wine". In 4.10 the Lover echoes this with "mah ṭōbû dōdayik miyyāyin "How much better is your love than wine". In both cases the comparison with wine is followed by one with oil: "lerêaḥ šemāneykā ṭôbîm" "Better than the fragrance of your oils / for fragrance your oils are sweet" (1.3); and "werêaḥ šemānayik mikkol beśāmîm" "And the fragrance of your oils than all spices" (4.10). Furthermore, there is paronomasia, in the phrase "ŠEMEN tûraq ŠEMEKA" "your name is golden oil" (1.3), and between "šemānayik" and "beśāmîm" in 4.10. Exum (73-74), using this and other parallels, suggests a structural relation between 1.2-2.6, 4.10-5.1, and 7.7-8.3; the last two she considers transitional sections. For instance, 1.12-14 has images of spices (nard, henna and myrrh) in common with the "pardēs" of 4.13-14; 4.10-5.1 and 7.7-8.3 share an outdoor setting and some items of vocabulary, such as "megādîm" "precious things", in 4.13 and 7.14, and "rêaḥ" "fragrance". I do not find these parallels convincing: most of the Song has an outdoor setting, and images of fragrance. Any reference to spices (e.g. 5.5, 5.13, 6.2) could be matched with the catalogue of 4.13-14. Furthermore, to obtain these units she breaks up coherent sequences, the wasf of 7.2-7, and the descent from Lebanon in 4.8-11.

112   Shea: 379-80 argues that the recapitulation is generally or at least frequently shorter than the exposition, both in the Bible and

Notes to Chapter One - Introduction

in ancient Near Eastern literature, giving among others the not altogether convincing examples of Job and Proverbs. However, he curtails the introduction unnecessarily, not seeing, for example, the parallels between 3.1-4 and 8.1-2, or 3.6 and 8.5, and thus allows himself space for a balanced central section.

113   Most critics perceive that 5.2-6.3 is one unit, beginning with the dream sequence 5.2-7 and continued through the dialogue with the daughters of Jerusalem. Since 6.1-12 has a clear concentric structure, that unit has to be extended: the Beloved's admission that the search is abortive, since the Lover has gone down into his garden, is complemented by his account of that descent. I will discuss this matter below.

114   Exum (65-66) has analysed this relationship very well. The sixty queens of 6.8 correspond to the sixty warriors of 3.8; the daughters of Zion who go out to gaze on Solomon in 3.11 now look in wonder at the Beloved (6.9); whereas at the climax of 3.6-11 Solomon's mother sets the seal on his wedding, in 6.9 the Beloved's mother is invoked at the moment of birth, in a context suggestive of a symbolic marriage of king and country, nature and culture. Finally, there is the echo of the question "Who is this?" (3.6) in 6.10.

115   Cook develops his notion of the sequence in pp. 132-151, but in my view achieves little more than a synopsis of the Song; in other words, he does not demonstrate an organic coherence.

116   The conative function of language is that which invokes the audience e.g. through vocatives or imperatives (Jakobson 1960: 355).

NOTES TO CHAPTER TWO
The Relationship of the Lovers

1   Krinetzki's 1981 commentary had not yet appeared when I wrote this chapter; in it the perceptions of his 1970 article are applied in depth to the exegesis of the Song.

2   1970: 406. This however is common ground between Freudians and Jungians (see, for example, Freud (1933: 147-9) ("On the Psychology of Women").

3   415-16. He constructs it, however, out of an array of not always convincing phallic images, often drawn from Jung's more abstruse alchemical researches, e.g. the identification of red lilies with masculinity and white lilies with femininity (1963, 265).

4   Rosemary Gordon (1978: 173) defines the collective unconscious as "the communal and collective heritage of the species, man", containing "impulses, dreams and fantasies ... characteristic of man in general". Fordham (145) contrasts the collective unconscious, which is equivalent to the archetypal shadow of an individual, with the conscious expressions of a society; it is often that which society denies in itself, and is potentially subversive. It is essentially a cultural acquisition, not an innate inheritance; this has been the source of much misunderstanding.

5   Falk (1982: 86) comments somewhat acerbically on the general attribution to a male poet; Lys (10) considers composition by a woman a possibility, an opinion widespread among biblical feminists. There is no decisive evidence, nor does it substantially affect the interpretation. In this work, however, I have related to a male poet, fictively identified with Solomon, who is beyond the threshold of the poetic world he contemplates; this is perhaps only relevant to my conclusion, considering 8.13-14.

6   Levinger (64) notes the slowness the repeated "'anî" "I" contributes to the verse; Krinetzki (1981: 160) suggests that the stress marks her disappointment and grief, and observes that it is followed by "dôdî" "my love", the occasion of grief, repeated in successive words: "pātaḥtî 'anî ledôdî wedôdî hāmaq 'ābār" "I opened to my love, but my love had vanished, gone ..." Pope (1976: 521), however, finds no evidence of stress in the redundancy, merely late Hebrew usage, citing Ecclesiastes. In Ecclesiastes, however, superfluous phraseology, and especially the repeated stress on "'anî" "I", is rhetorically very powerful, communicating the solipsistic and loquacious universe the speaker inhabits. Pope gives no reason for his dismissiveness.

7   Gerleman (201) and Rudolph (174) read "'ahabâ" "love" as "'ahûbâ" "the loved one", following the Vulgate. One need not take it as an abstraction for the Beloved, with Pope (1976: 632). As Gordis (1976: 96) says, it is "best taken as an apostrophe to the love-experience itself". The frequent emendation of "batta'anûgîm" "among delights" to "bat ta'anûgîm" "daughter of delights" (e.g. Pope

Notes to Chapter Two - The Relationship of the Lovers

1976: 632; J. B. White 47) is plausible but hardly necessary. On the basis of this verse, Fox (1981) suggests that the word "'ahabâ" is ambiguous, as in English, and may be an endearment. He draws a dubious parallel with Egyptian MRWT.

8   The palanquin, though made for <u>himself</u> ('āśâ lô), is clearly linked by the context to Solomon's wedding; with Winandy (1965) etc. I hold it to be parallel to Solomon's bed in 3.7, associated through the ambiguous question "mî zō't" "who is this?" with the Beloved.

9   Pope (1976: 408) and Gordis (1974: 83-84) assume that the phrase "until the day blows and the shadows flee" refers to the morning twilight, since they consider the context to betoken love-making. This, however, is unargued. Lys (130-32), after deliberating lengthily whether the shadows are those that stretch in the evening or disperse in the morning, contributes the original and elegant consideration that the scene (2.8-17) that this verse concludes is an invitation to a country walk, and could hardly be at night. Krinetzki (1964: 139-40) perceives, brilliantly, a metaphorical link between the flight of the deer and the fleeing shadows.

10   The relationship of art and architecture to the mother has been most extensively explored by Adrian Stokes (e.g. 1965, 1972), who illuminatingly alludes, for example, to the importance of the unitary breast principle in early Renaissance art (1965: 21-22), or to the varying significance of smoothness and roughness (e.g. "Smooth and Rough" 1972: 72). See especially his essay "Art and the Sense of Rebirth", 1972: 67-78.

11   Cf. Fox ("Love, Passion, and Perception": 12-14) whose analysis of the technique of the wasf is similar to mine. For Fox, the images communicate a metaphysics of love, a universal eros. He pays little attention, however, to their symbolic connotations, nor to the complex relationship between the parts of the body, with their attendant comparisons, in other words to overall structure. Falk (1982: 80-84) rightly maintains that the images of the wasfs are no more absurd than those of, for example, metaphysical and modern poetry, and biblical critics who have dismissed them as bizarre merely betray their own insensitivity. For a survey of interpretative follies, see Soulen (1967). Falk claims that only a little imaginative empathy is required to see the point of the images, and that most are visual though a few (e.g. our simile in 4.5) are tactile. This, however, is to limit them sensorily - in that often the comparison is exceedingly complex - and emotively, in that it denies the relative independence of their ostensible subject that Fox well defines.

12   As Jakobson argues (1960: 370) this is perhaps characteristic of poetry in general.

13   Cf. E. Kane "The Personal Appearance of Juan Ruiz" (106-7): "Most interesting of all these erotic folk beliefs is that which associates length of the nose with the proportions of the male generative member", and the further discussion by Dunn (81-82). I owe both these references to Dr Gutwirth. Ehrenzweig (1965: 210-12) provides some amusing examples.

14   Pope (1976: 470) astutely remarks on an implication of youthfulness in the image (cf. Krinetzki 1981: 137); his suggestion

that the breasts are small by analogy with the fawns is not impossible if a little too literal.

15   Pope (1976: 470) deletes "who feeds among the lilies" to conform to the parallel verse in 7.4; he holds that it has mistakenly been borrowed from 2.16-17. His objection to the image is not clear; he says nothing more than that there is "something wrong" with it. It is a good example of the technique whereby an image develops a life of its own, and is "presentational" as well as "representational", as Fox contends.

16   The comparison of the relationship of the fawns to the doe with that of the breasts to the beauty is well-perceived by Chouraqui (57), for whom the image expresses ideas of fecundity, maternity, beauty and innocence.

17   The "šôšannâ", like the "ḥabaṣṣelet" that is bracketed with it in 2.1, has not been conclusively identified. As Falk (1976: 214) sagely avers, "The particular flowers she calls herself are not important". This sentence is missing from her 1982 volume, where she claims that the identification of the flowers is crucial to the understanding of 2.1-2 (114-15), but fails to specify how, except that they are common wildflowers. Gerleman (116) cites Dalman's opinion that "šôšannâ" is a generic term for any flower with a calyx. The most widespread view is that of Feliks (28), that it is the "lilium candidum" "as the most beautiful, largest and most fragrant of the flowers of Israel". The objection is raised by Pope (1976: 368), that the "lilium candidum" is not red, and hence is inadequate as a metaphor for the Lover's lips; against this, Feliks considers that the analogy is of smell, not colour. Moreover, he is constrained to distinguish between "šôšannâ" and the "šôšannat hā'amāqîm", since the "lilium candidum" does not grow in valleys. One would have thought, however, that shape and colour are the most distinctive qualities of lips.

Pope's suggestion that the "šôšannâ" is to be identified with the Egyptian "šššn", the sacred lotus or water-lily, is attractive, and supported by much evidence of its symbolic sexual import, both near (e.g. Canaanite Astarte plaques) and far. Nevertheless, the naturalism does suggest the Israeli landscape ("lily of the valleys" etc.), where the lotus did not grow, except perhaps in the Jordan Valley.

Another suggestion, that it is the "anemone" (Robert and Tournay 436 and Wittekindt: 94f.) has generally fallen into disfavour, since the anemone is of little fragrance (Lys: 100).

18   As Krinetzki observes, citing Budde, the long-drawn out corresponding syllables articulate the dropping of the honey (1981: 143; 1964: 168). The verbal metaphor is enriched by alliteration and assonance: the repeated unvoiced labio-dental fricatives /f/ and /ś/ in "nōfet tiṭṭōfnâ śiftôtayik" "Your lips drop honey" trickle past the teeth and lips; the hard dental plosive /ṭ/ separates the syllables; the stressed compact /o/ rounds them, supported by the narrow unstressed drift of the /i/s: "nōfet tiṭṭōfnâ śiftôtayik ..."

19   Rudolph (150) soberly comments "Die Zungenkuss spielt in der 'ars amandi' vielen Völker eine grosse Rolle".

20   The best discussion is by Krinetzki (1981: 144). Falk (1982: 104)

considers that "milk and honey" is a fixed oral pair. Lys (186) citing Dussaud, adduces El's dream of the wadis flowing with honey as a portent of Baal's resurrection in the Baal-Anat Cycle (UT 49.III. 6-7, 12-13), to suggest that "milk and honey" have paradisal connotations. Avishur (516) sees wine and honey (npt) and oil and honey (npt) as conventional pairs, both in Ugaritic and Hebrew, and links wine in 4.10b with oil in 4.10c and honey in 4.11; he rightly points out that 4.10 and 4.11 are parallel tricola, and thus stylistically closer to Ugaritic. The exampla are not entirely unconvincing, since they are very few (two from Ugaritic, one from Proverbs), and unsurprising.

21 Krinetzki (1981: 169-170) compares 5.13 to the description of the Beloved as the spice-garden in 4.12-5.1, and thence to the feminine archetypal image of the vessel; he perceives also the infantile correlate, identifying the Lover with the "puer aeternus" who arouses the Beloved's maternal instincts. He notes too that the lips are closely linked to the genitalia, and proposes that manly youth and beauty derive from the archetype of the "Great Mother", suggesting this as an element in paedophilia.

22 Most commentators follow the Versions in reading "mgdlt" as a participle "growing" rather than as a noun "migdelôt" "towers", with the MT (Pope 1976: 540; Gordis 1974: 91; Lys: 225 etc.). NEB and others plausibly interpret "migdelôt" as "chests", following Mishnaic usage (Jastrow, Dictionary: 726). In either case, the essential comparison of the lover's cheeks with spices is unaffected. Gerleman (175), in line with his theory that the images of the wasfs are specific references to Egyptian conventions, explicates the towers as spice-cones worn at Egyptian feasts; it is of no consequence to him that spice-cones were worn on the head whereas the simile describes the cheeks (Pope 1976: 540; Krinetzki 1981: 279 n.397), since it is a literary "topos" to which incidental details are irrelevant. Levinger (70) provides no firm evidence for his contention that "migdal" may mean "balcony", clearly designed to conform to the extended metaphor he perceives between the Lover and a temple; the cheeks would comprise a window-box.

There is a beautiful paronomasia between "dāgûl mĕrebābâ" (DGL MR) "choice above ten thousand" in 5.10 and "migdelôt merqāḥîm" (GDL MR) in our verse.

23 Falk (1976: 214) derives an insinuation of toughness from the image; she is a plant that grows on all soils. Krinetzki (1981: 88) considers that the metaphor is an unassuming comparison with common wildflowers; hers is not an outstanding beauty. In 2.2, the Lover contradicts this. Falk's present interpretation (1982: 115) is very similar (cf. Rudolph: 129). Both of these interpretations lack the sensuous directness that is the primary quality of the image: the delicate loveliness of the flower, the familiar miracle of the spring, with its transience, combining pathos and uniqueness.

24 The fruit in question is uncertain. Apples did not grow wild in Ancient Israel; on the other hand, the same objection militates against the apricot (NEB), citron, and other fruits variously suggested. The quince, proposed in a note by Marcia Falk (1982: 115), is odourless (cf. 7.9) and sour. Feliks (32) suggests that it is a species

Notes to Chapter Two - The Relationship of the Lovers

of crab-apple with an unusually pleasant smell. Gerleman (116) and Rudolph (130) raise the possibility that the apple tree is precious because of its rarity.

25   The association is quite common in Romantic poetry, as illustrated in abundance by Praz. A wonderful 20th-century parallel is from Lorca's poem "Amnon y Thamar", in which Tamar is described as "agudo norte de palma" ("sharp pole-star of palm" - tr. Gili and Spender).

26   For the latter interpretation (cf. "kerem zayit" "olive grove" in Jud 15.5), see Pope (1976: 354) and Feliks (49). Pope gives a short account of the archaeological excavations of the perfume industry at Ein Gedi. According to Gordis (1974: 80), however, it was famous for its vineyards (cf. Krinetzki 1981: 245 n.100).

27   Krinetzki (1981: 81-2) sees in the Dead Sea and the flourishing oasis a symbol of the coexistence of life and death, that cannot exist the one without the other.

28   The preposition "be" in "bekarmê ʿēn gedî" "in the vineyards of Ein Gedi" is open to the reading from as well as the more usual in (Lys: 92, Pope 1976: 354 etc.). I would suggest that the ambiguity combines both localities in the movement: the henna is simultaneously visualised in its natural habitat and in the Beloved's possession.

29   Lys: 90 notes that a bag of myrrh (in fact a flask of spikenard or foliatum) is one of the items that a woman is forbidden to carry on the public domain on the Sabbath (Mishnah Shabbat 6.3). More or less all commentators mention the widespread use of this article; Pope remarks that it may still be bought (1976: 351).

30   Lys (91) suggests that the bag of myrrh is inseparable from the Beloved, worn at night when she is otherwise undressed.

31   Gordis (1974: 84) and Schoville (1970: 96-7), for example, interpret "ʾap" as "face". The less sober suggestion is that of Pope (1976: 636-7), who thinks it may refer to the vulva or clitoris, on the grounds that in Ugaritic the metaphor of a nose (ʾap) may refer to a city gate (2 Aqht V: 4-5). In Ugaritic, "ʾap" is attested as a term for the nipple, and this is more possible (Dahood: 1976). Nevertheless, if there is an extended metaphor of a kiss in this passage, as most commentators suppose, the most natural reference would still be to the nose, as the part of the face adjacent to the mouth.

32   For the Egyptian category of nose-kiss cf. Gerleman: 203, J. B. White: 138.   White believes the nose-kiss consists of breathing or sniffing round the partner's nose.

33   Krinetzki (1964: 222) conceives that they are forced to breathe through their noses since their mouths are stopped with kisses. Against this view, which seems somewhat contrived, Pope (1976: 636) objects that one breathes through one's nostrils the odour of the mouth. In his recent commentary, Krinetzki (1981: 201) has stressed the unification of the breath.

34   Levinger (83) sees a further allusion to "between my breasts he shall lie" in 1.13 in "And may your breasts be like clusters of grapes" in 7.9. Now he responds to her wish.

35   7.10 is a problematic verse, because of the change of speaker

in the middle. Gerleman (203) objects that this is unexampled in the Song, though 4.16 is possibly analogous. Gerleman accordingly redivides the sentences after "like fine wine"; considers that another comparison with wine is missing; and joins 7.10b to 7.11. Others drop "dôdî" "my love" (e.g. Pope 1976: 639), change it (e.g. to "lî" "to me": Rudolph: 174), repoint it (e.g. "dôday" "my caresses": Krinetzki 1981: 198), or reinterpret it (e.g. Gordis 1974: 97, who considers it to be a plural i.e. "flowing for lovers", or Schoville (1970: 98), who reads it as a Phoenician third-person suffix). There is no real objection to the change of speaker, however; cf. Lys (269) and J. B. White (132). Fox ("Love, Passion and Perception": 5) cites this as "a prime example of how the lovers' words balance each other".

36 The clarity of visual description is accentuated by the chiastic keyword "beautiful" that links the beginning of the wasf with the end. Nearly all critics, however, regard 7.7 as the beginning of the following sequence, but without explication. In view of the exact parallel with the wasf of chapter 4, that begins "Behold, you are beautiful, my friend" (4.1), and ends "You are entirely beautiful, my friend" (4.7), this is quite unjustified. A similar inclusion is to be found in the wasf of 5.10-16 (cf. Introduction p. 45).

37 The obscurity is increased by the hapax legomenon "dôbēb". The common interpretations are "flowing/stirring" (from ZWB) and the factitive "causing to murmur" from Aram. DBB "murmur" (cf. Jastrow, Dictionary: 226 for Talmudic and Midrashic usage, and Pope 1976: 643, for the alternative interpretations). Both are possible, though the first is simpler, and fits both meanings of "yšnym". Many critics follow the Sept. reading of "teeth" for MT "yešēnîm" "sleepers"; some attempt to adapt it to the MT, through enclitic Mems and the like. Pope (1976: 641) quotes a good suggestion by D. N. Freedman that the Yod before "šnym" be changed to Waw. Both readings are possible, though the MT "sleepers" is more interesting.

38 The Midrash and Rashi, following the allegorical interpretation, consider the "sleepers" to be the "dead". Pope (1976: 641) adopts this reading, and proposes that the reference is to libations to ancestors, since it suits his theory that the Song originated in funeral feasts.

39 Lys (269) and Gordis (1974: 97) hold that the predicate of "yešēnîm" is the lovers, presumably after their love has been satisfied; Levinger (84) considers it to be a conceit - extravagant in my view - for motionless lips. Goitein (1957: 289) remarks very beautifully that her wine "awakens the Lover to dream for ever of his Beloved". One may well associate wine and sleep, not to mention sleeping together. The referent of "yešēnîm" "sleepers" may be the lovers, in their mutual embrace; or it may be all lovers, as in 5.1, indulging in the wine that here stimulates their dreams; or it may be all those who are unawakened by love, as in 8.5. Delitzsch's comment, cited by Pope (1976: 641), that drinking in sleep is unknown takes the metaphor too literally: nor is the referent of palate, namely kisses, inappropriate, as Pope surmises. Kisses may be dreamt, whether "dôbēb" be taken to mean flowing over lips or causing them to murmur.

Notes to Chapter Two - The Relationship of the Lovers

40 Rashi expresses his astonishment as follows: "I cannot interpret this as a nose, neither literally nor metaphorically, for what sort of praise is this to say that she has a nose as large and erect as a tower? Therefore, I say, "ʾappek" is an expression for the face". Falk (1982: 127) interprets it similarly. However, Ibn Ezra, who had seen minarets, remarks that it is "a straight nose, without defects".

41 Krinetzki (1964: 216) linked the root meaning of Lebanon i.e. "white" with the colour of the ivory tower. Her remote beauty is reinforced by the snow-covered peaks. The suggestion is ingenious, if a little recherche. He has abandoned this interpretation in his recent commentary (1981: 191), where he stresses the aggressiveness of the image. Rudolph (173) considers that it may be a peak of Lebanon, and not a tower.

42 Cf. the articles on mediaeval chiromancy cited in n.29; the extraordinary attention with which antisemites scrutinise Jewish noses, connected with the fantasy of Jewish potency; the supposed nobility of Roman noses; the dominance of noses in cartoons. There is a splendid discussion and illustration of this in Ehrenzweig (1965: 213-14).

43 Also the nasal sounds /m/ and /n/, especially when they are non-phonemic i.e. purely emotive in function. /n/ for example tends to be associated with anger. We say "mmm" to convey appetite or wonder.

44 Krinetzki (1964: 160). The mention of David, in Krinetzki's current view (1971: 183 etc.), is one of the elements that serves to root the Song in a specifically Israelite and consequently religious setting. Though there may be a pun between "dāwîd" and "dôd", this does not justify Lys' translation "Tour-le-Cheri" (167).

45 For this practice see Ezekiel 27.10-11 (Pope 1976: 468). Only Levinger (53) raises the alternative provenance of the shields, whether they are captured from the enemy and hence displayed as a sign of victory, or else are hung in readiness by the troops, and thus a show of strength (53). Isserlin's suggestion that the verse is an extended simile of a necklace, comparable to a statue at Arsos, is very attractive and has been widely adopted.

46 Levinger (80) suggests an alliterative connection between "ṣebiyyâ" "doe" and "ṣawwāʾrēk" "your neck" to explain the omission of "hārôʿîm baššôšannîm". Refrains in the last two chapters are frequently condensed e.g. 7.11, 8.4 (cf. Introduction above). Furthermore, whereas the comparisons in the wasfs of ch.4 and ch.5 vary greatly in elaboration, those in ch.7 are generally of two clauses each. 7.4 thus parallels 7.2b, 7.3a, 7.3b etc. Pope (1976: 624) suggests that the last phrase is omitted so as not to duplicate "hedged with lilies" at the end of the previous verse (in 4.5, however, he excises "who feed among the lilies" to correspond to 7.4!). However, "lilies" appear at the end of 6.2 and 6.3 without apparent awkwardness.

47 "The many geographic metaphors (Kedar, Heshbon, Tirzah, Engedi etc.), by their repetition, persistently suggest identifying the contour of the country with the body of the beloved" (Cook: 127) cf. Krinetzki (1964: 216). The geographical allegory is itemised in considerable detail by Robert-Tournay; for example, the two breasts

Notes to Chapter Two - The Relationship of the Lovers

are identified with Mt. Ebal and Gerizim. Clearly, there is no cartographical exactitude in the Song; it is no criticism to say with Pope (1976: 626) that the eyes are misplaced. For what we have is a set of peripheral geographical landmarks. Gerleman (195) sees them as indicative of the predominant royal travesty.

48   Gordis (1974: 96), Ibn Ezra and others suggest that "karmel" should be "karmîl" "crimson" (II Chron 2.6 etc.), corresponding with "argaman" "purple". On the other hand, "Carmel" creates a far better visual image, in accord with the geographical sequence, contiguous with the sea and its produce. Levinger (80) believes there may be a deliberate pun between "karmîl" and "karmel", as does Lys (263-4).

49   According to the Talmud (T. B. Sukkah 49 a-b), the vagina of the Shekhinah - hence of the world and in particular the land of Israel - is the altar in Jerusalem. Robert-Tournay identify Jerusalem in this sequence with the navel or vulva of 7.3, basing themselves on such prophetic allusions as Eze 5.5, and the assumption that everything in the passage must have its geographic correlate.

50   Pope (1976: 630) writes that the emendations proposed for this phrase, especially the last word, are "scarcely worth reviewing"; "rehātîm", denoting "watering troughs" (Gen 30.38, 41, Ex 2.16) from Aram. RHT = run, is a straightforward metaphor for flowing or wavy hair, as Lys amusingly illustrates (265). Feliks (109), following some of the Versions, attaches the word "melek" "king" to the previous phrase i.e. "a king's purple, bound with threads" - cf. also Krinetzki 1981: 191. Not only does this make the last colon too short, as Pope observes (1976: 630), but the previous one is lengthened impossibly, quite apart from the abysmal anticlimax. Levinger (81) suggests, rather beautifully, that "rehātîm" and "rāḥîṭēnû" in 1.17 are variants of each other; that the runnels of "rehātîm" merge with the light fretwork of 1.17, woven into the fringe of the hair of the previous phrase, to which this is in apposition.

51   Jacob, cited by Levinger (80), draws attention to a Palestinian custom of decorating sheaves with flowers; Feliks (107) states that harvested wheat is normally protected by thorns, and the lilies are indicative of her beauty (cf. 2.2).

52   Opinions are divided whether the rare word "šorerēk" denotes "your navel" (cf. Eze 16.4, Prov 3.8) or "your vulva" (Arab. "śirr") cf. Pope (1976: 617). Krinetzki (1981: 192) suggests that the navel is a metonym for the entire genital region. The development of the image of the crater in which "the mingled wine may never be lacking" leads me to favour the second interpretation.

53   If the face symbolises the reality principle, the "face" we expose and submit to the world, the body represents the explosive pleasure principle, which we conceal under clothes (Paz 1975: 4).

54   For the suggestion that the wood is aromatic, see Feliks (33-34).

55   Pope (1976: 469) lists these; Gerleman (145) describes their elimination as pedantry. Schoville (1970: 75) notes that in Ugaritic the number often precedes the dual (e.g. for emphasis). As a zoologist, Feliks (14) observes that only one species of "ṣebî" commonly bears twins, namely the "gazella subgutturosa", now extinct in Israel.

Notes to Chapter Two - The Relationship of the Lovers

56   Pope (1976: 470) avers that the youthful fawns convey the small size of the "mammary orbs", according to the ideals of Arabic pulchritude. Other references to breasts in the Song contradict this supposed predilection, as we have seen.

57   In the Dogon religion, for example, as recorded by Marcel Griaule, the first human beings were four sets of twins; only with the fall from perfection, the menstrual cycle, and mortality, did single births begin to occur. Twins thus are a sign of original perfection, and in consequence are loaded with propitiatory gifts. In the Nuer culture, twins are quasi-divine, like birds, mediating between earth and heaven (Lévi-Strauss 1969: 151-54). The Dioscuri, according to Jung, represent a duality of mortality and immortality (1959a: 121-2). Frazer, inevitably, produces a multitude of examples of uncertain value.

58   As noted by Lys: 169.

59   E.g. Rudolph: 146. Lys (172) suggests that the thread may be tripled, or that the lips are like scarlet thread i.e as a material.

60   "A body of faience can quickly turn into the flame red of carnelian, leading a man to perdition, so warn the Wisdom Texts" (Alison Roberts, private communication).

61   In the Aqhat Epic (CTA 19 iv: 204-205) the heroine Pughat reddens herself with murex before avenging her brother's murder, thus disguising herself as Anat, who colours herself similarly before indulging her weakness for carnage (CTA 3 B: 2-3). Cf. de Moor 1968; 1971: 83-85; M. Dijkstra and de Moor 1975.

62   Fox ("Scholia to Canticles": 7-8) suggests an ingenious and attractive double pun: "midbar" may mean "desert" as well as "mouth" "nāʾweh" "lovely" may be read as "nāwê" "a pasture". Thus even a desert in her flourishes. Such an exegesis, though it seems incongruous in the wasf, with its progress through the parts of the body, would match the denial of barrenness in the previous verse: "And none is bereaved among them", and the evocation of landscapes. The vertical "synchronic" metaphor is an interesting variation on its sequential exposition, and intensifies the compression of v.3, in comparison with others in the wasf.

63   Contrary to popular opinion, however, there is no evidence of consanguineous marriages in the Egyptian royal house before the Ptolemies. Special sanctity was attributed to such marriage by Zoroastrians (Boyce: 54-5). In discussing the story of Amnon and Tamar, Fokkelman (1981: 103) argues that intercourse between half-siblings was not incestuous. This, however, might be another example of a royal family that feels itself too good for the world.

64   N. Waldman suggests a development from Akk. "lababû" "stir up, enrage", with a sexual connotation. Pope (1976: 479) considers that there may be a more specific reference to an erection concealed in the word "heart", citing Mesopotamian love charms. The two organs are not necessarily unconnected. However this may be, it is, I think, a reductive interpretation, since clearly more than the sexual organs are engaged, and the best sense is that closest to hand. Elsewhere LBB occurs as a denominative only in Job 11.25, in a singularly unhelpful context. Both privative and intensive functions

Notes to Chapter Two - The Relationship of the Lovers

have been proposed. Cf. Pope (1976: 478); Lys (180-1), etc.

65   Adopting the Qerê, with most commentators. The Ketîb "ʾaḥad" has found its protagonist in Gerleman (154) on account of the instability of gender differentiation among numerals. There are, however, no comparable examples. Gender in the Song nevertheless is sufficiently flexible to render assimilation to the following "ʾaḥad" possible. "ʿAnāq" and "ṣawwerōnāyik", though hapax legomena, are unproblematic as "bead" and "necklace" respectively. Pope (1976: 482-83) discourses on "eyestones" in Mesopotamian jewelry, possibly parallel to "one bead of your necklace". Rudolph (150) suggests that it is like a magic amulet; an interpretation similar to that of Chouraqui (59), that it is a talisman she gives him.

66   Chester-Beatty Papyrus 1.1a, stanza 2, uses for its keyword an analogous pun between "brother" and "two".

67   The Versions omit the comparative, followed by some commentators, e.g. Rudolph (178), who declares that the "k" is obviously the result of dittography with the previous "yittenekâ". Gordis (1974: 98) and others see in it an asseverative, which renders it virtually meaningless. This is to miss the subtlety of the simile, and its most natural import, that she wishes him to be <u>like</u> a brother, but more than a brother (Krinetzki 1981: 212).

68   Falk (1981: 104) considers that the possessive suffix emphasises that it represents her sexuality (cf. Pope 1976: 659). Commenting on 4.3, Krinetzki (1981: 136) maintains that the split-open pomegranate, with its red seeds, archetypally alluring (1970: 414), is a symbol for the substance of the woman herself.

69   Pope (1976: 658-59) argues on rhythmical grounds that "telammedēnî" is the corrupted remnant of a missing line, presumably using a synonym for the mother, as in 3.4, 6.9, and 8.5; he restores "to the chamber of the one who bore me" in 3.4. Rudolph (178) renders "tēledēni" "she bore me"; Gordis (1974: 98) suggests that "telammedēni" was substituted for the "bower of the one who conceived me" (horātî) under allegorical influence by a scribe who thought that "horah" meant "teach". These speculations are disregarded by others, who consider it to be a reference to sexual initiation; Gerleman (212) cites Egyptian parallels. Krinetzki (1981: 212), Gerleman and Lys (279) hold the subject to be the Lover; Falk (1982: 129) considers it to be the mother. Pope's objection to the rhythm of the verse lacks cogency; the semi-synonymous verbs, with one four-syllable nominal phrase interposed, give the line a gentle step-by-step dynamic progression, suggestive, Krinetzki (1964: 233) proposed, of solicitude.

70   Cf. Lys (278), who sees this as an example of the paradoxical desire of love for an unattainable unity. Edwards (89-90) writes "<u>like</u> is a mysterious door to a universe in the process of being unmade" - in this case the assumptions of kinship relationship. Similarly, Chouraqui (76) understands our image as a transcendence of all dualities and relationships.

71   5.1 lacks the symmetry of the other verses; repetition is subsumed in a succession of acts, each of which illustrates the consummation of the entry into the garden. Thus "I have <u>entered</u> my

Notes to Chapter Two - The Relationship of the Lovers

garden" is the general statement particularised in the cumulative sequence of verbs; to both of them "my sister, my bride" is in apposition, since she is the garden and also its produce.

72   Pope (1976: 474), J. B. White (45), etc., point MT "'ittî" "with me" as "'etî" "come", with the Sept. and other Versions. White considers this "necessary here to maintain a proper parallelism with "tāšûrî" (understood as a verb)". Such arguments are suspect in general, since they make unwarranted assumptions about the nature of parallelism (cf. Kugel 1981a), but here are incomprehensible. "Tābô'î" "come" is a perfect complement for "tāšûrî"; "'etî ...'etî" would simply overload the line. Gerleman (151) for his part draws attention to a beautiful chiasmus: "tābô'î tāšûrî" "come, hurry" cluster together on the peak of Lebanon. Gordis (1974: 87) suggests persuasively that "'ittî" "with me" is foregrounded for emphasis. Krinetzki (1981: 139) is constrained by the difficulties he encounters in reconciling distance in 4.8 with nearness in 4.9, to revocalise "'ittî" "with me" as "'ōtî" "me" and "tābô'î, tašûri" as "tābî'î" "bring" and "tāširî" "make me hasten", so that it is the Lover who is brought from Lebanon by the Beloved's fascinating eyes.

73   The two meanings of "ŠUR" "look, travel" (Köhler-Baumgartner: 957) are equally appropriate - cf. Gordis 1974: 87; Pope 1976: 474. The second (Aram. "šwr", Arab. "śara"), though, is otherwise unattested in the OT, and hence Levinger (56) suggests that ŠUR here means "look" in the sense of to "contemplate a descent", as in Gen 18.16.

74   According to the topographical note of Deut 3.9, Senir and Hermon are synonymous, though, as Pope (1976: 475) says, they may refer to different peaks. Amana is either the Amanus massif in the distant north, which seems improbable except perhaps for its symbolic association as the home of the gods ("sāpôn" = the north mountain), or else the source of the River Abanus (Qere "'Amanâ" II Kings 5.12) which flows through Damascus. According to Pope, in Assyrian sources this mountain was known as Umanum, Ammana and Ammun, now part of the Anti-Lebanon.

75   p. 178. Krinetzki (1964: 165) maintained that the mountains are mere symbols of coldness and solitude, hence their indistinctness. This is now developed (1981: 140) into an identification with the dazzling, catlike "devouring mother", from whom the Lover cannot free himself; this interpretation has an affinity with my own, that it is associated with the death and desolation (preexistence) from which life comes. Segal (480) thinks the whole passage is a joke.

76   Cf. Pope 1976: 475-7; Albright 1963: 3; Schoville 1970: 75-78. The latter consider it to be extremely ancient, since it contains a two-word ('itti millebānôn) and a one-word (mērö'š) parallelism. The flaws of this technique for dating poetry have already been discussed (Introduction p. 19 and n.30 above). Albright believes that it was originally a song for Adonis, who invited his beloved, a goddess identified with Aphrodite, to accompany him on his ill-fated hunt in the mountains of Lebanon; the Lebanon was sacred to Asherah, the "potnia thêrôn" "mistress of the beasts". Pope (1976: 477) asserts that the goddess of love and war was regularly associated with lions, and

Notes to Chapter Two - The Relationship of the Lovers

identifies the Beloved with her accordingly. This, however, is to confuse metaphorical connotation, since the Beloved in any case incarnates the forces of Eros, and is thus archetypally related to the goddesses Pope lists, with her actual fictional identity.

77 A beautiful analysis of the ambiguity of Aphrodite in Sappho's Ode, as a goddess from Olympus and a condition of the heart, and of the production of intense pressure e.g. through word-music, is to be found in Friedrich (108-125).

78 Cf. Lys (178). In the Ugaritic "rpum" texts, the deities feast on Lebanon. Stolz (esp.150) identifies Lebanon, "the cedar forest", with the dwelling of the gods in Gilgamesh, and postulates a whole series of related myths (see ch. 4 n.22).

79 Pope (1976: 488) declares that a locked garden denotes virginity; Rudolph (152) cites Catullus to this effect; in a previous article (Landy 1979: 518-520), I have discussed the assumptions behind this identification, and given further references. An insightful analysis is provided by Falk (1982: 122-23). For Krinetzki (1970: 409; 1981: 147), the garden and spring clearly refer to the vagina, and thus are primary symbols for the Great Mother. I have already discussed the virtues and limitations of this approach (above).

80 A number of commentators level "gan" and "gal" (e.g. Gerleman: 159; Müller: 1977: 158), following several versions and many ancient manuscripts. C. Schedl (167) notes that the Leningrad Codex keeps its options open by putting a meaningless Dagesh in the Lamed. The principal difficulty is that "gal" = spring in the singular is either a hapax or very rare (otherwise only in Job 8.17, where I think that the balance of probabilities suggests that it is some constant source of water, rather than a cairn). On the other hand, there is the parallel with "ma'yan" and the beautiful paronomasia, gan/gal as pointed out by Gordis (1974: 81), Lys (232), Levinger (60). There is a difference of opinion on the kind of fount signified - whether it is a "pool" (Pope 1976: 488; Good 1970: 94 n.44; Dahood 1964: 54), from the Ugaritic "gal" = cup, or whether it is a singular form of "galîm" = waves. As a "sealed spring", there would in fact be little difference.

81 Especially since it exploits the consonants of "nā'ûl": gaN Nā'ûl (gnnl) ... gaL nā'ûL (glnl).

82 The principal meanings adduced for "šelaḥayik" are "your shoots" (e.g. Lys: 189, Gordis 1974: 88), from "ŠLḤ" "to send out roots and branches" (Jer 17.8, Ps 80.12), and "irrigation canals" (cf. Neh 3.15). Pope (1976: 490) translates "groove", which allows him some pleasantries on "groovy groves"; it is unclear from his account whether he concurs with the view, for which he cites Haupt and others, that the conduit is a metaphor for the vagina. Levinger (60) suggests that the canals irrigate the far parts of the garden (see also Feliks, 83) - cf. below ch.4 p.194f.

83 Muller takes "nōzlîm" in 4.15 to be a noun "streams" (1977: 158, 162 n.7). Hence "nā'ûl" and "ḥātûm" are the only verbal forms.

84 Gordis (1974: 88), like Lys (196), noticing an apparent contradiction between the "sealed" spring and the one that is fed by the waters of Lebanon, puts this verse into the mouth of the Beloved, and changes "gannîm" into "gannî" "my garden", with BH, Rudolph

Notes to Chapter Two - The Relationship of the Lovers

(151). Lys inserts "je suis" before the unamended predicate, but it is hard to see how this can be read into the text. Schoville (1970: 81-82) proposes that the Mem is enclitic. Pope (1976: 495) is surely right in averring "it seems more likely that the two phrases simply continue the series of appositions". In my 1979 article (517 n.19) I contend that the garden is, as it were, all gardens; likewise, Gerleman (161) holds that it is a generalising plural.

85 Most critics attribute the whole verse to the Beloved; Pope (1976: 498), J. B. White (138) and Exum (64) assume that 16a is a continuation of the Lover's speech. Pope takes it for granted that the Lover invokes the winds, but comments on "my garden" that "the uncertainty here as to the speaker is not serious. Whether the bride or groom speaks, the scented garden clearly represents the lady's charms which are meant for her lover's enjoyment". Clearly there is an ambiguity; in my view, it makes better sense that the change of speaker should coincide with the sentence division, since 4.16 is internally coherent, moving from the coming of the south wind to the coming of the Lover. In contrast, in 7.10, where the parts change in mid verse, there is continuity of cadence with 7.9.

86 There is no need to cite the euphemism "bôʾ ʾel" for sexual intercourse common in narrative (e.g. Lys: 198). Euphemism is commonly a dessication of metaphor - it reduces it to a mere cipher - and is only applicable in particular literary contexts, where it is widely understood, part of the metalanguage of the genre.

87 Müller (1977: 159). He suggests, too, that the first person morpheme intensifies engagement in the situation - a very fine aperçu. I am less convinced by his further proposition that the verbs are performative, except insofar as all verbs are in poetry.

88 The tense is variously interpreted as past or present (Pope 1976: 504). Lys: 68, for instance, substitutes the present for the past throughout the Song. At all events the mode suggests a completed action, contrasting with the Beloved's wish in 4.16, implying either a simultaneity of wish and fulfilment, or word and action. The preterite (Levinger: 61) is sharper, more intensely reciprocal.

89 It would be tedious to examine in detail the various linguistic stratagems wherewith critics have preserved the privacy of the garden. Gordis (1974: 34) supposes that it is a rare plural for singular, that the Beloved addresses her Lover as "dôdî" and "rēʿî". Schoville (1970: 110) achieves the same result by turning the supposed plural suffixes into enclitic Mems. An attractive recent view is that "dôdîm" is a substantive, "love" or "caresses", as in 4.10 or 1.2 (Pope 1976: 508; NEB). Dahood (1963-74 X: 393) turns "rēʿîm" into a noun, to correspond to it. On the other hand, "rēʿîm" regularly means "friends", and "dôdîm" seems to parallel it. The ending of this section would thus accord with "zeh dôdî wezeh rēʿî" "This is my love and this is my friend" at the end of ch. 5.

90 Lys (202) rightly comments on the difference in tone; but it is hardly necessary to conjecture with him that the change of addressee implies a change of speaking subject.

91 Rosemary Gordon (71-72), after a survey of mythological aetiologies of death, concludes "This coupling of women with death ...

Notes to Chapter Two - The Relationship of the Lovers

is almost universal". She continues that in some myths this is quite explicitly the price she pays for giving birth: creativity and death are thus interlinked. The metaphorical association of the womb with death is a commonplace; like death, the womb represents a state of non-differentiation, relative unconsciousness, and fusion. Gordon traces how what she terms the "death" wish - the wish not to be - is a manifestation of the wish to revert to the womb (ibid.: 30-32).

92   Exum (63 n.44) joins 5.2 to the sequence of invocations of "bride" and "sister-bride", disregarding - or at least failing to interpret - the structural hiatus and the change of epithet to "my sister, my friend" in 5.2. In my view, after the celebration of her as sister and bride in 4.8-5.1, the chain of vocatives with which he wheedles her in 5.2 is partly ironic because rhetorical. In 5.1 the metaphors "sister" and "bride" were justified by his inclusion within the garden; now he is outside the door. The repetition spans the contrast.

93   Rabin (1973: 213) identifies the "mountain of frankincense" with the mountains of Southern Arabia, where the spices grow. The land of Punt was a vague designation for the lands south and east of Egypt (Lichtheim 1976: 38), and associated in the literature, including the love-poetry, with exotic spices, riches, and marvels. For example, in the Cairo love song no.1 st.6, the girl is compared to one from Punt (and associated consequently with Hathor).

94   Some critics (Gordis 1974: 87; Pope 1976: 471-72) take the twin mountains, like the parallel "hārê bāter" "cleft mountains" in 2.17, to be symbols of the breasts that the Lover sees in 4.5 (Krinetzki 1981: 137). As with 2.17, I consider the temporal clause to signify parting. "'Elek lî" "I will go", like "šôb" "turn" in 2.17, and "beraḥ" "flee" in 8.14, suggests a journey, away from the vision of the Beloved (cf. Falk 1982: 121).

95   This recognition gives rise to Pope's theory that the Song originated in funeral feasts (1976: 210-229). Fuerst (196) dissents from the view that 8.6-7 is the climax of the Song, appearing to find it dry and moralising; he warns against allowing it to dampen the eroticism of the rest of the book. In my view, this misses the point, that it is a statement of absolute value, whose authority derives from our experience of the book.

96   Krinetzki (1964: 144) understood the reference to conception to be a displacement of her own maternal desire; this has disappeared in his recent commentary, though in connection with 8.1-2 he remarks (1981: 212) that she gives birth to her Lover there. Chouraqui (54) sees it as a metaphorical superimposition, in that she leads the Lover to the roots of her being. Lys (147) proposes that it is a vestige of matrilochy, and suggests a correlation with Gen 2.24, on which the Song is a sort of commentary. There is no evidence for this archaic matrilochy, however; and in any event the interpretation seems far-fetched (see, though, Cook: 119). One may note in passing that at least on the evidence of the Egyptian love songs, the affairs of Egyptian households were controlled by the mother (cf. Chester-Beatty Papyrus I.l.a st.2 etc.).

97   Thus Krinetzki (1981: 95) holds that it is a compensatory

Notes to Chapter Two - The Relationship of the Lovers

memory, as does Falk (1982: 116); Lys (107) says that nothing prevents the verb being optative, even if the lovers are together; Pope (1976: 384), however, considers that there is no reason to think that it is not indicative, since the lovers are obviously in each other's arms. Rudolph (131), like Falk, thinks that it expresses a wish or fantasy. In my view, 2.6 contrast effectively with 2.5, whether as wish or memory; the lovers are only together if there is no continuity with the previous verse. The verb may be either optative or indicative.

98 So Gerleman (118), Rudolph (137), Gordis (1974: 51, etc.). However, Fox ("Scholia to Canticles" 3) thinks it may be any construction where wine is drunk, analogous to Egyptian beer houses. Pope (1976: 374-75) attempts to associate it with "marzēaḥ" feasts. Lys (202) ventures that the sign of love suggests a "cabaret" whose delights are more than bibulous; this proposal has won little favour, since the sous-entendu is in any case evident.

99 Pope (1976: 661), Lys (281). Lys has recourse to an indirect and wish-fulfilling quotation - she imagines her Lover speaking - in order to bolster his attribution of the refrain to the Lover in 2.7, based on her being in his arms in 2.6 (Lys: 111). Even if this were the case, however, it would not prevent the refrain being adopted by the other partner; examples are 2.16-17 = 4.5-6 and 2.10-13 = 7.12-14.

100 Most commentators infer that the oath is a request not to disturb the lovers (or Beloved) while they are sleeping, or until they are satisfied (e.g. Gordis 1974: 32). Pope (1976: 387) criticises this line of interpretation, noting that "ʾahabâ" "love" in the Song is an active subject: "love certainly has a will of its own, fickle as it may be".

101 Several commentators change the masculine suffixes to feminine: accordingly, it is the Beloved who is under the tree (J. B. White: 47; Rudolph: 180; Krinetzki 1982: 216),though they justify the alteration in only the vaguest terms e.g. Krinetzki avers that for the Beloved to awaken him there would be "most peculiar" (sehr sonderbar), Pope (1976: 663) incisively points out that the MT contradicts the allegorical interpretation and hence is most likely to be genuine, concluding spiritedly that "that this reading was preserved through centuries of allegorical interpretation suggests that it was so well-established and known that it could not be changed but was left to moderns to correct". Lys (283) adduces, moreover, that this is the culmination of the Beloved's searches. He excels himself in his discussion of this scene, lucidly examining the correlations between birth, death as symbolised by the desert, and sexual awakening. Our interpretations do not essentially differ, though I put more stress on the wider symbolic network, the relationship with 8.2, the theme of the apple-tree.

102 Budde's proposal to substitute "ṣamîd" "bracelet", for the second "ḥôtām", supported by Rudolph (180-81), has met with little welcome (e.g. from Gordis 1974: 99; Pope 1976: 667), because it is unsupported by the Versions, destroys the parallelism, and because, as Pope says, "zerôaʿ" may be a poetic synonym for "hand" and thus carry a seal. Pope (1976: 667) makes an interesting analogy with phylacteries, developed by Gordis (1974: 99) i.e. that she is bound on his heart and hand.

Notes to Chapter Two - The Relationship of the Lovers

103   Lys (286) succinctly summarises the functions of seals in ancient times:
   i)   they are engraved
   ii) authenticate documents
   iii) are a recognisance
   iv) seal a union.
Alter (1981: 9) describes them as equivalent to the major credit cards.

104   Levinger (90, 91) finely suggests that she hears his heart pounding as they walk with their arms round each others' shoulders. There is no need to insert a second "śîmēnî" with Albright (1963: 7) to create a two-word parallelism, even if one accepts his view that the verse is archaic, since double-duty verbs are quite frequent in ancient and Ugaritic poetry. (Schoville 1970: 107).

105   Hyam Maccoby (58) claims that "ᶜazzâ" really means "harsh", and deduces that the phrase "love is as strong as death" suggests valedictory sadness at frustration. However, a glance at the concordance (Mandelkern: 834) does not support Maccoby's contention. "ᶜAz" is used of such diverse entities as a well-protected border (Num 21.24), a powerful but beneficent wind (Ex 14.21), and a strong though dead lion (Jud 14.14).

106   UT 49.6.11-13; Pope 1976: 668-69; Albright 1963: 6. At the other extreme, D. Winton Thomas (221, 223) suggests that both "māwet" and "šeʾôl" may be unusual superlatives i.e. Love is extremely strong, Jealousy is hellishly bitter. However, his case is totally unargued. He does not consider "šalhebetyâ", and elsewhere in the article avers that there is no case where "ᵓēl/ᵓelōhîm", even if it is an intensive, quite loses its religious connotation. Why then "māwet" and "šeʾôl" should be drained of their meaning is unclear.

107   Pope (1976: 669), for instance, argues that "qinʾâ" "can designate a variety of strong emotions, anger, envy, jealousy, fury". All these are characterised by hatred for a third party. Gordis' (1974: 99) asseveration that it is not jealousy but passion "never being satisfied, hence showing no pity" is unargued. Lys (287-88) suggests that "qinʾâ" is the normal manifestation of divine love, on which human love is modelled; hence it does not refer to the love of God, as allegorical expositors devoutly suppose, but to the exclusive ardour of the Underworld. "QNᵓ", however, is essentially wrathful, possessive, intolerant of rivals; I cannot find any exception to this rule.

108   Gerleman (217) considers it to be simply an intensification, comparable to that of "ᵓahabâ" and "qinʾâ", and "môt" and "šeʾôl"; he cites Gen 49.6 where "ᶜaz" and "qāšâ" are coupled in a decidedly uncomplimentary context. He misses thereby the logical interplay of opposition and equivalence.

109   Lys (287) aptly describes it as "l'anti-monde, le non-monde". Descriptions of Sheol are too fragmentary and scattered to be easily summarised, nor are they entirely consistent - cf. Keel 1978: 63ff. Keel, after remarking that Israelite conceptions of the afterlife were less frightful than those of its neighbours, than the infernal city of Mesopotamia and the terrible judgement of the dead in Egypt, with its lurking crocodile monster, characterises the qualities of Sheol as darkness, silence, forgetfulness (cf. Job 10.21-22), disturbed only by

Notes to Chapter Two - The Relationship of the Lovers

the fall of emperors and stars (Isa 14, Eze 31).

110   Levinger (90) adduces its etymology from an Arab. root "to be dark red" i.e. the colour of fire (cf. Kohler-Baumgartener: 842).

111   Sexual fever and perpetual languishing in the Underworld are equated in an analogous source perplexingly overlooked by commentators, namely Prov 9.18, where Sheol is situated between the Lady of Folly's thighs; though with a markedly less charitable connotation.

112   Gaster (1975: 814; cf. Pope 1976: 670) supposes that in this context the "rešāpîm" are to be understood as fiends, emanating from the Ugaritic and Egyptian deity Resheph, the source of pestilence in Keret. The latter I understand to be a hypostasis, like Mot. It may still, however, have a chthonic colouring, and thus link Sheol, jealousy, and love, blending the contraries, as Krinetzki (1964: 243) observed. In his later commentary (1981: 220-221), the verse expresses most purely the coexistence of the "deadly" and the "bountiful" mother in the libido. "Rešāpîm" are associated with arrows, flaming or otherwise (Ps 76.4) and lightning (Ps 78.48) and some form of destructive visitation comparable with plague and famine (Deut 32.34, Hab 3.5); in no case is its meaning fully determinate. In any case, in this context, it clearly refers, whether as a metaphor or literally, to jets of flame.

113   Bachelard's study, The Psychoanalysis of Fire (esp. 43 ff.), is devoted to the working out of this metaphor in alchemy and myth.

114   E.g. Levinger: 90; Gordis 1974: 26 n.90. Gerleman (217) contends that the suffix "-yâ" (-yāh) is not the name of God at all but an emphatic particle, citing several examples (e.g. "maʾeppelyâ" "deep gloom" Jer 2.31) which, however, are equally easily adopted by Gordis to maintain his viewpoint (see likewise Krinetzki 1981: 290-1 n.562). While I concede that the name of God may sometimes be used idiomatically, as a vague connotation of grandeur, the instances most commonly referred to are not always convincing e.g. Nineveh was a very great city before God (Jonah 3.3); it is the concern of God for the great city that is the point of the parable. Likewise Stolz (148) argues that "harerêʾēl" "the mountains of God" (Ps 36.7) and "ʾarzêʾēl" "the cedars of God" (Ps 80.11) designate the divine domicile.

115   E.g. Pope (1976: 671) is constrained to eliminate it as a gloss, on the grounds of its rhythmical awkwardness. It is not clear to me why "rešāpeha" needs a gloss, especially with a more recondite term; indeed the postulation of glosses seems to me questionable, since it is uncomfortably like an excuse for eliminating anything inconvenient. Numerous and ungainly are the emendations proposed for "šalhebetyâ" - cf. Pope 1976: 670.

116   Pope (1976: 671) criticising Robert-Tournay's allegorical interpretation, writes "To seize upon the final consonants 'yh' as the sole reference to the God of Israel in the entire Canticle is to lean on very scanty and shaky support". However, it is equally valid to say that its uniqueness reinforces its solemnity.

117   References and comparisons to divinity are found in the love-literature of all ages. Rudolph (174), who holds that our phrase praises love as part of God's creation, and is the Song's supreme

expression, justly refers to Theocritus (Idylls, 2.134). It is a remarkable irony that just those commentators who populate the Song with concealed deities refuse to recognise his presence there when he comes to the surface.

118 Cf. Lys (289), who translates "un sacre coup de foudre" (282). As he says, in ancient times lightning was divine fire. Thus the interpretation would appear to be tautologous. Nevertheless, it limits the application unduly: it could refer to any sacred fire. There are only two other loci for "šalhebet" (Eze 21.3, Job 15.30), both of which could either refer to lightning or to a forest fire. As a probably Shaphal Causative of the root LHB, "flame", either interpretation is possible (cf. Dahood 1963-74 II: 407).

119 Cf. Landy 1981b: 166. Though there have been innumerable studies of the name of God, they add little in the way of insight beyond these two proximate meanings; cf. most recently, Gottwald (1980: 682) who, in accordance with his Marxist revolutionary theory of the origins of Israel, interprets it as "'el zu yahwi ṣeba'ot" "El who creates the armed hosts", developing Cross's (1973: 65-71) interpretation of the name as deriving from an epithet of "'el", "'el ḍu yahwî" "El who creates", parallel to the Ugaritic "el ḍu yakaninû" "El who creates". Childs (1974: 63-64) persuasively criticises this view in the context of Ex 3.13-15, in particular arguing that the emphasis on the novelty of the name would discourage seeking Ancient Near Eastern parallels; Gottwald should be sympathetic to this approach. Napier (52) rightly insists on the essential ambiguity of the name.

120 Prosody, being allophonic, is inevitably subjective, conditioned both by dialect (e.g. Anglo-Ashkenazi) and interpretation. Nevertheless, the number of possible variants, taking "shewas" and conjunctions into account, is limited; the basic pattern persists.

121 E.g. Ps 144.7, 32.6; Isaiah 17.13 (cf. Lys 290).

122 Lys (291) overstates in suggesting that in contrast to the equal struggle with death, love triumphs over chaos, since the lamp of love does no more than keep burning.

123 Levinger (91) suggests that the line is lengthened in order to stress the concluding word "'ahabâ", and to couple it with the end of the next sentence "bôz yābûzû lô" "they would surely despise him", producing a correlation with Prov 6.30-31, where the needy thief is not shamed, and gives all the wealth of his house. Zakovitch (1974: 368) points to the same association, but in my view fails to prove literary dependence. Many commentators note the prophetic resonance of 8.7a, citing especially Isa 43.2: "If you go through the waters, I will be with you; and through the floods, they will not overwhelm you".

124 Sadgrove considers that this verse was inserted by a Wisdom editor, through whose hands the Song passed; further evidence of his influence may be discerned, in Sadgrove's view, in the love of paradox and riddle that informs it, "(that) ... almost has the effect of making the entire work an extended riddle on the motif of love" (p. 247). Sadgrove here appears to be unduly influenced by a rigid compartmentalisation of genres. For example, he seems to take it as an adequate objection to an original association with wisdom lit-

Notes to Chapter Two - The Relationship of the Lovers

erature that the Song is part of the Ancient Near Eastern, and especially Egyptian, tradition of erotic poetry; but, as we have seen, the latter too has religious and sagacious elements.

125 The most plausible reading is that of Exum (75), according to whom the two "ʾahabâs" are correlated in a correspondence of long and short lines:

> mayim rabbîm lōʾ yûklû lekabbôt ʾet hāʾahabâ
> / ûnehārôt lōʾ yisṭepûhāh
> ʾim yittēn ʾîš ʾet kol hôn bêtô bāʾahabâ
> / bôz yābûzû lô

> Many waters cannot quench love
> nor will the Floods overwhelm it
> If a man were to give all the substance of his house for love
> they would surely despise him.

The numerous monosyllables and the long construct chain "ʾet-kol-hôn-bêtô" "all the substance of his house" flatten the line, however; it is a discordant echo of that which precedes it.

126 Levinger (90). Others read it as "it" (e.g. Lys: 292, Krinetzki 1981: 232). Pope (1976: 676) recognises the ambiguity, though he regards the line as prosaic and suspect. Zakovitch (1974: 368) even proposes that the redactor inserted the incommodious fragment 8.6-7 into the Song because of its association with "they would not shame me" in 8.1. In Tur-Sinai's interpretation (1943: 28-9) there is no contrast: 8.6-7 is a commentary on Prov 6.27-35 which warns against the perils of adultery. "ʾAhabâ" is parallel to "qinʾâ": it is jealous love, fierce and hard as Sheol, against which no restitution other than death suffices. "If a man were to give all his house" should in his view be an ineffective appeasement of the ire of a cuckolded husband, and not, as some hold, an avowal that love can be bought for no price (reading "lô" as "it") or, as I have construed it, an ironic reflection on social values.

127 After Death, Sheol, and Chaos, according to Lys (292), it is money that is the rival of Love. As Pope (1976: 676) says, this produces something of an anticlimax.

NOTES TO CHAPTER THREE
Beauty and the Enigma

1   "Nidgālôt" is a long-standing difficulty, since the Niphal of DGL occurs only here and in the parallel verse 6.10; the only other denominative form is "dāgûl", which we find in 5.10. The ancient versions, medieval commentators, and many moderns take the Niphal of "degel" = flag to be a "flagged" or "bannered" army (e.g. Levinger: 75; Krinetzki 1981: 277, n.426); Rudolph (162) observes that flags and banners are not necessarily military (cf. "diglô" "his banner" in 2.4), and suggests that they are constellations, in parallel with NEB, "majestic as the starry heavens", and Goitein (1965: 220-221), "stars of first-class magnitude". NEB, along with BH etc., omits the phrase in 6.4, presumably as a borrowing from 6.10. Goitein considers that DGL has a general connotation of "look, gaze", in common with Akkadian "dagalû"; of this "degel" = "flag, banner" is a particular instance, found almost entirely in the rollcalls of Numbers. The Niphal "nidgālôt" then means to be conspicuous. Further, in his view, the adjective "ʾayummā" has lost all connotations of terror, and becomes merely wondrous; a proposal motivated by the supposed incompatibility of beauty and wonder. Gordis (1969: 203-204) and others derive from the Akkadian "dagalû", "look, gaze", the sense "marvellous sights" ("frightening as visions" in Falk's poetic translation - 1982: 39), which is vague enough to fit both contexts, but consequently bathetic. There is a plethora of variations (e.g. Gerleman: 183).

Pope (1976: 561-562) has ventured the most spectacular interpretation of this ever-fecund word; simply from the root-meaning "gaze" he translates "trophies", developing an elaborate comparison with the terrible trophies of the goddess Anat, staggering under the heads and hands of her victims, and the adornments of other grisly deities, who combine the attributes of Beauty and Terror. His mythological supporting material, from India to Britain, is both very striking and extremely far from the text; as is the conjectural leap from root-meaning to precise definition.

The semantic field clearly covers all these possibilities. The terror of the army with banners is in perfect and dramatic apposition to the beauty of the cities; the constellations and stars complete the sequence of celestial similes in 6.10. Moreover, stars have a martial connotation, as the hosts of heaven. I have chosen to foreground its astral significance, since in this chapter I shall be primarily concerned with 6.10, where the meaning "constellations" is more applicable.

2   This translation of "hirhîbunî" is that of the NEB; Pope (1976: 564) has "drive me wild", and Lys (234) "car eux m'ensorcelent". The latter notes that it has the same root as the sea-monster Rahab, with a basic meaning of "importune, attack".

Notes to Chapter Three - Beauty and the Enigma

3   So they loved as love in twain
    Had the essence but in one;
    Two distincts, division none:
    Number there in love was slain.

    Hearts remote, yet not asunder,
    Distance, yet no space was seen,
    Twixt this turtle and his queen;
    But in them it were a wonder...

    Property was thus appalled
    That the self was not the same;
    Single nature's double name
    Neither two nor one was called.
                (Shakespeare, "The Phoenix and the Turtle")

4   Psychic distance as an aesthetic characteristic has been matter for contention since Bullough suggested it in 1912/13; it is associated with Kantian disinterestedness as pertaining to a detached aesthetic attitude. This has been criticised by Dickie and Wollheim (1971: 112) as one-sided, since it ignores intimate involvement with the work of art. Wollheim invokes Stokes' account of the "invitation" in art, its wooing of the senses through an appeal to unconscious fantasy to enter the dynamics of the composition. By the necessary aesthetic distance I mean simply the distance required to perceive and control a whole object, not a lack of involvement with it. I also refer to the Freudian concept of sublimation, the postponement of the immediate fulfilment of pleasure for a more lasting and socially more productive satisfaction. In Freudian theory, aesthetic feelings are associated with the genital phase, and attach themselves primarily to non-genital regions; alternatively, they result from anal repression (Rickman). Freud's references to aesthetics, like his criticism, are, however, disappointing, as Wollheim (1971: 135) remarks. The creative imagination is of more consequence for Jung, according to whom the artist finds fresh forms for the archetypes, and contributes to man's task of understanding and individuation. In the subsequent pages, Anton Ehrenzweig's works, The Psychonanalysis of Artistic Vision and Hearing, and The Hidden Order of Art, have been especially influential. Particularly exciting are the interplay of gestalt and thing-free perception, Apollonian and Dionysian principles, and the attention he gives to the inarticulate constituents of art e.g. textures, brush-strokes, overtones. Ernst Kris introduced the notion of aesthetic ambiguity, of an oscillation in the creative process, on the part both of the artist and the public, between absorption in the work and evaluation, between a creative phase and a critical phase. The Kleinians contributed greatly to aesthetic theory, introducing a more refined and also more human approach, especially in the volume, New Directions in Psychoanalysis. For them, the artist engages in a task of reparation, endeavouring to restore the integrity of the whole object, destroyed in the paranoid/schizoid and manic-phases, and grieved over in depression; there is thus a rhythm of regression and restoration. The writings of the art-critic Adrian Stokes complement these psychoanalytic re-

Notes to Chapter Three - Beauty and the Enigma

searches, as we have seen in the preceding chapters. More recently, there is Simon Stuart's study of reparation in literature, New Phoenix Wings. Anton Ehrenzweig's second volume, The Hidden Order of Art distinguished four levels on which the artist works, concluding on the level of the hermaphrodite or divine child. Other influences have been Winnicott's researches into play and transitional objects, between the self and the other, as the basis of culture, and especially Rosemary Gordon's very moving and thorough discussion of aesthetics in Dying and Creating: A Search for Meaning (1978).

Nietzsche's distinction between the Dionysian and Apollonian poles of aesthetic expression will be referred to from time to time; the motto for Dionysian beauty, from the demonic point of view, might well be Blake's proverb of Hell: "Exuberance is beauty"; its Apollonian aspect is its stillness - exuberance contained and controlled for a moment - expressed in aphoristic terseness.

5 Thus Falk (1982: 110), in contrast to most translations and commentaries, prefers to read the "wĕ" as "and", introducing a tension between the attitude of the Beloved and that of the daughters of Jerusalem. There are no positive grounds, however, for excluding either adversative or complementary meanings. Ibn Ezra alludes to commentators who refer to the beauty of negresses (possibly with reference to Moses' wife) and the fear that it will attract the "evil eye".

6 Pope (1976: 321) recognises the ambiguity. Schoville (1970: 103) follows a suggestion of Dahood (1965: 302) based on forced interpretations of Ps 49.7 and I Sam 18.9 that RʲH in this instance means "envy".

7 The opposition is already fully articulated in the Classical Pastoral, in Theocritus and Virgil (e.g. Idylls X.26-29, Eclogues II.16, X.38-9); and may be traced back to Homer (Odyssey XXIII. 240). In the Near East generally, however, skin tone as a signifier is replaced by skin-painting, for example, in the cosmetics of Anat ('nt II.2-3 and parallel passages; cf. de Moor (1971: 85).

A very interesting variation of the opposition white/black may be found in Egypt. Alison Roberts informs me that "if the Egyptians wanted to describe the colour of a beautiful female body they used 'thnw'. A 'body of thnw' = 'a body of faience' where the symbolic connotations are with the cool sleek glittering colour of the turquoise blue of Egyptian faience. This is contrasted with the red colour of carnelian in the texts, the colour of passion. A body of faience can quickly turn into the flame red of carnelian leading a man to perdition - so warn the Wisdom Texts" (letter).

In a late poem from Babylon, whiteness and darkness combine in a very earthy and Dionysiac image of the desired goddess:

> At the river crossing of Kar-bel-matati
> I saw my girl-friend and was completely overwhelmed.
> You are white like a gecko,
> Your skin is dusky like a pot,
> You are exhuberant [sic], you are made [happy].
>
> (Lambert 1975: 121)

Notes to Chapter Three - Beauty and the Enigma

Whiteness is here associated with the pullulant insect world, with dust and heat and disintegration. We now at the threshold of contra-indications of white complexion: leprosy, weakness, bloodlessness, based on the opposition healthy fairness/unhealthy pallor. The extremes are transformationally linked: too much shelter, too much repression, is deadly.

8   For the persistence of the motif in 19th-century fiction, see Frye (1957: 101).

9   I was fortunate enough to hear part of "The Spring of Memory" on (U.K.) Radio 4 recently. In this programme a hypnotised subject retraced his life, back to his birth and the womb. He was called upon to articulate these experiences; his account is extraordinarily convincing, and reminiscent of a Beckett prose. One of his most striking memories of birth was of intense pain in his eyes, and his first tear.

10 The substitution of the name of a tribe, Salmah, otherwise unrecorded in the OT, favoured by Gaster (1952: 322), Rudolph (123), Pope (1976: 320), and others, for the sake of an allegedly superior parallelism, is unnecessary, as Krinetzki (1981: 240) notes, as "überflüssig und entbehrlich". The manufacture of parallelisms has been responsible for much reductivism in poetry. Nor need we suppose "Solomon's curtains" to be a stylistic term, like "Louis Quatorze furniture", with Gordis (1974: 79).

11 Cf. André Neher: 169-171; and the further discussion in Blanchot, "La Question Littéraire", in Le Livre à Venir (99-107).

12 The metaphorical transition is underlined by complex punning. "Šeššezāpatnî" has been variously interpreted:

i)   as a Shaphal Causative of "zepet" "pitch" - to give "has made me black as pitch" (Dahood 1963-74 II: 406-407)

ii) "has gazed on me" - (cf. Job 20.8; 28.7) corresponding to the stare of the daughters of Jerusalem in the previous phrase (e.g. Pope 1976: 321).

iii) "has scorched me" - an Aramaicised form of ŠDP (cf. Gen. 41.6, 23 etc.), an image that merges with the subsequent rage of the brothers, as Lys points out (73).

"Niḥarû bî" is also a neat pun on ḤRH "to be angry", ḤRR "to be hot, scorched", and NḤR "to snort" (Driver 1933: 380), thus combining the ideas of human rage, solar heat, and possibly wounded satire, at the brothers' snorting irascibility.

13 BRR, whence "bārâ" "the radiant one" may refer to moral excellence (Ps 18.27; 24.4), to bright metallic sharpness (e.g. of arrows, Isa 49.2), or to physical choiceness e.g. of sheep (Neh 5.18). Marvin Pope translates it as "favourite" in 6.9 (1976: 570). As he admits, "It is no special distinction to be a favorite only child". Hence his choice is somewhat puzzling.

In Ps 19.9 "bārâ" plays the same rhetorical role of mediating between the brilliance of the sun and moral perfection; following the dramatic presentation of the sun in v.6-8 we have "The commandment of the Lord is <u>radiant</u> (bārâ) enlightening the eyes" (v.9). Hillers (1978) has noted a parallel to the word play in the present passage in an Ugaritic legal formula of emancipation:

Notes to Chapter Three - Beauty and the Enigma

> Km špš dbrrt kmt br ṣtqšlm
> As the sun is bright, so is Ṣitqashalim bright/free
> (UT. 10005.2-4)

The word "radiant" conveys the ambiguity in English.

14 "Šāḥar" "dawn" may also mean the morning-star (Dahood 1963-74 II: 412; Schoville 1970: 89-90); there is little to choose between the two interpretations. J. W. McKay (459) argues vigorously that Shahar here, without the article, is the feminine dawn goddess, matching the gender of "lebānâ" and "ḥammâ". Even if this is so, however, the Dawn-goddess merely personifies the dawn, itself personified by the Beloved; just as the morning star itself is the harbinger of the sun's rising ("the dawn's eye" in Marcia Falk's felicitous translation). This proposal introduces a note of false complexity.

15 Alison Roberts makes a most interesting comparison between the imagery of this section and that associated with the goddess Hathor, "the resplendent beauty who is the source of ecstasy", who is likewise manifest in the ladies of the royal entourage. A particularly close though inverted parallel is a speech of Hathor's to Rameses II at Karnak: "Come, come, O Lord of the Two Lands, possessor of sexual attraction, whose eyes are the sun and moon". As in our passage, a terrestrial dyad (the Two Lands; Jerusalem, Tirzah) is coupled with the cosmic complementarity of sun and moon.

16 Some critics argue that parable is essentially subversive, e.g. Crossan 1975: 54-61 and Harrison 1981: 196; they rely however excessively on the parables of revolutionary moralists, such as Jesus. There are parables affirmative of traditional values e.g. Nathan's parable, and, as indeed Harrison shows, Jesus' parables depend for their effectiveness on a conventional parabolic background, such as we find in Midrash. Frank Kermode (1979: 24-25) writes that "Parables are stories ... which are not to be taken at face value, and bear various indications to make this condition plain to the interpreter". At the simplest level, a parable is a narrative simile, whose comprehension is relative to the listeners' ability to apply it to a relevant situation. According to Harrison, a new moral concept can only be communicated through parable (1981: 206). However, insofar as it is a development of riddle, whose interpretation depends on knowing the key, it is more or less intelligible. A form that begins as a means of clarifying a difficulty uses its heuristic promise to compound bewilderment e.g. in the parables of Kafka and Borges. Kermode (1979: 25) writes in a crucial sentence "'narrativity' always entails a measure of opacity". We may perhaps correlate subversive parable with Williams' "Wisdom of Counter-Order" (and vice versa), as that which questions traditional concepts through paradox (James Williams 1981: 47-65 esp. 57ff.).

17 There have been various attempts to identify Baal-Hamon, either through emendation to "Baal-Hermon" or "Baal-Hammon" (BH, ed. Fr. Horst; Pope, 1976: 687-8), or with Balamon (Judith 8.3). As Gordis (1974: 101) remarks, "Many actual places do not occur in the Bible". Whether or not it is imaginary, as Krinetzki (1981: 228) and Gerleman (222) argue, its allegorical connotations are quite clear, and indicated by most commentators.

Notes to Chapter Three - Beauty and the Enigma

18 So Lys: 302, Krinetzki 1981: 228, Gerleman: 222, Rudolph: 185. Gerleman and Rudolph argue on the basis of a supposed parallel with 6.8-10 that the value of the Beloved is greater than that of Solomon's harem; the thousand pieces of silver correspond to his thousand wives. Even if this be granted, it is illicit to conclude that the young man is speaking, comparing his treasure to Solomon's concubines. It could equally well be the Beloved, asserting her own uniqueness. Likewise, Lys' argument on the basis of the complementarity of "lišlōmōh" "Solomon's" and "lepānāy" "mine" in 8.11 and 8.12 simply does not follow; nothing suggests that "lepānāy" refers to the Lover and not to the Beloved. On the contrary, the recapitulation of the issue of caring for her own vineyard in 1.5-6, using the very same phrases, makes it difficult to conclude that it is not the same speaker, as Exum affirms (76). Moreover, it is a very arbitrary procedure indeed to differentiate the Lover and his royal persona, as in the old-fashioned dramatic theory. In particular, Gerleman, who introduced the concept of "persona" into criticism of the Song, seems to have forgotten it in this instance.

19 Robert and Tournay: 318. Gerleman: 222 and Rudolph: 185 see it as a metonym for Jerusalem; Krinetzki (1981: 228) proposed that it may be restricted still further to the harem, which would reinforce its association with fertility. There is no reason to limit its application in this way; poetic figures have maximum resonance. No argument for identifying Baal-Hamon with Jerusalem does not apply with equal force to the whole of Israel.

20 So Levinger: 95, Rudolph: 184, Gerleman: 222; Lys: 301 holds that the reference is to each one of the keepers. A further ambiguity is that "yābi'" does not specify direction of transaction; the suffix of "piryô" may likewise be personal (his fruit) or impersonal (its fruit).

21 E.g. Lys: 301. Gordis (1974: 101) translates "tenants". Pope notes an exact equivalent in Ugaritic: "nǵr krm" as the title of a royal functionary (1976: 325).

22 Gordis (1974: 101-102) remarks that in Talmudic times a tenant-farmer received between a quarter and a half of the harvest; and suggests that either their conditions had improved since Biblical times, or else vine-tenders received less reward for less work. With the ingenuity of a Poirot, Tur-Sinai (1943: 11-12) reconstructs an elaborate and proverbial swindle by Solomon.

23 A correlation between anal eroticism and the character traits of orderliness, avarice, and obstinacy, was first made in Freud's paper "Character and Anal Eroticism" (1908) and elaborated in "On Transformations of Instinct as Exemplified in Anal Eroticism" (1917). Cf. Norman O. Brown (177-304) for a very full treatment.

24 There is the marvellous line "You are my short silvery girl" in Lambert (1975: 103).

25 Cf. Isa 47.13, Jer 10.2, ID 303. Charlesworth (185) states that the OT documents were not influenced by astrological beliefs, but he contradicts himself in the same breath, adding "but rather contains disputations against them". Refutation suggests a need for refutation, that astrological beliefs were current.

26 "Ṭîrâ" = "turret" (JPSA; Gordis 1974: 75; Falk 1982: 49);

"parapet" (NEB; Lys: 296); "Zinne" (Krinetzki 1981: 293), "Mauerfranz" (Gerleman: 219). Pope (1976: 680) favours "buttress". In Gen 25.6, Num 31.10 etc., "ṭîrôt" = "nomadic encampments"; in Eze 46.23 = "stone wall, row of stones". In Lys's view, the term basically refers to rows of protective stones, e.g. crenellated battlements. Gordis (1974: 75, 100) supposes that the turret is built against the wall, as a siege engine; he holds, with Tur Sinai (1943: 18), that the passage is spoken by desperate lovers, anxiously assailing the little one. "Sister" is then an endearment, as in 4.8, 5.2 etc. Lys sharply criticises this view.

Another reconstruction, proposed by Webster (1982: 81) is that instead of rivals the speakers may be friends of the Lover/bridegroom lightly questioning the Beloved's sexual development and/or chastity; 8.10-12 is her emphatic response. Symmetry suggests, Webster avers, a complementary situation in 1.5-7; there the friends of the Beloved/bride flirtatiously tease the virtuous lover. There is no evidence for the former being "a time-honoured ritual" before marriage (Fuerst: 197, quoted by Webster), nor for the speaker of 1.5-6 being other than the Beloved.

27 Pope 1976: 687. Marcia Falk (1976: 257) points out that it could be sisters, a possibility also suggested by Exum (1973: 75-76). The consensus of critics is that it is the brothers who speak in 8.8-9 and the Beloved who answers in 8.10. Gordis (1974: 75, 100) and Tur-Sinai (1943: 18) hold that 8.8-9 are the words of militant suitors. My view, that it is the Beloved who speaks throughout, is sustained by Delitzsch, cited by Pope, and taken for granted by Cook (149).

28 On this aspect of criticism of the Song, see Franz Rosenzweig (199-200): "... the infinity of such combinations as the curiosity of erudite eroticism is wont to excel in".

29 ṢWR: II "confine, bind, besiege"; IV "fashion, delineate" (BDB, 848-9). The Versions read it in the second sense; the former has been more common in recent times. In line with his interpretation, Gordis takes the meaning "besiege", while stressing that this is in fact homage or adornment, because of the delicacy and preciousness of the siege-weapons (1974: 100). Levinger (94) considers that the cedar is carved, as a decorative frame for the door.

30 At this point the divergent views, that 8.8-9 are the remembered words of the brothers, and that in them the Beloved sees a past image of herself, coincide for a moment.

31 Pope (1976: 678) summarises as well as anybody the various interpretations of the idiomatic usage of "DBR be":

    i)   as index of hostility (e.g. Ps 50.20)
    ii)   for a proposal of marriage (only I Sam 25.39).
    iii) Tur-Sinai suggests that it introduces an incantation (1943: 18-19).

In fact, verbs of speaking tend to be very versatile. In I Sam 25.39, "And David sent and spoke concerning Abigail (wayedabber be) to take her for himself as a wife", the verb speak does not necessarily function other than as an essential preliminary.

32 A question prevalent in Egyptian love poetry, in which the Beloved's door is frequently the subject of the poet's attention - e.g. Chester-Beatty Papyrus I c.6, 7; Papyrus 500. 7 (Lichtheim 1976: 188,

Notes to Chapter Three - Beauty and the Enigma

189). J. B. White (149-150) is over-cautious in adducing a comparison with similar scenes in the Song, on the grounds that lament is essential to the genre. Quite apart from the variety of treatments and moods associated with the motif in Egyptian love-poetry, this is indicative of an exclusive concern with classification at the expense of symbolic value. Gerleman (62) gives the motif proper emphasis.

33   "Môṣ'ēt" may be either the Qal Participle of MṢ' "find", or the Hiphil Participle of YṢ' "bring out, produce". The first would give to "find peace", analogous to the familiar idiom "mṣ' ḥēn be'ēn-"[+suffix] "to find favour in someone's eyes". The second would produce to "bring peace". The third meaning, "surrender", fits either derivation equally well; it is suggested by the conjunction of "peace" with the earlier military images. A recent proponent has been Levinger (94). Marcia Falk, on the other hand, takes it in reverse (1982: 132), holding that the Beloved's successful defence earns a truce.

34   Dahood 1963-74 IV: 416; Schoville 1970: 109. Dahood proposes that "môṣ'ēt" is formed from YṢ', to be found in Ugaritic (but see Cyrus Gordon UT: 415 where YṢ' does not appear in this sense). For Shalem as the Evening Star, cf. "The Birth of the Good and Gracious Gods" (UT 52).

35   A complementarity emphasised by the possible identification of "šaḥar" with the dawn-goddess, as advocated by McKay (459) cf. n.14.

36   The <u>conative</u> function is orientated towards the <u>addressee</u>. The <u>phatic</u> function is speech for the sake of speaking, for keeping the lines of communication open.

37   The attribution of the reply is disputed. Lys (80) holds that it is that of the shepherds/friends who politely invite the Beloved to join them. Another view is that of Gordis (1974: 80) and Tur-Sinai (1943: 17) who consider it to be a premonitory quotation in the mouth of Beloved of his friends' propositions. Gerleman (102) identifies it as an aside of the poet, whom he regards as an independent voice in the Song. Krinetzki assigns it to a male chorus (1981: 72).

On the face of it, as Krinetzki admits, the verse is the Lover's response, and it is thus that I leave it. The difficulties are not resolved by the various suggestions, but merely permutated. For instance, we still don't know whether "by the shepherds' huts" is parallel to or antithetical with "by your friends' flocks", and "If you know not" still appears nonsensical. The motive for these constructions is in fact a reluctance to accept the Lover's contrariness. As J. B. White elegantly remarks, this is just "joshing" (52, 129, 144-5).

If an utterance is specifically addressed to a particular person, it seems reasonable to assume that it is that person who responds, unless there are definite indications to the contrary. Failing these, I attribute it to the Lover, as do the NEB, White (see above), Levinger (27) and Cook (136).

38   Pope (1976: 330) argues strongly that "šallāmâ" does not mean "For why?" but "lest", equivalent to Aram. "dilmaʷ" and that "-mâ" is a negative particle. Gordis (1974: 80), Levinger (28), Krinetzki (1981: 242 n.79), all refer to the etymological connection, but interpret it

Notes to Chapter Three - Beauty and the Enigma

differently; as Lys (79) says, "for why" easily transposes itself into "lest". I retain it, as more petulant.

39   The following are the main lines of interpretation:

i) The most natural is as a participle of 'TH "cover, wrap" e.g. "veiled". This may be a sign of mourning (cf. Mic 3.7) or of a prostitute - cf. Tamar (Gen 38.14) (e.g. Meek IB; Pope: 1976: 330-31). This line of interpretation runs into difficulty, however, since veils are as often a sign of modesty as of wantonness (e.g. Gen 24.65); it is doubtful whether Tamar's was a disguise or an allure; and euphemisms for prostitutes are rare in Biblical Hebrew.

ii) As a metathesis of ṬʻH/ TʻH "wander" i.e. a vagabond. Marcia Falk ingeniously combines the two roots to give "go searching blindly", emphasising what she calls the "hide and seek theme" of the piece (1982: 111).

iii) A second possible denotation of ʻṬH is "pick lice" (Jer 43.12, Isa 21.17). Accordingly, NEB translates "that I may not be left picking lice". G. R. Driver defends this view vigorously, arguing both the insufficiency of the aforementioned interpretations and that lice-picking is a perfectly natural activity (1974). However, the etymology of ʻṬH as "picking lice" is very uncertain, since the other two loci, Jer 43.21 and Isa 21.17, are entirely obscure. Moreover, there is nothing to be gained by such a reading in context.

Sonia Grober (57) proposes an interesting and plausible derivation from ʻṬH = "swoop" (cf. I Sam 13.19); the Beloved imagines herself as unwelcome to the friends as a bird of prey.

40   In a somewhat restrained comment, Pope (1976: 333, 334-345) notes the sexual proclivity of goats in folklore, and quotes a long Sumerian poem in which Dumuzi and Geshtinanna possibly take their cue from watching the incestuous intercourse of flocks. This is hardly of relevance to our passage, where the kids are innocently grazing, and the lovers are not overtly consanguineous. The *general* analogy of nature and man in the Song, and its incestuous dimension, cannot be used to support a *particular* comparison in this case. Nevertheless, it may be an instance of the "lost shepherd" motif, found in numerous ancient Near Eastern texts, as suggested to me by Alison Roberts.

41   The only other instance is 4.1b-2, duplicated in 6.5b-6. Whereas the death of the divine shepherd poet is a traditional subject, both of ritual lamentation and the Classical Pastoral, one will look for it in vain in the Song. Cf. William Berg, Early Virgil: 15-22, 121-131, and passim. I have based much of the succeeding discussion on this superb book.

42   The absence of a sense of voice is one of the most extraordinary features of Roland Barthes' most sensitive study of the language of love, A Lover's Discourse: Fragments (1979), and is perhaps indicative of the one-sidedness of current French criticism; cf. Josipovici (1980). Roman Jakobson (1968: 16-17) has made some remarkable observations on infantile regression in sweettalk. For instance, in some Siberian languages women in intimacy regularly substitute phonemes from an earlier stage of childhood development for ones that are acquired later, especially j for the liquid l.

43   The quotation is from Robert Duncan's "Often I am Permitted

Notes to Chapter Three - Beauty and the Enigma

to Return to a Meadow", in The Opening of the Field (New Directions, 1973).

44   Alongside most modern commentators, I take the suffix of "lesusātî" to be a survival of the old genitive case, though the possessive might be a secondary ambiguity, as Levinger proposes (30). It would then be an expression of endearment, exactly parallel to "yōnātî beḥagwê hassela'" "My dove in the clefts of the rock" in 2.14

"Rekeb" "chariotry" is normally a collective noun: hence the plural form "rikbê" is anomalous. Accordingly, Dahood (1963-74 VIII: 347), Pope (1976: 337), and others, consider it to be synonymous with stallions. Gerleman (106) argues that until the time of the Ethiopian dynasty horses were normally harnessed to chariots. Alternatively, Krinetzki (1964: 293) and Lys (83) see in the phrase an idiomatic usage.

45   Gordis (1974: 48) seems to find the image somewhat embarrassing; a good example of how volatile are aesthetic values. A stanza from one of the most perfect of Egyptian Love lyrics is an extended comparison of the Lover with a horse (Lichtheim 1976: 186-7).

46   Similarly, McKay (459) argues that in 6.10 "lebānâ" "moon" and "ḥammâ" "sun" were chosen in preference to the more common "yārēaḥ" and "šemeš", so as to provide a correspondence of gender.

47   1976: 340 and passim. Also Hillers (1973: 71-80).

48   Pope's interpretation was presented in an expanded form in "A Mare in Pharaoh's Chariotry" (1970) and quite independently developed by Marcia Falk (1982: 112). The comparison is one of irresistable sex-appeal: the effect of the Beloved on the local males is like that of a mare on heat unleashed in a battle-field. To illustrate the use of this stratagem in ancient warfare, both refer to a ruse of the Prince of Qadesh, who thereby nearly brought disaster on the Egyptian army (Pope 1976: 338).

49   The proximity of the reference to him as king in 1.12, the richness of the ornaments in 1.10-11, and the royal metaphor in this verse, all contribute to the persona of Lover as king in this passage (Gordis 1974: 48).

NOTES TO CHAPTER FOUR
Two Versions of Paradise

1   Despite its ostensible date, Semeia 18 was only published in Summer, 1981.

2   This however is to misrepresent Lévi-Strauss, who stresses the dual nature of mythological thought, its diachronicity as well as its synchronic axis, for example in this passage (1970: 6, 16):

> Myth operates on the basis of a twofold continuum: one part of it is external and is composed ... of historical, or supposedly historical, events forming a theoretically infinite series from which each society extracts a limited number of relevant incidents with which to create its myths ... The second aspect of the continuum is internal and is situated in the psycho-physiological time of the listener, the elements of which are very complex: they involve the periodicity of cerebral waves and organic rhythms, the strength of the memory, and the power of the attention. Mythology makes demands primarily on the neuromental aspects because of the length of the narration, the recurrence of certain themes, and the other forms of back references and parallels which can only be correctly grasped if the listener's mind surveys, as it were, the whole range of the story as it is unfolded.

3   The narrative is semantically overloaded, as Jobling (41) argues. This does not mean, however, that one can abstract a pristine story by excising the aetiological elements, as A. J. Williams presupposes (1973: 73), though he recognises their relevance to the finished form of the tale (1973: 359). The supposition that a narrator begins with a story, to which aetiological details are affixed, rather than with a set of problems he endeavours to comprehend, is dubious. The form-critical assumption that first = simplest is fallacious, as Polzin has shown (1980: 14). Culley (1976: 40) argues that it is inaccurate to think in terms of an "original" story, at least in oral tradition; a point that Robert Alter (1981: 47-62) develops in his examination of Biblical type-scenes and their variations; cf. also James Williams 1979.

4   Leach (1969: 13-15), for example, interprets Gen 1 and Gen 2-3 as different parts of a structural set, addressing different aspects of the problem of unity and binarity, e.g. Eve corresponds to the "creeping things" of chapter 1. Freilich, on the other hand, in his structural analysis, sets the two creation stories on a narrative continuum, as does Brams in his application of game-theory to the Bible (11ff.). Several critics find unity on the level of redaction, as part of much larger units, e.g. Clines 1978: 65, 75; Anderson; Dahlberg. There is a literary comparison in Gros-Louis. Robert Alter summarises the potential relationship very precisely:

Notes to Chapter Four - Two Versions of Paradise

The differences between our two versions are so pronounced that by now some reader may be inclined to conclude that what I have proposed as a complementary relationship is in fact a contradictory one. If, however, we can escape the modern provincialism of assuming that ancient writers must be simple because they are ancient, it may be possible to see that the Genesis author chose to combine these two versions of creation precisely because he understood that his subject was essentially contradictory, essentially resistant to consistent linear formulation, and that this was his way of giving it the most adequate linear expression. (1981: 145)

5   Winnett dates it in the 6th cent. B.C.; Alonso-Schökel (1962: 315) proposes a date later than the ninth century. A. J. Williams (1973: 68) holds that the narrative underwent considerable evolution, and reached its final form in the late 8th cent. On the other hand, Haran dates P c.700. Wyatt (20) conjectures that the myth was composed as political allegory of the fall of the Northern Kingdom.

6   This view, common to 19th-century critics from Wellhausen onwards (cf. Skinner: 96) has been largely ignored in recent discussions. One exception is a stimulating essay by Bo Reicke "The Knowledge Hidden in the Tree of Paradise" (1956) who argues that agriculture was a traumatic development, conceived of as "a perilous and almost criminal interference with nature", a view shared by Lévi-Strauss and, on a factual plane, perhaps linked with Ronen's conclusion that living standards actually dropped with the Neolithic Revolution (A. Ronen 1976: 77). Hence the special ritual safeguards on eating the firstfruits, which are the vegetative equivalent of the firstborn. Reicke suggests that among other things, Gen 2-3 is an aetiological myth of the first fruits, the initiation into agriculture. Procreation is metaphorically identified with cultivation; and one remembers that the firstborn children die. Extending it further, the firstborn priests, Nadab and Abihu, also die, as part of the consecration of the sanctuary. Bailey (149) comments that J had a negative attitude towards civilization, compared to the Epic of Gilgamesh, where Enkidu revokes his curse of the harlot (herself an ambiguous figure) and substitutes praise. Thorkild Jacobsen, in his recent analysis of the Eridu Genesis (1981) observes the entirely positive evaluation of culture in the Sumerian myth, in contrast to the pessimistic conception in the P document of Genesis, with which he compares it. The structural correlates that Jacobsen adduces are very interesting. However, as Clines has shown (1978: 64ff.), the theme of the Primeval History is essentially ambivalent, e.g. the spread of sin is accompanied by the spread of grace, uncreation by recreation. The ambivalence of culture, dependent on man's natural goodness and contingent evil, is examined fully in Ricoeur's discussion (246-52).

7   Kessler (1982: 8) claims that only members of the same genre can be compared with each other. This is patent nonsense: Fishbane, for example, illuminatingly examines the transformation of the Eden motif in prophetic writings (111-20); Frye's whole oeuvre is devoted to the tracing of interconnections between different modes. But the

Notes to Chapter Four - Two Versions of Paradise

difference of genre does impose limits on possible comparisons, as will become apparent; this is to say no more than that each text is finally irreducible.

8   Most commentators interpret "miqqedem" as a geographical indication. Wyatt, however, argues that the temporal sense "seems altogether more satisfactory" (13), though he proceeds to propose a spatial meaning also. I concur with this perception of its ambiguity.

9   An example are the phrases "we will see/look if the vine has blossomed" and "the pomegranates are in flower", that link the garden of 6.11 to the fields of 7.13.

10   Uriel Simon has suggested to me that the literal translation of "pardēs" as "paradise" is misleading; nevertheless I consider that the connotation of felicity is appropriate, especially since it is clear from the context that it means no more than a splendid orchard or park.

11   Only saffron and cypress are native to Israel. The distribution of the others ranges from the East Indies to Abyssinia (Feliks: 23-28). Exum (64) avers that a chiasmus opposes "every incense tree" i.e. myrrh and aloes to "all species of spices" i.e. nard, saffron, calamus and cinnamon. Cinnamon, however, comes from the inner bark of a tree. According to Feliks (26 n.24), the cinnamon in current use was unknown in Israel in Biblical times; the plant that our text refers to is Sinaitic cassia, which likewise was extremely precious.

12   Rudolph (161) substitutes "lir'ot baggepānîm" "to look at the vines", following BH, on the grounds that the MT is striking (auffällig).

13   For Alonso-Schökel (1962: 303), however, this miniscule dissertation, as he calls it, is evidence for the "wisdom" component in the composition, the delight in knowledge for its own sake.

14   "A far away land or an area on earth that cannot be geographically pinpointed" (1974a: 80), cf. Speiser (1967b) for the view that the Gihon and Pishon are tributaries of the Euphrates and Tigris, that "mē'ēden" means "into Eden", and the garden was hence the land of Dilmun or Bahrein. Cassuto (1961: 117) suggests that they all emanated from the same subterranean source. Wyatt (13 n.9) dissociates himself from the view that no specific location is intended, and identifies Eden with the land to which the Israelites were exiled, though this is surely to invert its signification. Ibn Ezra has the charming idea that the garden was situated at the Equator, and hence was not subject to seasons.

15   L. P. Trudinger suggests that "beṭerem" means "recently, freshly" (root ṬRI) i.e. "All the grass of the field ... had recently sprouted" on the grounds that:

    i)   This interpretation of "ṭerem" fits most Biblical contexts.
    ii)   It dispenses with the absurdity that man was created before vegetation.
    iii) It reconciles the two accounts of creation.

In Trudinger's view, the next clause, concerning the rain, disposes of an objection, and 2.6 is an explanation "grass/herbs had just begun to spring up ... though the Lord God had not caused it to rain on the earth ... but a mist came up and watered the earth".

In my view, nowhere does "ṭerem" unambiguously mean "recently", and there are several instances where this meaning is

Notes to Chapter Four - Two Versions of Paradise

impossible (e.g. when Pharaoh's servants say "Do you not yet (haṭerem) know that Egypt is destroyed?"). None of the cases that Trudinger cites is especially convincing. In the second place, the absurdity is not that man should have been created before vegetation, but that he should have been thought essential to its existence (2.5b). The third difficulty is not really of concern to literary critics.

A more positive objection is that "Not Yet" is the logical beginning of the story, like the Babylonian Enuma Elish. Yet Trudinger does have a point - which is why I have given him so much consideration - "ṭerem" is wonderfully indeterminate, full of expectations, taking us right back to that earliest beginning.

16   Rashi glosses "tehôm", anticipating the dominant current interpretation as the subterranean freshwater stream, related to the Mesopotamian river-god Id, cf. Cassuto (1961: 104), W. F. Albright (1939: 102 n.25) that "ʼēd" = Ida. P. E. S. Thompson holds that Id/Edda is the dew that waters the whole face of the earth, a pattern of evaporation and condensation.

17   Following Pope 1976: 490 ("groove"), Levinger (60) et al. (cf. Neh 3.15; Jastrow, Dictionary 1580). Pope thinks it must refer to a part of the anatomy, hence his emphasis on its declivity, as "conduit" or "groove", rather than on its function of carrying water. Levinger, correctly in my view, connects it with "maʿyan ḥatûm" "the sealed spring", whose waters are dammed and exploited through the use of "šelāḥayik", irrigation canals.

Another common and plausible interpretation of this much-disputed word is "your shoots" (cf. Jer 17.8 etc.) - cf. Lys: 189, Gerleman: 158 etc. "Your shoots" are your extremities, tendrils, as well as those of the garden.

Other interpretations include "Your two cheeks", i.e. "šenê leḥayik" (NEB) and Rudolph's (151) extreme fragmentation: še (Rel. Part.) + leḥ (freshness, immaculateness) + -ah (her) + ke (like) ... (an orchard of pomegranates).

18   There is little necessity for the conjectural "palm tree" (Rudolph 166; BDB 636) as opposed to the regular "valley, wadi" (cf. Pope 1976: 579-80). The parallel in Num 24.17 carries no conviction.

19   Pope (1976: 497) suggests that "nōzlîm" is a noun, as in Prov 5.15 etc., while recognising that it could be an adjective complementing "ḥayyîm". In such a short sentence, to introduce a new synonymous subject where none is required by the syntax is simply otiose. I grant that spring torrents in Lebanon may be an impressive sight, as Pope says, but except in their gentler moments they would surely devastate gardens.

20   The precious stones (šôham) and excellent gold found there links this passage with the garden of Eden in Eze 28.13 and the garden of the gods in the Epic of Gilgamesh. A secluded land, encircled by rivers, is already half-removed from the world; its products are a sign of immense wealth, that grows from the soil. The supremacy of gold among metals may be accounted for perhaps only because it alone does not tarnish and is thus instinct with immortality (Nancy Sandars 1968: 159: "Yet from the first it possessed its symbolic "aura", its incomparable prestige, and this was probably

Notes to Chapter Four - Two Versions of Paradise

because of its incorruptibility"). Kush and Havilah are "fabled" lands, equivalent to Punt in Egyptian love poetry. It is interesting, however, that there, as in the Song, the imagery of El Dorado is replaced by that of spices; for instance, in the Song, the mountains of myrrh in 4.6.

21 Westermann suggests (1974b: 293) that the geographical information in 2.10-14 is a synchronic equivalent of genealogy, that localises the garden in our world; this does not however demythologise it. The garden is at the junction of the fabulous and the familiar, the symbolic and the empirical.

22 Hence surface water is associated with magic and healing (Keel 1978: 81, 140). Fishbane (17) likewise proposes that Eden was situated upon a cosmic mountain, adducing in addition to these considerations the streams' downward flow in our passage. Fritz Stolz, in a most stimulating article, has examined the references to the garden of God in the OT, and compared them with the Epic of Gilgamesh. In his view the myth of the garden of God was originally associated with Lebanon, cf. the "$arz\hat{e}^J\bar{e}l$" "the cedars of God" in Ps 81.20; the slaying of Humbaba in Gilgamesh is one version of this myth. The correlations are fascinating and need to be explored further. Stolz suggests, however, that the identification of Eden and Lebanon is Ezekiel's poetic synthesis.

23 The "$\bar{e}d$" and the river ($n\bar{a}h\bar{a}r$) might well be identical, if "$n\bar{a}h\bar{a}r$" be taken in its mythological sense as the world stream (Keel 1978: 21). In that case the impossibility of its being the fountainhead of the world's rivers is obviated. For Walsh (168) and Cassuto (1961: 114-15) likewise there is a rhetorical connection.

24 See the even more curious article by S. Bartino "Los cuatro vientos del Cantar y los cuatro rios del Paraiso" (1972). Bartino seeks to demonstrate that "$\hat{u}r\hat{\imath}$" and "$b\hat{o}^J\hat{\imath}$" are the east and west winds respectively, through analogy with "$meb\hat{o}^J\ ha\check{s}\check{s}eme\check{s}$". Even without resort to casuistic philology, one may suppose that North and South represent the totality of winds. Pope (1976: 498) cites Delitzsch's attractive suggestion that the east wind is not invoked because of its unfavourable aspect.

25 Alonso-Schökel (1962: 306) noting this fact, ignored by most critics, argues that it is consonant with the rhythm of sacred history that he finds epitomised in this narrative. Adam, born in the wilderness and transplanted to the garden, is the archetype of Israel, delivered from Egypt and given the Promised Land to "watch" and to "keep". Through this projection, Alonso-Schökel suggests, the Wisdom composer of the narrative could meditate on the origins of evil in history. The vocabulary "$wayyiqqah$ ... $wayyannih\hat{e}h\hat{u}$" "And he took ... and he set him down" underlines the association with the divine promise.

26 Lionel Trilling, quoted by Armstrong, 4.

27 Jobling (44) from a different perspective, argues its inherent instability, since it can only be spoken of using the language of "outside".

28 For the etymology of "$^Jeg\bar{o}z$" see Introduction (n.38). Pope (1976: 574-9) devotes a very long note to the sacred, sexual and

Notes to Chapter Four - Two Versions of Paradise

sinister significance of the nut, ranging from its "quasi-magical" popularity in organic food shops to its function in medieval medicine, and its Kabbalistic connotations, finally to infer that the nut garden is situated in the Qidron Valley (contemporary Wadi El-Joz) and is the entrance to the Underworld. While almost everything, and certainly every fruit, in the Song may have its cultic and sexual significance, given sufficient arcane assiduity, it is not clear from Pope's discussion that the nut is richer in its associated folklore than the pomegranate or apple.

29   Commentators have generally identified the garden with the Beloved, to conform to the application of the metaphor in chapter 4. The assumption that the garden can have but one reference is thus methodologically improper, besides grossly oversimplifying its function in 4.12-5.1, as I hope to have shown. In this case, the grounds for determining the value of the metaphor of the garden are purely contextual, viz. the exchange with the daughters of Jerusalem, which is only intelligible if the Beloved is not identified with it.

30   Exegetes hesitate between the two meanings of R'H: 1) to "pasture" (sheep) as in 1.7; 2) to "graze/browse" (BDB 944-5). Lys (129-30) indeed sees the ambiguity as essential to the verse and its parallel in 2.16. Gerleman (127-8), who understands the Lover to be in the guise of a shepherd, contrasts the first meaning here with the second in 4.5; this, however, is to beg the question whether the Lover is imagined as a fawn or shepherd, and is evidence for an over-dependence on the theory of literary personae. Rudolph (161) objects that sheep do not graze in gardens (though I once saw a whole flock of sheep trimming a lawn in Jerusalem) and emends "rō'eh" to "rōṣeh" "who desires" in conformity with this sedulousness to conserve gardens, changing also the previous "lir'ôt bagannîm" "to graze in the gardens" to "lir'ôt baggepānîm" "to look upon the vines". Since in discussing 2.16-17 he perceives the underlying image of the fawn, parallel to 2.8-9, in an idealised setting, such drastic disregard for the refrain in the service of realism seems unnecessary.

31   See Kawin p.43: "We attach new material to the refrain as it comes to us, as we would clip sail to a mast".

32   Levinger (76) attributes the verse to the Beloved, since: i) he assigns 6.12 to her; ii) it parallels her speech in 6.2-3 and her invitation in 7.13. There is no indication of speaker in 6.12, and frequently refrains are interchanged between the lovers (e.g. 2.10-13 // 7.12-14, 2.16-17 // 4.5-6). Gerleman (189) also attributes it to the Beloved, since 7.1 is addressed to her. Even granted the sequential unity of 6.11-7.1, this does not follow. As Pope says (1976: 579), the identity of the speaker cannot be syntactically determined. On the narrative level, the parallel with 6.2 "My love went down to his garden" (6.2) / "I went down to the garden" (6.11) would suggest that he is the speaker.

33   "Napšî" may be subject or object of "yāda'tî", or neither. Likewise, "śāmatnî" may or may not have it as predicate (cf. Pope 1976: 585).

34   6.12 is the most notoriously obscure verse in the Song, and I follow Falk (1982: 126) and Krinetzki (1981: 188) in not seeking to translate it. A very entertaining summary of interpretations is

Notes to Chapter Four - Two Versions of Paradise

provided by Pope (1976: 584-9). The principal problem is the syntax and meaning of "markebôt ʽammi nādîb" "chariots of my princely people". Driver (1950: 136), followed by NEB and Grober (verbal communication) read "mrkbt" as "mrbbt" "myriads", which does little damage to the text but results in a somewhat pale conclusion; others divide "mrkbt" into "mrk bt", taking "mrk" either as "your myrrh" (Tur Sinai 1943: 31; Gordis 1973: 95) or "fear" (Lys 248; cf. Lev 26.36). These exegeses are strained, as Fox has shown ("Scholia to Canticles" 9-10), and testify to desperation to extract some sense from the verse. For an extremely drastic recent reworking see Rudolph (166). Another view is that "nādîb" is a substantive "prince", not an adjective "princely", qualifying "ʽammî". Levinger (77) considers that poetic license permits the construct compound "nādîb ʽammî" "prince of my people" to be inverted, and cites examples; the Beloved is accordingly the chariot on which the prince rides. Pope (1976: 589) and Fox (Canticles 10) read "ʽam" "people" as "ʽîm" "with", with or without a paragogic Yod; on this interpretation the prince is taking her out in his chariot. Gerleman (190-1) identifies "ʽammî nādîb" as a possibly fictional personal name Amminadib (cf. Tournay 1959), equivalent to Prince Mehy in the Chester-Beatty Papyrus I.i; Pope growls at this "deus ex machina". The line of reasoning of Pope and Fox opens up other attractive possibilities, e.g. that it is he who is placed among the chariots, evoking the common metaphorical association of love and war in the Song. This is a guess at its connotative field rather than a precise interpretation, however; and this, I consider, is all that can be achieved with this verse.

35   Many commentators have invented meanings such as "make haste, turn" for "beraḥ dôdî" "Flee, my beloved", so as to avoid an untoward ending. I do not know of any instances where BRḤ can be convincingly translated as other than "flee" (contra Gerleman: 223, Rudolph: 186). Levinger (98-9) and Falk (1982: 133) remark that the separation of lovers forms a fit conclusion to the Song, though Falk suggests that it is a "false closure", a daylight dismissal concealing an anticipation of nocturnal union. Pope (1976: 698) advances an interesting suggestion and an ingenious translation. "Beraḥ", he contends, may mean "berîaḥ", a "bolt" (a screw?), with a sexual innuendo. It is not clear whether in Pope's view the Beloved is suggesting intercourse while she is singing to the friends in the garden, or merely promising future, not simply auditory, pleasures. Or perhaps she is being merely dismissive, as in the idiom "Screw yourself"?

36   "A heap of wheat hedged with lilies" in 7.3; the pastoral images of 4.1-2, 6.5-6; and the Pastoral dialogue of 1.7-8 (see p. 174).

37   A philological fashion for "pack" as the meaning of "paḥad" (Dahood 1964: 69; Albright 1957: 248) seems to be passing. The etymological flaws in the argument were exposed by D. R. Hillers (1972: 92 n.18). Pope comments very sagely "Fearsome as a pack of dogs may be, it does not seem likely that this alleged meaning is appropriate or adequate to the degree of dread suggested by the context" (1976: 437).

38   Many older critics refused to credit the poet's imaginative

Notes to Chapter Four - Two Versions of Paradise

daring, and employed their text-critical craft to suggest alternative meanings, readings, or constructions, e.g. "ʾahabâ" "leather" (NEB, Driver 1937: 160ff.) or "ivory" (Gordis 1974: 84 et al.). Pope (1976: 445) suggests that the interior of the palanquin is inlaid with a "love scene", like the royal bed of Ugarit (Pope 1976: Plate II). Lys (160) sees no necessity in changing the MT; cf. Levinger (48-49) and Cook (106).

There is accordingly no reason to assign "mibbenôt yerûšālāim" "of the daughters of Jerusalem" to the next verse, with Pope (1976: 445), for the sake of the parallelism "benôt yerûšālāim ṣeʾeynâ / ûreʾeynâ benôt ṣiyyôn "Daughters of Jerusalem, go out / And look, O daughters of Zion", since "ṣeʾeynâ ûreʾeynâ" "Go out and look" is an effective rhyming couplet as it stands, and it is readily comprehensible that the daughters of Jerusalem should be a qualification of "ʾahabâ" "love". Their attachment to the Lover is evident elsewhere, e.g. 1.3-4, as we have seen.

39   I may refer the reader to the excellent evocation of Oriental cities at night in Colin Thubron's Mirror to Damascus (Heinemann, London: 1967, 185-7).

40   John Armstrong's description (35) is perhaps worth quoting:

> It is the most long-surviving and stable of living things, though vulnerable and subservient to man, wholly predictable in its changes, a calendar whereon we may read the sure progress of the seasons, constant in formal outline, a landmark. It might stand in a churchyard, for it has associations which reach towards the idea of Eternity, yet not too far away from the security of the institutional fold; and it might mark the site of one such 'dear familiar place' as that in which Yeats's laurel tree is rooted.

41   For sources and argument see Westermann (1974b: 288-91) and A. J. Williams (1973: 62, 360-1). The main criteria are that the two trees appear in separate scenes, and the inconsistency over which tree is "in the midst of the garden". I would explain both by their complementary opposition, and through the intimate structure of the narrative; the Tree of Life appears in the peripheral episodes, from an externalised descriptive or divine perspective, one in other words that is objective and controls and focusses the narrative framework; the Tree of Knowledge is central to the characters within the garden, and is seen subjectively with their eyes. Genetic speculation is in any case academic, since both Williams and Westermann insist on the essential coherence of the final form of the text.

42   It is a pity that this article, published in 1975, is not more widely known, and for this reason I shall summarise it. Its significance is even more astonishing considering its brevity.

The Tree of Knowledge, Tsevat argues, has as one of its two functions that of a Tree of Death. This appellation would stylistically complement the Tree of Life. Why then did the narrator choose the much less obvious "Tree of Knowledge"? And why has no Biblical scholar asked this before? Two reasons, he suggests: 1) "Tree of Death" is unparalleled; 2) The assignment of the two trees to separate

Notes to Chapter Four - Two Versions of Paradise

traditions. He then introduces what he claims to be a misinterpreted Ugaritic parallel (UT 607, RS 24.244) in which there figure a Tree of Death, a serpent or serpents, and several unusual lexical correspondences with the Genesis myth. Complementing the Tree of Death is the "'r'r", the "tamarisk". See Tsevat (1980) for a full interpretation, as well as the contrary views of Young and Astour. To the question why the tree was called the Tree of Knowledge and not of Death, Tsevat suggests: i) narrative probability, since not even Eve would eat of a Tree of Death; ii) narrative economy, since a Tree of Death does not imply a gift of knowledge, while, according to the myth, mortality is consequent upon knowledge.

43   On Tsevat's exegesis, the text tells of the betrothal of the serpent god Horon with the mare goddess, and the dowry of serpents he bestows upon her. Planting the Tree of Death is one of the preliminaries.

44   Soggin 1975b: 104; Vawter 1977: 74; cf. Alonso-Schökel (1962: 303). For a comprehensive criticism of the view that "knowledge of good and evil" is sexual knowledge (e.g. Gordis 1957) see Bailey 145-47.

45   Vawter (1977: 72-3) says that "by 'the knowledge of good and bad' vs.17 did not envisage something immoral but rather something highly moral indeed, what other Biblical traditions would characterize as 'wisdom'. What man is being forbidden is simply what is not in his power to obtain and therefore what is not proper for him to aspire to." Vawter goes on to explain that it is not that Wisdom of a sort is not accessible to man, but that all his wisdom, as Job and Ecclesiastes show, will not locate him in the universe and in relation to God. For this we need faith, as St. Paul tells us. There is some circular reasoning here. According to Vawter, it would seem that man did not acquire "knowledge of good and evil" when he ate of the fruit of the Tree, since it is not in his power to obtain it. One need not posit an incessant conflict between prophets and sages, with McKane (1965), to realise that the morality of wisdom is in question throughout the OT, e.g. in II Samuel. Alonso-Schökel (1962: 301) has well observed that Biblical wisdom is precisely concerned with extremes of good and evil, experienced in Ecclesiastes and Job respectively; and that the philosophical mean is ironically linked with rebellion. He speculates that the narrative emanates from Wisdom circles, but is preoccupied with the limits and compromised nature of wisdom.

46   Cassuto (1961: 111) objects that such knowledge when posited of God is incomprehensible. A naive God who knows no evil is yet more absurd. The dark side of God, whose discovery is attributed to Jung but dates back to the Kabbalah and beyond, has been the subject of intense consideration by Gunn in most of his writings (1978, 1980, 1982), and some attention by other critics, e.g. Polzin (1980) and Jobling (1980) who makes God into the actantial "villain" of the tale. Crossan (1980: 110) well defines the "knowledge of good and evil" as "differentiated knowledge" i.e. of the world as a "disjunctive totality", including morality and sex.

47   Fortunately, Man did not die on that day, posing a little puzzle

Notes to Chapter Four - Two Versions of Paradise

for commentators. Cassuto (1961: 125) thinks God was exaggerating because man was childlike. Soggin (1975b: 172-3) shows that the "chronological tolerance" of "beyôm" "on the day" is great (Fishbane's translation "whensoever" is to be commended), and in a lengthy discussion (172-5) of "môt tämût" "You shall surely die" throughout the Bible demonstrates that it does not generally entail a mandatory death penalty, beyond possibility of repentance and mitigation. James Williams (1980: 58) so interprets this verse. In my view, it is important to retain the ambiguity: the prohibition may refer generally to mortality (so Vawter 1977: 73, Jobling: 47), but the stronger interpretation contributes dramatic tension in the ensuing crisis. One might add Jobling's comment (47):

> To be transferred from the sphere of immortality to that of mortality is not much different in the semantics of myth, from dying on the spot; and the man's instant death would be both a semantic and a narrative absurdity - the narrative would stop, and "outside" would be reduced to a single seme, death!

48 Crossan (1980: 109-10) links the alternatives to the contradiction whether the Tree of Life or of Knowledge is at the centre of the garden. God gave man eternal life but not differential knowledge; hence the Tree of Life was at the centre of the garden; but man chose differential knowledge for his centre.

49 Ricoeur (233) insists:

> The aetiological myth of Adam is the most extreme attempt to separate the origin of evil from the origin of good; its intention is to set up a radical origin of evil distinct from the more primordial origin of the goodness of things.

This however is an oversimplification, since both good and evil originate in the tree. The most extreme attempt to separate good and evil is in fact Zoroastrianism.

50 For the possible cultic significance of "ʾašîšôt" see Pope (1976: 378-9). It is not necessary, however, to follow his somewhat involved explanation, and Midrashic exegesis of Isa 16.12-17, in which he correlates the "ʾašîšôt" with the "persistent pastries" offered in the form of genitalia to the Queen of Heaven.

51 For lovesickness in Ancient Egyptian poetry see Chester-Beatty Papyrus I.i stanza 7, and Papyrus Harris 500 2a.6. (Lichtheim 1976: 185, 189; cf. J. B. White: 139-140; Gerleman: 119). In the former, for example, the loved one is the only patent remedy.

52 Various attempts have been made to integrate the two halves of the verse, to construct a story, e.g. that the Beloved is heard singing as she comes within earshot (Levinger 89; cf. Gordis 1974: 73). Others opine that there is no relationship between them, that they are bewildering little fragments thrown together (e.g. Falk 1982: 130). In my view, as I have argued in my introduction, contrast is a most important structural element; we need postulate neither narrative coherence nor total independence.

53 I owe this insight to Gabriel Josipovici (cf. Frye 1957: 212; Alter: 144).

Notes to Chapter Four - Two Versions of Paradise

54 Von Rad (89) holds that "God begins by giving man complete freedom". Similarly, Trible (1978: 86, 109) interprets permission as positive freedom. Westermann (1974b, 304) is more percipient when he notes that the form of the commandment (wayyeṣaw) has echoes both of the Decalogue and of apodictic legal formulae.

55 Walsh (161) notes that the technique of prolepsis, wherewith the dissonance at the end of this scene remains in suspense until 3.1, is reflected at its beginning by the anticipation of 2.10-14 in 2.6; and further, I would say, by the unresolved topic of rain. Thus the scene is left open, and its conclusion focusses attention on the central dialogue between the serpent and the woman.

56 Hugh C. White (1980: 95) argues that if the human being were immediately to break the prohibition, which he must do since the prohibition defines his subjectivity, it would reduce the conflict into an externalised conflict of good and evil, and nothing would convincingly absolve man from the divine wrath. The story would end very quickly. By introducing a third realm, neutral with regard to the prohibition, the narrator interposes ambiguity, and ensures that there is no authentic villain (cf. in contrast, Boomershine, where the serpent is characterised as the "opponent" and associated with fertility rites). One may compare Jobling's complementary suggestion, that it is God who is the ambiguous villain.

57 Gordis (1969: 203-4; 1974: 81) suggests that "diglô" means "his gaze" from Akk. "dagalû" (cf. NEB). Pope (1976: 376-77) specifies further that "diglû" = wish, intent, namely intercourse "a tergo". Rudolph (131) wonders why a loanword should be needed for such a common notion, as "gaze". "Degel" elsewhere only occurs in a limited range of national or military contexts; see Gerleman (118). Krinetzki (1964: 115) stresses the military metaphor; in his later work (1981: 91-2) he identifies the wine house with the fascinating but dangerous womb of the Great Mother; "Love" = the Lover is the sign that draws her there. He, Gerleman, and Rudolph suggest that "degel" has a non-military sense as a sign outside a tavern, citing Arab. "ğaya". Lys (105) seeks to retain the ambiguity, translating "enseigne".

58 Continuity with 2.6 and 2.8 would suggest that the speaker is the Beloved, though there is no indication of gender, and some have put it in the mouth of the Lover (Lys: 108-110, NEB etc.); especially since elsewhere only the Beloved addresses the daughters of Jerusalem (1.5-6, 5.8, 5.16). The parallel between our verse and 5.8 would seem to confirm the identification.

59 Rudolph calls it "the moral of the tale" (131).

60 Albright (1963: 6) and Schoville (1970: 105) see it as an actual mythological fragment associated with the myth of Shahar and Shalem. For the Albright-Freedman hypothesis, see Introduction p. 19. The evidence for a connection - the common word "šamm$\bar{a}$" "there", the two-word parallelism, the birth in the desert - seems tenuous indeed.

61 Clines (1974) argues that each of the epithets for the Torah in Ps 19. 8-10 is an allusion to the fruit of the Tree of Knowledge: i) it is "mešîbat nāpeš", a restorative of the soul, food that brings life; ii) "maḥkîmat petî", food that gives true wisdom; iii) "meśammeḥê lēb",

Notes to Chapter Four - Two Versions of Paradise

delightful; iv) meʾîrat ʿēnāyîm", enlightening the eyes, just as the fruit of the Tree of Knowledge opened the eyes, and v) "ʿōmedet lāʿad", enduring for ever. He concludes by remarking that the beginning of the Psalm is a meditation on Gen 1, and suggesting that the "great sin" and various other terms of the last verses refer to the garden of Eden. Altogether it is an impressive exegesis.

62   Only Good (1965: 83-4) seems to have acknowledged this. Others attribute the apparent inconsistency to a weakness of composition (e.g. Trible 1978: 132) or the blending of sources (e.g. A. J. Williams 1973: 375) or semantic overloading (Jobling: 43).

63   Pope (1976: 662) seems a little cool towards this hypothesis, perhaps because of its association with the allegorical interpretation of Robert-Tournay. However, the culmination of the parallel passage in Solomon's epithalamium; the invocation of the daughters of Jerusalem in the immediately preceding verse, and the centrality of Jerusalem in the symbolic geography of the Song, render the identification likely, especially here, at its climax.

64   See J. Navone (153): "Paradise (garden) is the archetypal symbol at the beginning and at the end of the pilgrim's path through the wilderness: it is the beginning and end of the human enterprise."

65   Only Trible (1978: 108) recognises the pun as "linguistic perversion"; "word play has become dis-ease" in contrast to the creative puns (ʾādām/ʾadāmâ, ʾîš/ʾiššâ) of chapter 2. She does not develop the linguistic implications of this perception.

66   Generally, if it is even noticed, it is interpreted rhetorically, as linking the two narratives (e.g. Vawter 1977: 76), and establishing a connection between the human couple and the serpent. An example is Cassuto (1961: 143), who takes it as meaning that although the human couple were naked, "the serpent within them was cunning". For Trible it suggests that animal power may prevail over human power (1978: 108). It is rarely mentioned by the Structuralists in the Semeia volume (only by Boomershine [117] who describes it as "playful" and does not consider its significance), who are too preoccupied with actantial oppositions, nor by Scriabine, though one would have thought it to be crucial to her argument, concerning the opacity of language. What is conspicuously lacking is any discussion of the pun as being of conceptual significance.

67   Perry and Sternberg (1968) have used the term "ironic" to describe the frequent detached objectivity of the Biblical narrator, e.g. in the David and Bathsheba story, as if he were the chronicler of events that did not concern him. Hugh C. White (1980: 96-97) considers that the narrator's direct intervention in the text is an infringement of Biblical narrative reserve - a somewhat dubious supposition borrowed from Auerbach. For the conventions of Biblical prose exposition, see Alter: 74-80; here its primary function is as a frame for the narrative, to summarise the past in 2.25 and introduce that which will destroy it.

68   Trible (1978: 105, 106 etc.) regards 2.25 as the beginning of the temptation sequence, so as to create a chiasmus with 3.7. Walsh (178), on the other hand, argues effectively that the creation of woman and the animals (2.18-2.25) corresponds to the ordering of

Notes to Chapter Four - Two Versions of Paradise

relations between the sexes and creatures (3.14-3.21); both end with two detached sentences. On a purely syntagmatic level, v.25 completes the description of the human couple; 3.1 introduces a new narrative agent, with his own initiative. Culley (1980: 30-31) is consequently right in identifying 2.4b-25 as an action sequence contra Jobling (43).

69   Crossan (1980: 110) links the phenomenon of shame with the beginning of language and awareness of differences. However, I do not understand his:

> Most of human history will seek to cover and deny this shameful fact that: In the beginning was the signifer, and the signifier was with the signified, and the signifier was the signified. Which if not shameful, is at least embarrassing.

Hugh C. White (1980: 96) interprets "shame" as evidence of an inner conflict, that ensures that the human figures remain ambivalent, and prevents closure of the narrative. In other words, (perhaps?), that they were unashamed then, but are now, keeps our interest alive, and ensures that we remain aware of them as strange but dynamic human beings, not as character-types.

70   Good 1965: 83 n.3: "the connotation of "ērom' and "ārûm' is not sexual but situational".

71   McKane (1970: 270); cf. Alonso-Schökel (1962: 302), who notes that the ambiguity poses the question whether the serpent is also wise, and Hugh C. White (1980: 97). Patte/Parker (74) characterise the quality of "'arûm" as denoting "an excessive freedom of choice".

72   The identity and provenance of this stone are unknown.

73   "Sappîrîm" are generally identified with lapis lazuli. Gk. "sappheiros" is commonly held to refer to lapis lazuli; cf. Gardiner (31), who justifies thereby translating the Egyptian word for lapis lazuli by "sapphire". This would be perfectly acceptable in the Song.

74   A fascinating summary is to be found in Pitt-Rivers. Trible (1973: 43, 46) characteristically overstates the matter when she claims that there is no shame in the Song, no sin and disobedience, though "not all the world loves a lover" (1978: 158-59). At least in the eyes of the watchmen there is sin and disgrace.

75   Scriabine (47) sees Adam as a co-creator: he gives the creatures God has formed their essential identity, a complementary action parallel to God's breathing into his nostrils the breath of life.

76   Trible (1978: 98) observes that "lir'ôt mah yiqrā' lô" "to see what he would call it" in 2.19 parallels "to work it and keep it" in 2.15, and that in each case man is made responsible for a different order of nature.

77   Some critics postulate a link with the encyclopaedic tendencies of ancient Wisdom schools (cf. e.g. Keel 1978: 59). Alonso-Schökel (1962: 303) thinks that Adam thereby establishes himself as a sage, a scientist, in contrast to the serpent; Scriabine (57) sees him as a mage, possessed of the "petits mystères", the full potentiality of human being. This accords with the view of Patte/Parker (73), that man has the power to order his own domain, i.e. the animals, to such an extent that it constitutes a limitation on God, but not to control

Notes to Chapter Four - Two Versions of Paradise

his own nature; this is done for him by God and the cherubim.

78 Westermann (1974b: 311) puts it very well: "der Mensch den Tieren Namen gibt und sie in diesen Namen seiner Welt zuordnet"; cf. also von Rad: 81. The assumption that name-giving is an exercise of sovereignty and should primarily be interpreted in terms of power (Trible 1978: 92-3; Walsh: 174 etc.) extrapolates too much from Oriental beliefs for which the evidence is uncertain. Man's control over the animals, except as part of his responsibility for the garden, is an open question in the text. As Hugh C. White (1980: 97) shows, they are not yet defined in relation to man. "The animal world constitutes a third person realm which is the symmetrical opposite of the divine realm". Only through the conflict with man, when it finds its voice, does a second person relationship develop, in which it is subordinated to him.

79 The best formal analysis is that of Walsh (164). Stuart (101, 105) obtains syllabic uniformity through textual reconstruction; the evidence for a consistent syllabic principle in Biblical poetry remains however slight indeed, despite distinguished advocates (see Halle and McCarthy 1981 for further discussion). For Alonso-Schökel (1962: 303), the well-constructed poem is indicative of Adam's aphoristic gift, characteristic of Wisdom literature. In my view, some caution is requisite; that v.23 has a definite poetic quality does not make it a poem. This would be to abstract it too much from the speech continuum. There is a tendency to find miniscule poems buried everywhere in Biblical prose. Though I differ from Kugel (1981b) who argues that the distinction between poetry and prose is alien to the Bible, it is not absolute, except when there are clear formal markers.

80 Brueggemann (1970) points out that the terms "flesh" and "bone" are associated with "weakness" and "strength" respectively. Hence the combination affirms relatedness in all eventualities, and a strength in weakness.

81 Walsh (164) has observed that this splitting is reproduced aurally through the staccato rhythm of the two-word phrases, the sharp caesurae, the doubling of the labials, p, m, and b.

82 Alter (31) points out that through its position at the beginning, end and centre of the verse man is syntactically surrounded by this new female presence. Trible (1978: 97-102) argues tortuously and at length that neither derivation nor appellation imply subordination.

83 Surprisingly, personal pronouns appear very late in a child's linguistic development, and correspondingly disappear very early in the agrammatical form of aphasia. A child, especially in regressive moods, e.g. bedtime soliloquys (cf. Weir), will use his proper name rather than a pronoun (some Hassidic rebbes do likewise). A personal pronoun, like a spatio-temporal marker (e.g. "when" or "where") is a "shifter", that is defined only in terms of its general message. A noun e.g. a name is autonomous; a shifter shifts from subject/object to subject/object, and is purely part of the grammatical superstructure (Jakobson 1971a; 1980: 103). A child may appropriate "I" or "me" as his unique possession and be angry or bewildered if others steal it.

84 Fishbane (19) notes that as well as differentiating man from his environment, enabling him to create a world with words, and fulfil

Notes to Chapter Four - Two Versions of Paradise

his task as steward of the garden, language is also "the shaper of syntaxes" on earth, wherewith man gives it (and each thing) meaning. Crossan is profoundly amiss (1980: 110) when he sees the gift of the garden as only differentiated knowledge, for it is knowledge that sees the connections between things. He holds that man and woman are not yet sufficiently differentiated: woman is still trapped within the male "my". This is to mistake the force of the partitive "min" in "MEʻaṣāmay" and "MIbbeśārî". If D. Stuart's proposal (105) is correct, that the naming is the climax of a lost poem on the designation of the animals, then the metaphorical, synthetic process began before the creation of the woman. But the only evidence for this is that "zōʼt happaʻam" "And now this" ("zōʼt paʻam" in Stuart's rendering) requires a poem to precede it. The names that Adam gives the animals and the intervening sleep the text supplies should surely be sufficient.

85   An old tradition associates the name "ḥawwâ" "Eve" with Aram. "ḥiwia'" "serpent" and the Phoenician serpent goddess "hawat"; cf. Westermann (1974b: 365) and A. J. Williams (1978: 357-66) for references; see also Vawter 1977: 87. Williams attempts to discredit the notion using the strictest positivist criteria (1978: 368-9). He assumes that the two meanings for Eve, "the mother of all that live" and "the serpent" are mutually exclusive, and that etymological derivation from the latter must be exact. Puns, and certainly the meaning of names in the Bible, are not noted for philological accuracy, to say the least.

86   Cf. Fishbane: 22-23: "The serpent represents that part of the world and man resistant to a fixed order."

87   A. J. Williams dissents strongly from Joines' view, waging vigorous war in the footnotes; his main criticism is that the division into categories (wisdom, chaos, regeration) is arbitrary and tailored to fit the Genesis account. Nevertheless in his own analysis he seems to me to justify amply Joines' characterisation, and in particular, the serpent's essential ambiguity.

88   Westermann (1974b: 327), for instance, argues that the issue is not whether God or the serpent lied, but the ambiguity of God's words, and the intrinsic connection between sapience and mortality; similarly, the serpent's claim that God is envious is not only to be evaluated per se, but for the realm of divergent possibilities and consequences it opens to consciousness. Similarly, White interprets the myth in terms of an open mode of subjectivity, one that will determine its own limits, and that projects itself externally. Thus the identity of the human being is no longer defined; the self becomes complex and ambiguous. Shame will cover over its intolerable sense of alienation, both from its "true" self (its "je" in Lacanian terms) and from others; hence the shame attached to inescapable sexual differences. In his response to White's article, Crossan claims that shame arises not from alienation but differentiation; insofar as a distinction can be made - and I think Crossan has misunderstood White - this is too general. Clearly the myth is saying something about the human condition. At the same time, White's terminology is confused: the "objective self" that seeks to identify with others is also, he says, the repressed narcissistic desire to become godlike

Notes to Chapter Four - Two Versions of Paradise

(101, 102); the serpent speaks for the secret wish of the woman/man. The narcissistic reaching for likeness in a world of differences (in what sense is this narcissistic?) is then most truly subjective, a repressed faith (such as Freud's oceanic feeling), not the alienating, but that from which we are alienated. Alter, in his brilliant comparison of Gen 1 and the beginning of the Gen 2 narrative, has shown that the author's syntax reflects his tangled, shifting, complexly interwoven view of the world. In other words, it is to the perspective of J that the serpent introduces woman. Or as Crossan (1980: 111) says, the author is in collusion with the serpent.

89   Cf. Westermann (327) on the ambivalence arising out of the realm of possibility, that can expand consciousness and threaten it.

90   For the intimate dependence between death - or the awareness of death - and creativity, between Eros and Thanatos, see Rosemary Gordon 1978; Ehrenzweig (esp. 1967); Hannah Segal 1971; etc. Ronen (1975: 101-2), who considers that the myth of the garden reflects the actual development of consciousness, traces the connection to prehistory (e.g. Neanderthal burials).

91   The only example of which I know is the disastrous compact between the eagle and the serpent in the myth of Etana.

92   Childs (1962: 46-50) explores the tension between the naturalness of the serpent and its magical/mythical background as expressing that between two views of evil: that it originates in man and is a chaotic principle in the universe; cf. Fishbane: 22-3. Boomershine's assertion (126) that the serpent is a competitive phallic deity ignores the textual emphasis that he was a creature made by God. Soggin (1975b) and Wyatt (1981) also view the myth as a polemic against fertility cults, whether of Baal or of El.

93   Freilich: 214: "Marginal systems are always lonely, striving, searching, pursuing the new to find satisfactions missing in their lives" (Note: "The marginal system best known to me is the anthropologist").

94   Robert Alter (30) cites the Midrash that Adam saw that all animals were paired, except himself alone, and then points out that in the text "ûleʾādām" "and for man" in 2.20 is in apposition to all the other creatures, as if to emphasise his solitude, which is not entirely appeased by the creation of woman.

95   "Jealousy fears to lose what it has; envy is pained at seeing another have what it wants for itself ... The envious man sickens at the sight of enjoyment. All endeavours to satisfy the envious man are fruitless" (Klein 1957: 8).

96   Cf. A. J. Williams' (1973: 21) totally unargued comment:

> There are no grounds ... for the idea that since YHWH brought the animals to the man, to see whether man recognised the association (ʿēzer kenegdô) he wanted, the Serpent, who belonged to the animals of Gen 2.19, later felt a grudge against the humans for his rejection in favour of the woman and therefore acted out of envy in Gen 3.1. There is a limit as to how far we may attempt to interpret the text as it is not intended to be a perfectly precise document with exact terminology and no loose ends.

Notes to Chapter Four - Two Versions of Paradise

Trible (1978: 111) also traces the serpent's motives to the discrepancies in the account of the animals' creation, though she refrains from specifying them. In my view, they can be adequately reconstructed from the available "bundle of qualifications" (Patte/Parker: 62-63).

97 Jobling argues that "the woman mediates between the man and the animals" (46). He cites the theme of naming as indicative of this mediation. Jobling's argument, imperfect though it is, in which he constructs opposed semantics for "inside" and "outside" along various isotopies (culture, society and sexuality etc.) to account for the transition between and coexistence of dream and experience, immortality (timelessness) and the life-cycle, the knowledge of "inside" and the facts of "outside", is rich in insight. The importance of middle terms - such as animals, the Tree of Knowledge, woman - that introduce the external forms into the inner space, and render it unstable, is perceptively delineated. I disagree with most of his conclusions, e.g. that the myth is patriarchal mythology, and likewise with the assertion that in a consistent monotheism, God can only be a character "to a limited extent" (49) (why the equivocation?), since he is the ultimate Sender. His actantial ambiguity, as villain as well as helper, surely does not mean that he has no character, no semantically significant relationship with man. One may note, as Hugh C. White (1980: 92) shows, there is no unambiguous ("closed") figure in the plot, since the conflict is internalised. James Williams' brief strictures, in his comment on Jobling's essay (1980: 51-53) do not substantially detract from Jobling's achievement.

98 A point very well made with reference to the Genesis creation myths by Duncan.

99 This association of philosophers, from Socrates onwards, with divinity is too well known to require illustration. What is perhaps less well-observed is the degree to which this survives, transmuted, into the twentieth century. Cf. the Introductory Memoir to Merleau-Ponty's posthumous volume, The Visible and the Invisible (Northwestern U.P., Evanston, 1968), and also several recollections of Wittgenstein; both had an otherworldly presence, an oracular speech (accounts of Wittgenstein's lectures are extraordinary), a self-effacing charisma. That even the most notoriously rationalistic of philosophers is associated with divinity and the occult quest has been shown by Michael Keefer in a study of Descartes' dreams in his remarkable thesis, This Fatal Mirror: Marlowe's Doctor Faustus, the Legend and Context (unpub. D.Phil. thesis, Sussex Univ., 1980).

100 Trible (1978: 156-7) contrasts the tension between men and animals in Gen 2-3, where the ambivalence of having "no helpmeet like him" turns to villainous hatred, with its disappearance in the Song. There they become "synonyms for human joy". She notes their use as metaphors for the lovers, without discussing the linguistic implications. Likewise, she does not appreciate the complexity of relationships with animals in the Song.

101 "Bisbā'ôt" "by the does" is homonymous with "sebā'ôt" = "hosts" (as in "the Lord of Hosts") while "aylôt" suggests "'ēlîm" or "'ēlôt", "gods" or "goddesses". Gordis (1974: 26-28) suggests that there is a

Notes to Chapter Four - Two Versions of Paradise

euphemistic echo of "ʾelōhê ṣebāʾôt weʾēl šadday" "by the God of Hosts and El Shaddai"; the mimicry of this most solemn invocation is in his view colloquial, analogous to the rhyming slang of European swear words. This I think is to reduce the symbolic force of does and hinds in the poem (above p. 77ff.); European swearwords are usually meaningless. The Septuagint translates "by the powers and forces of the field"; cf. NEB "by the spirits and goddesses of the field". Krinetzki (1981: 97) cites Wittekindt (cf. Rudolph: 132 and IB) that does and gazelles are sacred to the love goddess; Pope (1976: 386) adds, with Gordis (1974: 28) their efficacy against impotence in Mesopotamian incantations. Krinetzki (1981: 97; cf. 1970: 415) remarks on the significance of youthful grace, and that the association with divinity through word play discreetly reinforces that between love and God.

102 Falk (1982: 100) finds it hard to credit that the Beloved should warn the daughters against arousing passion. NEB and Lys, who attribute the verse to the Lover, interpret "ʾahabâ" as the Beloved - for Lys (110) she is the personification of love - so that the verse is simply asking them to be quiet, lest they wake her. Gordis cites and castigates Bruston for suggesting that it is a caution against aphrodisiacs; for him, as for Falk and Levinger (35), it is a plea for privacy, until love is finished (1974: 82). As Pope remarks (1976: 387), "the root ʿw/yr never has the sense of interrupt, but always refers to excitement". Feliks (15-16) proposes an underlying analogy, throughout the Song, with the sexual rhythm of does and gazelles; like them, the daughters should await their proper season. Pope (1976: 386) refers to Meek's proposal (IB) as "provocative", that the sympathetic stimulation of the gods of vegetation in an annual erotic rite is involved. As I have tried to show throughout this study, the attitude towards love in the Song is complex, since it is perilous as well as priceless; hence the Beloved's caution is not without reason.

103 Jobling (48) notes: "The Gnostics often made the serpent the hero of the story, for it typifies the characteristically gnostic knowledge - knowledge which is its own object (Jonas)."

104 Scriabine (50). Very astutely, she notes that this is one of the effects of Eve's paraphrase of the divine decree, that language is no longer absolute.

105 In a famous Egyptian poem (Chester-Beatty Papyrus I.i.b. Lichtheim 1976: 187) likewise the sister is a refuge where the hunted gazelle, an image for the lover as in the Song, finds safety.

106 Hezekiah describes himself in his sickness as sighing plaintively like a dove (Isa 38.14); cf. also Isa 59.11, Eze 7.16, Nahum 2.8. Also perhaps Ps 56.1, where it denotes a musical mode.

107 The significance of doves in the Ancient Near East generally is as divine messengers (Keel: 1977). The familiar association with the goddess of love, such as Ishtar or Aphrodite, may reflect not the dove's supposedly "prodigious amatory propensities" (Pope 1976: 400), but its homing instinct.

108 Moreover, ravens, like doves, are mediators between natural and human worlds, both in the Flood narrative (Gen 8.17) and in the legend of Elijah (I Kings 17.6). Krinetzki (1970: 415 n.59) claims the

Notes to Chapter Four - Two Versions of Paradise

raven as an archetypal male symbol, associated with the quality of "nigredo".

109 Trible (1978: 156-7) misreads the text badly when she claims "the lions and the leopards (4.8) also dwell in this garden where all nature extols the love of male and female".

110 In the very earliest literature, in fact, foxes are favourable creatures, cunning helpers of men or more often gods, associated however with trickery, great cleverness, and the crossing of boundaries; cf. Alster 1976: 125 n.52.

111 Aesop's Fables are the most familiar example. Rabbi Johanan Ben Zakkai is said to have been an expert in fables ('aggadot) of foxes (T. B. Baba Bathra 134a). There are many examples in the Talmud and Midrash. R. Meir knew 300! (T. B. Sanhedrin 38b). R. Akiba's famous parable in extremis, on the fox and the fishes, is an example of reputedly the most clever of creatures being the most foolish (T. B. Berakhot 61b). The proverbial folly of foxes, as well as their greed for grapes, may account for their premature incursion; Lys (126) suggests that it is the damage they cause that is feared ("leurs ébats et les terriers creusés") not their appetite while Lemaire (22-23, 26) uses the inappropriate timing to substantiate his contention that "zāmîr" (2.12) means "vendange", setting the scene in early summer (late June/early July), and giving it a cultic association. However, it seems to me that the description can only refer to spring, with the flowers covering the earth, the fragrance of vine and figtree, the voice of the turtledove. By late June or July the flowers have already faded.

A delicious example of the arrogant stupidity of foxes is this Sumerian proverb" "The fox having urinated into the sea / 'All the sea is my urine,' he said" (E. I. Gordon 1959: 222-23).

112 Various speakers have been proposed: Chouraqui (52) considers the question imponderable; Lys (127) assigns the text to the Beloved's solicitous mother; Gerleman (126) and Rudolph (135) etc. to the Beloved. I concur with the latter view, because:

    i) There is a clear syntactic break between 2.15 and 2.14, to which, Zakovitch proposes (1975: 292), it is a response.
    ii) The Beloved continues speaking in 2.16-17. Gerleman sees these verses as one unit.
    iii) "Vineyard" is always a symbol for the Beloved (1.6, 8.11) speaking for herself; its defence is required.
    iv) Poetic economy dissuades us from introducing extraneous characters.

113 Gordis (1974: 83) revocalises "'eḥezû" as "'aḥazû" to render "little foxes have seized us" and to deprive her of her chastity. His reason for doing this is not made explicit. He says "The verse is patently symbolic", and most recent commentators have provided their own more or less straightforward allegorical interpretation, robbing the poem of its suggestiveness and multiplicity of meaning.

114 Zakovitch (1975) compares 2.15 with Jud 15.4-5 in a remarkable and distinctive manner. It is a detailed inversion of our text: foxes are caught and sent to ravage vineyards, in vengeance for stolen love, not in defence of love. Furthermore, the context

Notes to Chapter Four - Two Versions of Paradise

associates it with Samson's riddle: just as our text has a riddling, folkloric quality.

115 For Trible (1978: 157) too the diminutive mitigates the danger, so that the foxes can be captured by love and serve Eros.

116 Westermann 1974a: 91. "'Ap kî" has been the subject of a variety of explanations. Walsh (164), for instance, maintains that it is an exclamation ("Indeed! To think that ...") since nowhere in the OT is it interrogatory; see also Speiser (1964, 23): "The serpent is not asking a question; he is deliberately distorting a fact". Westermann (1974b: 326) commonsensically remarks that the interrogative force emerges clearly from the context; in the Song of Songs 3.3 we have an example of a question omitting the interrogative particle. Cassuto (1961: 144) sees this as the function of "kî", as in post-Biblical Hebrew.

117 Walsh (165). See also von Rad (85) and Westermann (1974b: 326). Alonso-Schökel (1962: 307) points out that the serpent suppresses the positive side of God's command. Scriabine (50) observes that the serpent is already speaking our opaque language; for example, through suggesting and making us speculate on a background from which his question came. The very fact of his curiosity in this perfectly constituted world sets him rhetorically outside it; questioning already stimulates the desire for knowledge. Part of the innocent beguilement, as Hugh C. White notices (1980: 98), is that the serpent seems uninvolved: the command does not concern him!

118 Hugh C. White (1980: 98-100) suggests, however, that she is influenced by the illocutionary force of a third-person statement (i.e. an impartial outsider seems more authoritative than a party to an issue); though the risks of a mistake are enormous.

119 A point made by Boomershine (117-118) in his rhetorical analysis; he maintains that there is a maximum tension between the moral disapprobation of the audience and their identification with the character, that leads them ultimately to recognise her sin as their own. But culpability is not the issue; for example, in the story of David and Bathsheba every detail tacitly serves to magnify David's guilt (Perry and Sternberg 1968); here each phrase ironically reveals Eve's innocence. The narrative explains rather than blames.

120 Buber (25) wryly and accurately perceives the irony of this, that the fruit of knowledge is eaten in a state of suspension of choice: "The whole incident is spun out of play and dream; it is irony, a mysterious irony of the narrator that spins it. It is apparent; the two doers know not what they do ..." Trible (1978: 113), however, asserts that "She is fully aware before she eats". The words of the text do not support the view that it is a fully thought-out logical action, rather than a sensual association, that impels her.

121 Westermann (1974b: 339-340) disagreeing with von Rad and Gunkel who, following traditional doctrine, stress the "indescribable" nature of her unthinking, childlike deed, sees it as entirely normal and human, expressing the desire not only to break boundaries, but to open horizons, and to develop consciousness. The irony that Gunkel perceives is entirely accurate (and surely Westermann would not differ from his description of her action as "folgenschwerste",

Notes to Chapter Four - Two Versions of Paradise

fateful). The narrator's moral sympathies are thus divided (contra Boomershine); cf. Crossan 1980: 111. Alonso-Schökel (1962: 308) and Scriabine (52) very finely observe that she is looking at the same tree, but with different eyes, those of the serpent.

122   The concentrated doubled plosives are not so much difficult to pronounce (Walsh 166) as impart sharpness and intensity to the action, as well as focus attention upon it.

123   She still does not appear to "hear" the serpent's seditious insinuation "And you will be like God(s)". Hugh C. White (1980: 102) suggests that the admissable thought - it is good to become wise - cloaks the inadmissable one.

124   Cassuto (1961: 143, 146). Feminist critics have made too much fuss about Cassuto; he says little more than that the serpent represents an internal object, both in man and woman. Nevertheless, in his subsequent interpretation, he betrays somewhat startling views, e.g. "possibly, for the very reason that a woman's imagination surpasses a man's, it was the woman who was enticed first" (ibid.: 147); and stereotypes of the nature of "It is the way of the world for the man easily to be swayed by the woman". Higgins (1976) adds many delicious examples from the history of interpretation.

125   Lest I be misunderstood, I do accept the traditional view that there are archetypally masculine and feminine qualities, what Jung called "animus" and "anima", that exist in all of us, that there is a sense in which some women and men can be rightly and obviously described as very feminine or masculine, whether or not these attributes are culture-bound or inherent (whether indeed the question is meaningful), without detracting from our common humanity, and without considering one or other gender superior to the other. Moreover, the Bible frequently plays on these differences and evaluates them, for example in the interplay of feminine and masculine wisdom in II Samuel.

126   Trible (1978: 110), who calls the woman "hermeneut and rabbi" - evidently of the Reform persuasion - suggests that by her expansion of God's command she is following the rabbinical practice of "putting a fence round the Torah" (Aboth 1.1), in other words hedging major prohibitions with precautions designed to prevent the possibility of infringement. Von Rad (86) sees this as a sign of anxiety and vulnerability.

127   Namely: i) Is "^{ə}elōhîm" "God" or "gods"? ii) Does "yōd^{ʕ}ê" modify "^{ə}elōhîm" or define "wiheyîtem"? The second so-called ambiguity vanishes on examination: "yōd^{ʕ}ê" is governed necessarily by both words. Otherwise, "like God(s)" is meaningless. As for the first, that there is no clear distinction is manifest from 3.22, where God identifies himself as <u>us</u>, whom man now resembles (see above pp. 236ff.).

128   De Raedt's interesting criticism of Freilich's interpretation picks up this weakness (140), but still thinks exclusively in terms of symbolism "... She symbolises something more". Moreover, quite unjustifiably, he considers the woman to be subordinated to the man, as the later creation.

129   Crossan (1980: 109) adduces that God and the serpent share a

Notes to Chapter Four - Two Versions of Paradise

common consciousness, since the serpent does not use the first person, and has no "I" with which to answer God, or speak to woman. An undivided consciousness can only address itself as I-You, not as You-You or I-I. Further evidence is that the serpent shares God's knowledge, which he communicates to woman. Boomershine (126) assimilates the serpent's seduction to that of the tree, but assumes that they are in animistic opposition to God. Wyatt (17) identifies it with the Oak of the Teacher, at Shechem, of which the narrator allegedly disapproved.

130   Alster specifically bases himself on the work of Edmund Leach (1961: ix), whose emphasis differs from that of Lévi-Strauss. Leach stresses the problem of incest and human origins, Lévi-Strauss that of the emergence of culture from nature, man from animal. Leach adopts approvingly Ricoeur's observation that Lévi-Strauss ignores the whole area of Semitic or Indo-European thought:

> Virtually all the myths which Lévi-Strauss considers are those in which some or all the characters in the story are animals endowed with human characteristics.

This distinction, however, is too rigid, for the OT is, among other things, the story of the relationship of men and animals, which is connected with the incest motif. The prohibition of bestiality, for instance, is contextually associated with the laws of incest in Lev 18 and 20. R. Duncan has examined the various strands of the relationship with the animals in the Primordial History. A far more ambitious project, combining precise observation with a great deal of special pleading, is Jean Soler's "The Dietary Prohibitions of the Hebrews" (1979); using characteristically Levi-Straussian terminology, it endeavours to prove the centrality of the dietary laws to the code of the OT, an attempt harmless in itself but in the event reductive and complicated by over-generalisation and a multitude of errors. Both Lévi-Strauss and Leach agree that myth attempts the mediation of a contradiction, of continuous and discontinuous categories. This would be as true of the OT as it is of South American mythology.

131   Judges 16.7 may be another exception: "wehāyîtî ke'aḥad hā'ādām" "And I shall be like an ordinary man". But "man" here might simply mean "like an ordinary human being".

132   Cassuto (1961: 58), for instance, argues that Adam could not have been androgynous, since in 1.27 it says "male and female he created them". Leaving aside the separation of sources, which Cassuto does not accept, 1.27 is provocatively ambiguous. "'Ōtô" "him" in 1.27b is parallel to "'ōtām" "them" in 1.27c. Adam, like God, is both singular and plural.

133   Singer (1977): "the story of Adam and Eve is the archetypal myth of the new androgynous psychology" (p.90). Androgyny seems to be in vogue among feminist critics: Heilbrun is a good example. I have found them to be disappointing, however; Singer's book, for instance, is in my view diffuse, self-indulgent, and singularly lacking in original perception.

134   This no longer represents Trible's thinking:

Notes to Chapter Four - Two Versions of Paradise

> Elsewhere I have proposed an interpretation of "hā-ʾādām" as androgynous until the differentiation of female and male in Gen. 2:21-24 ... I now consider that description incorrect because the word "androgyny" assumes sexuality, whereas the earth creature is sexually undifferentiated. To understand the earth creature as either humanity or proto-humanity is, I think, legitimate. (1978: 141 n.17)

This would suggest that man was created asexual, rather than that both sexes were potentially present within him. One cannot claim this on the basis of a lack of sexual differentiation. That both femininity and masculinity originate in the primordial man is implied by the need for the two sexes to find their identity in each other. Trible herself implies this:

> His sexual identity depends upon her even as hers depends upon him. For both of them sexuality originates in the one flesh of humanity. (1978: 99)

For the image of the androgyne in early Christianity, see Wayne Meeks (1974).

135 I owe the observation of this ambiguity to my teacher, Rabbi Dr E. J. Wiesenberg. It is a curious exegetical phenomenon that Rashi and the other major medieval Jewish commentators only take the meaning "side" into consideration, whereas modern critics unanimously choose "rib". Trible (1978, 140 n.16), however, at least indicates the alternative. The Sumerian pun between "rib" and "life" (cf. "ḥawwâ"), referred to by many commentators, though it may be of antiquarian interest, as testifying to the origins of the story (Westermann 1974b: 314; Vawter 1977: 75), is of dubious significance for the interpretation. There is some speculation, which Westermann (1974b: 313) impugns, on the mechanics of the operation; he holds, and likewise von Rad (82), that the author was no longer very interested in aetiological details. It is hard to see why. As a metaphor, the rib is highly specific and fruitful; suggesting the intimacy of man and woman, the community of the upper half of the body, and the wondrous parsimony of God, for whom so little is necessary.

136 Trible (1978: 100-102) argues that differentiation does not imply derivation, that the phrase "kî mēʾîš luqoḥâ zōʾt" "for from man this was taken" does not refer to the creative process. That God took only the raw material from the man, and both man and woman originate in him, is no objection; man still provides the rib, man was still the medium. The analogy with man's being taken from the earth provides Trible with a delicious reductio ad absurdum:

> As "ʾiššâ" is taken from "ʾîš", so "hā-ʾādām" is taken from "hā-ʾadāmâ" (cf. 2.7). Yet "hā-ʾādām" is never portrayed as subordinate to the earth. On the contrary, the creature is given power over the earth so that what is taken from becomes superior to. By strict analogy, then, the line "this shall be called ʾiššâʾ because from ʾîšʾ was taken this" would mean not the subordination of the woman to the man but rather her superiority to him. (1978: 101)

Notes to Chapter Four - Two Versions of Paradise

Wisely, however, she maintains that both sexes are equal, that posteriority does not imply superiority.

137   Commentators, medieval and modern, somewhat over-literally limit the application of the title to human life. Only Westermann perceives an implicit connection with Mother Earth or some other primordial mother, though he takes it for granted that at the time of writing this original connotation had been lost (1974b: 365). There is no basis for such an assumption. My view is in agreement with that of Duncan (192), who writes:

> Adam calls his wife Eve because she is the "mother of all those who live". As it is peculiarly animals and men who are "living beings" in The Book of Genesis I see no reason why we should not interpret this passage as describing a family consisting of men and animals, with men in something of a parental role.

Kikawada (1972) compares the name of Eve to an epithet of the creatress Mami in the Atra-ḫasis Epic. As Eve is called "the mother of all that live" so Mami is "the Mistress of all the gods", and likewise this name is given to her before the birth of the first child. Kikawada concludes that Eve is demythologised: she is a creature, not the creatress, the mother of all the living, not of all the gods. Kikawada attempts to support his view that the figure of Mami is residually present in Eve by interpreting "qānîtî ʾîš ʾet yhwh" in 4.1 as "I created a man with YHWH". But Kikawada still restricts Eve's motherhood to the human race, despite the analogy with Mami, for reasons that are not apparent.

138   Patte/Parker (74) suggest that the designation alludes to sexuality as the source of life, and the archetypal human relationship, while the succeeding verse (3.21) confines the human domain to what they term "the world of living creatures". Thus the limits and potentialities of human existence are defined. This accords with their view that the myth is first about the power and will to create, for others not for oneself, and secondly about man's relational ambiguities. However, it is unnecessary to limit the reference of "the mother of all the living" to sexuality; it excludes the primary consideration of motherhood, and the woman's relationship with the earth.

139   Trible (1973: 41; 1978: 133), far from recognising the woman as mother, woman of respect, and in a position anterior and hence superior to that of man, holds that it subordinates the woman, and is the first direct and practical consequence of the "curse" in 3.16. It is the first step outside the garden. This is because she accepts unquestioningly the scholarly consensus that naming symbolises authority. There is no evidence for this, as Otwell (18) remarks drily: "mothers name children more often than do men in the Old Testament narratives, yet scholars have not taken this as evidence that mothers exercised more authority within the family than did fathers!" Patriarchs frequently name altars, such as Beth-El; do they thereby claim proprietary rights over them? Gal-ʿEd/ Yagur-Sahadutha is a good contrary example. Duncan (192) sensibly

approaches the issue not from a hypothetical significance in the Ancient Orient, as does e.g. von Rad (81) but from a contemporary perspective. Naming, he says, is a symbol of admission into a circle; it makes the object an "other", with whom we have a relationship.

140   Higgins exhaustively investigates Adam's motives and those of chauvinistic commentators through the ages. To these she could now add Brams (26) who thinks, like Milton, that Adam took the fruit out of his love for Eve. Alonso-Schökel (1962: 307, 308) sensitively interprets 2.24 as an anticipation of Adam's choice: just as man will forsake his parents and cleave to his wife, so will Adam forsake God; on the epic scheme, which the narrative foreshadows, this corresponds to Israel's apostasy. Walsh (166) argues that suspense is created by the redundant "gam" and "ʾimmāh" in the phrase "wattittēn gam leʾîšāh ʾimmāh wayyōʾkal" "and she gave <u>also</u> to her husband <u>with her</u> and he ate" (3.6), and by the continuant /m/s and long /a/s. But the phrase is nevertheless astonishingly short; there seems to be no reflection. Trible describes him contemptuously as "passive, brutish, and inept" (1978: 113), and "orientated towards his belly"; Bailey (148) also considers the woman more accessible to the serpent because more sensitive. Higgins (646) suggests that the man may have been with her throughout the dialogue; likewise Vawter (1977: 87), who cites the by no means universal Biblical convention that only two may speak in any one conversation. This would not solve the problem, however; the man stands idly by while the wife does the talking. For Hauser (1982: 26) this is evidence for the continued intimacy and quasi-identity of the man and woman (cf. Freilich: 215); this I find more convincing than Hugh C. White's assertion (1980: 102) that the silence suggests that each has his own private reasons.

141   J. B. Soloveitchik, in his interesting essay in Jewish orthodox existentialism (1974a; see also 1974b), sees in this evidence of man's failure to respond to the challenge of being an "ʿēzer kenegdô" "A helpmeet like unto him", an attempted reversion to the unproblematic condition of what he calls "majestic man", who masters the universe. Adam attempts to turn Eve into an objective fact, like the animals:

> The divine curse addressed to Eve after she sinned has found its fulfilment in our modern society. The warm personal relationship between two individuals has been supplanted by a formal subject-object relationship which manifests itself in a quest for power and supremacy. (1974a: 55-6)

142   The only exceptions being Ibn Ezra "obedience" and Rabin (1963) "fealty/loyalty". The unanimity of scholars is consequently impressive; cf. von Rad: 84, 90; Speiser 1964: 22; Steck: 106; etc.

143   See the discussion in Miller (27-31), and some sources there noted: Cassuto (1961: passim); A. J. Williams (1973: 262ff.), with the literature he draws on; and Walsh's intricate and precise analysis (171).

144   Miller (29) remarks that "it does not produce the kind of precise correlations that one finds in the judgement speeches to the snake and the man". Cassuto (1961: 165) follows Nachmanides in

Notes to Chapter Four - Two Versions of Paradise

interpreting it as a reversal of authority: "You influenced your husband and caused him to do as you wished; henceforth you and your female descendants will be subservient to your husbands". Miller objects, rightly, that she did not actively rule over her husband in 3.6 (30). Nevertheless, the approach is not totally misconceived, since the hierarchy of authority is one of the seminal issues in the narrative, as Walsh illustrates (174-176). Patte/Parker, judging by their formidable table of pertinent transformations (60) ingeniously add a second poetic punishment: whereas the woman, on her own initiative, incorporated pleasing fruit, she will now produce painful fruit subservient to the divine order. Hauser (1982: 32) suggests a pun between "ëṣ" "tree" and "ëṣeb" "pain" (cf. Cassuto 1961: 165ff.). Trible (1978: 139) like Walsh, understands the divine decrees to be a reestablishment of his authority, broken at the crisis; but only at the cost of estrangement.

145 Clines (1978: 126 n.30), however, sees no connection of content between "tešûqâ" in 3.16 and in 4.7. Westermann (1974b: 408-409) sees it as evidence that 4.6-7 is a later theological reflection on the Cain and Abel story, borrowing the terminology but not the content of 3.16. Fishbane (25-7), on the other hand, compiles a set of correspondences linking Gen 3 and 4.3-16, including "tešûqātô/ēk", the following phrase "wehû' yimšol bāk/ we'attâ timšol bô" "And he shall dominate you / But you can dominate it", and the dramatisation of the temptation through the serpent and the supposedly serpent-like image of sin "crouching at the door" (Gen 4.7).

146 Trible (1978: 158) notes this inversion, and adds perceptively that the woman completes the process precisely by taking the Lover back to her mother's house.

147 Some of the Versions read "his return", evidently reading "tešûbātô", or perhaps simply not understanding the word, as Lys (271) suggests. The relationship with Gen 3.16 has not gone unnoticed in criticism of the Song, though mostly this is limited to observing that the "tešûqâ" has passed from the woman to the man, and that the curse has changed to blessing (Gordis 1974: 97-8; Lys: 271; Rudolph: 107 and 175; Krinetzki 1981: 203-4). Krinetzki, for example, avers that the Song experiences sexual desire as pure and natural, as should the Church, in contrast to 3.16 and 4.7, where it is either the consequence of sin or its manifestation. Trible (1978: 154, 168) considers that whereas in Gen 3.16 the man did not reciprocate, and "her desire became his dominion", here male power vanishes, and "his desire becomes her delight". I am not certain, though, that this is not to mistake the slight ambivalence in the text, which, as I argue below, does not suggest perfect reciprocity.

148 Only Lys (278) remarks that the variation is weaker than the parallels in 2.16 and 6.3. He suggests that possibly in contrast to 2.16 and 6.3, where the refrain expresses sheer faith, there is now dynamic evidence of his attraction.

149 Some commentators give ḤBL the unusual meaning of "conceive" rather than "be in travail"; cf. Falk 1982: 130; Gerleman: 215; Rudolph: 180. There is little reason adduced for this, however; the only other instance of the verb, in Ps 7.15, does not provide a

Notes to Chapter Four - Two Versions of Paradise

clear meaning. Lys (285) interprets it as "was pregnant" (285); though an apple tree seems an improbable site for an entire gestation. Pope (1976: 664) remarks that all meanings and permutations of meaning are possible. Given the overwhelming preponderance of instances in which the root ḤBL means "travail" I take this to be its primary meaning. The Beloved then identifies with the Lover in his first consciousness. Feliks (117) proposes attractively that the second "hibbelâ" means to cut the umbilical cord (= hebel). Krinetzki's interpretation of the image is rather similar to my own (1981: 216), except that he puts the verse in the mouth of the Lover, as does J. B. White (47).

150   The mythological resonance of the verse, which I would grant to Albright (1962: 6) and Schoville (105) and which I have described above (n. 60) reinforces the association with divinity; the lyric as it were posits its own myth - cf. Müller 1976: 1977. Krinetzki cites various parallels from antiquity (1981: 217).

151   Somewhere, in another context, I have seen it objected that the orgasm of birth is not in the least like sexual orgasm (though it can be acutely pleasurable). Nor is the orgasm of death. It does not prevent death from having been a familiar sexual metaphor. Initiation, as also sexual initiation, is often associated with birth.

152   So Nachmanides; Sforno; Skinner: 68; Cassuto 1961: 133. Westermann objects that this is being over-rationalistic (1974b: 313). Vawter (1977: 74) likewise dismisses it as superficial, because "tardēmâ" is a divine sleep solely for miraculous purposes. The two explanations are not exclusive. My contention is that painful birth (3.16) thematically contrasts with painless parthenogenesis. Secondly, the narrative engages our sympathetic imagination; we wonder what it feels like.

153   Scriabine (52) observes that they open their eyes to the world of appearances.

154   Clines 1978: 75. Trible (1978: 120) remarks that the woman is quite alone, betrayed by the serpent on the one hand and her husband on the other.

155   Fretheim (91) observes that God's kindness, as a gesture of forgiveness, enables man to stand before God without shame - cf. Hugh C. White (1980: 103-105), for whom clothes provide a mode of intersubjective concealment, metonymic displacements of their illicit wishes.

156   Hauser (1982: 32) interprets the echo as a melancholy confirmation that their relationship will be quite different from its prelapsarian counterpart, emphasising their alienation from each other, their need to cover up; cf. Trible 1978: 134. Walsh (170) observes the correspondence of 2.24-25 and 3.14-21. Thematically 2.24 (+ 2.23) correponds to 3.20: the man leaves his parents for the mother embodied in Eve; 3.21 closes the subject of nakedness, advanced in 2.25.

157   Patte/Parker (74) suggest that ironically striving to appropriate the divine realm reduces the human couple to the vegetable domain: they hide among the trees and clothe themselves in figleaves. In 3.21 God restores them to their proper place in the

Notes to Chapter Four - Two Versions of Paradise

animal world, to which man gave names in 2.19-20, and with whose skins he now clothes them. Over this world he has limited authority, through his power to give order, and his freedom of choice.

158   Skinner (87) suggests that this is "the first departure from the Golden Age, mediating between the garden and the world outside"; cf. A. J. Williams 1978: 372; and Jobling: 47.

159   Brueggemann (1970: 538) argues that the natural partner of man is "ʾadāmâ", not "ʾiššâ". In fact, in the text "ʾādām-ʾadāmâ" and "ʾîš-ʾiššâ" are complementary pairs, and symbolically associated with each other.

160   Westermann (1974b: 359-60) sees this word as a structural link between the two curses.

161   For a good analysis of these correlations see P. D. Miller: 29.

162   Brueggemann (1972) argues that "raising from the dust" and reducing to the dust are formulaic metaphors for enthronement and deposition respectively, and that a conception of Adam as universal monarch underlies the narrative. But this, I think, is to reverse the relationship. Every monarch is symbolically Adam, in his grandeur and frailty, and personifies the kingdom. Brueggemann concludes with a fascinating discussion of the motif of man as dust in the Old Testament.

163   Westermann (1974b: 362-63) summarises scholarly dissension whether death should be considered part of the curse or merely a limit to the time of travail and sweaty diet; whether the subordinate clause "until you return to the earth from which you were taken, for dust you are and to dust you shall return" is merely an elegant poetic conclusion (Westermann holds that it was originally independent of the narrative) or the climax of the decree. Westermann alone recognises that there is a sombre positive note here:

> Darin klingt etwas Positives an, das Zurückkehren zur Erde am Ende der mühevollen Arbeit ja auch gut sein kann, ein Sterben Walt und lebenssatt. (363)

Walsh (168 n.20) asserts that the Waw in "weʾel ʿāpār tāšûb" "and to dust you shall return" is a "waw apodoseos". In my view, the prominence of the issue of death in the narrative (2.17, 3.3-4) means that its appearance here cannot be fortuitous, though it may be ambivalent, with an element of mitigation (cf. Clines 1978). Its introduction in a poetic subordinate clause, emphasising the symmetry of life, may be evidence of this. An irony I had not perceived is that the serpent eats the dust to which man returns (Trible 1978: 132).

164   Westermann (1974a: 102-3) holds that "toil" acquires a similar ambivalence: everything worthwhile is achieved through labour.

165   Critics have been singularly puzzled by the combination; as A. J. Williams says, all attempts to explain it are unconvincing (1973: 13ff.; cf. Westermann 1974b: 270). Speiser's ingenious theory is that it reverses the Babylonian custom of writing the determinative for god followed by the particular divine name, a practice unattested in the Bible and inappropriate to an alphabet (1964: 15-16). As Westermann writes, there must be a reason for its sole use here.

Notes to Chapter Four - Two Versions of Paradise

166 Westermann (1974b: 395-97) and von Rad (100) find after much discussion that the phrase "'et YHWH" is quite incomprehensible. Kikawada (35-7), who associates Eve with the creatress Mami (cf. n.135 above), suggests that it may be elucidated by a second parallel with the Atrahasis Epic. There Mami creates only with the aid of (itti) Enki; her Biblical counterpart mothers the human race together with (?et) YHWH. It suggests very sensitively the coexistence and cocreativity of man and God. Eslinger (1979: 68) is of the opinion that the exclamation is indicative of Eve's hubris, because she gives herself precedence over God. But the word order, with the prepositional phrase following the verb, is normal. On the contrary, it touchingly suggests that Eve recognises that she alone did not give birth to Cain.

167 Cf. A. J. Williams 1973: 361ff.; Walsh, etc. For Jobling (42), a cultivator is provided for the earth, and its lack fulfilled, despite the machinations of that "villain" God. An admirable discussion is that of Trible (1978: 137-39) who from the many correspondences between the beginning and end of the story (e.g. man keeping (šmr) the garden from within, the cherubim keeping (šmr) him out) traces the ironic dissonance between the formal symmetry and the semantic disintegration.

168 The ambivalence of the earth, man's alienation from his source (Hauser 1982: 29-30), is, according to Miller (40), "humankind's problem", but it is also the condition of his existence, not to be identified with any one element from which one originates (Patte/ Parker: 72).

169 Krinetzki develops this motif somewhat homiletically in his earlier work (1964: 217). In his recent commentary he interprets in terms of the feminine archetype of the vessel (1981: 193-94).

170 Robert Alter, however, argues that Biblical narrative often works through the tension it creates between two different traditions, each one of which foregrounds a different aspect of its subject (for example the stories about David's calling), that it is a composite artistry that like Cubist painting contrives to show us two aspects of a thing at the same time, thouugh they may be rationally irreconcilable, concluding his brilliant exposition of the creation stories as follows: (140)

> The creation story might have been more "consistent" had it begun with Genesis 2.4b, but it would have lost much of its complexity as a satisfying account of a bewilderingly complex reality that involves the elusive interaction of God, man and the natural world. It is of course possible, as scholars have tended to assume, that this complexity is the purely accidental result of some editor's pious compulsion to include disparate sources, but that is at least an ungenerous assumption and, to my mind, an implausible one as well.

Cf. also the discussion of Gros-Louis (1974a) and Clines (1978).

171 Sawyer (1974: 420) advances the interesting theory that "demût" was coupled with the older word "ṣelem" which was increasingly acquiring idolatrous connotations. The coupling of terms

Notes to Chapter Four - Two Versions of Paradise

for likeness (as in Eze 1.27), with the modifying particles "k" and "b", increases the sense of unfathomability. "Demut", derived from DMH (as in the Song 2.9), suggests that man is but a similitude (cf. von Rad: 56-7, Westermann 1974b: 202-203). Sawyer discusses at length what this resemblance might be, and whether it is with "ᵃelōhîm" as angels or God, concluding that the point is not the particular nature of the resemblance, but the fact that God allows us to participate in his transcendence. The most obvious resemblance immediately presented by the text is that man rules the earth as God rules the cosmos (cf. Clines 1979: 37). "The image of God is not man's bodily frame but his boundless spiritual being" (Raine: 14).

172 According to Robert Alter (158), such modes of indirection are the typical means of Biblical narrative for suggesting fragmentary and enigmatic insight into a contradictory but meaningful reality, a horizon of perfect knowledge possessed by the divine or human writer, but only partially accessible to the reader (cf. Perry [forthcoming]).

173 The subject of "mithallēk" may be either God or the voice/sound. This ambiguity in itself contributes a slight imprecision or doubt to the verse. Cassuto (1961: 152) considers the second alternative (Ibn Ezra) improbable since "mithallēk" generally refers to people who "walk about". Equally, however, it could refer to a sound going to and fro.

174 I agree with Patrick Miller's argument that the plural refers to the divine court, with the proviso that this need not exclude self-address, a dialogue within God, as Clines supposes (cf. Miller: 10, with references to various articles by Clines). Divine beings throughout the Bible are projections of God, only partially distinct from him (cf. Sawyer: 423-4): frequently we find that the text manipulates their identity; for example, an angel frequently turns into God himself (e.g. at the Burning Bush, or in Gen 18). Similarly, God is both multiple (ᵃelōhîm) and singular, and several texts insist on this indefinability. Hence the question whether man wished to become like angels, but not like YHWH himself, which preoccupies some critics, is besides the point. As Miller says, "The narrative speaks of a close relationship between divine world and human world: (19) and "the boundary between the divine and the human is not absolute" (Clines 1979: 37). God, in his aspect of "ᵃelōhîm", is a metonym for the divine.

175 Miller (19-26) shows that God speaks in the first person plural only when the human world impinges directly on the divine world (Gen 1.26, Gen 2.22, Gen 11.9, Isa 6.8). Miller suggests that in 1.26 it emphasises the exalted nature of man; since the likeness of or rivalry between the human and divine realms is at issue all the divine beings are convoked at this crisis; he cites analogies from Ancient Near Eastern literature. The paradoxical tension between 1.26 and 3.22 is, he considers, crucial to the Primeval History (and much else). This discussion is particularly fine. The use of the plural in the climax of 1.26 does seem to me to have exceptional rhetorical force, with its breathless audience; as does the sudden anxiety and appeal to the collective in 3.22.

Notes to Chapter Four - Two Versions of Paradise

176 Cherubim (Akk. karibû), guardians of temples or palaces, are composite hence liminal creatures: half-man, half-beast, semi-divine. They would thus add a partial resolution to the themes we have discussed (see Keel 1978: Plate VIII (or visit the British Museum)). Patte/Parker (66) perceive a relationship of contrariety with the "$^{y}\bar{e}$d" in 2.6. Whereas the "$^{y}\bar{e}$d" is a water mass with no power to give order to the cosmos or life to the earth, the cherubim, with their fire, separate the human and divine realms and perpetuate the order that was established in Eden, whereby man can only exist in relation to but separate from his origins. This would further confirm the symmetrical structure of the myth. One may add that whereas in 2.5 God's gift of rain complements human toil to make grass grow, here man leaves the garden to colonise the earth, while the cherubim protect the source of living waters. The interaction will continue despite estrangement.

177 According to Walsh (173), the Tale is an inversion of the "mythological universal of the quest for the centre", the locus of "absolute reality, sacred power and immortality (Eliade)"; in it, instead of fierce monsters who guard against access, we have the kindness of God and the faithlessness of man. But the issue is somewhat more complex, for the tree(s) are the repository of absolute reality, sacred power, and immortality, which man has in part appropriated. It is for this reason that they must be preserved, as Patte/Parker argue.

Addendum: Joel Rosenberg's altogether excellent essay on Gen 2-3, "The Garden Story Forward and Backward" - with which the journal Prooftexts was auspiciously launched - came to my attention too late for serious consideration. Narrative and non-narrative elements are correlated in this essay, from the material the composer might have used to the place of the story in the whole of the Bible. It is a most stimulating and welcome account, whose divergences from my own, which are considerable - in detail, in literary approach, and in the general conception of the tale - are less significant than our surprising coincidences and our complementarity.

NOTES TO CHAPTER FIVE
Conclusion

1   Fischel (1973: 25-32) argues vigorously that the passage is a brief anti-Epicurean parody; Scholem (1955: 52-53) is convinced, however, that it is an actual record of the visionary journey, and quotes a greatly expanded and dramatic version of this passage in the Hekhalot texts, in which the unfortunate aspirant is crushed by the deceptive plates. The evidence that Fischel accumulates from Epicurean sources does not in itself contradict Scholem, since, according to him, Epicureanism is associated with visions of light and water, celestial ascent, and semi-deification of its founder. He interprets R. Akiba's apothegm as a warning against Epicurean enthusiasm. I do not see why he regards it as a parody; the insistence that the mystic must not lose himself in his vision remained a distinctive characteristic of Jewish mysticism (Scholem 1955: 122-23).

2   For example, Jews cover mirrors in a house of mourning. This is rationally explained as the discouragement of vanity, but the emotional intensity that attaches itself to it suggests unacknowledged motives. Frazer (1922/74: 253) refers to the ancient Greek belief that a man who dreams of his reflection in a mirror will shortly die (cf. the myth of Narcissus; Alice Through the Looking-Glass).

3   From the blind beggar's tale in "The Tale of the Seven Beggars". At a wedding feast, the seven nights of which provide the external narrative framework, a blind beggar comes and gives the young couple a story as a gift; at the beginning of the tale, when the bride and groom were two children lost in a forest, he had blessed them with his blindness and his longevity; now he explains the meaning of his benediction: "Now you think that I am blind, but I am not blind at all, only the whole time of the world is to me less than the blink of an eye." A long narrative follows, in which the beggar shows that he is both infinitely young and inconceivably old.

4   From Wallace Stevens' poem "A Glass of Water" in the sequence, Parts of the World. The quotation comes from Gabriel Josipovici's novel, The Air We Breathe.

5   This is both true today, now that the Temple has been destroyed, and was true also of the Second Temple, since the Ark of the Covenant was lost when the First Temple perished.

6   At the beginning of Mythologiques, Lévi-Strauss explains that he selects one myth, more or less at random, which he calls his key myth, examines it in its ethnographic context and in relation to other myths in the same society, and expands the scope of the inquiry to embrace ultimately the whole of North and South America. In the same way, I chose one verse, more or less arbitrarily, examined it in relation to its setting, sought out its correlates, and thus came to see it as participating in a pattern of relations that implicates the entire poem.

LIST OF ABBREVIATIONS

AJSL	American Journal of Semitic Languages and Literatures
AB	Anchor Bible
AOAT	Alter Orient und Altes Testament
BA	The Biblical Archaeologist
BASOR	Bulletin of the American Schools of Oriental Research
Bib et Or	Biblica et Orientalia
BDB	Brown, Driver and Briggs (Hebrew and English Lexicon)
BH	Biblia Hebraica (cf. Horst)
BKAT	Biblischer Kommentar Altes Testament
BT	The Bible Translator
CBQ	The Catholic Biblical Quarterly
CTA	Corpus des tablettes en cunéiformes alphabétiques
ETL	Ephemerides theologicae lovanienses
HTR	Harvard Theological Review
IB	The Interpreter's Bible
IDB	The Interpreter's Dictionary of the Bible
JAAR	Journal of the American Academy of Religion
JANES	Journal of the Ancient Near Eastern Society of Columbia University
JAOS	Journal of the American Oriental Society
JBL	Journal of Biblical Literature
JCS	Journal of Cuneiform Studies
JEA	Journal of Egyptian Archaeology
JNES	Journal of Near Eastern Studies
JPOS	Journal of the Palestine Oriental Society
JQR	Jewish Quarterly Review
JSOT	Journal for the Study of the Old Testament
JSOTS	Journal for the Study of the Old Testament Supplement Series
JSS	Journal of Semitic Studies
KAT	Kommentar zum Alten Testament
MAD	Materials for the Assyrian Dictionary
NEB	New English Bible
PEQ	Palestine Exploration Quarterly
RB	Revue Biblique
SBLDS	Society of Biblical Literature, Dissertation Series
SMSR	Studia e Materiali di Storia della Religioni
SR	Studies in Religion
TQ	Theologische Quartalschrift, Tübingen
UF	Ugarit Forschungen
UT	Ugaritic Textbook (see under Cyrus H. Gordon)
VT	Vetus Testamentum
ZAW	Zeitschrift für die alttestamentliche Wissenschaft
ZDMG	Zeitschrift der deutschen morgenländischen Gesellschaft

BIBLIOGRAPHY

NOTE ON THE BIBLIOGRAPHY

This bibliography is not exhaustive, nor is it selective. I have not read everything that has been published, even recently, on the Song of Songs. Such would be an impossible labour; more important, the world is divided into readers and writers, hunters and gatherers. If I had spent my time collecting material, this book would never have been written. On this adventure, as will be apparent, I have had a few constant companions - Pope, Falk, Gordis, Lys, Krinetzki, Rudolph, Gerleman and Levinger - from whom I have learnt immeasurably, and for whom I have come to feel great affection. Living with a book over years is very different from reading it once. Other major recent commentaries (e.g. Robert-Tournay, Würthwein) have only been occasional visitors to these pages, for reasons that are contingent or temperamental. I have included in the bibliography all the works mentioned in the course of the book, save those I have not read, plus some that have been influential in its composition, or cited in previous articles. A special debt is owed to Michael Fox, Michael Goulder, Bernard Harrison and Menahem Perry for providing me with copies of unpublished work.

BIBLIOGRAPHY

Albright, W. F.
  1939 "The Babylonian Matter in the Primeval History (JE) in Gen 1-11" JBL 58: 91-103 [reply to S. Mowinckel: 87-91]
  1957 From the Stone Age to Christianity (Johns Hopkins U.P: Baltimore) (2nd edn.)
  1963 "Archaic Survivals in the Text of Canticles" in: Hebrew and Semitic Studies Presented to Godfrey Rolles Driver on the Occasion of his 70th Birthday, ed. D. Winton-Thomas and W. D. McHardy: 1-7
  1968 YHWH and the Gods of Canaan (Athlone: London)

Alonso-Schökel, Luis
  1962 "Motives sapienciales y de alianza en Gen 2-3" Biblica 43: 295-315
  1976 "Sapiential and Covenant Themes in Genesis 2-3" in: Studies in Ancient Israelite Wisdom (ed. James L. Crenshaw; Ktav: New York): 468-480 [tr. from 1962 article].

Alonso-Schökel, Luis & Zurro, Eduardo
  1977 La Tradducion biblica: lingüistica y estilistica (Ediciones Cristiandad: Madrid)

Alster, Bendt
  1972 Dumuzi's Dream: Aspects of Oral Poetry in a Sumerian Myth (Akademisk Forlag: Copenhagen)
  1975 Studies in Sumerian Proverbs (Copenhagen Studies in Assyriology 3; Akademisk Forlag: Copenhagen)
  1976 "On the Earliest Sumerian Literary Tradition" JCS 28: 109-126
  1978 "Enki and Ninḫursag: The Creation of the First Woman" UF 10: 15-27

Alter, Robert
  1981 The Art of Biblical Narrative (Basic Books: New York)

Anderson, Bernhard W.
  1978 "From Analysis to Synthesis: The Interpretation of Genesis 1-11" JBL 97: 23-39

Angenieux, Joseph
  1965 "Structure du Cantique des Cantiques" ETL 41: 96-142
  1966 "Les trois portraits du Cantiques des Cantiques" ETL 42: 87-140
  1968 "Le Cantique des Cantiques en huit chants à refrains alternants" ETL 44: 87-140

Armstrong, John
  1969 The Myth of Paradise (OUP: Oxford & London)

Astour, Michael
  1968 "Two Ugaritic Serpent Charms" JNES 27: 13-36

Audet, J. P.
  1955 "Le sens du Cantique des Cantiques" RB 62: 197-221

Auffret, Pierre
  1977 The Literary Structure of Psalm 2 (JSOTS 3; JSOT Press: Sheffield)

Bibliography

Avishur, Yitshaq
    1980   "Essai sur la structure littéraire du Psaume 137" ZAW 92: 346-377

Avishur, Yitshaq
    1973   "Lazziqa hassignonit ben shir hashirim wesifrut ugarit" Beth Miqra 19/4: 508-525

Avi-Yonah, Michael & Baras, Zvi
    1977   The World History of the Jewish People Vol.8: Society and Religion in the Second Temple Period

Bachelard, Gaston
    1964   The Psychoanalysis of Fire (tr. Alan Ross; Beacon: Boston).

Bailey, John A.
    1970   "Initiation and the Primal Woman in Gilgamesh and Gen 2-3" JBL 89: 137-150

Barker, Margaret
    1980   "Some Reflections on the Enoch Myth" JSOT 15: 7-29

Barth, Karl
    1958   Church Dogmatics Vol.III.1. The Doctrine of Creation (tr. Edwards, Bussey, Knight; ed. G. W. Bromiley & T. F. Torrance; Clark: Edinburgh)
    1960   Church Dogmatics Vol.III.2. The Doctrine of Creation (tr. Knight, Bromiley, Reid, Fuller; ed. G. W. Bromiley & T. F. Torrance; Clark: Edinburgh).

Barthes, Roland
    1971a   "Style and Its Image" in: Literary Style: A Symposium (ed. Seymour Chatman; OUP: London): 3-15
    1971b   "La Lutte avec l'ange" in: Analyse Structural et Exegese Biblique (ed. F. Bovon; Delachaux & Niestle: Neuchatel): 27-40
    1975   S/Z (tr. Richard Miller; Cape: London)
    1978   A Lover's Discourse: Fragments (Hill & Wang: New York)

Bartino, S.
    1972   "Los cuatros vientos del Cantar y los cuatro rios del Paraiso (Ct. 4.16)" Estudios Biblicos 35: 337-342

Berg, William
    1974   Early Virgil (Athlone: London)

Berry, Francis
    1962   Poetry and the Physical Voice (RKP: London)

Blanchot, Maurice
    1959   "La Question Littéraire" in: Le Livre à Venir (Gallimard: Paris): 99-107

Bloom, Harold
    1976   Poetry and Repression: Revisionism from Blake to Stevens (Yale U.P.: New Haven & London)

Boden, Margaret A.
    1970   Piaget (Fontana: London)

Boman, Thorleif
    1960   Hebrew Thought Compared to Greek (tr. Jules L. Moreau; SCM: London)

Boomershine, Thomas
    1980   "The Structure of Narrative Rhetoric in Genesis 2-3" Semeia 18: 113-129

Bibliography

Boyce, Mary
   1979 Zoroastrians: Their Religious Beliefs and Practices (RKP: London)

Brams, Steven J.
   1980 Biblical Games: A Strategic Analysis of Stories in the Old Testament (MIT: Cambridge, Mass. & London)

Bravmann, M. M.
   1975 "The Original Meaning of 'A Man Leaves His Father and Mother' (Gen 2.24)" Le Muséon (Louvain): 449-553

Broadribb, Donald
   1961-2 "Thoughts on the Song of Solomon" Abr-Nahrain 3: 11-36

Brown, Francis, & Driver, S. R., & Briggs, C. A.
   1907/1974 A Hebrew and English Lexicon of the Old Testament (Clarendon: Oxford)

Brown, John Pairman
   1969 "The Mediterranean Vocabulary of the Vine" VT 19: 146-170
   1981 "Proverb-Book, Gold Economy, Alphabet" JBL 100: 169-191

Brown, Norman O.
   1972 Life Against Death (Wesleyan U.P.: Middletown, Conn.).

Brown, Roger
   1958 Words and Things (Free Press: New York)

Brown, Stephen Glendon
   1980 The Serpent Charms of Ugarit (University Microfilms: Ann Arbor).

Brueggemann, Walter
   1970 "Of the Same Flesh and Bone (Gen 2.23)" CBQ 32: 532-540
   1972 "From Dust to Kingship" ZAW 84: 1-18
   1980 "Psalms and the Life of Faith: A suggested Typology of Function" JSOT 17: 3-32

Bryce, Glendon E.
   1980 "A Response to Patte and Parker" Semeia 18: 77-81

Buber, Martin
   1969 "The Tree of Knowledge" in: Biblical Humanism: Eighteen Studies by Martin Buber (ed. Nahum N. Glatzer; Macdonald: London): 14-21

Buchanan, George
   1956 "The Old Testament Meaning of Good and Evil" JBL 75: 114-120

Bullough, Edward
   1957 "Psychic Distance as a Factor in Art and an Aesthetic Principle" in: Aesthetics: Lectures and Essays (Bowes & Bowes: London)

Burrows, Millar
   1958 More Light on the Dead Sea Scrolls (Secker & Warburg: London)

Buss, Martin J.
   1979 "Understanding Communication" in: Encounter with the Text: Form and History in the Hebrew Bible (ed. Martin J. Buss (Fortress: Philadelphia; Scholars: Missoula): 3-44

Caquot, André, & Sznycer, Maurice, & Herdner, Andrée
   1968 Corpus des Textes Ougaritiques (du Cerf: Paris)

Bibliography

Cassuto, Umberto.
   1961   A Commentary on the Book of Genesis. Part I: From Adam to Noah (tr. Israel Abrahams; Magnes: Jerusalem)
   1967   A Commentary on the Book of Exodus (tr. Israel Abrahams; Magnes: Jerusalem)

Charlesworth, James H.
   1977   "Jewish Astrology in the Talmud, Pseudepigrapha, the Dead Sea Scrolls, and Early Palestinian Synagogues" HTR 70: 183-200

Childs, Brevard S.
   1962   Myth and Reality in the Old Testament (SCM: London)
   1974   Exodus: A Commentary (SCM: London)
   1979   Introduction to the Old Testament as Scripture (Fortress: Philadelphia)

Chouraqui, André
   1970   Le Cantique des Cantiques suivi des Psaumes (Presses Universitaires de France). Prefaces by André Neher, Rene Voillaume & Jacques Ellul

Civil, M.
   1964   "'The Message of Lu-dingir-ra to His Mother' and a Group of Akkado-Hittite Proverbs" JNES 23: 1-11

Clark, W. M.
   1969   " A Legal Background to the Yahwist's Use of 'Good and Evil' in Gen 2-3" JBL 88: 266-78

Claudel, Paul
   1963   Le Cantique des Cantiques (Oeuvres Completes Vol.22; Gallimard: Paris)

Clines, David J. A.
   1974   "The Tree of Knowledge and the Law" VT 24: 8-14
   1976   "Theme in Genesis 1-11" CBQ 38: 483-507
   1978   The Theme of the Pentateuch (JSOTS 10; JSOT Press: Sheffield)
   1979   "The Significance of the 'Sons of God' Episode (Genesis 6:1-4) in the Context of the 'Primeval History' (Genesis 1-11)" JSOT 13: 33-46

Coats, George
   1975   "God and Death: Power and Obedience in the Primeval History" Interpretation 29: 227-239

Cook, Albert S.
   1969   The Root of the Thing: A Study of Job and the Song of Songs (Indiana U.P.: Bloomington)

Cooper, Jerrold S.
   1971   "New Cuneiform Parallels to the Song of Songs" JBL 90: 157-162

Crim, Keith R.
   1971   "'Your neck is like the Tower of David' (The Meaning of a Simile in the Song of Solomon 4.4)" BT 22: 70-74

Cross, Frank Moore
   1973   Canaanite Myth and Hebrew Epic: Essays in the History of the Religion of Israel (Harvard U.P.)

Bibliography

Crossan, John Dominic
- 1975 The Dark Interval: Towards a Theology of Story (Argus: Niles, Illinois)
- 1980 "Response to White: Felix Culpa and Foenix Culprit" Semeia 18: 107-111

Culler, Jonathan
- 1971 "Jakobson and the Linguistic Analysis of Literary Texts" Language and Style 5: 53-66

Culley, Robert C.
- 1976 Studies in the Structure of Hebrew Narrative (Fortress: Philadelphia; Scholars: Missoula)
- 1980 "Action Sequences in Genesis 2-3: Semeia 18: 25-33

Dahlberg, Bruce
- 1977 "On recognising the unity of Genesis" Theology Digest 24: 360-367

Dahood, Mitchell
- 1963-74 "Hebrew-Ugaritic Lexicography I-XII Biblica 44 (1963): 289-303; 45 (1964): 399-412; 46 (1965): 311-332; 47 (1966): 403-419; 48 (1967): 421-438; 49 (1968): 355-369; 50 (1969): 337-356; 51 (1970): 391-404; 52 (1971): 337-356; 53 (1972): 386-403; 54 (1973): 351-366; 54 (1974): 381-393
- 1964 Ugaritic-Hebrew Philology (Bib et Or 17; Pontifical Institute: Rome)
- 1965 Psalms I 1-50 (AB; Doubleday: New York)
- 1968 Psalms II 51-100 (AB; Doubleday: New York)
- 1970 Psalms III 101-150 (AB; Doubleday: New York)
- 1976 "Canticle 7, 9 and UT 52, 61: A Question of Method" Biblica 57: 109-110

Daube, David
- 1968 Civil Disobedience in Antiquity (Edinburgh U.P.)

Derchain, Philippe
- 1975 "Le lotus, la mandragore, et le perséa" Chronique d'Egypte 50: 65-86

Derrida, Jacques
- 1974 "White Mythology: Metaphor in the Text of Philosophy" New Literary History 6/1: 5-74 [tr. F. C. T. Moore]
- 1978 Writing and Difference (tr. Alan Bass; RKP: London)

Detweiler, Robert E.
- 1980 " A Structural Reading of the Structural Exegeses of Culley, Jobling, and Patte/Parker" Semeia 18: 83-91

Dhorme, Eduard
- 1967 A Commentary on the Book of Job (tr. Harold Knight; Nelson: London) [first pub. 1926]

Dickie, George
- 1969 "The Myth of the Aesthetic Attitude" in: Introductory Readings in Aesthetics (ed. John Hospers; Free Press: New York; Macmillan: London): 28-45 [first pub. 1964]

Dijkstra, M.
- 1979 'Some Reflections on the Legend of Aqhat" UF 11: 199-210

Dijkstra, M. & de Moor, J. C.
- 1975 "Problematic Passages in the Legend of Aqhatû" UF 7: 171-216

Douglas, Mary
    1970   Natural Symbols: Explorations in Cosmology (Barrie & Jenkins: London)

Dressler, H. P.
    1979   "The Metamorphosis of a Lacuna: Is AT. AH. WAN ... A Proposal of Marriage" UF 11: 211-18

Driver, G. R.
    1933   "Studies in the Vocabulary of the Old Testament VI" JThS 34: 375-385
    1934   "Studies in the Vocabulary of the Old Testament VII" JThS 35: 380-393
    1936   "On Supposed Aramaisms in the Old Testament" JBL 55: 101-120
    1938   "Minor Prophets: Linguistic and Textual Problems I" JThS 39: 154-166
    1950   "Hebrew Notes on Song of Songs and 'Lamentations'" in: Festschrift für Alfred Bertholet zum 80 Geburtstage gewidmet von Kollegen und Freunden (ed. Walter Baumgartner et al.; Tübingen 1950): 134-156
    1974   "Lice in the Old Testament" PEQ 106: 159-160

Duncan, Roger
    1976   "Adam and the Ark" Encounter: Creative Christian Theological Scholarship 37: 189-197

Dunn, Peter N.
    1970   "De las figuras del Arcipreste" in: Libro de Buen Amore Studies, ed. G. B. Gibbon-Monypenny: 81-82

Dyke, Andrea
    1981   "Snakes in Dreams: Harvest 27: 45-60

Edwards, Michael
    1981   "Sublunary Language" Prospice 11: 66-96

Ehrenzweig, Anton
    1965   The Psychoanalysis of Artistic Vision and Hearing (Sheldon: London) (rev. edn.)
    1967   The Hidden Order of Art (Weidenfeld & Nicholson: London)

Eissfeldt, Otto
    1965   The Old Testament: An Introduction (tr. P. R. Ackroyd; Blackwell: Oxford)

Empson, William
    1965   Some Versions of Pastoral (Penguin: Harmondsworth)

Eslinger, Lyle
    1979   "A Contextual Identification of the bene ha'elohim and benoth ha'adam in Genesis 6:1-4" JSOT 13: 65-73

Exum, J. Cheryl
    1973   "A Literary and Structural Analysis of the Song of Songs" ZAW 85: 47-79

Falk, Marcia
    1976   The Song of Songs: A Verse Translation with Exposition (Ph.D. dissertation, Stanford Univ.)
    1982   Love Lyrics from the Bible: A Translation and Literary Study of the Song of Songs (Bible & Literature 4; Almond: Sheffield) [rev. version of 1976 Stanford diss.]

Bibliography

Feliks, Yehuda
  1980 Shir Hashirim - teba', 'alila we'alegoria (The Song of Songs: Nature, Epic and Allegory) (Keter: Jerusalem) (2nd rev. edn.)

Festinger, B. S.
  1981 "A Decade of German Psalm Criticism" JSOT 20: 91-103

Fischel, Henry A.
  1973 Rabbinic Literature and Greco-Roman Philosophy: A Study of Epicurea and Rhetorica in Early Midrashic Writings (Brill: Leiden)

Fishbane, Michael
  1979 Text and Texture: Close Readings of Selected Biblical Texts (Schocken: New York)

Fohrer, Georg
  1970 Introduction to the Old Testament (tr. David Green; SPCK: London)

Fokkelman, J. P.
  1975 Narrative Art in Genesis: Specimens in Stylistic and Structural Analysis (Van Gorcum: Assen)
  1981 Narrative Art and Poetry in the Books of Samuel. Volume I: King David (II Sam. 9-20 & I Kings 1-2) (Studia Semitica Neerlandica 20; Van Gorcum: Assen)

Fónagy, Ivan
  1971 "The Functions of Vocal Style" in: Literary Style: A Symposium (ed. Seymour Chatman; OUP: London): 159-176

Fordham, Michael
  1969 Children as Individuals: An Analytical Psychologist's Study of Child Development (Hodder & Stoughton: London)

Foster, Benjamin
  1974 "Humour and Cuneiform Literature" JANES 6: 69-85

Foster, John L.
  1971 "On Translating Hieroglyphic Love Songs" Chicago Review 23/2: 70-94
  1975 Love Songs of the New Kingdom (Scribner's: New York)

Fowler, Roger
  1975 "Language and the Reader" in: Style and Structure in Literature: Essays in the New Stylistics (ed. Roger Fowler; Blackwell: Oxford): 79-122

Fox, Michael
  1980 "The Cairo Love Songs" JAOS 100: 101-109
  1981 "'Love' in the Love Songs" JEA 67: 181-182
  ---- "'Love, Passion and Perception in Israelite and Egyptian Love Poetry" (forthcoming in JBL)
  ---- "Scholia to Canticles" (forthcoming in VT)

Frazer, James G.
  1974 The Golden Bough: A Study in Magic and Religion (abridged edn.) [first pub. in 1922]

Freedman, David Noel
  1980 Pottery, Poetry, and Prophecy: Studies in Early Hebrew Poetry (Eisenbrauns: Winona Lake, Indiana)

Freehof, Solomon B.
  1948-9 "The Song of Songs: A General Suggestion" JQR 39: 397-402

Freilich, Morris
 1975 "Myth, Method and Madness" Current Anthropology 16: 207-226
Fretheim, Terence E.
 1969 Creation, Fall and Flood (Augsburg: Minneapolis)
Freud, Sigmund
 1905 Jokes and Their Relation to the Unconscious (tr. James Strachey; Penguin Freud Library 6: 1976)
 1908 "Character and Anal Eroticism" Collected Works (stand. edn.) Vol.9: 167-177
 1917 "On Transformations of Instinct as Exemplified in Anal Eroticism" Collected Works Vol.17: 125-134
 1933 New Introductory Lectures on Psychoanalysis (Penguin Freud Library 2, 1979)
Friedrich, Paul
 1975 The Meaning of Aphrodite (Chicago U.P.)
Frye, Northrop
 1957 Anatomy of Criticism: Four Essays (Princeton U.P.) [3rd (paperback) edn. 1973]
 1970 The Stubborn Structure (Methuen: London)
 1976 The Secular Scripture (Harvard U.P.)
 1982 The Great Code: The Bible and Literature (Harcourt, Brace, Jovanovitch: New York)
Fuerst, Wesley J.
 1975 The Books of Ruth, Esther, Ecclesiastes, The Song of Songs, Lamentations (Cambridge Bible Commentary; Cambridge U.P.)
Gardiner, Alan H.
 1931 The Library of A. Chester-Beatty: Descriptions of a Hieratic Papyrus with a mythological story, Love Songs, and Other Miscellaneous Texts (The Chester-Beatty Papyri No. 1) (OUP: London)
Gaster, T. H.
 1952 "What the Song of Songs Means" Commentary 13: 316-322
 1975 Myth, Legend and Custom in the Old Testament. Vol.2 (Harper & Row: New York & London)
Gerleman, Gillis
 1965 Ruth. Das Hohelied. (BKAT 18; Neukirchener Verlag: Neukirchen-Vluyn)
Gevirtz, Stanley
 1976 Patterns in the Early Poetry of Israel (Chicago U.P.)
Ginsberg, H. L.
 1969 The Five Megilloth and Jonah: A New Translation (Jewish Publication Society of America: Philadelphia). Drawings by Ismar David
Ginsburg, Christian David
 1970 The Song of Songs (ed. S. H. Blank; Ktav: New York) [first pub. 1857]
Giordano-Orsini, Gian N.
 1975 Organic Unity in Ancient and Later Poetics: The Philosophic Foundations of Literary Criticism (Southern Illinois U.P.:

Carbonsdale & Edwardsville; Feffer & Simons: London & Amsterdam).
Goitein, Shlomo Dov
  1957 'Iyyunim Bammiqra' (Yavneh: Tel Aviv)
  1965 "'AYUMMA KANNIDGALOT (Song of Songs VI.10)" JSS 10: 220-221
Gollwitzer, Helmut
  1979 Song of Love - A Biblical Understanding of Sex (tr. Keith Crim; Fortress: Philadelphia)
Good, Edwin M.
  1965 Irony in the Old Testament (Westminster: Philadelphia; SPCK: London. Repr. Almond: Sheffield 1981 [Bible & Literature 3])
  1970 "Ezekiel's Ship: Some Extended Metaphors in the Old Testament" Semitics 1: 79-103
Goodenough, E. R.
  1953-68 Jewish Symbols in the Greco-Roman Period (Bollingen Series XXXVII; Pantheon: New York). Especially Vol.8: Pagan Symbols in Judaism (1958)
Gordis, Robert
  1957 "The Knowledge of Good and Evil in the Old Testament and the Dead Sea Scrolls" JBL 76: 123-138
  1969 "The Root DGL in the Song of Songs" JBL 88: 203-204
  1971 Poets, Prophets and Sages (Indiana U.P.)
  1974 The Song of Songs and Lamenations. A Study, Modern Translation, and Commentary (Ktav: New York) (rev. edn.)
Gordon, Cyrus H.
  1965 Ugaritic Textbook (Pontifical Institute: Rome)
  1978 "New Directions" American Bulletin of Papyrologists 15: 59-86
Gordon, E. I.
  1959 Sumerian Proverbs (Pennsylvania U.P.)
Gordon, Rosemary
  1978 Dying and Creating: A Search for Meaning (Society for Analytical Psychology: London)
Gottwald, Norman K.
  1978 "Sociological Method in the Study of Ancient Israel" in: Encounter with the Text (ed. Martin J. Buss; Fortress: Philadelphia; Scholars: Missoula): 69-82
  1980 The Tribes of YHWH: A Sociology of the Religion of Liberated Israel 1250-1050 B.C.E. (SCM: London)
Goulder, Michael D.
  1978 The Evangelists' Calendar: A Lectionary Explanation of the Development of Scripture (SPCK: London)
  1981 "Sequence and Precision in the Song of Songs" (unpublished)
Graves, Robert
  1973 The Song of Songs. Text and Commentary (Collins: London)
Greenfield, Jonas C.
  1964 "Ugaritic MDL and its Cognates" Biblica 45: 527-534
Grelot, Pierre
  1965 "Le Sens du Cantique des Cantiques" RB 71: 42-56
Griaule, Marcel
  1965 Conversations with Ogotommeli: An Introduction to Dogon Religious Ideas (OUP: London)

Bibliography

Grober, Sonia F.
   1980 Stylistic Features in the Song of Songs: A Sample Investigation to Show the Structural Coherence of the Poem (unpub. M.A. thesis: Witwatersrand Univ., Johannesburg)

Gros Louis, Kenneth R. R.
   1974a "Genesis 1-2" in: Literary Interpretations of Biblical Narratives (ed. Kenneth R. R. Gros-Louis, with James Ackerman & Thayer S. Warshaw; Abingdon: Nashville & New York): 41-51
   1974b "The Garden of Eden" in: Literary Interpretations of Biblical Narratives [see above]: 52-58

Guiraud, Pierre
   1971 "Immanence and Transitivity of Stylistic Criteria" in: Literary Style: A Symposium (ed. Syemour Chatman; OUP: London)

Gunn, David M.
   1978 The Story of King David: Genre and Interpretation (JSOTS 6; JSOT Press: Sheffield)
   1980 The Fate of King Saul: An Interpretation of a Biblical Story (JSOTS 14; JSOT Press: Sheffield)
   1982 "The Hardening of Pharaoh's Heart: Plot, Character, And Theology in Exodus 1-14" in: Art and Meaning: Rhetoric in Biblical Literature (ed. David J. A. Clines, David M. Gunn, and Alan J. Hauser; JSOTS 19; JSOT Press: Sheffield): 72-96

Halle, Morris & John J. McCarthy
   1981 "The Metrical Structure of Psalm 137" JBL 100: 161-167

Haran, Menahem
   1978 Temples and Temple Service in Ancient Israel. An Inquiry into the Character of Cult Phenomena and the Historical Setting of the Priestly School (Clarendon: Oxford)

Harrison, Bernard
   1980 "Metaphor and Interpretation" (unpublished)
   1981 "Parable and Transcendence" in: Ways of Reading the Bible (ed. Michael Wadsworth; Harvester: Brighton): 190-212

Hauser, Alan Jon
   1980 "Judges 5: Parataxis in Hebrew Poetry" JBL 99: 23-41
   1982 "Intimacy and Alienation in Genesis 2-3" in: Art and Meaning: Rhetoric in Biblical Literature (ed. David J. A. Clines, David M. Gunn, and Alan J. Hauser; JSOTS 19; JSOT Press: Sheffield): 20-36

Heilbrun, Carolyn G.
   1973 Towards Androgyny: Aspects of Male and Female in Literature (Gollancz: London)

Hengel, Martin
   1974 Judaism and Hellenism: Studies of the Encounter in Palestine in the Early Hellenistic Period (SCM: London)
   1980 Jews, Greeks and Barbarians: Aspects of the Hellenisation of Judaism in the pre-Christian Period (SCM: London)

Herion, Gary A.
   1981 "The Role of Historical Narrative in Biblical Thought: The Tendencies Underlying Old Testament Historiography" JSOT 21: 25-57

Bibliography

Hermann, Alfred
    1959   Altesägyptische Liebeslieder (Harrassowitz: Wiesbaden)
Higgins, J. M.
    1976   "The Myth of Eve - The Temptress" JAAR 44: 639-647
Hillers, D. R.
    1972   "Paḥad Yiṣḥaq" JBL 91: 91-92
    1973   "The Bow of Aqhat: The Meaning of a Mythological Theme" in: Orient and Occident. Essays Presented to Cyrus H. Gordon on the Occasion of His 65th Birthday (ed. Harry A. Hoffner Jr.; AOAT 22; Butzon & Kevelaer: Neukirchen-Vluyn): 71-80
    1978   "Běrit 'Am: Emancipation of a People" JBL 97: 175-182
Honeyman, A. M.
    1949   "Two Contributions to Canaanite Toponymy" JThS 50: 50-52
Horst, Fr.
    1966   Canticum Canticorum & Ecclesiastes in: Biblia Hebraica fasc. 13 (ed. R. Kittel etc.; Württembergische Bibelanstalt: Stuttgart)
    1967   "Die Formen des altehebraischen Liebesliedes" in: Gottes Rechte (ed. Hans W. Wolff; Kaiser: Munich) [first pub. in 1935]
Hrushovski, Benjamin
    1968   "Ha'im yeš lešělil mašma'ut: Do Sounds Have Meaning? The Problem of Expressiveness of Sound-Patterns in Poetry" Hasifrut 1: 410-420
Hutchinson, Arno
    1980   "Response to Paper by Robert Culley" Semeia 18: 35-39
Isserlin, B. S. J.
    1958   "Song of Songs IV, 4: An Archaeological Note" PEQ 90: 59-60
Iversen, E.
    1970   "The Chester-Beatty Papyrus no.1, Recto XVI, 9-XVII, 13" JEA 65: 78-88
Jabès, Edmond
    1963   Le Livre des Questions (Gallimard: Paris). [Tr. Rosemary Waldrop; Wesleyan U.P.: Middletown, Conn. 1977]
Jacobsen, Thorkild
    1976   The Treasures of Darkness: A History of Mesopotamian Religion (Yale U.P.: New Haven & London)
    1981   "The Eridu Genesis" JBL 100: 513-529
Jakobson, Roman
    1960   "Poetics and Linguistics: A Concluding Statement" in: Style and Language (ed. Thomas Sebeok; MIT: Cambridge, Mass.): 350-378
    1968   Child Language, Aphasia, and Phonological Universals (Mouton: The Hague)
    1971a   Studies on Child Language and Aphasia (Mouton: The Hague)
    1971b   "Shifters, Verbal Categories, and the Russian Verb" in: Selected Writings. Vol.2: Word and Language (Mouton: The Hague)
    1980   The Framework of Language (Michigan Studies in the Humanities; Michigan U.P.: Ann Arbor)
Jakobson, Roman & Jones, Lawrence
    1970   Shakespeare's Verbal Art in: "Th'Expense of Spirit'" (Sonnet 129) (Mouton: The Hague)

Jakobson, Roman & Lévi-Strauss, Claude
   1970 "Charles Baudelaire's 'Les Chats'" in: Structuralism: A Reader, ed. Michael Lane: 202-226

Jakobson, Roman & Halle, Morris
   1975 Fundamentals of Language (Janua Linguarum; Mouton: The Hague)(2nd edn.)

Jakobson, Roman & Waugh, Linda R.
   1979 The Sound Shape of Language (Harvester: Brighton)

James, E. O.
   1967 "The Tree of Life" in: Essays in Honour of Griffiths Wheeler Thatcher 1863-1953 (ed. by E. C. MacLaurin; Sydney U.P.): 103-118

Jastrow, Marcus
   1971 A Dictionary of the Targumim, the Talmud Babli and Yerushalmi, and the Midrashic Literature (Judaica Press: New York) [first pub. 1903]

Jastrow, Morris
   1921 The Song of Songs, Being a Collection of Love Lyrics of Ancient Palestine (Philadelphia)

Jay, Peter
   1975 The Song of Songs (Anvil: London). Introduction by David Goldstein

Jobling, David
   1980 "The Myth Semantics of Genesis 2:4b-3:24" Semeia 18: 41-49

Joines, Karen Randolph
   1975 "The Serpent in Genesis 3" ZAW 87: 1-11

Josipovici, Gabriel
   1979 The World and the Book (Macmillan: London) (2nd edn.)
   1980 "Text and Voice" Comparative Criticism 2: 3-25
   1981 The Air We Breathe (Harvester: Brighton)

Jung, C. G.
   1959a The Archetypes and the Collective Unconscious (tr. R. F. C. Hull; The Collected Works Vol.9, Part 1; RKP: London) [2nd edn. 1968]
   1959b Aion: Researches into the Phenomenology of the Self (tr. R. F. C. Hull; The Collected Works Vol.9, Part 2; RKP: London) [2nd edn. 1968]
   1963 Mysterium Coniunctionis (The Collected Works Vol.14; RKP: London) [2nd edn. 1970]
   1968 Analytical Psychology: Its Theory and Practice. The Tavistock Lectures (RKP: London) [1st paperback edn. 1976] [First delivered 1935]
   1972 Four Archetypes: Mother, Rebirth, Spirit, Trickster (tr. R. F. C. Hull; RKP: London).

Jung, C. G. & Kerenyi, C.
   1951 Introduction to the Science of Mythology: The Myth of the Divine Child and the Mysteries of Eleusis (tr. R. F. C. Hull; RKP: London)

Kane, E.
   1930 "The Personal Appearance of Juan Ruiz" Modern Language Notes 45: 103-109

Bibliography

Kawin, Bruce F.
- 1972 Telling it Again and Again: Repetition in Literature and Film (Cornell U.P.: Ithaca & London)

Keefer, Michael
- 1980 This Fatal Mirror: Marlowe's Doctor Faustus, The Legend and Context (unpub. Ph.D thesis: Sussex Univ.)

Keel, Othmar
- 1977 Vögel als Boten: Studien zu Ps 68, 12-14; Gen 8, 6-12; Koh 10, 20 und dem Aussenden von Botenvögeln in Ägypten Orbis Biblicus et Orientalis 14. (Vandenhoeck & Ruprecht: Freiburg & Göttingen).
- 1978 The Symbolism of the Biblical World: Ancient Near Eastern Iconography and the Book of Psalms (tr. Timothy Hallett; SPCK: London)

Kermode, Frank
- 1967 The Sense of an Ending (OUP: London)
- 1972 English Pastoral Poetry (Norton: New York) [first pub. 1952]
- 1979 The Genesis of Secrecy: On the Interpretation of Narrative (Harvard U.P.: Cambridge, Mass. & London)

Kessler, Martin
- 1982 "A Methodological Setting for Rhetorical Criticism" in: Art and Meaning: Rhetoric in Biblical Literature (ed. David J. A. Clines, David M. Gunn and Alan J. Hauser; JSOTS 19; JSOT Press: Sheffield): 1-19 [first pub. in: Semitics 4 (1974): 22-36]

Kidner, Derek
- 1967 Genesis: Introduction and Commentary (Tyndale Press: London)

Kikawada, I. M.
- 1972 "Two Notes on Eve" JBL 91: 33-37

Kirk, G. S.
- 1975 Myth (Cambridge U.P.)

Klein, Jacob
- 1981 The Royal Hymns of Shulgi, King of Ur: Man's Quest for Immortal Fame (Transactions of the American Philosophical Society: Philadelphia)

Klein, Melanie
- 1957 Envy and Gratitude (Tavistock: London)
- 1963 Our Adult World and Other Essays (Heinemann: London)
- 1975 "Notes on Some Schizoid Mechanisms" in: Envy and Gratitude and Other Works (Collected Works III; Hogarth: London): 1-24

Köhler, L. H. & Baumgartner, W.
- 1953 Lexicon in Veteris Testamenti Libros (Brill: Leiden)

Kramer, Samuel Noah
- 1969 The Sacred Marriage Rite: Aspects of Faith, Myth and Ritual in Ancient Sumer (Indiana U.P.: Bloomington)

Krauss, Samuel
- 1941-2 "The Archaeological Background of Some Passages in the Song of Songs" JQR: 115-137
- 1942-3 "The Archaeological Background of Some Passages in the Song of Songs II" JQR 33: 17-27
- 1944-5 "The Archaeological Background of Some Passages in the Song of Songs III" JQR 35: 59-78

Bibliography

Krinetzki, Leo (= Gunter)
    1964   Das Hohe Lied: Kommentar zu Gestalt und Kerygma eines alttestamentlichen Liebeslied (Patmos: Dusseldorf)
    1970   "Die Erotischen Psychologie des Hohenliedes" TQ 150: 404-416
    1971   "'Retractationes' zu früheren Arbeiten über das Hohelied" Biblica 52: 176-189
    1981   Kommentar zum Hohelied: Bildsprach und Theologische Botschaft (BET 16; Lang: Frankfurt & Bern)

Kris, Ernst
    1952   "Aesthetic Ambiguity" in: Psychoanalytic Explorations in Art (International U.P.: New York)

Kugel, James L.
    1981a   The Idea of Biblical Poetry: Parallelism and Its History (Yale: New Haven & London)
    1981b   "On the Bible and Literary Criticism" Prooftexts 1: 217-236

Lacan, Jacques
    1970   "The Insistence of the letter in the Unconscious" in: Structuralism (ed. Jacques Ehrmann; Doubleday: New York): 101-137 (Introduction by Jan Miel: 94-101). [Repr. from Yale French Studies 37-38 (1966-7)]

Lambert, W. G.
    1959   "Divine Love Lyrics from Babylon" JSS 4: 1-15
    1975   "The Problem of the Love Lyrics" in: Unity and Diversity: Essays in the History, Literature and Religion of the Ancient Near East (ed. H. Goedicke & J. M. Roberts; Johns Hopkins U.P.: Baltimore): 98-135

Landsberger, Franz
    1954   "Poetic Units Within the Song of Songs" JBL 73: 203-216

Landy, Francis
    1979   "The Song of Songs and the Garden of Eden" JBL 98: 513-528
    1980a   "Humour in the Bible" The Jewish Quarterly 28/1: 13-19
    1980b   "Beauty and the Enigma: An Enquiry into Some Interrelated Episodes of the Song of Songs" JSOT 17: 55-106
    1981a   "Structure and Mythology in the Song of Songs" Prospice 11: 97-117
    1981b   "The Name of God and the Image of God and Man: A Response to David Clines" Theology 84: 164-170
    1981c   "Irony and Catharsis in Biblical Poetry: David's Lament over Saul and Jonathan" European Judaism 15/1: 3-13

Leach, Edmund A.
    1961   Rethinking Anthropology (Athlone: London)
    1969   "Genesis as Myth" in: Genesis as Myth and Other Essays (Cape: London)

Lee, J. M.
    1971   "Song of Songs 5.10: My Beloved is White and Ruddy" VT 21: 609

Lemaire, A.
    1975   "Zāmīr dans la tablette de Gezer et le Cantique des Cantiques" VT 25: 15-26

Levinger, Eliezer
    1973   Shir Hashirim (Jerusalem)

Bibliography

Lévi-Strauss, Claude
  1963a Structural Anthropology (tr. Claire Jacobson & B. G. Schoepf; Basic Books: London & New York)
  1963b "Réponses à quelques questions" Esprit 11: 628-653
  1969 Totemism (Pelican: London)
  1970 The Raw and the Cooked: Introduction to a Science of Mythology Vol.1 (tr. John & Doreen Weightman; Cape: London)

Lichtheim, Miriam
  1975 Ancient Egyptian Literature. Vol.1: The Old and Middle Kingdoms (California U.P.: Berkeley, Los Angeles & London)
  1976 Ancient Egyptian Literature. Vol.2: The New Kingdom (California U.P.: Berkeley, Los Angeles & London)

Lloyd, G.
  1971 "The Creation Stories of Genesis: A Basis for a Theology of Nature and Environment" Japanese Religions 7: 11-28

Loewe, Raphael
  1965 "The Divine Garment and the Shiur Qomah" HTR 58: 153-160

Loretz, Oswald
  1971 Das althebraische Liebeslied: Untersuchungen zur Stichometrie und Redaktionsgeschichte des Hohenliedes und des 45 Psalms (AOAT 14/1; Butzon & Kevelaer: Neukirchen-Vluyn)

Lys, Daniel
  1968 Le Plus Beau Chant de la Creation (du Cerf: Paris)

Maccoby, Hyam
  1979 "Sex According to the Song of Songs: Review of Marvin Pope The Song of Songs" Commentary 32/6: 53-59

Magonet, Jonathan
  1975 "The Bush that Never Burnt: Narrative Techniques in Exodus 3 and 6" The Heythrop Journal 16: 304-311
  1976 Form and Meaning: Studies in Literary Techniques in the Book of Jonah (BET 2; Lang: Frankfurt & Bern; repr. Almond: Sheffield 1983 [Bible & Literature 8])

Mandelkern, Solomon
  1959 Veteris Testamenti Concordantiae Hebraicae et Chaldaicae (Schocken: Tel Aviv) (4th rev. & aug. edn.)

Margalit, B.
  1979 "Alliteration in Ugaritic Poetry: Its Role in Composition and Analysis" UF 11: 537-558

Marx, Karl
  1963 Selected Writings in Sociology and Social Philosophy (ed. T. B. Bottomore & Maximilien Rubel; Pelican: London)

May, H. G.
  1955 "Some Cosmic Connotations of Mayim Rabbim 'Many Waters'" JBL 74: 9-21

McKane, William
  1965 Prophets and Wise Men (Studies in Biblical Theology 44; SCM: London)
  1970 Proverbs: A New Approach (SCM: London).

McKay, J. W.
  1970 "Helel and the Dawn Goddess" VT 20: 451-464

Bibliography

McKenzie, J. L.
   1954 "The Literary Characteristics of Genesis 2-3" Theological Studies 15: 541-570

Meek, Theophile, J.
   1922-3 "Canticles and the Tammuz Cult" AJSL 39: 1-14
   1924a "Babylonian Parallels to the Song of Songs" JBL 43: 245-252
   1924b "The Song of Songs and the Fertility Cult" in: A Symposium on the Song of Songs (ed. W. H. Schoff; Oriental Soc. of Philadelphia): 48-79
   1956 "Introduction and Interpretation of the Song of Songs" IB V (Abingdon: New York): 98-148

Meeks, Wayne A.
   1974 "The Image of the Androgyne: Some Uses of a Symbol in Earliest Christianity" History of Religions 13: 165-209

Mendenhall, George E.
   1974 "The Shady Side of Wisdom: The Date and Purpose of Genesis 3" in: A Light Unto my Path: Old Testament Studies in Honour of Jacob M. Myers (ed. H. N. Bream et al.; Temple U.P.: Philadelphia): 319-334

Merleau-Ponty, Maurice
   1968 The Visible and the Invisible (tr. Alphone Lingis; Northwestern U.P.: Evanston)

Miller, Barbara Stoler
   1977 The Love Song of the Dark Lord (Columbia U.P.: New York)

Miller, Patrick D.
   1978 Genesis 1-11: Studies in Structure and Theme (JSOTS 8; JSOT Press: Sheffield)

de Moor, J. C.
   1968 "Murices in Ugaritic Mythology" Orientalia 37: 212-215
   1971 The Seasonal Pattern of the Ugaritic Myth of Ba'lu According to the Version of Ili-milku (AOAT 16; Butzon & Kevelaer: Neukirchen-Vluyn)

Muilenberg, James
   1969 "Form Criticism and Beyond" JBL 88: 1-18

Müller, Hans-Peter
   1976 "Die Lyrische Reproduktion des Mythischen im Hohelied" Zeitschrift für Theologie und Kirche 73: 23-41
   1977 "Poesie und Magie in Cant. 4:12-5" ZDMG Supp.III/1: 157-164

Murphy, Roland E.
   1949 "The Structure of the Canticle of Canticles" CBQ 11: 381-391
   1954 "Recent Literature on the Canticle of Canticles" CBQ 16: 1-11
   1961 The Book of Ecclesiastes and the Canticle of Canticles with a Commentary (Paulist Press: New York)
   1973 "Form-Critical Studies in the Song of Songs" Interpretation 27: 413-422
   1977 "Towards a Commentary on the Song of Songs" CBQ 30: 482-496
   1979a "The Unity of the Song of Songs" VT 29: 436-443
   1979b "Interpreting the Song of Songs" Biblical Theological Bulletin 9: 99-105
   1981 "Patristic and Medieval Exegesis: Help or Hindrance?" CBQ 43: 505-516

Bibliography

Nachman of Braslav
  1970   Sipporei Ma'asiot (Braslav: Jerusalem)
Napier, B. D.
  1963   Exodus (SCM: London)
Navone, John
  1975   "The Myth and Dream of Paradise" SR 5: 152-161
Neher, André
  1969   The Prophetic Existence (tr. William Wolf; Yosseloff: London)
Nietzsche, Fr.
  1956   The Birth of Tragedy and the Genealogy of Morals (tr. Francis Golffing; Doubleday: New York)
Nuttall, A. D.
  1980   Overheard by God: Fiction and Prayer in Herbert, Milton, Dante and St. John (Methuen: London)
Oesterley, W. O. E.
  1936   The Song of Songs: The Authorised Version Together with a New Translation, an Introduction and Notes (Golden Cockerel Press: London)
Ohmann, Richard
  1964   "Generative Grammar and the Concept of Style" Word 20: 423-439
  1966   "Literature as Sentences" College English 27: 261-266
Otwell, John H.
  1977   And Sarah Laughed: The Status of Women in the Old Testament (Westminster: Philadelphia)
Page, Denys
  1975   Sappho and Alcaeus: An Introduction to the Study of Ancient Lesbian Poetry (OUP: London) [first pub. 1955]
Pardee, Dennis
  1980   Review of Marvin H. Pope The Song of Songs, JNES 39: 79-82
Patte, Daniel
  1980   "One Text: Several Structures" Semeia 18: 3-22
Patte, Daniel & Parker, Judson F.
  1980   " A Structural Exegesis of Genesis 2-3" Semeia 18: 55-76
Paz, Octavio
  1961   The Labyrinthe of Solitude (tr. Lysander Kemp; Grove: New York)
  1971   Claude Lévi-Strauss: An Introduction (tr. J. & S. Bernstein; Cape: London)
  1974   Alternating Current (tr. Helen Lane; Wildwood: London). Especially "André Breton or the Quest for the Beginning": 47-59
  1975   Conjunctions and Disjunctions (tr. Helen Lane; Wildwood: London)
  1976   The Siren and the Seashell (Texas U.P.: Austin & London)
Perdue, Leo
  1977   Wisdom and Cult (SBLDS 30; Scholars: Missoula)
Perles, Felix
  1922   Analekten zur Textkritik des Alten Testament (Engel: Leipzig) [first pub. 1895]

Perry, Menakhem
---- "The Flexible Voice: Combined Discourse in Biblical Narrative" (forthcoming)
Perry, Menakhem and Sternberg, Meir
   1968 "Hammelek bemabbat 'ironi: (The King Through Ironic Eyes: The Narrator's Devices in the Biblical Story of David and Bathsheba and Two Excursuses on the Theory of the Narrative Text)" Hasifrut 1: 263-293
Pfeiffer, Robert
   1957 Introduction to the Old Testament (Black: London)
Pitt-Rivers, Julian
   1977 The Fate of Shechem and the Politics of Sex (Cambridge U.P.)
Polzin, Robert
   1980 Moses and the Deuteronomist: A Literary Study of the Deuteronomic History (Seabury: New York)
Pope, Marvin
   1970 "A Mare in Pharaoh's Chariotry" BASOR 200: 56-61
   1973 Job (AB 15; Doubleday: New York) (3rd edn.)
   1976 The Song of Songs (AB 7c; Doubleday: New York)
Popper, Karl
   1962 The Open Society and Its Enemies (Harper & Row: New York)
Praz, Mario
   1963 The Romantic Agony (Fontana: London)
Prickett, Stephen
   1981 "Towards a Rediscovery of the Bible: The Problem of the Still Small Voice" in: Ways of Reading the Bible (ed. Michael Wadsworth; Harvester: Brighton): 105-117
Pritchard, James B. ed.
   1969 Ancient Near Eastern Texts Relating to the Old Testament (Princeton U.P.: Princeton & London) (3rd. rev. edn.)
   1973 The Ancient Near East: A New Anthology of Texts and Pictures. Vol.1 (Princeton U.P.: Princeton & London)
   1975 The Ancient Near East: A New Anthology of Texts and Pictures. Vol.2 (Princeton U.P.: Princeton & London)
Rabin, Chaim
   1963 "Some Etymological Notes" Tarbiz 33: 114-117
   1973 "The Song of Songs and Tamil Poetry" SR: 205-219
von Rad, Gerhard
   1962 Genesis: A Commentary (tr. John H. Marks; SCM: London)
de Raedt, Jules
   1976 "On Freilich's Interpretation of Genesis 1-3" Current Anthropology 17: 139-142
Raine, Kathleen
   1982 The Human Face of God: William Blake and the Book of Job (Thames & Hudson: London)
Reicke, Bo
   1956 "The Knowledge Hidden in the Tree of Paradise" JSS 1: 193-201
Rendsburg, Gary
   1980 "Janus Parallelism in Gen 49:26" JBL 99: 291-293

Bibliography

Rexroth, Kenneth
  1969 "Classics Revisited LXXXV: The Song of Songs" Saturday Review of Literature (26th April): 16

Rickman, John
  1975 "On the Nature of Ugliness and the Creative Impulse" in: Selected Contributions to Psychoanalysis (Hogarth: London): 68-89 [first pub. 1940]

Ricoeur, Paul
  1969 The Symbolism of Evil (tr. Emerson Buchanan; Beacon: Boston)

Riffaterre, Michael
  1970 "Describing Poetic Structures: Two Approaches to Baudelaire's 'Les Chats'" in: Structuralism (ed. Jacques Ehrmann; Doubleday: New York): 188-230

Robert, André and Tournay, J-R.
  1963 Le Cantique des Cantiques: Traduction et Commentaire (Gabalda: Paris)

Ronen, Avraham
  1975 "The Garden of Eden and Prehistory" Israel Yearbook: 99-103
  1976 Introducing Prehistory (Cassell: London)

Rosenberg, Joel W.
  1981 "The Garden Story Forward and Backward: The Non-Narrative Dimension of Gen. 2-3" Prooftexts 1: 1-27

Rosenzweig, Franz
  1971 The Star of Redemption (tr. William Hallo; RKP: London)

Rowley, H. H.
  1939 "The Meaning of the 'Shulammite'" AJSL 56: 84-91
  1965 "The Interpretation of the Song of Songs" in: The Servant of the Lord and Other Essays (Blackwell: Oxford): 195-246 (rev. edn.)

Rudolph, Wilhelm
  1962 Das Buch Ruth, Das Hohe Lied, Die Klagelieder (KAT XVII, 1-3; Möhn: Gutersloh)

Rundgren, Frithiof
  1962 "'appiryon, Tragsessel, Sanfte" ZAW 74: 70-72

Ruwet, Nicolas
  1972 Langage, Musique, Poésie (du Seuil: Paris)

Sadgrove, M.
  1979 "The Song of Songs as Wisdom Literature" in: Studia Biblica 1978 I: Papers on the Old Testament and Related Themes (Sixth International Conference on Biblical Studies, Oxford 3-7 April 1978) (ed. E. A. Livingstone; JSOTS 11; JSOT Press: Sheffield): 245-248

Salzberger-Wittenberg, I.
  1970 Psychoanalytic Insight and Relationship: A Kleinian Approach (RKP: London)

Sandars, N. K.
  1968 Prehistoric Art in Europe (Penguin: London)
  1971 Poems of Heaven and Hell from Ancient Mesopotamia (Penguin Classics: London)
  1972 The Epic of Gilgamesh (Penguin Classics: London) (rev. edn.)

Sarna, N. M.
  1966 Understanding Genesis (Jewish Theological Seminary of America: New York)
  1971 "Bible: Canon, Text and Editions" Encyclopaedia Judaica (Keter: Jerusalem) IV: 814-839
Sasson, Jack M.
  1973a "A Further Cuneiform Parallel to the Song of Songs?" ZAW 85: 359-360
  1973b "The Worship of the Golden Calf" in: Orient and Occident: Essays Presented to Cyrus H. Gordon on the Occasion of his Sixty-Fifth Birthday (ed. Harry A. Hoffner; AOAT 22; Butzon & Kevelaer: Neukirchen-Vluyn): 151-159
Sawyer, J. F. A.
  1974 "The Meaning of 'běṣelem ʾĕlōhîm' ('In the Image of God') in Genesis 1-11" JThS 25 (New Series): 418-426
Schedl, Cl.
  1977 "Der Verschlossene Garten: Logotechnische Untersuchungen zum Hohelied, 4.12-5.1" ZDMG Supp. III/1: 165-177
Schmidt, Nathaniel
  1926 "Is the Song of Songs an Adonis Liturgy?" JAOS 46: 154-164
Scholem, Gershom
  1955 Major Trends in Jewish Mysticism (Thames and Hudson: London) (2nd edn.)
  1965 Jewish Gnosticism, Merkabah Mysticism, and Talmudic Tradition (Jewish Theological Seminary of America: New York). Appendix D: Mishnat Shir Hashirim by Saul Liebermann, 118-126. (2nd edn.)
Schoville, Keith N.
  1970 The Impact of the Ras Shamra Tablets on the Study of the Song of Songs (1969 Ph.D. thesis: Univ. of Wisconsin; Univ. Microfilms: Ann Arbor)
  1971 "Song of Songs" Encyclopaedia Judaica (Keter: Jerusalem) Vol.15: 143-150.
Scriabine, Marina
  1977 Au Carrefour de Thèbes (Gallimard: Paris)
Seale, Morris
  1975 The Desert Bible: Nomadic Tribal Culture and Old Testament Interpretation (Weidenfeld & Nicholson: London)
Segal, Hannah
  1964 Introduction to the Works of Melanie Klein (Heinemann: London)
  1971 "A Psychoanalytic Approach to Aesthetics" in: New Directions in Psychoanalysis (ed. Melanie Klein et al.; Tavistock: London): 384-405 [first pub. 1955]
  1979 Klein (Harvester/Fontana)
Segal, M. H.
  1962 "The Song of Songs" VT 12: 470-490
Shea, William H.
  1980 "The Chiastic Structure of the Song of Songs" ZAW 92: 378-396
Simpson, W. K. ed.
  1973 The Literature of Ancient Egypt: An Anthology of Stories, Instructions, and Poetry (Yale U.P.: New Haven & London)

Bibliography

Singer, June
   1977   Androgyny: Towards a New Theory of Sexuality (RKP: London)
Skehan, Patrick
   1965   "The Biblical Scrolls from Qumran and the Text of the Old Testament" BA 28: 87-100
Skinner, John
   1910   A Critical and Exegetical Commentary on Genesis (Clark: Edinburgh)
Smith, Morton
   1971   Palestinian Parties and Politics that Shaped the Old Testament (Columbia U.P.: New York)
Soggin, J. A.
   1975a "The Fall of Man in the Third Chapter of Genesis" Bib et Or 29: 88-111 [first pub. in SWSR 33 (1962): 227-256]
   1975b "Philological-linguistic Notes on the Second Chapter of Genesis" Bib et Or 29: 169-178 [first pub. in Biblica 44 (1963): 521-530]
Soler, Jean
   1979   "The Dietary Prohibitions of the Hebrews" New York Review of Books 26/19: 24-30
Soloveitchik, Joseph B.
   1974b "Confrontation" in: Studies in Judaica in Honour of Dr. Samuel Belkin as Scholar and Educator (ed. S. B. Stitskin; Ktav: New York): 45-67 [first pub. in Tradition 6/2 (1964): 5-29
   1974b "The Lonely Man of Faith" in: Studies in Judaica, 71-127 [first pub. in Tradition 7/2 (1965): 5-67]
Soulen, Richard N.
   1967   "The Wasfs of the Song of Songs and Hermeneutic" JBL 86: 183-91
Speiser, E. A.
   1964   Genesis (AB 1; Doubleday: New York)
   1967a "'Ed in the Story of Creation" in: Oriental and Biblical Studies (ed. J. J. Finkelstein & M. Greenberg; Pennsylvania U.P.: Philadelphia): 19-22 [first pub. 1955]
   1967b "The Rivers of Paradise" in: Oriental and Biblical Studies [see above]: 23-24 [first pub. 1954]
Steck, Odil Hannes
   1970   Die Paradieserzählung: Eine Auslegung von Genesis 2.4b-3.24 (Biblische Studien 60; Neukirchener: Neukirchen-Vluyn)
Stephan, S. H.
   1922   "Modern Palestinian Parallels to the Song of Songs" JPOS 2: 1-80, 198-278
Stokes, Adrian
   1965   The Invitation in Art (Tavistock: London)
   1971   "Form in Art" in: New Directions in Psychoanalysis (ed. Melanie Klein et al.; Tavistock: London): 406-420
   1972   The Image in Form. Selected Writings (ed. Richard Wollheim; Penguin: London)
Stolz, Fritz
   1972   "Die Baume des Gottesgartens auf dem Lebanon" ZAW 84: 141-156

Bibliography

Stuart, Douglas K.
   1976   Studies in Early Hebrew Metre (Scholars: Missoula)
Stuart, Simon
   1980   New Phoenix Wings - Reparation in Literature (RKP: London)
Thompson, P. E. S.
   1971   "The Yahwist Creation Story" VT 21: 197-208
Thompson, Thomas L.
   1978   "The Background of the Patriarchs: A Reply to William Dever and Malcolm Clark" JSOT 9: 2-43
Thubron, Colin
   1967   Mirror to Damascus (Heinemann: London)
Tournay, J-R.
   1959   "Les Chariots d'Amminadab" VT 9: 288-309
   1975   "Abraham et le Cantique des Cantiques" VT 25: 550-558
   1980   "The Song of Songs and its Concluding Section" Immanuel 10: 5-14
Trible, Phyllis
   1973   "Depatriarchalizing in Biblical Interpretation" JAAR 41: 30-48
   1978   God and the Rhetoric of Sexuality (Fortress: Philadelphia)
Trudinger, L. P.
   1975   "'Not Yet Made' or 'Newly Made': A Note on Gen.2.5 (beterem)" Evangelical Quarterly 47: 67-69
Tsevat, Mattiteyahu
   1975   "Šĕnê hāʿēṣîm ʾăšer bĕtôk haggan" ("The two trees that were in the garden") Eretz Yisrael 12: 40-43
   1980   "Der Schlangentext von Ugarit UT 607 - KTU 1.100 - Ug. V.564ff. RS. 24.244" UF 12: 759-778
Tsur, Reuven
   1971   A Rhetoric of Poetic Qualities (unpub. Ph.D. thesis: Sussex Univ.)
Turner, Victor
   1974   Dramas, Fields, and Metaphors (Cornell U.P.)
Tur Sinai, H.
   1943   Shir Hashirim (Tel Aviv) [repr. in: Hallašon wehassefer The Language and the Book. Essays in Biblical Hebrew. Vol.2 (Bialik: Jerusalem 1950): 351-388]
Ullendorf, Edward
   1977   Studies in Semitic Languages and Civilisations (Harrassowitz: Wiesbaden)
   1979   "The Bawdy Bible" Bulletin of the School of Oriental and African Studies 42: 425-456
Urbach, Ephraim E.
   1975   Our Sages: Their Concepts and Beliefs (tr. Israel Abrahams; Magnes: Jerusalem)
Vater, Ann M.
   1978   "The Rhythm of Communication in the Hermeneutical Process" in: Encounter With the Text (ed. Martin J. Buss; Fortress: Philadelphia; Scholars: Missoula): 173-187
Vawter, Bruce
   1977   On Genesis: A New Reading (Chapman: London)
   1980   "Prov 8:22: Wisdom and Creation" JBL 99: 205-216

Bibliography

Waldman, N. M.
  1970 "A Note on Canticles 4:9" JBL 89: 215-217
Walsh, Jerome T.
  1977 "Genesis 2:4b-3:24: A Synchronic Approach" JBL 96: 161-177
Waterman, Leroy
  1925 "The Role of Solomon in the Song of Songs" JBL 44: 171-187
Webster, Edwin
  1982 "Pattern in the Song of Songs" JSOT 22: 73-92
Weir, Ruth
  1962 Language in the Crib (Mouton: The Hague)
Weiss, Meir
  1962 Hammiqra kedemuto. The Bible and Modern Literary Theory (Bialik: Jerusalem)
Wellek, Rene & Warren, Austin
  1978 Theory of Literature (Penguin: London) [first pub. 1949]
Wertheimer, S. A.
  1955 Batei Midrashot (Mossad HaRav Kook: Jerusalem) (rev. edn.)
Westenholz, A.
  1972 Review of MAD 4 & 5 by I. J. Gelb in: JNES 31: 380-382
Westenholz, J. & A.
  1977 "Help for Rejected Suitors. The Old Akkadian Love Inscription MAD V.8" Orientalia 46: 198-219
Westermann, Claus
  1974a Creation (tr. John J. Scullion; SPCK: London)
  1974b Genesis 1-11 (BKAT 1/1; Neukirchener Verlag: Neukirchen-Vluyn)
Wetzstein, J. G.
  1873 "Die Syrische Dreschtafel" Zeitschrift fur Ethnologie 5: 270-302
White, Hugh C.
  1978 "Structural Analysis of the Old Testament Narrative" in: Encounter with the Text (ed. Martin J. Buss; Fortress: Philadelphia; Scholars: Missoula): 45-66
  1980 "Direct and Third Person Discourse in the Narrative of the 'Fall'" Semeia 18: 91-106
White, John B.
  1978 A Study of the Language of Love in the Song of Songs and Ancient Egyptian Literature (SBLDS 38; Scholars: Chico, Ca.)
Widengren, Geo.
  1955 Sakrales Königtum im Alten Testament und im Judentum (Kohlhammer: Stuttgart)
Wifall, W.
  1974 "The Breath of His Nostrils: Gen.2.7b" CBQ 36: 237-240
Williams, A. J.
  1973 The Significance of the Genesis Three Serpent with Reference to OT And Ancient Near Eastern Traditions (unpub. Ph.D. dissertation: Univ. of Manchester).
  1977 "The Relation of Gen.3.20 to the Serpent" ZAW 90: 357-374
Williams, James G.
  1980a "The Beautiful and the Barren: Conventions in Biblical Type-Scenes" JSOT 17: 107-119

Bibliography

   1980b "Response to Jobling: The Necessity of Being 'Outside'" Semeia 18: 51-53
   1981 Those Who Ponder Proverbs: Aphoristic Thinking and Biblical Literature (Bible & Literature 2; Almond: Sheffield)

Wimsatt, W. K.
   1967 The Verbal Icon: Studies in the Meaning of Poetry (Kentucky U.P.: Lexington)

Winandy, Jacques
   1965 "La litière de Salomon (Cant.3.9-10)" VT 15: 103-110

Winnett, Frederick V.
   1965 "Rethinking the Foundations" JBL 84: 1-19

Winnicott, Donald Woods
   1962 The Family and Individual Development (Tavistock: London)

Winton-Thomas, D.
   1953 "A Consideration of Some Unusual Ways of Expressing the Superlative in Hebrew: VT 3: 209-224

Wittekindt, W.
   1926 Das Hohelied und seine Beziehung zum Istarkult (Orient Buchhandlung: Hannover)

Wittgenstein, Ludwig
   1974 Tractatus Logico-Philosophicus (tr. D. F. Pears & B. F. Guinness. Introduction Bertrand Russell; RKP: London)

Wittig, Susan
   1977 "A Theory of Multiple Meaning" Semeia 9: 75-103

Wollheim, Richard
   1969 Art and Its Objects (Harper & Row: London) (2nd edn.)

Würthwein, Ernst
   1969 Die Fünf Megilloth (HAT 18; Mohr: Tübingen)

Wyatt, Nicolas
   1981 "Interpreting the Creation and Fall Story in Gen.2-3" ZAW 93: 10-21

Yamauchi, E. M.
   1964 "Tammuz and the Bible" JBL 84: 283-290

Young, Dwight B.
   1979 "The Ugaritic Myth of the God Horan and the Mare" UF 11: 839-848

Zakovitch, Yair
   1974 "Shir Hashirim (8.6b-7) wĕziqatô lĕmišlê 6.20-31" (The Song of Songs [8.6b-7] and its Relation to Prov 6.20-31) Beth Miqra 20: 366-368
   1975 "Ben Shir Hashirim lesipporei shimshon" (The Song of Songs and the tales of Samson) Beth Miqra 21: 292-294
   1980 "A Study of Precise and Partial Derivations in Biblical Etymology" JSOT 15: 31-50

INDEXES

INDEX OF REFERENCES
TO BIBLICAL AND CLASSICAL JEWISH SOURCES

[* = principal discussions]

GENESIS		2.19-20	*233-4, 354n157	3.15	264
1	187, 191, 257-63, 324n4, 338n61, 342n88	2.20	234, 343n94	3.16	*248-55, 351n139, 353n145/147, 354n152
		2.21	247, 252		
		2.21-2	*247-8		
1.1	279n5	2.21-4	349n134	3.17	255, 257
1.26	259-62, 357n175	2.22	247, 357n175	3.17-9	200, 246, 253
1.27	349n132	2.23	*227-8, 242, 243, 253, 341n79, 354n156	3.18	201
1.28	262			3.19	255-6, 257
2	186-7, 339n65, 342n88			3.20	*228-9, *247-8, *253, 255, 254n156
		2.24	219, 222, *248-50, 252, 260, 312n96, 352n140, 354n156		
2.1-4	187			3.21	*253-4, 351n138, 354n156/157
2.4	*262, 356n170				
2.4-7	187			3.22	210, 212, 218, *219, 260, *261-2, 348n127, 357n175
2.4-15	189	2.24-5	354n156		
2.4-25	339n68	2.25	220-3, 254, 339n67/68, 354n156		
2.5	194, 197, 200-1, 257, 331n15, 358n176				
		2.25-3.1	*220-3	3.23	200, 257
		2-3	5, 184, 188, 246, 252, 257, 160, 328n4, 344n100	3.24	*262-3, 265
2.6	194, 338n55, 358n176			4.1	*219, 248, 257, 351n137
				4.2-16	363n145
2.7	146, 246, 253, 257, 350n136	3	186, 257, 353n145	4.6-7	353n145
				4.7	250-1, 353n145/147
2.8	*190, 196, *198-9, 200	3.1	187-8, 220-1, *229-33, 242, 255, 338n55, 339n68, 343n96	8.17	345n108
				11.9	357n175
2.8-9	*190-1			18	357n174
2.9	*191, *210-3, 218, 243			18.16	309n73
		3.1-6	*241-4	24.65	326n39
2.10	194, 197	3.3	244	25.6	324n26
2.10-4	*193-6, 199, 322n21, 338n55	3.3-4	355n163	29.10-1	79
		3.4	212, 242, 244	30.38,41	306n50
				38.14	326n39
2.15	196, *199-201, 229, 255, 340n76	3.5	*236-7, 260	41.6,23	321n12
		3.6	*242-4, 248, 353n140/144	49.6	314n108
2.16-7	*215-6, 247				
2.17	244, 336n45, 355n163	3.7	253, 339n68	**EXODUS**	
		3.8	253, *261	2.16	306n50
2.18	189, 199, 205, 259	3.9-16	257	3.13-5	316n119
		3.12	253, 255	14.21	314n105
2.18-25	187, 339n68	3.14	255	15	130
2.19	*226-7, 257, 340n76, 343n96	3.14-3.21	339n68, 354n156	**LEVITICUS**	
				18	349n130

Index of References

19.18	71	**EZEKIEL**		6.30-1	316n123
20	349n130	1.27	356n171	9.18	315n111
26.36	333n33	5.5	306n49	17.27-8	292n78
		7.16	345n106	25.19	28
NUMBERS		16.4	306n52	26.4-5	292n78
21.24	314n105	21.3	316n118	26.10	201
24.17	331n18	27.10-1	305n45	27.30	125
31.10	324n26	27.21	148	29.19	31
		28.13	331n20	30.16	125, 132
DEUTERONOMY		31	315n109	31.30	145
3.9	309n74	31.3-9	196		
4	127	46.23	323n26	**JOB**	
6.6	279n6			8.17	310n80
32.34	315n34	**JONAH**		10.21-2	314n109
		3.3	315n114	10.22	126
JUDGES				11.25	307n64
5.7	282n27	**MICAH**		15.30	316n118
14.14	314n105	3.7	326n39	17.14	98
15.4-5	346n114			20.8	321n12
15.5	303n26	**NAHUM**		28.7	321n12
16.7	349n131	2.8	345n106	31	32
				31.26-7	293n80
I SAMUEL		**HABAKKUK**			
13.19	326n39	3.5	315n112	**SONG OF SONGS**	
18.9	320n6			1	55
25.39	324n31	**PSALMS**		1.1	*16, 74
		7.15	353n149	1.1-4	92
II SAMUEL		8.4	159	1.1-5	51
	336n45,	18.27	321n13	1.1-8	52, 55
	348n125	19	218	1.1-2.7	44
		19.6-8	321n13	1.2	38, 53, 74,
I KINGS		19.8-10	338n61		207, 311n89
17.6	345n108	19.9	321n13	1.2-3	297n111
5.12	309n74	24.4	321n13	1.2-4	49, 55,
		32.6	316n121		296n99
ISAIAH		36.7	315n114	1.2-7	296n99
5.1	28, 154	49.7	320n6	1.2-2.6	297n107/111
6.8	357n175	50.20	324m31	1.2-2.7	40
14	315n109	56.1	345n106	1.3	56, 297n111
16.12-7	337n50	76.4	315n112	1.3-4	334n38
17.13	316n121	78.48	315n112	1.4	71,122, 286
21.16	147	80.11	315n114		n49, 291n73
21.17	326n39	80.12	310n82	1.5	49, 51, 68,
38.14	345n106	81.20	332n22		*142-8, 151,
43.2	316n123	93	130		163-6, 174,
47.13	323n25	96-100	281n19		178, 202,
49.2	321n13	137.6-7	283n27		238, 296n99
59.11	345n106	137.8-9	282n27	1.5-6	49, 51, 118,
		144.7	316n121		*142-52,
JEREMIAH		148	281n19		156-7, 160,
2.31	315n114				162, 166,
10.2	323n25	**PROVERBS**			169, 172,
17.8	310n82,	3.8	306n52		174, 224,
	331n17	5.15	331n19		250, 274,
43.12,21	326n39	6.27-35	317n126		296n99/100,

[389]

Index of References

	323n18, 324 n26, 338n58	2.2	217, 296n100 196n100, 302 n23, 306n51		297n106, 327n44, 346n112
1.5-7	324n26	2.2-3	39, 297n109	2.15	27, 42-3, 48-9. 207, *240-1, 346 n112/114
1.5-8	56	2.3	39, 50-4, 58, 78, *81-2, 84-5, *213-4, 217- 8, 264, 296 n100, 329n6		
1.6	66, 142-4, *148-9, 151, 153, 155-6, 167, 173, 198, 207, 213, 226, 241, 256, 346n112			2.16	42, 53, 57, 78, 238, 251, 291n73, 294n92, 333 n30, 353n148
		2.3-6	116		
		2.3-7	55, 214, 217		
1.7	51, 198, 226, 254, 333n30	2.4	116, 214, 318n1	2.16-7	42-3, 55, 57, 112, 301 n15, 313n99, 333n30/32, 346n112
		2.5	54, 69, 85, 116, 214-7, 313n97		
1.7-8	49, 51, 72, *169-76, 224, 274, 296n99, 334n36	2.6	52, 116, 312n97, 313 n99, 338n58	2.17	42, 72, 77, 112, 203, 261, 312n94
		2.7	52, 117, 214, 216, *236, 313n99	3	52, 57, 91, 204
1.8-11	40, 250			3.1	45, 114
1.9	49, 70, *176-7, 239	2.7-3.5	40	3.1-2	46
1.9-17	50	2.8	41, 77, 238, 296n102, 338n58	3.1-4	*44-7, 52, 57, *114-6, 118, *208, 297n112
1.9-2.3	55				
1.9-2.7	50	2.8-9	42, 43, 84, 297n106, 333n30		
1.10	177			3.1-5	57
1.10-1	55, 70, *177, 327 n49	2.8-!7	40, 41-4, 48, 53, 55, 57, 124, 300n9	3.1-6	55
				3.2	45, 114, 208, 297 n105
1.12	281n25, 327 n49				
1.12-4	297n111	2.9	41-2, 203, 296n102n, 356n171	3.2-3	46
1.13	54, *83, 84, 303n34			3.3	45, 114, 208, 225, 347n116
1.13-4	51, 53-4, 82-4	2.10	41, 43, 297n106	3.4	40, 46, 66, 114, 116, 146, 208, 250, 380n69
1.14	54, *82-3, 282n26	2.10-3	51, 53, 57, 62, 69, 70, 72,195, 207, 313n99, 333n32		
1.15	55, 177, 228			3.5	52, 117, *236
1.15-6	*177-8, *228			3.6	49, 52, 118, 209, 297n112, 298n114
1.15-7	54, 297n109	2.11	41, 195, 198, 296n102		
1.16	177, 228, 297n110	2.12	41-3, 53, 72, 213, 238, 296n102, 346n111	3.6-11	*44, 56-8, 118, *209, 214, 220, 282n26, 298n114
1.16-7	54, 116				
1.17	91, 213, 306n50	2.13	41, 43		
2	52, 202, 296n101	2.14	42-3, 70, 72, 80, 206, 237, *238, 296n102,	3.6-5.1	40
2.1	*81, *83, 203, 301n17			3.7	209, 282n27, 300n8
2.1-2	40, 78, 296 n100, 301n17			3.8	113, 298n114
2.1-3	50, 54, *81,			3.9	19, *91,

Index of References

	154, 195, 213, 282n26		*98-9, 101, *103, 109, 111, 123,		198, 205, 224-5, 312 n92, 324n26
3.11	19, 49, 58, 66, 76, 118, *120, 146, 154, 209, 298n114	4.10	139, 309n72 38, 55, 92, 101, 108, 111, 297 n111, 302	5.2-6 5.2-7 5.2-8	56 44, 47, 55, 57-8, 72, 298n113 56-7
4	55, 57, 75, 85, 202, 204-5, 207, 304n36, 305 n46, 310n82	4.10-1 4.10-5.1 4.11	n20, 311n89 108, 302n20 297n111 79, *90-3, 103-11, 195,	5.2-6.3 5.3 5.4 5.5	40, 296n103, 298n113 254 68 68, 80, 297n111
4.1	44-5, 55, 96, 304n36	4.12	254 58, 65, 80,	5.6 5.7	47 47, 146, 208,
4.1-2	76, 326n41, 334n36		101, 104-5, 122, 192,	5.8	225-6, 254 58, 69, 116,
4.1-3 4.1-5	43, 57, 96 50, 57, *75-6, 89,	4.12-5 4.12-5.1	194, 218 105, 109 26, 29, 40,	5.9	338n58 44-5, 174, 226, 297n105
4.1-7 4.2-5 4.3	111 45, 55-7 *94-6 *94-6, 254, 258, 307n62, 308n68		44, 56, 76, 101, *104- 11,*201-2, 206, 215, 217, 302n20, 333n29	5.9-16 5.10 5.10-16	55-6 302n22,318n1 13, 26, 44- 5, 57-8, 71, 80, 285 n39, 287n55,
4.4	57, 76, 82, 87, 89, 96, 161, 282n26	4.13	82, 100, 107, 111, 201, 281n25,	5.12 5.12-3	304n36 80, 132, 239 80
4.4-5 4.5	57 *74-8, 80, 83-4, 87-9, *92-6, 99, 101, 111, 237, 273,	4.13-4 4.14	282n26, 297n111 80, 106, *192-3, 281 n25, 297n111 213, 281n25	5.13 5.14 5.15	*77-81, 83, 239, 297 n111, 302n21 *224-5 81, 90, 195, 213
	300n11, 305 n46, 312n94, 333n30	4.15 4.16	*105-8, 132, *194-5, 310n83 *106-8, 183,	5.15-6 5.16	91 44-5, 79, 338n58
4.5-6	42, 55, 112, 313n99, 333n32		197-8, 201, 304n35, 310 n85, 311n88	6 6.1	55-7, 194, 202, 205 45, 57, 174,
4.6	*72-3, *112, 261, 332n20	4.16-5.1	109-10, 201, 206	6.1-12	297n106 40, 56,
4.7	44, 86, 304n36	5	55, 201,305 n46, 311n89		296n103, 298n113
4.8	45, 58, 76, *101-4, 106, 109-11, 195, 239, 240, 309n72, 324 n26, 346n109	5.1 5.2	44, 51, 71, 101, *108-11, 156, 192, 206, 304 n39, 308n71, 312n92 51, 56, 69,	6.2 6.2-3 6.2-12	78, 80, 193, 195, *202-4, 296n103, 297 n111, 305n46, 333n32 43, 333n32 43, *201-5, 217
4.8-9 4.8-5.1 4.8/12-5.1 4.9	283n30 57-8, *97- 112, 312n92 56 55, 58, 69,		70, 80, 97, 111, 132,	6.3	57, 78,

[391]

Index of References

	*203, 238, 251, 291n73, 294n92, 305n46, 353n148	7.2-7	44-5, *85-90, 297n111	7.13-4	53
		7.3	70, *88-90, 95, 225, 269, 282n26, 305n46, 306n49, 334n36	7.14	54, 297n111
				8	167-9
6.4	43, 88, 138-9, 174, 204			8.1	38, 53, 58, 99, 101, 116-7, 132, 208, 225-6, 317n126
6.4-8.3	40, 296n103				
6.5	44, 204	7.3-4	*89-90, 92		
6.5-6	326n41, 334n36	7.3-5	96	8.1-2	52-3, 79, *99-101, 107, 111, *114-6, 118, 120, 297n112, 312n96
		7.4	87, 89, 94-5, 237, 301n15, 305n46		
6.5-7	43, 50, 57				
6.6	94				
6.7	254, 258	7.4-5	50, 57		
6.8	150, 291n73, 298n114	7.5	82, 85, *86-9, 91, 95, 154, 283n28		
				8.1-3	132
6.8-9	43, 156			8.1-5	52, 55, *114-21, *124-5
6.8-10	56-7, *150-151, *160, 166, 173-4, 275, 323n18	7.5-6	*88-9, 92		
		7.6	45, 69, 88, 139, 251, 281n25		
				8.1-7	40, *113-33
6.9	44, 66-7, 71, 80, 119, 150-1, 154, 172, 237, 239, *245, 252, 298n114, 308n69, 321n13	7.7	69, 297n110, 304n36	8.2	40, 66, 79, 99-100, 119-20, 146, 208, 250, 313n101
		7.7-8.3	297n111		
		7.8	54, 83, 87, 213	8.3	52-3, *116-7, 120
		7.8-9	39, 75, *82, 119, 218	8.4	52-3, *117, 124, 216, 305n46
		7.8-10	44, 47-8, 54, 56, 85, 88, 92		
6.9-10	*159, 172			8.4-14	40
6.10	23, 43-4, 71, *118, 138, 150, 165, 251, 283n28, 285n39, 298n114, 318n1, 327n46	7.8-11	56	8.5	40-3, 52-4, 66-7, 81, 85, 116, *117-24, 132, 146, *214, 216-8, 220, *252, 264, 297n112, 304n39, 308n69
		7.7-14	54-6		
		7.9	48, 54, *84-6, 92, 303n34, 311n85		
		7.10	44, 48, 79, *85-6, 286n49, 303n35, 304n35, 311n85		
6.11	51, 56-7, 106, 193, 195, 206, 281n25, 290n68, 296n103, 330n9, 333n32				
		7.10-1	304n35	8.6	58, 113, *121-9, 214, 284n37
		7.11	53, 57, *251-2, 304n35/46		
6.11-12	43, *204-5				
6.11-7.1	333n32	7.11-4	44, 53-4	8.6-7	40, 51-2, 55, 58, 114, *121-33, 258, *273-4, 296n100, 312n95, 317n126
6.12	*205, 217, 333n32/33	7.11-8.5	40		
		7.12	54, 90, 209, 282n26		
7	57, 296n101, 305n46	7.12-3	54		
7.1	45, 69, 333n32	7.12-4	51, 53, 207, 313n99, 333n32		
				8.6-14	40
7.1-7	55-6	7.13	54, 56-7, 330n9, 333n32	8.7	53, 117, 121, *129-33, 225-6, 296n100, 316n123
7.2	254, *258-9, 305n46				
7.2-3	224, 254				

Index of References

8.8	160, 167-9	3.15	310n82, 331n17		Hagigah	
8.8-9	324n27/30				12a	279n5
8.8-10	49, 51, 66, *160-70, 173, 177-8, 274, 283n28	5.18	321n13		14b	16, *269-70
					15b	17
		II CHRONICLES				
		2.6	306n48		Ketuboth	
8.8-12	56				62b-63a	279n6
8.8-14	44, 52, 55	**JUDITH**				
8.9	91, 160, 164, 168-9	8.13	322n17		Nedarim	
					50a	279n6
8.9-10	209	**BEN SIRA**				
8.10	68, 74-5, 87, 154, 160-2, *164-5, 168-9, 258, 324n27	17.7	281n21		Baba Bathra	
					134a	346n111
		MISHNAH				
		Shabbat			Sanhedrin	
		6.3	303n29		38b	346n111
8.10-12	324n26				101a	280n7
8.11	19, 28, 40, *152-5, 206-7, 323n18	Avot				
		1.1	348n126		Shebuoth	
		1.16	280n12		35b	280n10
8.11-12	49, 51, 153, 160, 163, 165, 169, 172, 178, 216, 274, 296n99, 346n112	2.18	14			
		3.9	293n80		Menahot	
		5.1	281n15		29b	279n5, 280n15
		Sotah				
		9.14	282n26		**TALMUD P.**	
					Yeb 14b 279n6	
8.12	*152-7, 209, 323n18	Kelim				
		15.6	279n1		**ABOTH de R Nathan**	
8.12-14	296n99					291n70
8.13	31, 49-51, *133, 154, 207, 238, 296n99	Yadaim				
		3.2-5	279n1		1.2	279n2
		3.5	*13-8, 279 n2, 280n13		6.15	279n6
8.13-14	49, *206-7, 297n99, 299n5				**SIFRE**	
		TOSEFTA			Kedoshim	
		Sanhedrin			4.12	14
8.14	72, 77, 133, 203, *271, 312n94	12.10	280n8			
					MIDRASH	
		TALMUD BAB.			Gen. Rabbah	
		Berakhot			1.14	279n5
ECCLESIASTES		55a	280n15			
1.13	33	61b	279n6, 346n111		Lev. Rabbah	
2.5	281n25				28.1	280n14
3.11	33, 200					
4.3	15	Shabbat			Shir Hashirim Rabbah	
7.5	28	30b	280n14		1.2.1	280n10
7.28	247	89a	279n5		1.10	281n17
9.6	125					
11.9	280n14	Eruvin			**MISCELLANEOUS**	
		13.b	280n11		Midrash of the Alphabet	
ESTHER						280n15
7.8	202, 290n68	Sukkah				
		49a-b	306n49		Shiur Qomah 279n4	
NEHEMIAH						
2.8	281n25				Pereq Shirah	
						183, 281n19

INDEX OF MODERN AUTHORS

Albright, W.F.	19, 282n26, 283n30, 309n76, 314n104/106, 331n16, 334n37, 338n60, 354n150	Childs, B.S.	31-2, 291n70, 316n119, 343n92
		Chouraqui, A.	301n16, 308n65/70, 312n96, 346n112
Alonso-Schökel, L.	187, 283n33, 329n5, 330n13, 332n25, 336n44/45, 340n71/77, 341n79, 347n117/121, 352n140	Civil, M.	287n55
		Clines, D.J.A.	33, 187, 218, 255, 328n4, 329n6, 338n61, 353n145, 354n154, 355n163, 356n170/171, 357n174
Alster, B.	246, 265, 346n110, 349n130		
Alter, R.	187, 314n103, 328n3/4, 337n53, 339n67, 341n82, 342n88, 343n94, 356n170, 357n172	Coats, G.	187, 215, 242
		Cook, A.S.	36-7, 57, 76, 97, 138, 161, 171, 184, 289n63, 298n115, 305n47, 312n96, 324n27, 325n37, 334n38
Anderson, B.W.	328n4	Cooper, J.S.	26, 284n34, 287n53-5
Angénieux, J.	40, 296n97	Cross, F.M.	316n119
Armstrong, J.	230, 332n26, 335n40	Crossan, J.D.	322n16, 336n46, 337n48, 340n69, 341n84, 342n88, 347n121, 348n129
Astour, M.	335n42		
Auffret, P.	282n27		
Avishur, Y.	283n29, 294n91, 302n20		
		Culler, J.	295n95
Bachelard, G.	315n113	Culley, R.C.	328n3, 339n68
Bailey, J.A.	329n6, 336n44, 352n140	Dahlberg, B.	328n4
		Dahood, M.	165, 281n25, 303n31, 310n80, 311n89, 316n118, 320n6, 321n12, 322n14, 325n34, 327n44, 334n37
Barker, M.	187		
Barth, K.	184		
Barthes, R.	27, 289n61, 326n42		
Bartino, S.	332n24		
Berg, W.	26, 176, 190, 290n64, 291n71, 293n84, 326n41	Daube, D.	187-8
		Derchain, P.	22, 38, 284n37, 285n41/43, 486n45/47, 288n57
Blanchot, M.	321n11		
Bloom, H.	27	Derrida, J.	27, 36, 273, 289n61, 293n80
Boomershine, T.	185, 187, 338n56, 339n66, 343n92, 347n119/121, 348n129	Dhorme, E.	293n80
		Dickie, G.	319n4
		Dijkstra, M.	307n61
Boyce, M.	307n63	Driver, G.R.	321n12, 333n33, 334n38
Brams, S.J.	215, 328n4, 352n140		
Broadribb, D.	40, 295n96	Duncan, R.	187, 202, 235, 344n98, 349n130, 351n137/139
Brown, N.O.	323n23		
Brueggemann, W.	341n80, 355n159/162		
Buber, M.	280n9, 347n120	Dunn, P.N.	300n13
Bullough, E.	319n4	Dyke, A.	230
Cassuto, U.	243, 330n14, 331n16, 332n23, 336n46, 336n47, 339n66, 347n116, 348n124, 349n132, 352n143/144, 354n152, 357n173	Edwards, M.	308n70
		Ehrenzweig, A.	141, 144, 146, 295n95, 300n13, 305n42, 319n4, 320n4, 343n90
		Eissfeldt, O.	288n58, 294n87-8
		Eslinger, L.	356n166
Charlesworth, J.H.	323n25	Exum, J.C.	40, 50, 289n59, 296

Index of Authors

Exum (cont.) n101-3, 297n105-11, 298n114, 311n85, 312n92, 317n125, 330n11, 323n18, 324n27

Falk, M. 37-40, 66, 78, 106, 109, 159, 204, 294n87-8, 296n101/103, 299n5, 300n11, 301n17/20, 302n23-4, 305n40, 308n68-9, 310n79, 312n94/97, 318n1, 320n5, 322n14, 323n26, 324n27, 325n33, 326n39, 327n48, 333n33, 334n35, 345n102, 353n149

Feliks, Y. 76, 301n17, 302n24, 303n26, 306n50, 306n51/54-5, 310n82, 330n11, 345n102, 353n149

Festinger, B.S. 291n74
Fischel, H.A. 279n6, 280n14, 359n1
Fishbane, M. 187-8, 196, 215, 329n7, 332n22, 336n47, 341n84, 342n86, 343n92, 353n145

Fohrer, G. 294n87
Fokkelman, J. 36, 307n63
Fordham, M. 64, 67, 115, 299n4
Foster, J.L. 285n40, 288n56
Fowler, R. 295n95
Fox, M. 21-4, 284n37, 285n38/40/43, 286n44/47, 299n7, 300n11, 301n15, 303n35, 307n62, 313n98, 333n33

Frazer, J.G. 307n57, 359n2
Freedman, D.N. 19, 283n28, 304n37, 338n60
Freilich, M. 186, 233, 244, 328n4, 343n93, 348n128, 352n140

Fretheim, T.E. 354n155
Freud, S. 73, 221, 299n2, 319n4, 323n23
Friedrich, P. 310n77
Frye, N. 35, 141, 147, 154, 184, 187, 237, 321n8, 329n7, 337n53
Fuerst, W.J. 291n72, 312n95, 324n26

Gardiner, A.H. 340n73
Gaster, T.H. 315n112, 321n10
Gerleman, G. 20, 86, 109, 112,

Gerleman (cont.) 281n22, 282n26, 284n34/37, 289n59, 294n87-8, 299n7, 301n17, 302n22/24/32, 304n35, 306n47/55, 308n65/69, 309n72, 310n80, 311n84, 313n98, 314n108, 315n114, 318n1, 322n17, 323n18-20/26, 325n32/37, 327n44, 331n17, 333n30/32, 334n33/35, 337n51, 338n57, 346n112, 353n149

Gevirtz, S. 294n92
Ginsberg, H.L. 281n24
Giordano-Orsini, G.N. 38, 293n85, 295n93
Goitein, S.D. 28, 50, 68, 279n3, 281n22-3, 284n34, 304n35/39, 318n1
Gollwitzer, H. 30
Good, E.M. 222, 310n80, 339n62, 340n70
Gordis, R. 18, 93, 97, 161, 279n1/3, 282n26, 283n31, 286n49, 288n58, 291n70, 292n76, 294n87-8, 299n7, 300n9, 302n22, 303n26/31/35, 304n39, 306n48, 308n67/69, 309n72-3, 310n80/82/84, 311n89, 312n94, 313n98/100/102, 314n107, 315n114, 318n1, 321n10, 322n17, 323n21/22/26, 324n27/29, 325n37-8, 327n45/49, 333n33, 334n38, 336n44, 337n52, 338n57, 344n101, 345n102, 346n113, 353n147

Gordon, C.H. 42, 281n25, 294n92, 325n34
Gordon, E.I. 346n111
Gordon, R. 299n4, 311n91, 320n4, 343n90
Gottwald, N.K. 290n67, 316n119
Goulder, M.D. 281n25, 291n72, 292n76
Graetz, H. 281n24, 282n26, 288n57
Graves, R. 288n57
Grelot, P. 284n34

Index of Authors

Griaule, M.	307n57	Kikawada, I.M.	351n137, 356n166
Grober, S.F.	326n39	Kirk, G.S.	291n74
Gros-Louis, K.R.R.	187, 328n4, 356n170	Klein, M.	223-4, 343n95
		Köhler, L.H.	309n73, 315n110
Guiraud, P.	295n95	Kramer, S.N.	286n49
Gunn, D.M.	336n46	Krinetzki, L.(=G.)	63-5, 72, 89, 107, 110, 115, 138, 161, 184, 207, 289n59, 291n70/72, 294n87, 297n105, 299n1/6, 300n9/14, 301n18/20, 302n21-3, 303n26-7/33/35, 305n41/44/46, 306n50/52, 308n67-9, 309n72/75, 310n79, 312n94/96-7, 313n101, 315n112/114, 317n126, 318n1, 321n10, 322 n17, 323n18-9/26, 325n37-8, 327n44, 333n33, 338n57, 344 n101, 345n108, 353 n147/149, 354n150, 356n169
Halle, M.	341n79		
Haran, M.	329n5		
Harrison, B.	184, 322n16		
Hauser, A.J.	186, 352n140/144, 354n156, 356n168		
Heilbrun, C.G.	349n133		
Hengel, M.	290n65-8, 291n71, 292n77/79, 293n81-3		
Herion, G.A.	289n58		
Hermann, A.	284n35		
Higgins, J.M.	348n124, 352n140		
Hillers, D.R.	321n13, 327n47, 334 n37		
Horst, F.	322n17		
Hrushovski, B.	295n95		
Isserlin, B.S.J.	282n26, 305n45		
Jabès. E.	62		
Jacobsen, T.	25, 288n56, 329n6		
Jakobson, R.	34-6, 38, 58, 73, 139, 227, 295n95, 298n116, 300n12, 326n42, 341n83	Kris, E.	319n4
		Kugel, J.L.	283n30, 294n91, 295 n92, 309n72, 341n79
		Lambert, W.G.	26, 95, 288n56, 320 n7, 323n24
James, E.O.	210		
Jastrow, Marcus	302n22, 304n37, 331n17	Landsberger, F.	294n87
		Landy, F.	37, 39, 220, 310n79/84, 316n119
Jastrow, Morris	289n59		
Jay, P.	288n57	Leach, E.	186, 328n4, 349n130
Jobling, D.	185, 210, 328n3, 332n27, 336n46-7, 338n56, 339n62, 339 n68, 344n97, 345n103, 355n158, 356n167	Lemaire, A.	346n111
		Levinger, E.	117, 123, 204, 240, 281n17/22, 282n26, 294n87, 296n103, 297n106, 299n6, 302 n22, 303n34, 304 n39, 305n45-6, 306 n48/50-1, 309n73, 310n80/82, 311n88, 314n104, 315n110/114, 316n123, 317 n126, 318n1, 323n20, 324n29, 325n33/37-8, 327n44, 331n17, 333 n32-3, 334n35/38, 337n52, 345n102
Joines, K.	230-2, 342n87		
Jolles, A.	284n37		
Jones, L.	295n95		
Josipovici, G.	326n42, 337n53, 359n4		
Jung, C.G.	230-1, 299n3, 307n57, 319n4, 336n46, 348 n125		
Kane, E.	300n13		
Kawin, B.F.	331n31		
Keefer, M.	344n99		
Keel, O.	130, 196-7, 314n109, 332n22-3, 340n77, 345n107, 358n176	Lévi-Strauss, C.	185-6, 273, 295 n95, 307n57, 328n2, 329n6, 349n130, 359n6
Kerenyi, C.	231		
Kermode, F.	26, 174, 271, 322n16	Lichtheim, M.	24, 285n38/40, 286 n46, 295n94, 312n93,
Kessler, M.	329n7		

Index of Authors

Lichtheim (cont.)	324n32, 327n45, 337 n51, 345n105	Navone, J.	339n64
		Nietzche, F.	146, 320n4
Lieberman, S.	13-4	Ohmann, R.	93
Loretz, O.	294n91	Otwell, J.H.	351n139
Lys, D.	79, 97, 101-2, 117, 123, 160, 163, 184, 195, 209, 257, 279 n3, 281n17-8/25, 291 n70, 294n87-8, 299 n5, 300n9, 301n17, 302n20/22, 303n28-30 /35, 304n39, 305n44, 306n48/50, 307n58-9 /64, 308n69-70, 310 n78/80/82/84, 311 n86/88/90, 312n96- 97, 313n98-9/101, 314n103/107/109, 316n118/121-2, 317 n126-7, 318n2, 321 n12, 323n18/20-1/26, 325n37-8, 327n44, 331n17, 333n30/33, 334n38, 338n57-8, 345n102, 346n111-2, 353n147-9	Page, D.	103
		Parker, J.F.	See Patte & Parker
		Patte, D.	18, 185
		Patte, D. & Parker, J.F.	185-6, 196, 215, 340n71/77, 343n96, 351n138, 352 n144, 354n157, 356 n168, 358n176-7
		Paz, O.	61, 67, 73, 142, 144, 223, 306n53
		Perdue, L.	290n69, 293n80
		Perry, M. & Sternberg, M.	339n67, 347n119, 357n172
		Pfeiffer, R.	294n87-8
		Pitt-Rivers, J.	340n74
		Polzin, R.	328n3, 336n46
		Pope, M.	31, 37, 77, 79, 86, 93, 97, 110, 117, 129, 130-1, 137, 147, 176-8, 279n3, 281n17 /25, 282n27, 283n28 /33, 286n49, 288n57, 290n66, 291n72, 292 n75, 293n80, 299n6-7, 300n9/14, 301n15/17, 302n22, 303n26/28-9/ 31/33/35, 304n37-9, 305n45-7, 306n50/52/ 55, 307n56/64, 308 n65/68-9, 309n72-4/ 76, 310n76/79-80/82 /84, 311n85/88-9, 312n94-5/97, 313n98- 102, 314n106-7, 315 n112/115-6, 317n126- 27, 318n1-2, 320n6, 321n10/12-3, 322n17, 323n21/26, 324n27/31, 325n38, 326n39-40, 327n44/47-8, 331n17- 19, 332n24/28, 333 n32-3, 334n35/37-8, 337n50, 338n57, 339 n63, 344n101, 345 n102/107, 353n49
Maccoby, H.	281n23, 314n105		
Magonet, J.	293n81		
Mangelkern, S.	314n105		
Marx, K.	159		
May, H.G.	129		
McCarthy, J.J.	341n79		
McKane, W.	336n45, 340n71		
McKay, J.W.	322n14, 325n35, 327 n46		
Meek, T.J.	326n39, 345n102		
Meeks, W.A.	349n134		
Mendenhall, G.E.	187, 250		
Merleau-Ponty, M.	344n99		
Miller, B.S.	283n33		
Miller, P.D.	187, 254-5, 352n143- 44, 355n161, 356 n168, 357 n174-5		
Moor, J.C.de	307n61, 320n7		
Muilenberg, J.	38		
Müller, H.P.	20, 25, 27, 29, 62-3, 105, 108, 113, 138, 257, 283n32, 286n48, 310n80/83, 311n87, 354n150		
		Popper, K.	212
Murphy, R.	36-8, 50, 74, 291n72, 249n89, 297n108	Praz, M.	302n25
		Prickett, S.	34
Nachman of Bratslav	270, 281n20	Pritchard, J.B.	200
Napier, B.D.	316n119	Rabin, C.	28, 281n22, 282n26, 283n31, 312n93, 352
Neher, A.	321n11		

Index of Authors

Rabin (cont.)	n142	Scriabine (cont.)	354n153
Rad, G. von	211, 253, 338n54, 340n78, 347n117/121, 348n126, 350n235, 351n139, 352n142, 356n166/171	Seale, M.	283n33
		Segal, H.	143, 343n90
		Segal, M.H.	281n22, 309n75
		Snea, W.H.	40, 50, 296n98-101, 297n112
Raedt, J. de	348n128	Simpson, W.K.	285n40, 295n94
Raine, K.	356n171	Singer, J.	349n133
Reicke, B.	329n6	Skinner, J.	329n6, 354n152, 355 n158
Rickman, J.	319n4		
Ricoeur, P.	187-8, 244, 329n6, 337n49, 349n130	Smith, M.	290n65/69, 293n81
		Soggin, J.A.	210-1, 336n44/47, 343n92
Riffaterre, M.	295n95		
Robert, A. & Tournay, J.-R. 279n3, 283n28, 284n34, 301 n17, 305n47, 306n49, 315n116, 323n19, 339 n63		Soler, J.	349n130
		Soloveitchik, J.B.	187, 352n141
		Soulen, R.N.	89, 300n11
		Speiser, E.A.	330n14, 347n116, 352 n142, 355n165
Ronen, A.	211, 329n6, 343n90	Steck, O.H.	352n142
Rosenzweig, F.	121, 324n28	Sternberg, M.	339n67, 347n119, 357 n172
Rowley, H.H.	18, 286n49, 291n72, 294n87		
		Stokes, A.	64-5, 300n10, 319n4
Rundgren, F.	282n26	Stolz, F.	310n78, 315n114, 332n22
Rudolph, W.	35, 288n58, 289n59, 294n87, 297n105, 299 n7, 301n19, 302n23-4, 303n35, 305n41, 307 n59, 308n65/67/69, 310n79/84, 312n97, 313n98/101-2, 315 n117, 318n1, 321n10, 323n18-20, 330n12, 331n17-8, 333n30/33, 334n35, 338n57/59, 344n101, 346n112, 353n147/149	Stevens, W.	67, 359n4
		Stuart, D.K.	341n79/84
		Stuart, S.	320n4
		Thompson, P.E.S.	331n16
		Thompson, T.L.	290n67
		Thubron, C.	335n39
		Tournay, J.-R.	294n87, 334n33 See also Robert & Tournay
		Trible, P.	66, 172, 184-7, 200, 213, 243, 246-7, 249, 338n54, 339n62 /65-6/68, 340n74/76, 341n78/82, 343n96, 344n100, 346n109, 347n115/120, 348n126, 349n134, 350n135-6, 351n139, 352n140, 353n144/146-7, 354 n154/156, 355n163, 356n167
Sadgrove, M.	316n124		
Salzberger-Wittenberg, I. 143			
Sandars, N.K.	331n20		
Sasson, J.M.	25		
Sawyer, J.F.A.	356n171, 357n174		
Schedl, C.	28-9, 310n80		
Schmidt, N.	31, 186n49		
Scholem, G.	13, 279n4, 281n16/ 19, 359n1		
		Trudinger, L.P.	330n15
Schoville, K.N.	165, 281n25, 283 n29, 294n91-2, 303 n31, 304n35, 306n55, 309n76, 310n84, 311 n89, 314n104, 320n6, 322n14, 325n34, 338 n60, 354n150	Tsevat, M.	211, 335n42, 336n43
		Tur Sinai, H.	161, 282n26, 286n49, 289n63, 317n126, 323 n22/26, 324n27/31, 325n37, 335n33
		Urbach, E.E.	279n6, 280n7/15
		Vawter, B.	211, 260, 336n44-5/ 47, 339n66, 342n85, 350n135, 352n140, 354n152
Scriabine, M.	185, 237, 260, 339 n66, 340n75/77, 345 n104, 347n117/121,		

Index of Authors

Waldman, N.M. 307n64
Walsh, J.T. 186, 244, 254-5, 332 n23, 338n55, 339n68, 341n78-9/81, 347n116-17, 348n122, 352n140/143-4, 354n156, 355n163, 356n167, 358n177
Weir, R. 341n83
Wertheimer, S.A. 280n15
Webster, E. 40, 291n72, 324n26
Westenholz, J. & A. 25, 37, 286n50, 287n51, 289n59
Westermann, C. 187, 215, 222, 242, 253, 332n21, 335n41, 338n54, 340n78, 342n85/88, 347n116-7/121, 350n135, 351n137, 353n145, 354n152, 355n160/163-5, 356n166/171
Wetzstein, J.G. 291n72
White, H.C. 185-6, 210, 338n56, 339n67, 340n69/71, 341n78, 342n88, 344n97, 347n117-8, 348n123, 352n140, 354n155
White, J.B. 22-2, 31, 38, 283n29/34, 284n35-7, 285n38-9/43, 289n59, 291n70/73, 294n87-8/91, 299n7, 303n32/35, 309n72, 311n85, 313n101, 324n32, 325n37, 337n51, 353n149
Widengren, G. 282n26
Williams, A.J. 186, 230, 254, 328n3, 329n5, 335n41, 339n62, 342n85/87, 343n96, 352n143, 355n158/165, 356n167
Williams, J.G. 153, 292n78, 322n16, 328n3, 336n47, 344n97
Winandy, J. 300n8
Winnett, F.V. 329n5
Winnicott, D.W. 320n4
Winton-Thomas, D. 314n106
Witterkindt, W. 282n26, 301n17, 344n101
Wittgenstein, L. 141, 233, 344n99
Wollheim, R. 319n4
Würthwein, E. 291n72
Wyatt, N. 329n5, 330n8/14, 343n92, 348n129
Young, D.B. 334n42
Zakovitch, Y. 289n60, 297n106, 316n123, 317n126, 346n112/114

INDEX OF SUBJECTS

[* = principal discussions]

Abel	251, 353n145	Androgyny (see also Hermaphrodite)	
Adam	188, 206, 209, 219, 226, 227, 228, 235, 242, 243, 246, 253, 261, 332n25, 340 n75/77, 341n78, 343 n94, 350n137, 352 n140/141, 355n162		63, 73-92, 112, 119, 195, 239, 246-48, 260, 273, 349 n132/133, 350n134
		Anemone	301n17
		Angels	357n171/174
Adam & Eve, Life of	279n3	Animals/Fauna	184, 186, 188, 219, 221, 226, 233-4, *235, 236-41, 242, 254, 257, 261, 264, 284n37, 339n66, 340 n68, 341n78, 343n96, 344n97/100, 349n130, 350n137/138
Adam Kadmon	273		
Adonis	309n76		
Aesop	346n111		
Ahasuerus	32, 202, 290n68		
Akiba, Rabbi	13, 14, 15, 16, 17, 18, 28, 269-70, 271, 279/3, 4, 5, 6, 280 n7, 346n111, 359n1		
		Animus/Anima	63, 68, 230, 348n125
Akkadian	282n26	Anthropomorphism	260
Alienation, Concept of	159, 185, 186, 342n88	Aphasia	341n83
		Aphrodite	309n76, 310n77, 345 n107
Allegorical Interpretation	13, 14, 16, 203, 294n87, 296n97, 305n47, 313 n101	Apollonian/Apollo	145, 157, 162, 164, 174, 179, 191, 319-20n4
Allegorical Place Names	154	Apple	39, 50, 52-5, 81, 83-7, 90, 92, 116, 118, *119, 120-1, 213-4, 216-8, 264, 303-4n24, 313n101, 354n149
Alliteration, discussion of	93-96, 103, 112, 125, 128-9, 131, 138, 169, 175, 271, 282 n26, 301n18, 302n22, 305n46, 310n81		
		Arcadia	26
Alabaster	224	Archetype	62-4, *65-7, 202, 204, 273, 284n37, 319n4, 332n25
Alexandria	32, 288n57		
Alphabet, Letters of	280n15	Aristotle	35, 293n79, 294n86
Altar	127, 306n49	Asherah	309n76
Amana	309n74	Ashkenazi Jews	292n76, 316n120
Ambiguity	35, 139-40, 142, 170, 171-2, 222, 244, 245, 262, 269, 273, 274, 316n119, 317n126, 319n4, 320 n6, 333n30, 337n47, 338n56, 340n71, 342 n87/88, 348n127, 350n135, 351n138	Assyria	196, 288n56
		Astrology	159, 323n25
		Atra-Ḥasis Epic	351n137, 356n166
		Baal	123, 302n20, 343n92
		Baal-Hamon	153-5, 206, 322n17, 323n19
		Babylon	289n62
		Bahrein	330n14
Amminadib	334n34	Balcony	302n22
Amnon	307n63	Banner	216, 318n1
Amplification	64	Bathsheba (see also David)	120
Anat	95, 138, 147, 307 n61, 381n1, 320n7	Beauty	30, 112, *137-42, 143-5, 147-8, 150-3, 157-8, 161-2, 165-6,

[400]

Index of Subjects

	169, 172-9, 188, 191, 193, 210, 230-2, 235-6, 238, 241, 243, 258, 263-4, 270, 274, 318n1, 320 n4/5/7	Chaos	129-30, 132, 230-31, 233, 238, 264, 269, 316n122
		Character	61, 67-73, 264, 323 n23, 340n69, 347n119
Belly	89, 224	Chariot (see also Horse/Mare) 327 n44, 334n34	
Beloved, as Observer	68-72	Cheeks	302, 22
Bezalel	280n15	Cherubim	262-3, 271, 341n77, 358n176
Birth	53, 58, 115, 119-21, 124, 150-51, 205, 208, 214, 216-7, 219, 223, 230-1, *252-3, 354n151	Chiasmus, as a Structural Principle 40, 42, *44-7, 108, 131, 199-201, 207, 227, 296, n98/99/101, 309n72, 330n11, 339n68	
Black Madonna	138, 147	Child	64, 67, 90, 164-5, 190, 202, 216, 231, 237, 243, 245, 320n4
Blessing	257, 262, 353n147		
Blindness	359n3		
Bolt, Screw	334n35		
Bone	341n80	Chiromancy	305n42
Borges, Jorge Luis	322n16	Cinnamon	330n11
Bowl	224	City	46, 88, 116, 120-1, 124, 144-5, 147-9, 162, 165, 169, 174, 178, 207-9, 274, 288 n58, 335n39
Brahmin Philosophy	293n79		
Breast(s)	45, 48, 54, 64, *74-78, 81-5, 91, 93, 100-1, 111, 114-6, 160, 162, 164, 237, 239, 300n10, 301n14/ 16, 303n34, 307n56, 312n94		
		Clearchus	293n79
		Cliché	295n92
		Climax	*44-5, *51-2, 58, 269, 273, 296n100
Breathing/Breath	84-7, 92, 256, 262-3, 265, 303n33, 340n75	Cloak (kuttōnet)	254
		Clothes	91-2, 107, 112, 226, 253-4, 306n53, 355 n157
"Bricolage"	289n61		
Brother	97, 99-100, 110, 114, 116, 308n66	Collective Unconscious 299n4	
		Comedy	147
Brothers	149, 151, 160-1, 250, 321n12, 324n27/30	Conception	115-6, 312n96
		Condescension, By Lover 70	
		Conjunction of Opposites 64	
Burning Bush, The	127, 357n174	Constellations/Stars	151, 159, 258, 318n1
Cain	251, 257, 353n145, 356n166		
		Contempt	141, 143-4, 147-8, 174, 264
Carmel	88, 89, 306n48		
Cassia	330n11	Corn/Wheat	96, 225, 306n51
Castration Fantasy	70, 177	Cosmic Mountain	196, 332n22
Catharsis	45	Crocodile	285n40/41, 314n109
Cedars	54, 81, 90-1, 161-4, 213, 315n114, 324 n29, 332n22	Cultic Interpretation 286n49	
		Culture	88, 120, 127, 187-8, 190-1, 193, 201, 208, 222, 226, 231, 235, 254, 264, 329n6
Centre	*36, *51, 56, 58, 111, 133, 186, 206, 210, 212, 221, 243, 250, 252, 263, 269, 273, 289n61, 337n48, 358n177		
		Curse (in Genesis) 249-50, 255-7, 265, 351n139, 352 n141/144, 353n147, 355n160/163	
Ceylon	20		

[401]

Index of Subjects

Cynicism 32, 291n71
Cypresses 54, 213
Dance/Ritual Courtship 57
Darkness 130, 143-6, 149, 158, 165, 179, 209, 224, 265, 274, 320n7
Date of Song 18ff, 27ff, 37
Dates (Palm, Fruit) 25, 39, 48, 54, 74, *82, 83-5, 90, 119, 213
Daughters of Jerusalem/Zion 55, 57, 91, 124, 143-7, 149-52, 154-58, 164, 166, 174, 179, 204, 207, 215-6, 226, 296n99, 297n106, 298n113/114, 320n5, 321n12, 333n29, 335n34, 338n58, 339n63, 345n102
David 153, 305n44, 324n31, 356n170
David and Bathsheba 339n67, 347n119
Dawn/Dawn Star/Šāḥar 165, 285n39, 322n14, 325n35, 338n60
Day 209
Dead Sea 82, 303n27
Death 58, 110, 112-5, 118, 120-1, *123, 124-28, 130-2, 142, 146-7, 158, 186, 191-2, 194, 198, 209, 211-13, 218-9, 229, 232, 236, 238-9, 241, 255-6, 258, 262, 265, 269, 273-4, 309n75, 311-12n91, 336n42, 337n47, 343n90, 354n151, 355n163
Deconstruction 33, 295n95
Deictics 185
Delphic Oracle 231
Desert 88, 118, 120-1, 147-48, 150, 178, 214, 216-7, 219, 238, 275, 307n62
Despair 117, 125, 199
Dew 198, 331n16
Diaspora 29, 289n62
Dilmun, Land of 330n14
Dionysiac/Dionysus 120, *145, 146-9, 151, 157-9, 162, 164-5, 173-9, 191, 193, 205, 230-31, 235, 239, 245, 251, 264, 274, 319n4
Divine Court/Assembly 261-2, 357n174
Diving/Divers 286n43/45
Dogon 307n57
Donne, John 21
Door 160ff. 325n32
"Double" (Doppelganger) 93
Dove/Turtledove 39, 42-3, 70-2, 150, 179, 237, *238-39, 245, 250, 258, 265, 296n102, 327n44, 345n106/107/108
Drama, Interpretation as 294n87, 323n18
Dumuzi/Tammuz 25, 97, 286n49, 326n40
Dust 255-8, 355n162/163
Eagle 342n91
Earth/Earth Mother 88, 119, 145-46, 176, 197, 200, 246-7, 252-3, *254-56, 257, 262-3, 265, 270, 350n136, 351n137, 356n167/168, 358n176
Ecclesiastes 15, 18, 20, 29-32, 125, 212, 279n2, 280n13, 282n27, 291n70, 292n77/78, 299n6, 336n45
'Ed (Mist, Flood) 194, 196, 330n15/16, 358n176
Ego 67, 108, 123, 127, 179
 Altera Ego 164
Egyptian Art 284n34
Egyptian Dialogue on Death 113
Egyptian, Love Lyrics *20-24, 38, 97, 284-6n34-47, 295n94, 296-97n104, 308n69, 312n93/96, 317n124, 324n32, 327n45, 332n20, 337n51, 345n105
 Chester-Beatty Papyrus 1a 21, 23-4, 38, 285n39, 296-7n104, 308n66, 312n96, 324n32, 334n34, 337n51
 Chester-Beatty Papyrus 1b 327n45, 345n105

[402]

Index of Subjects

Cairo Obtracon Love Songs 21-3, 38, 285n37/40-43, 286n44-5, 312n93
Papyrus Harris 500 24, 38, 284n37, 285n38, 324n32, 337n51
Ein Gedi 290n66, 303n26
El 343n92
Elijah 345n108
Elisha ben Abuya 17
Enigma 140-41, 148, 152-3, 157, 160, 167-9, 174, 178, 224, 237, 263, 274
Enki 356n166
Enkidu 329n6
Enuma Elish 331n15
Envy 143-4, 148, 150, 157, 174, 225, 234, 237, 240, 264, 275, 320n6, 343n95/96
"Evil Eye" 320n5
Epicureanism 32, 291n71, 359n1
Equator, the 330n14
Eridu Genesis, the 329n6
Eschatology 289n62
Esther 32, 202, 279n12, 282n27, 290n68, 292n77
Etana, Myth of 343n91
Ethiopic Dynasty 327n44
Eunuchs 155
Euphrates 195, 330n14
Eve 188, 219, 229, *241-45, 247, *248-49, 253, 255, 257, 261, 265, 336n42, 342n85, 345n104, 347n119, 351n137, 352n140/141, 354n156, 356n166
Evening Star, Shalem 165-66, 325n34, 338n60
Excretion/Anal Character 146, 158; 323n23
Exile 19, 271
Eye/Eyes 89, 132, *165-66, 178-9, 191, 222-3, 239, 253, 258, 270, 284n34
Fable 346n111
Faience 307n60, 320n7
Fate 159
Father 66, 83, 119, 251-2, 255

Fawn/Gazelle 25, 39, 42-3, 52, 69, 72-4, 76-7, 82, 84, 89, 92, 96, 111-12, 117, 202-3, 216-18, 236, *237-39, 256, 259, 265, 271, 300n9, 301n16, 306n55, 307n56, 333n30, 344, 345n101/102/105
Feminism, Feminist critics 184, 243, 246, 299n5, 348n124/125, 349n133
Fifteenth Ab, Dances of 31
Fig Tree 213
Fig Leaves 223, 254, 354n157
Fire 58, 121, 123, *126-28, 129, 131-2, 233, 256-8, 262-3, 265, 269, 270, 314n106, 315n112/113, 316n118
Flesh 341n80
Flood Narrative, the 345n108
Flowers *193, 202-4, 209, 296n102, 346n111
Folk Poetry, Song as 289n59
Forest 54, 116, 121
Form-Criticism 285n37, 291n72, 328n3
Foxes 48-9, *240-1, 265, 346n110/111/113/114, 347n115
Frankincense 112, 312n93
Fruit 191-2, 209, 232, 248
Funeral Feasts, (see also Marzēaḥ) 292n75, 312n95
Gal-Ed/Yagur-Sahadutha 351n139, Rabban Gamaliel 13
Game-Theory 328n4
Garden, Metaphor of 51, 55/7, 70-1, 80, 102-111, 114, 116, 133, 156, 179, 183, *189-210, 213, 215-9, 221, 225, 238-9, 240, 243, 251, 253, 255, 262-4, 269-70, 273, 290n68, 308n71, 310n79/84, 333n29
Garden of Eden 51, 98, 178, 183-84, 187-89, *190-91, 192, *193-210, 202, 205, 210, 212, 216-20, 226, 228-9, 233, 239, 240, 248, 257, 260, 264, 271, 274-

[403]

Index of Subjects

	75, 330n14, 331n20, 332n22, 339n61, 343n90, 358n176	Hathor	22/3, 285n42, 312n93, 322n15
Garden of the Gods	331n20	Hatshepsut	281n23
Gematria	29	Havilah	195, 332n20
Genealogy	332n21	Head	224
"The Gentry", Theory of	293n81	Heart	58, 98, 103-4, 109, 122-3, *124, 126, 132, 205, 217, 271, 286n43, 307n64
Geshtinanna	97, 326n40		
Gihon	195, 330n14	Hecataeus	293n79
Gilgamesh, Epic of	309n78, 329n6, 331n20, 332n22	Hekhalot Literature	279n4, 359n1
		Hellenism	19, 28-30, 32-3, 283n31
Gita Govinda, the	283n33		
Gnostics, the	345n103	Henna, Camphire, Cypress	53-4, *82-3, 84, 90, 282n26, 303n28, 330n11
God	14, 17, 21, 32-3, 58, 121, *127/28, 129-32, 178, 186, 188, 190, 198-99, 201, 205, 212-13, 215, 219, 221, 226-27, 231-37, 242, 244, 246, 248, 250, 252-5, *256-62, 263-5, 269-70, 272-75, 314n106/107, 315n114/116/117, 316n119, 336n46, 337n47/48, 338n54, 340n75/77, 343n92, 344n97/101, 348n123/126/127/129, 350n135/136, 352n140, 354n155/157, 356n166/167/170, 357n171/173/174/175, 358n176/177	Hermaphrodite (see also Androgyny	320n4
		Hermon	309n74
		Heshbon	88, 283n28
		Hezekiah	345n106
		Hillel, School of	15, 280n11/13
		Hittite	287n53
		Holy of Holies	13, 16-17, 271
		Honey	25, 79, 104, 109, 192, 302n20
		Horon	336n43
		Horse/Mare	50, *176-77, 239, 241, 250, 284n37, 327n44/45/46, 336n43
		House, Mother's	52, 55, 110, 114-6, 118-9, 208, 250, 353n146
		Houses, Lovers'	54, 91, 116, 213
Gold	177, 224, 331n20	Houyhnhnms	221
Golden Age, the	138, 355n158	Humbaba	332n22
Gongoresque Poetry, Spanish	142	Hyperbole	103, 127, 159
Good News Bible	34	Id/Edda, Ida	331n16
Grass	201, 257, 330n15, 358n176	Idealisation, by Lover	69-70
		of Pastoral	145
Great Synagogue, Men of the	279n2	of Nomads	147
Greek		Immortality	188, 210, 212-14, 218-19, 230, 261-2, 264, 273, 358n177
Anthology	18		
Hegemony	19		
Loan Words	18-9, 282n26	Impurity	279n1
Songs	17	Inanna	287n54
Education	29	Incestuous Imagery	97ff., 149, 163, 186, 225, 273, 307n64, 349n130
Observers	32, 292n79		
(See also Hellenism)			
Hair	83, 89, 239, 306n50	India	29, 283n31
Hamlet	244	Individuation	64, 319n4
Hassidic Masters	17, 281n20, 341n83	Innocence	146-9, 151, 157, 174, 187, 202-3,

[404]

Index of Subjects

	235, 239, 242-3, 245, 249, 251, 275, 347n119	Ketubim (the Writings)	16, 279-2, 291n70
Integration	73, 148, 186, 226, 265, 271-2, 274	Kids	173-4, 326n40
Intentional Fallacy, the	183	King	25, 69, 70-71, 89, 92, 98, 102, 127, 145, 148, 150, 154-56, 165, 177-8, 202, 204, 206, 209, 226, 238-9, 251, 284n37, 327n49, 355n162
Iranian (see Persian)			
Iron Age	290n67		
Irrigation Canals, Systems	198, 201, 290n67, 310n82, 331n17		
Ishtar	95, 138, 147, 197, 287n51, 345n107	Kingdom	88, 92, 98, 102, 120, 127, 148, 154-56, 165, 206, 251
Israel	17-18, 20, 29, 127, 154, 159, 269, 305 n44, 316n119, 332n25, 352n140,	King Lear	142
		Kiss	79-81, 84, 91, 99, 103, 114-15, 297 n111, 301n19, 303 n31/32/33, 304n39
Israel, Land of	67, 88-9, 102, 256, 306n49, 323n19		
Israelites	228, 290n67, 330n15	Knowledge	142, 188, 210-14, 216-19, 223, 225, 231-33, 257, 261-62, 264, 274, 336 n42/44/45/46, 337 n48, 342n84, 345 n103, 347n120
Israel, Northern Kingdom	329n5		
Ivory	224, 335n38		
Jackal	284n37		
Jaguar	233		
Janus-parallelism	42-43		
Jealousy	*125, 126, 128, 149, 163, 234, 314n106/ 107/108, 315n110, 343n95	Koan	215
		Kush	195, 332n20
		Language	15, 190, 226-27, 232, 247, 264, 272-73, 281n16, 342n84, 345 n104, 347n117
Jerusalem	29, 32, 88, 139, 145, 174, 219, 258, 282n28, 290n65, 232 n19, 339n63		
		Language, of Song	139-40, 178, 263, 270-71
Jesus	292n78, 322n16	Language of Job	293n80
Jewellery, Precious Stones	174, 254, 331n20	Law	166-7, 225
		Leather	335n38
Jewish Mother	250	Lebanon	86, *90-92, 102-107, 109-10, 112, 114, 120, 195-6, 239, 269, 273, 305n41, 309n72/ 76, 310n78/84, 331 n19, 332n22
Jews	282n28, 289n62, 292-93n79		
Job	32, 113, 212, 279-2, 290n70, 292n77, 298 n112, 336n45		
		Levites	293n81/82
R. Johanan ben Zakkai	346n111	Light	270
Jonah	292n77, 293n81	Lily, Lilies	39, 42/3, 78, 80, *81-83, 89, 92, 96, 193, 202-4, 225, 237, 251, 301n17, 302n24, 306n51
Judea	290n65		
Jungian Psychology	64, 67, 230, 299n2		
Kabbalah	13, 16, 29, 31, 138, 258, 281n16, 292n76, 333n28, 336n46		
		Lions and Leopards	103, 110, 113, 192, 239-41, 309n76, 346n109
Kafka, Franz	322n16		
Kalba Sabua	279n6		
Kali	138, 147	Lion	270
Keats, John	113	Lips	78, 81, 87, 91-2, *95-6, 302n21, 304
Kedar	147-8, 192, 219, 238		

[405]

Index of Subjects

	n39, 307n59
Literary Criteria for Dating	19
Lotus	301n17
Love-magic, Incantations	286n49, 307n64, 345n101
Love Sickness	85, 214, 216-17, 337 n51
Lover, as Character	69-72, 250
Lyric, the	*35-6, *63, *67-8, 138-9, 263-4
Magic Mushrooms	288n57
Malebolgia, Dante's	230
Mami	351n138, 356n166
Mandala	196
Mandrakes	53-4
Mantle (redid)	226
"Many Waters"	*129-31
Marble, Place of, Stones of	269-70
Marginal Systems	343n93
Mari	196
Marriage	115, 158, 163, 166, 249, 324n31
Marriage Week Theory	291n72, 295 n96
Marzēah Feasts (see also Funeral)	31, 313n98
Matrilochy	312n96
Megasthenes	293n79
R. Meir	346n111
Merkabah Mysticism	279n4, 281n19
Mesopotanium Poetry	20, *24-6, 211, 286/8n49/56, 307n64
Sacred Marriage Hymns	25
Divine Love Lyrics	25-6, 96, 288n56, 320n7
MAD V.8	25, 286-7n50/2
The Message of Ludingira to His Mother	25-6, 287-8, 53-55
Messiah, the	280n6
Metalwork	188
Metamorphosis	230, 237
Metaphor	35, 56, 62, 75, 98, 104, 111, 115, 129, 139, 140, 153, 157, 160, 167, 176, 178, 183, 190-1, 205, 207, 211, 222, 224, 228, 236, 241, 257, 260-4, 269-70, 273, 284n37, 289n61, 305 n47, 307n62, 309n76, 311n86, 333n29, 342 n84, 344n100
Metonymy	62, 76, 82, 104, 113, 120, 148, 162, 176, 191, 222-4, 354n155
Midwife	253
Milk	79, 83, 92, 101, 104, 192, 302n20
Mirror	270, 359n2
Mistress of the Mountains	103, 309n76
Moon	151, 159, 258, 293 n80, 327n46
Moses	14, 279n5, 293n79
Mot	123
Mother	19, 53, 63-4, *65-7, 77, 83-4, 91-2, 99-100, 107, 109-12, 118-20, 126-7, 133, 138, 146, 151, 208, 214, 216-17, 229, 239, 245, 247-8, 250-56, 264-5, 272-73, 287n52, 298n114, 300n10, 302n21, 309 n75, 310n79, 315n112, 338n58, 350n137/138/ 139, 355n156
Mountains of Spices	271
Mouse	285n41
Mouth	79, 307n62
Murex	88, 307n61
The Muse	15, 270-1, 273
Music	188, 281n20
Mycenaean	282n26
Myrrh	54, 78-80, 83-4, 303n29/30, 332n20
Mystery	141, *142, 212, 228, 231, 238, 260, 271, 274
Myth-and-Ritual School	291-2n74
Nachman of Bratslav	281n20
Nadab and Abihu	329n6
Nahum of Gimzu, Akiba's teacher	279n5
Nakedness	212, 219-26, 231, 235-6, 241, 253, 257, 264, 354n156
Narcissism	62, 67, 342n88
Nard	281n25
Nathan's Parable	153, 322n16
Navel	306n52
Neanderthals	343n90
Neck	55, *87
Necklace	55, 98-9, 305n45, 308n65
Negev	290n67

Index of Subjects

Negresses 320n5
Nehemiah 290n65
New Critics 295n93/95
New Year Festival 295n96
Night 208, 239
Nineveh 315n114
Nipples 76, 83, 303n31
Nirvana 113
Non-sequitur 242
Nose 75, 84, *85-7, 90, 300n13, 303n31/32/33 (see also Kiss), 305 n40/42/43
Numerical Symbolism 290n64
Nuts, Nut Garden 191, 202, 281-2 n25, 332n28
Oak of the Teacher, at Shechem 349n129
Oceanic Feeling, Freud's Concept 73, 166, 342n88
Oil 297n111, 302n20
Oniads 289n62, 290n69
Onomastica 227
Onomatopoiea 129
Organic Unity 34-5, 58, 295n93
Orgasm 132, 252, 354n151
Orphic poetry 29, 187
Othello 126
Oxymoron 97
Pack (paḥad?) 334n37
Paedophilia 302n21
Pain 252-3, 255, 253n144
Palace 148
Palanquin 58, 70, 91, 118, 120, 124, 207-9, 213-14, 219, 282n26, 300n8, 335n38
Palestinian, Modern Love Poetry 283n33
Parable 153-4, 157, 270-71, 315n114, 322n15
Paradigm *39, *51, 189, 190, 193, 206-7, 209, 233, 238, 284n37
Paradise 33, 100, 111, 184, 202, 206, 214, 216, 219, 237-39, 241, 252, 264, 269/70, 272, 339n64,
Pardēs, Paradeisoi 16, 18, 29, 281n25, 282n26, 290 n68, 330n10
Parallelism 227, 283n29/30, 294 n91, 302n20, 314 n104, 321n10

Pargod or Divine Veil 279n5
"Parole Originaire" 289n61
Parthenogenesis 354n152
Passover 31, 292n76
Pastoral 25, *26-7, 28-33, 49, 76, 96, 113, 144-5, 147, 149, 157, 171, 174-6, 179, 190, 239, 241, 275, 288n57, 289n58, 293n84, 326n41, 334 n36
Pathetic Fallacy 62, 226
Pentecost 292n76
Pereq Shirah 281n19
Persia(n), Iranian 18-20, 27, 281-2n25/26, 289 n62, 290n66/68
Personal Pronouns 341n83
Pharaoh 130, 176
Pharisees 290n69, 293n82
Philosophers, Philosophy 289n61, 293n79/82, 344n99
Phoenicia 282n27
Phylacteries 313n102
Pishon 195, 330n14
Plants/Flora 184, 186, 354n157
Plato 30, 34, 212
Poet, as Character 62, 66-7, 109, 112, 121, 127, 139, 154, 175, 207, 259, 270-71, 299n5, 325n37, 326n40
Poetic Function 34
Poetic Unity 33/40 et seq.
Poirot, Hercule 323n22
Pomegranates (see also "Paradise") 96, 100, 115, 201-2, 213, 258, 308n68
Pre-Islamic Love Poetry 283n33
Primeval History, the 329n6, 349 n130, 357n175
Prince Mehy 334n34
Projection, Mechanism of 90, 273
Prophets, the (Nebi'im) 16
Prophetic Writings 131, 187, 235, 259, 282n27, 329n7
Proverbs 32, 279/2, 284n35, 291n70, 292n77/78, 298n112, 302n20
Psalms 17, 281n19, 293n81
Psychoanalysis 272
Ptolemies 290n66, 307n63
"Puer Aeternus" 302n21
Pughat 307n61

[407]

Index of Subjects

Puns	142, *220-22, 223, 226, 229, 264, 307n62, 308n66, 321n12, 339n65/66, 342n85	Samaritans	283n28
		Samson's Riddle	347n114
		Sandals	254
		Sanskrit	281n25, 282n26, 283n33
Punt, Land of	112, 312n93, 332n20	Sapphires	224-5, 340n73
Purity	146/7, 149, 158, 239, 245	Sappho	33, 103, 310n77
		Scarlet	*95, 96, 307n59
Purple (’argāmān)	282n25	Schadenfreude	234
Qadesh, Prince of	327n48	Sea	88, 130-1
Qidron Valley (Wadi El-Joz)	333n29	Seal	58, 122-3, 272, 284n37, 313n102, 314n103
Queen of Heaven	337n50		
Queen of Sheba	281n23	Self	64-5, 196, 201, 270, 272
Rachel, Akiba's wife	279n6		
Rain	194-5, 197-8, 201, 209-10, 257, 261-2, 330n15, 338n55, 358n176	Senir	309n74
		Sephardi Jews	292n76
		Sequence, as Structural Element 35, 51, 57, 74	
Raisin Cakes	214, 216, 337n50	Serpent	178, 183, 186, 188-89, 210-11, 215, 221, *229-36, 237-45, 250, 255, 261, 264-5, 275, 336n42/43, 338n55/56, 339n66, 340n71/77, 342n85/86/87/88, 343n91/92, 344n96, 347n116/117, 348n121/123/124, 349n129, 352n140, 353n144/145, 354n154, 355n163
Rape, Fantasies of	240		
Raven	239, 345n108		
Re	22		
Rechabites	147		
Regression	73, 115, 175, 248, 252, 319n4, 326n42, 341n83		
Relative Particles	282-3n27		
Renaissance Poetry	37-8		
Renaissance Art	300n10		
Repetition, as Structural Element 36-8, 46-8, 93, 122, 170, 297n106/7		Servant	284n37
		Shame	116-17, 169, 208, *222-3, 224-6, 253-54, 263-4, 340n69/74, 342n88, 354n155
Repression	97, 124, 141, 143, 145-7, 158, 167, 172, 208, 225, 263, 274, 319n4		
		Shammai	280n12
Resheph, rešāpîm	315n112	Shammai, School of	15, 280n11/13
Rhetorical Criticism	184-6	Sheep	94, 170-1, 173-4, 241, 333n30
Rhyming Slang	345n101		
Rib or "Side" (ṣēlāʿ)	247, 350n135, 336	Shekhinah	17, 138, 306n49
		Sheol, Underworld	121, *125-6, 128-9, 131-2, 211, 257, 314n107/109, 315n111/112, 333n28
Rift Valley	219		
"Rivers"	129/31		
Rivers of Eden, the	194-6, 198, 331n20, 332n22/23/24	Shepherd, Shepherdess	25, 94, 170-71, 173-4, 274, 284n37, 325n37, 326n40/41, 333n30
River	48		
Romantics	289n59, 303n25		
Ruth	32, 292n77	Shifters	228, 341n83
Sabbath, the	31, 188	Shiur Qomah	13, 279n4
Sadism	238	Siddhartha	113
Saffron (Karkom)	83, 281n25, 330n11	Sight, Sense of	86, 162, 173, 258, 270, 296n102
Sages, the	284n35		
Salmah	321n10	Silver	155-6, 158-67, 173, 177, 274, 323n24
Samaria	282n28		

Index of Subjects

Simile	35, 99-100, 147, 308 n67/70, 322n16
Sin	188, 339n61, 347n119, 353n147
Sirens, the	130
Sister	55, 67, 70, 97-9, 101, 110-11, 116, 225, 309n79, 312n92, 324n26, 345n105
Little Sister	49, 160-8, 177, 198, 247
Sisters	160, 324n27
Sky	257, 262
Sleep	85-6, 115, 119, 171, 173, 252, 304n37/38/39, 354n152
Smell, Sense of	86, 89-90, 162, 258
Snow	195, 305n41
Socrates	344n99
Solomon	14, 18-19, 26, 28-30, 51, 91, 118, 120, 124, 126-7, 147-8, 153-6, 159, 163, 209, 219, 238, 250-1, 281n17/23, 282n26, 283n31, 290 n68/70, 299n5, 321 n10, 323n18/22, 339 n63
Solomonic Enlightenment	281n22
South American Myths	232-3, 349 n130, 359n6
Southern Arabia	312n93
Spain	284n33
Speech	95-6, 120
Spice-cones (Egyptian apparel)	302n22
Spices	82-3, *192-3, 203
Spring (Season)	42, 53, 55, 57, 119-20, 139, 190, 192-3, 195, 205-7, 210, 238, 256, 265, 331n79, 346n111
Spring (of Water)	*105-6, 107, 109, 122, 132, 192, 194-5, 197, 201, 205-6, 216, 237, 269-70, 310n79/80/ 84, 331n17
Stoicism	32, 291n71
Structuralism	183, 185-6, 221, 246
Subordination of Woman	69-70
Subtlety	220-29, 231, 236, 242, 253, 264
Suckling, Lactation	53, 75-80, 92, 99, 104, 107, 116, 191, 248, 273
Suen, Father of Ishtar	287n51
Sugar, Sweetness	79, 83, 191, 243
Sweettalk	326n42
Sumerian	287n53, 346n111, 350 n135
Sun	142, 147-51, 159, 169, 173, 198, 213, 258, 321n12/13, 327 n46
Surrealism	30
Sword, Twisting	262
Synaesthesia	285n38
Synecdoche	74, 75, 164
Syntax, Discussion of	151-2, 167-9
Tablets of Stones, Shattered	17
Taggim or Tittles	279n5
Tamar (Gen.)	326n39
(II Sam.)	307n63
Tamarisk	336n42
Tamil Poetry	28, 283n31
Tapir	233
Tavern (House of Wine)	116, 313 n98, 338n57
Teeth	94
Second Temple	19, 290n69, 293n82, 359n5
Temple, Solomon's	127, 170, 359n5
Ten Commandments, the	281n15, 338 n54
Terror	137-8, 144, 147, 151, 159, 176-7, 274, 318n1
Theocritus' Idylls	26-7, 144, 288 n57, 316n117
Theophrastus	281n25, 293n79
Thighs	224, 258-9
Thorns	257
Tigris	195, 330n14
Tikkun, Kabbalistic Concept of	281n20
Tilapia Fish	22, 285-6n43
Tinneius Rufus, (Roman Governor)	280n6
Tirzah	18, 89, 139, 145, 174, 258, 283n28
Tobiads	289n62, 290n68
Tongue	91
Topoi, of Egyptian Love Poetry	284n36, 302n22
Torah	14-19, 32, 279n5, 280 n9, 338n61, 348n126
Towers	*74-5, *87, 88-9, 96

Index of Subjects

Trauma 186
Tree, Metaphor of 183, 188-92, 199, 201, 205, *210-19, 243-4, 252-3, 255, 263-4, 335n40/41-42, 349n129, 353 n144, 354n157, 358 n177
Tree of Life 210-11, 214, 218-9, 252, 254, 256, 262-4, 335n41, 337n48
Tree of Knowledge 211-16, 218-9, 221, 235, 237, 242-43, 256, 264, 335n41/42, 337n48, 338, 339 n61, 348n121
Turret (ṭîrâ) 323-4n26
Twins 66, 92-4, 99, 101, 119, 124, 273, 307n57
Ugarit 18, 37, 123, 282n25, 287n53, 302n20, 310 n78, 314n104, 321n13, 323n20, 335n38, 336 n46
  Baal-Anat Cycle 302n20
  Aqhat 302n61
  Rpum texts 310n78
  UT607 RS24 244, 336n42
Ugliness 141-2, 144, 174
Umbilical Cord 354n149
Vagina/Vulva 77-8, 83, 88, *89-90, 115, 149, 162-3, 224, 269, 303n31, 306n49/52, 310n79/82
Veil 258, 326n39
Vendange 346n111
Vessel, Archetypal Symbol of 63, *64-5, 107, 302n21, 356n169
Vines, Vineyards, Wine 42, 44, 48-49, 53-4, 83, 85, 100, 104, 115, 123, 149, 152-9, 163, 165, 173-4, 178, 192, 206-207, 209, 240-1, 269, 297n111, 302n20, 303 n26, 304n39, 313n98, 323n18/22, 346n111/112/114
Virgil 26, 29, 144
Virginity, Chastity 73, 104, 106, 144-5, 240, 310n79, 324n26, 346n113
161, 164, 209, 302 n22, 305n41/44/45
Voice 44, 175, 206-7, 245, 265, 271, 289n61, 326n42
Wall 160ff.
Wanderer (tōteyâ) 171, *172, 173-5, 219, 254, 274, 326n39
Warriors 57
Wasf, Technique of 44, 55-7, 69, 71, 73-4, *75-6, 78, 80-1, *85-6, 88, 94-95, 111-12, 224, 288 n55, 300n11, 302n22, 304n36, 305n46, 307 n62
Watchmen 46, 55, 57, 115, 124, 146, 207-8, 225-6, 250, 340n74
Water (See also Spring) 132, 269, 270
  Surface Water 332n22
Weather 198, 257
Whiteness 95-6, 144, 158-9, 179, 265, 320, 321 n7
Winds, Wind 107, 109, 198, 201, 210, 261, 311n85, 332 n24
Wisdom
  Tradition and Literature 29-33, 131, 187-8, 211-12, 223, 290-1 n69/70, 292n78, 316-317n124, 330n13, 332 n25, 336n45, 340n77, 341n79, 342n88, 348 n125
  Ophidic/Chthonic Wisdom 230-1, 233, 238, 241, 255, 264
  Hermetic Wisdom 236-8
Wittgenstein, Ludwig 344n99
Wolf 284n37
Womb 110, 115, 132, 146, 178, 195, 213, 248, 264, 273, 312n91, 338n57
Wonder 58, 117-8, 121, 141, 159, 163, 178, 243, 258, 318n1
Work 200, 206, 255, 355 n164
Yahwist, the 188
Zoroastrianism 307n63, 337n49